World Political Innovators

World Political Innovators

Volume 2

Volume 2

SALEM PRESS
A Division of EBSCO Information Services
Ipswich, Massachusetts

GREY HOUSE PUBLISHING

World Political Innovators, 2016, published by Grey House Publishing, Inc., Amenia, NY, under exclusive license from EBSCO Publishing, Inc. Majority of the content originally appeared as articles in various issues of *Current Biography* magazine, published by H. W. Wilson. New profiles and other materials have been added for this work.

∞ The paper used in these volumes conforms to the American National Standard for Permanence of Paper for Printed Library Materials, Z39.48 1992 (R1997).

Library of Congress Cataloging-In-Publication Data

Names: Salem Press.
Title: World political innovators / [edited by] Salem Press.
Description: [First edition]. | Ipswich, Massachusetts : Salem Press, a division of EBSCO Information Services; Amenia, NY : Grey House Publishing, [2016] | Includes bibliographical references and index.
Identifiers: ISBN 978-1-68217-161-5 (set) | ISBN 978-1-68217-163-9 (vol. 1) | ISBN 978-1-68217-164-6 (vol. 2)
Subjects: LCSH: Politicians—Biography. | Heads of state—Biography. | World politics—20th century. | World politics—21st century.
Classification: LCC D412 .W67 2016 | DDC 324.2092/2—dc23

PRINTED IN THE UNITED STATES OF AMERICA

CONTENTS

VOLUME 1

VOLUME 2

Appendixes

Indexes

M

WINNIE MANDELA

South African Political Activist; Social Worker

Born: September 26, 1936; Transkei, South Africa
Affiliation: Independent

INTRODUCTION

South Africa's black leader Nomzamo Winnie Mandela has been called "the incarnation of the Black spirit." She and her husband, Nelson Mandela, the national hero who is serving a life term in prison for sabotage and treason, "have become a symbolic couple with their incredible strength and refusal to be broken," according to South African Bishop Desmond Tutu, the 1984 Nobel Peace Prize winner. A social worker by profession, she has struggled for black liberation during a quarter of a century as a "banned" person who is forbidden a public life and, as virtually without rights, is subject to sometimes brutal harassments by security forces. Mrs. Mandela, whose African name Nomzamo means "trial," has also served several prison terms under South Africa's peculiarly legalistic system of white racial supremacy, usually for suspected participation in the African National Congress, the outlawed revolutionary group most blacks look to for leadership.

Because the banning orders are intended to silence Winnie Mandela, detailed information about her life and work was spotty until the 1985 publication in English of Part of My Soul Went with Him (Rowohlt, 1984; Penguin; W. W. Norton), a collection of interviews with her conducted by Anne Benjamin and adapted by Mary Benson, and the appearance of Miss Benson's recent biography, Winnie Mandela *(Braziller, 1986). After her house in Brandfort, the isolated town to which she was "banished" in 1977, was burned down in August 1985,*

Winnie Mandela.

she openly broke her ban, appearing at political events and making public statements. Her renewed prominence shows her to be a militant defender of her people who envisions a multiracial, democratic but socialist society where South Africa's 73 percent black majority will have their rightful role in governing. "[I would] gladly go and water that tree of liberation with my own blood, if it means that the children I am bringing up under [present] conditions will not lead my kind of life," she has declared. "...I find myself strength from the knowledge that each step I take the nation is behind me."

431

EARLY LIFE

Winnie Mandela is a descendant of the Xhosa, a traditional African people whose official "homeland," since 1963, has been the eastern Transkei region of the Cape Province, bordering the Indian Ocean. Born in 1936 in the mountainous Pondoland district of the Transkei, Nkosikazi Nobandle Nomzamo Madikizela (her full Xhosa name) was one of the nine children of Columbine Madikizela, a history teacher in government service, and his wife, a domestic science teacher. The father added "Winifred" to his daughter's name out of admiration for the industriousness of the Germans and respect for Christian missionaries. He refused the position as a minor chief of the Tembu tribe in their village of Bizana that could have been his by blood right, toiling instead on his meager salary and instructing his children about the valiant history of the Xhosa and their subjugation by the white colonists. His wife died, at the age of about forty, when Nomzamo Winnie was nine, and the girl then had to leave school for six months to harvest crops in the fields and tend the family's sheep and goat.

The poverty of village life was such that finding simple necessities like food was a constant struggle and going barefoot was the norm for Nomzamo Winnie until she reached high school. Nevertheless, she received a formal education in subjects like Latin, English, the sciences, and mathematics—a regimen few black South Africans could expect nowadays, since the Bantu Education Act of 1953 radically lowered school standards and funding for them and, until recently, mandated only the local African language as the medium of instruction. Her leadership qualities emerged early: while attending Shawbury High School on the outskirts of the Transkei she organized church services, served as chief-prefect for supervising younger girls, and won high grades in class and sports trophies at regional festivals. During her senior year, in 1952, she heard about the Defiance Campaign being led in the cities by Nelson Mandela and the Youth League of the African National Congress (ANC), South Africa's oldest black liberation organization, to oppose pass laws and other color-bar regulations that were instituted as part of the comprehensive policy of apartheid after the Afrikaner National party came to power in 1948. Winnie Madikizela was by then well aware of the white insistence on superiority over blacks: "There is an anger that wakes up in you when you are a child and it builds up and determines the political consciousness of the black man," she told Anne Benjamin.

LIFE'S WORK

Winnie Madikizela moved to Johannesburg in 1953 to study at the Jan Hofmeyr Social Centre, which counted Nelson Mandela among its patrons. Perhaps the only student from a rural area at the school, she lived at the Helping Hand hostel, where her fellow residents included many black workers involved in the multiracial South African Congress of Trade Unions (SACTU) and the ANC. "We found ourselves discussing political issues all the time," she has recalled. She received top marks in her course in pediatric social work, becoming, on her graduation in 1955, the country's first black medical social worker, according to several reports. That December she began her clinical training at Baragwanath Hospital for Africans in Johannesburg. A colleague from that period remembers her as a young woman with "a highly developed social conscience" who would tour the city's black townships looking for the destitute and others with no one to care for them. Meanwhile, through her activities with the multiracial Federation of South African Women and other women's groups she learned speechmaking and other political skills.

In June 1955 an historic Congress of the People, composed of 3,000 delegates from the ANC, the Indian Congress, the Coloured People's Organization, the white Congress of Democrats, and the SACTU, adopted a Freedom Charter calling for democracy and equality across racial lines and denouncing "government founded on injustice and inequality." Authorities responded by imposing further repressive legislation, ultimately arresting 156 people of all races in December 1956 and charging them with a treasonous, Communistic conspiracy to overthrow the government by violence. Nelson Mandela was among those indicted, but in the early stages of the trial he continued his law practice in Johannesburg. It was there that Winnie Madikizela met him around Christmas of 1956 through Adelaide Tsukudu, her friend who was then engaged to Oliver Tambo, Mandela's law partner and a cofounder with him of the ANC's Youth League.

Although Nelson Mandela was fifteen years her senior and already a hero to his people, while she was just a "country bumpkin," in her words, she fell in love with him immediately. But, she has said, "even at that stage, life with him was life without him." She "never had any frivolous romance with him—there was never time for that," as Mandela was busy with consultations "twenty-four hours a day." In 1957 she joined the Women's League of the ANC and soon rose to become chairwoman both of its local branch and of its counterpart in the Federation of South African Women (or Women's Federation). Her social work activities expanded to include visits and aid provision to families whose members were held in jail as political prisoners. In June 1958, while Mandela's treason trial still dragged on, he was allowed to leave Johannesburg for four days, and the couple were married at her home in Bizana in an abbreviated ceremony that combined traditional and Western elements. (Mandela had been divorced from his first wife a year before.) They set up house in an undistinctive three-room shack in the black township of Orlando outside Johannesburg.

In 1958 Winnie Mandela joined the mass protests that were organized by the Women's Federation against the pass laws, which had been extended two years before to require black women as well as black men to carry documents approving their movements in restricted white areas. She was imprisoned, along with thousands of other women, for two weeks in September 1958, despite her pregnancy, and she attributes the saving of her first child, Zenani, to the care that friends gave her during the detention. As a result of her protest activity she was dismissed from her job at Baragwanath Hospital.

Following the March 1960 massacre in Sharpeville near Johannesburg of seventy people nonviolently protesting the pass laws, the ANC was outlawed, but in March 1961 Mandela and some thirty codefendants were found not guilty of treason. Jubilation was short-lived, however, as he went underground as a fugitive almost immediately afterward, in the aftermath of his public speech calling for a general strike on the occasion of South Africa's independence from the British Commonwealth, which was set for May 31, 1961. Winnie Mandela and their two young daughters, often relying on white accomplices, were able to visit him at numerous hideouts, most frequently at a farmhouse used as the ANC's secret headquarters at Lilliesleaf in Rivonia, an outer suburb of Johannesburg. Sometimes she resorted to ruses in order to meet him, once successfully feigning labor pains to slip through a police cordon. She worked meantime for the Child Welfare office, doing field work in Johannesburg's black township of Soweto. When Mandela was captured in August 1962, "it was the collapse of a political dream," Winnie Mandela told Anne Benjamin. "At that moment I wasn't only shocked for myself. I was shocked for the struggle and what it meant for the cause of my people....I knew at that time that this was the end of any kind of family life." Nelson Mandela

was sentenced that November to five years' imprisonment with hard labor for inciting the general strike and leaving the country without valid documents.

Within two months of her husband's conviction Winnie Mandela was served with her first banning order, the ostensible provocation being her membership on the national executive of the Women's Federation. Promulgated under the Suppression of Communism Act of 1950, the ban, to last for two years, forbade her to leave Johannesburg and restricted her participation at public and private meetings. In 1963 she was acquitted of a charge of breaking the ban by attending a gathering.

The police scored a key tactical point when they arrested seven ANC leaders at Lilliesleaf in July 1963, and Nelson Mandela was placed among the accused at what has since become known as the "Rivonia trial." Pleading not guilty, he eloquently used the courtroom as a forum for his cause, but without avail, for in June 1964 he and six others were sentenced to life in prison for sabotage, treason, and violent conspiracy. On the day of the pronouncement, Winnie Mandela, who had obtained special permission to attend the trial sessions, which were held in Pretoria, emerged from the provincial supreme court building flashing a smile that "dazzled." Writing for the London Observer (March 20, 1983), Allister Sparks recalled that when she came out to them the crowd of blacks thronging the courthouse square "cheered, perhaps the only time black people have ever summoned the courage to cheer in that place." A photograph of her at one of Mandela's trials shows her talking to white policemen and smiling brilliantly, with the insolence of royalty.

Winnie Mandela acknowledges that the period immediately following Nelson Mandela's remanding to Robben Island prison, offshore from Cape Town, was a time of political and personal "desperation....Solitude, loneliness, is worse than fear." With the ANC leadership behind bars, she has said, "the difficult part was finding myself with a spotlight on me. I wasn't ready for that....And I had to think so carefully what I said...." Yet she began to develop into a strong public figure in her own right, partly through her friendship with an Anglican priest, Father Leo Rakale, who "hauled" her "out of [her] shattered self." "I rediscovered the value of my soul in relation to my religious beliefs and most of all to the cause of my people....I had ideas and views of my own. I had my own commitment and I wasn't just a political ornament."

The integrity of that commitment was borne out repeatedly in the next years. Mrs. Mandela was deeply but quietly involved in political work, helping to organize study groups and history lectures especially for educating the youth about conditions in South Africa. In 1965 a more stringent banning order was imposed on her, and because it restricted her to Orlando she lost her position with the Child Welfare society. She embarked on a long series of temporary jobs, including shoe repair, dry cleaning, and work in a furniture shop, and was forced out of each one and denied others as the security police intimidated the employers. New prohibitions added in 1966 barred her from preparing, printing, or publishing "any document, book, pamphlet, record, poster, [or] photograph." Her daughters were expelled from a number of schools, until they went to Swaziland in 1967 for their schooling. Family friends and others who came to her aid were harassed or punished on minor charges. Winnie Mandela was found not guilty of resisting arrest during a 1967 incident in which she threw to the floor a policeman who had entered her bedroom unannounced, and that same year she spent four days in jail on a charge of ban violation.

South Africa's Terrorism Act of 1967, which mandated the arrest of persons suspected of committing acts that endangered the maintenance of law and order or of inciting others to do so, was applied against Winnie Mandela and twenty-one others in May 1969. Ninety-nine counts under the Suppression of Communism Act were brought against the group, most having to do with their purported efforts to reestablish the ANC. Like most of the accused, Winnie Mandela was held incommunicado and in solitary confinement at Pretoria Central Prison. "The whole thing is calculated to destroy you, not only morally but also physically," she has observed. For nine months, she was subjected to harsh and filthy conditions that left her fevered, swollen, and malnourished and underwent arduous interrogations, sometimes blacking out on the fourth or fifth day of questioning. Her jailers told her she could go free if she publicly called upon the ANC to surrender.

In February 1970 the state withdrew the case and the defendants were all acquitted, only to be instantly re-detained on nearly identical charges under Section 6 of the Terrorism Act, which provided for indefinite detention. Their imprisonment continued. Winnie Mandela was by then actively inspiring her block-mates to agitate for better treatment, and a fellow prisoner recalls that she stopped the white prison matrons from hitting other prisoners and sent reports to their lawyers. Finally, in September 1970, after enduring seventeen months

as unconvicted detainees, all but one of the accused were acquitted. A congratulatory essay that appeared in Sechaba (November-December 1970), the official organ of the ANC, applauded the group for holding out "against the relentless vindictiveness of the prosecution in its determination to get a conviction. [The authorities] more than met their match in the inner strength of Winnie Mandela's group." In two weeks a new five-year banning order was decreed against her and many of her confreres, this one forbidding visitors and placing her under house arrest at night and on weekends. The Lutheran Bishop Manas Buthelezi, president of the South African Council of Churches, wrote in his tribute to Nomzamo Winnie Mandela that appears in Part of My Soul Went with Him: "She is a window through which even the most uninitiated eye is introduced to the obscure, twilight existence of the banned and detained.... She was silenced all right, but I heard her strengthening message and I was able to survive [my own] banning order."

Although from 1970 to 1974 Winnie Mandela had frequent occasion to appeal convictions and sentences for violating her ban, appeal against the order itself was not provided for in law. She served a reduced six-month term in Kroonstad Prison in 1974-75 for meeting with her children in the presence of a banned person, the photographer Peter Mugabane. Her ten short months of freedom when the current ban expired, in 1975-76, ended in the wake of the Soweto uprising in June 1976, when black schoolchildren protested the introduction of the Afrikaans language into their classrooms and 500 persons lost their lives. Because she helped to form the Black Parents Association, a now-banned group that offered assistance to the hundreds of families affected by the riots and that unsuccessfully requested negotiations with the minister of police, she was arrested the following month under the Internal Security Act of 1976 (which incorporated the Suppression of Communism Act). The police accused her personally of organizing the uprising. Immediately after her release from a Johannesburg jail in December 1976, she was again placed under ban.

More severe punishment was meted out to Winnie Mandela in May 1977, when she was banished for an indefinite period to the rural Afrikaner town of Brandfort, located forty miles north of Bloemfontein, the provincial capital of the Orange Free State. That dictate landed her and her daughter Zindzi in Brandfort's depressed black ghetto known as "Phatakahle"—"Handle with care"—in tiny shack Number 802, without an indoor toilet or running water. Although Winnie Mandela called her exile "totally dispiriting...a living grave," she also said she felt "honored to be brought home" to the region where the ANC was founded, in Bloemfontein in 1912. The conditions of her ban, which barred her from meeting with more than one person and forbade South African newspapers to quote her, even after death, still held, and besides being under constant surveillance she was required to report weekly to the police station. During the following years she underwent countless arrests and many legal proceedings for violations, once on a charge of conversing with neighbors about the price of a chicken and, on another occasion, for receiving two white women as visitors. She was acquitted in 1978 of inciting the Soweto riots and awarded compensation for defamation.

Writing in *The New York Times* (August 18, 1985), Sheila Rule described Winnie Mandela's work as a community leader in Brandfort: "Each morning, she makes her rounds, gathering scores of children and taking them to the nursery school she operates in the hall of a Methodist church....From there, Mrs. Mandela begins her work at the clinic. She sees many infants [and] victims of stabbings and other violence. [She] visits the elderly....someone is always coming by for advice or guidance..." Other projects she started include a soup kitchen, women's self-help groups, and a youth club. Meanwhile she refused to acknowledge "whites only" signs at the police station, post office, and local shops, organized boycotts and, at some stores, gained entrance for blacks. Although at first she operated the clinic out of her house, she eventually received donations to erect a separate building for it in her garden. In 1982 her ban was renewed for five years.

When in late 1983 the South African government adopted a new constitution giving "coloureds," or mixed-race persons, and Indians, but not blacks, limited parliamentary representation, Winnie Mandela condemned that policy as "the best recipe for the worst violence, the worst possible confrontation between blacks and whites." Events proved her right, and in July 1985 a state of emergency was declared in many districts, eventually totaling around forty. That action only escalated both the violence and international disapproval of it, and more than 900 deaths due to racial strife, mostly of blacks, were recorded for 1985. In August the government intensified its negotiations with Winnie Mandela, Nelson Mandela, and their advisers, begun several

months before, for his release from prison, but later that month she announced her husband's rejection of the amnesty terms that were offered. "The only thing that is left to be discussed by the people of this country and the ruling Afrikaners is the handing over of power to the majority," she quoted him as saying, suggesting that he would be prepared to talk when apartheid was abandoned, the ban on the ANC was lifted, political prisoners were released, and exiles were allowed re-entry. "[South African President P. W.] Botha is speaking of my husband's freedom," she said, as quoted by her lawyer, Ismail Ayob. "My husband speaks of the people's freedom." Following Botha's widely publicized speech that month, which disappointed hopes of significant reforms, she decried the president's remarks as having "disastrous consequences for South Africa."

On August 14, 1985 Winnie Mandela's house and clinic in Brandfort were firebombed, following an incident in which young black demonstrators took refuge and were arrested there. She publicly blamed the police Security Branch for the arson and returned to her house in Orlando, where she remained as of December 1985 in defiance of the government's so far unenforced order to return to exile. She refused an offer of $10,000 for reconstruction from the United States Embassy in South Africa, in keeping with her belief that United States policy "echoes the programs of the racist regime." In October 1985 members of the diplomatic community at the United Nations in New York City privately donated $100,000 to her. Since making her move to Orlando, Winnie Mandela has also defied her banning order, giving interviews and occasionally speaking in public, including at the October 1985 hanging of the black poet Benjamin Maloise, who was convicted of murdering a black policeman. Her boldest flouting of the authorities came when she addressed a rally of some 2,000 blacks that was held after a mass funeral outside Pretoria in early December for victims of police violence. "The day is not far when we shall lead you to freedom," she told the people. "In the same way as you have had to bury our children today, so shall the blood of these heroes we buried today be avenged."

On June 12, 1986, in anticipation of mass demonstrations commemorating the tenth anniversary of the 1976 Soweto uprisings, the South African government imposed a new state of emergency that prohibited, among other activities, visits by journalists to black areas, press coverage of police actions, and publication of "subversive" statements. Less than a month later, on

July 8, 1986, all special restrictions on Winnie Mandela were lifted in what seemed to be a counterbalancing public relations gesture as well as a tacit admission that the state's attempts to destroy her politically had gone down to defeat. Members of the international press corps were officially permitted to quote her on condition that her statements, in keeping with the rules of the state of emergency, did not seem to further the ends of the ANC and were not otherwise "subversive."

In the first quotes to appear from her in the South African press in eleven years, Mrs. Mandela wasted no time in calling for "immediate and total" economic sanctions against South Africa and condemning President Ronald Reagan and British Prime Minister Margaret Thatcher for continuing "to call themselves friends of the black people, while, in effect, they are friends of the racists." Limited economic sanctions against South Africa were imposed by the United States Congress on October 2, 1986.

Winnie Mandela's irregularly allotted visits each year to Robben Island and, after her husband was moved in 1982, to Pollsmoor Prison outside Cape Town have often been a target for police restrictions and harassment. She and her two daughters, Zindziswa Mandela, twenty-four, and Zenani Mandela Dlamini, twenty-six, received permission to visit Nelson Mandela as a family for the first time in early November 1985 in Cape Town, where he underwent surgery for removal of his prostate. Zindzi, a poet who published the collection Black As I Am in 1978, has often served as her mother's spokeswoman, while Zenani, an accountant, lives in Swaziland with her three children and her husband, the son of that country's late King Sobhuza.

PERSONAL LIFE

Nearly every description of Nomzamo Winnie Mandela remarks on her beauty of facial expression and her spirited courage. Although she told Anne Benjamin that she "ceased a long time ago to exist as an individual" and renounced any expectation of personal happiness, she is capable of deep laughter and retains her habit of welcoming anyone who turns to her for help. She is noted to have "a hell of a temper." She says she "couldn't live without" the Canadian Air Force exercises she first practiced during her 1969-70 imprisonment, and she reads widely to keep her "sanity." A video documentary of her life, entitled I Shall Never Lose Hope, which was produced by the Kenmerk company in the Netherlands, won the Tyneside Festival prize in England for best video in 1985. She was honored, in absentia, with the Robert F. Kennedy Humanitarian Award in November 1985.

FURTHER READING

Chicago Tribune II p17 O 16 '83 por; The New York Times Ag 18 '85 por; Washington Post A p1 Ag 26 '85 pors; Benson, Mary. Winnie Mandela (1986); Mandela, Winnie. Part of My Soul Went with Him (1985); Thompson, Leonard and Prior, Andrew. South African Politics (1982)

MAO ZEDONG (ALSO KNOWN AS MAO TSE-TUNG) (MA'O DZU' DOONG')

Former President of the People's Republic of China

Born: Dec. 26, 1893; Shaoshan, Hunan, China
Died: September 9, 1976; Beijing, China
Affiliation: Chinese Communist Party Leader

INTRODUCTION

For more than two decades, the leader of 930.7 million Chinese at the time of his death in 1976, (now it is more than a billion) was Mao Zedong, Chairman of the Communist Party of the People's Republic of China and "Supreme Leader." A soldier, politician, poet, and scholar, he was considered by many as the leading interpreter of Marxist-Leninist doctrine. Of peasant origin, Mao deviated from orthodox Marxism by placing the peasantry rather than the urban proletariat in the vanguard of the revolutionary struggle, in accordance with existing realities in China.

Like many of the Chinese Communist leaders, Mao Zedong came from an area of Central China where militarism had made itself most harshly felt, where relations between landlords and peasants were at their worst, and where Western ideas were looked upon with disfavor.

He also spent decades fighting for survival against warring factions in China, including the Nationalist Party (also known as the Kuomintang, of which he was briefly a member), and against the Japanese invasion. One of his wives was executed by the Nationalist Party. This need for survival fuelled his need for purges; a quick search of the Internet lists links asserting that millions of Chinese died during the years of the Great Leap Forward (between 1959 to 1962, 20 million people were estimated to have died of starvation) and the Cultural Revolution (between 1966 to 1976; with the worst of it occurring between 1966 and 1971, when more than 1.5 million people were killed). During the Cultural Revolution, millions of people also suffered imprisonment, seizure of property, torture or general humiliation. A generation of people was uneducated because of the closures of schools.

Mao also was a popular philosopher, with several books to his credit, which included the "Little Red Book," officially known as Quotations of Chairman Mao Zedong, *a must-have item for the Chinese and trendy outside of China as well. Five billion copies were printed in 500 different editions and 50 languages, more than the entire population of 3 billion in the 1970s.*

Yet Mao could be a cruel man, demonstrated by his purges and his long-term relationship with his "right-hand man," Zhou Enlai, whom he denied treatment for cancer. His detractors equated Mao with Adolf Hitler and Joseph Stalin, citing systemic human rights violations, and claimed that the number of deaths in China through starvation, forced labor and executions was closer to 40 to 70 million people.

EARLY LIFE

Mao was born on December 26, 1893, in the village of Shaoshan, Hunan, China, the eldest of four children of Mao Jensheng. His mother's family name was Wen. He had two brothers: Tse-min (using the Wade-Gile's spelling), who died in a Nationalist prison in 1941, and Tse-t'an, who was killed in the early 1930s; he also had one sister. His father, once a poor peasant, paid off his debts after serving in the army, and gradually acquired three and a half acres of land and a rice-trading business. He treated his family and his servants harshly, providing them with only the barest means of sustenance. Mao's mother, a devout Buddhist, gave charity to the poor behind her husband's back, and hoped that her son might eventually enter the priesthood.

Mao, a frail child, began to work in his father's fields at seven. He sympathized with his father's farm laborers and with the poverty-ridden, but rebellious, peasants of Hunan. In his youth, he engaged in a "dialectical

struggle" against the authority of his father, forming a "united front" with the other members of his family. On at least two occasions he ran away from home.

Entering the local private elementary school at the age of eight, Mao studied the Confucian classics, but grew to dislike Confucius, whom he identified with the authoritarianism of his father and his teachers. He much preferred the romantic novels of ancient China. After completing elementary school at 13, he returned to the farm, where he helped his father with accounts.

In September 1907, Mao entered middle school at Xiangxiang, 15 miles from home, with the reluctant approval of his father, who wanted to apprentice him to a rice merchant. At the school, he studied science and other modern subjects and came into contact with the ideas of the reform movement of Kang Youwei and Liang Qichao, who sought to modernize the Manchu dynasty. During vacations, Mao and a schoolmate became wandering scholars, exposing their bodies to the elements and earning their way by writing scrolls.

In 1911, Mao entered secondary school at Changsha, where he wrote anti-Manchu political essays. Although he had not yet fully accepted the policies of Sun Yat-sen's revolutionary Kuomintang movement, he decided, in late 1911, to join the Nationalist regular army, where he served as an orderly to the younger officers. He was discharged in the summer of 1912.

In late 1912, Mao, who no longer received an allowance from home, entered the tuition-free teachers' training college at Changsha, and remained for six years. There he first became influenced by Socialist writings, although his understanding of Socialism was superficial. He also founded the New People's Study Organization, many of whose members later joined the Communist movement.

Graduating in 1918, shortly after his mother's death, Mao did not return home but went to Beijing, where he helped to organize a "work and learn" program for students who wished to study in France. Subsequently he took a menial position as an assistant at the Beijing University library, while studying in his spare time. During this period, he had no great ambition and would have been satisfied with eventually taking a minor government post. In 1919, he returned to Hunan province, where he edited the *Hsiang River Monthly Review*, and organized Hunanese students in an effort to overthrow a corrupt military governor. In 1920, he became a teacher in the first normal school at Changsha.

Affiliation: Chinese Communist Party Leader

Having in the meantime become a convinced Marxist, Mao was caught up in the May Fourth movement, which originated in student demonstrations in Beijing on May 4, 1919, protesting against the provisions of the Treaty of Versailles that granted Japan the former German concessions in China. This movement formed the core of the Chinese Communist Party, which held its founding congress in Shanghai in the summer of 1921. Mao, representing a small group of Communists in Hunan, was one of the 12 founding members of the Party. The congress rejected affiliation with the Communist International in Moscow, and it was not until 1922 that the Party established formal relations with the Comintern. After the founding congress, Mao returned to Hunan, where he set up the provincial branch of the Communist Party and organized a number of trade unions.

After the Communist Party decided, in 1923, to collaborate closely with the Kuomintang in a united front against the northern militarists, Mao became a member of the Kuomintang, while continuing to serve as a member of the Central Committee of the Communist Party. He was regarded at this time as representing the extreme right wing of the Communist Party. He continued to be active in both the Communist Party and the Kuomintang until 1927, when Chiang Kai-shek's massacre of the Shanghai workers brought about the break between the two parties.

In the spring of 1925, Mao had come to recognize the potential revolutionary role of the peasants, and began to organize peasant unions in Hunan. In 1927, under Party instructions, he wrote *Report of an Investigation into the Peasant Movement in Hunan*, ascribing a central role to the peasantry in the revolutionary class struggle. At first, the report was tabled by the Central Committee of the Party, but, later in the year, it was published in the Central Party organ.

In September 1927, Mao led some 2,000 Hunan peasants in the abortive Autumn Harvest Uprising, and he was removed from his Politburo position and from the Hunan Provincial Committee. He then retreated with the remnants of his forces to Chingkanshan Mountain in Jiangxi province, where he was joined in April 1928 by Zhu De, a former warlord who had gone over to the Communists. Together they established the Fourth Workers' and Peasants' Red Army, with Mao as political commissar and Zhu De as military commander. During his years in the mountains, Mao continued to develop the tactics of guerilla warfare.

In November 1931, the First National Congress of Soviets was held at Juichin in Jiangxi province, marking the formal establishment of the China Soviet Republic, and Mao was elected Chairman of the Provisional Soviet government. Meanwhile, in late 1930, Chiang Kai-shek had begun his "extermination campaigns" against the Communists. Four of these campaigns were successfully repulsed by the Red armies, but in the fifth campaign, which took up the greater part of 1934, the Communist forces were severely defeated.

In October 1934, the Communists, pressed by Kuomintang forces, began the Long March of some 6,000 miles northward from Jiangxi to Shaanxi province. This legendary march was marked by heroism on the part of the Red (later known as the People's Liberation Army, or PLA) forces, only a fraction of whom survived. In its course, Mao greatly increased his stature and, at the Party conference held at Zunyi in Guizhou province from December 1934 to January 1935, his authority was virtually unchallenged.

Arriving at northern Shaanxii province in October 1935, Mao re-established the Soviet Republic of China, with headquarters first at Pao An, and later at Yan'an. Meanwhile, the pressure of the Japanese, who had invaded Manchuria in 1931, was mounting and, in March 1936, Mao called for an anti-Japanese united front with the Kuomintang. As a result of Mao's efforts, an agreement was reached in the spring of 1937 after the Communists had pledged to abandon the agrarian revolution.

During the Japanese War, Mao lived in a cave in Yan'an, where he raised his own tobacco and spent his nights studying and writing political essays. By 1938, he was universally recognized as the authoritative leader and theoretician of the Communist movement. His primer on guerilla warfare was published in 1937. In *The New Democracy* (1940), Mao justified the compromise between the Kuomintang and the Communists and depicted democracy as an interim stage between feudalism and Socialism. In *Coalition Government, 1945*, he called for a government reflecting the will of the people.

Although Mao had acquired a reputation of being merely an agrarian reformer, in practice he tended to be increasingly influenced by the policies of Stalin. From 1942 to 1944, he instituted a far-reaching "rectification" program aimed at tightening Party discipline and purging undesirable elements. At the Seventh Party Congress, in April 1945, Mao was elected Chairman of the Central Committee and of the Revolutionary Military Council.

LIFE'S WORK

When the war with Japan ended in August 1945, the Communists were in a strong position. For a time they made attempts to reach an agreement with the Kuomintang. Following a conference between Mao and Chiang Kai-shek shortly after the Japanese surrender, Mao complained with some bitterness that Chiang had treated him "like a peasant." Mao was said to have been strongly criticized, in late 1945, by some of the more radical elements of his Party for his willingness to grant too many concessions to the Kuomintang, in the effort to form a coalition government. During this period, he was still looked upon by many Western observers as an agrarian reformer with strong democratic tendencies.

After the failure of efforts by General George C. Marshall, representing the United States government, to bring about a coalition government, the Chinese Civil War resumed in the summer of 1946. The Communists constantly increased the number of their peasant adherents by promising them land redistribution. When the Red armies crossed the Yangtze River on April 21, 1949, the end of Kuomintang rule on the Chinese mainland was in sight. A few months later, Mao Zedong was virtually the supreme ruler of China. On October 1, 1949, a week and a half after the Republic had been proclaimed by the Chinese people's political consultative conference, Mao Zedong was elected chairman of the new Central People's government, and an organic law and common program were adopted.

In December 1949, Mao left China for the first time to visit Moscow for Soviet Premier Joseph Stalin's 70th birthday. The visit resulted in the negotiation, in February 1950, of a 30-year treaty of "friendship, alliance, and mutual assistance" between China and the Soviet Union. On the domestic scene, Mao proceeded with great vigor to transform the face of his war-torn nation. During the early 1950s he instituted a series of rectification campaigns against waste, bureaucracy, and corruption. Against the landlords he began a reign of terror that lasted until 1954. Mao himself admitted later, in 1957, that during these early years some 800,000 persons were liquidated. (Other estimates of the number of persons killed by the Communists run much higher.)

The First Five-Year Plan, providing for large-scale industrialization and collectivization of agriculture, was launched in November 1952. By 1956, about 83 percent of all Chinese peasants were on collective farms.

Under the constitution of September 1954, emphasizing a unified state and setting up the basic organs of government, Mao was installed as Chairman of the People's Republic of China and of the National Defense Council. He was also made honorary chairman of the National Committee of the Chinese people's Consultative Conference and was elected a deputy to the National People's Congress. At the same time, he retained his Communist Party positions as Chairman of the Central Committee, Chairman of the Politburo, and member of the Politburo Standing Committee. He was re-elected to these positions in the Party in September 1956.

On February 27, 1957, fearing the possibility of revolts such as occurred in Hungary in 1956, and noting the adverse economic conditions prevailing in China at the time, Mao gave a major speech on "the correct handling of contradictions among the people." He conceded that contradictions could and did exist within a Socialist society and said that these could best be resolved, not by the terror that had marked the early years of Communist rule, but by means of free discussion and criticism. "Let a hundred flowers blossom! Let a hundred schools of thought contend!" he declared. Although the new policy was received with great enthusiasm, criticism of the government far exceeded the expectations of Mao Zedong. By June 1957, the government again instituted police rule and suppressed its critics by force.

Under an economic program designated as the "Big Leap Forward," Mao, in April 1958, launched a model commune, which he named "Sputnik." A few months' later, people's communes were established on a nationwide scale. Unlike the earlier collective farms, which were economic institutions under county administration, the communes were political units under Party rule and controlled virtually every phase of an individual's life. However, the communes failed to alleviate the adverse economic situation and, by mid-1961, the government was forced to grant farmers a greater degree of freedom and some measure of free enterprise. Meanwhile, millions of Chinese had died from starvation.

In late 1958, Mao requested that he not be re-elected as head of state in the elections of January 1959 so that he could concentrate more fully on questions of Marxist-Leninist theory and policy matters. Many historians now say he was pressured to remove himself from the limelight by other members of the government, because of the failures of the Great Leap Forward. Mao was replaced as Chairman of the People's Republic of China by Liu Shaoqi on April 27, 1959. Most observers agree that Mao's position of leadership remained undiminished, in view of the fact that he retained his Chairmanship of the Communist Party, where the real power in China continued to reside. Liu later held the title of "President," and eventually clashed with Mao, who reasserted himself during the Cultural Revolution. Lui was later branded a traitor and "disappeared" in 1968. Lin Biao took Lui's place, also a victim of the Cultural Revolution and accused of planning a coup d'état. Biao died in a plane crash over Mongolia (many claimed he was trying to escape to the Soviet Union) and was posthumously removed from the Party and all offices he had held.

Unlike Premier Nikita S. Khrushchev of the Soviet Union, Mao Zedong had expressed little fear of the possible consequences of a nuclear war and had maintained that China could absorb hundreds of millions of casualties and emerge victoriously. He believed that the threat of global conflict could be removed only by the victory of the Communist Revolution over "the United States reactionaries and their lackeys." On the other hand, he had conceded that compromises between "imperialist" and Socialist countries could occur under certain circumstances.

Within the Communist bloc, Mao's stature had steadily grown, especially since the death of Stalin in 1953, and he was regarded by many as overshadowing Khrushchev as the ideological leader of the Communist world. His prestige was greatly enhanced when, at a meeting of world Communist leaders in November 1957, he was instrumental in bringing about the adoption of an "Anti-Revisionist" Manifesto aimed at Marshal Tito of Yugoslavia.

In the 1960s, relations between Communist China and the Soviet Union had become increasingly strained. Mao did not like Khrushchev's denunciation of Stalin; he thought it was disrespectful. In private correspondence and at international conferences Chinese Communist spokesmen had accused the Soviet Union of

having abandoned orthodox Marxist-Leninist doctrine and of having adopted a revisionist policy. Khrushchev, on the other hand, had accused Mao of seeking to incite a global conflict. After Khrushchev left office, heightened tension between China and the Soviet Union led to the Sino-Soviet border conflict, a seven-month undeclared military conflict over land the Soviets retained that had been seized by Imperial Russia that was not resolved diplomatically until 1991.

Many observers have stated that deteriorating relations between China and the U.S.S.R. contributed to the onset of the Cultural Revolution that started in 1966. Others state that the root cause of it was Mao's revenge against those who criticized him for the failures of the Great Leap Forward.

Mao's second in command, Zhou Enlai, the Premier of China, fought against the worst of Cultural Revolution without alienating Mao. Mao had declared the official end of the Cultural Revolution in 1969. Historians, however, state that it continued until after his death in 1976, when members of the "Gang of Four," which included Jiang Qing, Mao's fourth wife, were arrested by Hua Guofeng (Mao's hand-picked successor of Biao as President), tried, convicted, and imprisoned. The other members of the "Gang" were Wang Hongwen, Yao Wenyuan, and Zhang Chunqiao. They took advantage of Mao's failing health (he suffered from a stroke, in 1971, as well as other ailments), and continued the policies of the Cultural Revolution. They had engaged in a power struggle with Zhou Enlai and his supporters, and once they were removed from power, China was able to move on from the excesses of the Cultural Revolution.

Although Mao Zedong had renounced the ideas of Confucius, he was considered a scholar in the classical tradition of China. A five-volume English translation of his writings was published by Lawrence and Wishart Ltd., and by International Publishers, under the title *Selected Works of Mao Zedong (1954-62)*. As a poet, Mao relied heavily on ancient classical forms, although he maintained that all art and literature must serve the revolution. In 1957, he reluctantly permitted the publication of some of his poems, in spite of his fears that they might have an adverse influence on Chinese youth.

Many of his contemporaries later asserted that Mao developed a personality cult during the Cultural Revolution. Among the people of Communist China, Mao Zedong was regarded as a "living Buddha" hailed in song and story as "the people's great savior." His portrait was displayed everywhere and his theories were considered infallible. On the other hand, it has been said that he was a poor administrator. Although he had acquired some wealth through royalties on his writings, he avoided worldly vanities except for good food, wine, and cigarettes. He often traveled among the peasants, wearing a simple uniform without insignia of rank.

Despite his ill health, Mao still appeared in public, such as when then U.S. President Richard M. Nixon visited China in 1972. It was the only meeting between the two heads of states, and it helped move China further away from the U.S.S.R. and into the American sphere of influence. Other meetings with Nixon were headed by Zhou Enlai.

Mao, at the age of 82, died on September 9, 1976, of ALS (amyotrophic lateral sclerosis, better known as "Lou Gehrig's Disease") and lung problems due to heavy smoking. Many observers said he also had Parkinson's Disease.

His body lay in state at Beijing's Great Hall of the People for one week, and was viewed by thousands of people. On September 18, three-minutes of silence were formerly observed throughout China. Millions crowded Tiananmen Square for the final service, which was concluded with Hua Guofeng's 20-minute-long eulogy atop Tiananmen Gate. Mao's body was permanently interred in a Beijing mausoleum.

PERSONAL LIFE

Mao Zedong was first married at the age of 14 to a 20-years-old peasant girl, in a traditional ceremony that had been arranged by his parents. This marriage was never consummated. In 1920, he married Yang Kaihui, the daughter of a professor at Peking University who bore him two sons. She was executed by the Nationalists during the early part of Chiang Kai-shek's anti-Communist campaigns. Mao's third wife, He Zizhen, a former schoolteacher, was reportedly divorced by him and relocated to the Soviet Union. She bore him five children, some of whom had to be abandoned to peasants during the Long March of the 1930s. His eldest son, Mao Anying, was reportedly killed in the Korean War in November 1950. Mao's fourth wife was Jiang Qing (stage name, Lan Ping), a former stage and motion picture actress, by whom he had two daughters.

FURTHER READING

Atlan 204:56+ D '59; Asia Who's Who (1960); Dean, Vera Micheles. Builders of Emerging Nations (1961); Elegant, Robert S. China's Red Masters (1951); Payne, Robert. Portrait of a Revolutionary: Mao Tse-Tung (1961); Tang, Peter S.H. Communist China Today vol I (1961), Who's Who in Modern China (1954)

ANTE MARKOVIĆ

Prime Minister of Yugoslavia

Born: November 25, 1924; Konjic, Kingdom of Yugoslavia (now Bosnia and Herzegovina)
Died: November 28, 2011; Zagreb, Croatia
Affiliation: League of Communists of Yugoslavia

INTRODUCTION

Although it enjoys a higher standard of living than most of the other Eastern European countries now struggling, with varying degrees of success, to convert to Western-style democracies with free-market economies, Yugoslavia faces a unique set of problems brought on by the long-standing ethnic rivalries among its six republics and two autonomous provinces. Those rivalries, long suppressed or ameliorated during the thirty-five-year regime of Marshal Josip Broz Tito, resurfaced following his death in 1980 and have recently pushed the nation into civil war.

Leading what some observers believe is a futile effort to save the Yugoslav union is Ante Marković, a former electrical engineer who, since becoming prime minister in March 1989, has overseen sweeping and largely successful economic reforms that have earned him international recognition. His plans to integrate Yugoslavia into the European Community, however, have been undermined by the intransigence of the Communist-led republic of Serbia, the Serbian-dominated Yugoslav army, which has slipped from the grasp of civilian control, and burgeoning independence movements in the republics of Slovenia and Croatia.

EARLY LIFE

Ante Marković was born on November 25, 1924 in Konjic, in the Yugoslav republic of Bosnia and Herzegovina.

Ante Marković.

He joined the League of Communist Youth in the 1930s and served for a time as its leader. During World War II he fought with the partisan forces organized by Josip Broz Tito and the Communist party to resist the German and Italian occupation of Yugoslavia. After receiving a degree in electrical engineering from Zagreb University in Zagreb, the capital of Croatia, Marković took a job designing heavy machinery at the Rade Koncar factory in that city. He later became head of the company's test department, and from 1961 to 1986 he was director general of the plant. Meanwhile, Marković had risen through the ranks of the local Communist party to become, in 1982, president of the executive council of the republic of Croatia. From 1986 to 1988 Marković served as president of Yugoslavia's collective presidency, the eight-member body that is responsible chiefly for defense, foreign affairs, and internal security. (Yugoslavia's legislature, the Federal Assembly, elects the nation's cabinet, the Federal Executive Council, which oversees economic affairs. The president of the council, the prime minister, is the head of government.)

> ## Affiliation: League of Communists of Yugoslavia
>
> The League of Communists of Yugoslavia was a major Communist party in Yugoslavia. The party was founded in 1919 as an opposition party in the Kingdom of Serbs, Croats and Slovenes. After initial successes in the elections, it was denounced by the royal government. It remained an illegal underground group until World War II.

LIFE'S WORK

After Tito broke off relations with the Soviet Union in 1948, Yugoslavia emerged as the most open of the totalitarian states of Eastern Europe. So, when the Iron Curtain began to lift in the late 1980s, it was widely expected that Yugoslavia would be among the first Communist-bloc nations to adopt a Western-style democracy and market-driven economy. Although Prime Minister Branko Mikulic was not thought to be among the progressive members of his government, he appeared determined to be just that when, in 1988, he implemented an IMF-sponsored economic-austerity program that called for restricting government spending, placing a ceiling on wages, and gradually lifting price controls on consumer goods and services. But Mikulic failed to convince liberal members of parliament of his commitment to reform, and, on December 30 of that year, he and his entire cabinet resigned following a vote of no confidence. In its search for a successor, the collective federal presidency considered Ante Marković and Borisav Jovic, then the president of the executive council of Serbia. On January 19, 1989 the collective presidency elected Marković, in the belief that he would provide greater leadership than his predecessor had in the government's drive to reform the economy. The Federal Assembly confirmed Marković's appointment on March 16, 1989, and he was sworn in as prime minister later that day.

After Tito's death, the six republics had begun to assume greater control over their own affairs, making it difficult for the prime minister to fashion economic policy without the cooperation of the leaders of the republics. When Marković took office the Yugoslav economy was spinning out of control. The inflation rate for 1988 exceeded 250 percent (despite government subsidies that partially offset the true cost of staple crops), one out of six Yugoslavs was unemployed, foreign debt stood at $21 billion, the Yugoslav dinar was worthless on world markets, and most state-run businesses were losing money.

In Marković's view, the only solution was a head-long rush toward a free-market economy. To that end, he encouraged foreign investment, allowing overseas investors to purchase Yugoslav companies and eliminating restrictions on the importation of hard currency. He also expanded the areas in which private enterprise was allowed to operate and kept government bureaucrats from harassing the fledgling entrepreneurs. In the process, Marković hoped to entice Yugoslav emigres who had prospered in the West to reinvest in their homeland. As one Western diplomat told William Echikson of the *Christian Science Monitor* (May 16,1989), regarding Marković's bold opening of the private sector, "This one measure is worth more than all the other economic reforms. Just imagine all those Yugoslavs in Germany, with $15 billion to $20 billion tucked away in banks, coming home and setting up businesses."

In the meantime, to cover the losses of state-run businesses, Yugoslav banks printed more and more currency, driving the inflation rate to nearly 2,000 percent by the end of 1989. With wages lagging, the average Yugoslav's purchasing power plummeted to the lowest level in nearly twenty-five years. In a cordial meeting with President George Bush in Washington, D.C., in October 1989, Marković stressed that, to overcome the crisis, his country needed access to Western technology and training as well as loans from the World Bank. Marković's hopes for reforming the Yugoslav economy, however, were threatened by several factors, including the country's largely inefficient "worker self-management system," under which employees, not the state, own and operate companies, and conflicts between the wealthier northern republics of Slovenia and Croatia and the poorer southern republic of Serbia, whose leader, Slobodan Milosevic, wields considerable power.

In his first months in office, Marković proved reluctant to take on Milosevic and request more authority to restructure the economy, but on December 18, 1989 he unveiled a bold new economic plan, more comprehensive than anything before tried in the Communist bloc. Scrapping the worthless dinar, he created a new currency, the first in Eastern Europe to be fully convertible with all Western currencies, and he freed interest rates, which had been set, to that point, by the National Bank. As a temporary measure to curb inflation, he ordered a six-month wage freeze and placed government controls on the prices of housing, electricity, medicine,

postal services, gasoline, and rail transportation. By the spring of 1990, inflation was less than 10 percent, foreign debt had been trimmed by 16 percent, currency reserves and exports were up, and the new Yugoslav dinar was gaining respect on Western markets. Investor confidence could be measured in the 300 Yugoslav companies purchased by foreigners and the even more numerous joint ventures that had sprang up.

Despite those improvements, Marković confronted serious problems. Although unemployment had dipped to 13 percent by the summer of 1990, industrial production was down, and looming on the horizon was the prospect of a significant increase in unemployment when the government stopped subsidizing unprofitable businesses. Perhaps most ominous was the possibility of rekindled inflation once wage and price controls were removed. Nevertheless, in the spring of 1990, Marković, buoyed by his initial success, was enormously popular both at home and abroad as the principal architect of free enterprise in Yugoslavia.

The only significant criticism in the West of Marković's leadership was his failure to open up his country's political system as a corollary to the economic reforms. Marković initially resisted calls for an end to one-party rule, and, in response to his critics, he insisted that economic reforms must come first. Besides, he argued, Yugoslavia had long held contested elections for public office, even if the only candidates allowed on the ballot were Communists. To reconcile Marković's seemingly inconsistent political caution with his economic boldness, longtime observers of the Yugoslav political scene pointed to the centuries-old ethnic rivalries simmering beneath the country's surface. The westward-leaning republics of Slovenia and Croatia, for example, have long resented Serbian domination of the nation's affairs, and Yugoslavia's Albanian population has often complained of Serbian oppression, especially in the province of Kosovo, which, although it lies within Serbia, has an Albanian majority. In an interview with Henry Kamm of *The New York Times* (October 9, 1989), Marković himself hinted that democratic pluralism in Yugoslavia could break down along ethnic lines and exacerbate tensions. "Our reality is very complex," he said. "We are one country with two alphabets, three religions, four languages, five nationalities, six republics, and twenty-three million incorrigible individualists."

Nevertheless, on January 22, 1990 the Communist party ended a bitterly divided congress by renouncing its constitutionally guaranteed political monopoly and encouraging the parliament to create a multiparty system. On April 22 of that year, Marković returned to Croatia to take part in the first multiparty elections since World War II. The non-Communist Croatian Democratic Union won a clear majority. Elections in 1990 in Slovenia, Bosnia and Herzegovina, and Macedonia also ended Communist rule in those republics. Voters in Serbia and Montenegro, however, retained their Communist governments.

In the months that followed, the restive northern republics began demanding more autonomy. They urged that Yugoslavia be reconstituted into a loose confederation of independent states modeled on the European Community. Serbia, on the other hand, called for a stronger federation but continued to oppose Marković's economic reforms. Recognizing that increased ethnic tensions could undermine those reforms, Marković, too, urged the creation of a strong central government and warned of the dangers of continued squabbling among the republics. "The acts of the highest state organs of Slovenia, Serbia, and, partly, Croatia inevitably lead to a straining of political relations in Yugoslavia and directly threaten the country's survival," he declared in a speech on November 15, 1990, as quoted in *The New York Times* (November 28, 1990). "The situation is characterized by growing nationalism and separatism and an alarming worsening of ethnic relations, all of which is expressed in violence, a drastic threat to public order, peace, and citizens' safety." He went on to denounce Serbia for its recently instituted policy of imposing duties on goods imported from the northern republics. Marković's speech contributed to a dire assessment of the situation by the United States Central Intelligence Agency, which forecast the likelihood of a full-scale civil war in Yugoslavia by the spring of 1992.

Croatia's determination to declare its independence was complicated by the militant Serbian minority in that republic, which did not want to sever ties with the central government. Violence flared in Borovo Selo, a predominantly Serbian community in Croatia, on May 3, 1991, resulting in the deaths of more than a dozen Croatian police and Serbian civilians. Six days later Marković arrived at the scene, to the jeers of Serbs in the streets, who were touting a plan recently adopted by the collective presidency that called for the disarmament of all paramilitary groups and the creation of a commission to investigate the cause of the disputes between the two ethnic groups. Although the plan was accepted by both sides, it proved difficult to enforce and eventually gave way to renewed fighting.

The deepening ethnic divisions in the streets spilled over into the parliament on May 17, as Serbian lawmakers blocked what was supposed to be the routine election of Stipe Mesic, a Croat, to the office of president, as prescribed by the Yugoslav constitution, which mandates the rotation of the leadership of the collective presidency among the republics. The Serbs managed to delay Mesic's election for six weeks. Meanwhile, Marković embarked on a last-minute effort to forestall a declaration of independence by the northern republics. In an address to the Croatian parliament on June 24, he pleaded with his fellow citizens to rise above petty ethnic differences and to unite in making a stronger, economically self-sufficient Yugoslavia. "We must find a way of living together," he declared, as quoted in *The New York Times* (June 25, 1991). "We face the collapse of society. . . . We could find ourselves sitting on a bomb, which could blow us all up." Despite Marković's plea and stern warnings of the dangers of disunion from United States secretary of state James A. Baker 3d and several European foreign ministers, both Croatia and Slovenia voted to secede on June 25, although each continued to insist that a loose confederation was still an acceptable alternative to outright independence.

Some observers have argued that the West's attempts to discourage Slovenia and Croatia from seceding may have emboldened the Yugoslav army, which is dominated by a largely Serbian officer corps, to try to crush the rebellion by force. The army attacked swiftly on June 27, sending tanks, armored personnel carriers, and aircraft equipped with air-to-ground missiles into Slovenia. In short order the army seized the republic's main airport at Ljubljana and most of Slovenia's twenty-seven border posts. The army's lightning-fast crackdown fueled rumors that the Marković government had been toppled in a military coup. Although that turned out to be untrue, events seemed to be spinning out of the prime minister's control. "When you let the genie out of the bottle, it starts to act on its own," France Bucar, the president of the Slovenian parliament, complained, as quoted by Chuck Sudetic of *The New York Times* (June 29, 1991). "We're dealing with the fact that Mr. Marković, who in the world had the image of backing a peaceful resolution of the crisis, played the role of ordering the attack on Slovenia." But others questioned whether Marković had, in fact, sent the troops into

Slovenia, and most observers concluded that hard-line Serbian generals had masterminded the operation.

During a cease-fire negotiated with the help of the European Community, the Yugoslav army, without government authorization, delivered an ultimatum to Slovenia to abandon control of its borders with Italy, Austria, and Hungary. On June 30 Marković went on national television to declare that the army had acted on its own and that the troops had been ordered back to barracks. Although fighting erupted again on July 2, a three-month truce was arranged five days later, in which the Slovenes agreed to suspend all moves toward independence, deactivate their paramilitary forces, and allow army troops to withdraw to secure bases. In exchange, the government agreed to negotiate a new federal structure. Meanwhile, the Slovenian declaration of independence remained in effect, and Slovenian police were to operate the customs posts on the three foreign borders, with all duties to be shared with Belgrade.

With the crisis in Slovenia averted, at least temporarily, attention shifted to the other breakaway republic, Croatia. After the Croatian Democratic Union came to power in 1990, the republic's Serbian minority began mounting an armed resistance. Serbian president Milosevic at first only tacitly supported the rebellion with repeated criticisms of Croatia's treatment of the Serbs, but, as the insurrection gained momentum, he openly encouraged it. In a televised speech on July 6, 1991, Milosevic vowed to defend the rights of Serbs throughout Yugoslavia, even if Croatia succeeded in maintaining its independence. The Serbian rebellion in Croatia has been remarkably successful. In early August insurgents, possibly with the help of the Serbian-dominated Yugoslav army, captured many of the Croatian towns that border Serbia, and Croatian leaders acceded to rebel demands for greater autonomy.

PERSONAL LIFE

Ante Marković was a distinguished-looking man, with swept-back silver hair and dark bushy eyebrows. Little is known about his personal life. During his rare meetings with members of the Western press corps, reporters have invariably found him to have an ingratiating manner and a welcome sense of humor. "I am lifting Yugoslavia's optimism," he told David Binder in an interview for *The New York Times* (March 5, 1990). "I just hope I don't get a hernia."

Following the breakup of Yugoslavia, Marković disappeared from the public eye. He instead dedicated himself to a business career, working as an economic advisor to the Macedonian government. Marković died on November 28, 2011, after a short illness.

FURTHER READING

Christian Sci Mon p6 My 16 '89 por; *The New York Times* A p3 fa 20 '89, A p16 fe 25 '91 por, E p5 fe 30 '91 por; *International Who's Who*, 1991-92

VLADIMIR MECIAR (METCH-YAR)

Political Leader and Prime Minister of Slovakia

Born: July 26, 1942; Zvolen, Slovakia
Affiliation: People's Party Movement for a Democratic Slovakia

INTRODUCTION

Vladimir Meciar, "the man most responsible for the breakup of Czechoslovakia," according to Gareth G. Cook and Tim Snyder, writing in the Christian Science Monitor *(January 12, 1993), is a former lawyer and amateur boxer who joined the pro-democracy movement in his native Czechoslovakia in 1989, when communist regimes throughout Eastern Europe were in a state of collapse. While serving as prime minister of Slovakia,* historically the least industrialized and poorest region of Czechoslovakia, from June 1990 until April 1991, he was one of several politicians who supported the establishment of an autonomous Slovakia within the context of a loosely confederated state. Following the 1992 elections, in which he was returned to the prime ministership, he emerged as the most vocal advocate of this goal and went on to help craft the republic's independence and the dissolution of the Czechoslovak Federation—the so-called velvet divorce—which went into effect on January 1,1993. In March 1994 his opponents in parliament joined forces, and Meciar, after losing a vote of confidence, was removed from power.

Since he emerged in 1990 as Slovakia's popular politician, Meciar has always presented himself as a selfless public servant committed to improving the welfare of his people. While the Slovak electorate has bought this image, many Western observers as well as his opponents have viewed him as a political opportunist whose commanding presence and populist rhetoric serve to mask his demagogic personality, intolerance for dissent, and lack of respect for democratic institutions. "Meciar is not interested in constitutional government," Jan Carongursky, who served as Slovakia's prime minister in the period between Meciar's two terms in that office, was quoted as saying in the National Review *(July 6, 1992). "He wants to govern absolutely." Further tarnishing Meciar's record are allegations that he has ties to the state secret police and the KGB. Notwithstanding such charges, he has remained a popular figure in Slovakia—more popular, in fact, than the policies he has espoused. Few of his opponents are therefore willing to write him off, in spite of his recent fall from power. And as it turned out, Meciar, who repeatedly expressed confidence in his ability to win the 1994 election, which was held on September 30 and October 1, captured a plurality of the vote in the balloting, though whether he would succeed in forming a government was uncertain.*

EARLY LIFE

Vladimir Meciar was born on July 26, 1942, in Slovakia. According to one source, the place of his birth was Zvolen; others variously cite Trencin and Ziar nad Hronom as his hometown. At the age of seventeen, Vladimir Meciar became a clerk in the District National Committee in the same town. He later attended Komensky University, in Bratislava, the capital of Slovakia, and studied for a time in the Soviet Union.

LIFE'S WORK

Meciar got his first important positions in the Communist Party in the late 1960s, when he served as a senior official in the Communist Youth Movement in Slovakia and vice-chairman of the People's Control and Auditing Committee in Ziar nad Hronom's District National Committee. This period has become known as the Prague Spring, during which the then-Communist Party leader Alexander Dubcek launched a campaign to liberalize the country. Meciar was among those Communists who supported the reforms, and in 1970, two years after Warsaw Pact troops invaded the country in

an effort to crush the movement, Meciar and many other reformers were expelled from the Communist party. At about that time, Meciar entered law school. According to one source, in 1973 he became a lawyer for a company called Skloobal, in Nemsova, a position he held until 1990. Another source reported that he pursued his legal career in Trencin. He was also an amateur boxer. Like other supporters of the aborted reform movement, Meciar is said to have kept his politics to himself during these years, patiently awaiting the collapse of the Communist regime.

Meciar returned to political life in late 1989, during Czechoslovakia's democratic revolution, which is known as the 'Velvet revolution" because it was carried out peaceably, not violently, as was the case in the other East European countries then shedding their communist pasts. During this period thousands of Czechoslovaks, under the direction of dissident intellectuals, most notably the playwright and future federal president Vaclav Havel, demanded an end to Communist rule and the establishment of democracy in their country. For his part, Meciar joined Public Against Violence, a newly formed Slovakia-based party that, with its Czech counterpart, the Civic Forum, led the demonstrations that helped bring about the fall of the Communist regime.

In January 1990 Meciar was appointed interim minister of the interior—at Dubcek's suggestion, he has claimed. Following the June 1990 elections, the first democratic elections held in post-Communist Czechoslovakia, in which Public Against Violence won a plurality of the vote in Slovakia, Meciar was named prime minister of the Slovak republic. His principal task and greatest challenge was to manage Slovakia's transformation into a capitalist and democratic society. This required him to engage in negotiations with the federal government and the Czech republic on the future status of the nation and its constituent republics.

While the Slovaks and the Czechs agreed that one-party rule and their socialist-style economic system had to be abandoned in favor of a democracy with a market-based economy, they disagreed over how to carry out the transformation. Meciar, for instance, advocated implementing free-market principles gradually, while the Czechs wanted to charge rapidly into a capitalist future. Meciar was also concerned about the powers and rights of Slovakia vis-a-vis those of the federal government, and, to accommodate what he perceived as his fellow Slovaks' desire for a measure of self-rule, he proposed the establishment of a federation of two sovereign republics. The Czechs, on the other hand, wanted the federal government to remain the country's principal governing authority. "Once the children of the revolution had to define themselves, they started to go their separate ways," Theodore Draper wrote in the *New York Review of Books* (January 28, 1993).

Several months into Meciar's term, the Czech negotiators—and some Slovaks as well—began to view him as the principal obstacle to reaching an agreement. His opponents were also disturbed by what they saw as the increasingly authoritarian nature of his administration. As evidence, they pointed to Meciar's demand that his interior minister resign because of his efforts to dismantle the former communist secret-police networks at the ministry. When the minister refused, Meciar took steps to reduce his powers, and when that move failed to silence him, Meciar himself threatened to resign. At that point the public rallied to Meciar's defense and, in the end, the minister was forced to step down.

There were also allegations, made public by the parliamentary Slovak defense and security commission in 1991, that, during his tenure as interim interior minister, Meciar had destroyed secret-police files identifying him as a "right-wing extremist," that he had compiled information that could be used to blackmail his enemies, and that he had collaborated with the State Security police and the KGB. These charges, combined with Meciar's unwillingness to compromise with the Czechs over the country's future and his reputation for being manipulative and power-hungry, prompted the legislature of the Slovak republic, the Slovak National Council, to dismiss him as prime minister in April 1991, during a secret meeting from which he had been excluded.

As it turned out, Meciar's fall from power only enhanced his reputation among the Slovak masses. As Paul Wilson observed in the *New York Review of Books* (August 13,1992), "Meciar became a martyr to backroom politics directed from Prague—perhaps even from the Castle itself—and far from dislodging him from power, it strengthened his hand and won him widespread sympathy in Slovakia." And while he was stripped of nominal authority, Meciar was not rendered powerless. Following his discharge from office, he and his supporters formed a new political organization, the Movement for a Democratic Slovakia (Hnutie za Demokraticke Slovensko, or HZDS). By early 1992 it had emerged as the most popular political party in Slovakia, and Meciar, the republic's most popular politician.

The public's enthusiasm for Meciar was due at least in part to his renewed commitment to Slovakian self-determination. While he had long advocated a constitutional arrangement that would give the republic greater autonomy, he became increasingly outspoken in his support for this goal following his dismissal from the premiership. In so doing, he touched on a potentially explosive issue among Slovaks. Before World War I, when Slovakia was part of the Hungarian side of the Austro-Hungarian empire, the Slovak minority had been "Magyarized," or forced to adopt the cultural traditions of their Hungarian rulers. Following the war, the Czechs and Slovaks united to form Czechoslovakia, whose capital, and seat of power, was situated in Prague, in the Czech republic. Although the arrangement did little to ease the Slovaks' collective sense of inferiority, until the late 1980s their desire for self-determination for the most part lay dormant; they were apparently placated by the Communist regime's success in raising the standard of living of a majority of Slovaks, largely by establishing weapons manufacturing factories in the region, thus providing jobs.

The collapse of communism in Eastern Europe and the Soviet Union changed all that, for the Slovaks were thenceforth free to express their pent-up resentment of the Czechs. Moreover, the disintegration of the Soviet Union, Slovakia's principal market, and the closure of the republic's unprofitable arms factories exacerbated their anxiety over what appeared to be a bleak economic future. While Slovakian fears were real, Meciar's critics charged that he was not merely giving voice to the aspirations of the Slovak people; rather, in their view, he was ruthlessly exploiting Slovaks' insecurity over the economy and their collective identity for the sole purpose of gaining power. Perhaps because of his hold over ordinary Slovaks, his critics viewed Meciar, who was not alone in advocating that Slovakia be granted greater autonomy, as the most dangerous proponent of this position.

Meciar and his Movement for a Democratic Slovakia were still riding high in the polls when the campaign for the June 1992 elections got underway. His party's electoral prospects were enhanced by the fact that the federal government's economic plan had done little to improve economic conditions in the republic. Indeed, the unemployment there had risen to 12 percent, or four times the level in the Czech republic. The Czechs were also attracting significantly larger levels of foreign investment and experiencing a much higher rate of economic growth than were the Slovaks. This state of affairs seemed to confirm Meciar's contention that his fellow Slovaks were being given short shrift by the Czechs.

During the campaign, Meciar repeatedly assured his supporters that "Prague will no longer tell us what to do." He even led them in a version of Czechoslovakia's national anthem that omitted the first verse, which refers to the Czechs. While he stopped short of proposing that Slovakia become fully independent, he told his listeners that the prospect of a more autonomous Slovakia was considerably less frightening than that of a Slovakia continuing to chafe under an economic plan that, in his view, had been cavalierly imposed on them by the Czechs. "In [Meciar's] eyes, all Czechs melt down into the single image of the arrogant businessman who has little time for the honest, if slow, Slovak peasantry," Misha Glenny wrote in *New Statesman & Society* (June 19, 1992).

Adopting the same argument that he had used during his first term as prime minister, Meciar proposed that each republic become an autonomous entity, united by a central government whose powers would be restricted to dealing with common economic, defense, and foreign policy issues. His vision of Czechoslovakia's future was thus at odds with that promoted by federal president Vaclav Havel, who remained committed to a unified nation and who, on the eve of the election, in a thinly veiled reference to Meciar, urged Slovak voters to "resist all cheap and seductive appeals to nationalist emotion" and reject "people for whom power is more important than the fate of the nation." Havel's entreaties apparently had little effect. HZDS won a plurality of the vote—37 percent—and Meciar was named prime minister, replacing his old rival, Jan Carongursky. Apparently in retaliation for Havel's lack of support for Meciar, in July a majority of Slovak deputies blocked Havel's re-election to the federal presidency.

During the next few weeks, Meciar and the newly elected prime minister of the Czech Republic, Vaclav Klaus, a conservative economist who had been the driving force behind the federal government's radical economic reforms, tried to reach an agreement on the relationship between the two republics. Although neither had voiced support for the dissolution of Czechoslovakia during the 1992 election campaign, the policies to which each was committed were so incompatible that a formal separation soon emerged as a likely prospect. For instance, whereas Meciar argued that he had been

elected with the mandate of acquiring international recognition for an autonomous Slovakia, Klaus maintained that he could consider either a "reasonable and functional" federation or outright partition, nothing in between. And while Klaus wanted a central bank to pursue monetary policy and was committed to privatizing state-owned enterprises, Meciar demanded that each republic have its own central bank and that the state remain in control of industry.

The outcome of the negotiations seemed certain in August, when the two sides agreed to a formal separation of the country, scheduled to take place on January 1, 1993. Ironically, many Slovaks did not subscribe to Meciar's position on either the autonomy issue or economic reform, but they supported him nevertheless. As a Slovak businessman told Leslie Chang for the *Christian Science Monitor* (August 3, 1992), "You ask someone, 'Are you happy with Meciar's economic policy?' 'No.' 'Are you happy with his separatist policy?' 'No.' 'Who would you vote for if the election were tomorrow?' 'Meciar.'"

Meanwhile, Meciar was once again drawing the ire of his political opponents. They were troubled, for instance, by his decision to hold a by-invitation-only press conference following his party's 1992 electoral victory. Even more disconcerting was his renationalization of the company that prints every major newspaper in the republic and his attempt to strong-arm Slovakia's one television network into giving him a regular ten-minute spot during which he would address his fellow Slovaks. There were also concerns about his apparent insensitivity to the rights of Slovakia's Hungarian minority.

Following the dissolution of Czechoslovakia, members of Meciar's own party joined his critics in opposing his leadership. Increasingly, Meciar's government appeared to be mired in petty infighting and unable to deal with the country's enormous economic problems. His relations with several key government officials, including Michal Kovac, Slovakia's president, were especially strained. "The Movement [for a Democratic Slovakia]'s power stemmed from a destructive program; they were always against something," Karol Jezik, the editor of an opposition newspaper, told David Rocks in an interview for the *Chicago Tribune* (March 4,1993). "But to come up with a positive program now to rebuild Slovakia, that's beyond the capabilities of Vladimir Meciar and the Movement."

By early 1994 economic conditions in Slovakia had worsened. Inflation stood at 22 percent, economic activity had declined, unemployment had increased to more than 15 percent, and the privatization of state-owned enterprises was proceeding at an excruciatingly slow pace. According to political observers, much of the blame lay with Meciar, who had insisted on holding the government's key economic posts himself. He also insisted on formulating Slovakia's foreign policy and on representing Slovakia abroad whenever possible. The increasingly authoritarian nature of his rule prompted members of parliament to hold a vote of confidence. Meciar lost, seventy-eight to two, with seventy abstentions, and was forced to resign on March 11, 1994. Even his opponents acknowledge that he nonetheless remains a formidable political force. And, indeed, in the 1994 election, Meciar won 35 percent of the vote—more than any other candidate but not enough to form a government on his own.

Although Meciar made several more presidential bids, the Party was dissolved in 2014.

PERSONAL LIFE

Mark Frankland, writing in the London *Observer* (March 31,1991), described Vladimir Meciar as a "dark-haired, solidly built, and florid" man who "looks like a shrewd farmer, ... a bruiser with brains and humor." While Anthony Robinson and Patrick Blum, who interviewed him for the *Financial Times* (November 2,1993), acknowledged that he came across as a compelling and entertaining figure on the hustings, they found him in private to be "extraordinarily immobile, big but not tall, with a strong handshake and expressionless face in which only his eyes seem to move." With his wife, he has two sons and two daughters.

FURTHER READING

Financial Times pll N 2 '93 por; *Nat R* 44:22+ fl 6 '92; *New Statesman & Society* pl4+ Je 19 '92; *International Who's Who,* 1994-95

GOLDA MEIR

Prime Minister of Israel

Born: May 3, 1898; Kiev, Ukraine
Died: December 8, 1978; Jerusalem
Affiliation: Mapai; Labor Party

INTRODUCTION

In 1921 a young woman left her home and emigrated to Palestine because she felt that "the Jewish people had the right to one spot on earth where they could live as a free, independent people." As Premier of Israel, Golda Meir stood at the head of the Jewish homeland that she helped to create. After succeeding the late Levi Eshkol as Premier in March 1969, she directed her efforts toward maintaining the national security while seeking ways to establish a lasting peace settlement for the Middle East.

EARLY LIFE

Golda Meir was born Goldie Mabovitz (or Mabovich) in Kiev, the Ukraine, on May 3, 1898, one of the eight children of Moshe and Bluma (Neiditz) Mabovitz. Her five brothers all died in childhood. She also has two sisters. Recalling the fears of Cossacks and peasant mobs bent on pogroms that haunted her during her childhood in Czaxist Russia, Mrs. Meir has said: "If there is any logical explanation . . . for the direction which my life has taken ... [it is] the desire and determination to save Jewish children . . . from a similar experience."

When Golda was five her father, a skilled carpenter and cabinetmaker, decided to seek his fortune in the United States and sent his family to Pinsk, the mother's hometown. In 1906 the family was reunited in Milwaukee, where they lived in a poor Jewish neighborhood. While the father looked for work, often without success, the mother operated a small grocery store. Even after the father found steady employment as a railroad worker, the family barely subsisted on the combined incomes. At Milwaukee's Fourth Street elementary school, Golda soon headed her class. She attended North Division High School for one term but left after an argument with her parents, who objected to her ambition to become a schoolteacher, and went to Denver to live with her married sister, Shana.

In Denver she attended high school, helped out in her brother-in-law's dry-cleaning establishment, and listened with fascination to the young Socialists and Zionists who congregated at her sister's home. At

Affiliation: Israeli Labor Party

The Labor Party is associated with supporting the Israeli–Palestinian peace process, pragmatic foreign affairs policies and social democratic economic policies. The Party, established in 1968, is a social democratic and Zionist political party. Until 1977, all Israeli Prime Ministers were affiliated with the Labor movement. Isaac Herzog has been its leader since 2013.

sixteen, having obtained her parents' approval of her plans to become a teacher, she returned to Milwaukee and reentered North Division High School where she graduated as vice-president of her class. She then attended the Milwaukee Teachers' Training College while working as a librarian at a local branch library and teaching part time in a neighborhood Yiddish folk school.

LIFE'S WORK

Meanwhile, her interests in Socialism and Zionism had begun to crystallize. Rejecting both anarchism and Marxist ideology, she was drawn to the democratic Socialism of Eugene V. Debs. In 1915 she joined the Poale Zion, a small, Yiddish-speaking faction of the Socialist-oriented Labor Zionists, and she soon became an eloquent street-corner speaker for the Zionist cause. Her father, who recoiled at the thought of his daughter speaking on street corners, threatened on one occasion to drag her off the platform "by her braid," but recanted after hearing her speak. Although she graduated from Teachers' Training College in 1917, she gave up her dream of a teaching career and became a full-time staff member of Poale Zion at a salary of $15 a week.

Golda Mabovitz was married on December 24, 1917 to Morris Myerson (or Meyerson), a sign painter, whom she had met in Denver. (The name Meir, which she adopted in 1956, is a Hebraicized version of Myerson.) By that time she had become convinced that her future lay in the Jewish homeland. A meeting with David Ben-Gurion, who was touring the United States in behalf of Zionism, was a major factor in her decision. In 1921 she persuaded her reluctant husband to sail with her to Palestine as a member of the third *aliyah,* or wave of immigration. The Myersons joined the Kibbutz Merhavia, ten miles south of Nazareth, in a marshy, malaria-ridden region. There

Golda Meir picked almonds, raised chickens, took care of children, and studied Hebrew and Arabic. "My first impression of Palestine was discouraging," she admitted in an interview with Michael J. Berlin in the New York *Post* (March 8, 1969). "Quinine was served daily with each meal. But in the moonlit evenings we would dance the Hora and sing songs of pioneer Palestine." Although she soon became a respected member of the kibbutz community, her husband chafed under its pressures.

By 1923 Morris Myerson had become convinced that he could never adjust to kibbutz life, and the couple moved to Tel Aviv, where Golda Meir took an office job with the Office of Public Works of Histadrut (Israel Labor Federation). In 1924 she was made treasurer of the agency—which later became Solel Boneh, Histadrut's contracting company. After the birth of their first child the Myersons moved to Jerusalem. To make ends meet, Golda Meir had to take in laundry, while her husband worked for a pittance as a bookkeeper. She looks back upon the years 1924 to 1928 as the most wretched of her life.

In 1928 she went back to work for the labor movement as secretary of the Moetzet Hapoalot (Women's Labor Council) and as its representative on the Vaad Hapoel, the executive committee of the Histadrut. During her two decades with the council she was its representative at international conferences. In 1928-29 she was a delegate to the council's American Zionist counterpart, the Pioneer Women's Organization, and from 1932 to 1934 she lived in the United States while serving as the organization's national secretary.

Mrs. Meir became active in the World Zionist movement in 1929, when she was elected a delegate of the Ahdut Haavoda faction to the World Zionist Congress. After Ahdut Haavoda merged with another labor group in 1939 to form the Mapai labor party she served as a Mapai delegate to the international congresses. During the 1930's she went on a number of missions to Europe and the United States in behalf of the World Zionist Organization and the Jewish Agency for Palestine. She also served in the executive of the Vaad Leumi (National Council), the chief organ of Jewish self-government under the British mandate. In addition, she was on the executive boards of several Histadrut enterprises, including a medical fund, an aviation company, and a shipping concern. By 1936 she was in charge of all of the Histadrut's mutual aid programs and was chairman of the board of directors of Kupat Holim, which provided medical services for almost half of Palestine's Jewish population. In 1940 she was named head of the

Histadrut's political department, which dealt with foreign relations. During World War II she also served on the British War Economic Advisory Council.

In the post-World War II struggle to establish a Jewish homeland, Mrs. Meir sided with the activist faction headed by Ben-Gurion, who insisted that Jews should act as though an independent Jewish state were already in existence. When the British, in June 1946, arrested most of the executive members of the Jewish Agency, Golda Meir became acting head of the agency's political department—he top position of authority in the Jewish community of Palestine. She occupied that post for several months in the crucial period that preceded Israeli independence. In January 1948 she went to the United States and collected some $50,000,000 for Israel. On the eve of independence Mrs. Meir, in an unsuccessful effort to allay Arab opposition to the establishment of the Jewish state, dressed as an Arab woman and secretly crossed the border into Jordan to meet with King Abdullah.

On May 14, 1948 Mrs. Meir was among the signers of the proclamation of independence of the state of Israel and became the only woman member of the provisional council of state, its first legislature. In September 1948 she was sent to Moscow as Israel's first minister to the Soviet Union. Her simple act of going to Moscow's only synagogue for Rosh Hashanah services set off a spontaneous pro-Israel demonstration by more than 40,000 Jews. She was elected to the first Knesset (Parliament) in January 1949 as a candidate of the Mapai, Israel's strongest political party. Returning from Moscow in April 1949, she took office as Minister of Labor and Social Insurance in Premier David Ben-Gurion's government and remained in that post until 1956. An architect of Israel's national insurance plan, Mrs. Meir was also responsible for providing employment and housing for hundreds of thousands of new immigrants to the young nation. She remembers her seven years with the Labor Ministry as "the happy days," pointing out that "building modem housing for people who have lived in huts, even in caves," was "something to live for."

When Moshe Sharett-Israel's Premier from 1953 to 1955—resigned as Minister for Foreign Affairs in June 1956, Ben-Gurion, who had again become head of the government, appointed Golda Meir as Sharett's successor. Her staunch support of Ben-Gurion's policy of swift retaliation against Arab attacks prompted the Premier to call her "the only man in my Cabinet." Mrs. Meir recalls that one of her saddest duties was to stand before the United Nations in 1957 during the Suez crisis and announce that Israel would comply with a demand by the great powers to withdraw her troops after a victorious sweep through the Sinai peninsula.

Although Israel was originally neutral in the cold war, the growing hostility of the Soviet Union and the unwillingness of "third world" nations to accept the Jewish state caused the country to turn more and more to the West. One area in which Israel met with some success was in its program of technical aid to emerging nations of Africa, which developed into a major feature of Israel's foreign policy. In 1965 Israel established diplomatic relations with the Federal Republic of Germany, a step that, as Mrs. Meir remarked at the time, produced a debate "between the head and the heart" for every Israeli, From 1953 to 1966 she also served each year as chairman of the Israeli delegation to the U.N. General Assembly.

In early 1966 Mrs. Meir resigned her Cabinet post and accepted the less challenging position of secretary general of the Mapai party. With the merger of the major labor factions—Mapai, Rafi and Ahdut Haavoda—into the united Israel Labor party in February 1968. Mrs. Meir became secretary general of the new organization. Meanwhile, the Middle East situation again exploded. After hostilities broke out on June 5, 1967 the Israelis defeated the armies of Egypt, Syria, Jordan, and Iraq and captured the Gaza Strip, the Sinai Peninsula, the eastern section of Jerusalem, the west bank of the Jordan, and the Golan Heights of Syria. A cease-fire, arranged by the U.N., halted the fighting on June 10, 1967.

In July 1968 Mrs. Meir resigned her party post. Although her decision may have been partly motivated by poor health and advancing age, the main reason for her resignation may have been the fact that she had been outvoted on important political issues. Her retirement was short-lived. In February 1969 Levi Eshkol, who had succeeded Ben-Gurion as Premier in 1963, suffered a fatal heart attack. Although she no longer held any official position, Mrs. Meir, a friend and confidante of the late Premier, was summoned to an urgent meeting of Cabinet members and leaders of the Labor party to help choose an interim Premier who would serve until the general elections scheduled for October. The leading candidates were Defense Minister Moshe Dayan and Deputy Prime Minister Yigal Allon. Mrs. Meir favored Allon, considering the flamboyant Dayan a maverick.

Fearing that a power struggle might split the party, the delegates bypassed Allon and Dayan and chose Golda Meir. On March 17, 1969 Mrs. Meir was sworn in by

Israeli President Zalman Shazar as the fourth Premier of Israel. In her inaugural address she asserted that Israel would continue to demand "face to face talks" with the leaders of Arab nations as a prerequisite for a peace settlement and expressed the hope that friendly nations would understand that "our fate cannot be determined by others." In her first few months Mrs. Meir infused the office of Premier with new vigor and took steps to forge unity within the faction-ridden Labor party.

In the general elections of October 28, 1969 the Labor party lost its majority, although it remained the strongest party, with fifty-six of the 120 seats in the Knesset. Mrs. Meir continued as Premier but was forced to form a new, twenty-four-member Cabinet, which included representatives of six parties, ranging from the leftist Mapam to the right-wing Gahal party. It was approved by the Knesset on December 15, 1969. Meanwhile, the 1967 cease-fire had become virtually nonexistent. In September 1969 Mrs. Meir visited President Richard Nixon in Washington, D.C. in an effort to obtain needed armaments. She reiterated Israel's insistence on direct talks with the Arabs and rejection of any peace plan that might be imposed by the great powers.

On July 31, 1970 the Israeli Cabinet, urged by Premier Meir and Defense Minister Dayan, finally accepted a United States formula for a limited cease-fire and the opening of peace talks with the United Arab Republic. The Israeli leaders, who had been unresponsive to previous American peace initiatives, reportedly agreed to the proposal after receiving assurances of Israel's security from President Nixon. The agreement prompted the six members of the Gahal faction to resign from the Cabinet. After a ninety-day cease-fire went into effect on August 7, 1970 Mrs. Meir told the Knesset that the U.N.-sponsored peace talks would try to achieve "a contractual peace established on defensible, agreed borders" between Israel and Egypt Addressing the U.N. General Assembly on October 22, 1970, Mrs. Meir declared that Israel was willing to continue the cease-fire "without a time limit." She appealed to Arab leaders "to recognize once and for all that the future of the Middle East lies in peace and this must be achieved by the Israelis and Arabs themselves."

Although 92 percent of Israelis approve of her foreign policy according to a 1970 public opinion poll, Mrs. Meir has riot been immune to criticism. Her repudiation of World Jewish Congress president Nahum Goldmann's effort to meet with Gamal Abdel Nasser in April 1970 touched off a wave of controversy, as did her declaration of support of President Nixon's Southeast Asian policy in November 1969. Convinced that the Arab nations bear the primary responsibility for the Palestinian refugee problem, she feels, nevertheless, that the problem could be resolved within the context of a general peace settlement. As for Israel's "image," Golda Meir has said: "If we have to have a choice between being dead and pitied, and being alive with a bad image, we'd rather be alive and have the bad image." A volume of her selected papers, *This Is Our Strength*, with a foreword by Eleanor Roosevelt, was published by Macmillan in 1962. She held honorary degrees from the Reform Jewish Hebrew Union College and the University of Wisconsin.

PERSONAL LIFE

Golda Meir was separated from her husband in 1945; he died in Tel Aviv in 1951. Her son, Menachem Myerson, is a concert cellist who studied with Pablo Casals. Her daughter, Mrs. Sara Rehavi, lives at Revivim, a kibbutz near Beersheba. Mrs. Meir, who dotes on her five grandchildren, is affectionately called "Golda Shelanu" ("Our Golda") by Israelis. Five feet five inches tall, she dressed simply, disliked makeup, and wore her dark gray hair in a bun. Her favorite recreations included reading and listening to her large collection of classical recordings. She was fond of cooking, and often at late Cabinet meetings she prepares omelets or chicken soup for her aides. In 1969 she ranked fourth on the list of women most admired by Americans.

Meir resigned as Prime Minister in 1974 and died of lymphoma in 1978.

FURTHER READING

The New York Times Mag p52 + O 26; '69 pors; *Time* 94:28+ S 19; '69 por; Shenker, Israel and Mary. *As Good as Golda* (1970); Syrkin, Marie. *Golda Meir; Israel's Leader* (1969); *Who's Who in Israel, 1968*; *Who's Who in World Jewry* (1965)

ADNAN MENDERES

Prime Minister of Turkey

Born: 1899; Ottoman Empire
Died: September 17, 1961; Turkey
Affiliation: Democrat Party Founder

INTRODUCTION

Prime Minister Adnan Menderes was a key figure in the development of his country into a bulwark for the free world in the strategic Mediterranean area. Menderes, a lawyer and progressive farmer, was appointed to the Premiership by Turkey's President Celal Bayar after the elections of May 1950 when the Democratic party defeated the long-dominant Republican People's party. He was renamed Prime Minister after the May 1954 elections and was active in fostering collective measures for military security of the Balkan countries and also through the North Atlantic Treaty Organization (NATO).

The overwhelming victory of the Democratic party in the 1954 general election has been regarded as a clear endorsement of the policies of the Menderes' government during the past four years to encourage private enterprise at home and to cooperate with the Western powers in international affairs. At the invitation of the U.S. government, the Turkish Prime Minister visited the United States in June 1954 for conferences on American aid to Turkish military and economic growth. The fostering of close Turkish-American relations in collective security undertakings, Menderes said, was based upon "the mutual trust and identity of viewpoint" which exists between the two countries.

EARLY LIFE

Adnan Menderes was born in a small town near Izmir (Smyrna), Turkey in 1899. Following his graduation from the American College in Izmir, he studied at the University of Ankara, where he received a degree in law. He then returned to his family farm and introduced modern methods of agriculture.

While working as a political organizer in his district, Menderes came to the attention of Kemal Ataturk, who in 1923-1924 had created the Republic of Turkey on the ruins of the Ottoman Empire and had become President of the new state. Elected to the National Assembly in 1930, Menderes took part in the government controlled by Ataturk's Republican People's party, a totalitarian political organization which sought to extend Turkey's Westernizing revolution through a system of state capitalism.

LIFE'S WORK

The sweeping victory of the Democratic party candidates for the National Assembly in 1950 brought to an end the twelve-year tenure of President Ismet Indnii, Ataturk's successor. Soon after he was named President of Turkey by the assembly, Celal Bayar appointed Menderes as Prime Minister. The new party program that Menderes announced to the assembly on May 29 included granting workers the right to strike, passage of a liberal press law, curtailment of government expenditures, transfer of state-controlled industries to private enterprise, and encouragement of foreign investments in developing the country's resources. In the by-elections of 1951 the Democratic party won eighteen out of twenty contested seats in the National Assembly.

Because of a dispute over internal matters in March 1951, Menderes submitted the resignation of his

---

Affiliation: Democrat Party Founder

In 1946, Menderes joined Celal Bayar and other political associates in organizing the Democratic party, thus introducing a genuine two-party system into the country. For the next four years he was one of the leaders of the opposition in the National Assembly. A speech by him in 1947, charging fraud in certain elections to the assembly, made him the center of a free-press controversy. The trial which followed publication of his speech in several newspapers vindicated freedom of the press. As Menderes' new party gained in popularity, it attracted the support of the Turkish peasantry.

Claiming political descent from Ataturk (who had died in 1938), the Democrats remained attached to the reforms instituted by the beloved national hero, at the same time that they advocated a system of free enterprise to replace the state-owned business operations of the Republican People's party. This difference in objectives was the chief issue between the two political groups in the general election of May 14, 1950.

Cabinet, but was at once asked by President Bayar to form a new government. The Associated Press stated at this time that Menderes' administration had been criticized for presenting a deficit budget and for failing in its election promise to reduce the cost of living. An unfavorable attitude toward what it considered the inflationary policies of Menderes' government has also reportedly been held by the International Bank for Reconstruction and Development, whose mission in Ankara was closed in March 1954 on the demand of Turkey (*The New York Times,* March 21, 1954).

The Democratic party's first four years in power saw the standard of living in Turkey reach a point hitherto never achieved. In an interview with Joseph Fromm of the *US. News & World Report* (December 7, 1951) Menderes discussed his party's goal of securing the development of free enterprise and of transferring state-owned industrial plants to private business. "I am convinced that free and private enterprise," the Prime Minister emphasized, "is the only system which can give the greatest impetus to economic development."

As part of its program to encourage private initiative the Menderes government provided facilities and guarantees for the investment of foreign private capital in Turkey; it also passed a law permitting foreign groups to share in the development of the country's petroleum resources. Through financial, economic and technical aid from abroad—especially from the United States—Turkish agricultural production and mineral output have been increased and new roads have been built throughout the nation. Turkey is now the fourth largest wheat exporting country in the world.

Consistent with its policy of cooperation with the West, soon after the outbreak of the Korean War Menderes' Cabinet decided to send Turkish troops to Korea to fight with United Nations forces. Menderes believes that "those who fought in Korea for the security of the free world were also defending their homelands.... The struggle in Korea has shown that the great principles behind the United Nations are something more than mere words."

Turkey's application for admission to NATO in the summer of 1950 was also viewed by some observers as evidence of the government's greater initiative in matters of military preparedness and collective security. Reviewing Turkish foreign policy of the past four years, Fuat Koprulii, Minister of Foreign Affairs in Menderes' Cabinet, disclosed in February 1954 that the United States had given Turkey $954,000,000 in military aid since 1950 and $237,000,000 in economic grants. He

also announced that NATO had approved expenditures of $135,458,000 for building military bases and installations in Turkey during the next few years.

"The real directing force behind the Democratic party"—these are the words used by Welles Hangen of *The New York Times* (May 2, 1954) to describe the Prime Minister's political power. "He is uncontested master of the party today," Hangen continues, "although he has won many enemies by his ruthless suppression of opposition." Menderes was criticized at home and abroad in 1952 for proposing a bill to protect his Cabinet ministers from insult by making adverse criticism punishable by law.

The National Assembly in March 1954 adopted a measure prescribing prison sentences and fines for newspaper reporters whose published statements "could be harmful to the political or financial prestige of the state." Defending the bill, the Prime Minister, who denied an attempt to curb freedom of the press, maintained that restraint was necessary against excessive vilification of officials.

The general election of May 2, 1954 returned the Democratic party to power with 58.4 per cent of the votes cast. In the National Assembly, which will remain in session until 1958, the Democrats gained 503 seats, while other parties won a total of thirty-eight. (The Communist party, outlawed in Turkey, is not represented in this group.) Menderes, who was renamed Prime Minister, interpreted the election results primarily as an endorsement of his government's foreign policy.

An important aspect of this policy has been Menderes' efforts to improve collective measures for peace and security. On a visit to Greece in May 1952 he stopped at the island of Spetsai, once a stronghold of resistance against the Ottoman Turks. "The suave Turkish leader," reported the *Christian Science Monitor* (May 3, 1952), "won all hearts, when, speaking in excellent Greek he told the islanders he brought 'greetings, love and friendship from Turkey to Greece....' "

Since strengthening Turkey's ties with Greece and Yugoslavia through the Balkan "friendship and collaboration" pact of February's, 1953, Menderes has been interested in integrating the Balkan agreement with NATO, thus militarily allying Italy and Yugoslavia in common defense. "Collective security," the Prime Minister said, "can be effective only when it presents a continuous front without gaps" (*The New York Times,* June 6, 1954).

An editorial in the *Washington Post* (June 4, 1954) has expressed the view that if Menderes "is able to lay the groundwork for a Trieste settlement he will have established his country as the diplomatic as well as the military leader of the Mediterranean area." On August 9, 1954 a twenty-year treaty was signed by the foreign ministers of Turkey, Greece and Yugoslavia, agreeing that an act of aggression against one or more of them would be considered against them all, and providing for political and military cooperation and mutual aid. This treaty had the effect of linking Yugoslavia indirectly with NATO of which both Turkey and Greece are members. *Time* magazine (August 23, 1954) commented: "The new Balkan pact, in effect, closes the last gap in NATO's ring around Europe, which begins in Iceland and extends to Mount Ararat."

With another neighbor, Pakistan, in early April 1954, Turkey signed a mutual defense and economic cooperation pact, in an attempt to create a collective security system in the Middle East. Menderes and Mohammed Ali, Prime Minister of Pakistan, met at Ankara in June to discuss measures to "widen the scope" of the treaty, "presumably by adding such neighbors as Iraq and Iran" *(Newsweek,* June 21, 1954).

The Turkish statesman made his first trip to the United States in early June 1954 when he was invited to confer with government officials on American aid for Turkey's future economic and military development. Maintenance of a large defense force, it has been pointed out, imposes an economic burden upon the country that it cannot bear without external assistance (Turkey has a standing army of about 450,000). At the end of Menderes' four-day visit in Washington it was announced that the United States would grant Turkey about $200,000,000 in military aid during the coming year and about $70,000,000 in economic aid, and would speed up movement of $500,000,000 worth of military equipment "in the present pipeline" (*The New York Times,* June 6, 1954).

PERSONAL LIFE

Prime Minister Menderes was married and the father of a son, Aydin, and two other children. He was said to be an eloquent speaker, with great personal power over political and governmental affairs. A New York *Herald Tribune* editorial (June 2, 1954) described him as "a Liberal in the old tradition and a doughty champion of his own principles."

In 1960, a military coup organized by officers deposed the government, and Menderes was arrested along with the leading party members. Charged with violating the constitution and embezzling money, Menderes was put on trial and sentenced to death. He was executed on September 17, 1961, despite pleas from several world leaders including President John F. Kennedy and Elizabeth II of the UK.

FURTHER READING

N Y Herald Tribune p22 Je 2 '54; II pi Je 6 '54 por; *The New York Times* pl7 My 2 '54; p26 Je 1 '54; *Reporter* 10:22 Ja 19 '54; *International Who's Who,* 1954

PIERRE MENDÈS-FRANCE
Prime Minister of France

Born: January 11, 1907; Paris, France
Died: October 18, 1982; Paris, France
Affiliation: Radical Socialism

INTRODUCTION

Upon the resignation of the Laniel Government in June 1954, President Rene Coty of France called on Pierre Mendès-France, a Radical Socialist, to assume the premiership. A brilliant lawyer, economist and the mayor of Louyiers, Mendès-France was known as "the pitiless gadfly of French politics", frequently criticizing the policies of various Cabinets of the Fourth Republic.

Believing France's position in world affairs depended upon her withdrawal from the war in Indochina and the renovation of her antiquated economy, Mendès-France made these two issues the cornerstone of his policy. He also placed emphasis upon establishing peace and: sequrity in North Africa, and upon giving the Western powers France's answer on the European Defense Community (EDC).

EDC, designed to rearm West Germany within a European army, was rejected by the French National Assembly on August 30, 1954 by a vote of 319 to 264 to postpone indefinitely further debate. After the vote, Premier Mendès-France said that he had "long warned . . . friends and allies" that there was no majority for the treaty in the Assembly, and that "new solutions should be studied rapidly" (The New York Times, August 31, 1954).

At the nine power conference in London held shortly afterwards, Mendès-France and other Western leaders signed, on October 3, 1954, the Final Act of London which is designed to integrate, Germany politically and militarily in Western Europe. On October 13 the National Assembly gave Mendès-France a vote of confidence to continue negotiations to carry out the Final Act.

EARLY LIFE

Pierre Mendès-France was born on January 11, 1907 in Paris to a dress manufacturer who was descended from a long line of Sephardic Jewish dealers of cloth. His mother was the former Palmyre Calin. His maternal grandmother, a devout Orthodox Jew, was responsible for Pierre's religious training. There are several theories about the origin of Mendès-France's hyphenated name. A cousin believes that it derives from Mendoza, and that upon expulsion from Spain in 1492, the French branch of the family added "France" to differentiate themselves from those who settled elsewhere. Pierre Mendès-France believes that his name originates from an alliance between the Mendès and Franco families in either Spain or Portugal prior to the fourteenth century.

Young Mendès-France attended public schools and the College Turgot. Later he matriculated simultaneously at the Faculte de Droit and the Ecole des Sciences Politiques of the Universite de Paris. At the age of eighteen he received the doctor's degree in law, first in a class of 800. He also received a diploma in political science.

During his student days he was the leader of a group at the Faculte de Droit, which became involved in a street fracas with Royalist students, from which he emerged with a misshapen nose. By passing his bar examinations at the age of twenty-one, he became the youngest lawyer in France.

At sixteen, Mendès-France had enrolled in the Radical Socialist party (comprised of conservative business men) to which his father belonged. He established residence in Louviers, with a view to entering politics when he became legally eligible for office. He wrote an economic study, *UOeuvre Financiere du Gouvernment Poincare* (published in 1928), which favorably impressed then Premier Raymond Poincare.

LIFE'S WORK

Running on the Radical Socialist ticket in 1932, he became the youngest member of the Chamber of Deputies. When Leon Blum formed his second Popular Front ministry in 1938, the young Radical Socialist was named Under Secretary of State to the Treasury, a position which brought him into contact with Georges Boris, Blum's chief of cabinet, who is today Mendès-France's closest adviser. After four weeks of tenure, the Cabinet fell when a measure for economic mobilization prepared by Mendès-France was rejected. (He has consistently been a member of the French parliament, except through the World War II period.)

In September 1939 the politician entered the French air force as a lieutenant, and was assigned to Syria. On leave in Paris when the Germans entered the city in June 1940, he accompanied his family to Bordeaux, and then went to North Africa. There he was arrested (on a charge of desertion from the French Army) by officials of the Vichy Government, and sentenced to six years in prison. He escaped by climbing down a rope of bed sheets and took refuge in Grenoble. Later he joined General Charles de Gaulle's Free French forces in London, and participated in raids over Germany and France.

Summoned to Algiers by General de Gaulle in November 1943, Mendès-France was named commissioner of finance of the Committee of National Liberation. In its behalf he signed the Franco-British monetary agreement of February 1944. Six months later, he headed the French delegation to the Bretton Woods Monetary Conference. He represented France on the board of governors of the International Monetary Fund, and also served as an alternate governor of the International Bank for Reconstruction and Development.

Following the liberation of Paris, Mendès-France in September 1944 was appointed Minister of the National Economy, in de Gaulle's Provisional Government, a post he held until January 1945, when the rejection of his economic plan—stringent rationing, suppression of the black market, ceilings on wages and prices, limitation of paper money, capital levies on profits, and blockage of bank accounts—caused him to resign. Mendès-France's anti-inflationary policies were in conflict with the inflationary measures of Rene Pleven, the Finance Minister. De Gaulle at first sought to make peace between them, and refused Mendès-France's resignation, but ultimately, in April 1945 accepted it.

For a long period Pierre Mendès-France refused offers of ministerial posts, and confined himself to opposing the inflationary policies of successive Cabinets and to serving on technical missions for the French government, as delegate to the 1946 Savannah monetary conference, and as member of the French delegation to the United Nations Economic and Social Council from 1947 to 1950.

When it became apparent that the disorganized French economy and the drain on it by the war in Indochina required a new policy, Mendès-France in June 1953 was invited to form a Cabinet, but upon presenting his program to the National Assembly, he missed the necessary approval by a margin of only thirteen votes—301 to 119, with 205 abstentions. When Premier Joseph Laniel resigned on June 12, 1954, Mendès-France, as the foremost opponent of the outgoing ministry, was asked by President Rene Coty to form a new Cabinet. Six days later, he achieved the necessary majority vote of 419 to 47 with 143 abstentions. Although he had categorically refused to accept the premiership if it depended upon Communist votes, he received ninety-five ballots from Communists. These votes were not needed to give him the required number of supporters.

Genet in the *New Yorker* (July 10, 1954) declared that "the poorer class, and the topmost educated class, are the most enthusiastic about him, the middle class the least." He created a new portfolio for Moroccan and Tunisian affairs, and, deciding to retain the foreign affairs ministry for himself, called upon relatively young and new men for his twenty-nine member Cabinet "instead of playing musical chairs as other postwar premiers have done" (*Business Week,* June 26, 1954). He also required rigorously efficient methods for the operation of his staff, and put a stop to the traditional practice of leaking Cabinet secrets to the press prematurely.

Immediately after accepting the premiership, Mendès-France went to Geneva to discuss the essential points of a cease-fire agreement in Indochina with Chou En-lai, Premier and Foreign Minister of Communist China. He again went to Geneva in July to pursue the major part of the negotiations, in which Great Britain's Foreign Minister Anthony Eden also participated (U.S. Under Secretary of State Walter Bedell Smith was present at the request of the French Premier). Mendès-France had, said *Commonweal,* "a unique factor of strength behind him: the remarkably united support of the French people." France, Viet-Nam, Laos, and Vietminh signed an agreement effective July 22, while Cambodia signed a separate agreement effective July 23. In reporting to the French Assembly the Premier said: "I have no illusions ... as to

the contents of the agreements. Their text is sometimes cruel . . . but the best we could hope for under the circumstances" (*Christian Science Monitor,* July 23, 1954).

The agreement, approved by a 462 to 13 vote of the National Assembly, provided for the division of Viet-Nam roughly along the seventeenth parallel, thus leaving the city of Hanoi and the port of Haiphong in the Communist area, for the free passage to the South of any of the northern area's 12,000,000 inhabitants who preferred not to remain under Communist rule, for general elections in 1956, and for supervision of the implementation of the truce by Canada, India, and Poland. Hanson W. Baldwin of *The New York Times* characterized the truce as "a personal triumph for the French Premier but also a national defeat."

Turning slightly more than a week later to what he called "the next act of the drama," Mendès-France "flew to Tunisia, and this, together with his offer of a program of genuine internal autonomy to the Tunisians . . . had the appeal of the spectacular." On July 30, his Cabinet had approved the Premier's plan to turn over the administration of all internal affairs to the Tunisians, while the control of defense and foreign affairs would remain under French jurisdiction.

Approved by the Tunisian Bey Sidi Mohammed al-Amin and the interned leader of the nationalist Neo-Destour party, Habib Bourguiba, the Tunisians immediately began formation of a Cabinet to negotiate the details of the autonomy which they had demanded since 1947, all negotiations to be contingent, as Mendès-France had specified, on the restoration of order and suppression of the prevailing terrorism against French colonists in the region.

To recoup France's perilous economic condition, the Premier on August 10 presented what he characterized as his "New Deal" to the National Assembly, which by a vote of 361 to 90 thereupon granted him extensive economic powers, effective until March 31, 1955. Based primarily on the necessity for modernizing France's antiquated industrial plants, the long-range plan also provided for the elimination of unnecessary subsidies, the liberalization of foreign and domestic trade, agricultural reforms, reorganization of the social security system and of nationalized industries, increased housing, diminished protectionism, freer competition, elimination of marginal businesses, and establishment of governmental funds for the aid of relocated workers.

Toward the middle of August, the Premier undertook the solution of the long-existent deadlock in the Assembly on ratification of EDC which had already been ratified by the parliaments of four other nations. Visiting Brussels at that time, Mendès-France laid before the representatives of Western Germany, the Netherlands, Belgium, Luxembourg, and Italy a number of modifications which would be more acceptable to the National Assembly. The proposals included a veto for each nation in the administration of the European army, the right of France to maintain its own separate army in addition to its forces in EDC, and the denial of such a right to Germany.

Rejection of his modifications by the five ministers led the Premier to fly to England on August 23 in order to obtain Sir Winston Churchill's assurance that Great Britain would join EDC or an alternate organization as well as France; this, too, met with rejection. When the matter came up for debate before the French National Assembly on August 28, the Premier disassociated the vote on the measure from one on confidence in his Government. In his three-hour speech to the Assembly that day, Mendès-France, who maintained his personally objective attitude to the problem, pointed out that failure to approve the EDO provisions for a supranational army would require an alternative vote to approve the Bonn treaty, which would allow sovereignty to Western Germany.

The New York Times (August 31, 1954) called the defeat of EDC by the National Assembly "the greatest postwar triumph for Soviet policy," and stated that "the primary responsibility" must rest on Premier Mendès-France, "who refused to fight for the Community project." However, *The New York Times* pointed out that the Premier "has recognized that neither German sovereignty nor German rearmament can be delayed indefinitely." Three of his Cabinet members resigned before the Brussels conference and three more have resigned since the vote on EDC.

Nine powers—Belgium, Canada, France, German Federal Republic, Italy, Luxembourg, "Netherlands, Britain, and United States—signed the Final Act on October 3, 1954.

The agreement provides that the occupation of the German Federal Republic will be ended, the Brussels treaty will be expanded to include Germany and Italy and its signatory powers will establish an agency for control of armaments on the Continent for its members, and the eight members of the North Atlantic Treaty Organization that were present agreed to recommend that Germany be invited to become a member of NATO. Britain gave assurances that she will maintain four divisions and a tactical air force on the Continent.

The Final Act was considered by many observers a victory for the French Premier. It received the implied approval by the National Assembly on October 13, 1954 by a vote of confidence that will enable the Mendès-France Government to complete the negotiations in accordance with the agreement of October 3. The vote was 350 to 113 with 152 abstentions.

His cabinet fell in February 1955. In 1956 he served as Minister of State in the cabinet headed by Guy Mollet, but resigned over Algeria, which was beginning to dominate French politics. He then resigned as party leader in 1957.

In 1967 he returned to the Assembly as a PSU member for the Isère, but again lost his seat in the 1968 landslide election victory of the Gaullist party. When François Mitterrand formed a new Socialist Party in 1971, Mendès France supported him, but did not attempt another political comeback of his own.

PERSONAL LIFE

On December 26, 1933 Mendès-France married Lily Cicurel, a talented portrait painter; they have two sons, Bernard and Michel. He was said to have few amusements, other than skiing and playing the piano; he rarely went to the theatre or a concert, and was seldom seen in Paris society.

Theodore H. White described Mendès-France as a "short, stocky, heavy-set man, jet-black of hair, broad of nose, and blue-black of jowl, who looks far more like one of the blue trousered workers in the Paris Metro than one of the most eminent and scholarly intellectuals in French life" (*Reporter,* December 22, 1953).

According to Theodore H. White, Mendès-France believed that the first duty of the French government is to choose what shall be given up, for only by abandoning part of its claim to global greatness now can France withdraw, regroup its forces and energies for counterattack, and then return to its rightful power.

FURTHER READING

Le Monde p2 Je 18 '54 Life 37:84 J1 19 '54; *N Y Herald Tribune* II p3 Je 20 '54; II p2 Je 27 '54; *The New York Times* p2 Je 18 '54; *The New York Times* Mag p1O Je 27 '54; *N Y World-Telegram* p7 Je 26 '54; Time 63:27+ Je 28 '54 por; *U S News* 37:47+ J1 2 '54 por; *Dictionnaire Biographique Frangais Contemporain* (1954); *Who's Who in France,* 1953-54; *Who's Who in the United Nations* (1951); *World Biography* (1954)

ANGELA MERKEL
Chancellor of Germany

Born: July 17, 1954; Hamburg, Germany
Affiliation: Christian Democratic Union (CDU)

INTRODUCTION

As the Chancellor of Germany and leader of the Christian Democratic Union (CDU), Germany's largest opposition party, Angela Merkel is Germany's most prominent politician. Her considerable political stature has come in the context of being a woman and a Protestant, marking her as an unlikely leader of a party traditionally helmed by Catholic men. She also grew up in East Germany, a rarity in the CDU, which contributes to her unique position within the party. Often compared to former British prime minister Margaret Thatcher, Merkel has gained a reputation for being a no-nonsense strategist and an ambitious politician.

EARLY LIFE

Merkel was born Angela Dorothea Kasner on July 17, 1954 in Hamburg, West Germany. Her father was a Protestant minister, and her mother was a teacher. When she was very young, the family moved to the communist German Democratic Republic (East Germany); her father took a position in a parish in Bradenburg. Merkel's father is said to have "regarded the Stalinist regime benevolently," according to Ludwig Niethammer's profile of Merkel, as posted on the World Socialist Web Site (April 28, 2000), and she was involved in the Free German Youth (FDJ)—the Stalinist youth organization of East Germany. She studied physics at the University of Leipzig and went on to complete a Ph.D., which she was awarded in 1986, in quantum physics at the Academy of Sciences in Berlin.

LIFE'S WORK

The fall of the Berlin Wall in 1989, which began the unification process between East and West Germany, prompted Merkel's first foray into politics; she joined the Demokratische Aufbruch—Democratic Awakening (DA)—a group with its roots in the Evangelical Church. Merkel had been appointed as the DA press spokeswoman, but the group disbanded when it was revealed that its head, Wolfgang Schnur, was really an East German secret service agent. The pro-capitalist faction of the DA switched as a body to the CDU, and following the East German parliamentary elections in the spring of 1990, Merkel became a deputy government spokeswoman under Lothar de Maiziere, East Germany's last leader prior to German reunification. A common argument by her critics is that Merkel's assignment was due to luck rather than political aptitude. "The scene was East Germany in 1990," Charles P. Wallace reported for *Time* Europe (April 3, 2000, on-line), "a chaotic moment after the fall of the Berlin Wall when an interim government was trying to steer the country from communism to democracy. Lothar de Maiziere . . . was shuttling almost daily between Washington, London and Moscow. A crisis arose behind the scenes: de Maiziere's press spokesman turned out to have a crippling fear of flying. In desperation, the East German leader asked an unfamiliar assistant in his office named Angela Merkel to join him before the television cameras as history unfolded." Merkel's fortuitous role in this pivotal chapter of Germany's history placed her squarely in the political arena she had been eyeing for a year. "For me, three things were immediately clear after the reunification," Merkel recalled for the Berliner Morgenpost in 1998, as quoted by the World Socialist Web Site. "I wanted to get into the Bundestag (parliament), I favored rapid German unity and I supported a free-market economy." With the help of de Maiziere, she successfully ran for the Bundestag as a representative of the Stralsund/Ruegun constituency. De Maiziere also convinced Chancellor Helmut Kohl to consider Merkel for a political post. According to Wallace, Kohl had contacted de Maiziere, "looking for a young woman whom he could bring into his cabinet as a sign of his solidarity with the newly reunited east." Kohl named Merkel as the federal minister for Women's Issues and Youth in January 1991. At the end of that year, she became deputy chairperson of the CDU. In 1994 Merkel relinquished her position as minister for Women's Issues and Youth to become the Secretary of Environment, Conservation and Nuclear Safety. She continued her rise within the CDU as well-she was elevated to the position of General Secretary for the party in 1998.

Merkel's detractors have often argued that her rise to political prominence was due more to her function as a syncophant for Kohl than any real political abilities. Ludwig Niethammer wrote that under Kohl, Merkel "remained colourless and avoided any conflict with her political mentor," adding, "It is well known that ex-chancellor Helmut Kohl built up 'the girl,' as he called her, in his own interests. People close to him could only advance if they were considered adaptable and obedient. Angela Merkel was both." Kohl was Merkel's prime mentor during her political youth; as chancellor from 1982 to 1998, he was the venerated patriarchal figure of the CDU. Kohl's pet name for Merkel, "the girl," further compounded what later critics would argue about her: that, despite supporters' claims that she represented the fresh face of a rejuvenated party, in fact she was a product of the old establishment, molded by Kohl and with little original political thought. Kohl lost the chancellorship to Social Democrat Gerard Schroder in 1998, and Kohl's political career was ended with a campaign finance scandal. Merkel at first defended her boss, dismissing the charges—that Kohl had amassed one million dollars in undeclared donations using a network of secret accounts—against him as "totally absurd," as quoted by Rob Broomby for the BBC (March 20, 2000, on-line). But as Kohl's case unraveled, revealing a trail of corruption and deceit, Merkel made headlines for being the first member of his cabinet to break ties with him and condemn his actions. In an open letter published in the Frankfurter Allgemeine Zeitung in December 1999, Merkel criticized her former patron for refusing to name the illicit donors. She called Kohl's reign "irretrievably" over and excoriated him for the damage he had inflicted on the CDU—and, while maintaining, "Perhaps it is asking too much to demand that Helmut Kohl resign from politics," Merkel wrote, as quoted in the *Australian* (December 24, 1999, on-line). "There is no escaping the fact that [the CDU has to] take the future into our own hands."

In 2000 the CDU was again shaken when Wolfgang Schauble, Kohl's successor, was forced to resign after being implicated in the same scandal that had ruined his former boss. With Schauble's departure, Merkel was unexpectedly next in line to lead the CDU. In March 2000 Merkel was nominated to chair the CDU. As Christoph Neshover wrote in a report for the American Institute for Contemporary German Studies (March 21, 2000, on-line), "Merkel's nomination by the party leadership makes it very unlikely . . . that any other candidates will run. If elected, Merkel will be the first woman to chair a major German party since 1949." Merkel ran unopposed at the April 2000 party convention and was approved by 96 percent of the delegates. Charles Wallace

noted: "Party leaders clearly hoped that choosing a pastor's daughter who is also a scientist with a specialty in quantum physics would demonstrate the CDU's desire for a clean break with its besmirched past." Although Merkel provided a fresh face for the CDU, her nomination was also the result of a capacity to remain focused amid political turmoil. In addition to her supporters, political observers singled her out as someone who could rescue the embattled CDU. Winning the support of party members spanning the party's various factions, Merkel was carving out a leadership persona. Ute Schmidt, an expert on the CDU at the Hannah Arendt Institute for Research on Totalitarianism in Dresden, Germany, told Lucian Kim for the *Christian Science Monitor* (April 10, 2000), "Merkel isn't burdened with the past. She is bringing a new form of communication to the CDU. She is showing more openness and none of the arrogance. I think her own self-image will change the party." Others, like Karl Feldmeier, a senior correspondent at the Frankfurter Allgemaier Zeitung newspaper, called her "convincing," as quoted by the BBC (March 20, 2000, on-line), but questioned her political abilities beyond mere public appeal. "[Merkel] doesn't have a group of close allies in the party. . . . She is supported by the sympathy of a growing part of the membership of the party—and that's all."

Merkel's rise in 2000 provided a solid foundation from which to build a candidacy for chancellorship in 2002, but she spent those two years strengthening her weakened and fragmented party. She backed Edmund Stoiber, the prime minister of Bavaria—one of Germany's richest, most conservative states—as the 2002 challenger to incumbent Gerhard Schroder. Stoiber, leader of the Christian Social Union, another German conservative group, was shown in polls to have the best chance of beating Schroder, and in January 2002, at a news conference in Magdeburg, Merkel vowed to support Stoiber's candidacy, announcing, as quoted by CNN (January 12, 2002, on-line), "Together with Edmund Stoiber, I will make my contribution." Stoiber lost the October 2002 election, however, and within weeks Merkel had reignited her critiques of the chancellor, whom she accused of deceiving voters about the extent of the country's economic woes. At the CDU's party conference that month, Merkel announced, as quoted by the Deutsche Welle (November 11, 2002), "This government has blatantly and cold-bloodedly lied into the faces of the German people." She claimed that the country had reached a "post-war lowpoint." Many conference attendees were impressed with Merkel's bold words and commanding presence and several questioned whether Stoiber had been the right candidate in the election after all. "There are many within the CDU who overtly opine that the feisty 48-year-old from the eastern German state of Brandenburg would indeed have made a better chancellor candidate than Edmund Stoiber," the Deutsche Welle reported. "The most vociferous in the pro-Merkel camp say that her eastern roots would have guaranteed the party a high percentage of votes from women in eastern Germany, an area which Stoiber dramatically failed to tap into at all."

In 2003 Merkel became increasingly vocal about international issues, causing a stir when she wrote an opinion piece for the *Washington Post* (February 20, 2003), supporting the United States' imminent invasion of Iraq and criticizing Europe's almost collective refusal to aid the military effort. Titled "Schroder Doesn't Speak for All Germans," the article stressed the importance of preserving Germany's ties with the United States while exhorting other countries to recognize that "the danger from Iraq is not fictitious but real." She wrote, "the determination and unity of the free nations will, in the Iraq conflict, have a decisive effect not only on the outcome of the crisis but on the way in which we shape the future of Europe and its relationship with the United States. They will have a decisive effect, too, on how we guarantee peace, freedom and security, and how we find appropriate answers to the new threats of our time." Merkel had also been a proponent of the American War on Terror launched after September 11, 2001, endearing her to the administration of President George W. Bush. Schroder's party members were angered; besides the faux pas of criticizing her government in a foreign newspaper—violating an "unwritten rule of international diplomacy," according to M. N. Hebbar in an editorial for Al-Jazeerah (March 8, 2003, on-line)—Merkel won further enmity from the Social Democrats by traveling to the United States soon after the article was published, meeting with senior officials and speaking out about the war. "It is not every foreign leader who, in 48 whirlwind hours in Washington, gets to meet with the vice president, the secretary of defense, the national security advisor, the deputy secretary of state, the United States trade representative, influential senators and the chairman of the Federal Reserve," Todd S. Purdum wrote for *The New York Times* (February 26, 2003). "When the visitor is leader of her country's opposition party, such treatment is all but unheard of. But that was

the schedule today and Monday of Angela Merkel . . . perhaps the Bush administration's favorite official these days." Schroder's party denounced Merkel's transatlantic networking; the Social Democrat party secretary Olaf Scholz explained, as quoted by Deutsche Welle, (February 26, 2003), "Merkel is making foreign policy against the will of a majority of Germans without any mandate from the voters . . . and would be better advised to keep quiet." With Schroder's growing unpopularity at home, however, a poll completed in February by the German magazine Stern found that voters would support Merkel in an election over Schroder by a five percent margin.

On September 16, 2003 the Agence France Presse released an article headlined "Germany Dares to Dream of a Woman President," which speculated that Merkel had a good chance to be chosen as the conservative candidate for Germany's 2006 general election. James Mackenzie, writing for Reuters (December 2, 2003), reported on a CDU meeting at which some reforms she backed were approved by a wide margin, dramatically altering the party's stance on such issues as health and welfare reform, as well as introducing major changes to the tax system. Though the party's positions will only effect change if the CDU returns to power, Merkel's support of radical initiatives proved to her fellow conservatives that she is a bolder politician than previously thought. "Ms. Merkel has sorted herself out, found her style and gained in authority," Urlich Hesse-Lichenberger reported for the liberal German newspaper, Suddeutsche Zeitung, as quoted by the *London Guardian* (December 5, 2003, on-line). Insofar as the CDU convention functioned as a "barometer of public opinion," Hesse-Lichenberger wrote, Merkel had "passed with flying colors."

Merkel assumed office as Chancellor of Germany in 2005. She narrowly defeated Chancellor Gerhard Schröder, winning by three seats. After the CDU agreed to a coalition deal with the Social Democrats (SPD), she was declared Germany's first female chancellor. Merkel is also the first former citizen of the German Democratic Republic to lead the reunited Germany and the first woman to lead Germany since it became a modern nation-state.

When she accused the U.S. National Security Agency of tapping her cell phone in 2013, she made headlines. At a summit of European leaders she chided the United States for this privacy breech, saying that "Spying among friends is never acceptable." Later reports revealed that the NSA may have been surveilling Merkel since 2002. Merkel was sworn in for a third term in December 2013.

In November 2015, *Forbes* magazine ranked Chancellor Merkel the second most powerful person in the world—the highest ranking ever achieved by a woman—and later that year she was named *Time* magazine's "Person of the Year." Merkel has played a leading role in Europe's reaction to the migrant crisis, announcing that Germany would welcome refugees fleeing Syria's civil war. The German government says 1.1 million people claimed asylum in the country in 2015.

The decision to welcome Syrians won her plaudits in some quarters but sparked a backlash in others, with some senior officials openly questioning the approach. Street protests organized by the right-wing Pegida movement has drawn thousands opposed to "Islamisation" of Germany. With anxiety over migration rising,

Merkel's approval ratings have plummeted, and in late 2015, they were at an all-time low of 54 percent.

PERSONAL LIFE
Merkel divorced her first husband in 1982. She married chemist and professor Joachim Sauer in 1998. They have no children together, but Sauer has two adult sons from a previous marriage. Merkel is a football fan, and she likes attending national team games in her official capacity. Her hobbies include reading, hiking, and gardening. In 2002 an opera based on Merkel's life, *Angela—A National Opera*, was mounted for a brief run in Berlin.

FURTHER READING
BBC News (on-line) Mar. 29, 2000, with photo; *BusinessWeek* (on-line) Mar. 10, 2003; *The New York Times* A p10 Feb. 26, 2003, with photos; *Time Europe* (on-line) Apr. 3, 2000; *Washington Post* A p39 Feb. 20, 2003

HO CHI MINH
President of North Vietnam

Born: May 19, 1890; French Indochina
Died: September 2, 1969; Hanoi North Vietnam
Affiliation: Communist Party of Vietnam

INTRODUCTION
President Ho Chi Minh of North Vietnam—familiarly known to his countrymen as "Uncle Ho"—was a legend among North and South Vietnamese alike. One of the last remaining Old Bolsheviks, Ho was a founder of the French Communist party and helped to organize Communist cadres and guerilla forces in China and Southeast Asia in the 1920's and 1930's. During World War II he co-operated with Allied forces in fighting the Japanese invaders in Indo-China, but after the war his guerillas engaged in an eight-year independence struggle against France.

The Geneva agreement of 1954 that followed the defeat of the French divided the former French protectorate at the seventeenth parallel between the Democratic Republic of Vietnam in the north, presided over by Ho Chi Minh, and the Republic of Vietnam in the south, which continued to be tied to the West. In recent years, as a result of its aid to antigovernment Viet Cong

guerilla forces in South Vietnam, Ho Chi Minh's regime has come increasingly into conflict with the United States, which is determined to prevent the spread of Communism in Asia. Despite stepped up American military aid to South Vietnam and air raids against strategic targets in the north, Ho Chi Minh has declared his intention to carry on the struggle until victory.

EARLY LIFE
Ho Chi Minh is a native of the village of Kim Lien, in the province of Nghe An, in central Vietnam (then a part of French Indo-China) near the Tonkin border, an area noted for widespread anticolonial activity. Accounts of his birthdate differ, but May 19, 1890 is believed to be the most accurate. (Some sources give July 15, 1892 as his birth-date, while others give 1891.) He was originally named Nguyen That Thanh or Nguyen Van Thanh, and before adopting the name Ho Chi Minh (meaning "most enlightened one") in the early 1940's he had been known by various aliases, including Nguyen Ai Quoc, Nguyen Sinh Chin, Nguyen O Phap, Song Man Tcho, and Ly Thuy. His father, Nguyen Sinh Huy, a descendant of mandarins, was a civil servant of modest means,

Ho Chi Minh.

who was well-versed in the Confucian classics, and who later practiced Oriental herb medicine after being dismissed from his government post for anti-French activities. The youngest of three children, Ho had a sister, Thanh, and a brother, Khiem. Both of them took part in the independence movement, and both were said to have died in the early 1950's. Little is known of his mother, who is believed to have been of peasant background.

Exposed to revolutionary activities at an early age, Ho was acting as a messenger for an anticolonial organization by the time he was nine. He obtained a traditional Sino-Vietnamese education, studying Confucianism, Buddhism, and Christianity among other subjects. Tutored by his father, he was educated at a village school and at the French *lycee* in Cap Vinh. Later he studied at the Lycee Quoc Hoc at Hue, which was regarded as the best secondary school in the country, and which counted several revolutionary leaders among its alumni. Because of his anti-colonial views, Ho was forced to leave the school in 1910 without graduating. Moving to the south, he served for a time as an adjunct teacher at the Lyce Dac Than in Phan Thiet, South Annam, an institution where anti-French sentiments predominated. In 1911 he attended a trade school in Saigon for three months.

In the summer of 1912 (some sources give 1910 or 1911) Ho Chi Minh shipped out as a galley hand on the French merchant ship *Latouche-Treville*, reportedly to escape from French authorities in his homeland. During the next few years he traveled throughout the world. By 1914 he was in London, where he worked as a snow-cleaner and as an apprentice to the noted chef Escoffier at the Carlton Hotel. In London he joined the Lao Dong Hai Ngoa (Overseas Workers' Association), a Chinese-led anti-colonial group that championed Irish independence. Later he visited the United States, living for a time in New York's Harlem and in Boston.

LIFE'S WORK

Ho settled in Paris, where he worked as a gardener, cook, and laundryman and later established his own studio for retouching photographs. Impressed by the intellectual life of Paris, Ho attended university lectures and political discussions and studied die works of Karl Marx and other Socialists. During the Versailles Peace Conference that followed the end of World War I, Ho rented a dark suit and tried to obtain an audience with United States President Woodrow Wilson to present the case for Indo-Chinese independence, but his efforts failed.

Although essentially a nationalist, Ho Chi Minh became more and more convinced that the road to liberation of his homeland lay in the direction of Communism. In 1919 he joined the French Socialist party. In the following year, after a split in Socialist ranks, he joined other members of its left wing in founding die Communist party of France and aligned himself at the time with its anti-Moscow independents. As the party's expert on colonial affairs, Ho traveled through Europe, speaking at party congresses and writing anti-colonial tracts. The most important was the pamphlet *Le procds de la colonisation frangaise* (Paris, 1926?; Hanoi, 1962), which was widely distributed and even found its way to Vietnam, where Ho (who was then known as Nguyen Ai Quoc, or Nguyen the Patriot) was hailed as a hero. Upon the urging of Jean Longuet, the son-in-law of Karl Marx, Ho also contributed articles to his radical Paris newspaper *Le Popidaire*. Later, Ho served as editor of *Le Faria* (The Outcast), a weekly Indo-Chinese exile newspaper published in Paris. He also wrote plays for cabarets, including the anti-French comedy *Le dragon de bambou* (The Bamboo Dragon).

In 1922 Ho Chi Minh went to Moscow as a French delegate to the fourth World Congress of the Communist International, and in the following year he represented the French Communist party at the Congress of International Peasantry, also in Moscow. He remained in the Soviet Union from 1923 to 1925 for indoctrination and training in revolutionary techniques at the University of the Toilers of the East, and was said to have become a Russian citizen. During this period he became closely acquainted with the top Soviet leaders, including Lenin, Stalin, and Trotsky.

In 1925 Ho went to China to serve at the Soviet consulate in Canton as a translator and aide to Mikhail Borodin, the Soviet adviser to Chiang Kai-shek's Kuomintang government, which at the time was allied with the Chinese Communists. There he helped to train Communist cadres at Whampoa Military Academy and recruited Vietnamese political refugees for a guerilla force that aimed at eventual liberation of Vietnam from French rule. After Chiang Kai-shek broke with the Communists in 1927, driving them underground, Ho fled to Moscow. As director of the Asian bureau of the Communist International in Shanghai in the late 1920's and early 1930's, Ho was responsible for Communist affairs in an area that encompassed India, China, Southeast Asia, and Japan.

Continuing meanwhile to build up his liberation force, which had been forced to shift its base of operations from Canton to Hongkong, Ho spent some time in Thailand, where he established an organization of Indo-Chinese exiles and published a newspaper. In 1929 French authorities in Vietnam, aware of his revolutionary activities, sentenced him to death in absentia. On January 6, 1930 Ho Chi Minh, operating from his headquarters in Hongkong, drew together his forces of Communists and nationalists into a single organization that became the Communist party of Indo-China. Later in the same year those forces infiltrated into northern Vietnam, where they staged an abortive peasant revolt that was ruthlessly suppressed by the French. Ho was imprisoned by British authorities in Hongkong in 1930, but he was released after a few months, reportedly because of a tubercular condition.

During most of the 1930's Ho Chi Minh remained a shadowy figure in the background. He helped to organize a Communist party in Singapore and moved clandestinely through Southeast Asia, coordinating revolutionary activities, and turning up, according to some accounts, in various places in the disguise of a Buddhist monk, a beggar, or a business tycoon. For a time he was rumored to have died of tuberculosis. With the outbreak of World War II and the occupation of much of Southeast Asia by the Japanese, Ho went to South China. There, in the village of Chingsi, on May 19, 1941, he and his military aide, Nguyen Vo Giap, organized Indo-Chinese Socialist and Nationalist exile forces into the Vietnam Doc Lap Dong Minh Hoa (League for the Independence of Vietnam), popularly known as the Viet Minh, which was aimed against both the French and the Japanese invaders. To emphasize national unity, Ho dissolved the Indo-Chinese Communist party at the time.

Arrested in late 1941 at Liuchow by Chinese Nationalists on charges of being a French spy, Ho was released in the following year, after persuading General Chang Fa Kwei, the local warlord, that he could be of service to the Chinese in the struggle against the Japanese enemy. Adopting his present name to hide his earlier identity, Ho remained in China for a time, where he trained his forces under Chinese Nationalist sponsorship. In December 1944 he returned to Vietnam after an absence of more than three decades and organized his guerillas into formal military units, setting up bases and establishing combat zones. During the latter stages of the war, Ho Chi Minh's forces worked closely with the United States, rescuing downed American fliers and furnishing intelligence information to the Office of Strategic Services in return for American supplies. For a time, Ho also worked as a translator for the United States Office of War Information in Chungking. At that time Ho was favorably disposed to Americans, hoping that the United States would help the Vietnamese achieve independence after the war.

On August 19, 1945 Ho Chi Minh's Viet Minh forces marched victoriously into Hanoi, driving out the Japanese, and forcing the puppet Emperor, Bao Dai, to abdicate. On September 2, 1945 Ho proclaimed the Democratic Republic of Vietnam, which claimed to represent the entire country. When nationwide elections were held on January 6, 1946, Ho Chi Minh was elected president, and 230 of the 300 seats in the new national assembly were filled by Viet Minh members. In May 1946 the Lien Viet, or National United Front, representing the political parties of the country, was organized. Two months later, a liberal constitution was adopted, modeled in part on the United States constitution, and proclaiming Vietnam "an indivisible whole."

Meanwhile, on March 6, 1946 France, unwilling to give up Vietnam entirely, recognized its former protectorate as a free state within the French Union. To clarify the status of Vietnam, Ho and twelve associates traveled to Fontainebleau, France, where a *modus vivendi,* but no real agreement, was reached. Disagreements over the status of Vietnam and the control of the territory of Cochin China led to charges and countercharges of violations. On December 20, 1946 Ho declared a "national war of resistance" and called on his countrymen to "drive out the French colonialists and save the fatherland."

Although Ho Chi Minh's government proceeded ruthlessly against opponents of the regime and former collaborators with the Japanese, the Democratic Republic of Vietnam at first took on more of a nationalistic rather than Communist orientation. In 1948 Ho was quoted as saying that he was no longer a Communist. After the victory of the Chinese Communists in 1949, the Ho Chi Minh regime tended to turn more toward Communism. In early 1950 the Communist governments of Eastern Europe and Asia recognized the republic, and on March 3, 1951 the Communist party of Indo-China was revived as the Lao Dong (Workers party) of Vietnam. Soon afterward, agrarian reform measures were introduced.

Meanwhile, General Giap's guerilla forces were gaining the advantage over French expeditionary forces. On July 21, 1954, following the defeat of the French in a fifty-five-day siege at Dienbienphu, a cease-fire agreement was signed at Geneva. The Geneva agreement divided Vietnam at the seventeenth parallel and provided, among other things, for elections in two years, to settle the future of the divided country. North Vietnam, of which Ho Chi Minh was now both president and Premier, comprises an area of 63,344 square miles and a population estimated in 1965 at 17,600,000. Although North Vietnam has mineral resources and a promising industrial potential, it lacks the abundant rice lands of the south and thus depends on Communist China or the Soviet Union for economic support.

On September 20, 1955 Ho Chi Minh relinquished the Premiership to Pham Van Dong, but he retained the presidency and the chairmanship of the Lien Viet. Meanwhile, from 1954 to 1956, the North Vietnamese government ruthlessly pursued its land reform program, during whose course an estimated 50,000 people were said to have been executed. Charging the radical faction of the party with responsibility for the uprising, he dismissed the pro-Chinese Truong Chinh as secretary-general of the Lao Dong and assumed that post himself.

A new constitution, adopted in i960, gave Ho almost unlimited power and placed a greater emphasis on Communist principles than the 1946 constitution had done. In September i960 Ho was re-elected president but relinquished his post as secretary-general to Le Duan.

Meanwhile, in 1959, there had emerged in South Vietnam the Communist-oriented Viet Cong guerrilla force, which was unofficially aided by the North Vietnamese government. Ho Chi Minh justified the existence of the Viet Cong (and its political arm, the National Liberation Front) on the grounds that the South Vietnamese government, then headed by Ngo Dinh Diem, had refused to permit elections, as specified in the Geneva agreement, to bring about reunification of Vietnam. The United States, which was committed to aid the South Vietnamese government, sent military aid and advisers to help the Saigon government cope with the guerrillas. Over the next few years, military commitments on both sides multiplied, and the war escalated.

In August 1964 a North Vietnamese attack on American ships in the Gulf of Tonkin led to retaliatory air raids by the United States. Acting on evidence of increased direct aid in the form of troops and supplies from the Hanoi regime to the Viet Cong, President Lyndon B. Johnson in February 1965 inaugurated a policy of bombing raids against military targets in the north. He also greatly increased American ground troops in South Vietnam. Although the United States maintains that North Vietnam's actions constitute aggression against a sovereign state, Ho Chi Minh contends that Vietnam is a single nation, that the Saigon government is an artificial creation of the Americans, and that the United States by its intervention is violating the Geneva agreement and is preventing the reunification of Vietnam.

In a speech in April 1965 President Johnson declared his willingness to enter "unconditional negotiations" to end the Vietnam conflict. In reply, Ho Chi Minh said that the United States could obtain "peace with honor" only if it withdrew its troops from South Vietnam and ended its raids on the north; if North and South Vietnam agreed to ban foreign troops from their territory; if the Viet Cong would have the decisive voice in South Vietnamese affairs; and if the country were reunited without foreign interference. Subsequent efforts by world leaders, including Pope Paul VI and United Nations Secretary-General U Thant, failed to bring the two sides to the negotiating table or to prevent the escalation of the conflict in 1965 and 1966. That escalation has tended to bring Hanoi closer to Communist China.

In the summer of 1966 Ho Chi Minh, apparently acting in response to world opinion, rescinded an earlier threat to try captured American airmen as war criminals. On the other hand, Ho ordered a partial mobilization of North Vietnamese forces in July 1966 in response to American bombing attacks on oil depots near Hanoi and Haiphong, and pledged to fight on to victory "even though this war should go on . . . twenty years or more."

PERSONAL LIFE

Little is known of Ho Chi Minh's private life. "An old man likes to hold on to his little mysteries," he once told Bernard B. Fall, as quoted in the *Saturday Evening Post* (November 24, 1962). Although it was rumored that in the 1930's he took a wife or concubine who bore him a daughter, he denied such reports. A frail man with a wispy beard and with what Peggy Durdin once described in *The New York Times Magazine* (May 9, 1954) as a "thoughtful face with reflected intelligence, subtlety and serenity," A man of moderation and nonviolence, Ho, who has never commanded troops in combat, was said to favor compromise over conflict. He was fond of children and gallant to women. On the other hand, a reporter for the New York *Post* (August 9, 1964) has contended that "his benign exterior hides one of the most singleminded, skillful, and ruthless Communists."

Although Ho Chi Minh lived modestly, in the gardener's cottage of the former French governor-general's palace, and dressed simply, in sandals and a mandarin-style tunic, he was something of a gourmet and fond of English and American cigarettes. A skilled poet, painter, and calligrapher, Ho was also fond of football. He spoke French, English, German, Russian, Czech, Japanese, and some Portuguese, in addition to several Chinese and Vietnamese dialects. A four-volume collection of his writings and speeches, entitled *Selected Works* was published in Hanoi in 1960-62. The British journalist James Cameron noted in his book *Here Is Your Enemy* (Holt, 1966) that Ho Chi Minh has a quality rarely found in Communist leaders: "the gift of fun, of detachment, fantasy, of rising above the grey desert of dogma—in short, of being what he claims to be, the Universal Uncle."

Ho Chi Minh died in September 1969 from heart failure at his home in Hanoi, at the age of seventy-nine. News of his death was withheld from the North Vietnamese public for nearly forty-eight hours because he had died on the anniversary of the founding of the Democratic Republic of Vietnam.

FURTHER READING

For Affairs 33:86+O'54 Look 30:32+ Ag 9 '66 pors; *Nat Observer* pi8 Ag 23 '65 pors; *Reporter* 12:11 + Ja 27 '55 por; *Asia Who's Who* (1960); Fall, Bernard B. *The Two Viet-Nams* (1963); *International Who's Who, 1965-66; International Year Book and Statesmen's Who's Who,* 1966; Library of Congress. Legislative Reference Service. *Who Are They?* pt 6 (1957)

ISKANDER MIRZA

President of Pakistan

Born: November 13, 1899; Murshidabad, British India
(now West Bengal, India)
Died: November 13, 1969; London, United Kingdom
Affiliation: Republican Party

INTRODUCTION

Pakistan became an Islamic republic on March 2, 1956 and Major General Iskander Mirza, then Governor General, signed the bill which created the republic as crowds in Karachi cheered. The Constituent Assembly passed a resolution approving continued membership in the British Commonwealth of Nations (India is the only other republic in the Commonwealth). Mirza was elect-
ed the new republic's first and provisional President by the Assembly on March 5. When he was nominated by the Moslem United Front coalition he promised to hold general elections "within the shortest possible time." He took office on March 23.

Mirza had been Governor General of Pakistan since 1955 after Ghulam Mohammed resigned. "A major general who speaks the tribesmen's language and plays a profitable game of bridge with diplomats" is the way he was described in The New York Times *when he assumed the duties of his predecessor temporarily on August 7.*

General Mirza was emerging more and more as the country's strong man during a series of internal and international crises that have marked the history of Pakistan since it was constituted as a Dominion on August 14, 1947. Content with power behind the scenes when Pakistan became independent, he had been more recently the instrument through which his predecessor ruled.

According to Time *(August 15, 1955) and* Reporter *(January 27, 1955), Mirza had little patience with the politicians he has handled so often and successfully and does not subscribe to the founders' concept of a Moslem nation, although he himself is a Moslem. As Governor General, he had believed that he should have "extensive and clearly defined powers, including the power to dismiss governments." He regarded democracy as something for which Pakistanis still must be educated.*

EARLY LIFE

Iskander Mirza was born on November 13, 1899, the son of a wealthy Bengali landowner. While studying for his B.A. degree at Ephinstone College, Bombay, he was appointed to Sandhurst, Britain's military college, at Camberley, England. There he distinguished himself as a crack rifle shot and earned his cricket "blue."

The first Indian cadet to become a British army officer, he won distinction as a military and civil servant of the rulers of his native land. He fought with the Cameronians (2nd Scottish Rifles) at Kohat in 1922 and with the 17th Poona Horse in Waziristan in 1924. For twenty years he was Britain's "top policeman" in the Khyber Pass northern frontier area.

LIFE'S WORK

He entered the Indian Political Service in 1926, serving as assistant commissioner at Abbottabad, Bannu, Nowshera and Tank and as deputy commissioner at Hazara and Mardan. His understanding of tribal affairs won him appointment as deputy commissioner at Peshawar (1940-45), after which he became political agent for the Orissa States.

In 1946 he was appointed joint secretary to the Ministry of Defense of the government of India. On India's partition the following year, he became the first Defense Secretary of the Pakistan government. In 1954 he was sent to restore order in East Pakistan, where formation of a provincial government by an avowed secessionist had been followed by rioting. He suspended the newly elected popular Parliament and, with only one army division at his disposal, kept order among 44,000,000 people (*Reporter,* January 27, 1955).

While serving as Governor of East Bengal (East Pakistan) he was mobbed by cheering crowds, grateful for his prodigious efforts in behalf of sufferers in a flood disaster. "Mirza," commented a prominent Pakistani, "has done more for the common man whom he says he despises than all the politicians who promised a new heaven on earth to get votes" (*Time,* August 15, 1955).

When he was appointed a Minister in the central government of Pakistan in October 1954, his portfolios were the Interior, and States and Frontier Regions. In June 1955 he was elected to the Constituent Assembly on the Moslem League ticket. Never before a party member, he chose "the party which was responsible for the creation of Pakistan."

Mirza's views on the nature of the state owe much to Mustapha Kemal Ataturk, founder of the Turkish republic, according to correspondent John P. Callahan, writing in *The New York Times* (August 7, 1955). Kemal's fifteen-year rule was marked by a steady trend away from the political influence of religious leaders toward a secular state.

Mirza's views were more specifically formulated in a statement to foreign correspondents read by the secretary of Pakistan's Ministry of Information and Broadcasting on December 4, 1954:

"The head of a parliamentary government after his election manages, through the party system, a complete hold on governmental machinery. The delegated power is entirely for the purpose of controlling the people themselves and regulating their life and conduct in accordance with established customs, law and usage."

Writing in the *Reporter* (January 27, 1955), Philip Deane recounts that he asked General Mirza, during pacification operations in East Bengal, what he would do if a certain renowned holy man and allegedly leftist agitator should return from England to make trouble. According to Deane, Mirza expressed the hope that the holy man's supporters would demonstrate at the airport, in the event of his return, so that "I can have one of my crack marksmen shoot him." Asked if the interviewer might quote him, the general is reported to have replied: "Please do. Our friend might read your report and decide to stay out of the country."

The general is described by Deane as one of the hierarchy chosen to run the country by its founder, Mohammed Ali Jinnah. Jinnah gave the hierarchs much power but, as a born autocrat, knew how to control them. After

Jinnah's death in 1948 and that of his successor, Liaquat Ali Khan, in 1951, politicians and religious leaders began to make their influence felt in Pakistan.

Then came strained relations with India over the control of Jammu and Kashmir, near war with Afghanistan over independence agitation among border tribesmen, and riots and secessionist threats in East Pakistan. Governor General Ghulam Mohammed reasserted the authority of the hierarchy, dismissing the Constituent Assembly. Confined by paralysis, however, he handed over the reins to Mirza.

Mirza was sworn in as President of the world's first Islamic Republic on March 23. "An outspoken critic of religious fanatics," according to *The New York Times*, "he has pledged complete freedom and equality for Pakistan's Hindu minority. The population is predominantly Moslem."

President Mirza is described as "tough, intelligent, Western-minded" and "colorful enough to attract legend." He is "dapper in his Savile Row suits, gallant in the presence of ladies." He "loathes intrigue and is staunchly loyal to those who trust him" (*Time*, August 15, 1955).

Democracy, to his mind, is a fine ideal, but what does it mean? "Power to the people. Power to choose. Choice, however, presupposes knowledge. You have seen these illiterate peasants. What do they know? They certainly do not know more about running an administration than I do" (*Reporter*, January 27, 1955).

In 1958, Mirza illegally appointed Army Commander General Ayub Khan as Prime Minister. The two men had an intense rivalry. He then tried to make himself more secure by getting the support of Khan's rivals within the Army and Navy. Forced to resign in October 1958, Mirza was exiled to London.

PERSONAL LIFE

Mirza occupied a large house in Karachi with spacious grounds and a white portico, which was both his official residence and office. His second wife was a Persian. Humayun, a son by Mirza's first wife, was married in 1954 to Josephine Wing Hildreth, a graduate of Vassar College and the daughter of U.S. Ambassador to Pakistan Horace A. Hildreth. Mirza was fond of riding, shooting and horse racing.

Mirza was living in exile in London when he died of a heart attack in November 1969. He reportedly struggled financially while living in London, most of the time in poverty.

FURTHER READING

The New York Times pl4 Ag 7 '55 (por); *Pakistan Affairs* 7 :2 Ag 29 '55 (por); *Pakistan News Digest* pi—f—Ag 15 '55 (por); *Reporter* 12 :30+ Ja 27 '55; *Time* 66:17 Aug 15 '55 por; *Who's Who*, 1955

FRANÇOIS (MAURICE) MITTERAND (ME-TA-RAN')
Former President of France

Born: Oct. 26, 1916; Jarnac, France
Died: January 8, 1996; Paris, France
Affiliation: Socialist Party

INTRODUCTION

François Mitterrand was a life-long politician of France, and served as President of France under the Fifth Republic. His election as the Socialist Party candidate, on May 10, 1981, marked an historic turning point for that country; the end of 23 years of Gaullist rule (referring to the governments led by Presidents Charles de Gaulle, Georges Pompidou, and Valéry Giscard d'Estaing), and the first leftist government of the Fifth Republic. For Mitterrand, who defeated the in-cumbent, Valery Giseard d'Estaing by 51.76 percent to 48.24 percent, the election capped the most spectacular political comeback in a long career marred by many reversals of fortune.

Mitterrand had served as a Cabinet minister in various governments of the ill-fated Fourth Republic (which collapsed after Algeria's fight for independence), and he had made his first try for the Presidency in 1965, when he ran as the candidate of the left and forced de Gaulle into a humiliating runoff. But it was not until 1971, when he was elected head of a splintered and moribund Socialist Party, that Mitterrand began the ten-year drive that would eventually transform French politics. Pursuing a strategy of "unity of the left"—that

François Mitterand.

foreign policy, he broke with Gaullist precedent by moving closer to NATO, disagreeing sharply with the United States over its El Salvador policy and other Third-World issues, and adopting a friendly stance towards Israel.

Mitterrand, possibly because of his experiences in politics during the Fourth Republic, when governments changed frequently, was able to adapt to changes of the electorate. He was twice forced by the loss of a Parliamentary majority into "cohabitation governments" with conservative cabinets led, respectively, by Jacques Chirac (1986–1988), and Édouard Balladur (1993–1995).

Mitterrand also was one of the founders of the European Union. Both he and Helmut Kohl, the Chancellor of Germany, negotiated the Maastricht Treaty, which was signed on February 7, 1992, and birthed the European Union.

EARLY LIFE

François Maurice Adrien Marie Mitterrand was born on October 26, 1916, in the small historic town of Jarnac in the Charente department of western France, the fifth of eight children born to Joseph and Yvonne (Lorrain) Mitterrand. The father was a railroad station master at Angouleme before he inherited a profitable vinegar distillery, and the family was frugal, Roman Catholic, and petit bourgeois. He had, however, one unusual trait for a man of his social milieu, which were his liberal political views. They profoundly influenced his son François. The other key element in François' intellectual makeup, his passionate love of literature, he inherited from his mother. All three of François' brothers became prominent: One was a professor of literature, another a leading industrial manager and, the third, was a former Air Force general who ran one of France's largest aerospace companies.

After a brilliant scholastic career at the College Saint-Paul in Angouleme, Mitterrand went on to study at the University of Paris, where he received an advanced law degree and a diploma from the Ecole Libre Des Sciences Politiques. In 1939, he enlisted in the colonial infantry and, in June 1940, was wounded in the chest and captured by the Germans near Verdun. In December 1941, he escaped from a prison camp on his third attempt, and returned to France, where he joined the Resistance and organized a small group of former P.O.W.'s, the National Movement of War Prisoners and Deportees. For a time, Mitterrand also worked as a minor government official for the Vichy regime. He even received a medal from the Petain government, an honor that political opponents have used to challenge

is, an alliance with the Communist party—Mitterrand built the Socialists into the strongest party in France. In 1981, he capitalized on his country's deep desire for change and, by brilliantly out-maneuvering the Communists, took the Presidency.

As President, Mitterrand moved rapidly to fulfill the promises summed up in one of his campaign slogans, "le changement" (or "the change"), while maintaining a basically pragmatic approach. For the first time since the 1930s, the French Cabinet included Communist ministers. His most sweeping reforms were a nationalization program under which the government took control of virtually all French banking and several of the country's largest industrial firms, and a decentralization program that revolutionized French local politics by transferring power from Paris to the provinces and towns. Mitterrand had elected to buck the trend of most Western governments by spending lavishly to spur economic growth. In the integrity of his war record, but Mitterrand contended that his Vichy post merely supplied him with a cover for his activities with the Resistance.

In 1944, Mitterrand served briefly as Secretary General for War Prisoners and Deportees in the provisional government for liberated France under Charles de Gaulle. Running under the banner of the center-left Democratic and Socialist Resistance Union (UDSR), he was elected Deputy, in November 1946, to the first postwar National Assembly from the department of Nievres, which he represented until 1981 (except for the years from 1959-1962). When, in 1947, he was named Minister of War Veterans and Victims in the Cabinet of Paul Ramadier, he took over the first of nearly a dozen Cabinet posts that he was to hold in the revolving-door governments of the Fourth Republic. Those posts included: Secretary of State to the Presidency of the Council in Charge of Information (1948-1949); Minister for Overseas Territories (1950-1951); Minister of State (1952-1953); Minister of the Interior (1954-1955); and Minister of State for Justice (1956-1957).

Mitterrand was one of the few non-Communist politicians who took an uncompromising stand against the constitution that established the Fifth Republic, in 1958, which invested the new President, Charles de Gaulle, with overwhelming powers for a seven-year term. His intransigency cost him his seat in the National Assembly in the 1958 elections, which were swept by the Gaullists, but in, April 1959, he was elected to the less powerful Senate, where he served until he returned to the Assembly in November 1962. Now established as a major figure in the opposition, he maneuvered for the next few years through the "byzantine intrigues" of the fractured French left, advocating an alliance of the moderate left with the French Communist Party (PCF). On September 9, 1965, he declared himself a candidate in the Presidential election of that year and, on the following day, it was announced that the small group that he headed, the UDSR, had joined with the Socialists, Radicals, and other factions to form the Federation of the Democratic and Socialist Left (FGDS). Soon the Communists also agreed to support the FGDS, thus enabling Mitterrand to run in the election as the candidate of the united left. On the first round of voting, he astonished observers by winning 32.2 percent of the vote, preventing de Gaulle from achieving an absolute majority and forcing him into an embarrassing second-round runoff. De Gaulle won the runoff by 54.5 percent to 45.5 percent for Mitterrand.

As head of the FGDS, Mitterrand labored to strengthen the leftist alliance. It scored major gains in the Parliamentary elections of 1967, but, in 1968, Mitterrand made a miscalculation that caused its standing to take a plunge. During the student and worker rebellion of 1968, he dramatically offered to head a provisional government, apparently acting on a conviction that de Gaulle would soon resign. The rebellion fizzled out, however, and in the parliamentary elections of June 1968, the left was decimated by a Gaullist landslide that eventually led to dissolution of the FGDS in November. In May 1969, an attempt to unify the center-left groupings into a new Socialist Party collapsed. Mitterrand's group, the Convention des Institutions Republicaines (CIR), refused to join the reconstituted party, but, after two more years of maneuvering, Mitterrand saw his chance and led the CIR to the Socialist Party Congress at Epinay-sur-Seine in the middle of June 1971. By mustering the support of two other factions for his platform, which argued that the Socialist Party should develop its own detailed program before entering upon negotiations with the Communists, Mitterrand triumphed at the Congress. On June 16, the Central Committee voted to name him the First Secretary of the Socialist Party [French Parti Socialiste (PS)], to which he had never before belonged.

LIFE'S WORK

The campaign began in March, with six minor candidates and four major ones: Mitterrand, Giscard, Marchais, and Jacques Chirac, the Mayor of Paris and Giscard's right-wing competitor. Giscard was vulnerable, for France longed for a change from too many years of Gaullist rule and Giscard's remote, patrician manner. Mitterrand tried to position himself correctly, adopting as his slogan the phrase "*la force tranquille*," or "quiet strength." Campaigning in a low-keyed manner, he played down some of the Project Socialiste's more extreme proposals and indicated that the Communists would play a minor role if he won. His campaign was largely based on criticism of Giscard's record, particularly his failure to combat high unemployment and inflation, his cozy relationship with the U.S.S.R., and what Mitterrand saw as his Presidential abuses of power. Mitterrand promised the social welfare improvements, nationalization, and third-world foreign policy that the Socialists had long advocated, to which Giscard responded by branding his proposals as impractical and inflationary, and by stressing the economic growth that France had enjoyed during his own term.

Affiliation: Socialist Party

When Mitterrand took over, the Socialist Party was a negligible amalgam of hostile fiefdoms whose candidate had received only five percent of the vote in the 1969 Presidential election, and whose membership was down to 80,000 from the 355,000 it had numbered in 1946. To that fractious and weakened party, Mitterrand brought a strategy based on his conviction that the Socialist Party could only win power through the "unity of the left." It must, he felt, also "rebalance the left" by increasing its strength in relation to the Communists, thus offering the French a genuine alternative to Gaullism, and one less terrifying than that of Communism. Mitterrand supervised the preparation of a Party Program called *"Changer la Vie"* (or "Change Life") and then entered into the bruising negotiations with Georges Marchais, Secretary General of the Communist party, which eventuated on June 27, 1972, in the historic "Common Program," (an electoral program under which both parties pledged to run). The Common Program provided for improvements in social welfare, including higher minimum wages and pensions; nationalization of private banking, insurance, and certain major industrial firms; constitutional reforms reducing Presidential powers; and, France's continued membership in both NATO and the European Economic Council (EEC).

The dividends of the Common Program immediately became apparent. In the Parliamentary elections of March 1973, the left polled 45.8 percent of the vote, its highest total since 1956, and the PS-MRG alliance polled 20.8 percent, only 0.6 percent less than the PCF. The Socialist Party's rapid growth was spurred even more by the presidential elections that followed the death of Georges Pompidou on April 2, 1974. Announcing, on April 8, that he would be the candidate of the united left, Mitterrand pledged himself to campaign for a more just society, greater defense of civil liberties and structural changes that would give the Prime Minister, more power as a check on the President.

In the first round of voting, on May 5, Mitterrand led eleven other candidates with 43.4 percent of the vote, while Valery Giscard d'Estaing, a Gaullist former finance minister, ranked second. In the week of frenetic campaigning between the first and second rounds, both men claimed to be advocates of change, so that the contest focused on images rather than issues. The aristocratic Giscard presented himself as a

Kennedyesque liberal, doing his best to excite popular fears of a government with Communist participation. Mitterrand projected a cool and moderate image, although he was not above denouncing Giscard as the minion of "these princes, these dukes, these millionaires [who] have not had a new idea in fifteen years." On May 12, a huge voter turnout elected Giscard by the slim margin of 50.7 percent to Mitterrand's 49.3 percent.

Mitterrand's near-victory severely strained the alliance of the left, especially the Communists who, aghast at the rapid growth of the Socialist party, began to attack Mitterrand constantly. Mitterrand angrily responded, and the sniping continued throughout 1975 as the Socialists continued to improve their vote in by-elections. The departmental elections of the spring of 1976 confirmed the trend: The combined left polled a stunning 56.4 percent on the first round, with the Socialists surpassing the Communists by 26.5 percent to 22.8 percent. And the municipal elections of early 1977 gave political observers a feeling of *deja vu*, when the left again defeated the right, by 49.3 percent to 37.9 percent. Since the Socialists were now the largest political party, opinion polls predicted that the left would win the parliamentary elections in March 1978.

Shortly after the municipal elections, the Communists demanded a much more radical Common Program, including more nationalization, a higher minimum wage, and more posts for their party in a projected left government. Acrimonious talks proceeded throughout 1977, with Mitterrand arguing within his party for compromise, but, on September 22, 1977, the Communists rejected the Socialists' offer, and the talks broke down. When the campaign began on February 20, opinion polls still predicted a victory for the left. However, the widespread disillusionment over the breakdown of the alliance and the Communists' vituperative attacks on the Socialists revived the traditional French fears of intransigent Communists, with the result that the government parties won a comfortable majority in the National Assembly, with 291 seats to 200.

Although most observers believed the Communists had sabotaged the Common Program out of their reluctance to be junior partners in a Socialist regime, the 1978 elections nevertheless represented a cata-

---

Affiliation: Socialist Party *(Continued)*

strophic setback for Mitterrand, who was now viewed as a loser. But he persevered. At the Socialist Party Congress at Metz, in April 1979, he was challenged by the rightist Michel Rocard; although Mitterrand won, the resolution expressing his viewpoint failed to obtain a clear majority of the votes for the first time in his tenure. During the summer of 1979, he proposed a new Common Program to the Communists, but Marchais stalled for time. At the Party's annual convention, held at Alfortville in January 1980, delegates approved a new program, the so-called "Project Socialists." There was considerable dissatisfaction with Mitterrand in the party, both among those who felt he could not win in the Presidential election scheduled for 1981, and those who disliked his centralized style of leadership. But when Mitterrand finally announced his candidacy in November, Rocard and other prospective Party candidates dropped out, and the Socialist Party overwhelmingly supported Mitterrand at its January 1981 convention.

In the first round of voting, on April 26, both Giscard and Mitterrand fared slightly better than expected, by coming in first and second respectively, with 28.3 percent and 25.8 percent of the vote. Chirac took 18 percent and Marchais polled 15.3 percent, a devastating drop from the Communists usual 20 percent. Marchais' poor showing provided the key to the election, for it lulled French fears that Communists would be a major influence in a left government. During the two weeks between rounds, Giscard resorted to Red Menace scare tactics, while Mitterrand used his acerbic wit to skewer the President with such phrases as "the monarchy that dares not speak its name." On May 10, 1981, the French elected Mitterrand with a healthy margin of 15,714,598 to 14,647,787.

Thousands of leftists danced in the streets of Paris, prices on the bourse plunged, and the franc plummeted on foreign exchange markets. One source of anxiety was that France now had a divided government, with a Socialist President, but a rightist-controlled National Assembly. One of Mitterrand's first official acts, therefore, was to dissolve Parliament and call for new elections in June. In the two rounds of voting on June 14 and 21, the Socialists and their ally the Movement of Radicals of the Left (MRG) or *"Mouvement des Radicaux de Gauche,"* won a stunning majority of 285 seats in the 491-seat Assembly, with the Communists taking 44 seats (half their former total) and the combined right taking 157.

When Mitterrand was inaugurated on May 21, he asked somewhat rhetorically in his brief address: "In today's world, can there be a loftier duty for our country than to achieve a new alliance between Socialism and liberty, a more noble ambition than to offer it to tomorrow's world?" On the next day he announced his Cabinet, which was dominated by members of the moderate or rightist wings of the Party such as Pierre Mauroy as Prime Minister, Gaston Defferre as Interior Minister, Jacques Delors as Minister of Economy and Finance, and Claude Cheysson as Foreign Minister. However, several left-wingers also were given Cabinet posts, and all other factions of the party were represented among the full and junior ministers. The Cabinet immediately imposed emergency measures to halt the decline of the franc and the flight of capital from the country. A number of significant, but not radical social measures were also decreed during Mitterrand's first month in office. These included a ten percent increase in the minimum wage to $3.10 an hour; a hike of about 25 percent in payments to the poor, aging, and handicapped; a mandatory fifth week of paid vacation for all salaried workers; the creation of some 50,000 government jobs; and, a reduction in the work week. To raise money for those benefits, the Socialists said they would ask Parliament to impose an array of new taxes on the rich and on corporations.

The 1982 budget Mitterrand proposed to the Assembly, in September 1980, contrasted sharply with those of most other Western governments in that it was frankly expansionary, calling for a 27 percent increase in spending to reduce unemployment, which the Socialists regarded as their primary task. Reforms involving criminal justice were quickly enacted, including the abolition of the death penalty and of the draconian State Security Court. But the two centerpieces of Mitterrand's First-Year Program were his plans for decentralization and nationalization.

Formally proposed in July 1981, the decentralization plan would abolish one of the main features of Napoleonic government, the system under which virtually every local decision must be approved by a prefect appointed by the central government. Prefects would be replaced by regional and departmental councils with full power over projects and budgets. The nationalization plan, on the other hand, was viewed by Mitterrand as a way to increase the central government's leverage over the economy. When it was finally passed by the Parliament on December 18, it provided for the takeover of 36 private banks and nine huge firms in the electronic, metallurgical, chemical, and armaments fields. The government was to pay some $7-billion in compensation. Mitterrand, to the relief of the business community, promised the newly nationalized firms full autonomy of action and left some of their original executives in place.

In foreign policy, Mitterrand startled some observers with his fervent support for NATO and his sharp anti-Soviet stance. At a meeting held in Luxembourg, in July 1981, of the EEC heads of state he denounced "the dangers of galloping neutralism in Western Europe" and strongly supported the NATO plan to deploy American Pershing and cruise missiles in Europe. He substantially increased the French defense budget, announced that France would develop the neutron bomb, and, during his first official visit to the United States in October, spoke favorably of President Reagan's plans for a military buildup. He did, however, urge the Americans to begin serious arms control talks with the Russians. In January, ignoring intense pressure from the United States, he signed a major contract to buy natural gas from the Soviet Union. On issues involving developing countries, he repeatedly differed with the Reagan Administration. At the Cancun, Mexico, summit meeting in October 1981, for example, he argued for a more accommodating attitude towards the demands of poor countries. He particularly disagreed with Reagan on the causes and solutions for turmoil in Central America. Mitterrand told an interviewer for *Time* (October 19, 1981): "The reality is that El Salvador lives under an unbearable, dictatorial oligarchy. ... We believe that the prolongation of those outdated systems in Latin America is a danger for the whole world. Do we speak of Communism? This is how it is introduced!" Departing from the pro-Arab tilt of previous French governments, Mitterrand was an ardent friend of Israel, and, in March 1982, he journeyed there for an emotional two-day visit, the first by a French president. While in Israel, he spoke before the Parliament, chiding both the PLO for not recognizing Israel's right to exist, and the Israelis for not recognizing the Palestinian right to an independent state.

A year after Mitterrand took office, it was clear that his administration would mark a watershed in French history, although pragmatism dictated that some reforms be delayed or toned down. For example, a much publicized tax on various forms of wealth emerged from the Assembly in November 1981, with so many exemptions that it was expected to bring in less than one percent of government revenues. In April 1982, the government actually cut corporate taxes in an effort to stimulate investment, and decided to postpone further reductions in the work week.

Such concessions provoked squabbling within the Party between moderates and radicals, creating an impression that the government lacked direction. In January, the Socialists lost four Parliamentary by-elections, and, in local voting in March, the left lost to the right by two percent of the vote. Worst of all, the economy remained in a parlous state: By mid-1982, unemployment had actually increased, partly because of political opposition from businessmen, who were refusing to invest, and inflation still ran at about 14 percent. That high rate caused Mitterrand to devalue the franc twice, in October 1981 and June 1982, in order to ease speculative pressure on foreign exchange markets.

Nevertheless, Mitterrand remained determined to stay the course with his expansionary policy, which included improving pensions for the elderly; paid parental leave; increasing the amount of family allowances; increasing the number of child-care facilities; and dropping fees for some medications. While hosting an economic summit meeting at Versailles in June for the leaders of the seven largest industrial nations of the West, he called for more state investment and planning for new technologies "to make sure that technology will not destroy jobs at a faster rate than it can create them."

During the nine years he served as President, Mitterrand worked with seven Prime Ministers, two of whom represented opposition parties. The zigzags of his long political career had given rise to one of his epithets as "the chameleon," and he demonstrated his practicality and adaptability throughout his career as President of France.

He consistently, however, criticized the U.S.S.R., although he was a Socialist. France became more distant from the U.S.S.R., after the expulsion of 47 Soviet diplomats and their families from the country in 1982 (they had been accused of large-scale industrial and military espionage). Mitterrand also sharply criticized the Soviet intervention in Afghanistan as well as the country's nuclear weapons buildup.

He also was concerned about the developments in East Germany and in the Balkans, fearing that there would be "violent outbursts" in the former Yugoslavia, with the recognition of Croatia and Slovenia.

During his second term as President, his government expanded social welfare domestically, which included the creation of the Insertion Minimum Revenue (RMI), which ensured a minimum level of income to those deprived of any other form of income; restoration of the Solidarity Tax on Wealth; the institution of the Generalized Social Tax; the extension of parental leave up to the child's third birthday; the introduction of a private child-care allowance; the extension of the age limit for family allowances to 18 years in 1990; the 1989 Education Act which, amongst other measures, obliged local authorities to educate all children with disabilities; the reform of the Common Agricultural Policy; and, the 1990 Gayssot Act on hate speech and Holocaust denial.

Mitterrand also was concerned about the Anglicization of French speaking Africa, the former colonies of France, and he reached out to their current governments with mixed results.

After the signing of the Maastricht Treaty, Mitterrand and Kohl also were able to get their respective nations to move on from the tragedy of World War II. Although Mitterrand at first opposed the reunification of the two Germanies, his relationship with Kohl eventually made him supportive of a reunited Germany. Both heads of states believed that a Europe with countries that cooperated with one another and shared a common currency was necessary to prevent another major European war.

The most negative event during Mitterrand's tenure was the bombing of a Greenpeace U.K., vessel by French intelligence operatives. The *Rainbow Warrior*, which was used by the organization to support whaling, seal hunting, nuclear testing, and nuclear waste dumping campaigns, during the late 1970s and early 1980s, exploded in the Auckland harbor in New Zealand. After the first explosion, a photographer went back to the ship to retrieve photographic equipment and was killed. The ship was on its way to protest French nuclear testing on the island of Moruroa. In mid-1985, the French Defense Minister, Charles Hernu, was forced to resign after the discovery of French involvement. Two agents pleaded guilty to manslaughter and were sentenced to ten years in prison, but only served two years before being released. In 2006, after Mitterrand's death, it was revealed that he had personally authorized the bombing.

Mitterrand died of prostate cancer, which he had chosen to not disclose to the public, in Paris on January 8, 1996. His private physician, Dr. Claude Gubler, wrote a book called *Le Grand Secret* ("The Great Secret"), which revealed the late President's cancer and the falsification of medical reports to hide it from the public. Mitterrand's family then prosecuted the doctor and his publisher for violating medical confidentiality.

His private funeral was held in the town of his birth, Jarnac. He was buried in the family tomb in the southwestern French town, after a private mass. Twenty thousand people converged on the town. Media reports stated that his wife, Danielle Mitterrand, was joined by her children and grandchildren while watching the funeral procession to the cemetery. His mistress, Anne Pingeot, and their 21-year-old daughter, Mazarine, stood next to his wife and children. A Requiem Mass also was held in Paris at the Notre Dame Cathedral. *CNN* (January 11, 1996) reported that German Chancellor Helmut Kohl, Mitterrand's partner in more than a decade of robust European interaction, shed tears, as did as Cuban President Fidel Castro.

PERSONAL LIFE
Mitterrand had married the former Danielle Gouze (died, 2011), on October 24, 1944. He met her while they were both in the Resistance. The couple had three sons: Pascal Mitterrand (who did in infancy); Jean-Christophe, a journalist; and, Gilbert, a law professor. Mitterrand also had a daughter, Mazarine Pingeot-Mitterrand, by his mistress Anne Pingeot, and a son Hravn Forsne (with whom he fathered with Swedish journalist Christina Forsne).

Mitterrand was an officer of the Legion of Honor, and for his World War II service he received the Croix de Guerre and the Rosette de la Resistance. He wrote ten books of political and literary essays, which include, *La Chine au Defi*, 1961; *Le Coup d'État Permanent, 1964; Un Socialisms du Possible, 1971*; *La Rose au Poing, 1973; La Faille et le Grain, 1975; L'Abeille et L'Architecte, 1978;* and *lei et Maintenan, 1980.* Mitterrand's autobiography, *Ma Part de Verite,* was published in 1969. He worked on a novel for over a decade, and selections from his journals were published in English as *The Wheat and the Chaff, 1982.*

FURTHER READING
International Who's Who, 1982-1983; Nugent, Neill, and Lowe, David. The Left in France, 1982; International Year Book and Statesmen's Who's Who, 1982; Who's Who, 1982-83; Who's Who in France, 1979-1980.

KIICHI MIYAZAWA

Prime Minister of Japan

Born: October 8, 1919; Fukuyama, Japan
Died: June 28, 2007; Tokyo, Japan
Affiliation: Liberal Democratic Party

INTRODUCTION

The prime minister of Japan, Kiichi Miyazawa, is a veteran bureaucrat with fifty years of experience behind him in a wide variety of government positions. From his first assignment in the Finance Ministry during World War II to his ascendancy to the office of prime minister on November 5, 1991, he has played a significant role in the creation of modern Japan. Within the private councils of the ruling Liberal Democratic party he has been a contender for prime minister at least since the late 1970s. His career was thought to have ended in December 1988, when he was forced to resign as finance minister after being implicated in the Recruit Company influence-peddling scandal. He owes his swift return to favor to the failure of his predecessor, Toshiki Kaifu, to muster support in the Japanese parliament for his policies and to the public's unwillingness to punish the ruling party for the scandal in the 1990 elections.

The first Japanese prime minister to speak fluent English, Miyazawa has long had extensive relations with the United States. As minister of international trade and industry, he negotiated a complex textile accord with the administration of President Richard Nixon. As foreign affairs minister, he quarreled publicly with the administration of President Jimmy Carter over energy policy, and as minister of finance, he engaged in protracted negotiations over trade and currency rates with the Ronald Reagan administration. Such longstanding ties with the United States, coupled with his unabashed admiration for Americans, have drawn criticism from some Japanese, who fear that he may cave in to American demands on trade and economics. (He "stinks of butter," his detractors sneer in reference to Western influence.) His admirers dismiss such fears. "He knows America and he speaks English extremely well, but that does not mean he is pro-American," an unidentified Japanese diplomat told Steven R. Weisman of The New York Times (October 28, 1991). "He might even be more blunt than Americans are used to. It's something he is going to have to watch."

Kiichi Miyazawa.

EARLY LIFE

Kiichi Miyazawa was born on October 8, 1919 in Tokyo, Japan. His father, Yutaka Miyazawa, represented the Hiroshima Prefecture in the Japanese parliament, and his mother, Koto Miyazawa, also was from a prominent political family. One of his younger brothers serves in the upper house of parliament; the other was an ambassador. Miyazawa was educated at Tokyo Imperial University, and he was a representative at the Sixth Japan-America Student Conference, held in the United States in 1939.

LIFE'S WORK

In 1942 Miyazawa joined the Finance Ministry and within seven years rose to become the minister's private secretary. Like many Japanese, he recalls the American occupation with distaste, especially the arrogance of General Douglas A. MacArthur. As a delegate to the San Francisco Peace Conference, Miyazawa was present on September 8, 1951 when forty-nine nations concluded the peace treaty with Japan, restoring its "full sovereignty" but permitting the continued presence of American forces on Japanese soil.

From 1953 to 1965, Miyazawa served in the House of Councillors the largely ceremonial upper chamber of the Japanese Diet, of parliament. He was vice-minister of education during 1959 and 1960. In 1967 he was elected to his father's seat in the House of Representatives. Miyazawa served three separate stints as director general of the Economic Planning Agency: 1962 to 1964; 1966 to 1968; and 1977 to 1978. In the last instance, under Prime Minister Takeo Fukuda, the appointment reportedly was the result of political infighting, in which the supporters of Masayoshi Ohira, the secretary-general of the ruling party, perceived Miyazawa as a potential threat to Ohira's ambition to succeed Fukuda. In denying Miyazawa a more prominent cabinet post, Ohira's supporters hoped to undermine any plans he might have had to challenge Ohira. During his last year as chief economic planner, Miyazawa organized a new policy council to deal with the burgeoning trade dispute with the United States.

Before Miyazawa's career path was diverted by Ohira, he had served in two key cabinet posts: he was minister of international trade and industry from 1970 to 1971 and foreign minister from 1974 to 1976. In the former position, during the administration of Prime Minister Eisaku Sato, he oversaw construction of the Japanese World Exposition (Expo '70) at Senri Hills outside Osaka and engaged in protracted negotiations with the Nixon administration over a textile treaty. In June 1970 he flew to Washington, D.G., for talks with Secretary of Commerce Maurice Stans in an attempt to iron out technical differences between the two countries, but he returned to Tokyo empty-handed. A textile agreement was finally reached in the following year. As foreign minister during the oil shortage of the mid-1970s, Miyazawa was unusually outspoken in his criticism of the Carter administration for losing control of the American economy and for failing to respond to the energy crisis. In a country that reveres harmony and where even serious differences can be cloaked in euphemism, Miyazawa startled some observers by denouncing Washington for "dragging its feet on energy."

From 1980 to 1982 Miyazawa served as minister of state and chief cabinet secretary. In 1984, while serving as chairman of the ruling party's executive council, he was mugged at a Tokyo hotel, to which he had been lured by a man posing as a campaign contributor. Despite a blow to the head, Miyazawa managed to wrestle his assailant to submission and gained favorable attention in the press for his courage. By November of that year he had emerged as the main challenger to Prime Minister Yasuhiro Nakasone's reelection. Because Nakasone had ignored Miyazawa in choosing his cabinet, Miyazawa was able to exploit his position as an outsider to offer an economic alternative to Nakasone's austere budget. That was Miyazawa's so-called asset doubling plan, which called for more public-works spending and less emphasis on foreign trade. "We should do what we can now, not so much to export our products more but to improve what we are lacking," he declared, as reported in *The New York Times* (July 8, 1984).

In a country where, despite its growing wealth, half the people were without flush toilets, Miyazawa's plan hit a responsive chord. Although Nakasone won reelection, Miyazawa's political standing was enhanced significantly. By the next election, in 1986, he had inherited from Zenko Suzuki the leadership of Nakasone's main rival faction within the Liberal Democratic party. Again Miyazawa pressed for more public-works projects, this time under a plan to be financed from bonds and the sale of government shares in Japan Air Lines and Nippon Telegraph and Telephone. Although he failed to muster enough support from other faction leaders to deny Nakasone a third term that year, Miyazawa's growing popularity induced Nakasone to bring him into the cabinet as his finance minister. During 1987 and 1988 he also served concurrently as deputy prime minister.

Miyazawa's two years as finance minister were dominated by negotiations with the United States over trade and currency exchange rates. In the face of an alarming trade deficit, Secretary of State James A. Baker 3d engineered a steep slide in the dollar on world currency markets, beginning in February 1985. The objective was to render American goods cheaper abroad and foreign goods more expensive to import, thus letting the marketplace correct the trade imbalance without resort to the protectionist legislation then under consideration in Congress. At a secret meeting in San Francisco in September 1986, Miyazawa and Baker laid the foundation for a broader agreement, reached on October 31 of that year, which sought to stabilize the dollar and offset the Japanese trade surplus. Under its rather vague terms, the United States agreed to end its efforts to drive down the dollar in return for Japan's promise to lower interest rates and otherwise fuel a domestic expansion, which, in turn, would increase demand for imported goods and thus reverse, or at least slow, its trade surplus. For a time, the agreement seemed to be working, as the dollar began to firm against the yen, but by the end of the year, the dollar's slide had resumed.

Although the Reagan administration apparently was not deliberately weakening the dollar, neither was it doing anything to check its decline, reportedly because of disappointment in Tokyo's apathetic expansionist policy. On January 22, 1987, a few days after the yen hit a thirty-eight-year high against the dollar, Miyazawa flew to Washington for an emergency meeting with Baker. The two-and-a-half-hour session produced another vaguely worded communique, in which Baker held out the possibility of intervention to prop up the dollar but pointedly refrained from making an outright commitment. Although Miyazawa tried to put the best construction on the meeting, he returned to Tokyo without the assurances for American intervention that he had sought. Finally, at a Group of Six meeting in Paris on February 22 of that year, Miyazawa was able to persuade Baker and his counterparts in Britain, France, West Germany, and Canada that a coordinated effort to stabilize world currencies was crucial to the achievement of a healthy world economy.

In a clear change in American policy, Baker asserted that he would cooperate in checking any further fall in the dollar. "I . . . am happy, very happy with the results of this meeting," Miyazawa said. For its part, Japan reasserted more forcefully its pledge to "follow monetary and fiscal policies which will help to expand domestic demand and thereby contribute to reducing the domestic surplus." In an interview with Hobart Rowan of the *Washington Post* (April 17, 1988), however, Miyazawa refueled old skepticism concerning Japan's sincerity on trade issues. "I really don't know how far we can go," he said, "how far we are willing to go—and how quickly. It may be that Japan is such a country [of] consensus that once set on the way [to lower surpluses], it may go all the way. . . . That's just possible. Then one day, we will be suffering from a trade deficit."

In the race to succeed Nakasone in 1987, Miyazawa competed against rival faction leaders Noboru Takeshita, the party's secretary-general and a former finance minister; Shintaro Abe, the leader of the party's executive council and a former foreign minister; and Susumu Nikaido, a party gadfly with little traditional support.

The "New Leaders," as the candidates were dubbed in the press, kicked off their genteel intra-party campaign on October 8 following months of closed-door maneuvering. In typical Japanese fashion, Miyazawa spoke in language that by Western standards sounded like false humility. "My colleagues are just as good as I am," he was reported as saying in the *Washington Post* (October 9, 1987). "All I can say is I will try my best depending upon my past experience. But my colleagues also have their great merits. . . . Being a Japanese, that's the extent of my modest answer." As expected, Takeshita was elected prime minister. Continuing as finance minister, Miyazawa pushed an innovative plan to restructure Third World debt, elements of which were incorporated in the Latin American debt-relief package worked out with United States secretary of the treasury Nicholas F. Brady in 1988.

In the same year, Miyazawa's dream of becoming prime minister evaporated in the Recruit scandal. Executives of Recruit, an aggressive information-services and real-estate conglomerate, tried to curry favor with politicians and bureaucrats by selling them shares of stock at a sharp discount from market value just before the stock was to be sold to the general public for the first time. Among those offered the risk-free opportunity to buy the discounted shares on the eve of the public offering was Miyazawa's secretary. Moreover, his secretary purchased the stock in Miyazawa's name—apparently with an interest-free loan from a Recruit financial subsidiary. Although none of that behavior is illegal under Japanese law, it certainly was unseemly for the nation's finance minister to profit at the public's expense.

Miyazawa compounded his problems by changing his explanation with each fresh disclosure. At first he insisted that his secretary had bought the stock in his own name without his knowledge. Faced with evidence to the contrary, the minister conceded that he had authorized the purchase in his name, but only as a favor to the salesman, who claimed that he needed to use a politician's name to be assured of getting in on the deal. When a parliamentary investigation contradicted Miyazawa's version of events, he tailored his story yet again to fit the existing evidence. As one of the few targets of Recruit brazen, or foolish, enough to register the stock in his own name, Miyazawa was particularly vulnerable to charges of impropriety. He apologized publicly but resisted calls for his resignation until December 9, 1988, when party leaders insisted that he step down.

To cleanse the party of the scandal, faction leaders proposed Toshiki Kaifu, one of the few senior party members untouched by impropriety, as prime minister in August 1989. The Liberal Democratic party, which has ruled Japan since its inception in a merger of the Liberal and Democratic parties in 1955, then braced for the elections of February 18, 1990, the first chance voters would have to punish the party directly. Perhaps because Recruit's reach had extended into the opposition parties as well, voters seemed unwilling to single out the Liberal Democrats for special blame. The ruling party won 275 seats, a comfortable majority, which, together with support from allied parties, constituted a loss of just ten seats. Only one member implicated in the scandal was defeated. Despite his humiliating resignation, Miyazawa, too, was reelected to a seat in parliament.

By September 1991 Miyazawa was confident enough of his rehabilitation within the party to begin jockeying to succeed Kaifu, who was in trouble for his timid posturing amid Iraq's aggression against Kuwait and the abortive coup in the Soviet Union as well as for his failure to enlist support in parliament for the political reforms he had promised upon taking office. "This is an exceptional time, where we do need leadership," Miyazawa said, in an obvious slap at Kaifu, as reported in *The New York Times* (September 26, 1991). "Our indecision at the time of the gulf war was a case in point. You know, our civil servants cannot establish goals for Japan. They look to the prime minister's office for decisions, which were not forthcoming." At a private party meeting on October 4, the Takeshita faction withdrew its support from Kaifu, forcing him to renounce another term as prime minister.

Miyazawa quickly emerged as the front-runner over former finance minister Michio Watanabe and former transportation minister Hiroshi Mit-suzuka. The Takeshita faction (led by Shin Kane-maru, who resigned as vice-chairman of the Liberal Democratic party in August 1992) invited one of its own, Ichiro Ozawa, to run, but when he declined for health reasons, it finally agreed to support Miyazawa. The endorsement, announced on October 11, assured his victory. In Japanese fashion, he accepted with the obligatory self-deprecation: "I do not believe I am worthy of the honor." In a pro-forma vote of Liberal Democratic members of parliament and local party officials on October 27, Miyazawa received 285 of 492 votes cast, to 120 for Watanabe and 87 for Mit-suzuka, thus paving the way for his formal appointment as prime minister on November 5, 1991.

Miyazawa vowed to coordinate economic and foreign policy closely with the United States. Although economic and trade differences deeply divide the two countries, he has consistently professed admiration for the United States. In the interview with Hobart Rowan, for example, he said, "To many Japanese minds, America is a great country, and they probably—if you really forced the question—would say, in essence, that they believe in America. This is still a great country." But he also vowed as prime minister to speak "frankly" about those differences. And he is known to resent the Japan-bashers in the United States and elsewhere who blame all their economic problems on Tokyo.

The chief challenges facing the new prime minister were the extent to which he could open up the Japanese rice market to cheaper imports without incurring the wrath of the country's powerful rice farmers; working out a World War II-related territorial dispute with the Soviet Union over the Kuril Islands; exerting greater Japanese influence in foreign affairs, particularly within Asia; and following through on Kaifu's unfulfilled promises of campaign reform. He formed a cabinet composed largely of veteran politicians, many of them returning to power for the first time since the Recruit scandal. He also named his erstwhile rival, Michio Watanabe, as foreign minister and deputy prime minister.

Meeting with President Bush in Tokyo and New York City in January 1992 and in Washington, D.C., in July of that year, Miyazawa indicated a willingness to use "every possible means" to stimulate the Japanese economy. Between July 1991 and July 1992 the Bank of Japan lowered the discount interest rate five times at Miyazawa's urging in order to halt an economic downturn, which was partly responsible for an increase in Japan's trade surplus with the United States. Miyazawa also took steps to assuage the fears of those who criticized Japan for practicing "checkbook diplomancy" during the Persian Gulf war—that is, for supporting the war effort financially but not with personnel. On June 15, 1992 Japan passed a controversial peacekeeping-operations bill that would allow the deployment of troops overseas for the first time since World War II. In the elections of July 26, 1992, which were widely perceived as a referendum on that bill, the Liberal Democratic party gained a working majority in the upper house of the Diet, winning sixty-eight of the 127 contested seats. Not long afterward, on September 8, 1992, Miyazawa announced that 1,800 troops would be sent to Cambodia as part of the United Nations peacekeeping forces there.

PERSONAL LIFE

Kiichi Miyazawa was a short, balding man who was described as imaginative, intelligent, mild-mannered, soft-spoken, and courtly, but also as aloof, arrogant, and overbearing at times. His fluency in English engendered resentment among some Japanese, including a cabinet minister who once criticized him for debating Henry Kissinger in English. "What's wrong with Japanese?" the minister asked. "Is he ashamed of his own language?" Miyazawa seemed baffled by such criticism. He and his wife, Yoko, whom he met in the United States at the Japanese-American student conference and whom he married in 1943, have a son, Hiro, an architect, and a daughter, Keiko, who is married to an American State Department official, Christopher J.

Lafleur. Miyazawa enjoyed reading and attending performances of No plays, the highly stylized Japanese dance-drama. He was the author of *Tokyo-Washington Secret Talks* (1956) and *Challenge for Beautiful Japan* (1984), both in Japanese. Miyazawa died in Tokyo at the age of 87 on June 28, 2007.

FURTHER READING
The New York Times A p5 O 12 '91 por, A pl+ O 28 '91 por; *International Yearbook and Statesmen's Who's Who,* 1990; *International Who's Who,* 1991-92; *Who's Who in the World,* 1991-92

VIACHESLAV M. MOLOTOV
Communist Party Leader

Born: March 9, 1890; Kukarka, Russian Empire
Died: November 8, 1986; Moscow, Soviet Union
Affiliation: Communist Party of the Soviet Union

INTRODUCTION
The Western world knows Viacheslav M. Molotov primarily as the chief spokesman for Soviet policy during World War II, and during the postwar period when Communist expansion in eastern Europe and parts of Asia led to growing deterioration in East-West relationships. As Commissar (later Minister) for Foreign Affairs from 1939 to 1949, and since early 1953, Molotov attended most of the important international meetings of the time, including the Conference on International Organization in San Francisco in 1945 to establish the United Nations.

He was the member of longest standing in the presidium of the Central Committee of the Communist party (formerly the politburo) and one of the leaders in the U.S.S.R. who had a major part in the Bolshevik Revolution of 1917. For more than thirty years he was considered the man closest to Joseph Stalin, as the chairman of the Council of the People's Commissars (Premier) from 1930 to 1941 and deputy chairman (Vice-Premier) since 1941.

In Berlin in early 1954 Molotov conferred with the western Foreign Ministers on problems relating to Germany and Austria which remained unsolved almost ten years after World War II and which continued unsolved at the end of these talks.

Later at the Geneva conference, convened on April 26, 1954, Molotov, reiterating the position of Chinese Communist Premier and Foreign Minister Chou En-lai, asserted that the "peoples of Asia have the full right to settle their affairs themselves." The New York Times editorial (April 30, 1954) noted: "Unfortunately the Asian peoples who have thrown off foreign rule . . . to become free and self-governing are not yet strong enough to resist by their own forces the new imperialism that threatens to engulf them in the name of communism. They need the help of the older democracies to save them from being submerged in the totalitarian flood"

The Soviet Foreign Minister on May 11, 1954 bitterly attacked the Southeast Asian defense pact proposed by the United States, and also denounced the United Nations as a "belligerent" in Korea. His attack was answered by Paul-Henri Spaalc, Foreign Minister of Belgium, who declared: "We cannot allow the justifiable intervention, of the United Nations in Korea to be depicted as an act of aggression."

EARLY LIFE
Born Viacheslav Mikhailovich Skriabln on March 9, 1890, Molotov is a native of the village of Kukarka in the Vyatka (now Kirov) region. His father, Mikhail Skriabln, a shopkeeper, was able to afford music lessons and some formal education for his children. When the boy was about twelve years old he left school in Nolinsk to attend a Czarist secondary school in Kazan,

where he joined a students' Marxist group and took part in the revolution of 1905. As a member of the Bolshevik wing of the Russian Social Democratic Labor party, he became a leader in a Kazan Marxist youth organization in 1906. Still in his teens, the young Bolshevist was arrested by Czarist police and deported to Vologda in north European Russia. Here he proceeded to organize railway workers. During his years of exile, jailings, escapes and re-arrests, he used a number of pseudonyms, one of which, Molotov (hammer), he came in time to adopt permanently.

Life's Work

His two-year sentence of exile in Vologda completed in 1911, Molotov entered the Poly-technical Institute of St. Petersburg (later Leningrad). While carrying on underground activities in St. Petersburg schools, he continued studying the theories of Marx, Engels and Lenin. He contributed to the Bolshevik journal *Zvezda* and in May 1912 became part-founder, with Stalin, of *Pravda,* an official party paper illegally published in. St. Petersburg.

After being expelled from the city for his political activities, he conducted party work from the suburbs and in Moscow. Molotov was exiled to Irkutsk in Siberia in 1915, but the following year he escaped and returned to St. Petersburg to become a member of the Russian Bureau of the Bolshevik Central Committee. While many party leaders were in exile in Siberia or abroad, Molotov took a prominent role in directing preparations at home for the November 1917 Revolution which brought the Bolsheviks to power.

In 1917 he became a member of the executive of the Petrograd (Leningrad) Soviet and, with Stalin, of the military revolutionary committee. After decrees had been issued for nationalization of industry, he was made chairman in 1918 of the People's Economy Council, northern region. During the next two years he was sent to various parts of the country, to direct restoration of areas conquered by the Red Army and devastated by civil war.

Molotov's political duties increased in 1920 when he was chosen secretary of the central committee of the Communist party of the Ukraine. Upon becoming a member of the Central Committee of the Soviet Union a-year later, he was named by Lenin as the committee's responsible secretary (Stalin was general secretary of the secretariat). At the age of thirty-one (1921) he was also admitted as a candidate member of the party's

politburo (political bureau), influential in formulating Soviet government policy. In December 1925, he gained full membership on the politburo, the youngest member this body has ever had.

In the struggle for party leadership after Lenin's death, Molotov sided with Stalin against Trotsky, worked in Leningrad in 1926 against the Zinovievists (Trotsky supporters) and in Moscow in 1928 against Bukharin and Rylcov. Some of his titles at this time were member of the central executive committee of the Russian Soviet Socialist Republic (1927), member of the presidium of the central executive committee of the U.S.S.R., and member of the executive committee of the Communist International (1928-1934).

With Stalin's control of the party secure, Molotov in 1930 succeeded Rylcov as chairman of the Council of People's Commissars of the U.S.S.R., thus becoming Premier at the age of forty. "The secret of Molotov's success," wrote Walter Duranty (*Stalin & Co.,* 1949) "was that every step up the ladder, he left behind him the record of a difficult task efficiently performed." The new head of the government spoke proudly in his acceptance speech of the guidance he had received from Stalin.

As Premier he was largely concerned with the industrial and agricultural phases of the Five Year Plans, "helping Stalin to force the country through its industrial revolution and to crush all domestic opposition" (*The New York Times Magazine,* February 11, 1951). In 1935 he served on the committee for drafting reforms to the constitution. Early in the same year he made his first important speech on foreign affairs when he addressed the All-Union Soviet Congress, soon after Russia had joined the League of Nations.

In May 1939 Molotov succeeded Maxim M. Litvinov as Commissar for Foreign Affairs. His first important act in this office was the signing in August 1939 of the Russo-German nonaggression pact. While the Nazis subsequently overran the democracies in central and western Europe, the Soviet Union absorbed the Baltic Republics and engaged in war with Finland, In a continuing effort to remain at peace with Germany, the Russian diplomat visited Berlin in November 1940 for consultation with Nazi leaders, reportedly on his first trip outside his own country.

When Germany invaded the U.S.S.R. in June 1941 Molotov turned his efforts to negotiating a mutual-aid pact with Great Britain, in which both nations agreed not to make a separate peace with Germany. After a visit to England in the summer of 1942, he flew to Washington, where he arranged for an increase in lend-lease aid from the United States. The Soviet Foreign Commissar at this time also occupied the position of vice-chairman of the Council of People's Commissars, Stalin having taken over the premiership from him in May 1941. Molotov became as well in 19J-1 a member of the five-man State Committee of Defense (with Stalin, Malenkov, Beria and Voroshilov) formed to prosecute the war.

The Soviet official had an important part in the international conferences among Allied leaders during and immediately after World War II, including the historic meetings at Tehran, Yalta and Potsdam. In 1945 he headed the Soviet delegation to the Conference on International Organization in San Francisco. Here and at subsequent early sessions of the U.N. General Assembly first appeared the differences between the U.S.S.R. and the West.

While failing to reach agreement with Western powers on many details of the treaties affecting the defeated nations of World War II and on other world problems such as control of atomic energy, Molotov was able to conclude a series of trade and nonaggression pacts with eastern European nations. The satellite countries became in 1947 participants in the Council for Economic Mutual Assistance (Molotov plan). This program to integrate Soviet and eastern European economies was effected after the June 1947 Paris conference, where Molotov rejected the Marshall plan.

"The stalling, obstructionist tactics Molotov employed at the Italian peace treaty parley in 1946 and at every council of foreign ministers which he has attended are also characteristic," wrote Donald Robinson *(The 100 Most Important People)*. "By long-winded speeches impugning the democracies' motives, devious parliamentary maneuvers calculated to stall the sessions, and by an adamant refusal to compromise a single point, he either has gotten . . . what he has wanted or has seen to it that no agreement of any kind was reached."

Molotov's was "the dominant Soviet voice in the East-West debate" during the years between the end of World War II and 1949 (Anne O'Hare McCormick in *The New York Times,* July 25, 1951). Not merely Stalin's mouthpiece, he came to be regarded "more than any other man" as responsible for Soviet aggressiveness *(The New York Times Magazine,* February 11, 1951). The announcement on March 4, 1949 that he had been replaced by Andrei Y. Vishinsky as Foreign Minister gave rise to speculation in the West as to Molotov's future role in Russia. One conjecture was that he was preparing to assume, the "premiership in the event of Stalin's death. A report from Formosa in March 1952 stated that from a base in Siberia he was directing operations for an expanded Communist underground in the Far East.

After the death of Stalin on March 5, 1953, Molotov resumed his' position as Minister of Foreign Affairs. Georgi M. Malenkov, who became Premier, is believed to be a member of a committee dictatorship which supplanted the one-man rule. According to the *U.S. News & World Report* (February 26, 1954), some experts say that Molotov urged the rule by committee and is an influential member of the group.

Time (April 20, 1953) reported that the British Foreign Office sees four objectives in present Communist foreign policy: "(1) the breakdown of NATO, (2) the neutralization of Germany, (3) the end of Nationalist China, and (4) a break between the United States and her foreign allies." When the big-four Foreign Ministers met in Berlin in early 1954, Molotov attacked the European. Defense Community (EDC) and NATO as a course to another world war and proposed a collective security treaty for European countries that would exclude U.S. participation. At the Berlin conference, which failed to produce agreement on issues relating to Germany and Austria, the ministers decided to meet again, in late April in Geneva, to discuss problems of Korea and Indochina. The Chinese Communist government was invited to take part at the Geneva meeting on a basis that would not imply U.S. recognition of that government.

On two occasions (January 30 and February 13) during their stay in Berlin, Molotov and Secretary of State John Foster Dulles met in secret sessions to talk about President Dwight D. Eisenhower's proposal of an international pool of atomic energy for peacetime uses.

Molotov is the author of a number of publications (in Russian): *The Party's Policy in the Villages, Elections to the Soviets, On the Lessons of Trotskyism, On the Success and Difficulties of Socialist Building, Fighting for Socialism* and others. Among his writings available in English translation are *The Communist Party of the Soviet Union* (Modern Books, 1929), *Food for All; the Abolition of the Bread Card System in the Soviet Union* (International Publishers, 1934) *and Stalin and Stalin's Leadership* (Foreign Languages Publishing House, 1950).

Many attempts have been made by Western observers to evaluate the position of the Soviet Foreign Minister, who was also a member of the Supreme Soviet of the U.S.S.R. John Gunther expressed his opinion in *Inside Europe* that Molotov "is by no means a mere figurehead, but a man of considerable intelligence and influence." To E. Crankshaw (*The New York Times Magazine,* February 11, 1951) he is a "dangerous man . . . because of the limitations of his thought and imagination." Partly because Lenin reportedly called him "the best file clerk in Russia," Molotov was the butt of some humorous and disparaging comments in his own country and abroad. His career, as W. Duranty has pointed out, belies any idea of him as a "dull, unenterprising fellow, a plodder, who could be trusted to do a job competently but would never set any stream on fire."

PERSONAL LIFE

In 1922 he married Polina Karpovskaya, a "handsome woman noted for her charm as a hostess." She is a Ukrainian-born Jewess who worked in the Communist party of the Ukraine under the name of Zhermchuzhina (pearl) Semyanovia.

While director of the Soviet perfume and cosmetics trust, she visited the United States in 1936 to study American methods. She later (1937-1939) served as Commissar of the fish industry. The Molotovs have a daughter, Svetlana, and an adopted daughter, Sonia. The diplomat received the Order of Lenin in 1940, 1943, 1945, and 1946. He also held the Hammer and Sickle Gold Medal and the title of Hero of Socialist Labor, among other honors.

The Soviet leader was a scholarly looking figure, a stockily built man with a round face, broad forehead and trimmed mustache. He played the violin, was interested in the arts and literature, and enjoyed tennis and skiing. In manner he is methodical, precise and somewhat pedantic. Sir Winston Churchill (*Time,* April 20, 1953) once said of him, "He was above all men fitted to be the agent and instrument of ... an incalculable machine."

According to Donald Robinson in *The 100 Most Important People,* Molotov is "a very suspicious man. When he stayed at Winston Churchill's country home, he kept a loaded revolver by his bedside. He brought his own food when he stayed with President Roosevelt at the White House. He did sneak off on a secret trip to see the sights of New York. And he has no antipathy to vodka."

Molotov died on November 8, 1986. He was 96 years old at the time of his death, and was buried at the Novodevichy Cemetery in Moscow.

FURTHER READING

N Y Herald Tribune II p3 O 24 '43 por; p5 Mr 5 '53 por; *The New York Times* plO Mr 6 '53; p6 Mr 9 '53; *The New York Times* Mag pl2+ S 22 '46; p8+ F 2'47;p5+ F 11'51 por; *Newsweek* 43 :34+ F 8 '54 P M p9 Jl 9 '41 por; *Time* 61:34 Mr 16 '53; 61:32+ Ap 20 '53 por; Coates, W. P. and Z. K. *A Biographical Sketch in Soviet Peace Policy* (1941); Duranty, W. *Men Who Make Your World* (1949); Stalin & Co. (1949) Steel, J. *Men Behind the War* (1942); *Who's Who,* 1954; *Who's Who in America,* 1954-55; *World Biography* (1948)

ROBERT (GABRIEL) MUGABE (MOO-GA'BA)

President of Zimbabwe

Born: February 21, 1924; Kutama, Rhodesia (Zimbabwe)

Affiliation: African National Union, Zimbabwe African National Union, Zimbabwe African National Liberation Army, Zimbabwe African National Union-Patriotic Front

INTRODUCTION

Robert Mugabe is the current President of Zimbabwe, serving since December 22, 1987. As one of the lead-ers of the rebel groups against white-minority rule, he was elected as Prime Minister, head of government, in 1980, and served in that office until 1987, when elected the head of state. Since 1975, he has led the Zimbabwe African National Union–Patriotic Front (ZANU–PF).

Mugabe belonged to several African national movements. One of them, the Zimbabwe African National Union (ZANU), got him internationally known. He was the most militant of the black leaders in opposition to the white supremacist government of former

Rhodesian Prime Minister Ian Smith. After Smith was replaced on May 31, 1979, by Bishop Abel T. Muzorewa under a new constitution that changed the country's name to Zimbabwe Rhodesia, and ostensibly turned the government over to its black majority (but, left substantial power in the hands of the white minority), Mugabe vowed to fight on with his Mozambique-based guerrilla force for true black majority. "Genuine independence," he believed, "can only come out the barrel of a gun."

Upon release from being a political prisoner between 1964 and 1974, Mugabe and his associates left for Mozambique in 1975, to launch the fight during the Rhodesian Bush War from bases there. He emerged as a hero in the minds of many Africans. After calling for reconciliation between the former belligerents, he won the general elections of 1980, and became Prime Minister of an independent Zimbabwe.

To consolidate his power, he had to fight internal dissidents, including former allies aligned with rival Joshua Nkomo, leader of the minority Ndebele tribe, in the province of Matabeleland. He sent the Fifth Brigade, soldiers trained by North Koreans, to Nkomo's stronghold. Between 1982 and 1985, at least 20,000 people died in ethnic cleansing and were buried in mass graves. He invited the dissidents to join forces with his party, successfully ushering in a one-party, authoritarian government. In 1987, the office of Prime Minister was eliminated and Mugabe became head of state, head of government, and Commander-In-Chief of the armed forces, with powers to dissolve Parliament and declare martial law. In 2008, Mugabe entered a power-sharing deal with Morgan Tsvangirai and Arthur Mutambara, both members of opposition parties. Although this power sharing agreement reduced violent incidents in the country, it did not curtail them. Dozens of members of the opposition, and human rights activists, later had been abducted and tortured. In 2013, despite numerous accounts of electoral fraud, Mugabe won his seventh term as President.

More than a decade ago, Mugabe and his supporters were targeted with sanctions by members of the European Union and the United States. Although the European Union has lifted most of the sanctions, the U.S. has not. According to the Voice of America website, The United States, along with many other Western countries, imposed sanctions on Zimbabwe's leadership in 2002, following reports of election rigging and human rights abuses. Despite the sanctions (which also include travel bans to certain countries), the United States remains one of the major providers of humanitarian aid to Zimbabwe.

Mugabe was elected as the Chairperson of the African Union (AU) on January 30, 2015. He has announced his intention to run for re-election in 2018, at the age of 94, and has been accepted as the ZANU-PF candidate. In February 2016, Mugabe said he had no plans for retirement.

EARLY LIFE

The son of a village carpenter, Robert Gabriel Mugabe was born on February 21, 1942, at Kutama, northwestern Mashonaland, in the former British colony of Southern Rhodesia. He is a member of the Shona tribe, which now makes up over 75 percent of the population of Zimbabwe, and he belongs to the Zezuru clan. Educated in Roman Catholic mission schools in Kutama and Empenden, Mugabe began his career as a teacher at the Kutama mission in 1942, while still in his teens. In 1943 he moved on to the Dadaya mission, where he taught under superintendent Garfield Todd, who later became Prime Minister of Southern Rhodesia. Mugabe had his first clash with authority when he threatened to "box" Todd because of a deduction from his scanty teacher's pay. According to a profile in the London Observer (October 31, 1976), he "raised quite a hell of a row," before the amount deducted was restored. From 1946 to 1949, he taught at the Hope Fountain Mission.

In 1950, Mugabe went to South Africa to attend the University of Fort Hare, a training ground for black political leaders. There he qualified for a B.A. degree after a year's study, and it was there, too, that he first became seriously interested in politics. Returning to Southern Rhodesia, he obtained a teaching job in 1952 at the Drifontein Roman Catholic school in Umvuma, about ninety miles south of Salisbury (now Harare, Zimbabwe). In 1953-1954, he was a teacher in the government service, first at the Salisbury South Primary School, and then in the midlands town of Gwelo. Mugabe moved to Northern Rhodesia (now Zambia), in 1955, to teach at the Chipembe Teacher Training College. From the autumn of 1956 until the spring of 1960, he was in Accra, Ghana. There he married, taught at St. Mary Teacher Training College, and fell under the influence of the radical politics of President Kwame Nkrumah. According to Who's Who in Africa (1973), his experience in Ghana gave him "a breadth of vision on African nationalism [that] few of his compatriots developed."

Life's Work

It wasn't until a cease fire was negotiated, in September 1979, at Lancaster House, where Smith, Mugabe, Nkomo, and others were attendance that the fighting stopped. The concerned parties also agreed on a new constitution for a new Republic of Zimbabwe, with elections in February 1980. The Lancaster Agreement saw Mugabe make two concessions: He allowed 20 seats to be reserved for whites in the new Parliament; and, he agreed to a ten-year moratorium on constitutional amendments.

His return to Zimbabwe in 1979 was well received, and he became Prime Minister in the 1980 elections and President in 1987.

Besides ethnic cleansing, during 1982 to 1985; continual human rights violations and violence; election fraud; and, involvement of Zimbabwe's troops in the Democratic Republic of Congo's civil war; Mugabe, beginning in 2000, encouraged the takeovers of white-owned commercial farms, leading to economic collapse and runaway inflation. Although his referendum to develop a new constitution that would allow the government takeover of white farms did not pass, groups of individuals calling themselves "war veterans" invaded white-owned farms, causing many whites to flee the country. As a former schoolteacher, Mugabe did not neglect education in his nation; however, an observer had noted that schools throughout the country had close.

Reports also have surfaced that his second wife, Grace Marufu Mugabe, is a "lavish" spender in a country that is so impoverished that it cannot keep its schools open. Her sometimes lavish international shopping sprees have led to the nickname "Gucci Grace," and she has been targeted with travel sanctions, along with Mugabe, since 2002. It remains to be seen if the infamous 94-year-old President will run in the 2018 elections.

Back in Southern Rhodesia, Mugabe immersed himself in the nationalist struggle against the white supremacist government of Prime Minister Edgar Whitehead. In 1960-1961, he was Publicity Secretary (or information minister) in Joshua Nkomo's newly formed National Democratic Party (NDP), which sought to bring about "one man, one vote" rule by means of moral persuasion, civil disobedience, and propaganda abroad. Mugabe's education enabled him to bridge the gap between the grassroots peasantry and the intellectuals in the nationalist movement, and he insisted on involving the largely illiterate rural population in the drive for African rights and majority rule. "It will be necessary for graduates, doctors, lawyers, and others who join the NDP to accept the chosen leaders, even if they may not be university men," Mugabe declared in a speech on June 11, 1960.

As its publicity secretary, Mugabe was charged with the task of announcing the NDP's initial assent to a new constitution on February 7, 1961, following a constitutional conference with British authorities at Salisbury. Although the constitution admitted blacks to the Southern Rhodesian Parliament for the first time, Mugabe opposed it, since it granted 50 of the 65 Parliamentary seats to whites, who comprised only about one twentieth of the colony's population. Largely as a result of Mugabe's influence, the constitution was rejected by an NDP congress at Bulawayo, on February 17, and, by an unofficial referendum organized by the Party in July 1961, a few days before the predominantly white electorate approved it by a two-to-one margin.

After increasing restiveness among the black population led to the banning of the NDP on December 9, 1961, Mugabe became Acting Secretary General and Publicity Secretary of the Zimbabwe African People's Union (ZAPU), established in its place by Nkomo. Continued racial unrest led to a ban on ZAPU and the arrest of Mugabe and other nationalist leaders in September 1962. After his release in December, Mugabe went to Northern Rhodesia, where, in March 1963, he delivered a fiery speech at a meeting of the United National Independence Party, and was again arrested along with his wife. He escaped the following month and fled to Dar es Salaam, Tanzania.

Meanwhile, the Rhodesian Front, which demanded independence for Southern Rhodesia from Great Britain on the basis of white-minority rule, won decisively in the December elections. By that time the neighboring colonies of Northern Rhodesia and Nyasaland, with which Southern Rhodesia had been linked in the Central African Federation since 1953, were well on their way to becoming the independent black-ruled states of Zambia and Malawi, respectively. But the British authorities resisted Southern Rhodesian demands for independence, insisting that the white minority of that colony must first grant greater equality to the black majority.

A split in the leadership of ZAPU occurred in July 1963, when Mugabe, then still in Tanzania, joined with the Rev. Ndabaningi Sithole in breaking with Nkomo to form a more radical organization, the Zimbabwe African National Union (ZANU). In an interview in *The New York Times* (November 5, 1976), Mugabe recalled: "We broke with Nkomo . . . because we believed he was not for armed struggle [and] was half-hearted about it at the time." On his return to Salisbury in August, Mugabe was named Secretary General of ZANU, ranking second to party leader Sithole. He was immediately arrested again as a result of a speech he had broadcast from Dar es Salaam, but was permitted to go free on bail.

As the highest-ranking African nationalist official then at large, Mugabe was interviewed by Robert M. Hallett of the *Christian Science Monitor* (August 19, 1964), at ZANU's modest Salisbury headquarters. "As far as we are concerned, the time has come for African rule," he declared. "We are not for gradualism..., It is an insult to the African people. There is no compromise on the one-man, one-vote issue." He called for a "nonracial society," but one that must be ruled by the African majority. Although willing to negotiate with the British, Mugabe rejected what he called "useless talks" with Southern Rhodesia's white leaders. After delivering a speech in which he denounced the leaders of the Rhodesian Front as "dangerous cowboys" and ridiculed their wide-brimmed bush hats, Mugabe was once more arrested, in August 1964, and remained in detention, or restriction, for the next decade. With the African nationalist movement divided and in disarray, with its top leaders in prison, and with negotiations with British authorities a failure, Ian Smith—who had become Prime Minister in April 1964—unilaterally declared Southern Rhodesia (now called Rhodesia) independent of Great Britain on November 11, 1965.

During his years in confinement, Mugabe became a convinced Marxist. Devoting much of his time to teaching young black political prisoners, he continued his own education by correspondence and private study. He was for a time an external student with the University of London, passed three law examinations, and eventually held a half dozen university degrees, in education, administration, economics, and law.

Meanwhile, black, nationalist guerrilla forces began in the late 1960s to carry out raids against the Rhodesian government, considered an outlaw regime by the United Nations. The Smith regime responded with increasing repressions and adoption, in 1969, of a new constitution known as the "white man's charter." In December 1970, some of the lower echelon leaders of ZANU and ZAPU, while in confinement, proposed a merger of their organizations, suggesting that both Sithole and Nkomo step down to make way for a united front under Mugabe's leadership. Although it ended in failure, the attempt made clear Mugabe's acceptability to both sides. Later, Mugabe led a group of his fellow prisoners in an effort to depose Sithole as leader of ZANU, accusing him of "selling out."

Mugabe was among 16 black, nationalist leaders released by the Smith regime, in early December 1974, at the urging of South African Prime Minister John Vorster and Zambia's President Kenneth Kaunda. Growing friction between Rhodesia and Zambia, as well as the overthrow, in April 1974, of Portugal's right-wing dictatorship, launching that country's African colonies of Angola and Mozambique on the road to independence, had caused Vorster to fear for his country's security and motivated him to enter negotiations with Kaunda and other African leaders. At Kaunda's invitation, Rhodesia's black leaders met at Lusaka, Zambia, later in December, and agreed to form a common front for negotiations with Smith under the African National Council (ANC), then Rhodesia's only legal black political organization, which had been founded by Bishop Abel Muzorewa in 1971.

Alone among the black leaders meeting at Lusaka, Mugabe refused to accept the unified ANC. His insistence on being acknowledged as leader of ZANU was rebuffed by Kaunda, who continued to recognize Sithole. After quarreling openly with Kaunda, Mugabe went briefly to Tanzania and then to Mozambique. There, the new Marxist Frelimo government eventually permitted him to play a major role in organizing the thousands of young, black Rhodesian exiles who began to cross the border into Mozambique in early 1975, to form a guerrilla force that became known as the Zimbabwe African National Liberation Army [ZANLA). Mugabe helped to establish three guerrilla training camps in Mozambique and directed guerrilla raids into Rhodesia, personally taking part in at least one of those skirmishes. His guerrilla constituents soon recognized him as the leader of ZANU. Mugabe's account of the nationalist struggles of that period was circulated in what became known as "The Mugabe Diary."

In the wake of the failure of South African-Zambian détente efforts, in August 1975, and the breakdown, in March 1976, of constitutional talks between Smith and Nkomo, a new peace initiative was begun, in the summer of 1976, by United States Secretary of State Henry Kissinger, who was concerned about possible Soviet and Cuban intervention in the turbulent Rhodesian situation. On September 24, 1976, Smith announced that he accepted in principle the Kissinger proposals for black majority rule within two years. In preparation for the Geneva talks, Nkomo (who had broken earlier with Bishop Muzorewa) met with Mugabe at Maputo, Mozambique, on October 5, 1976, to form a tactical alliance that would enable the two leaders to present a united front at the conference, and eliminate the threat of future civil war between their rival nationalist organizations. Amid revolutionary fanfare, the Patriotic Front was announced at Dar es Salaam five days later and was promptly denounced by Sithole, who had never relinquished the leadership of ZANU.

But the Geneva conference, which opened on October 29, 1976, under the chairmanship of British U.N. delegate Ivor Richard, seemed doomed from the start. Hostility between the Patriotic Front leaders, on the one hand, and the delegations led by Muzorewa and Sithole on the other, precluded any semblance of black unity. While Smith insisted that the Kissinger proposals for a two-year interim racially-mixed government dominated by whites, pending adoption of a constitution based on majority rule, must be accepted as a whole, Mugabe and Nkomo maintained that those terms were not binding, since they had not been party to them. Looking upon the Smith regime as illegitimate, even before the conference opened, the Patriotic Front leaders demanded that the theme at Geneva must be the immediate and total "transfer of power from . . . the United Kingdom ... to the people of Zimbabwe" and declared their intention to "intensify the armed liberation struggle until... victory." Mugabe especially opposed the Kissinger proposal to leave the police and defense establishments in the hands of whites, during the interim period. When the Geneva conference ended on December 12, 1976, the only principle that had been agreed upon

was the setting of March 1, 1978, as the tentative date for black rule.

In April 1977, Mugabe engaged in talks about Rhodesia's future with visiting British Foreign Secretary David Owen, in Dar es Salaam, and was rebuffed in his argument that Smith and rival black nationalists be barred from future talks. A few months later, Owen presented his proposals for the vesting of executive power in a British commissioner and for an international peacekeeping force to all interested parties, but they were opposed both by Smith, unwilling to relinquish his authority, and by the Patriotic Front leaders, who demanded full power for their guerrilla forces. The talks were, for the time being, stalemated.

Toward the end of 1977, Smith entered negotiations with Sithole, Muzorewa, and Chief Jeremiah Chirau that resulted, on March 3, 1978, in what became known as the "internal settlement." Although it promised "majority rule" by the end of the year (later postponed to April 1979), it granted 28 of the 100 parliamentary seats to whites for at least ten years, and it gave them the power of veto. United States Ambassador to the U.N. Andrew Young called it a "recipe for civil war" and *The New York Times* editorial (March 5, 1978), described it as "little more than a device for keeping real power in the hands of Rhodesia's small, white minority." Addressing the U.N. Security Council in New York City later that month, Mugabe called the "internal settlement" a fraud perpetrated by the Smith regime, "with the active assistance of African stooges and traitors."

Meanwhile, Mugabe and Nkomo, fearing that the "internal settlement" might leave them isolated, had resumed talks with Owen and other British officials at Malta in January 1978, and succeeded in narrowing the gap between their own positions and the Anglo-American proposals. In a meeting with Owen and United States Secretary of State Cyrus R. Vance at Dar es Salaam, in April, Mugabe and Nkomo indicated that they might assent to British and American demands for an impartial U.N. force to ensure free elections in Rhodesia. Nor did they reject the prospect of taking part in a conference of all parties to the Rhodesian conflict, including the Smith regime. They continued, however, to insist on a dominant role for the Patriotic Front during the transition period.

Although several authorities had predicted an impending break in the tactical alliance between his Chinese-backed ZANU and Nkomo's ZAPU, supported by Cuba and the Soviet Union, Mugabe had denied the possibility. While conceding that some differences between the two organizations had arisen, he told Godwin Matatu, in an interview in *Africa* magazine (October 1978), that "there are no differences of a nature that can split the Patriotic Front." Convinced of his strength, he asserted in his U.N. speech, in the spring of 1978, that the Patriotic Front controlled over two-thirds of his country's territory and had the solid backing of the Zimbabwean masses.

Following national elections, in April 1979, that were boycotted by the Patriotic Front, Muzorewa was inaugurated in May as Prime Minister under the new Zimbabwe Rhodesian constitution. Mugabe and Nkomo remained in determined opposition to the government and rejected amnesty offers, but also indicated that they were receptive to a settlement more in line with Patriotic Front demands. In September 1979, Mugabe and Nkomo met in London, under British auspices with Muzorewa, Smith, and other leaders of the Salisbury government, to discuss constitutional changes aimed at giving greater power to the black majority, but differences over proposed safeguards for the white minority and other matters remained as obstacles to settlement.

PERSONAL LIFE
Robert Mugabe had married his Ghanaian-born wife, the former Sally Heyaffron (or Sarah Haytron) in Salisbury in 1961. They had a son who died at the age of four, during his father's imprisonment. His first wife died in 1992; Magabe married Grace Marufu in 1996. Observers state that prior to their marriage, she had been his mistress. They have three children: a daughter, Bona; and, two sons, Robert Peter, Jr., and Bellarmine Chatunga. He has one stepson, Russell Goreraza.

FURTHER READING
Guardian O 2 '76; London Observer p7 O 31 '76 por; People 11:36+ My 7 '79 por; Africa Contemporary Record, 1976-77; Africa South of the Sahara, 1978-79; International Who's Who, 1978-79; Who's Who in Africa (1973)

BENITO MUSSOLINI
Italian Fascist Leader

Born: November 11, 1869; Naples, Italy
Died: December 28, 1947; Alexandria, Egypt
Affiliation: National Fascist Party

INTRODUCTION
Mussolini's critics have found it something of a feat to change their minds about him as fast as he changed his mind about himself. More often than not, the political commentators have found themselves several policies behind or several shades too indignant or conciliatory as the case may be. Those who, like Winston Churchill, by their early adulation contributed materially to the world's former high opinion of the twentieth century Roman conqueror, have had to eat their words. Actually only ex post facto prophets have been able to predict the course of Mussolini's activities, chiefly because the Roman dictator's only thread of consistency was his opportunism.

EARLY LIFE
Benito Amilcare Andrea Mussolini was born on July 29, 1883 in the village of Dovia, commune of Predappio, the son of Alessandro and Rosa (Maltoni) Mussolini. His mother had been graduated from the Normal School at Forli and was the teacher of the elementary school at Dovia. His father was a blacksmith and ardent labor leader, and Benito was named for Benito Juarez, the liberator of Mexico. In his early Socialist days Benito

Affiliation: National Fascist Party

The National Fascist Party was created by Mussolini as the political expression of fascism. The Party ruled Italy from 1922 to 1943, when Mussolini was deposed by the Grand Council of Fascism. The Party was rooted in nationalism and the desire to expand and restore Italian territories. Italian Fascists felt this was necessary for Italy as a nation to assert its superiority and strength, claiming that modern Italy is the heir to ancient Rome and its legacy.

wrote of his father: "His house always offered shelter and friendship to those pursued by the authorities. Later, when the Socialists had come to take part in municipal politics, my father became Mayor of Predappio. In 1892 he formed in Predappio the first labor union. . . In 1902 he was again arrested. . . He left me no material heritage, but he left me a moral one—his treasure: the ideal."

According to his own accounts, Mussolini was an unruly child. He would crawl under the benches in his mother's schoolroom above the forge and pinch the legs of the pupils. When he grew older he often came home bloody from bouts with his contemporaries, with the police, and with the irate owners of apple trees and fishing nets which Benito, and the young band of marauders which he led, raided. His mother was nevertheless determined to make a schoolteacher of him and prepared him for the school of the Silesian Friars at Faenza, from which he was sent home as incorrigible after a number of incidents climaxed by Benito's stabbing of a fellow pupil. He entered the Normal School of Forlimpopoli, however, and took his diploma as a primary schoolteacher at the age of eighteen.

Benito Mussolini taught elementary school at Gualtieri Emilia. It is said that he heartily detested his profession and transferred that hatred to his pupils, so that they frequently returned from school weeping and trembling. From the towns in which he taught have come rumors that he drank, gambled, and engaged in bouts that had to be broken up by the police. In 1902, however, in order to avoid military service, Mussolini decided to emigrate from Italy. He wanted to go to America, but his mother could lend him only the equivalent of about $9, which took him as far as Switzerland. When he reached the Swiss border he learned that his father had been arrested for Socialist activity. He was about to turn back, but a

message from his mother urged him to go on, and he made his way to Lausanne.

LIFE'S WORK

Benito spent two years in Switzerland, penniless and at first friendless. He found comfort, assistance, and an audience among the Swiss and expatriate Italian Socialists, and managed to attend some of the courses at Lausanne University. In June 1903 he organized a stoneworkers' strike in Bern (he had been working as a mason) and was expelled from the city for his efforts. In 1904 the Swiss authorities discovered a falsification in his passport and threw him out of Geneva. In the meantime he had ignored the call to the Italian Army and was listed as *Renitente de Lava* (deserter). The general amnesty which accompanied the King's birthday in 1904, however, gave him the opportunity to return to Italy, and he was immediately inducted into service with the "jaunty, quick-stepping 10th Bersaglieri." According to his own testimony he enjoyed his period of service, but it was cut short by the death of his mother.

Mussolini returned to schoolteaching and remained in that profession for three years. He had learned French and studied at the university in Switzerland. This enabled him to get a post in a middle instead of an elementary school. He taught at Tolmezzo and Oneglia, but did not remain long at either school. He was always getting into trouble for his political opinions or his too-free use of the knife in arguments. He led a mob against the Mayor at Forli in July 1908, demanding a reduction in the price of milk, and was sentenced to eight months' imprisonment and fined 200 *lire* for "armed revolt." This was his first arrest in Italy. Before the sentence expired he was fined 100 *lire* more for "revolutionary expression."

In March 1909 Mussolini went to the Italian speaking province, Trentino, then apart of Austria. Here he engaged in Socialist activity and wrote for the Italian papers. For a signed article in *Il Popolo di Trento* supporting the Italian claim to Trentino he was expelled from Austria, and he returned to his father's house in Forli. His father by this time had given up his blacksmith's shop and opened a kind of tavern which provided wine, spaghetti, and radical conversation. Assisting him in running the tavern was a widow, Anna Agostini Guido, and her daughter, Rachele, who was later to become Benito's wife.

In Forli, Mussolini plunged once more into revolutionary activity. He became the salaried secretary of the Forli Socialist Party and was editor of a radical paper called *La Lotta di Classe* (The Class Struggle). He wrote voluminously denouncing war, the Church, and capitalism. In September 1911 he was sentenced to five months' imprisonment for organizing an armed uprising against the Tripoli war. He was convicted on numerous counts, including inciting riots, stopping work in war factories, halting streetcars, hampering recruiting, and the like.

By the time the Italian Socialist Congress convened at Reggio Emilia, Mussolini was nationally known. He was elected the director of the Socialist Party in July 1912 and editor of the Socialist organ, *Avanti!,* in December of the same year. He continued his anticapitalist and anti-clerical writings, and in 1913 wrote a book on John Huss in which he attacked the Church in the preface. He was the author also of an anti-clerical historical novel, *The Cardinal's Mistress*, in which he remarked: "The people is blind, like all simple folk. It loves and hates without discernment. It sacrifices its victims only to mourn and adore them when the hour of bestial fanaticism has ceased."

In June 1914 he led a mob to Cathedral Square, Milan, in the unsuccessful attempt to seize the municipal buildings during the "Red Week Revolution." In August, Mussolini was fighting against Italian intervention in the First World War. "Italian Proletariat," he pleaded, "resist the war menace. . . For us Belgium is nothing but a belligerent power just like the others. . . All the powers at war are of the same degree of guilt, and it is our right, our duty, to cause a revolution of the working class against them." But in November of the same year Mussolini resigned the editorship of the *Avanti!* and started a new newspaper, *Popolo d'Italia,* which immediately came out for entrance into the War on the side of the Allies.

When the Socialist Party convened in Bologna, November 25, Mussolini was invited to defend his action. As he entered the hall, "the Congress shouted as one man: *Chi pagaf* [Who paid?]" The only explanation that has been advanced for Mussolini's *volte-face* has been the temptation held out by French propaganda money, and even Mussolini's apologists have not denied that he was subsidized by a "loan" which was paid back, they say, after the War was over. In his farewell speech to the Socialist Party, Mussolini said: "Do not think that in taking away my membership card you will be taking away my faith in the cause, or that you will prevent my still working for socialism and revolution."

Four men led the movement for Italian entrance on the side of the Allies, Mussolini, D'Annunzio, Battisti, and Corradini, and in April 1915 Mussolini was arrested in Rome for organizing the interventionists. On May 24, 1915 Italy entered the War, and in September Mussolini was called up by his regiment, the 10th Bersaglieri. Mussolini spent fifteen months at the front except for time out in the hospital for what has variously been described as typhoid fever and gastroenteritis. In February 1917 a prematurely exploded bomb wounded him with about forty steel splinters. He was taken to the hospital at Ronchi and underwent twenty-seven operations to extract the pieces of shell. He tells that he refused to accept an anesthetic while doctors were probing his wounds despite the fact that he was in such a high fever that he could not be moved even when the building in which he was hospitalized came under Austrian fire. In August 1917, discharged from further military service, he went back to his *Popolo dTtalia,* in whose pages he lauded the war effort and cheered Italy on to greater triumphs.

After the Armistice, Mussolini and his friends, feeling that Italy had been cheated in the *post-bellum* division of spoils, plotted to get Fiume for their fatherland. With D'Annunzio, the poet who had won fame during the War as an aviator, and others, Mussolini formed the *Fasci Italiani di Combattimento* which was later to become the Fascist Party. The name was taken from the *fasces* or bundle of sticks with an axhead bound up in them which had been the symbol of the power of the Roman consuls. Through the columns of his paper Mussolini raised funds for the *coup.* Forty or fifty veterans, wearing the black shirt of the Italian *Arditi,* or shock troops, led by D'Annunzio, occupied Fiume on September 12, 1919, and remained there for more than a year in defiance of both the Italian Government and the Paris Peace Conference. Mussolini threatened to lead a national uprising if the Italian Government attempted to take action against D'Annunzio. Despite this apparent success, when Mussolini ran as independent candidate for Parliament at Milan in the general election of November 16, 1919 he polled only 5,000 votes, and not a single Fascist candidate was elected to the Chamber. Premier Francesco Nitti, fearing another *coup*, jailed Mussolini, but freed him in twenty-four hours.

The year 1920 was a year of famine and unemployment, when strikes spread over Italian industry. Sharecropping tenant farmers refused to harvest the proprietors' shares, factories were seized, and a state of anarchy was swiftly growing in both political and economic life. Apologists for the Fascist regime report that Mussolini's Fascist squads stepped in to combat a Bolshevik revolution, and that in wresting control of the factories from the Communists they succeeded in saving Italy from the morass of anarchy and Communism. Other observers report, however, that Mussolini actively supported the strikes of 1920, and that despite his turncoat international policy he still considered himself a Socialist and a foe of dictatorship. It was only when Mussolini, ready as ever to be on the winning side, thought that the socialist cause would never gain complete control over the Government because of the Party's internal strife and differing ideologies that he chose to throw his lot in with the Right and turned his now armed Fascist *squadristi* against his former labor friends.

During 1921 the Fascisti and various socialist and labor groups had frequent clashes, and although the Government arrested troublemakers on both sides, the number of Fascisti arrested was disproportionately small. By the summer the "Red menace" had all but disappeared. The Socialist Party had expelled the Communists in January. Mussolini had been elected to Parliament in May and had started his legislative career by making peace with labor and with the Socialists. In November, however, he officially organized the National Fascist Party.

During the year 1922 Mussolini changed his tactics again. Either his peaceful resolutions were a ruse to cover up his efforts to consolidate his position, or else the violence of the Fascist movement was too strong by now even for him to keep in check. He was forced to follow its revolutionary activity or lose the position he had gained. In any case, by October the Fascists were ready to march on Rome. Actually the revolution was a bloodless one, and Mussolini remained in his newspaper office until he received a telephone call from the King on October 29, inviting him to form a Cabinet. He left the following day, by train, for Rome. Commentators looking back on the "March on Rome" invariably point out how easily it could have been stopped had the King and the Premier declared martial law as they were on the verge of doing. Although the actual Fascisti were few in numbers, the Government was afraid that the police and the Army, if not in actual connivance with the Fascisti, would not act against them.

In less than a month Mussolini demanded and received dictatorial powers, and by February of the following year he had created a powerful Fascist militia. He established a secret police second only to the Gestapo and the G. P. U., and in March reorganized the state economy into what he called the "Corporate State." Mussolini and his economists have given the designation of Corporate State to the organization of economic classifications into Fascist groups. In 1927, for instance, he organized a national confederation of employers' syndicates, including industry, agriculture, commerce, navigation, land transportation, and banking, and six equivalent confederations of labor which, with a thirteenth "Federation of Fascist Syndicate of Intellectuals," acted together as a corporation. No other labor unions or employer associations were allowed. The Ministry of Corporations, presided over by Mussolini, was the ruling body "from whose decisions there is no appeal."

In the summer of 1923 Mussolini had his first international disagreement. General Tellini and his staff were murdered on the Albanian side of the Albano-Greek border. Mussolini, nevertheless, demanded 50,000,000 *lire* indemnity of Greece, death to the murderers, and military honors for the victims. Refusing League of Nations arbitration, Mussolini meanwhile ordered the Italian Fleet to bombard the Island of Corfu, causing 100 casualties among the civilians, the only residents of the Island. It was only after a great deal of diplomatic pressure that Mussolini finally withdrew from Corfu.

The same year Mussolini was appealed to by Sicilian businessmen to stop the activities of the gangster mob known as the "Black Hand," "the most powerful criminal oligarchy that ever existed." The organization had branches all over the world, notably in Chicago and New York, furnishing the United States with most of the Italian bootleggers and racketeers. Mussolini's reaction to this plea was to incorporate the efficient "Black Hand" into his "Black Shirt" militia.

During 1924 and 1925 Mussolini spent most of his efforts consolidating his position. By a treaty with Yugoslavia in 1924 Mussolini secured Fiume for Italy. The assassination on June 11, 1924 of the Socialist deputy, Matteoti, Mussolini's strongest opponent in Parliament, for a time bid fair to turn not only the foreign press but many of his own adherents against him. Mussolini has claimed that Matteoti was the Thomas a Becket of his regime, and that he is guiltless of all complicity in the murder. Several assassins were convicted, among them an Italian gangster, Dumini, from Chicago. But whatever Mussolini's part in the crime, he was the one who profited most (despite the bad press) from the removal of his strongest contender for popular favor.

It was during this period of consolidation that Mussolini crushed various organizations, including the Freemasons who had contributed millions of *lire* to his cause. He did away with municipal elections, abolished freedom of the press, and tried to send Hitler arms. (Austrian officials stopped eleven freight cars loaded with guns and ammunition.) In 1926 three unsuccessful attempts to assassinate Mussolini were_ made, the first by Zanziboni, a youth in Fascist uniform; the second by the Honorable Violet Gibson, "whose shot so disfigured the nose of Italy's idol that it displayed strips of plaster the next day"; the third by Lucetti, who threw a bomb that injured eight persons, Mussolini not among them. The following year Mussolini announced the "end of the epoch of reprisals, devastations, and violence." He suppressed the Catholic Boy Scouts and aroused the Pope's protestations against the "Fascist monopolization of youth." A "Fascist Labor Charter" abolished strikes. Manhood suffrage was eliminated by decree, and the stabilization of the *lire* on a gold basis was announced.

In 1928 Mussolini celebrated the anniversary of the Corporate State. During the same year he was expelled from the National Press Club of Washington for "suppression of the press and the denial of personal liberty," and five carloads of munitions bound for the Hungarian Fascists were intercepted by Austria. (In September, Fascism was made the permanent government. The Grand Council, and not the King, was to appoint future Premiers.) In February 1929 Mussolini and Cardinal Gasparri signed a Vatican peace treaty which gave the Pope temporal power within the Vatican State. The outside world was inclined to acclaim Mussolini's improved relations with the Vatican as well as the improved railway service, the decrease in unemployment, the stabilization of the foreign and domestic debts, and the revaluation of the *lire.* There were some even then, however, to point out that the lack of parliamentary opposition meant that only Fascist figures were available and that much of the progress was only on paper and the rest of it was a result of lowering wages and lengthening the working day. It was also pointed out that Mussolini had been a militant atheist and that the accord with the Pope was one the latter would one day regret, although the Catholic Church had supported the crusade for nationalism and "against Bolshevism." A French writer at the time felt that Mussolini and the Pope were working to establish an "International Catholic State." These fears were dispelled when Mussolini later suppressed the Vatican newspaper and dissolved Catholic youth groups.

From 1931 to 1934 Mussolini destroyed all last vestiges of opposition, extended the activities of the secret service, and began to arouse the protests of civil liberties groups all over the world. Several more unsuccessful attempts to assassinate him were made, and several more carloads of arms to various international Fascist groups were intercepted by Austria. In March 1934 Mussolini announced "a plan not for five years or ten, but for sixty years . . . at which time Italy will have primacy in the world. . . . Our future lies in Asia and Africa." The same year a book, *Fontamara,* by Ignazio Silone, appeared in which the expatriate Italian writer accused the Fascisti of a continuous and ruthless war against the Italian peasantry, of murder, rape, oppression, and suppression. The peasant had no court to which to appeal; he was allowed no organ in which to express his opinions. He had no escape except to leave his home and country, and even in leaving he encountered almost insurmountable obstacles.

With Marshal de Bono, who had aided in his March on Rome, Mussolini worked out a plan for an Ethiopian campaign, and in October 1935, 170,000 Italian troops and workmen passed through the Suez Canal. Despite halfheartedly applied sanctions and unimplemented opposition by the League of Nations, Mussolini's conquest of Ethiopia was absurdly swift. In May 1936 Mussolini's troops reached Addis Ababa, and the Emperor Haile Selassie (who had decorated the Duce with the Grand Order of Solomon) sought refuge in England. Mussolini then announced that Ethiopia was an Italian colony and that King Victor Emmanuel was an Emperor. His reasons for the conquest included the altruistic desire to bring civilization to a barbaric slave-owning people as well as to provide room for Italian expansion and colonization. It has been generally assumed that Mussolini had the fortitude to defy England and the League after a careful analysis of the 1931 Manchuria incident, which convinced him not only that the League of Nations offered its members no protection, but also that England would not fight unless her commercial interests were at stake.

In 1934 Mussolini had stopped Hitler's attempt to annex Austria by sending Italian divisions to the Brenner Pass. But in 1937 Mussolini joined with Hitler to form the Rome-Berlin Axis, and both partners sent military aid to the Fascist insurgents in Spain. England officially deplored the arrangement but did nothing to prevent it. Confident now that his deductions concerning British policy were correct, Mussolini seized upon the excuse of a second massacre of Italians by Albanian bandits in 1939 to conquer Albania and annex it to the Italian Empire.

From September 1939, when the Second World War began, until June 1940, when Mussolini entered the War, there were some who hoped that Italy might be persuaded to enter on the side of Britain or at least to stay out of the conflict completely. As a matter of fact, the tone of the Allied press toward Mussolini was beginning to soften a bit. It was made quite clear that if Mussolini would betray his Axis partner all might be forgiven. It was the Russo-German treaty (very unpopular in Italy, where the justification for the Axis had been its anti-Communism) which, the Allies hoped, would keep Italy from fighting on the side of Germany. Either following what he conceived to be his own interests or succumbing to German pressure, Mussolini declared war on the Allies shortly after the Nazi invasion of France, on June 10, 1940. On June 17 the French asked Germany for an armistice, and Mussolini's proclamation of victory referred to a "break-through" by the Italians across the Alps. The Italian claim to Nice, Corsica, and Savoy was pushed aside, however, and Mussolini later waged his African and Greek campaign with Germany's guidance and assistance. Although Greece fell, military observers generally conceded that the Italian Army was unequal to its self-imposed task and that Hitler's technical and military assistance in Italy had reduced Mussolini to the position of Italian *Gauleiter*.

Even Italian Fascists were soon disillusioned by the fruits of war. Mussolini acquired Dalmatia, in Yugoslavia, only by taking it by force after the Nazis had double crossed him. Rommel's desertion of the Italians in Africa is only one illustration of the true relationship between the Axis "partners." As unrest and hatred of the Germans increased in Italy, Hitler has been forced to station increasing numbers of troops there. Italian industrialists, whose power expanded under Fascism, hate the Nazis as much as the man in the street, for Italian heavy industry has suffered severely through German encroachment. Mussolini himself is a veritable prisoner of the Nazis: the German Ambassador in Rome, who sees him nearly every day, has been called the real ruler of Italy. Italy is not even well protected by the Nazis:

according to one source, up to the summer of 1942 her northwest coast had "only a few coastal batteries, pill-boxes, and a few outmoded fighting planes," and in the fall of 1942 the Duce pleaded in vain for greater help in the Mediterranean.

After the American invasion of North Africa Italian morale, never good, naturally fell to a new low. Churchill promised that the African cleanup would give the Allies a springboard of attacking Italy, and the devastation of Turin, Genoa, Milan, Savona, and other cities in northern Italy began. Mussolini called his Party chiefs to Rome, urged "merciless severity" with rumor-mongers, defeatists, petty chiselers, and Allied sympathizers, and begged his people to stand up under their punishment at least as well as the British. But his speech of December 2 (given under "the impression that the Italian people wished to hear my voice") hardly seemed an adequate answer to Churchill. Since Italy had entered the War the Duce had made very few speeches, and none of them had carried the swashbuckling confidence and sarcasm of his earlier oratory, but this time he sounded actually ill as he assured his people that he was not a hyena, but "a thousand times more a gentleman than Churchill is"; that the invincibility of Japan was the absolute guarantee of an Axis victory; that they were marching side by side with Germany in a unity "that is becoming our common way of life, the fusion of all interests." On December 19 Mussolini signed a decree naming a new national directorate of the Fascist Party. By this time bomb-panicked refugees were thronging Italian roads; there were reports that Rome, which had heretofore been spared by Allied bombers in spite of the fact that its railroad terminals were used by the Nazis, might be declared an open city; and peace demonstrations were commonplace throughout Italy. It was rumored that Mussolini had fired his Army chief of staff and a one-time Governor of Libya for "unprincipled pacifism," and it was also rumored that the Nazis had assumed full control of all Italian railroads and ports without consulting the Italians.

It is undeniable that the alliance with National Socialist Germany changed the character of Italian Fascism in another way. The Jews in Italy, for instance, had been divided into Fascists and anti-Fascists like the rest of the population, and had been treated more or less according to their political activities. The chief financier of the march on Rome had been Jewish—the president of the Banca Commerciale. Important academicians as well as military men in Italy were Jews, and Mussolini had verbally objected to the anti-Semitic pogroms, although his anti-socialist and antidemocratic pogroms had been models for German Storm Troopers, and the castor oil and other coercion methods of the Black Shirts had from the start been the last word in persecution methodology. Union with Hitler, however, brought to the Italians the privilege of calling themselves Aryans and the duty of outlawing the non-Aryans, according to Hitler's system of ethnology. Anti-Semitic decrees were issued, and a Jewish exodus from Italy began. Among the exiles was Donna Margherita Sarfatti, an early biographer of Mussolini credited with having introduced Mussolini to art, music, and belles-lettres. She left for Paris when her Jewish ancestry came to light.

PERSONAL LIFE

Mussolini's bald head, protruding chin, and increasing girth graced the rotogravure sections of most newspapers after his rise to power. Only five feet seven inches tall, he tried to carry himself so that he looked taller. He wore spectacles in private, but when he made his public appearances he discarded them and rolled his eyes while talking so that the whites show and his eyeballs pop with emotion. In 1942 Mussolini was described as a "sick, neurotic" man suffering from stomach ulcers, and rumors circulated that his heart and brain were affected by syphilis. A victim of claustrophobia, his office in the Palazzo Venezia was tremendous, and when he was driven in his automobile he insisted on excessive speed because he couldn't stand being confined for any length of time. It had also been bruited about that he is an "almost certifiable" paranoiac. In 1940, on his fifty-seventh birthday he invited newspaper correspondents to his riding ring at the Villa Torlonia, where he demonstrated that he was still fit. According to the official Italian reports he cleared nineteen post-and-rail jumps, including one five-feet-two inches high, and defeated two well-known Italian tennis players at their game. According to American correspondents at least this last feat was a fake, however, and by the winter of 1941 it was known that he had stopped playing tennis and had cut down on his horseback riding.

The stories of the women in Mussolini's life were numerous and more or less scandalous in proportion to the violence of the raconteur's antipathy to *Il Duce*. He was married to Rachele Guidi, by whom he had five children in two sets which he humorously dubbed "series one" and "series two." (The interval between the two groups is a result of his wife's having remained in the provinces while Mussolini was consolidating his position at Rome.) His favorite daughter, Edda, was married to Count Ciano, his Foreign Minister. Of his two elder sons, Vittorio and Bruno, "lethargic stubborn fellows who were not always careful of their behavior or the kind of friends they chose," Bruno was killed while testing a bomber in Pisa, Italy in 1941, and Vittorio does not seem likely to make a name for himself in either political or military affairs, although lie made the front pages during the Ethiopian War by describing his bombing activities as "exceptionally good fun," and war as "the most beautiful and complete of all sports."

It was said that Mussolini attempted at one time, without success, to educate his peasant wife to her position as First Lady of Italy. In the end, she led a secluded life, emerging occasionally only to officiate at the marriage of one of her children or to dedicate a new maternity home or hospital. Outwardly she became more worldly. She employed good dressmakers, had her hair and nails done, and occasionally went on reducing diets.

In the final days of World War II on April 28, 1945, Mussolini was executed, likely by Italian Communists. In the years since then, the facts surrounding his death have been questioned in Italy. Theories have been presented that Mussolini's death was part of a British special operation, but most accept that he was shot by Walter Audisio, a Communist partisan.

FURTHER READING

Collier's 104:11+ Ag 5 '39 pors; 105: 12-13+ Mr 9 '40; *Cur Hist* 52:7-9 Ap '41; *Forum* 98:170-4 O '37; 98:sup 10-11 D '37; *Ladies' H J* 55 :20 O '38; *N Y Post* pl2 Mr 23 '40 por; *The New York Times* VII pl8+ D 6 '42; il *Newsweek* 10:7-10 S 27 '37; 18:20 S 8 '41; *Read Digest* 31:49-51 D '37; *Time* 38:16 Ag 18 '41 il; 37:27-9 Je 9 '41 pors; Bainville, J. *Dictators* p206-25 1936; Crain, M. *Rulers of the World* pl05-32 1940; Gunther, J. *Inside Europe* p 171-89 1940; *International Who's Who* 1942; Kain, R. S. *Europe: Versailles to Warsaw* pl05-32 1940; Megaro, G. *Mussolini in the Making* 1938; Mussolini, B. *My Autobiography* 1936; Packard, R. and E. *Balcony Empire* 1942; Salvemini, G. *Fascist Dictatorship in Italy* 1927; Sarfatti, M. G. *The Life of Benito Mussolini* (Preface by Mussolini) 1925; Seldes, G. *Sawdust Caesar* 1937

ALI HASSAN MWINYI (AH-LEE HAH-SAHN MWIN-YEE)
President of Tanzania

Born: May 18, 1925; Kivure, Pwani Region, Tanzania
Affiliation: Chama Cha Mapinduzi (CCM)

INTRODUCTION

Although Africa has to a large extent retained its image in the West as a continent plagued by nepotism, ethnic strife, and chronic economic disarray, the reality is, according to many observers, in some ways more benign, for in recent years an increasing number of African politicians have committed themselves to reforming their countries not only economically but politically as well. The challenge confronting Africa's present-day leaders, many of whom belong to the so-called second generation of African politicians, is that of transforming their countries' state-run economies into free-market ones and of relaxing the restrictions on political freedom imposed by their socialist-minded predecessors. "There are few tasks more difficult, and more important, than those that face the second generation of African leaders," John Storm Roberts, a former editor of the newsmagazine Africa Report, *told* Current Biography.

One of these politicians is Ali Hassan Mwinyi, who became the president of Tanzania in 1985. He succeeded Julius Nyerere, who remains a respected figure in Tanzania because of his role in the country's struggle for independence but whose fidelity to his own distinctive brand of socialism contributed to its economic decline. In addition to improving his country's rickety economy, Mwinyi has permitted a free press, denationalized the country's formerly state-run businesses, and improved civil liberties. His staying power, as well as his success in instituting various reforms, has come as something of a surprise, for although he assumed the presidency through legitimate means, he was at the time of his election widely seen as a transitional figure, and he lacked a strong power base of his own.

EARLY LIFE

Ali Hassan Mwinyi was born on May 8, 1925 in Kivure, in the then-British trusteeship territory of Tanganyika. His parents, who were Muslims, moved to the almost entirely Islamic island-group of Zanzibar and Pemba, just off Tanganyika's coast, when he was very young. Mwinyi trained as a teacher, completing his studies in England, at the University of Durham, in the last year of

World War II. On his return to Zanzibar, he joined the staff of the Zanzibar Teacher Training College, of which he eventually became director.

LIFE'S WORK

Zanzibar, a British protectorate then ruled by a hereditary sultan, was and remains the heartland of the Afro-Arab Swahili culture. The inhabitants identified themselves as either Arabic or Afro-Shirazi (African), and the latter resented the politically and economically dominant Arab group. As a Muslim African whose mainland roots distanced him somewhat from the tangled ethnic/political conflicts of the time, Ali Hassan Mwinyi was politically valuable, and he was appointed permanent secretary to the minister of education when Zanzibar achieved independence from Great Britain in late 1963.

In January 1964 the Zanzibari government was overthrown. President Julius Nyerere of neighboring Tanganyika, also newly independent from Great Britain, sent security forces to the island nation to restore order, and soon after that the two countries joined to form the United Republic of Tanzania. Mwinyi spent the next six years as assistant general manager of the government-run Zanzibari State Trading Company. In

---

Affiliation: Chama Cha Mapinduzi (CCM)

The Chama Cha Mapinduzi Party is the ruling party in Tanzania and the longest ruling party in Africa. Formed in 1977 as a merger between Tanganyika African National Union (TANU) and the Afro-Shirazi Party (ASP), the CCM has retained its popularity over time, winning in landslide elections. The CCM was originally for African socialism, and now believes that economic modernization and free market policies will raise living standards. Goals of the CCM include obtaining new and modern technology and increasing employment and productivity.

The CCM's foreign policy focus has been primarily economic diplomacy within the international system, as well as peacefully coexisting with neighbors. The Party has a strong political base in rural Tanzania. Mwinyi was the Party Chairman from 1990-1996.

1970 he was appointed minister of state in the Tanzanian President's Office. He later became Tanzania's ambassador to Egypt, and in the early 1980s he served as minister of health and home affairs and minister of natural resources and tourism. During these years he gained a reputation as a moderate who was respected by both ideological socialists and those who were eager to reform the economy along free-market lines. Then, in 1984, Mwinyi was unexpectedly thrust into the most powerful political post in Zanzibar.

Mwinyi's emergence as a key player in Tanzanian politics was precipitated in part by the increasingly fragile relationship between the country's mainland and island constituents. The union had in fact been strained since its establishment two decades before, though official intolerance of dissent masked the tension in the early days. One source of discord was the lack of a common history and culture: while Zanzibar's history and Swahili culture were closely linked with that of the Tanganyikan coast, they were quite alien to those of the "upcountry," or inland, regions, from which many of Tanzania's politicians had come. Another was that while Zanzibaris were permitted to hold union government jobs, mainlanders were barred from working for the Zanzibari government. Zanzibar's semiautonomous status extended to the fact that mainland travelers to the island portion of the ostensibly united nation had to pass through customs, though the same was not true for islanders visiting the mainland.

Zanzibaris, too, were dissatisfied with the union. The defining document of Tanzanian socialism, the 1967 Arusha Declaration, had mandated the establishment of collective farms. The system, known as ujamaa, was said to reflect the traditional African extended family system, which was foreign to Zanzibaris. Particularly irksome to the Zanzibaris was the fact that the collectivization program had proved disastrous for the island's (as well as the union's) economy. By January 1984—ironically, the twentieth anniversary of the Zanzibari revolution and creation of the union—unrest on the island had become so serious that President Nyerere felt compelled to send troops to maintain order there.

In this tense climate, Mwinyi was elected president of Zanzibar and chairman of the Zanzibar Revolutionary Council. Later in 1984, as a result of a change in the constitution that made the Zanzibari president a vice-president of the union, he assumed the latter post as well. Mwinyi's position was further strengthened in August, when he won the vice-chairmanship of the

country's sole political party, Chama Cha Mapinduzi (CCM, which in English means the Revolutionary Party), with 96 percent of the vote. Immediately after his election as president, Mwinyi tried to ease Zanzibari discontent by introducing economic reforms that gave private enterprise and free-market forces more of a role than the party traditionally permitted.

Mwinyi's rise to power came at a crucial period not only in Zanzibar's political history but Tanzania's as well, for Nyerere, the country's first and only leader, was then preparing to step down from the presidency. Partly as a result of the impending change in leadership, the positions of president and CCM chairman—both of which had been held by Nyerere—were separated, and that of the prime minister was strengthened. As Roger Yeager observed in *Tanzania: An African Experiment* (1989), those changes "made the national executive more potent without the CCM's ultimate control over public policy being sacrificed." They also allowed Nyerere to resign as president while retaining his overriding influence as party chairman, a position he said he planned to hold until 1987 but did not relinquish until 1990.

Mwinyi was a principal beneficiary of these events. On August 15, 1985, following a power struggle within the CCM between economic liberals and centrists, the delegates to a special convention of the CCM elected Mwinyi the sole candidate to succeed Nyerere as president of Tanzania. In October of that year, 92 percent of the Tanzanian electorate confirmed the party's choice, and on November 5 Mwinyi was sworn in as Tanzania's second president for a five-year term.

Because of his relative obscurity and his lack of a strong power base, Mwinyi was expected to be a transitional figure. And as might be imagined, given Nyerere's domination of Tanzanian politics for the previous two decades, most Tanzanians expected Mwinyi to defer to Nyerere, who would remain Tanzania's ultimate arbiter of power. This view was expressed by a businessman during an interview with Edward Girardet for the *Christian Science Monitor* (March 21, 1985) a few months after the election: "In this country, the party is the real government. Nyerere may have stepped down as president, but the landlord has not changed." Samuel M. Wangwe, a professor and dean of arts and sciences at the University of Dar es Salaam, agreed, telling Edward A. Gargan in an interview for *The New York Times* (November 3, 1985), "The party is the main policy-making organ. Mwinyi will not, cannot, make any major changes in the next two years. His principal problem is how to improve the performance of the economy, how to make people accountable for their performance."

Improving the economy ranked as the most daunting challenge any Tanzanian politician could have faced. As a Reuters reporter observed, as quoted in the *Guardian* (November 6, 1985), Mwinyi "inherited appalling economic problems, including sagging agricultural output partly due to poor government planning and excessive state intervention," which were compounded by an ambitious but unaffordable social agenda. An *Economist* (August 23, 1986) writer's assessment of the country's circumstances was even grimmer: "Tanzania is in a mess even by black Africa's gloomy standards." The economic crisis in which Tanzania found itself was generally attributed to "the failed system of ujamaa," as the Economist writer put it, which had been instituted and perpetuated by Nyerere. Under that system, some thirteen million peasants who had previously worked their own land had by 1976 been resettled, many of them forcibly, into eight thousand cooperative villages. Their crops were bought and distributed by the government, and the country's major industries were nationalized and operated by state-run companies. But because Tanzania lacked experienced civil servants, the nationalized economy had little chance of being managed efficiently. The net result was that following independence Tanzanians became progressively poorer, economic growth slowed, and the country became increasingly dependent on foreign aid. The nation even had difficulty feeding itself; between 1970 and 1984 agricultural output dropped dramatically—by 25 percent.

One of Mwinyi's first important moves as president—which also turned out to be one of his first successes—was to conclude an agreement with the International Monetary Fund according to which Tanzania would begin to introduce free-market reforms in return for new loans from the bank. As part of the reform effort, Tanzania's troubled state marketing organization, the Agricultural Products Export Corporation, was dissolved; the notoriously low prices that the government paid farmers for their crops were raised; some state-run businesses were privatized, and others were closed down; interest rates were raised; price controls on many consumer items were lifted; government spending was cut; and the country's overpriced currency was devalued. For its part, in 1986 the International Monetary Fund agreed to extend to Tanzania a standby loan of seventy-eight million dollars. The IMF agreement, the first such

accord in six years, was welcomed by the international lending community, and in 1986 the World Bank, which had suspended assistance to Tanzania because the country was so far behind in its payments on previous loans, agreed to lend one hundred million dollars.

By 1987 ordinary Tanzanians were beginning to feel optimistic about their future. As Sheila Rule observed in *The New York Times* (April 15, 1987), Mwinyi "has gained popularity in this impoverished country as his government moved ahead with initiatives that moderated Mr. Nyerere's socialist principles and slowly eased economic decline. . . . Tanzanians credit Mr. Mwinyi's economic recovery program with much of what they are experiencing today, including higher crop prices, a greater role for private enterprise and more goods in the market. Even though prices remain out of reach of the ordinary Tanzanian, the people say they like to see more goods in the shops. There is a psychological benefit in this, they say."

Predictably, the reform effort was opposed by some members of the ruling party's socialist old guard. In 1987 these hardliners retaliated by excluding Cleopa Msuya, Tanzania's chief negotiator with the IMF, from the CGM National Executive Committee. They also launched a campaign among village party chairmen to persuade them to oppose grassroots reform. Popular support for Mwinyi's economic recovery program, too, dissipated somewhat, as Tanzanians began to realize that their circumstances were unlikely to improve significantly in the near term. (Indeed, in some respects their conditions worsened.) Despite these difficulties, Mwinyi's liberalization policies prevailed, to the extent that Tanzania's intellectuals and policy leaders became more accepting of them. As Yeager put it, "Even the former radical Abdulrahman Babu has extolled 'the dynamic practices of capitalism.'"

Another challenge confronting Mwinyi was the resurgence of hostility between Zanzibaris and mainlanders. Tensions flared in 1988, when, at a conference on women and development, Sophie Kawawa, the wife of the CCM secretary-general, said that Muslim law would be modified wherever it discriminated against women, particularly in regard to polygamy and inheritance. In Zanzibar, Muslim, conservative, and anti-mainland sentiment converged, culminating in a protest march to the State House by four thousand demonstrators. In the ensuing melee, two people were killed and dozens were wounded. Mwinyi flew to Zanzibar and promised that any changes in the nation's laws would be subject to constitutionally established procedures; he warned, though, that "any further threats to the union's peace and internal security would be vigorously prosecuted."

The year 1990 marked another watershed in Tanzanian political history, for in that year Nyerere relinquished the chairmanship of the CCM. Some political observers suggested that Nyerere's declining influence would provide Mwinyi, who succeeded Nyerere as party chairman, with an opportunity to take bolder steps in reforming the economy. As a writer for the *Economist* (June 2, 1990) observed, Mwinyi's "fragile economic improvements of recent years, including real growth of 4 percent a year since 1986, were achieved in the face of persistent meddling by his predecessor." By the time Mwinyi was reelected to a second term as president later in 1990, some observers were beginning to feel that Mwinyi's approach to Tanzania's problems had become less cautious. He took an important step in October 1993, when he opened a branch of the Meridien Biao bank, thus ending the government monopoly of the banking system.

In the 1990s Mwinyi began to liberalize Tanzania's political system. In 1991 he appointed a special commission on political reform, and in the following year the CCM leadership adopted the commission's recommendation that the government permit the formation of opposition parties. Another of the commission's recommendations—that a Tanganyikan government parallel to the Zanzibari government be established to ease the mainlanders' persistent resentment of the Zanzibaris—was ignored, however, and the mounting tension between the two sides in turn laid the groundwork for the worst crisis of Mwinyi's tenure as president.

The imbroglio was precipitated by the revelation that Zanzibar had secretly joined the Organization of the Islamic Conference (OIC) in clear violation of the union's secular constitution. Mwinyi at first tried to condone the move; he even went so far as to suggest that the union government might also join the OIG. But the fact that Mwinyi, a Muslim with strong ties to Zanzibar,

appeared to be taking a partisan stand infuriated mainlander politicians, who in 1993 revived the proposal that a Tanganyikan government be established. When Nyerere was consulted for his views, he was openly critical of the government, and by implication, of Mwinyi. "Many observers were predicting the fall of Mwinyi and his top leadership within days," Louisa Taylor observed in *Africa Report* (May/June 1994). The crisis passed after the CCM leadership agreed to solicit the views of party members on the matter of forming a Tanganyikan government.

The debate over the relationship between the union's constituent parts is likely to feature prominently in the campaign leading up to the first multiparty presidential elections, scheduled for 1995. Louisa Taylor has said that "for all sides the elections have become the deadline for reform." The elections may also prove to be a turning point in

As one Zanzibari official predicted in an interview with Taylor, "If the present structure is not changed, the union will break as soon as Mwinyi steps down. The pressure is coming from the mainland. They want him out; some people just can't stand the thought of Zanzibaris in State House."

PERSONAL LIFE

Ali Hassan Mwinyi, who has a stocky build, is of medium height and has a predilection for conservative dark suits. A devout Muslim, he is said to be a modest, incorruptible man with a reputation for honesty and flexibility. Since 1960 he has been married to Siti A. Mwinyi, with whom he has five sons and four daughters.

FURTHER READING

Guardian p9 O 18 '85 por; The New York Times A p4 Ap 15 '87 por; Toronto Globe and Mail p4 Ag 16 '85 por; Washington Post A p29 N 6 '85; Contemporary Black Biography vol 1 (1992); International Who's Who, 1994-95

N

GAMAL ABDEL NASSER (NA'SER)

2nd President of Egypt

Born: Jan. 15, 1918, Bakos, Egypt
Died: September 28, 1970, Cairo, Egypt
Affiliation: Arab Socialist Union

INTRODUCTION

Gamal Abdel Nasser, the President of Egypt until his death in 1970, was known for his Pan-Arab vision and his cunning political and military strategy. He was the leader of the military junta (known formally as the Revolutionary Command Council, or RCC), a bloodless coup d'état of July 23, 1952, that overthrew King Farouk I. Nasser, who had selected Major General Mohammed Naguib as the "front man" for the revolt, became Prime Minister in April 1954. Following a 1954 attempt on Nasser's life by a Muslim Brotherhood member, who was acting on his own, he cracked down on the organization. Mohammed Naguib was put under house arrest; Nasser eventually abolished the Revolutionary Command Council to remove opposition to his consolidated power, and became President in 1956. He also continued in the office of Prime Minister until 1962.

When Nasser assumed control of the government, Egypt and the surrounding region had a bright outlook: Nasser had gone far toward accomplishing two of the revolution's major goals: Social reform and settlement of the Suez Canal Zone dispute with Great Britain. In 1953, as Deputy Prime Minister, Nasser introduced far-reaching land reforms. In 1954, as Prime Minister, Nasser negotiated the Anglo-Egyptian Agreement, under which British troops were to be evacuated gradually from the Canal Zone. The agreement had been described in a New York Herald Tribune *editorial as,*

Gamal Abdel Nasser.

"one of the more important diplomatic feats of the postwar period."

Nasser's political cunningness was demonstrated during the 1956 war with Israel, after he nationalized the Suez Canal and closed it to Israel shipping. The Israelis attacked the Sinai Peninsula while, in a coordinated attack by France and Great Britain, French and

British troops invaded Port Said in the Canal Zone. Egypt technically lost this war, as Israel was able to occupy the entire Sinai and France and Great Britain easily took Port Said in the Canal Zone, despite Egyptian resistance. Nasser was repeatedly urged to surrender by his advisors, especially by Abdel Hakim Amer, the Egyptian Minister of Defense, but refused. He was relying on the U.N. Security Council's decision that Egypt had a right to seize the Canal, which was backed by the Administration of U.S. President Eisenhower. The U.S. demanded Israeli, French and British withdrawal. Nasser, technically the aggressor and also the loser, was able to turn the Suez Canal Crisis into a victory because Egypt kept the Suez Canal.

To counter the Baghdad Pact, which was an alliance of some Arab nations with the United States, Nasser was able to persuade other Arab nations, most notably Saudi Arabia and Syria, into remaining in the political and defense pact of the Arab League with Egypt. At the height of his power, Nasser achieved a step toward his goal of Pan Arabism when Egypt and Syria joined together to create the United Arab Republic (U.A.R.), in 1958. The union between the two nations was short-lived, however; Syria left the U.A.R. after a coup d'état in 1961.

Until his death of a heart attack in 1970, Nasser continued to hold out hope for Pan Arabism, which was dashed by the 1967 Six-Day War (the Arab forces sustained heavy military casualties and lost territory in the Sinai, the West Bank, and the Golan Heights).

EARLY LIFE

The oldest of four sons of an Upper Egypt middle class family, Gamal Abdel Nasser was born on January 15, 1918, in the small town of Beni Mor in Asyut Province. The senior Nasser, who was of Arabian stock, was a Post Office Civil Servant. After the death of his first wife in 1926, he remarried and fathered eleven children. Illustrative of Gamal's early rebellious traits is the story that, at the age of seven, when forbidden to dig in the garden, he dug a hole so large that his father fell into it.

Young Nasser is said to have been closely attached to his mother, the daughter of an Alexandrian building contractor. Her death increased the contemplative tendencies of the eight-year-old boy, who was then living in Cairo, where his father had sent him to be educated.

In his early schooling, Gamal was an indifferent pupil, preferring American motion pictures to his classes. At the age of 16, he organized and led the students of Cairo's Al Nahda Al Misria School in a demonstration against British domination in Egypt. Soon becoming a serious student, interested especially in law and in biographies of the great men in history, he was awarded his secondary school certificate with distinction.

While attending the Royal Military Academy, which he entered in 1937, as one of 40 applicants chosen out of 400, he was known for his outspokenness against colonialism. After his graduation at the age of 20, Nasser joined the Third Rifle Brigade and was sent to Mankabad in Asyut, where he served as an infantry platoon commander. "The senior officers were very bad," Life (March 8, 1954) quotes him as recalling. "I organized all the junior officers into a group against [them]."

About this time the young officer came to know some of the men who were later to be his political colleagues. At the Asyut barracks he met Anwar Al Sadat and Zakaria Mohie El Din, and Ahmed Anwar. In 1939, while stationed in Alexandria, he met Abdul Hakim Amer.

Nasser was transferred in 1942 to El Ala-mein. He soon returned to Alexandria for a brief period of duty as lieutenant with the Fifth Infantry Brigade, and was then sent to the Sudan, where he served in Jabal El Awlia with Abdul Hakim Amer. In the same year, he received an appointment as a teacher at the Royal Military Academy.

In Cairo, he also studied at the Army Staff College, from which he graduated with honors. As part of his instruction there, states an Egyptian Embassy biographical sketch of Nasser, he learned how to protect the capital city and its approaches from ground and air enemy forces, information that he put to use when he undertook the coup d'état that dethroned King Farouk I.

For several years, Nasser had been distressed by conditions in the Army, widespread inefficiency in the government, and the ferment throughout Egypt arising from opposition to British influences. While closely observing the tension of the period, he began clandestinely to organize a group to plan for revolution, hand-picking each member from the men he met in the Army. "I was patient and never despaired," he later told James Bell (Life, March 8, 1954). "I chose them one after another and tested them without their ever knowing it."

Sent to Palestine in 1948 to fight against Israel, Nasser became more than ever determined to overthrow the Farouk regime, which had failed to supply adequate munitions for the Army. His heroism in battle brought him a shoulder wound and the nickname "Tiger of Faluja."

Affiliation: Arab Socialist Union

The coup that Nasser had been planning for ten years was staged on July 23, 1952. It forced the abdication of King Farouk I (his 17-month-old son was made King) and set up a ruling military junta, the RCC, with Naguib taking over as Prime Minister in September. In a move ending the reign of Farouk's son, King Ahmed Fuad II, Naguib, in June 1953, proclaimed Egypt a republic and formed a new cabinet.

Lieutenant Colonel Nasser at that time became Deputy Prime Minister. He also was named Minister of the Interior, with control over internal security, a key post that he held until October 4, 1953. During this time, he instituted land reforms in Egypt. Another of Nasser's titles was Secretary General of the Liberation Rally, a quasi-political mass organization established and directed by the young officers (in May 1954, he assumed leadership of the rally's High Council). He was the dominant figure in the RCC (the Army junta), and the chief policy maker of the Naguib regime.

Growing dissension between Naguib and Nasser came to a climax on February 25, 1954, when Naguib was charged with demanding "absolute and autocratic power" and was forced to resign as Prime Minister, President, Military Governor of Egypt, and chairman of the Revolution Command Council. By March 15, 1954, the popular general had been restored to all his offices; and Nasser had relinquished the post of Prime Minister that he had temporarily filled. On April 18, Nasser again replaced Naguib as Prime Minister. This time Naguib, whose prestige with the people Nasser was regarded as having previously underestimated, retained the Presidency—then largely a figurehead position. Nasser reshuffled his 22-man cabinet, which included eight members of the junta, apparently to oust ministers who had sided with Naguib.

During Nasser's time as Prime Minister, he was Egypt's chief negotiator in efforts to settle the long-standing dispute with Great Britain over the Suez Canal. In general, he pursued a policy of compromise, with violence as a last resort, and is credited with having done much to clear the ground for eventual accord. On July 27, 1954, Egypt and Britain representatives initialed an agreement embodying the general principles for withdrawal of British forces and supplies from the Canal Zone within 20 months, thus bringing to an end Britain's 72-year-old occupation. In case of an attack on Egypt, any other member of the Arab League or Turkey, Great Britain would be permitted, according to the agreement, to put the base on a "war footing" and would consult with the Egyptian government on other steps to be taken.

The settlement of the Suez dispute was viewed in the United States press as a personal victory for Nasser and a triumph for the moderate leadership he has given Egypt. To Nasser, the Anglo-Egyptian agreement was "the turning point in the history of Egypt." He spoke also of "a new era of friendly relations based on mutual trust, confidence and co-operation [opening] between Egypt and Britain and the Western countries," (*Manchester Guardian*, July 28, 1954). Political observers expected that removal of Egypt's resentment toward the West would result in increased military collaboration between Egypt and the free world and would pave the way for foreign economic aid needed to finance the social reforms of the Nasser Administration.

It was at Faluja that he called the first meeting of his Free Officers Movement, an organization described by *Newsweek* (April 26, 1954) as "a masterpiece of secrecy." Men from this group, whose total membership of 700 was known only to Nasser, infiltrated the government and King Farouk's palaces, as well as the military high command, to gather information to aid underground preparation for the Army revolt. Realizing that the public would be reluctant to accept seizure of power by young, inexperienced revolutionists, the Free Officers chose for the movement's "front man" Major General Mohammed Naguib, a highly respected hero of the war in Palestine.

LIFE'S WORK
Following a 1954 attempt on Nasser's life by a Muslim Brotherhood member (who was acting on his own), Nasser cracked down on the organization. The Nasser government withdrew Egyptian citizenship from five leaders of the anti-Western Moslem Brotherhood on September 23, and from Mahmoud Abdul Fath, owner of a suspended Cairo newspaper. They were accused of "treasonous actions abroad harmful to Egypt's prestige and strength" (*The New York Times*, September 25, 1954).

On November 14, 1954, Major General Naguib was deposed from the Presidency by the junta, thus ending the struggle for power between Nasser and Naguib. One cause of conflict between the two rival factions was over the question of how long the "transition period" from monarchy to full democracy should last. Naguib and his supporters advocated an early parliamentary election and the return of the government to civilian rule. Nasser maintained that the junta should remain in power until it had accomplished its aims of bringing social justice to Egypt's workers and peasants, and of freeing the Suez Canal Zone from British occupation. After having rescinded Naguib's promise to restore parliamentary government, the junta announced, in May 1954, that the National Consultative Assembly, when elected, would have only an advisory role.

In 1956, Nasser announced in Alexandria that he was nationalizing the Suez Canal, which was his reaction to the withdrawal of the United States and Great Britain from funding the Aswan Dam project. Nasser stated that he intended to use the profits from the Suez Canal to fund the dam. It was a breach of the international agreement he had signed with the UK on October19, 1954, although he ensured that all existing stockholders would be paid for their investment. A hidden agenda was to disrupt Israeli shipping. The same day of the announcement of nationalization the canal, Egypt closed it to Israeli shipping.

Nasser greatly underestimated the majority shareholders of the Suez Canal, France and Great Britain. He had gambled that Great Britain, in particular, was in no condition to respond, but he was wrong. Although the U.S. Security Council affirmed that Egypt had the right to the Canal as long as it allowed international shipping to continue, France and Great Britain secretly made an agreement with Israel to take over the Canal, occupy the Canal Zone, and topple Nasser's dictatorship. The Israelis attacked Egyptian posts in the Sinai Peninsula and, two days later, British and French planes bombarded Egyptian airfields in the Canal Zone. Nasser was more concerned about protecting the Canal than the Sinai Peninsula, so he ordered the armed forces to protect the Canal, which allowed Israel to seize most of the Sinai Peninsula. This move angered Abdel Hakim Amer, the Minister of Defense, who later accused Nasser of starting a needless war. Egyptian forces retreated and blocked the canal by sinking three ships.

Nasser assumed command of the armed forces and traveled to Port Said in the Canal Zone, where the Egyptian forces battled the French and British forces after they landed, in early November. Although Egypt was clearly losing and French and British forces easily were the victors, Nasser ordered the head of the Egyptian militia not to surrender. U.S. President Eisenhower's Administration, however, strongly condemned the French, British and Israelis because the U.S. backed the U.N. Security Council's decision. French and British forces left the region by the end of December; Israel left the Sinai in March of 1959, and returned all prisoners of war. Nasser tightened rules of qualifications for Egyptian citizenry, resulting in several French, British and Jewish sympathizers' expulsions from Egypt. Despite heavy military losses, Nasser was able to turn the 1956 war into a political victory in Egypt.

Nasser continued his promotion of Pan-Arabism. He agreed to the proposal to unite with Syria to create the United Arab Republic (U.A.R.), in 1958, to stabilize that country. The formation of the United Arab Republic had hopes of other Arab countries joining the new state, which never happened. Then head of state of Syria, Al-Quwatli, resigned his office in favor of Nasser. Nasser tried to replace Syrian institutions with their Egyptian counterparts, including land reforms. Since the culture of the two countries was significantly different, the experimental United Arab Republic failed with a 1961 Syrian secessionist coup d'état.

Nasser ignored warnings from the Soviet Union that Israel planned to attack on Syria in 1967, days before the Six Days War. His Defense Minister, Abdel Hakim Amer, used the Soviet intelligence as a pretext for sending troops to the Sinai without authorization. He concealed another communication to Nasser from Jordan's King Hussein that the U.S. and the Israelis were involved a ploy to "drag Egypt into the impending war" until the troops were in the Sinai. Amer urged Nasser to block the Straits of Tiran (also known the "Gulf of Aqaba"), which Nasser thought Israel would see as a cause for war with Egypt. Amer assured Nasser that Egypt was prepared for conflict, and he anticipated an Israeli attack due to his intelligence. Nasser was confident that if Egypt were attacked, they were ready and a cease fire would come immediately to Egypt's aid, as it had in 1956. He eventually blockaded the straits. On May 26, Nasser declared, "our basic objective will be to destroy Israel." On May 30, King Hussein committed Jordan in an alliance with Egypt and Syria.

On June 5, Israel attacked. Its Air Force struck Egyptian air fields, destroying much of the Egyptian Air

Force, and its ground troops captured the town of el-Arish. The next day, Amer ordered Egyptian forces to withdraw from the Sinai, causing most of the Egyptian casualties. Israel quickly captured Sinai and the Gaza Strip from Egypt, the West Bank from Jordan, and the Golan Heights from Syria. It wasn't until it was too late, observers said, that Nasser took the Soviet warning seriously.

In the war's aftermath, Nasser tried to resign, but Egyptians took to the streets in protest, so he remained in office. Nasser launched what has been called the "War of Attrition" with Israel, in 1968, as an attempt to regain the land Israel took from Egypt during the Six-Days War. Egypt shelled Israel from the Canal Zone. Israel retaliated with commando raids, artillery shelling and air strikes; Egyptian citizens left the cities in the Canal Zone. Nasser stopped all military activities to regroup, and the war resumed in March 1969. He brokered an agreement with the Palestinian Liberation Organization (PLO) and Lebanon to attack Israel from Lebanon.

In June 1970, Nasser accepted the US-sponsored Rogers Plan, under pressure from the Soviet Union (which was concerned about further escalation), although the other parties involved rejected it. Following Nasser's acceptance, Israel agreed to a ceasefire and Nasser used the lull in fighting to move missiles towards the Canal Zone.

Meanwhile, the other Arab participants were getting ready to head into Lebanon to attack the PLO. Nasser held an emergency Arab League Summit on September 27 in Cairo, where he forged a ceasefire agreement.

Nasser was a heavy smoker. As the summit closed on September 28, 1970, and the last Arab guests left, he suffered a heart attack. He was immediately taken home, and died there several hours later. Nasser suffered from arteriosclerosis, and diabetes. Nasser's funeral procession through Cairo on October 1 was attended by at least five million mourners. All Arab heads of state attended, with the exception of Saudi's King Faisal; Soviet Premier Alexei Kosygin and French Prime Minister Jacques Chaban-Delmas also attended. The final destination of the procession was the Nasr Mosque, later renamed Abdel Nasser Mosque, where Nasser was buried.

Nasser, despite being a military dictator, a socialist, turning Egypt into a "police state," and his war losses, still is revered in the Arab world because he was successful in removing the British permanently from Egypt. He also was very charismatic and able to motivate Arabs unlike other Arab leaders.

PERSONAL LIFE

In 1944, Nasser married Tahia Kazem, and they had two daughters, Mona and Hoda, and two sons, Khaled and Abdul Hamid. Reports state that Nasser was successfully able to compartmentalize his family life away from his life as the military dictator of Egypt.

FURTHER READING

The New York Times p 1+ Mr 30 '54; p 1+ Ap 18 '54; The New York Times Mag pl2+ S 19 '54 pors; N Y World-Telegram p7 Jl 31 '54 por. Time 63 :30 Mr 8 '54 por; 63 :38 Ap 26 '54; U S News 34:44+ My 22 '53 por; 36:16 Mr 5 '54 por; World Biography,1954.

JUAN NEGRÍN

Spanish Republican Leader; Scientist

Born: February 3, 1892; Las Palmas, Gran Canaria
Died: November 12, 1956; Paris, France
Affiliation: Spanish Socialist Workers' Party (PSOE)

INTRODUCTION

With the growing international opposition to the Franco dictatorship in Spain, Juan Negrín, the Premier of the Republic, was a cohesive force among Spanish Republicans within the country and in exile in England, France, the United States, and Mexico. The Socialist

Negrín worked throughout his own exile toward the reestablishment of a democratic Spain.

EARLY LIFE

Juan Negrín was born in the Canary Islands, the Spanish possession in the Atlantic Ocean off the coast of Africa; one source gives the date as 1892. Educated largely on the Continent, he studied medicine at several German universities. It was in these student years that he came into contact with the leaders of German socialism and his political ideology developed. When he had completed his studies in Germany, Negrín studied in other European capitals. Returning finally to Madrid, he became one of the youngest professors in Spain. (Negrín was one of the founders of University City, which was later reduced to rubble in the fight for the capital.) He served as professor of physiology at the Medical Faculty of Madrid University, and was also at different times director of the Physiological Institute and director of the Madrid Chemical Laboratory. In addition to his scientific prominence, the Spanish intellectual gained a reputation as an expert in economic and financial affairs and as a political philosopher. The professor's practical ability was also demonstrated, as for example, in his formation of *Editorial Espana,* described as "that great nursery of Spanish contemporary thought." A member of the Socialist Party for many years, he actively entered politics in September 1936 when he became Minister of Finance in the Largo Caballero Cabinet. One of his first acts upon assuming office was to reassure American investors concerning their holdings in Spain.

LIFE'S WORK

In April 1931 the people of Spain had voted for a republic and King Alfonso had fled into exile. Thus by a bloodless revolution the Bourbon monarchy was replaced by moderate Republican leaders, with a new constitution which provided for universal suffrage, sweeping social legislation, the separation of Church and State, and cooperation with the League of Nations. As Minister of Finance Negrín survived many Cabinet changes in the swiftly flowing current of Spanish politics. In May 1937 the professor-politician was made Premier, a fact which is said to have caused some surprise since he was considered a mediator rather than a leader. Jacques Ambrun, writing in *Living Age* (October 1938), pronounced Negrín's election "a good thing in many respects, and, indeed, [it] marks a new era in Spanish politics." He emphasized that Negrín, "the leading spirit of Republican Spain," was a man whose "patriotism is not marred by overexcessive, foaming-at-the-mouth nationalism and to whom Europe is a reality. . . . By education and conviction, he is primarily a European."

Negrín retained the portfolio of Minister of Finance and Economy in his own Cabinet, and in April 1938 assumed the added responsibility of the Ministry of National Defense. Spain, in the grip of a bloody civil war since July 1936, was ravaged as the Loyalists fought for the Republic against German and Italian arms under Franco's command. For almost three years the struggle raged. William C. Atkinson, writing in the British *Fortnightly* in January 1939, stated that the Republican resistance "belied all the prophets, even the dictators; it will be remembered when the history of human values in the twentieth century comes to be written." To the claim of Franco sympathizers in the United States that he was fighting bolshevism, one reporter stated, "There was not a single Communist in the Popular Front Government when the Franco forces launched their rebellion," and *Time* Magazine pointed out that Negrín's Cabinet was "no more and no less Red than that of French Premier Leon Blum."

Negrín and the Republicans appealed to the world for help, but the non-interventionist policy of the democracies and increasing German and Italian aid to Franco doomed the Republic. At Geneva in 1938 in one of his many calls for action by the League of Nations, the Spanish Premier stated, "Once foreign intervention in Spain has been eliminated, I can assure you a policy of national conciliation, conducted under the firm, energetic direction of an authoritative government, will make it possible for all Spaniards to forget these years of conflict and cruelty and will rapidly re-establish the domestic peace." Negrín also announced at that time the evacuation of foreign volunteers from the Republican ranks—those men who had come from many countries to fight in the international brigades beside the Loyalists, Treatment of Spain's case by the League was described by one reporter as "power politics in the raw and at their worst." In those stormy years Negrín once told reporters, "Gas masks today are worth more than all the protests to Geneva. We will fight in the language the enemy understands."

On May 1, 1938, Negrín announced a long-term program, addressed to all Spaniards on both sides asking them to cooperate in the building of a new, peaceful Spain. Among the Premier's "Thirteen Points" were: 1) the absolute independence and territorial integrity of the country ; 2) the ejection of all foreign elements, military and economic, "who since July 1936 have invaded Spain and sought to dominate her economic life in their own interests"; 3) a republic of the people, based on the principles of pure democracy, with a strong executive power dependent at all times on the will of the people, plus provisions for social legislation, agrarian reform, and amnesty of prisoners. But Franco's troops continued their advance, and the closing phase of the struggle was marked by upheavals within the Loyalist regime itself. When President Manuel Azana resigned in February 1939 Negrín became active head of state. A month later Madrid was delivered to the Nationalists by a military coup d'etat, and the Government leaders fled to France. There Negrín remained until June 1940 when he went to live in England.

Living in exile in London, Negrín has maintained contact with his ministers, many of whom are in Mexico. (Meanwhile, in Madrid in 1941 a Franco court stripped him of his citizenship and imposed a fine of one hundred million pesetas.) The Spanish leader is said to have retained the optimistic confidence which distinguished him even in the hopeless days of the civil war as he now plans for the restoration of the Republic. In 1941, in his first speech after the end of the civil war, Negrín told a group of Loyalists in London of the continuing resistance within their country. He called for an end to "squandering precious energies in back-room recriminations and personal knife-play," and urged all to join in the common struggle against fascism and nazism. Early in 1942 the press carried reports of Negrín's fight on another front, the scientific—he assisted in experiments carried on by the eminent British scientist J. B. S. Haldane, among them, the testing of the effects of gases on submarine crews.

With the military defeat of fascism in Europe the anti-Franco forces have gained power, and predictions are made of impending trouble for the Falangist leader. In January 1945, writing in *PM,* Alexander H. Uhl declared, "The battle for Spain is going on right now." That same month a meeting in New York's Madison Square Garden under the sponsorship of Nation Associates and other liberal groups urged the United States to break relations with Franco Spain. The rally was scheduled to hear an address by Negrín broadcast from London, but British authorities refused the Spaniard permission to use the radiotelephone service, an action which caused adverse comment in Britain and America. Negrín's speech was, however, read at the meeting and was thereafter reprinted in various periodicals. The Spanish Premier, who had broken his five-year silence, self-imposed because he "did not want to add fuel to the political bickerings within the Spanish emigration," emphasized his belief that the Spanish people were ready and able to conduct their own affairs without intervention, but would welcome the help of friends.

In February Ted Allan in a *Collier's* article, "Battle For Spain," wrote that he found Spain industrially under German "occupation" and that more people died from starvation and disease in Spain from 1941 to 1944 than in any other country in Europe. Allan told of the underground movement directed by a broad anti-Franco group, the Junta Suprema de Union Nacional, whose leaders still repeat their war slogan, "Madrid will yet be the tomb of fascism." Negrín, Allan stated, "may be the hope of Spain—for he alone may be able to unite all the various factions. Once before all the anti-Franco factions fought under his leadership during the civil war, and Spain's underground is hoping that he will again emerge to head a national coalition." In March Negrín spent five weeks in conference with Spanish leaders in France, winning the support of the Communists. A few months before that he had conferred with anti-Franco political groups m Paris, where the French press had welcomed him. In March Clifton Daniel reported in *The New York Times,* "Dr. Negrín's prestige has grown enormously in the past six months."

In May 1945 Negrín arrived in America, stopping in Washington and New York on his way to the United Nations Conference on International Organization. His presence in San Francisco at that time was interpreted by the liberal press as a hopeful sign for Spain. A *PM* editorial lauded the San Francisco rejection of the Franco regime and applauded Ne-grin's plan for establishing a government in exile. By July Negrín was in Mexico working with Republicans there. Meanwhile, anti-Franco sentiment continued to grow on an international scale. The Potsdam conference decision on Spain was considered a major blow to Franco's reign. The joint communique of the Big Three barred the admission of Spain to the United Nations organization because the Spanish Government, "having been founded with the support of the Axis powers, does not, in view of its origin, its nature, its record, and its close association with the aggressor states, possess the qualifications necessary to justify such membership."

The New York *Herald Tribune* carried a series of articles in August 1945, "Spain Under Franco," in which the author, John Chabot Smith, stated, "It is said in Spain that 95 per cent of the people are opposed to the Franco regime." J. Alvarez del Vayo, last Republican Foreign Minister, discussed Negrín's plan for Spain in the *Nation* (July 21, 1945). "His dominating concern," said del Vayo, "is to bring about the restoration of the Republic with a minimum of violence and to establish rapidly the peace and order necessary for reconstructing the country." In August he told a Republican meeting in Mexico City that he would be willing to resign to expedite unity. Later that month when Diego Martinez Barrio was installed as provisional President of the Spanish Republic before the exiled Cortes (Parliament), Negrín urged a government of all parties to work toward the restoration of the Republic, and he and his Cabinet resigned, according to custom. A few days later when Jose Giral became Premier, it is reported that his first act was to call on Negrín to induce him to join the new Cabinet as Foreign Secretary. Negrín's refusal caused considerable speculation as to dissension within the Republican bloc. However, Negrín is not opposed to the Giral Government; and according to an article by Owen Roche (*PM,* September 5, 1945), his absence is due to the following reasons: "1) to remove any cause for redbaiting; 2) to eliminate the fears of British and other investors in Spain; 3) to enable him and his followers to return to Spain in the best position to accept a mandate from the Spanish people themselves." In her book *Smouldering Freedom,* published in early September 1945, Isabel de Palencia stated that there can be no doubt that Negrín "has the support of the majority of Spanish Republicans in exile and probably of those within Spain also."

After having consulted with Under Secretary Dean Acheson at the State Department in late December 1945, Negrín proceeded to Paris where members of the Spanish republican Government-in-exile were gathering. He has steadfastly insisted on the legitimacy of the present Government-in-exile, but in the opinion of many observers he will use his influence to make it more representative of the Spanish resistance groups than it has been.

PERSONAL LIFE

The Spanish democrat, a man of vigor and "exceptional versatility," was described by one writer as "that strange phenomenon, an active scholar, a curious mixture of scientist and businessman, an intellectual and an organizer." A fluent linguist, Negrín spoke English, French, and German, and understood Russian. He wrote little, but did contribute an article to *Free World* in January 1943, "Science and Statesmanship," in which he stressed the necessity for a union between science and statesmanship in order to achieve reconstruction and a lasting peace. A man of modest manners with a lively sense of humor, Negrín was reported to have appeared to Churchill as "one of the ablest statesmen in Europe."

Negrín's wife Maria and son Miguel were in New York City to greet him when he arrived in May 1945. Another son, Juan, is a brain specialist in a New York hospital. Negrín died in Paris in 1956.[45]

FURTHER READING

Liv Age 355:138-40 O '38; *PM* pl2 D 18 '42 por; *International Who's Who,* 1942

JAWAHARLAL NEHRU
Indian Nationalist Leader

Born: November 14, 1889; India
Died: May 27, 1964; Kashmir
Group Affiliation: All-India Congress Party

INTRODUCTION
Under the Defense of India Act "preaching pacifism" was forbidden. In the autumn of 1940 Gandhi, in seeking some method to campaign for Indian independence without embarrassing the British war effort, hit on the method of "token civil disobedience." Selected leaders in the Indian Nationalist movement were to brave arrest so that the people of India might remain aware that the movement had not been abandoned. Jawaharlal Nehru was one of the two men selected to start the campaign; both were immediately arrested and sentenced to prison. Nehru (known in India as "Jawaharlal," sometimes as "Pandit" or "wise man") received a jail term of four years, having refused to testify at his own trial. This sentence one British Laborite called "harsh in the extreme," and predicted it would have serious repercussions in India, Great Britain and the Americas. Parliamentary debates indicated that England was concerned with growing Indian unrest, and the New Republic announced: "British policy toward India seems without a spark of enlightenment, understanding or justice.... Men like Mr. Churchill and Lord Halifax can apparently imagine no alternative to terrorization." In December 1941, however, the Pandit and 500 other members of the All-India Congress Party were released.

Jawaharlal Nehru.

Prison was no novelty to Jawaharlal Nehru. According to John Gunther, he spent seven terms in prison and had been previously sentenced to an aggregate of ten and one-half years, although he served only five and one-half years of them. His previous sentence was in 1934, after a "seditious" speech in Calcutta. It was in prison that political study led him to merge socialism with his nationalism; it was in prison that he wrote a history of the world in the form of letters to his daughter; and it was while serving a prison sentence that he wrote his autobiography, which was published in England in 1936 and hailed as the Indian "Education of Henry Adams." An American edition appeared early in 1941 under the title Toward Freedom, with two new chapters added.

EARLY LIFE

He was born in Allahabad November 14, 1889, the son of Motilal Nehru, a Kashmiri Brahman (equivalent to a Cabot or Lowell in the United States), a millionaire and one of India's most distinguished lawyers, yet a liberal who used to discuss with his son the conduct of the white man in India. In 1905 he took young Jawaharlal to England and put him in Harrow. There he stayed for three years, and then went on to Cambridge, took his

degree in 1910 and remained in London for two more years, studying law and passing his Bar examinations. At that time Nehru called himself a "Cyrenaic," read Pater and Wilde and tried, he said, "to ape the prosperous but somewhat empty-headed Englishman who is called a 'man about town.'"

It was 1912 before Jawaharlal returned to India with a vague desire to enter politics. His father was already active; it was at his house that in 1916 the coalition was made between the Moslem League and the Indian National Congress (a political mass organization of Indians at that time seeking Dominion status, later complete independence). Jawaharlal joined the Nationalist movement. During the First World War, he says, "There was little sympathy with the British in spite of loud professions of loyalty," and when the end of the War brought "intense repression, martial law in the Punjab and the famous Amritsar massacre" in place of the promised independence, Gandhi's doctrine of nonviolent resistance found followers everywhere. During the non-cooperation campaign, hundreds actually fought for the privilege of being arrested; in the month of December 1921, 30,000 persons were imprisoned. Jawaharlal, who had become interested in the peasant movement, who was beginning to feel "shame at my own easygoing and comfortable life and our petty politics of the city . . . [and] sorrow at the degradation and overwhelming poverty of India," followed Gandhi in spite of his father's disapproval. And within a year, Motilal joined him, to work and fight with his son for nine years, devoting his fortune to the cause of India's independence, and losing his health in British prisons. Even Jawaharlal's mother was to be beaten in demonstrations; his wife, Kamala, who died in 1936, was to follow her husband to jail; and in December 1940, his sister was arrested.

LIFE'S WORK

Making speeches, traveling all over the country and even to Sri Lanka investigating conditions, taking part in protest processions, agitating against the salt tax or other repressive measures, entering forbidden territory in defiance of the British, periodically imprisoned and released, Jawaharlal finally gave up his law practice to devote himself entirely to politics. He was elected to the headship of the Allahabad municipality and to Congress. Loyal to Gandhi and one of Gandhi's staunchest defenders, nevertheless Jawaharlal was, by this time, beginning to wonder if the "diapered saint" went far enough. He did not approve of Gandhi's glorification of poverty and renunciation; he himself was becoming convinced that India's problem was as much economic as political, that the land system must be changed and that the "vested interests"—brown as well as white—must be removed before this could come about.

In 1929, Gandhi pushed Jawaharlal forward for the Presidency of Congress, and he was elected. His popularity with the masses and with Indian youth, as well as with the intelligentsia, reached such disturbing heights that after 1930 his playfully iconoclastic wife, and his daughter Indira began to address him: "Oh Jewel of India, what time is it?" "Oh Embodiment of Sacrifice, please pass the bread." For ten years, Jawaharlal was either Secretary or President of Congress; he was President three times. It was he who made Gandhi come out for complete independence; it was he who, in 1931, persuaded the Working Committee of Congress to accept a few planks that smacked a little of socialism. For a long time many of those in the Nationalist movement had been more radical than their leaders; Gandhi was accepted as a saint, but they did not all share the saint's patience. Now Jawaharlal, generally conceded to be Gandhi's successor, aroused India's 350 millions in a way that Gandhi never had. In the spring of 1936, he openly preached socialism to follow complete independence, and urged that his followers organize into workers' and peasants' unions. Reports that Gandhi had proclaimed his lifework ruined by this deviation were denied, and the two continued to work in close collaboration.

Before the elections to the Federal Legislature in February 1937, Jawaharlal, then Chairman of the Congress Party Executive Committee, traveled 110,000 miles in 22 months, in one week made 150 speeches and brought 33,000,000 persons to the polls. The fighting slogan was one of political independence, of resistance to Sir Samuel Hoare's new Federal Constitution of 1935, which Jawaharlal called a "charter of bondage," because it handed most of the control of the Chambers to Indian princes and landlords ("Britain's Fifth Column in India") and, in addition, gave Britain the power to veto any measures passed by the Indians. The Nationalists received an absolute majority in six key provinces and the largest single-party representation in the five remaining provinces, but in protest against the Constitution, six Congress members refused to become cabinet ministers in their provinces. Although they came to

terms within a few months, they pledged themselves to continue their opposition.

Early in 1939, Jawaharlal was faced with a dilemma. Bose, the Bengal Leftist leader, was elected to the Presidency of Congress in spite of Gandhi's opposition. At that time, Jawaharlal was a member of its Working Committee, and, although probably sympathetic to many of Bose's avowed aims, his loyalty to Gandhi made him withdraw his support from the organization. The resignations of many others followed. Bose was out and Jawaharlal back on the Committee before the year was out, however; and, when in September 1939 Britain declared India belligerent without any formal reference or intimation to Indian representatives and rushed the Indian Constitution Amending Bill through Parliament, he was the author of a protest by the Working Committee. It asserted that war or peace was an issue that the Indians should be allowed to settle, that India's resources were not to be exploited for "imperialist ends," and that Britain must state her war and peace aims before she could expect cooperation. The answer to this protest, he said, "indicated sufficiently clearly that there was no intention and, so far as that government was concerned, no possibility of the ending of the imperialist structure in India." Therefore as intensely as the Indians detested Fascism and Nazism, they were not convinced that Britain was really fighting for any "new world order." In the meantime, the Congress governments in the provinces had resigned, parliamentary government had been suspended, and in India there was "full-blooded dictatorship and authoritarianism."

Jawaharlal concluded sadly: "The way of cooperation does not lie for us; the hundred-year-old hostility will remain and grow in future conflicts, and the breach, when it comes, as come it must, will also not be in friendship but in hostility." He would hope for a British victory in the present conflict, but he would not cooperate actively with India's rulers.

Nehru's release from prison found his position somewhat changed. "India," he said, "is prepared to go for an all-in aid in the war, if her political aspirations are satisfied." He told a group of students that India's warm regard for China, Russia and America justified war with Japan. But he also tried to make Britain aware that as long as the democratic aspirations of the Indian people remain unrealized ("the four freedoms" do not apply to India, Churchill had said), they cannot play their proper role in bringing about an Axis defeat.

John Gunther described Jawaharlal as "an Indian who became a westerner; an aristocrat who became a socialist; an individualist who became a great mass leader." Unlike Gandhi, he emphasized economics, believed in the industrialization and urbanization of India, advocated normal marriage and sex relationships, was a "devout rationalist" and, while not anti-religious, has said "the spectacle of what is called religion, or at any rate organized religion, in India and elsewhere, has filled me with horror." He was not concerned with Indian problems alone. During the Spanish War he visited and spoke for Loyalist Spain, and he had also visited and organized aid for China. He not only favored a classless, planned society but was convinced that anything that comes in its way "will have to be removed, gently if possible, forcibly if necessary." "Socialism is for me not merely an economic doctrine which I favor; it is a vital creed which I hold with all my head and heart." He was not a Communist chiefly because he resisted "the Communist tendency to treat Communism as holy doctrine." He was in Moscow only once, with his father in 1927, to see the tenth anniversary festivities. Nor was he a member of the Congress Socialist Party. In Congress his position would probably be described as Left center, just as Gandhi's was Right center. The relationship between the two men was a very close one, if strange. Gandhi said: "There is a heart-union between us which no intellectual differences can break," and Jawaharlal called him "Bapu" (father). He had never underestimated what Gandhi had done for India: "Reactionary or revolutionary, he [had] changed the face of India, given pride and character to a cringing and demoralized people, built up strength and consciousness in the masses, and made the Indian problem a world problem." Yet Nehru could also say of Gandhi: "What a problem and puzzle he has been!"

Once Japanese aggression was curtailed, India finally had her chance to be a free, independent nation. In 1947, Nehru and his colleagues were released from confinement and the British proposed plans for transfer of power. Once elected, Nehru headed an interim government, which was impaired by outbreaks of communal violence and political disorder, and the opposition of the Muslim League led by Muhammad Ali Jinnah. The Muslim League demanded a separate Muslim state of Pakistan. Nehru tried several times to create a coalition government with the Muslim faction, but failed. He reluctantly agreed to the partitioning of India into India and Pakistan. Nehru was elected Prime Minister of the new government on August 15, 1947.

On January 30, 1948, Gandhi was shot while he was walking to a platform from which he was to address a prayer meeting. His death acted as a catalyst to solidify the creation of the new nation of India. Nehru and his supporters suppressed several non-supporters of the new government; it was estimated that 20,000 people were arrested.

Nehru turned to his daughter, Indira, for comfort and support [his wife had passed away in 1936]. He easily led the Congress to an overwhelming majority in the elections of 1952. His daughter moved to his official residence and acted as his Chief of Staff. In the 1957 elections, he also led the Congress to a major victory, but his government was facing rising problems and criticism. Nehru contemplated resigning, but continued to serve. Although he had been against Indira's official entry into politics, she ran in the election against his wishes. The election of his daughter as Congress President in 1959 aroused criticism for alleged nepotism. Nehru and his daughter also were butting heads over policy. Nehru also led the Congress to victory in the 1962 elections, but with a diminished majority.

With the passage of the new Constitution of India, which came into force on January 26, 1950, India became a sovereign democratic republic. Nehru declared the new republic to be a "Union of States". He and his supporters re-drew the country's states along linguistic lines. The Constitution, which Nehru helped write, clearly stated, "The State shall endeavor to secure for the citizens a uniform civil code throughout the territory of India." Nehru worked hard to ensure that everyone was treated equally under the new government, but his critics claimed that the new laws were enforced unevenly. The caste system and other archaic social structures were prohibited, including the practice of polygamy by Muslims. Hindi was adopted as the official language of India, in 1950, with English continuing as an associate official language for a period of 15 years, after which Hindi would become the sole official language. (The elimination of English as an associate official language later failed.) Education was improved. Under Nehru's leadership, the government attempted to develop India quickly by embarking on agrarian reform and rapid industrialization. A successful land reform law was introduced that abolished giant landholdings, but efforts to redistribute land by placing limits on landownership failed. Agriculture production increased during his tenure in office, as more land was put into production and irrigated.

Nehru's foreign policy was uneven. His policy of non-alignment left the country eligible for aid from countries aligned with either the Western or Eastern bloc. He was a strong supporter of pacifism on the international stage. In 1954, he and China signed a treaty known as the Five Principles of Peaceful Coexistence; it was called in India the Panchsheel (from the Sanskrit words, panch: five, sheel: virtues). Although he was a pacifist, Nehru believed in the necessity of a national defense and advocated that India become a nuclear power. His government established outposts in territory along the Chinese-India border in places where there previously had not been any military presence. This situation resulted in the 1962 Sino-Indian War, which India lost. The aftermath of the war saw sweeping changes in the Indian military to prepare it for similar conflicts in the future. Nehru, felt pressured, because he was seen as responsible for failing to anticipate the Chinese attack on India. Nehru ordered the raising of an elite, Indian-trained "Tibetan Armed Force" composed of Tibetan refugees.

Nehru's health declined steadily after the Sino-Indian War, which many attributed to the shock of the Chinese betrayal and attack on India. He spent some time in Kasmir, recuperating, in 1963. On May 26, 1964, he collapsed from what was thought to be a heart attack and never recovered. His death was announced the following day. Nehru, on May 28, was cremated in accordance with Hindu rites on the banks of the Yamuna River.

PERSONAL LIFE

Nehru considered himself a "Hindu Agnostic," because he saw religious taboos as preventing India from going forward and adapting to modern conditions. He married Kamala Kaul (died, 1936) in the early 1900s, when she was age 17. Their only living child, Indira, was born in 1917.

FURTHER READING

Asia 36:354-9 Je '36; 36 :614 S '36; 36: 626-30 O '36; 37 :341 My '37;. 39:92-6 F '39 il por; 39:252-5 My '39; 39:555-6 O '39; 39:662-3 N '39 il pors; 40: 595-9 N '40; Christian Cent 53:1139 Ag 26 '36; 57: 1404 N 13 '40; Christian Sci Mon Mag p3 Mr 2 '38 il por; Cur Hist 45:81-4 Mr '37 por; 54:44-6+ My '41; New Repub 103:677 N 18 '40; 104:538-9 Ap 21 '41; The New York Times p4 N 8 '40; IV p2 N 10 '40; Pacific Affairs 13:17-29 Mr '40; Read Digest 36:79-83 F '40; Survey G 26:481-4 S '37 il por; Time 30:18 Jl 19 '37 por; 33:23 Mr 6 '39 por; 37:102-4 F 24 '41; Bartlett, R. M. They Did Something About It p44-60 1939; Gunther, J. Inside Asia p408-25 1940; International Who's Who; Nehru, J. L. Autobiography 1936; Nehru, J. L. Eighteen Months in India, 1936-37: Being Further Essays and Writings 1938; Nehru, J. L. Toward Freedom 1941; Singh, A. Nehru: the Rising Star of India 1939.

BENJAMIN NETANYAHU (NEH-THAN-YAH-HOO)

Prime Minister of Israel

Born: October 21, 1949; Tel Aviv; Israel
Party Affiliation: Likud

INTRODUCTION

By a margin of less than one percentage point, Israeli voters in May 1996 elected Benjamin Netanyahu, the leader of the right-of-center Likud Party, prime minister. A relatively young, telegenic politician who went to high school and college in the United States, Netanyahu inspires devotion from his supporters, who applaud his tough stand on matters of Israeli security, and provokes despair among his opponents, who fear his leadership will derail the peace process undertaken by his Labor Party predecessors. He began his political career fairly

recently, in 1988, when he captured a seat in Israel's parliament, after having pursued careers in the Israeli military, in business, and in government. During the 1991 Persian Gulf war, he gained international renown when he was interviewed live on CNN as Iraqi missiles fell on Israel. His grace under fire helped win sympathy for his country around the world.

A year later Netanyahu became Israel's chief spokesman at the Middle East peace conference in Madrid, where he earned praise—and criticism—for his ability to "spin" information to his government's best advantage. Elected leader of the Likud Party in 1993, he emerged as a fierce critic of Israel's land-for-peace agreement brokered by the Labor prime minister Yitzhak

509

Benjamin Netanyahu.

Rabin and representatives of the Palestine Liberation Organization. After Rabin's assassination by an Israeli fanatic, in November 1995, Netanyahu was widely criticized for not having done enough to stop the rancorous antigovernment protests that had preceded the killing, a charge he vigorously denied. A national election the following May pitted Netanyahu against Rabin's successor, Shimon Peres. Four deadly Arab terrorist attacks against Israelis in the weeks prior to the election fanned support for the Likud leader's firm stand against the PLO.

Following his election to the prime ministership, Netanyahu pledged to continue the peace process. One of the first actions of his right-wing coalition government, however, caused a rift in the process—the announcement of the expansion of Jewish settlements in the occupied West Bank and Gaza Strip. The move infuriated the Palestinians, as did the prime minister's decision to open an entrance to a tunnel in Jerusalem that is close to Muslim holy sites. Violence erupted in the territories in late September, resulting in the deaths of 79 people. At an emergency meeting arranged in October by President Bill Clinton in Washington, D.C.,

Netanyahu refused to yield on the issue of the tunnel. He also insisted that the redeployment of Israeli troops in the ancient city of Hebron, which had been agreed to by the previous government, be delayed until new security provisions for the Jewish settlers there could be arranged. In the opinion of the columnist Thomas Friedman, writing in The New York Times *(September 29, 1996), "Netanyahu can have real negotiations between leaders or a real war between peoples. Those are his choices. There is nothing in between. There never was."*

EARLY LIFE

The second of the three sons of Cela (Segal) and Benzion Netanyahu, Benjamin Netanyahu was born Binyamin Netanyahu on October 21, 1949 in Tel Aviv, Israel, and he grew up in Jerusalem. He is widely known in Israel by his nickname, Bibi. His father, a professor of Jewish history who has written on the subject, often told Benjamin and his brothers, Jonathan and Iddo, about the struggle to create the Jewish state and the competing views among Zionists over the best way to achieve success. On the one hand, there was the so-called revisionist movement, to which Netanyahu's father adhered, which evolved into the Likud Party after Israel declared its independence in 1948. The revisionists believed that some revenge attacks against Arab civilians and the British mandatory government were justified, and that the borders of the Jewish state should extend eastward to include the land that is now Jordan. On the other hand, the mainstream movement, led by David Ben-Gurion (who eventually founded the Labor Party and became Israel's first prime minister), favored a more measured military strategy and demonstrated a greater willingness to compromise on territory for the sake of peace.

When Benjamin was 14, his father accepted a teaching position at Dropsie College (now known as the Annenberg Research Institute), in Philadelphia. Initially despondent over leaving Israel with his family, the young Netanyahu adjusted quickly to American life and schooling. An excellent student, he mastered idiomatic English, "complete with baseball metaphors," according to Geraldine Brooks, who profiled him for GQ (May 1992). During the spring of 1967, when he was in his senior year of high school, Israel was on the verge of war, and Netanyahu persuaded his teachers to let him take final exams early so he could return to his homeland. A little too young to fight in the Six-Day War that June, he was nevertheless there to bask in the country's pride at its victory. In less than a week, the Israeli military had defeated the forces of five Arab countries and had captured land that more than tripled its size: the West Bank (including the Old City of Jerusalem), the Sinai peninsula, the Gaza Strip, and the Golan Heights. Two months later, Netanyahu entered the army and was accepted into a secret unit called Sayeret Matcal (which means "border reconnaissance"), an elite antiterrorist force skilled in staging raids behind enemy lines. Acceptance into "the unit," as the force is sometimes called in Israel, is a mark of prestige. To qualify, soldiers must pass challenging intelligence and psychological tests and withstand the rigorous training, which, as Geraldine Brooks noted, includes "80-mile forced marches, with 50-pound packs and no stops for 24 hours; runs through waist-deep, freezing mud; solo navigations without a map, in stinging sandstorms; never enough food, never enough water, never enough sleep." Recalling his experience, Netanyahu told Brooks, "It's torture—things you look back on and can't believe you did."

LIFE'S WORK

One of Netanyahu's first missions with Sayeret Matcal was in 1968, when his team blew up 13 unoccupied planes parked at Beirut International Airport, in Lebanon. The action was taken in retaliation for the hijacking of an El Al airplane by Palestinian terrorists operating out of Lebanon. Another important mission occurred in 1972, after a Sabena Airlines jet was hijacked by two men and two women and was forced to land at Lod Airport (now called Ben-Gurion Airport), outside Tel Aviv. Dressed in mechanics' overalls, the Sayeret soldiers approached the plane as if to refuel it and then stormed inside. Netanyahu went in through a wing door, and after wrestling a female hijacker to the ground, he pounded her head against the floor of the plane and demanded, "Where are the explosives?" Another Sayeret commando saw Netanyahu struggling and took aim at the woman. As Netanyahu raised his hand to wave his comrade off, he was shot in the upper arm. The injury turned out not to be serious, and the mission ended in success—all 100 people aboard were rescued.

After receiving several army promotions, Netanyahu became a captain and recruited his elder brother, Jonathan, into the antiterrorism unit. Later, their younger sibling, Iddo, joined them, and for a short while all three brothers served together. Considering the elite status of the force, this was quite a coup for the Netanyahu family, and the story of "the three brothers, fighting like lions," as Shimon Peres, Israel's former prime minister, once described them, became something of a legend in the country.

After his army service ended, in 1972, Netanyahu returned to the United States and enrolled at the Massachusetts Institute of Technology (MIT), in Cambridge, where he majored in architecture. A year later he interrupted his studies to fight for Israel in the Yom Kippur War, participating in battles in the Sinai and the Golan Heights. At the war's end, he resumed his studies at MIT, and by 1976 he had earned a B.A. degree in architecture and an M.B.A. degree in business management. After completing his education, Netanyahu got a job at Boston Consulting Group as a management consultant. While listening to the radio on July 4, 1976, he heard about a daring Israeli raid at Entebbe Airport, in Uganda, which resulted in the rescue of 100 Israeli passengers on a hijacked Air France plane. Assuming (correctly) that his brother Jonathan had led the mission, Netanyahu called his parents in Jerusalem and learned that Jonathan had been the only Israeli commando who was killed. "Yoni," as Jonathan was called in Israel, instantly became a national hero and a symbol of the army's bravery.

Netanyahu took his brother's death hard: he could not swallow food for weeks, according to one source. Moving back to Israel, he founded the Jonathan Institute in Jerusalem, whose mission was to study the origins of terrorism and come up with ways for governments to combat it. He organized two international conferences on terrorism, one in 1979 and another in 1984, which were attended by scholars and politicians from all over the world. In further tribute to his brother's memory, Netanyahu collected letters Jonathan had written from 1963 through 1976 and had them published in the book *Self-Portrait of a Hero: The Letters of Jonathan Netanyahu* (1981), which he edited.

Meanwhile, Israel was undergoing major political changes that resulted from the 1977 election, when the Labor Party was voted out of power for the first time in the country's history and was replaced by the Likud Party. One of those changes involved a feverish building policy to increase Israeli settlements in the occupied West Bank. Prime Minister Menachem Begin (who negotiated a peace treaty with Egypt in 1979 that resulted in Israel's subsequent relinquishment of the Sinai peninsula) deemed the return of the West Bank unthinkable because of the area's military and historical value. The wave of Jewish settlements disturbed the native Palestinian population; many left-wing Israelis also opposed the building policy as unnecessarily provocative.

Aligning himself with the Likud, Netanyahu became acquainted with some of the party's leaders, including Moshe Arens, through his work at the Jonathan Institute. Arens was appointed ambassador to the United States in 1982, and he astonished many people in Israel by choosing Netanyahu, who had no diplomatic experience and was then working as a marketing manager for a furniture company, to serve in the important position of deputy chief of mission at the Israeli mission in Washington, D.C. According to one source, Arens found Netanyahu's political views "more to his taste than the professionals in Israel's dovish foreign ministry."

Netanyahu proved to be an unconventional diplomat who had little patience with bureaucratic red tape. After two effective years in Washington, Netanyahu was named Israel's permanent representative to the United Nations. An articulate speaker, he was often sought out by American journalists for comments on Middle Eastern issues. His bluntness sometimes sparked controversy, as happened when he was quoted by a reporter for the New York *Daily News* (January 28, 1985) as saying that the international pressure on Israel to withdraw from the West Bank was tantamount to asking the Jewish state "to commit suicide . . ., [because] there are now 10,000 tanks on our eastern border." At that time, a national unity government was in place in Israel, run jointly by representatives of the Likud and Labor parties. High-ranking Labor members charged that Netanyahu's remarks contradicted the official government position that the ultimate status of the West Bank was subject to negotiation; Likud members defended him and disputed the Labor interpretation of government policy.

In 1988 Netanyahu resigned his United Nations post and announced his intention to run for a seat in the Knesset, Israel's parliament. In order to qualify for a position on the Likud's ticket, he had to do well in the party primary held that July. He surprised many observers by placing first among the long list of candidates, an unusual feat for a political newcomer. Following the election Prime Minister Yitzhak Shamir appointed Netanyahu deputy foreign minister, a post he held (until 1991) in addition to his seat in the Knesset. Through his work in the foreign ministry, Netanyahu became adept at talking to members of the international press corps, a skill that was to prove of particular importance in January 1991. It was then that Iraqi president Saddam Hussein, in an effort to draw Israel into the Persian Gulf war, ordered the launching of Scud missiles into the Jewish state. During the crisis, which lasted for several weeks,

Netanyahu became "the TV voice—and face—of his beleaguered nation," a writer for *People* (Spring/Summer 1991) noted. "In more than 200 live interviews, his flawless English and calm demeanor helped muster support around the world for Scud-weary Israel." Impressed by Netanyahu's performance (and perhaps his telegenic good looks as well), people from all corners of the globe sent him fan mail and love letters. Indeed, according to the *People* article, an Israeli magazine named Netanyahu the man with whom women most wanted to share a bomb shelter.

Netanyahu was so prized as a spokesman during the Persian Gulf war that Prime Minister Shamir put him in charge of the government's contacts with the foreign press during the Madrid peace conference in October 1991, the historic meeting between Israel and its Arab neighbors. The results were "dazzling," according to Geraldine Brooks. Netanyahu won praise from many for his gracious manner toward reporters, including those from Arab countries, and for his talent in expressing the Israeli point of view in succinct sound bites. Others, however, deemed his "spin" on events superficial and blasted his interpretation of Arab-Israeli history as untrue. Meanwhile, Netanyahu was involved in a behind-the-scenes feud with his boss, Foreign Minister David Levy. Soon after the Madrid conference, at the behest of Shamir, Netanyahu moved on to a new position as deputy minister in the prime minister's office.

The June 1992 election in Israel was won by the Labor Party, with Yitzhak Rabin as its leader. Rabin was able to form a government with smaller, left-wing parties, leaving the Likud out of power for the first time in 15 years. Soon after the election, Shamir, then 77, said that he would step down as his party's leader, and a scramble began within the Likud to assume the party's helm. Netanyahu promptly announced his candidacy, and, to the dismay of some older and more experienced politicians, it was immediately apparent that his chances for success were excellent. A new system had been put in place allowing the Likud's 145,000 members to vote directly for their leader; previously, the choice had been made by the party's small, cliquish central committee. Netanyahu's polished on-camera presence gave him a clear advantage in a primary campaign that emphasized American-style television interviews and political advertisements.

Netanyahu's electoral prospects dimmed considerably in January 1993, when the revelation that he had had an extramarital affair became the number-one topic of discussion in Israel. An associate of a senior Likud politician had reportedly called his wife, Sara, and told her that unless her husband withdrew from the party's race, a videotape of him in "compromising romantic situations" with another woman would be made public. Using a preemptive strategy, Netanyahu went on television to admit to the affair and to state that it had ended a few months before. His wife stood by him, and he went on to beat three other contenders in the March 1993 primary with 52 percent of the vote. At the age of 43, he became the youngest person to lead a major Israeli political party.

As the official spokesman for the opposition, Netanyahu often lashed out at the policies of the Labor-led government. He was particularly incensed by Prime Minister Rabin's decision to recognize the PLO, considered by many in Israel to be a terrorist group, as the legitimate representative of the Palestinian people. In 1993 Rabin and PLO leader Yasir Arafat concluded a peace agreement that outlined territorial concessions by Israel in the Gaza Strip and the West Bank in accordance with Palestinian self-rule. Many Israelis favored the land-for-peace policy, believing, as Rabin did, that the Jewish state could not remain a democracy while maintaining military control over 1.5 million native Palestinians. Others, like Netanyahu, argued that the Palestinians ought to be offered autonomy over their civilian affairs but that Israel's security depended on its continued military presence in the disputed areas.

Arab extremists from the Islamic movement Hamas were also unhappy about the peace accord; denouncing it as too limited, the group launched a series of attacks against Israeli civilians. To Netanyahu, the wave of terror confirmed the Likud's contention that the government's policy of conciliation and concession toward the Palestinians was foolhardy and mortally dangerous to Israel. On September 28, 1993, the day Rabin and Arafat made history by signing the peace accord in Washington, D.C. (an act for which they, along with Shimon Peres, won the 1994 Nobel Peace Prize), Netanyahu attended an "alternate signing" in Israel that had been staged by the Likud as a declaration of loyalty to the Jewish state.

In 1994 Netanyahu praised the Rabin government for negotiating a peace treaty with Jordan's King Hussein. "Across the Jordan River there is no safe refuge for terrorists as there is now in PLO-controlled Gaza," he wrote in an op-ed article published in *The New York Times* (November 21, 1994). "With Jordan we have a

genuine peace, not a tactic whose sole purpose is to seize land to be used as a launching ground for still another war against Israel." Throughout 1994 and 1995, as more and more West Bank towns came under PLO control, in accordance with the 1993 peace agreement, the debate among Israelis over whether it should have been concluded grew increasingly heated, with right-wing extremists introducing a particularly acrimonious tone. Rabin, who had been one of the country's greatest military heroes, was denounced at political rallies as a traitor by extremists, some of whom also constructed placards that depicted the prime minister in an Arab headdress or a Nazi armband. As he left a peace rally in Tel Aviv on November 4, 1995, Rabin was assassinated by Yigal Amir, a right-wing fanatic.

Rabin's murder shook Israel to its core, and along with grief, there was widespread anger at Likud leaders for not controlling the extremist, right-wing fringe. Netanyahu in particular was put on the defensive by Rabin's widow, who refused to shake his hand at her husband's funeral. In several subsequent interviews, Leah Rabin blamed him directly for not quelling the climate of hate that she believed had inspired Amir to act. Many political commentators agreed and accused Netanyahu of fanning the feelings of extremists for his own political gain. Fighting back, Netanyahu insisted that he had reproached those who had defamed Rabin in his presence, and maintained that his own arguments against the prime minister's policies had always been civil. "This is sheer McCarthyism," he told Serge Schmemann of *The New York Times* (November 10, 1995). "What you are witnessing is a classic case of guilt by association."

After Rabin's death, Foreign Minister Shimon Peres took over the prime ministership with no challenge from the Likud. The next election was scheduled for November 1996, but Peres decided to move it up to May 29, to take advantage of the wave of popular support for him and the Labor Party. That support dropped sharply in the wake of four Arab suicide attacks against Israelis between February 28 and March 4, which killed a total of 62 people, among them the assailants. While Peres took strong steps to reestablish security, including closing the borders of the West Bank and Gaza Strip indefinitely, the toll of the bombings caused many Israelis to reevaluate the terms of the 1993 peace accord as well as the Labor leadership. In a nationally televised debate with Peres three days before the election, Netanyahu charged that the Labor leader's negotiations with the PLO had brought "neither peace to Israel nor real security. It brings us fear." Netanyahu promised to be tougher than Peres on matters of security, although he offered no specifics.

Voting directly for their prime minister for the first time, Israelis chose Netanyahu by the razor-thin margin of 50.4 percent to 49.5 percent, for a plurality of about 29,000 votes out of almost 3 million cast. The deep division in Israel over the election was made apparent by the contrast between the ecstatic victory rallies staged by Likud supporters, who chanted "Bibi, king of Israel" in the streets, and the mournful gatherings of Labor supporters (at the spot where Rabin had been shot), who were convinced that the peace process, too, had been killed. Netanyahu insisted that he was committed to peace, but his opponents remained skeptical. After a few weeks of political wrangling, the new prime minister established a right-wing coalition government, with several religious parties and a party of Russian immigrants providing his Likud base with a Knesset majority.

In August 1996 the new government took one of its first steps toward reversing the policies of the previous Labor coalition when it lifted the four-year-old freeze on the expansion of settlements in the West Bank and Gaza Strip. Denouncing the new policy as a "flagrant violation" of the 1993 Oslo agreement, Arafat called for a general strike in the territories on August 29 to protest the Israeli government's "declaration of war on the Palestinian people." In an attempt to cool tensions, the Israeli prime minister agreed to meet face to face with Arafat—whom he had reviled throughout his election campaign—and the two posed for a grim handshake.

Passions flared anew, however, at the end of September, over a new entrance to an ancient tunnel in Jerusalem that is near sites considered holy to both Muslims and Jews. The Labor government had indefinitely delayed opening the entrance, in deference to Palestinians' fears about its effect on their holy places. After determining that no damage would be done to any site, Netanyahu approved the opening of the new entrance. Rioting immediately erupted in the territories, resulting in the deaths of 79 people. President Bill Clinton called for an emergency summit at the White House on October 2 that was attended by Netanyahu, Arafat, and King Hussein of Jordan. By that time the bloodshed in the territories had stopped, and the central issue was Israel's long-delayed withdrawal of its troops from the West Bank city of Hebron, as stipulated by the 1993 peace accords. Although he insisted that he was "committed" to redeploying troops in the ancient city, Netanyahu refused to commit to a date for doing so. He also refused to close the tunnel's entrance, even temporarily as a gesture of goodwill, arguing that to do so would "reward" those who had provoked the violence. The Israeli leader was hailed by his supporters at home for his strong stands, but his policies were denounced throughout the Arab world and by his opponents in Israel, including Peres, who declared Netanyahu wanted "peace for nothing." Soon after the Washington summit, a new round of negotiations about Hebron began in Israel. The talks dragged on as Israeli negotiators argued that stronger security measures had to be established to protect the 400 Jewish settlers, who live among 100,000 Palestinians, before troops could be withdrawn, while PLO representatives insisted that the Oslo accords had already provided the necessary framework for withdrawal.

PERSONAL LIFE

Benjamin Netanyahu and his third wife, Sara, a child psychologist whom he married in 1991, live in Jerusalem. They have two sons, and he also has a daughter from his first marriage, which, like his second, ended in divorce. In 2009, Netanyahu became a grandfather, and he now has three grandchildren.

He is the author of *Terrorism: How the West Can Win* (1986), *A Place Among Nations: Israel and the World* (1993), *Fighting Terrorism: How Democracies* Can *Defeat Domestic and International Terrorists* (1995), and *A Durable Peace: Israel and its Place Among the Nations* (1999).

FURTHER READING

GQ p142+ My '92 pors; New Republic *p19-h fe 21 '93; People p42+ Spring/Summer '91 pors;* The New York Times *Ap3 Jl7 '88 por, p4 Ja 16 '93 por, A p8 N 10 '95 por, A p1+ Je 1 96 pors ; International Who's Who, 1996-97*

RICHARD NIXON

President of the United States

Born: January 9, 1913; Yorba Linda, California
Died: April 22, 1994; New York, NY
Group Affiliation: Republican Party

INTRODUCTION

An extraordinary series of victories, defeats, and recoveries, the career of Richard Nixon, the thirty-seventh president of the United States, is unparalleled in American history. He is the only politician in the United States to have been elected twice as vice-president and twice as president, and the only president to resign. Just six years after his election to the House of Representatives, in 1946, the staunchly anti-Communist Republican from California became, at the age of thirty-nine, the country's second-youngest vice-president-elect. After serving ably and conspicuously under President Dwight D. Eisenhower for eight years, he narrowly lost his first presidential campaign, in 1960, to John F. Kennedy. By all appearances, Nixon's political career seemed to be over, especially after he was defeated in the gubernatorial election in California two years later, but in 1968 he made a stunning comeback when he was elected president of the United States on a pledge to end the Vietnam War, which had polarized the country. Characterized by the sometimes violent suppression of antiwar demonstrations and social protests, urban unrest in the wake of the assassinations of the civil rights leader Martin Luther King Jr. and the Democratic presidential candidate Robert F. Kennedy, and rising crime, the Nixon era was also marked by astonishingly liberal domestic programs and historic overtures to the People's Republic of China and the Soviet Union.

His diplomatic achievements notwithstanding, Nixon was for many years—and may well remain—one of the most despised public figures of all time. Berated by some for his failure to bring to a speedy end American involvement in the Vietnam War (a goal he finally achieved in 1973), he was widely reviled during the final months of his presidency, after congressional investigations into the burglary of Democratic National Committee headquarters in the Watergate office-apartment complex and the White House's subsequent cover-up of the scandal revealed a president who was capable of wrongdoing on an unprecedented scale. Under the threat of impeachment, Nixon resigned the presidency

Richard Nixon.

on August 9, 1974. "Greatness comes not when things go always good for you," he said in his televised farewell address to the nation, "but . . . when you take some knocks, some disappointments, when sadness comes, because only if you have been in the deepest valley can you ever know how magnificent it is to be on the highest mountain."

For the remaining two decades of his life, Nixon endeavored to attain the heights once again, by writing books on foreign policy, visiting world leaders, and holding informal meetings with journalists at his home. At the time of his death, in 1994, he was regarded as a well-respected elder statesman by some, while to others he remained what one analyst called "the most colossal disaster in the history of the American presidency." Commenting on Americans' enduring fascination with the former president, Jonathan Alter wrote in Newsweek *(May 2, 1994), "He dominates our political consciousness not because of what he did—for good or ill—but because of who he was. . . . His character came to represent political character generally. .. . Nixon helped make people skeptical not just of individual politicians (a stout American tradition) but of the legitimacy of politics and government as a means of addressing their problems."*

EARLY LIFE

Named for King Richard the Lion-Hearted of England, Richard Milhous Nixon was born on January 9, 1913 in Yorba Linda, California, the second of the five sons of Francis Anthony ("Frank") Nixon, a former Methodist who had converted to the Quaker faith around the time of his marriage, and Hannah (Milhous) Nixon, a devout Quaker throughout her life. An undemonstrative woman, Hannah Nixon rarely, if ever, displayed physical affection toward her children, but she cared for them with a saintly stoicism, ministering tirelessly to two of her sons during periods of fatal illness. Her fourth son, Arthur, died of meningitis in childhood, when Richard was twelve. The Nixon boys, including Donald, born in 1915, and Edward, born in 1930, grew up in Whittier, California, where their father, who had tried unsuccessfully to grow lemons for a living in Yorba Linda, was first an oilfield worker, then the owner of a gas station and general store.

Rising at 4:00 A.M. every morning to buy fresh fruit and vegetables for the family store, young Richard Nixon spent most of his time working or studying. He excelled at Fullerton High School and, later, Whittier High School. When he was fifteen, his older brother Harold, then eighteen, came down with tuberculosis; Hannah Nixon repeatedly traveled with her son to the drier, less polluted environment of Prescott, Arizona, where it was hoped he would recover. To pay for Harold's medical expenses, she began taking in other consumptive boarders and was soon operating what amounted to a hospice in Prescott. Richard Nixon joined his mother and brother in Arizona in the summers, finding odd jobs as a janitor, carnival barker, and chicken plucker. (After five years during which his health alternately deteriorated and improved, Harold Nixon died at the age of twenty-three.)

Upon his graduation from Whittier High School, in 1930, Nixon was honored with a Harvard Club award as "best all-around student" and offered a scholarship to Harvard University, in Cambridge, Massachusetts. Because the traveling and living expenses he would have incurred attending Harvard—or Yale University, in New Haven, Connecticut, which had also expressed interest in him—were more than he could afford, Nixon turned down the scholarship and enrolled at Whittier College, which he could attend while living at home. A skilled debater and an accomplished actor, he served as president of his freshman class and, in his senior year, as president of the student body. Second in his class academically, Nixon received a B.A. degree in history, with honors, from Whittier College in 1934; he continued his education on a full-tuition scholarship to Duke University Law School, in Durham, North Carolina. Barely able to make ends meet as a graduate student, he lived first in a toolshed without heat, then in a five-dollar-a-month room, which he shared with a roommate. Nicknamed Gloomy Gus for his usually dour countenance, he did not go out on a single date in his three years at Duke. Instead, as his other campus sobriquet, Iron Butt, indicated, he spent most of his time rooted to his seat in the library, studying. A member of the Duke Bar Association and the Order of the Coif, an honorary society, he graduated third in his class of 1937, with an LL.B. degree.

Despite his solid academic credentials, Nixon was turned down by prestigious law firms in New York City as well as by the FBI. Already interested in a career in politics, he returned to California to practice law in his hometown with the firm of Wingert & Bewley, which soon became Bewley, Knoop & Nixon, so that he could begin to establish a political base there. To increase his chances of meeting potential clients, he joined various civic groups and clubs, including the local community theatre troupe, where, in 1938, he met Thelma Catherine Patricia ("Pat") Ryan, a schoolteacher, whom he married on June 21, 1940. In December of the following year, shortly after Japan attacked Pearl Harbor, the Nixons moved to Washington, D.C., where the young lawyer had a higher-paying job waiting for him in the tire-rationing section of the Office of Price Administration; he worked there from January 1942 to August 1942. Although he was entitled to a draft deferment on two counts (the pacifism of the Quaker religion and his government job), Nixon nonetheless obtained a commission in the United States Navy, allegedly because he recognized that avoidance of military service in World War II would adversely affect his hoped-for political career. During his three years in the navy, he served as a supply officer in the South Pacific, first in New Caledonia, then in the Solomon Islands.

LIFE'S WORK

Returning to Whittier after his discharge in 1946, Nixon launched his first political campaign with half of the estimated $10,000 he had won playing stud poker with his fellow sailors while in the navy. Endorsed as a candidate for the House of Representatives from the Twelfth Congressional District by local Republican business leaders, Nixon conducted what some have called his first smear campaign—against Jerry Voorhis, the five-term Democratic incumbent. One of Nixon's ads said, "Remember, Voorhis is a former registered Socialist and his voting record in Congress is more socialistic and communistic than Democratic." Winning with 56 percent of the vote in an across-the-board Republican landslide that returned both houses of Congress to that party for the first time since 1929, Nixon had seized upon the issue—redbaiting—that would bring him national attention in his first four years in Congress and would characterize several of his campaigns in the future. He was reelected with 86 percent of the vote in 1948.

In exchange for being assigned a coveted membership on the Education and Labor Committee during his freshman term in Congress, Nixon agreed to serve on the House Un-American Activities Committee, which was looking into alleged Communist influences in labor unions and other American organizations. The committee's investigation in 1948-49 of Alger Hiss brought Nixon national prominence, for he arranged a confrontation between Hiss, a former State Department official with a sterling career record, and Whittaker Chambers, a senior editor of *Time* who had confessed to spying for the Soviet Union and who said he had met Hiss in a communist cell. Hiss at first denied knowing Chambers but was convicted on perjury charges. Having made a name for himself, Nixon declared his candidacy for the Senate in the 1950 election. Capitalizing on his reputation as a staunch anti-Communist, he conducted a ruthless campaign against his opponent for the seat, Helen Gahagan Douglas, a Democratic member of the House whom he dubbed "the pink lady" for her zealous New Dealism. In return, Douglas, who was to lose the election by the largest plurality of any senatorial candidate that year (59 percent to 41 percent), began calling her opponent Tricky Dick, a label invented by an editorial writer for the *Independent Review*.

In the eyes of some political observers, Nixon seemed to be living up to that label in 1952, when, after having pledged to support Governor Earl Warren of California for the Republican presidential nomination, he persuaded California delegates at the Republican National Convention to back a resolution intended to break an apparent deadlock between two candidates, conservative Senator Robert A. Taft of Ohio and the more popular General Dwight D. Eisenhower, in favor of the latter. In the event of such an impasse, the nomination might have gone to Warren as a compromise, but Nixon preferred Eisenhower, who had already approached the young senator about being his running mate.

Nixon was indeed chosen as his party's vice-presidential nominee, and no sooner did the campaign begin than he resorted to mudslinging, saying that the Democratic presidential candidate, Adlai E. Stevenson (whose running mate was Senator John Sparkman of Alabama), held a Ph.D. from Secretary of State Dean Acheson's "College of Cowardly Communist Containment." In retaliation, the Democrats exposed an $18,000 slush fund that Nixon had received, and they falsely implied that he was using the money for personal as well as political purposes. Nixon's credibility was so severely damaged by the accusations that Eisenhower seriously considered dropping him from the ticket. It was then that Nixon delivered his famous, televised "Checkers" speech, in which he pointed to his wife's "respectable Republican cloth coat" as evidence of his thrift and honesty and declared that the only gift he had accepted was a cocker spaniel named Checkers. Although the speech might have secured his position on the Eisenhower ticket, it brought him few converts, according to Stephen E. Ambrose, who noted in the first book of his three-volume biography of Nixon that "despite the flood of telegrams [that arrived in support of Nixon after the speech], a majority in the audience [of an estimated fifty-eight million people] found the speech objectionable, if not nauseating."

Having weathered that crisis—the second of those turning points (the first was the Hiss case) in his early career that he described in his first book, *Six Crises* (1962)—Nixon was elected vice-president of the United States when he and Eisenhower won the general election in November 1952 by an impressive margin of 55 percent to 44 percent. The team was reelected in 1956, triumphing with 59 percent of the vote over Stevenson and his vice-presidential candidate, Senator Estes Kefauver of Tennessee. In the aftermath of Eisenhower's heart attack in September 1955, which Nixon identified as the third of his six crises, Nixon was from time to time called upon to perform some of the president's ceremonial and executive duties, particularly during

Eisenhower's illnesses in 1956 and 1957. By all accounts, he fulfilled those obligations competently.

The fourth crisis came midway through Nixon's second term as vice-president, during a goodwill tour of South America in 1958. Toward the end of the trip, he found himself in the midst of an angry, anti-American mob in Caracas, Venezuela. While standing at attention during the playing of the Venezuelan national anthem at one official function, he and his wife were spat upon by hundreds of people standing above them on a balcony. On their way out of the city, the Nixons' motorcade was ambushed on the road, and their cars stoned while they were trapped in a rigged traffic jam. Secret Service men managed to fight off the crowd, and no one was killed on either side, perhaps because Nixon had ordered his bodyguards to hold their fire. In a similar incident earlier on the same trip, during his visit to Lima, Peru, Nixon had walked into a crowd of thousands of rock-throwing students shouting epithets in Spanish. Forced to retreat to his car, he faced the mob and shouted, "Cowards! Are you afraid of the truth?"

The fifth crisis explored in Nixon's book was no less confrontational but was far less dangerous physically, although the diplomatic repercussions could have been far-reaching had Nixon lost his temper. The setting was the kitchen of an American model home at a trade show in Moscow, where Nixon engaged in an impromptu tit-for-tat discussion with Soviet leader Nikita S. Khrushchev, who had been haranguing his American guest about the superiority of Communism. Finally, Nixon had had enough. As he recalled in *Six Crises*, he told Khrushchev, "To me, you are strong and we are strong. ... For us to argue who is the stronger misses the point. If war comes we both lose." The two men concluded the "kitchen debate," as it became known, by agreeing that their nations both wanted peace. When the story was reported in the American newspapers, the general consensus was that Nixon had held his own against the Soviet leader. The subsequent surge in Nixon's popularity so enhanced the prospects for his being chosen to lead the Republicans to the White House in the presidential election of 1960—the sixth crisis—that Governor Nelson A. Rockefeller of New York decided not to run for president that year.

Although Nixon had no trouble clinching his party's presidential nomination in the summer of 1960, the campaign against his Democratic opponent, Senator John F. Kennedy of Massachusetts, proved to be difficult and exhausting for both candidates. Appearing with Kennedy in the first televised presidential debate in history, on September 26, 1960, Nixon, who had refused help from the makeup staff (except for an ineffectual "beard stick" to cover his perpetual five o'clock shadow), appeared pale, thin, and haggard. In contrast, the charismatic Kennedy looked tanned and well rested. Thus, although radio listeners thought Nixon had won the debate, the record-breaking eighty million television viewers came to the opposite conclusion.

The three subsequent televised debates that followed failed to erase the negative impression Nixon had made in his first encounter with Kennedy. Later, he acknowledged his mistake, writing in Six Crises, "I believe that I spent ... too little time on appearance: I paid too much attention to what I was going to say and too little attention to how I would look." Nixon and his running mate, Henry Cabot Lodge of Massachusetts, lost the election to Kennedy and his running mate, Senator Lyndon B. Johnson of Texas, by the narrowest margin in American history, about 113,000 popular votes out of 68 million cast. (The electoral margin was greater—the Democrats won 303 electoral votes to the Republican ticket's 219.)

In such a close election, television may well have been the deciding factor, but among the many other aspects that might have contributed to Nixon's defeat was the fact that he had run an uncharacteristically clean campaign, devoid of personal attacks on Kennedy's Catholicism or on his father's reputation for womanizing and bootlegging. Eisenhower, too, may have proved detrimental to Nixon's candidacy, for when he was asked at a news conference to name one major initiative of his vice-president that the administration had adopted, he replied, "If you give me a week, I might think of one." Although he was urged by some of his advisers to contest the results of the election, Nixon accepted his defeat gracefully in the interest of national unity and returned to California where he accepted a position with the law firm of Adams, Duque & Hazeltine of Los Angeles. In what some observers have labeled a rare—to that date—miscalculation, Nixon decided to run for governor of California against the popular Democratic incumbent, Edmund G. ("Pat") Brown, in 1962. After losing to Brown by 5 percentage points, he snapped at reporters, whose allegedly unfair coverage of the campaign he partially blamed for his defeat, "You won't have Nixon to kick around anymore, because, gentlemen, this is my last press conference."

Moving in 1963 to New York City, Nixon joined the law firm of Mudge, Stern, Baldwin & Todd, which eventually became Nixon, Rose, Guthrie, Anderson & Mitchell. In 1964 he stumped on behalf of Senator Barry M. Goldwater of Arizona, the Republican nominee for president. Setting himself the task of rebuilding the Republican Party in the wake of Lyndon Johnson's rout of Goldwater, Nixon campaigned indefatigably in 1966 for congressional and gubernatorial candidates, picking up countless political IOU's along the way. Two years later, he easily captured his party's nomination for president at the Republican National Convention in Miami Beach, vanquishing the more liberal Nelson Rockefeller and the more conservative Governor Ronald Reagan of California, With the Democratic Party driven by dissent over the Johnson administration's policy on the Vietnam War (Johnson himself had announced on March 31 that he would not seek reelection), the time seemed right for a Republican resurgence. Pledging to end the war in Vietnam, Nixon and his running mate, Governor Spiro T. Agnew of Maryland, narrowly defeated the Democratic standard-bearers, Vice-President Hubert H. Humphrey, who had not distanced himself enough from Johnson, and Edmund S. Muskie, with 43.4 percent of the vote to the Democrats' 42.7 percent; 13.5 percent of the voters supported Governor George C. Wallace of Alabama, who ran on the American Independent Party ticket.

Inaugurated as the thirty-seventh president of the United States on January 20, 1969, Nixon set in motion a broad range of domestic policies that were praised by President Bill Clinton, a Democrat, in his eulogy at Nixon's funeral a quarter-century later, for having served as "an inspiration to us today as we seek to place the 'American dream' within the grasp of all of our citizens." Although Nixon's accomplishments in welfare and health-care reform fell far short of his goals, among which were a guaranteed family income and housing allowances, he and his chief urban-affairs adviser, Daniel Patrick Moynihan, proposed one of the most generous, far-reaching family-assistance plans in legislative history. In an attempt to explain such an apparent paradox, Jacob Weisberg wrote in a retrospective assessment of Nixon's political career for New York (May 9,1994) that Nixon believed his guaranteed-income strategy would actually hurt liberals by dispensing with the need for social workers, "a group he singularly despised," in Weisberg's words, because government entitlements would depend solely on income. "Under Moynihan's influence," Weisberg wrote, "Nixon became so obsessed with screwing the liberals that he didn't notice he had become one himself."

The Nixon administration expanded the food stamp program, built an unprecedented number of subsidized housing units, established the Environmental Protection Agency, lowered the voting age to eighteen, tied Social Security increases to the cost of living, cut military spending, and instituted revenue-sharing with local and state governments. A less successful act was the imposition of wage and price controls in August 1971, in an effort to curb inflation. Although it was a popular decision at the time, prices rose dramatically after the controls were lifted following Nixon's landslide victory in November 1972, when he and Agnew were returned to office with 60.7 percent of the vote, trouncing the Democratic nominee, George S. McGovern, a liberal, antiwar senator from South Dakota, and R. Sargent Shriver.

In the area of civil rights, to which the president initially gave limited support by reserving a fixed percentage of federal contracts for businesses owned by minorities, Nixon backed off considerably from certain other programs in the interests of winning back disaffected southern conservatives. Among other measures taken, he eased up on the highly controversial program of busing students to schools in other neighborhoods to achieve racial balance in public education. "By the 1972 election," Weisberg wrote, "Nixon was campaigning against the unfairness of the very programs he had put in place, trying to drive a wedge between middle-class white ethnics and the Democratic Party." Nixon also packed the Supreme Court with four appointees chosen for their conservative views: Chief Justice Warren E. Burger and Associate Justices Harry A. Blackmun (who, by the time of his retirement, in 1994, was known as an outspokenly liberal jurist), Lewis F. Powell Jr., and William H. Rehnquist.

It was in the area of foreign policy that Nixon achieved his greatest successes. Chief among them was his historic trip to the People's Republic of China to meet Premier Zhou Enlai in February 1972, an unprecedented visit that Nixon had initiated by sending his national security adviser, Henry A. Kissinger, on a secret mission to that country in July 1971. His overture paved the way for President Jimmy Carter's restoration, in 1978, of full diplomatic relations between China and the United States, which had recognized Taiwan, or the Republic of China, as the only legitimate Chinese government ever since the Communists, under Mao Zedong, had conquered the mainland in 1949. In geopolitical terms, Nixon's playing of the "China card" gave his administration greater leverage vis-a-vis the Soviet

Union, with whom the United States had been engaged in a war of ideologies for more than twenty-five years. Fighting the Cold War on all fronts—especially scientific, economic, and military—had proved to be expensive as well as dangerous, and Nixon and Kissinger were determined to reach what the latter termed a more comfortable "world equilibrium" with the Soviet Union. To that end, Nixon inaugurated the Strategic Arms Limitation Talks (SALT) in 1969, which would continue for ten years and produce two treaties, the first of which Nixon and Soviet leader Leonid I. Brezhnev signed in 1972. Putting a mutually verifiable limit on antiballistic missiles led to an overall lessening of international tensions and a brief period of detente.

Fulfilling his campaign promise to end the war in Vietnam proved to be an elusive goal, and his first term passed, during which the conflict widened and intensified, before Nixon finally obtained what his administration hailed as "peace with honor" with the conclusion of the Paris peace accord of January 27, 1973, which provided for the return of American prisoners of war. (Two years later Saigon, the capital of South Vietnam, fell to the Communists.) As early as June 1969, under his so-called Vietnamization policy, Nixon had begun withdrawing American troops from Indochina while continuing to aid the South Vietnamese government in its struggle against the Communist-led North Vietnamese. His announcement on April 30, 1970 of imminent military incursions into Cambodian territory, where the Communist guerrillas were finding sanctuary, drew a firestorm of criticism, as did the "Christmas bombing" of Hanoi, in December 1972. Despite Nixon's efforts to reduce American involvement in the war by delegating more responsibilities to the South Vietnamese, American fatalities continued to mount. At the time he took office, the death toll had stood at just over thirty thousand; by 1973, 27,557 more Americans had died. The ever-rising number of casualties provoked intensified antiwar protests, which in turn created a siege mentality at the White House. On May 5, 1971, a year and a day after Ohio National Guardsmen fatally shot four students during a demonstration at Kent State University, Nixon expressed the hope that the teamsters' union could provide "thugs" to deal with enemies of the war effort, according to John Herbers of *The New York Times* (April 24,1994). "They've got guys who'll go in and knock their heads off," Nixon told his aides in a taped conversation that was later released.

Historians and former Nixon aides agree that the quagmire in Vietnam precipitated the Watergate scandal, which can be said to have begun when Daniel Ellsberg, a former, low-level government staffer, leaked the Pentagon Papers (a study of American policy in Southeast Asia commissioned by Robert S. McNamara, President Johnson's secretary of defense) to *The New York Times* in 1971, fueling antiwar demonstrations and so infuriating Nixon that he began authorizing illegal methods to discredit Ellsberg and others whom the president placed on his notorious "enemies list." Among the many petty burglaries carried out by operatives directed from the White House was the one perpetrated by five men employed by the Committee for the Reelection of the President (popularly—and derisively—known by the acronym CREEP) on June 17, 1972 at the Democratic National Committee headquarters in the Watergate office-apartment complex in Washington, D.C. Although Nixon's denial of involvement was generally accepted at the time, a full-blown scandal erupted in March 1973, when federal judge John J. Sirica extracted fuller confessions from the Watergate burglars by threatening to impose stiff sentences. Some members of the White House staff were implicated, and for the next year and a half the nation was consumed with finding out how much the president knew and what else he had done in the name of extending his executive powers. "It was like living in an oversized mystery novel," John Herbers recalled.

Thanks to an elaborate taping system installed in the White House at Nixon's direction (shortly after he had ordered the dismantling of the one set up by Johnson), and after much legal wrangling that encompassed the resignation of the attorney general Elliot L. Richardson and the dismissal, on October 20, 1973, of his deputy, William D. Ruckelshaus, and of special prosecutor Archibald Cox in what became known as the "Saturday Night Massacre," congressional investigators eventually obtained more than sufficient evidence of Nixon's involvement in the Watergate cover-up and in other illegalities, such as abuse of campaign funds and corruption of government agencies. Meanwhile, on October 10, 1973, Vice-President Agnew had resigned under the threat of prosecution for fraud in an unrelated scandal; Representative Gerald R. Ford of Michigan, the House minority leader, was appointed vice-president two days later. Support for Nixon eroded rapidly as published transcripts of the White House tapes revealed a sordid side to the president, whose use of vulgar language was indicated by the numerous "expletive deleted" references in the transcripts. Following weeks of nationally televised hearings, the House Judiciary Committee voted, in the final days of July 1974, to recommend impeachment of Nixon on three counts: obstruction of justice, abuse of power, and defiance of congressional subpoenas.

Facing almost certain impeachment by the full House, on August 9, 1974 Nixon became the first American president to resign his office. In a tearful farewell speech to his cabinet, he said, "Always give your best, never get discouraged, never be petty; always remember, others may hate you, but those who hate you don't win unless you hate them—and then you destroy yourself." Once again it seemed that Nixon's political career was over, but the long, painstaking resurrection of his reputation began only a month later, on September 8, 1974, when he was pardoned unconditionally by President Ford for all crimes he "committed or may have committed or taken part in" while in office. In contrast, many of Nixon's aides and associates served prison terms. In a series of televised interviews with David Frost in 1977, Nixon, who never confessed to anything more than errors in judgment, declared, "When the president does it, that means it is not illegal." Years later, in another television interview with a former aide, he said that no apology to the American people could be "more eloquent, more decisive, [or] more finite" than the act of his resignation.

On the day he was pardoned by President Ford, Nixon was diagnosed as having phlebitis. Hospitalized until November 14, 1974, he was excused from testifying at the Watergate trial, which lasted from October 5 to December 28, 1974, and he did not make a public appearance until the following year, when he attended a fund-raiser in New York City. Painfully aware that the nation was not yet ready to forgive him for Watergate, Nixon seldom ventured far from his home in San Clemente, California, where he began trying to salvage his reputation by writing books that combined memoirs and ruminations on foreign policy. In his *New York* magazine article, Jacob Weisberg described those books as being, "for the most part, banal compendiums of conventional wisdom that fluttered from left to right with prevailing winds." *RN: The Memoirs of Richard Nixon* (1978), Nixon's first work after leaving office, sold well and impressed critics with what one reviewer called its "sometimes brilliant" analyses of Mao, Khrushchev, and Brezhnev. (Nixon's impressions of those men and other world figures were recorded in his book *Leaders*, published in 1982.) Stephen Ambrose described *RN* as "readable but unreliable," explaining that in place of

insights and revelations there were defenses, omissions, and even, in some cases, lies.

After moving into a three-story townhouse on the Upper East Side of Manhattan in 1980, Nixon published *The Real War*, in which he cast the Cold War as World War III, "the first truly total war." Anticipating by three years President Reagan's designation of the Soviet Union as the "Evil Empire," the former architect of detente observed in *The Real War*, "It may seem melodramatic to treat the twin poles of human experience represented by the United States and the Soviet Union as the equivalent of Good and Evil, Light and Darkness, God and the Devil, yet if we allow ourselves to think of them that way, even hypothetically, it can help clarify our perspective on the world struggle." In *Real Peace: A Strategy for the West* (1983), a hastily written, self-published 107-page essay, however, Nixon seemed to be implicitly criticizing Reagan's single-minded military buildup. "To keep the peace and defend our freedom," he argued, "we need to adopt a policy of hard-headed detente," or "detente with deterrence." "Whatever one's position on specific foreign and military policy debates," Stephen Ambrose noted in the third volume of his biography of Nixon, "you could find a Nixon quote in Real *Peace* to support it."

Nixon's subsequent books did little to mollify critics of his literary style, which was judged more suitable for speechifying than for writing books, and the quality of his research; his ideas were predictably applauded by conservatives and derided by liberals. *No More Vietnams* (1985) was a defense of his policies during the war there and an argument for intensified involvement in Central America, particularly where aid to the Nicaraguan contras, or right-wing rebels, was concerned. The lesson of Vietnam, he contended, was not to know when to stay out of other countries' civil wars, but to know how to win the next time around. Billed as a how-to manual for the president, *1999: Victory without War* (1988) was described by Stephen Ambrose as "the best and worst of Nixon." Ambrose singled out his "long, sensitive section" on Soviet leader Mikhail Gorbachev and his arguments for arms-control negotiations and international involvement for special praise, although he decried the book's frequent contradictions. Furthermore, no one could adequately explain the strange logic by which the Communists ruling the Soviet Union were bad whereas those in Beijing were good.

Reviewing Nixon's *Seize the Moment: America's Challenge in a One-Superpower World* (1992) for *New*

York Newsday (January 12,1992), Steven V. Roberts called the book "a marvelously clear and thoughtful analysis of the foreign policy challenges facing America," but he noted that "this is a 'one-superpower world' only when it comes to counting missiles, not money." In his last book, *Beyond Peace* (1994), Nixon made a final stab at countering the isolationist sentiments that threatened to overwhelm certain elements of the American body politic at a time when foreign policy initiatives in such conflict-ridden areas as the former Yugoslavia seemed ineffectual at best and counterproductive at worst. "Because we are the last remaining superpower," Nixon warned, "no crisis is irrelevant to our interests. If the U.S. had been willing to lead, a number of steps short of the commitment of ground forces—for instance, revoking the arms embargo—could have been taken early in the Bosnian crisis to blunt Serbian aggression."

In between writing projects, Nixon traveled throughout the country and the world, meeting with foreign leaders abroad and journalists and former colleagues at home. From 1981 to 1990 he lived in Saddle River, New Jersey, a suburb northwest of New York City; in 1990 he moved to nearby Park Ridge, New Jersey. Although Nixon's official political rehabilitation could be said to have begun in January 1979, when President Carter invited him to a state dinner at the White House at the insistence of the guest of honor, Deputy Prime Minister Deng Xiaopeng of China, his name was apparently taboo at Republican national conventions for another thirteen years. It was not until the 1992 convention in Houston that an image of Nixon's face, shown on the giant screen at the convention center, elicited cheers from the party faithful. Accustomed to giving advice to Ronald Reagan on foreign policy, in March 1992 Nixon launched what U.S. *News & World Report* called "a carefully orchestrated campaign" to prod President George Bush into helping Boris Yeltsin, the beleaguered president of the newly democratic Russia. By 1994 Nixon's foreign policy advice was being sought out by President Bill Clinton, symbolizing the extraordinary level of esteem in which Nixon was held twenty years after Watergate.

PERSONAL LIFE

Richard Nixon died at New York Hospital-Cornell Medical Center in New York City on April 22, 1994 after a devastating stroke left him in a coma; in accordance with the dictates of his living will, no life-support systems were employed to prolong his life. Nixon's body was buried next to that of his wife, Pat, who had died of lung cancer in 1993, on the grounds of the Richard M. Nixon Library and Birthplace in Yorba Linda. Opened in 1990, his is to date the only presidential library erected without federal financing and the only one not housing the original copies of the presidential papers, which remain at the National Archives by order of a law passed by Congress in the wake of the Watergate scandal. The former president is survived by his two daughters, Tricia Nixon Cox and Julie Nixon Eisenhower, and four grandchildren.

FURTHER READING

The New York Times pl+Ap 24 '94 pors; New York 27:38+ My 9 '94 pors; Newsweek 123:20+ My 2 '94 pors; Time 143:26+ My 2 '94 pors; U S News 116:24+ My 2 '94; Aitken, Jonathan. Nixon: A Life (1993); Ambrose, Stephen E. Nixon: The Education of a Politician, 1913-1962 (1987), Nixon: The Triumph of a Politician, 1962-1972 (1989), Nixon: Ruin and Recovery, 1973-1990 (1991); Anson, Robert Sam. Exile: The Unquiet Oblivion of Richard M. Nixon (1984); Hoff, Joan. Nixon Reconsidered (1994); Morris, Roger. Richard Milhous Nixon: The Rise of an American Politician (1990); Nixon, Richard. RN: The Memoirs of Richard Nixon (1978), In the Arena: A Memoir of Victory, Defeat, and Renewal (1990); Who's Who in America, 1994; Who's Who in American Politics, 1993-94; Wicker, Tom. One of Us: Richard Nixon and the American Dream (1991)

MANUEL ANTONIO NORIEGA (MORENA)

Panama Military Dictator

Born: February 11, 1934; Panama City, Panama
Group Affiliation: G-2 Intelligence Service

INTRODUCTION

Since taking command of the Panamanian army in 1983, General Manuel Antonio Noriega has remained entrenched as the dominant power in Panama and, to the chagrin of the Reagan administration, has demonstrated little willingness to return that Central American republic of two million people to the control of a duly elected civilian government. Critics, including former officers in his command, have charged—and United States intelligence confirmed—that Noriega has engaged in or fostered election fraud, drug trafficking, money laundering, espionage against the United States, and even murder. Yet, at a time when the United States has successfully used its influence to help topple such corrupt dictatorships as those in the Philippines and Haiti, Noriega has withstood widespread calls for his ouster. His core of support remains the Panamanian military, which has thrived under his rule. Whether that will be enough to ensure his survival in the face of growing American pressure and unrest at home is problematical. "His days are numbered," an unidentified American policymaker was quoted as saying by Don Oberdorfer of the Washington Post *(July 23, 1987). "But that number could be dozens, hundreds, or even thousands of days."*

EARLY LIFE

Manuel Antonio Noriega Morena was born in 1934, in one of the poor barrios of Panama City, into a family of Colombian background. Educated at the Instituto Nacional, Panama's premier high school, he had planned to study medicine but when his family found itself unable to afford such costs, he accepted a scholarship to the Military School de Chorrios in Lima, Peru. On his return to Panama, he was commissioned a sublieutenant in the National Guard and was stationed at Colon, where he became a favorite of Captain Omar Torrijos. By 1968 Noriega had been promoted to the rank of first lieutenant and had been reassigned to Chiriqui province. In October of that year he joined the rebel "Combo" forces who were resisting the military reorganization undertaken by President Arnulfo Arias. During the coup on October 11 that brought down the Arias government and ushered in the era of military rule that survives today, Lieutenant Noriega swiftly seized the radio and telephone centers in the provincial capital of David, effectively cutting off all communication with Panama City.

LIFE'S WORK

In the ensuing power struggle Omar Torrijos emerged as the dominant figure. His relationship with Noriega was cemented in December 1969, when three rightist colonels staged a counter coup while he was in Mexico. Torrijos risked a night flight into Chiriquí province, where Noriega, now a major in command of the provincial National Guard, loyally awaited his return. Because the crude David airstrip was not equipped with landing lights, Noriega lined up every available motor vehicle along either side of the runway and at the first sound of approaching aircraft ordered all the headlights turned on. Torrijos landed safely and, with Noriega's troops, marched east to retake the capital.

Noriega was richly rewarded with a promotion to lieutenant colonel and an appointment as chief of military intelligence. In that position, he emerged as Torrijos's right-hand man and made his first contacts with the American intelligence community. At the request of the Nixon administration in 1971, Noriega was dispatched to Havana to secure the release of the American crews of two Miami-based freighters, which Cuba had seized and steadfastly refused to return directly to American authorities. Despite that aid and other such assistance, the Nixon administration was so upset at persistent reports that Noriega was heavily involved in drug trafficking that in 1972 it considered but ultimately rejected a proposal to assassinate him, according to a Senate Intelligence Committee report that was confirmed for *The New York Times* (June 13, 1986) by John Ingersoll, who was then director of the Bureau of Narcotics and Dangerous Drugs.

Following Torrijos's death in a plane crash in 1981, a lengthy power struggle between civilian and military leaders ended with the emergence of General Dario Paredes as the new strongman in charge of the National Guard and Colonel Noriega as his chief of staff. In August 1983 Noriega succeeded Paredes and promoted himself to general. Later that year the National Guard

Affiliation: G-2 Intelligence Service

As head of Panama's dreaded G-2 intelligence service, Noriega kept close tabs on dissidents and often resorted to harassment and intimidation. In a major sweep in 1975, G-2 agents rounded up selected businessmen and broadcast executives critical of the government, confiscated their possessions, and exiled them to Ecuador. In the next year G-2 cracked down on the Union Patriótica Feminina, a women's group outspoken in its opposition to the oppressive measures of the Torrijos government. Among those arrested was Alma Robles, the daughter of a former leader of the National Assembly. She was held incommunicado for days in a filthy jail cell while charges of stealing clothes were trumped up against her. That treatment shamed even some officials in the Torrijos government.

By the late 1970s, Noriega had acquired a reputation as the most feared man in Panama. "I know that I have an image problem," he conceded in an interview with Sally Quinn of the *Washington Post* (March 8, 1978). "Mine is a position that doesn't attract sympathy. But somebody must do this job. And it's a normal position in all the armies of the world. In Panama there is only one force that has control. That's my job."

was combined with the smaller navy and air force to form the Panamanian Defense Forces, which under Noriega now numbers about fifteen thousand men.

In 1984 Noriega's candidate for president, Nicolás Ardito Barletta, won a narrow victory over former President Arnulfo Arias, amid charges that the military had tampered with the ballots. Noriega had chosen Barletta, an economist and former planning minister in the Torrijos regime, because he needed someone to grapple with Panama's staggering national debt and prodigious bureaucratic waste in order to satisfy restrictions placed on the government by the International Monetary Fund and other foreign holders of nearly $4 billion in Panamanian notes. But Barletta's program of lowering tariff barriers and slashing wages drew protests from business and labor alike that culminated in a forty-eight-hour general strike in July 1985. Two months later, Barletta was forced to resign, ostensibly because Noriega disapproved of his handling of the economy, but it was learned later that Noriega removed him because he was pressing an investigation into the government's role in the grisly murder of Dr. Hugo Spadafora.

Spadafora had been criticizing Noriega without serious consequences since the two served together in the Torrijos regime, but in 1984 he had charged publicly for the first time that Noriega was involved in drug trafficking. Spadafora was last seen alive being dragged off a bus near the Costa Rican border by G-2 agents. In September 1985 his tortured, decapitated body was discovered crammed into a United States mailbag just inside the Costa Rican border. The investigative reporter Seymour Hersh, in a wide-ranging expose on the front page of *The New York Times* (June 12, 1986), cited Defense Intelligence Agency information that linked Noriega to the murder. "I want that guy's head," Noriega was quoted as telling his subordinates just days before Spadafora's corpse was found.

The American government sharply protested the removal of Barletta, the first directly elected president of Panama since the 1968 coup, and grew increasingly alarmed over the impropriety of Noriega's actions. The Reagan administration slashed economic aid to Panama by 85 percent, and National Security Adviser John M. Poindexter was dispatched to Panama City to warn Noriega to stay out of drug trafficking. Noriega, in turn, denounced Washington for meddling in Panamanian affairs and proceeded to name Vice-President Eric Arturo Delvalle, an heir to a sugar fortune, to replace Barletta. Although Delvalle's economic policy differed little from that of his predecessor, he did not pursue the Spadafora investigation and thus posed no direct threat to Noriega.

The day on which the Hersh expose appeared, Noriega was in Washington, D.C., to attend a meeting of the Inter-American Defense Board. In addition to the Spadafora murder, the article implicated Noriega in a variety of other crimes. Citing a classified Defense Intelligence Agency report and information from unnamed White House officials, Hersh reported that Noriega had exacted protection money from drug dealers for the use of Panamanian soil as a transshipment point for narcotics bound for the United States and as recently as the early 1980s had had a personal financial stake in a drug-processing laboratory near the Colombian border. Estimates of Noriega's yearly take ran into the millions of dollars. Panama's strict banking laws limiting disclosure of private accounts have made it a haven for illegal income. Huge drug profits, as much as $500 million annually, reportedly are wire-transferred from Panamanian accounts to banks in the United States or elsewhere. Noriega and other Panamanian officers are said to have taken part, at least indirectly, in such money-laundering schemes.

The Hersh article also disclosed that Noriega had long worked as a double agent, and that while cooperating with American intelligence agencies for more than a decade, he also aided Communist governments. In the mid-1970s, while he was the head of Panamanian intelligence, Noriega purchased from an American army sergeant stationed in Panama highly classified technical manuals of the National Security Agency, the supersecret agency responsible for electronic eavesdropping around the world. Noriega, in turn, released them to Cuba. Moreover, Noriega is said to have facilitated the sale of restricted American technology to the Eastern bloc, earning for himself an estimated $3 million. He also reportedly sold arms to the M-19, Cuban-backed guerrillas fighting to overthrow the democratic government in Colombia.

The Hersh article touched off a firestorm of criticism against Noriega both in the United States Congress and in Panama, prompting the general to cut short his scheduled stay in Washington, D.C. Back in Panama, he categorically denied all charges and went on the attack, challenging *The New York Times* to name its sources and denouncing his domestic critics as traitors who were trying to destabilize the government and seize power. He attributed the leaked stories to hardline conservatives in the United States, who, he charged, were looking for an excuse to abrogate the 1978 treaty in which the United States pledged to return the Panama Canal to Panama in the year 2000.

Over the next twelve months the furor seemed to subside, but in June 1987 Colonel Roberto Díaz Herrera, Noriega's former chief of staff, who had been forced into retirement, publicly charged that Noriega had rigged the 1984 election, masterminded the murder of Spadafora, and even had a hand in the plane crash that killed Torrijos. Díaz Herrera admitted that he himself had bribed polling officials to tip the election to Barletta in 1984 and that he and other high-ranking officers had grown rich by exacting fat fees from Cubans applying for Panamanian visas. The charges touched off a wave of violent street demonstrations and fresh calls for Noriega's ouster. Responding swiftly and sharply, Noriega declared a state of emergency, suspended the constitution, banned public demonstrations, closed down newspapers and radio stations, and detained or drove into exile key opposition leaders. In a massive show of force, between forty and sixty of Panama's riot

troops—known as "the Dobermans"—staged an early-morning raid, under the cover of two helicopter gunships, on the house of Roberto Díaz Herrera. Anticipating the attack, Díaz Herrera had gathered a small army of supporters and had prepared for a siege, but after a four-hour fire fight he and forty-four of his supporters were captured. Once in custody, Díaz Herrerra recanted his charges and confessed to "inciting antigovernment violence."

Meanwhile, the National Civil Crusade, a coalition of the Roman Catholic Church, the Chamber of Commerce, and other business, civic, and student organizations, launched a successful two-day general strike to protest the state of emergency and to call for a return to civilian government. Dressed in white, their symbol of protest, the dissidents banged pots and pans together in a loud show of defiance and sporadically assembled until broken up by riot police.

On June 26, 1987 the United States Senate passed with broad bipartisan support a resolution calling on the Panamanian government to remove Noriega and investigate the charges against him. Four days later, Noriega abruptly lifted the nine-teen-day-old state of emergency to permit a group of 5,000 government-inspired protesters to attack the American embassy. The Panamanian police quietly withdrew their embassy guard just moments before the mob stoned the embassy and painted anti-American slogans on its walls, inflicting more than $100,000 in damage and prompting the State Department to close the embassy's consular section and library in protest. A few days later, pro-Noriega demonstrators destroyed a prominent statue of Franklin D. Roosevelt that had overlooked the capital city for forty years.

The attack on the embassy marked a turning point in relations between Panama and the United States. Over the next few weeks, the Reagan administration began signaling its eagerness to find a successor to Noriega. The administration suspended all military and economic aid to Panama, and the armies of the two countries, which had worked closely for years in connection with the Panama Canal and the United States Southern Command based in Panama, stood at arm's length. The United States Army was forbidden even to supply routine maintenance to Panamanian forces. Noriega's requests to purchase tear gas from American stockpiles were rejected. In an interview with Lally Weymouth of the *Washington Post* (October 11, 1987), Noriega complained bitterly of being abandoned by the United States after years of cooperating with the CIA and other American intelligence agencies. "When the Americans need something," Noriega said, "they picture it very nicely and say you're a hero, but when they don't need you anymore, they forget you."

Meanwhile, the unrest in Panama created a crisis of confidence within the Panamanian banking community, further undermining Noriega's position. Banking profits account for nearly 10 percent of the Panamanian gross national product. Nervous depositors have withdrawn billions of dollars since the state of emergency was imposed. The strain of such capital flight is especially hard on Panama as it struggles to service its $3.9 billion foreign debt.

Noriega has lost virtually all support outside the Defense Forces, and even that has shown some signs of cracking. His predecessor, retired General Dario Paredes, broke his silence in July 1987 to support the charges of corruption against Noriega and to call on the strongman to resign. Gabriel Lewis, a former ambassador to the United States, whom Noriega had recruited to try to mediate an end to the crisis, fled to Costa Rica just ahead of arrest and from exile vowed to wage an international campaign to depose the general.

Nevertheless, Noriega insisted that there was not "a shred of evidence" against him and showed little readiness to step down or share power with the civilian government. He has said that he might even run for president himself in Panama's next elections, which are scheduled for 1989. In August 1987 he adopted the slogan "Not one step back" and intensified his condemnations and attempts to discredit the United States, the National Civil Crusade, and the Roman Catholic Church. He also expelled a handful of foreign correspondents.

Surprisingly enough, in December 1987 Noriega's government announced the reopening of the opposition newspapers and radio stations that it had shut down the previous July. According to José I. Blandón, then consul general of Panama in New York, Noriega even flirted behind the scenes with the idea of giving up power. In an interview with Elaine Sciolino for *The New York Times* (January 26, 1988), Blandón asserted that he had drafted, at Noriega's request, a plan that would have permitted the strongman and his associates to relinquish power without fear of facing criminal prosecution either in Panama or in the United States. Although he approved a preliminary version of Blandón's "Thoughts on a Panamanian Political Solution" in early December, Noriega abruptly condemned the plan and fired the consul general a few weeks later. Blandón's response was to threaten to reveal documents and notes that would

conclusively link Noriega to drug trafficking, money laundering, and the murder of Hugo Spadafora unless the general agreed to step down. "Noriega can kill me, that's the risk," Blandón told Elaine Sciolino in *The New York Times* interview, "but he can't kill what I know." Blandón was quickly placed under American protection and was subpoenaed to testify before a Miami grand jury that had been investigating charges against Noriega but had been having difficulty in obtaining documentary evidence. In late January of 1988, while Blandón was testifying in Miami, a convicted American drug smuggler, Stephen M. Kalish, testified before the Senate committee investigating Noriega that in exchange for help with the Panamanian branch of his drug business, he had given the general millions of dollars in bribes. Even as the Miami grand jury prepared to indict Noriega, however, some officials were wary of forcing the strongman from office. "Noriega is bad," one former American official told Lally Weymouth, "but he keeps the lid on. Don't corner him. He will fight and he holds the trump [the Panama canal]. We've got a catastrophe in Nicaragua. Do we need another one in Panama of our own making?"

In two indictments returned by federal grand juries in Miami and Tampa, Florida on February 4, 1988 and made public the following day, the United States Department of Justice charged Noriega with having violated United States racketeering and drug laws by providing protection to international narcotics traffickers in return for millions of dollars in bribes, allowing the laundering of drug profits by Panamanian banks, and turning Panama into a center for international cocaine smuggling. But because of existing limits in extradition treaties it seemed unlikely that Noriega could be brought to trial in the United States as long as he remained in power.

In late February 1988 Panama's elected president, Eric Arturo Delvalle, tried to dismiss Noriega but was himself ousted by the army-dominated national assembly and replaced by the former education minister, Manuel Solis Palma. Meanwhile, economic sanctions imposed by the United States seriously hampered Panama's economy, as did a series of strikes staged by Noriega's domestic opponents. On March 18, 1988 the Panamanian government declared a "state of urgency," and five days later, Noriega thwarted a coup attempt by dissident army officers. But despite growing pressure for his departure, Noriega tenaciously clung to power. By late May 1988 the Reagan administration conceded failure of its efforts to persuade the Panamanian strongman to step down. Although in the campaign for the forthcoming United States presidential elections the Democratic party tried to make an issue of Vice-President George Bush's alleged past dealings with Noriega, by the fall of 1988 the Reagan administration acted, at least publicly, almost as though the Panamanian general did not exist.

In 1988, Noriega was indicted by the United States on drug trafficking charges and in the 1989 U.S. invasion of Panama he was removed from power, captured, detained as a prisoner of war, by the United States and flown to the United States. Noriega was tried on eight counts of drug trafficking, racketeering, and money laundering in April 1992. On September 16, 1992, he was sentenced to 40 years in prison (which was later reduced to 30 years).

Noriega's U.S. prison sentence ended in September 2007. France was granted its extradition request in April 2010. He arrived in Paris in April 2010, was retried, found guilty, and sentenced to seven years in jail on July 2010. A conditional release was granted on September 23, 2011, for Noriega to be extradited to Panama to serve 20 years. He returned to Panama on December 11, 2011.

PERSONAL LIFE

The stocky, five-foot-five-inch Manuel Antonio Noriega has dark wavy hair, broad eyebrows and guarded, close-set eyes, a bull neck, and a swarthy complexion so pockmarked that behind his back he is called *cara de piña, or* "pineapple face." Noriega is married to Felicidad Sierio, and the couple has three daughters. He is said to have an illegitimate son by a mistress. He enjoys reading, dancing, and judo. Visitors are struck by the collection of beautiful secretaries that seem to be in constant attendance in his office. He collects portraits of children and porcelain statuettes of toads, whose Spanish name, *sapo,* is Panamanian slang for "informer." Paradoxically, in light of his reputation as a brutal dictator, Noriega is a vegetarian because, he said, "I don't believe men should eat the flesh of other animals." He converted to Buddhism in about 1974. Although officially he draws only a modest military pay, he has amassed a fortune estimated in the hundreds of millions of dollars.

FURTHER READING

Cur Hist 85:421+ D '86; *Harper's* 275:57+ D '87 pors; *Vanity Fair* 51:140+ Je '88 pors; *Washington Post* D p1 Mr 8 '78 por, H p2 O 11 '87; *Sea of Greed: The True Story of the Investigation and Prosecution of Manuel Antonio Noriega;* McCullough, D. J., Pendleton, L., Deer Hawk Publications, S, 2014

O

BARACK OBAMA (BA-RAHK OH-BAHM-UH)

President of the United States

Born: Aug. 4, 1961; Honolulu, Hawaii
Affiliation: Democratic Party

INTRODUCTION

Barack Obama is the 44th President of the United States. As the current President, nearing the end of his second term, President Obama presses on to settle age-old animosities between nations while the War on Terrorism, which he inherited from the former President, George Walker Bush, continues. In March, 2016, he visited Cuba and President Raúl Castro, to heat up what has been termed, "the Cuban thaw." In May 2015, as the first sitting U.S. President to do so, he visited the site of the U.S. atomic blast at Hiroshima with Japan's Prime Mister, Shinzo Abe. As the 2009 winner of the Noble Peace Prize (October 9, 2009), Obama was cited for his work in nuclear non-proliferation and for reaching out to the Muslim world. Obama continues to work for world peace.

A February 2015, Washington Post *article reported a poll of 391 members of the American Political Science Association's Presidents & Executive Politics section, the premier organization of experts of the American Presidency. They rated President Obama as the 18th best American President: He ranked ahead of Presidents Gerald R. Ford, Jimmy Carter, Richard Nixon, and George W. Bush; but behind Presidents Clinton, Eisenhower, Reagan, Johnson, Kennedy, and George H.W. Bush. His legacy still remains to be seen, however, as he is the sitting U.S. President.*

Besides being the only American President to win the Nobel Peace Prize during his first term in office,

Barack Obama.

President Obama also is the first African-American to be elected to the highest office in the nation.

"If there is anyone out there who still doubts that America is a place where all things are possible; who still wonders if the dream of our founders is alive in our time; who still questions the power of our

democracy, tonight is your answer," Democratic U.S. Senator Barack Obama of Illinois said to a crowd of 125,000 supporters in Grant Park, in Chicago, on November 4, 2008, shortly after he was pronounced the winner of the 2008 Presidential election. Obama handily defeated the Republican nominee, John McCain, the senior U.S. Senator from Arizona, with 365 electoral votes to McCain's 173, and 69,456,897 popular votes (52.9 percent of the total) to 59,934,786 (45.7 percent) for his G.O.P. opponent. He was the first Democrat to win more than 50 percent of the popular vote since Jimmy Carter. Obama and his Vice-Presidential pick, Senator Joseph R. Biden of Delaware, won majorities in six of what were considered battleground states: Ohio, Pennsylvania, Indiana, Florida, North Carolina, and Virginia (the last of which had not voted for a Democratic Presidential candidate since 1964). With Obama's victory and a significant number of Democratic wins in the House and Senate, on January 20, 2009, when Obama took the Presidential oath of office, all three branches of the federal government returned to Democratic control for the first time since 1994.

During much of his Presidential campaign, he went against the political grain by focusing on his ideas and positions, rather than attacking the Republican nominee, although he expressed many criticisms of the policies and actions of the Administration of the incumbent, Republican President, George W. Bush. He and his advisers took full advantage of the Internet to organize existing voters and register new ones (young people and people of color in particular), and used the Web to raise a record-breaking amount of money for his campaign from an unprecedented number of individual contributors. With his slogans—"Change We Can Believe In" and "Yes We Can"—Obama worked to instill a feeling of hope in the electorate at a time when a severe economic recession, prolonged wars in Afghanistan and Iraq, serious damage to the U.S.'s image overseas, and dire warnings about global warming had weakened morale and confidence among many Americans. That hope, and extraordinary excitement about his victory among large segments of the population in and beyond the U.S., led well over a million people to stand in freezing temperatures on the National Mall to witness Obama's swearing-in as the 44th president of the United States.

Within days of his entering the White House, Obama signed executive orders that called for the closing of the Guantanamo Bay prison camp within a year; banned torture in interrogations of prisoners and ordered that only techniques described in the Army Field Manual may be used in handling suspected terrorists or prisoners of war; prohibited the practice of so-called extraordinary rendition, in which suspected terrorists were sent for interrogation in Syria or other countries known to condone torture; froze the pay of senior White House staff members earning more than $100,000 annually; imposed rules regarding lobbyists that were far stricter than existing regulations; and reversed several policies put in place during the Bush Administration that discouraged labor-union activities and "tilted toward employers," in the words of David Stout, writing for The New York Times (January 30, 2009). Obama also reinstated a policy in effect during the Administration of President Bill Clinton, whereby the U.S. would continue to help fund international family-planning agencies deemed worthy of support and would not withhold financial aid from such groups, as did the Bush Administration, solely on the grounds that they provided information about or performed abortions. On January 29, 2009, Obama signed the so-called Lilly Ledbetter Fair Pay Act of 2009, which removes certain barriers to women seeking to challenge pay discrimination where they work. One day earlier, the House of Representatives had approved the President's $819 billion economic recovery plan, which included the so-called "bailouts" of the automobile makers, G.E. and Chrysler, troubled banks and Wall Street. Five days later, he signed the reauthorization of the State Children's Health Insurance Program (SCHIP) to cover an additional four million uninsured children.

His time in the Oval Office started out strong, but he has continued to run into the oppositional policies of the Republican Party. His first Administration continued, with the help of his fellow Democrats in Congress, to pass domestic legislation to lift up the poor and middle class. His most notable accomplishment was on March 24, 2010, when Obama signed into law the Patient Protection and Affordable Care Act (ACA), which was passed by the Senate, in December, and by the House by a vote of 219 to 230 on March 23, 2010.

The November 2, 2010, midterm election, when the Democratic Party lost 63 seats in, and control of, the House of Representatives, entrenched the Republican opposition. Obama called the election results "humbling" and a "shellacking."

However, the political climate turned in his favor when President Obama and the Navy SEALS caught up with the mastermind of the September 9, 2001, terrorists *attack on New York's World Trade Center and the Pentagon. Osama Bin Laden, the founder and head of the Islamist group Al-Qaeda, was killed in Pakistan on May 2, 2011, by United States Navy SEALS of the U.S. Naval Special Warfare Development Group.*

On November 6, 2012, Obama won 332 electoral votes, exceeding the 270 required for him to be re-elected as President. Obama became the first Democratic president since Franklin D. Roosevelt to twice win the majority of the popular vote.

Since that time, the President has exercised his Executive Powers to keep the government running because of the oppositional Republican-controlled Congress, to the point that he has been accused of abusing his Executive powers.

EARLY LIFE

Barack Hussein Obama was born on August 4, 1961, in Honolulu, Hawaii. He was named for his father, who was born in the town of Alego, Kenya, on the shore of Lake Victoria. The elder Obama proved to be a gifted student. He won a scholarship to study in Nairobi, Kenya's capital, before being selected for a government sponsorship to go, in 1959 at age 23, to study econometrics at the University of Hawaii. The school's first African student, he established himself among its intellectual and social leaders, serving as the first President of the International Students Association, which he helped organize, and graduating at the top of his class in only three years. In 1959, he took a Russian class, in which he met an 18-year-old, white, Kansas-born anthropology major, Stanley Ann Dunham, known as Ann. The two married in 1960.

The elder Barack Obama received a scholarship to pursue a Ph.D. at Harvard University, in Cambridge, Mass.; the scholarship covered only his own expenses, however, and he left Hawaii alone when his son was two. He and his wife later divorced, and young Barack would see his father only once more, at age ten. When the younger Obama was six, his mother remarried; her second husband, named Lolo, was an Indonesian-born fellow student of hers at the University of Hawaii. The family moved to Jakarta, the capital city of Indonesia, where Obama's half-sister Maya was born. Ann taught English to Indonesian businessmen at the U.S. Embassy, while Lolo ascended from government surveyor to executive with an American oil company. When Ann and Lolo's relationship—which eventually ended in divorce—began to deteriorate, Ann sent Obama to

Honolulu to live with her parents, who enrolled him in the prestigious Punahau Academy, a college-preparatory school attended by children of the islands' elite.

One of only a handful of black students in the academy, Obama grew more conscious of issues regarding race and identity. While his skin color and hair texture set him apart from most of his schoolmates, his home life made him socially, if not economically, similar to them, as he had been raised by a white mother and grandparents in a middle-class environment. He sought black role models from among the men he played basketball with on the local public courts and his grandfather's poker buddies. "I learned to slip back and forth between my black and white worlds, understanding that each possessed its own language and customs and structures of meaning, convinced that with a bit of translation on my part the two worlds would eventually cohere," Obama wrote in his memoir, *Dreams from My Father: A Story of Race and Inheritance*, published in 1995 and in a modified edition in 2004. In that book he recalled becoming unpleasantly aware that his race affected the way others responded to him: "The feeling that something wasn't quite right stayed with me, a warning that sounded whenever a white girl mentioned in the middle of conversation how much she liked Stevie Wonder; or when a woman in the supermarket asked me if I played basketball; or when the school principal told me I was cool. I did like Stevie Wonder, I did love basketball, and I tried my best to be cool at all times. So why did such comments always set me on edge?" "I engaged in self-destructive behavior," he told Sandy Banks for the *Los Angeles Times* (March 13, 2005). "Sometimes I lashed out at white people and sometimes I lashed out at black people."

Amid his confusion, Obama experimented with drugs and alcohol and let his grades slip. He nonetheless graduated with his peers from Punahau, in 1979, and later that year he enrolled at Occidental College, in Los Angeles, California. After two years he transferred to Columbia University, in New York City, to study political science with a specialization in international relations. "Mostly, my years at Columbia were an intense period of study," Obama told Shira Boss-Bicak for *Columbia College Today* (January 2005). "When I transferred, I decided to buckle down and get serious. I spent a lot of time in the library. I didn't socialize that much. I was like a monk."

One morning, during his first semester at Columbia, in November 1982, he received a call from Nairobi, informing him that his father had been killed in a car accident. "At the time of his death, my father remained a myth to me, of both more and less than a man," he wrote in his memoir. (His mother later died from ovarian cancer.)

LIFE'S WORK

In the period leading up to his graduation from Columbia, in 1983, Obama had sought work as a community organizer, writing letters of application to progressive grassroots organizations across the nation. His letters went unanswered, however, so he took a job as a research analyst for a financial consulting company. He was soon promoted to financial writer. "I had my own office, my own secretary, money in the bank," Obama wrote in *Dreams from My Father*. "Sometimes, coming out of an interview with Japanese financiers or German bond traders, I would catch my reflection in the elevator doors— see myself in a suit and tie, a briefcase in my hand—and for a split second I would imagine myself as a captain of industry, barking out orders, closing the deal, before I remembered who it was I had told myself I wanted to be and felt pangs of guilt for my lack of resolve." He ultimately quit his job and worked on a campaign to promote recycling in New York City, while sending out a second round of letters in search of community work. He eventually landed a job with the Developing Communities Project, a nonprofit coalition of secular and church groups on the South Side of Chicago. For three years, he canvassed door-to-door and met with local business and political leaders in efforts to save manufacturing jobs, launch job-training programs, and improve city services in South Side housing projects.

During Obama's time in Chicago, his older half-sister Auma, the child of his father's first marriage (to a Kenyan woman) and one of seven half-siblings with whom he shares a father, came to the United States for an extended visit, during which she told Obama some of the details of their father's life. In the mid-1980s, when Obama was working as a community organizer and preparing to attend law school, he traveled to Kenya to see his father's homeland. "There, he managed to fully embrace a heritage and a family he'd never fully known and come to terms with his father, whom he'd long regarded as an august foreign prince, but now realized was a human being burdened by his own illusions and vulnerabilities," the lawyer and novelist Scott Turow, who is a friend and political supporter of Obama, wrote for *Salon* (March 30, 2004, online).

In 1988 Obama entered Harvard Law School, where he gained national attention in 1990 as the first African-American to be elected President of the *Harvard Law Review,* the nation's most prestigious academic law journal. He earned his J.D. degree, magna cum laude, in 1991. While in law school, Obama worked as a summer associate at Sidley Austin, a Chicago firm; Michelle Robinson, an associate attorney who had graduated from Harvard Law the year before, supervised him. Although she was hesitant to date someone with whom she was working, Obama eventually persuaded her to join him for a movie. The pair married in 1992.

In 1992, Obama led a voter-registration drive that added approximately 150,000 new people to Chicago's voter rolls and helped Bill Clinton, the Democratic candidate, win Illinois in that year's Presidential election. Obama turned down an offer to clerk for Abner Mikva, then Chief Judge of the U.S. Court of Appeals for the Washington, D.C., circuit, to accept a position at the Chicago firm of Miner, Barnhill & Galland. There, he focused on civil rights law, representing victims of housing and employment discrimination and working on behalf of voters' rights. Shortly thereafter, he began lecturing part-time on constitutional law at the University of Chicago Law School. "Teaching keeps you sharp," Obama told William Finnegan for the *New Yorker* (May 31, 2004).

In 1996, the Illinois Democrat Alice Palmer decided to give up her seat in the Illinois State Senate to run for U.S. Congress. Seeing an opportunity, Obama, who harbored political ambitions, sought and secured Palmer's blessing to run for her seat, which represents Chicago's 13th District, covering the South Side, Hyde Park, and the University of Chicago. Palmer lost her bid for Congress and asked Obama to step aside so that she could run for re-election in the State Senate, but Obama refused and, without a Republican opponent, easily won the election. He quickly gained a reputation as an effective legislator, skilled at working with the Republican majority. He sponsored and passed a bill requiring Illinois to share its data on its welfare program with researchers, and he helped to push through the first campaign-finance-reform legislation to pass in his state in a quarter-century.

In 1999, Obama suffered two major political setbacks. The first involved a year-end vote on a controversial gun-control bill that was coming to the floor of the Senate. The bill, forged in a bipartisan coalition between Chicago's Democratic Mayor, Richard M. Daley, and the Republican Illinois Governor, George Ryan, faced intense opposition from the National Rifle Association (NRA), one of the nation's most powerful lobbies, and State Senate Republicans. Obama, who supported the measure, was visiting his extended family in Hawaii. Despite pleas to return, he was absent for the vote. The bill was defeated, and the local press and his Senate colleagues excoriated Obama. Around the same time, Obama made an ill-advised run for the U.S. House of Representatives, against fellow Democrat Bobby Rush. Obama thought Rush was an ineffectual lawmaker, but the four-term representative and former leader of the local Black Panther Party was very popular. In the 2000 Democratic primary, Rush defeated Obama by a two-to-one margin.

Obama bounced back emphatically in the following years. When Democrats took control of the Illinois State Senate in 2003, he successfully ushered 26 bills through the Legislature, including a large tax credit for the working poor and expanded in 2008.

Obama entered the 2004 race to become the junior U.S. Senator from Illinois as one of several Democratic contenders. His popularity grew as he successfully spread his populist message to a base beyond Chicago, and he was soon the second-place favorite behind Blair Hull, a well-liked and wealthy businessman. Hull consistently held the lead for much of the race, but as the primary neared, a revelation that he had abused his ex-wife during their marriage caused his campaign to crumble. Obama went on to win the Democratic nomination, capturing 53 percent of the vote, in March 2004. He faced Republican Alan Keyes, a former United Nations ambassador and Presidential candidate, in the general election. Obama's campaign built so comfortable a lead in the polls that he was able to take time to stump for Democratic candidates in Wisconsin, Colorado, South Carolina, and other states, thus increasing his national profile and garnering favor among fellow Democrats. He was selected to give the keynote speech at the 2004 Democratic National Convention, held in July in Boston, Mass. (The decision met with curiosity by national politicians who knew little about him.)

The defining characteristic of the contentious 2004 Presidential campaign had been—and continued to be—the division between so-called "Red" and "Blue" America: red being the pundits' blanket signifier for the allegedly Republican, conservative, and religious denizens of southern and Midwestern states, and blue connoting the supposedly Democratic, liberal, secular

population of the Northeast and West Coast. Amid this talk of red and blue, Obama delivered a message of shared values that crossed all color lines, racial and electoral. "Now even as we speak, there are those who are preparing to divide us, the spin masters, the negative ad peddlers who embrace the politics of anything goes," he declared to an energized crowd. "Well, I say to them tonight, there is not a liberal America and a conservative America—there is the United States of America. There is not a Black America and a White America and Latin America and Asian America—there's the United States of America. . . . We worship an awesome God in the Blue States, and we don't like federal agents poking around in our libraries in the Red States. We coach Little League in the Blue States and yes, we've got some gay friends in the Red States. There are patriots who opposed the war in Iraq and there are patriots who supported the war in Iraq. ... In the end, that's what this election is about. Do we participate in a politics of cynicism or do we participate in a politics of hope?"

Obama's speech immediately made him the political equivalent of a rock star. That November, carried on a wave of good will and media attention, Obama went on to trounce Keyes, with 70 percent of the vote, to become the first male African-American Democrat (and the fifth African-American) to serve in the U.S. Senate. Assuming office in January 2005, Obama kept a low profile and focused on learning the procedures of the Senate and carefully choosing his public appearances. (Despite his attempts to stay out of the spotlight, that year he won the N.A.A.C.P. Image Award and the Newsmaker of the Year Award from the National Newspaper Publishers Association, and he was named one of *Time's* most influential people of the year.) Obama was appointed to three top Senate panels: the Committee on Environment and Public Works, which provides oversight of the Department of Transportation and the Environmental Protection Agency (E.P.A.); the Committee on Veterans Affairs, which has jurisdiction over compensation, pensions, and medical treatment for veterans of the U.S. military; and the Committee on Foreign Relations, which has responsibility for some aspects of U.S. foreign policy. Obama contributed to several key debates before the Senate in the 109th Congress and showed an independent streak that sometimes defied party lines. Stating that President George W. Bush should be allowed some latitude in the appointment of his Cabinet, Obama voted "yes" regarding the confirmation of Condoleezza Rice as Secretary of State. However, he registered a minority vote of "no" in the confirmation of Alberto Gonzales as U.S. Attorney General; as White House counsel, Gonzales had been responsible for setting guidelines for the treatment of suspected terrorists held in U.S. military prisons—directives seen by many as overly harsh and therefore illegal.

On August 30, 2005, as a result a mission in late August 2004 when Obama accompanied the Chairman of the Senate Committee on Foreign Relations, Richard Lugar of Indiana, to Russia, Ukraine, and Azerbaijan, the U.S. and Ukraine signed an agreement placing safeguards on the storage or transport of potentially lethal pathogens and other such materials, the existence of which dated back to Soviet-era biological-weapons programs.

The media soon began to speculate on a possible Obama run for the U.S. Presidency. He had already become a favorite among many political insiders. (In 2005, he won a poll conducted by the Washington, D.C., magazine *National Journal* in which members of Congress, many lobbyists, and other movers and shakers in the world of politics were asked which politician had the greatest potential to become president in 20 years.) Thanks in part to his second book, *The Audacity of Hope*, his national status continued to rise in 2006, as he made appearances on television programs, including *Oprah* and *Larry King Live*. Tickets for his book-tour appearances sold out within minutes in such big cities as Seattle, Boston, and Philadelphia. The columnist David Brooks, known for his conservative slant, wrote a commentary in *The New York Times* (October 19, 2006), entitled "Run, Barack, Run." "I should note that I disagree with many of Obama's notions and could well end up agreeing more with one of his opponents," Brooks wrote. "But anyone who's observed him closely can see that Obama is a new kind of politician. As [Joe] Klein [of Time] once observed, he's that rarest of creatures: a mega-hyped phenomenon that lives up to the hype. It may not be personally convenient for him, but the times will never again so completely require the gifts that he possesses. Whether you're liberal or conservative, you should hope Barack Obama runs for President." Days later, Obama was featured in the cover story, titled "Why Barack Obama Could Be the Next President," of the October 23, 2006 issue of *Time*. For the remainder of 2006, however, Obama focused his attention on that year's Senate elections, traveling the country to help raise funds and campaign for Democrats.

After months of mounting rumors and speculation, Obama formed a Presidential exploratory committee in January 2007. The following month, in Springfield, Ill., (where Abraham Lincoln lived from 1837 to 1861), he officially announced his candidacy for the U.S. Presidency. During the Springfield speech, he introduced his campaign's overall theme of change: "For the last six years we've been told that our mounting debts don't matter, we've been told that the anxiety Americans feel about rising health care costs and stagnant wages are an illusion, we've been told that climate change is a hoax, and that tough talk and an ill-conceived war can replace diplomacy, and strategy, and foresight. And when all else fails, when [Hurricane] Katrina happens, or the death toll in Iraq mounts, we've been told that our crises are somebody else's fault. We're distracted from our real failures, and told to blame the other party, or gay people, or immigrants. And as people have looked away in disillusionment and frustration, we know what's filled the void. The cynics, and the lobbyists, and the special interests who've turned our government into a game only they can afford to play. They write the checks and you get stuck with the bills, they get the access while you get to write a letter, they think they own this government, but we're here today to take it back. The time for that politics is over. It's time to turn the page." Obama's entry into the presidential primaries placed him among several Democrats vying for the nomination, including U.S. Senator and former First Lady Hillary Rodham Clinton, Senator Biden, and former North Carolina Senator and 2004 Democratic Vice-Presidential nominee John Edwards.

From the start of his campaign, Obama's limited political experience was called into question. The Democratic Illinois state senator Ray Miller, for example, said to Gilbert Price for the *Columbus, Ohio, Call & Post* (February 15-21, 2007), "[Obama] has only been a member of the United States Senate for two years. I'm not aware of any significant accomplishments he's had in his two years. Quite frankly, that is not my standard for pursuing the Presidency of the United States. We don't have a lot to measure him by at this point." By contrast, another Democratic Illinois State Senator, Donne Trotter, argued that Obama's intellect was more than sufficient to qualify him. "[Obama] is a reader, a learner of different approaches and philosophies. He has the brainpower to absorb the facts . . . and make good decisions," he told Judy Keen for *USA Today* (January 17, 2007, on-line). David Axelrod, Obama's political strategist and media adviser, told Keen, "Campaigns themselves are a gantlet in which you get tested. People get to see how you handle pressure and how you react to complicated questions. It's an imperfect and sometimes maddening system, but at the end of the day it works, because you have to be tough and smart and skilled to survive that process."

The Democratic primaries became increasingly heated as the year progressed. Clinton had been the favorite before Obama entered the race, and soon the two were in a head-to-head battle for what was bound to be, in either case, a history-making nomination. By the end of Super Tuesday, February 5, Obama led the race with 847 delegates. Clinton, with 834 delegates, had narrowly won the popular vote, 46 to 45 percent.

Amid accusations that the mainstream media had been soft in their coverage of Obama, Clinton's campaign began to focus on Obama's character. In March 2008, footage surfaced showing Obama's former pastor and spiritual mentor, Jeremiah Wright, Jr., giving sermons at Chicago's Trinity United Church of Christ. (The source was reportedly not connected to the Clinton campaign.) In those sermons, Wright proclaimed his disgust with the U.S. government for mistreating minorities; he accused those in power of purposefully flooding black neighborhoods with drugs and suggested that the country's international policies and activities were to blame for the 9/11 terrorist attacks. The sermons immediately sparked controversy; Clinton used the opportunity to question Obama's integrity. Shortly after the footage began to air on national news programs, Obama condemned Wright's remarks and delivered an impassioned speech on the topic of race in America. "As imperfect as [Wright] may be, he has been like family to me. He strengthened my faith, officiated [at] my wedding, and baptized my children. ... I can no more disown him than I can disown the black community," Obama said in Philadelphia on March 18, 2008. "The profound mistake of Reverend Wright's sermons is not that he spoke about racism in our society. It's that he spoke as if our society was static; as if no progress has been made. . . . But what we know—what we have seen—is that America can change. That is the true genius of this nation." He added, "I would not be running for President if I didn't believe with all my heart that this is what the vast majority of Americans want for this country. This union may never be perfect, but, generation after generation has shown that it can always be perfected."

The speech, titled "A More Perfect Union," received widespread praise, and as the months passed, Obama began to widen his lead. On June 3, 2008, the day of the final primaries, in South Dakota and Montana, he garnered 60 super-delegate endorsements. Obama ultimately accumulated 2,154 delegate votes, enough to become the presumptive Democratic nominee and the first major-party African-American Presidential nominee in U.S. history. A few days later, Clinton suspended her campaign and announced her support of her former rival.

Obama decided to pick Joe Biden, a devout Roman Catholic raised in a working-class family, a politician with years of experience in international as well as national affairs, in hopes of silencing or at least muting those who complained that he was seriously deficient in those areas. Biden had been a member of the U.S. Senate since 1973 and had chaired the Senate Committee on Foreign Relations, and he was widely recognized for his expertise on foreign policy and national-security issues. He was also known, however, for his tendency to be long-winded and for his verbal gaffes, which had become somewhat legendary on Capitol Hill. (In February 2007, for example, when he had thrown his own hat into the Presidential ring, he had said of Obama, "I mean, you got the first mainstream African-American who is articulate and bright and clean and a nice-looking guy." Though, by his own account, Biden had not meant to offend African-Americans and later apologized to Obama, the remark is said to have soured his chances to become the Democratic nominee.)

Obama officially accepted the Democratic Presidential Nomination at the 2008 Democratic National Convention, held in Denver, Colo. Senator John McCain, who was nominated soon afterward at that year's Republican National Convention, was a former Navy pilot who had been held prisoner for over five years during the Vietnam War and had been elected to the Senate in 1987. A self-described "maverick," McCain became known for dissenting from his Republican colleagues on several important issues and working with Democrats more closely than many of his GOP colleagues to pass legislation. Though he had become popular with people across the political spectrum, his age (72) and his past, serious health problems became matters of concern during the race. (His win would have made him the oldest person ever elected to a first term as President.) For his running mate, McCain chose Sarah Palin, the Governor of Alaska since 2007, who had previously served as Chairperson of the Alaska Oil and Gas Conservation Commission and as mayor of her hometown, Wasilla, Alaska. Outside Alaska, Palin was virtually unknown.

As the first female Republican Vice-Presidential nominee, she soon became a focal point in the Presidential race. Though she brought youth and excitement to the Republican ticket, inquiries into her political past and family life raised questions about the campaign's vetting process and, by extension, about McCain's judgment. (The public soon learned, for example, that her unwed, teen-age daughter was pregnant, and allegations surfaced that Palin had used her influence as Governor to get her former brother-in-law fired from his job as an Alaska state trooper.)

The McCain campaign tried to capitalize on the public's uncertainty about Obama's history, character, religion, friends, and experience. During the Republican National Convention, Palin, touting her tenure in Wasilla and sarcastically casting aspersions on Obama's work at the community level, said, "I guess a small-town mayor is sort of like a community organizer, except that you have actual responsibilities." While the line got a laugh from party loyalists, it did no lasting harm to Obama, who has often said that his work on Chicago's South Side taught him many of the skills he would need later.

More damaging to him was his rivals' repeated insinuations about his connection to William Ayers, which had first been mentioned during the Democratic primary campaign. Ayer was a founding member of the Weather Underground, a militant activist group seeking to end U.S. involvement in the Vietnam War in the late 1960s and early 1970s. Underground members had been responsible for several bombings, including explosions at the Pentagon and the U.S. Capitol. Obama and Ayers lived in the same Chicago neighborhood and had served on several boards together. Ayers had also hosted a gathering at his home to introduce Obama to community members during his first run for political office. Although Ayers had long ago become a respected member of the Chicago community and an honored Professor of Education at the University of Illinois, his activities with the Underground (which dated from when Obama was a young child) led Palin, during an Englewood, Colo., event on October 4, 2008, to accuse Obama of "palling around with terrorists." Obama dismissed the accusation at a campaign stop in Chillicothe, Ohio, on October 10, saying, "Nothing's easier than riling up a crowd by stoking anger and division, but that's not what we need now in the United States. The American people aren't looking for someone who can divide this country; they're looking for somebody who will lead this country. Now more than ever, it is time to put country ahead of politics." (Following the election, Ayers spoke out about the accusations, writing for the December 6, 2008, edition of *The New York Times*, "[Obama and I] didn't pal around, and I had nothing to do with his positions. I knew him as well as thousands of others did, and like millions of others, I wish I knew him better.")

Obama's campaign, for the most part, limited attacks on McCain to his stance on political issues and his voting record. It focused on policies Obama sought to implement as President: tax cuts for middle-class Americans, reform of the health-care system, emphasis on renewable energy, fiscal discipline, and the withdrawal of troops from Iraq.

After three televised Presidential debates, polls showed Obama pulling into the lead. He received endorsements from many celebrities and major newspapers, including the *Washington Post*, the *Los Angeles Times*, and the *Chicago Tribune*, the last of which had never before endorsed a Democrat for President. "Many Americans say they're uneasy about Obama. He's pretty new to them," the editors of the *Chicago Tribune* wrote (October 19, 2008). "We can provide some assurance. We have known Obama since he entered politics a dozen years ago. We have watched him, worked with him, argued with him as he rose from an effective State Senator to an inspiring U.S. Senator to the Democratic Party's nominee for President. We have tremendous confidence in his intellectual rigor, his moral compass and his ability to make sound, thoughtful, careful decisions. He is ready."

In its endorsement, the *Washington Post* (October 17, 2008) explained, "The choice is made easy in part by Mr. McCain's disappointing campaign, above all his irresponsible selection of a running mate who is not ready to be President. It is made easy in larger part, though, because of our admiration for Mr. Obama and the impressive qualities he has shown during this long race. Yes, we have reservations and concerns, almost inevitably, given Mr. Obama's relatively brief experience in national politics. But we also have enormous hopes." Obama even gained the support of such well-known Republicans as former Secretary of State Colin Powell, who, in endorsing him on the October 19, 2008, edition of the TV show *Meet the Press* (October 19, 2008), called him "a transformational figure."

Obama's first Presidential campaign was described as arguably the best-organized in recent history. His campaign workers set up "Camp Obama" events—training courses for volunteers, lasting several days, about the political process and organizational techniques. Unlike most other campaigns, Obama's focused on recruiting college students and young adults, Hans Riemer, Obama's national youth-vote director, told David Shaper for *National Public Radio* (June 13, 2007, on-line), "Historically, campaigns have looked at young people as the hardest demographics to mobilize. In reality, if you know what you're doing, they can be one of the easiest to mobilize." (On Election Day, according to exit polls, some 66 percent of voters ages 18 to 29 cast their ballots for Obama.) Also, Obama used the Internet skillfully to rally voters. His presence on social networking web sites, including Facebook and MySpace as well as the video-sharing site YouTube, helped spread his message, as did the My.BarackObama.com web site launched by his campaign, with the help of Facebook's co-founder Chris Hughes. "From controlling the canvassing operations to corralling e-mail lists, organizing meetings and overseeing national phone drives, Obama's web network is the most ambitious, and apparently successful, Internet campaign effort in any Presidential race in the web's short history," Sarah Lai Stirland wrote for *Wired* (March 3, 2008, on-line). In October 2008, Obama and his team won *Advertising Age's* Marketer of the Year Award.

Obama was also an extraordinarily successful fundraiser. McCain's campaign, which opted for public financing, was thus barred from accepting private donations after his official nomination and was limited to about $84 million in U.S. Treasury funding; Obama's campaign managers, however, decided to forgo public financing and continue raising money as they had during the primaries. Obama was the first Presidential candidate from a major party to decline public financing since 1976, when the public-financing system was launched. (McCain later criticized Obama for that decision, pointing out that the year before he had said that he would accept public financing.) By Election Day, thanks in large part to millions of individual small donations, the Obama campaign had accumulated a reported $770 million. Obama spent a record $240 million on television advertisements, including a half-hour, prime-time infomercial broadcast during the final week of the campaign.

Obama's election to the Presidency sparked jubilation all over the nation as well as around the world. Mwai Kibaki, the President of Kenya, declared November 6 a national holiday in honor of Obama's victory.

According to BBC News (November 5, 2009, on-line), the President of France, Nicolas Sarkozy, said, "At a time when we must face huge challenges together, [Obama's] election has raised enormous hope in France, in Europe and beyond. France and Europe . . . will find a new energy to work with America to preserve peace and world prosperity."

After his election, Obama quickly named his choices for his Cabinet. Most were confirmed without controversy by the Senate. Exceptions included New Mexico Governor Bill Richardson, Obama's first choice for Commerce Secretary, who withdrew his name from consideration, citing a probe into allegations that his administration had given contracts to a political donor; Timothy F. Geithner, who was sworn in as Treasury Secretary despite having failed to pay $34,000 in federal taxes (which he later paid with interest); and Tom Daschle, whose own tax issues led him to withdraw his name from consideration for the post of Secretary of Health and Human Services. The Daschle episode, in particular, led to accusations that Obama had gone back on his pledge to apply strict ethical rules to appointments in his Administration, especially when it was revealed that Obama had urged Daschle to seek confirmation in spite of the tax situation. Obama quickly admitted that he and others involved in the process had "screwed up."

Meanwhile, Obama and his team worked to come up with detailed solutions to some of the nation's economic problems. On December 6, 2008, Obama announced his plans for a public-works program, the largest since President Dwight D. Eisenhower signed the legislation that launched the Federal Interstate-Highway System, in 1956. Obama's program, which would create millions of new jobs, sought to make public buildings more energy efficient, repair the nation's highways and bridges, and modernize classrooms and hospitals. The program was part of Obama's larger economic-stimulus package, passed by the House on January 28 and by the Senate on February 10.

In his first months in office, Obama concentrated on boosting the U.S. economy and creating jobs. As of the end of October 2009, the overall effect of the Administration's stimulus plan remained unclear; although the nation's Gross Domestic Product (GDP) grew by 3.5 percent during the third quarter (July through September of 2009), its best performance in two years, some economists maintained that the recession was far worse than the Administration had anticipated and that the stimulus would not accomplish its aims.

Obama also focused on health-care reform. His promise to pass health-care legislation by the end of 2009 had been complicated by the actions of Republicans and a few Democrats who have balked at his call for an affordable, government-run insurance option for Americans who lack employer-provided insurance. An onslaught of conservative opposition to the health-care legislation, during the summer of 2009, prompted the President to defend his plan against false claims, including the assertion that mandatory end-of-life counseling (by "death panels") would deny health care to sick senior citizens and children with birth defects. Some Republicans also accused Obama of starting down the slippery slope toward a socialist government. Health-care experts, even those who did not support the proposed plan, denied such allegations. In August 2009, while the health-care debate was raging in the media, Obama's approval ratings sank to 50 percent for the first time during his Presidency.

On other fronts, shortly after he took office, Obama lifted the ban on most stem-cell research, imposed by George W. Bush, and had repeatedly addressed the issue of global warming. Obama worked to make his Administration more transparent to the public and banned members of his Administration from receiving gifts from lobbyists. He increased the nation's military involvement in Afghanistan; in the fall of 2009, he grappled with the request by General Stanley McChrystal, the commander of the International Security Assistance Force and of U.S. forces in Afghanistan, for 40,000 additional troops to ensure "success" in Afghanistan.

On October 28, 2009, Obama signed into law a bill that expanded the definition of federal hate crimes to include those committed against individuals based on sexual orientation or gender identity. The law was hailed by gay-rights activists, who at the same time harshly criticized the President for his failure to act on his promise to abolish the "Don't Ask, Don't Tell" policy, which bars from military service homosexuals who reveal that they are gay. (This law later was repealed September 20, 2011.) The following day, Nancy Pelosi, the Speaker of the House, introduced the Affordable Health Care for America Act, a bill crafted by House Democrats that would provide insurance to 36 million uninsured Americans by 2019. Obama praised the bill, calling it "a historic step forward."

In his first interview for an overseas news outlet, Obama told an interviewer for Al-Arabiya, a Dubai-based television-news service, as quoted by *marketwatch.com* (January 26, 2009), "My job to the Muslim world is to communicate that the Americans are not your enemy. We sometimes make mistakes. . . . But if you look at the track record . . . America was not born as a colonial power, and that the same respect and partnership that America had with the Muslim world as recently as 20 or 30 years ago, there's no reason why we can't restore that." In October 2009, in a controversial development, Obama received the Nobel Peace Prize.

One of the most important acts as President in his first term was the capture and death of Osama Bin Laden, the founder and head of the Islamist group, Al-Qaeda, who was killed in Pakistan on May 2, 2011, by United States Navy SEALS of the U.S. Naval Special Warfare Development Group, as well as other troops. "Operation Neptune Spear," was carried out in a Central Intelligence Agency-led operation (C.I.A.). There are varying accounts of how Bin Laden was fatally shot. His body was taken to Afghanistan for identification before being buried at sea. Al-Qaida operatives later vowed to get revenge for his death, Pakistani's engaged in a huge outcry, and Amnesty International questioned why Bin Laden was killed when he was unarmed. Most of the American public approved of the operation and its outcome, as did the United Nations, NATO, the European Union, and a large number of governments.

President Obama was easily re-elected for his second term in 2012. He addressed supporters and volunteers at Chicago's McCormick Place after his re-election and said: "Tonight you voted for action, not politics as usual. You elected us to focus on your jobs, not ours. And in the coming weeks and months, I am looking forward to reaching out and working with leaders of both parties."

During his second term, Obama's Administration campaigned for better gun control laws. At the end of January, 2013, he called for comprehensive immigration reform, including a path to citizenship for 11 million illegal immigrants. After his push for gun control failed (the U.S. Senate rejected his bid for an assault-weapons ban and expanded background checks), I.R.S. official Lois Lerner admitted that conservative groups seeking tax-exempt status were targeted by the I.R.S.

Complaints of long patient wait times at V.A. Health Care Facilities, with allegations surfacing of "secret appointment lists" to hide the length of the waiting times, became a scandal for the Obama administration in 2013. (In some cases, veterans died without being seen or receiving treatment.) V.A. Secretary Eric

Shinseki resigned amid the scandal. A day later, Obama secured the release of Bowe Bergdahl, a U.S. prisoner of war in Afghanistan, which was made in exchange for five Taliban commanders. But the move, made without informing Congress, sparked controversy, and there were allegations that Bergdahl was captured after deserting the army.

In September 2014, the President approved a plan allowing unaccompanied migrant children to apply for refugee status and provide more money for immigration lawyers. During the November midterm elections, Republicans held the House and seized control of the Senate. On November 20, the President moved to defer deportations for as many as four million illegal immigrants, sparking Republican Party indignation. Republicans vowed to defund the action. On December 17, the President announced plans to normalize relations with Cuba.

In June 2015, the Supreme Court recognized a right to same-sex marriage nationwide. In the same month, Obama unveiled plans to expand overtime pay for millions of workers, and signed legislation granting him fast-track trade authority after a long fight, clearing the way for the Trans Pacific Partnership.

In the first quarter of 2016, President Obama announced an executive order on gun control: The Bureau of Alcohol, Tobacco, Firearms and Explosives would require that people who sell guns at stores, at gun shows or over the Internet be licensed and conduct checks. The ATF also would finalize a rule requiring background checks for buyers of dangerous weapons from a trust, corporation or other legal entity, and would require purchased guns to undergo background checks.

In March 2016, the President and his family visit Cuba, the first visit of a sitting U.S. President to Cuba in 88 years, and, the following day, held a joint press conference with the Cuban President, Raúl Castro, at the Palace of the Revolution in Havana. Many travel restrictions of Americans to Cuba were lifted.

Obama is endorsing 2016 Democratic Presidential candidate Hillary Clinton, the former Secretary of State, for President. In May, the NBC News/Wall Street Journal poll showed that President Obama hit his highest approval rating since his second inauguration: Fifty-one percent of registered voters said they approved of the job Obama was doing as President, compared to 46 percent who disapproved. In the years after his Presidency ends, historians may upgrade the legacy of President Obama beyond his current ranking as the 18th greatest American President.

PERSONAL LIFE

President Barack Obama and his wife, Michelle Obama, were married in 1992. The Obama's, which include two daughters, Malia, (age 17) and Sasha (age 14), remained in Chicago's Hyde Park neighborhood during Barack Obama's years in the U.S. Senate. He commuted back and forth between Washington, D.C., and Chicago. Michelle Obama left her job, as Vice President of Community and External Affairs at the University of Chicago Medical Center, to help campaign during her husband's run for the Presidency. She said that, as First Lady, she hoped to be an advocate for the nation's working women and military families. Her top priority, however, would be to continue to raise Malia and Sasha. "Our girls are the center of Barack's and my world," she wrote for *U.S. News & World Report* (October 27, 2008). "They're the reason he is running for President—to make the world a better place for them and for all children."

Michelle Obama's mother also moved into the White House to supervise Malia and Sasha. Malia has been accepted into Harvard University.

FURTHER READING

Chicago Tribune C pi Mar. 2005, C p37 Oct. 19, 2008, *(on-line)* Dec. 5, 2008; *Columbia College Today* p14+ Jan. 2005; *Ebony* p196 Nov. 2004, p16 Nov. 2008; *New Republic* p21 May 31, 2004; *The New York Times* A p21 Dec. 6, 2008, A p1+ Nov. 5, 2008, A p1-h Jan. 2009; *New Yorker* p32+ May 31, 2004; *Newsweek* p74 Dec. 27, 2004; *Salon* (on-line) Mar. 30, 2004; *Time* p74 Nov. 15, 2004, (on-line) Aug. 23, 2008; *Washington Monthly* (on-line)Nov. 2004; *Washington Post* C pi Feb. 24, 2005, A pi Oct. 17, 2008; *whitehouse.gov Selected Books*: *Dreams from My Father: A Story of Race and Inheritance,* 1995; *The Audacity of Hope: Thoughts on Reclaiming the American Dream,* 2006; *Change We Can Believe In: Barack Obama's Plan to Renew America's Promise,* 2008

MILTON OBOTE

President of Uganda

Born: December 28, 1925; Apac Distract, Uganda
Died: October 10, 2005; Johannesburg, South Africa
Affiliation: Uganda People's Conference

INTRODUCTION

After spending nine years in exile, Dr. Milton Obote returned to his native Uganda from neighboring Tanzania in 1980 to resume the leadership of his country of some 13,000,000 people from which he had been ousted in 1971 in a coup led by army commander Idi Amin. One of the architects of Ugandan independence in the 1960's, Obote served as his country's Prime Minister and then as its President but failed in his efforts to forge unity in the strife-torn nation. After his reelection to the Presidency in December 1980, Obote proceeded with characteristic optimism to undertake the formidable task of repairing the devastation inflicted on his country by Amin's reign of terror. "The pearl of Africa will rise and shine again," Obote has predicted, borrowing a metaphor once applied to Uganda by Winston Churchill.

EARLY LIFE

Apollo (or Apolo) Milton Obote was born about 1925 (some sources give the year as 1924 or 1926) in the village of Akokoro on Lake Kwania in Lango district, in what was then the British protectorate of Uganda. He was the third of the nine children of Stanley Opeto, a farmer and minor chieftain of the Lango tribe. His mother, Pulisikira, was one of his father's four wives. "I was born of a ruling family," Obote told Edward R. F. Sheehan, as quoted in *The New York Times Magazine* (January 22, 1967). "My grandfather, great-grandfather, and great-great-grandfather were all rulers." While tending his father's flocks of sheep, goats, and cattle, Obote would fantasize that they were human beings. "I tried to talk to them and to pretend that I was myself a chief governing men," he has recalled.

After a spear wound that he suffered at the age of twelve ended his career as a herd boy, Obote entered a local primary school. In the early 1940's he attended the Lira Protestant mission school and Gulu high school, both in northern Uganda, and from 1945 to 1947 he was at Busoga College, a breeding ground for African nationalism, at Mwiri, in the eastern part of the country. Although he did not distinguish himself as a student, former schoolmates remember him as being strong-willed and independent. In 1948 Obote entered Malcerere University College in Kampala, where he studied political science, economics, and English but dropped out after two years. Bent on a career in law or politics, he obtained a scholarship to study law in the United States, but his plans were rejected by the British authorities in Uganda on the ground that American law would be of little use in his country. After his efforts to study in London or at Gordon College in Khartoum were also turned down, Obote completed his formal education with a number of correspondence courses.

LIFE'S WORK

Determined to enter public service through the trade union movement, Obote went to neighboring Kenya soon after leaving Makerere and took a menial job as a laborer in the sugar works near Kisumu. Later he worked for a construction company and took jobs as a clerk and as a salesman. At the same time he became increasingly active as a labor organizer, to the dismay of the British colonial authorities.

Obote started in-politics as a member of elder statesman Jomo Kenyatta's Kenya National Union. It was banned in 1952 because of its alleged links with the terrorist Mau Mau, but there was no evidence that Obote was involved in its activities. During his stay in Kenya, Obote helped the lawyer and politician Argwings Kodhek to found the African District Congress and worked with Tom Mboya in the Peoples' Convention party. After political parties were banned in Kenya he helped to organize so-called "social clubs" that conducted clandestine political meetings.

Returning to Uganda in the mid-1950's, Obote organized the Lango branch of the Uganda National Congress (UNC), one of the preindependence political parties, of which he had been a member since 1952. In 1957 he was named by the Lango district council to represent his district in the pre-independence Uganda Legislative Council, where he was noted for his outspokenness with colonial authorities and, in the words of Edward R. F. Sheehan* "soon became a skillful craftsman in the black Byzantium of Ugandan tribal politics." He was returned to the Uganda Legislative Council as a member of the UNC in Uganda's first popular elections, held in October

1958. After a factional dispute in 1959 split the UNC, Obote led his followers into a merger with the Uganda People's Union to form the Uganda People's Congress (UPC) in 1960, with himself as president-general.

As British rule in Uganda neared its end, a major obstacle to national unity was the rivalry between the new nationalist parties, as exemplified by Obote's UPC, and the hereditary rulers of Uganda's four traditional tribal kingdoms, who resisted independence. The strongest and most advanced of these kingdoms was Buganda, whose Kabaka, or king, was Sir Edward Frederick Mutesa II, popularly called "King Freddie." A boycott of the March 1961 general election by Buganda enabled the predominantly Roman Catholic Democratic party under Benedicto Kiwanuka to form a government, while the UPC was relegated to second place and Obote became leader of the opposition.

During the months that followed, Obote shrewdly negotiated with the leaders of Buganda and of the other three kingdoms, Bunyoro, Toro, and Ankole, eventually winning them over to the cause of national independence by promising them federal autonomy. In September 1961 Obote's UPC concluded an alliance with the newly established Kabaka Yekka ("King Only") party of Buganda. The national election of April 25, 1962 brought the UPC forty-three seats and the Kabaka Yekka twenty-four, giving the governing coalition under the new Prime Minister, Obote, a solid majority in the ninety-one member unicameral National Assembly. At the constitutional conference held at Marlborough House in London in June, Obote played a major role in drafting the new compromise constitution, which made due allowances for the separatist aspirations of the kingdoms.

Amid festivities, on October 9, 1962 Uganda ended sixty-eight years as a British protectorate, as the black, yellow, and red Ugandan flag replaced the Union Jack, In a news conference that same day, Obote declared that his country was ready to take its place in the British Commonwealth and the United Nations, determined to remain neutral between East and West, and prepared to support all African nationalist movements while emphatically rejecting the white supremacist regimes of South Africa, Rhodesia, and the Portuguese colonies. He announced amnesty for thousands of political prisoners and praised the contributions of Uganda's white and Asian minorities, assuring them that they had nothing to fear from the African majority.

The alliance between nationalism and traditionalism in Uganda formally took effect in October 1963, after a year of independence, when the Kabaka of Buganda was installed in the ceremonial office of President, an arrangement that Obote had persuaded his reluctant party colleagues to accept in the interest of national unity. Meanwhile, Obote at first managed to maintain the precarious balance of forces within his country. In the spring of 1963 he succeeded in suppressing a separatist movement in Uganda's western province, and early in 1964 he enlisted British aid in quelling a mutiny in the army. Despite his stated preference for a socialist one-party state and his efforts to establish cordial relations with Moscow and Peking, he encouraged private investment and development aid from the United States and other Western nations. In May 1963 he joined thirty other African heads of government in signing the original charter of the Organization of African Unity. His government's $250,000,000 economic development plan, announced in July 1963, was based on a program drafted by a World Bank mission. In addition to the Prime Ministership, Obote assumed responsibility for the ministries of defense and foreign affairs from 1963 to 1965.

The uneasy alliance between the UPC and Buganda's Kabaka Yekka party broke up in August 1964 over the long-standing "lost counties" issue, which involved the return of territory taken by the British from the kingdom of Bunyoro and given to Buganda in the late nineteenth century. The transfer of the lands in question, following a popular referendum, fueled Buganda's opposition to the central government. Meanwhile, defections from the other parties during 1964 and 1965 gave the UPC a substantial majority in the National Assembly, ostensibly moving Uganda toward the status of a one-party state. At the same time, however, the unity of the UPC was increasingly threatened by tribal, ideological, and religious divisions.

The Obote government underwent a major crisis in early 1966 when an opposition spokesman charged the Prime Minister, along with deputy army commander Idi Amin and others, with having misappropriated some $350,000 in proceeds from gold and ivory captured during the 1964-65 revolt in the former Belgian Congo. Denouncing the charges as a frameup, Obote accused his opponents of plotting with foreign nations against him. On February 22, 1966 he assumed all powers of government and ordered the arrest of five members of his Cabinet who had supported the allegations. To forestall a move by the opposition to unseat him, he suspended the 1962 constitution two days later.

On April 15, 1966 Obote" was installed in the office of executive President for a five-year term under a new constitution that greatly expanded the powers of the central government. The Kabaka of Buganda called the Prime Minister's seizure of the government illegal and ordered the Obote government in Kampala out of Bugandan territory. In May 1966 Obote surrounded the Kabaka's palace on Kampala's Mengo Hill with government troops under Idi Amin, who was now the army commander. After much bloody fighting, Bugandan forces were subdued, the Kabaka was forced into exile in London, and emergency regulations were imposed in Buganda. On September 8, 1967 Uganda formally became a republic after the National Assembly officially adopted the new constitution, which abolished the four hereditary kingdoms and concentrated powers over state, government, and armed forces in the Presidency. By August 1968 the parliamentary opposition had dwindled to six out of eighty-nine National Assembly seats.

Under Obote's virtual one-man rule, Uganda for a time experienced relative political stability and economic prosperity. In mid-1966 his government launched a new five-year economic development plan to diversify agricultural production and expand industry. Although he resorted to repression when he thought it necessary, he encouraged communication between the government and the people and devoted much effort to reconciling tribal and religious differences. In December 1967 he led his country into an East African Economic Community with Kenya and Tanzania. Obote enhanced his international prestige by serving as a mediator in the Nigerian civil war of 1968-69 and by acting as host to Pope Paul VI, whose trip to Uganda in the summer of 1969 made him the first pontiff to visit an African nation.

A "move to the left" was launched by Obote in October 1969, when he introduced a "Common Man's Charter" aimed at "creating a new political culture and . . . way of life," with the means of production in the hands of "the people as a whole." On December 19, 1969, at the close of a UPC conference that unanimously approved the charter, an attempt was made on the life of Obote, who suffered facial wounds. A state of national emergency was declared, and six persons were arrested for their part in the assassination plot, allegedly instigated by a member of the Bugandan royal family.

Once recovered from his wounds, Obote went ahead with his plans for socialization and "Ugandanization" of the economy during 1970. In January his government imposed restrictions on merchants who were non-citizens.

On May Day he announced that most of the country's import and export trade would be nationalized and that the government would acquire a 60 percent interest in manufacturing and other industries. In July 1970 Obote introduced new electoral laws aimed at eliminating voting along tribal lines, and in August the UPC passed a resolution that the party president would also be the President of Uganda, thus ensuring that Obote would be returned to office without opposition. But Obote's centralization and modernization efforts failed to take root in the essentially pluralist and traditionalist Ugandan society, and discontent was mounting on all levels.

Although Obote had at first maintained harmonious relations with Idi Amin, whom he promoted to major general in 1968, he soon regarded the army commander as a potential rival. The President steadily built up the strength of his own special corps of loyal Langi troops, and while Amin was visiting Cairo in September 1970, he moved to consolidate his control over the Army. But Amin, on his return, took advantage of the discontent with Obote's rule and took steps to ensure the support of the key elements of the army and police for himself.

On January 25, 1971, while Obote was attending a Commonwealth Prime Ministers' conference in Singapore, Amin staged a coup and installed a military regime in Kampala. At first the overthrow of Obote was welcomed by many Ugandans, after Amin assured them that he had no personal political ambitions. But before long, Amin seized absolute power and launched an eight-year reign of terror seldom equaled in world history, during which thousands were massacred, executed, or driven into exile. The steady deterioration of the economy was aggravated by Amin's expulsion of noncitizen Asians, who had dominated Ugandan commerce and industry, and Uganda's formerly friendly relations with Great Britain, the United States, and Israel were in a shambles.

Meanwhile, Obote, who still considered himself President of Uganda, had been granted asylum in Tanzania by President Julius Nye-rere, along with some political supporters and about 1,000 loyal soldiers. While living quietly with his family in a beach house near Dar es Salaam, he kept abreast of events in Uganda, hoping for an opportunity to topple the Amin regime. In September 1972, following a year of tension between Uganda and Tanzania, Obote's exile forces, with the approval of Nyerere, launched an unsuccessful attack on Uganda. Breaking an eighteen-month silence, in May 1973 he sent a letter addressed to African heads of state, in which he accused the Amin regime of killing tens of thousands of Ugandans. Little was heard from him again until January 1979, when he denounced "the fascist dictator" Amin, who, he contended, had transformed Uganda into "a human slaughterhouse."

Renewed border clashes between Uganda and Tanzania prompted Nyerere, urged on by Obote and his supporters, to invade Uganda wi h Tanzanian and exile troops in February 1979. On April 12 Kampala fell to the invaders, and Amin fled to Libya. Obote had been regarded as the most likely successor to Amin, but there was considerable opposition to him among the political parties that had been formed in exile. The most important was the Uganda National Liberation Front (UNLF), a broad-based coalition, whose leaders felt that an early return to Uganda by Obote might promote disunity. Following Amin's downfall, the UNLF installed Dr. Yusuf K. Lule, a nonpolitical academician, as provisional President, and when he proved unable to cope with the problems of the ravaged country, he was replaced in June 1979 by the lawyer Godfrey Binaisa.

In May 1980, following the ouster of Binaisa by a six-member military commission, whose chairman, Paulo Muwanga, was a close ally of Obote, the former President returned to Uganda after a nine-year absence and launched his campaign for the Presidency under the banner of his own UPC. In the months that followed, he campaigned throughout the country, promising to promote peace and prosperity and to weed out poverty, corruption, and tribalism, while playing down his earlier socialist views.

In the midst of the campaign, on September 17, 1980, the ruling military commission expelled all non-UPC members from the twenty-eight member Cabinet. Obote was further aided in his campaign by the military, Which made its planes, vehicles, and security troops available to him. His position was also enhanced by the fact that electoral districts were drawn up in such a way as to give a clear advantage to the northern region from which he drew his strength. Furthermore, in seventeen districts opposition candidates were disqualified, permitting UPC members to be elected unopposed in those constituencies.

Surrounded by chaos and maladministration, on December 9, 1980 Ugandans went to the polls for the first time in eighteen years. When it appeared that the rival Democratic party, led by Paul Ssemogerere, might be winning, the military commission chairman Muwanga personally took charge of the vote-counting. The election results, announced on December 13, gave the UPC a clear majority in the 126-member Parliament. A sixty-member Commonwealth observer team conceded that the elections had been fair, although some of its members expressed skepticism. As the leader of the winning party, Obote was sworn in as President for a five-year term on December 15, 1980 and promised a government of national conciliation in which his opponents would be invited to join.

During the first few months after his return to the Presidency, Obote tried to bring Uganda gradually back to normalcy by cementing relations with other African countries, seeking aid from the International Monetary Fund and the United Nations Development Program, devaluing the currency, and curbing the power of the military. But by the spring of 1981 Uganda seemed to be once more on the road to chaos, largely because of the actions of such dissident groups as the Popular Resistance Army and the Uganda Freedom movement, which attacked police and army installations, wrecked communications, and sabotaged the country's vital coffee crop.

The disorder was exacerbated by tribal unrest, economic instability, crime, the lack of discipline in the armed forces, and the exodus of the 10,000 Tanzanian peace-keeping troops that had remained in Uganda after the downfall of Idi Amin. The Obote government responded by reactivating the dreaded State Research Bureau, which had been Amin's chief agency of repression, by arresting and executing the opponents of the regime, and by closing down the newspapers of the opposition.

PERSONAL LIFE

Dr. Apollo Milton Obote—who once quipped, "I'd rather have Milton's brains than Apollo's good looks"— had several children by three marriages. His third marriage, to Miria Kalule, a Buganda tribeswoman and a former secretary at Uganda's U.N, mission, took place on November 9, 1963. Obote's doctorate is an honorary LL.D, awarded to him in 1963 by Long Island University in New York, apparently by arrangement with the United States State Department. He also held an honorary degree from New Delhi University in India. Little is known of Obote's personal life, except that he was a voracious reader, and that he sometimes went for days without food as a form of self-discipline. His church was the Uganda Anglican.

In August 2005, Obote announced that he was stepping down as leader of the UPC. In October of the same year, Obote died of kidney failure in a hospital in Johannesburg.

FURTHER READING
African Index 3:39+ *Je 25 '80; The New York Times Mag* p36+ *Ja 22 '67 pars; Africa Yearbook and Who's Who, 1977; Daggs, Eliza. All Africa (1970); Gingyera-Pinycwa, A.G.G. Apollo Milton Obote and His Times (1978); International Who's Who, 1981-82; Mittelman, James H. Ideology and Politics in Uganda (1975); Who's Who in Africa (1973)*

MANUEL A. ODRÍA
President of Peru

Born: November 26, 1896
Died: February 18, 1974
Affiliation: Union Nacional Odriista

INTRODUCTION
A career Army officer, Odría was appointed Chief of Staff by President Jose Luis Bustamante y Rivero in 1946. A year later, he was named Minister of the Interior. Bustamante's policies caused Odría to resign from the Cabinet in July 1948. Since assuming the presidency in October 1948 he has abolished many state controls on Peru's economy, and encouraged foreign capital to invest in his country.

EARLY LIFE
Manuel Apolinario Odría Amoretti was born in Tarma, Department of Junin, Peru on November 26, 1897, son of Arturo Odría y Alvarez and Zoila Amoretti de Odría , and the grandson of Colonel Manuel Odría , a nineteenth century war hero. His father died during Manuel's childhood, and his mother, who became a dressmaker, managed to finance his early military education. He entered the Escuela de Off dales de Chorrillos (Military School) in 1915, and was commissioned a second lieutenant in 1919. He remained as an instructor at the school until he advanced to the rank of captain.

In 1927, he entered the Escuela Superior de Guerra (War College) from which he was graduated in 1930; he was promoted to the rank of major. Later he studied at the Escuela Superior de Guerra Naval (Navy School).

LIFE'S WORK
The officer was made a lieutenant colonel in 1936 and became chief of staff of the Fourth Division stationed at Cuzco. He served as chief of the third section of the Army General Staff and chief of staff of the First Division at Piura. This was near the unmarked boundary between Peru and Ecuador, which has been in dispute for more than a hundred years. During a skirmish, Odría distinguished himself in action and was made a full colonel. Returning to the Escuela Superior de Guerra, he became assistant director. Later, as director of the college, he made a study tour in the Panama Canal Zone and the United States.

The legislature confirmed Colonel Odría 's promotion to the rank of brigadier general in 1946, and he was made Chief of Staff of the Army. President Bustamante appointed him Minister of Interior and chief of police in January 1947, when the country was stirred by the assassination of Francisco Grana Garland, publisher of *La Prensa,* one of Lima's newspapers.

At this time the country was undergoing a period of inflation which *Newsweek* (November 16, 1953) attributed to state controls and severe restrictions placed on imports and exports. The government of Peru was heavily in debt and. printing-press money flooded the country. General Odría urged Bustamante to outlaw the Alianza Popular Revolucionaria Americana (Apra), whose members, the Apristas, Odría blamed for the country's economic crisis. General Odría resigned as Minister of Interior because of his disagreement with official policy in regard to this issue.

An uprising against the government by the Apristas in Callao on October 3, 1948 was quickly defeated by the Army, after which Apra was outlawed. A second uprising began in the Army garrison at Arequipa on October 27. General Odría assumed command and requested Bustamante to resign because of the danger of seizure of the government by radical elements. *Time* (November 8, 1948) reported that the President "waited stubbornly" until escorted to Limatambo airfield. He went into exile in Argentina.

General Odría flew to Lima on October 31 and was greeted by a military band and cheering crowds. The revolution, called the "Restoration Movement," was without bloodshed. Odría promptly dissolved the legislature, established an all-military government and was proclaimed provisional President by the Army, pending a constitutional government. He said he would remain in power only long enough "to call an election and install a truly democratic government" (*Newsweek,* November 22, 1948). Victor Raul Haya de la Torre, leader of Apra, took refuge in the Colombian Embassy in Lima, and was forced to remain there until April 1954 when negotiations between Colombia and Peru permitted him to seek asylum in a foreign country.

President Odría promised to re-establish the economy of the nation and its credit abroad but the prospect seemed remote, since the country was said to be on the verge of bankruptcy. One of his first acts was to hire Klein and Saks, a U.S. firm of economic consultants. Recommendations of the economists were put into effect by special decree on November 11, 1949.

Business Week (December 31, 1949) reported that the decree released the sol, the Peruvian monetary unit, from the official exchange, removed state subsidies except those for the import of wheat, granted increases in wages, and cancelled price controls except on fuel and breadstuffs. The government was ready with restraining orders if industry jumped prices. Odría also repealed a law that required exporters to surrender dollars for sols, and instituted a mining code eliminating taxes on minerals for a period of twenty-five years.

Most business executives felt that Odría had cleared the way for a stable government. A hydroelectric works and two large irrigation projects were built. U.S. companies invested about $90,000,000 in oil, metal industries and agriculture. Further investments were thought risky until a constitutional government was established.

General Odría resigned as provisional President on June 1, 1950 to become a candidate for the presidency in the national elections of July 2, when many seats in parliament were to be filled. During the interim, General Zenon Noriega was President. Odría's only opposition candidate was General Ernesto Montagne. Robert K. Shellaby (*Christian Science Monitor,* June 27, 1950) reported that on June 11 the electoral tribunal disqualified Montagne as a candidate after his petitions were declared fraudulent.

This was followed by uprisings of students at the Arequipa and San Marcos universities. Order was restored by government troops on June 15, and General Montagne and leaders of the outlawed party, Apra, were arrested.

Odría and his followers won the election, with two minority parties—Socialist and Independent—trailing in the parliament. General Odría assumed the office of President on July 28, 1950 for a six-year term. In his inaugural speech, he said that health, education and labor were the principal concerns of the government and announced plans for new hospitals, schools, low-cost housing and social insurance. A public works program called for a highway system and completion of irrigation projects.

The New York Times (January 4, 1952) reported that foreign trade increased 50 per cent during the first half of 1951 over the same period in 1950. Production of minerals had increased 20 per cent during 1951, and the American Smelting, and Refining Company was engaged in preliminary work in copper deposits. *Reader's Digest* (April 1954) noted that in the Sechura Desert, there are hopeful indications of oil deposits. The government has invited investors in that area on the basis of a fifty-fifty split in earnings and forty-year renewable concessions. "As a result, Peruvian, Canadian and U.S. firms have begun large-scale operations. Peru may become a major source of oil for the Western Hemisphere."

Arrangements for Le Tourneau del Peru, Inc., a subsidiary of Le Tourneau Institute of Longview, Texas, to build a colony called Tournavista on a 1,000,000-acre tract in the jungle of the Pucalpa area was approved by the Peruvian Senate on January 22, 1954. In return, Le Tourneau del Peru will build thirty-three miles of paved highway connecting the colony with the Trans-Andean Highway, a water supply, sewage disposal and other public services.

During a good-will visit to Brazil in August 1953, President Odría issued with the late President Getulio Dornelles Vargas of Brazil, a declaration of their joint determination to defend democratic and Pan-American principles. The two nations signed five agreements to strengthen their trade and economic relations. Odría has stated that "political cooperation among the American nations also requires economic cooperation" (New York *World-Telegram and Sun,* January 9, 1954).

PERSONAL LIFE

Odría married Maria Delgado de Odría in 1927. They have two sons, Cesar and Manuel. The family is Roman Catholic. The President was of average build "with a weatherworn face . . . and a steady gaze." He has sandy hair and blue eyes. For relaxation, he enjoyed chess, bullfights and the opera. He has been decorated by the governments of Argentina, Nationalist China, Ethiopia, Spain, and Venezuela as well as Peru. *Time* (November 8, 1948) quoted General Odría as saying: "Party politics poisons the hearts of the people and sickens their minds."

After the military coup that overthrew Belaúnde in 1968, Odría kept a low profile in Peruvian politics. He died in 1974.

FURTHER READING

Time 52:40 N 8 '48 por; *New Century Cyclopedia of Names* (1954); *World Biography* (1954)

DANIEL ORTEGA

President of Nicaragua

Born: November 11, 1945; La Libertad, Nicaragua
Group Affiliation: Frente Sandinista de Liberación Nacional (FSLN)

INTRODUCTION

In Nicaragua in 1979 the guerrilla avengers of the martyred nationalist hero Augusto César Sandino (1895-1934) brought to an end the American-backed Somoza dynasty, the longest and, in the eyes of many, the most corrupt dictatorship in Latin American history. The first among equals in the victorious Sandinista leadership was Comandante Daniel Ortega, a patriotic pragmatist without whose wide popular following the otherwise doctrinaire leftist revolution might never have succeeded. Confronting the gargantuan task of rebuilding an impoverished country devastated by the civil war and bled bankrupt by the Somoza oligarchy, the Sandinista junta, as coordinated by Ortega, set up a Government of National Reconstruction that was originally pluralistic as well as socialistic. Ironically, that government's efforts to maintain its diversity and to nurture a mixed economy domestically and remain non-aligned internationally have been hampered by economic sabotage and cross-border military raids carried out by United States-supported "freedom fighters." Ortega saw hope for a change in the American perception of Nicaragua as an epicenter of Communist influence in Central America in bilateral discussions held partly under Mexican auspices in the summer of 1984. The Reagan administration's hostility to the Sandinistas remained implacable, however. After Nicaragua agreed to sign a regional peace treaty drafted by the Contado-

Daniel Ortega.

Fernanda LeMarie—Cancillería del Ecuador

ra group (Colombia, Mexico, Panama, and Venezuela) in September 1984, Representative Michael Barnes of Maryland, the chairman of the House subcommittee on hemispheric affairs, said, "The administration's objections to the treaty reinforce my belief that it's never had any real interest in a negotiated settlement."

EARLY LIFE

Daniel Ortega Saavedra was born on November 11, 1945 into a lower middle-class family in the town of La Libertad, Nicaragua. He has a younger brother, Humberto,

545

now the minister of defense in the Sandinista government. Another younger brother, Camilo, who was also a leader in the Sandinista revolution, was reported killed in 1978. One of the Ortega brothers' chief revolutionary role models was their father, a veteran of the peasant army of Augusto César Sandino, after whom the Sandinistas are named. After United States Marines occupied Nicaragua (for the third time in seventeen years) in 1926, Sandino and his men waged protracted guerrilla warfare against the invaders. Stalemated, the American force withdrew in 1933, leaving behind as surrogate the infamous National Guard (Guardia Nacional), native mercenaries trained and supplied by them and headed by Anastasio Somoza García, a graduate of West Point military academy. After the American withdrawal, Sandino laid down his arms and accepted an invitation for "peace talks" with Somoza. Following one of the talks, he was seized and assassinated. Thus began the Somoza dynasty, which, with American support, for more than four decades would rule Nicaragua as if it were a family estate, taking as its own up to 30 percent of the arable land, exercising a monopoly control of the economy, protecting American interests, and repressing political opposition. After Anastasio Somoza García was assassinated in 1956, his older son, Luis, became president. Luis' rule was almost benevolent in comparison with those of his father and his younger brother, Anastasio Somoza Debayle, who succeeded to the presidency in 1967.

LIFE'S WORK

Although at least ten years younger than most of the FSLN's leaders, Daniel Ortega won rapid promotion in the organization. He was in charge of the FSLN's urban resistance campaign by 1967, when he was captured and jailed by the National Guard. He remained incarcerated for seven years, until December 30, 1974, when he and some dozen other Sandinista prisoners were released in exchange for high-level Somocista hostages. Ortega and the other released prisoners were flown into exile in Cuba, where he received military training under veterans of Fidel Castro's guerrilla campaigns. After a few months, he secretly returned to Nicaragua and rejoined the FSLN's guerrilla war against Somoza.

There were three "tendencies," or factions, within the FSLN, held together under Carlos Fonseca Amador's strong leadership. The two smaller factions, one of which was led by Tómas Borge Martínez, were doctrinaire Marxist-Leninist. The Terceristas, or Third Party, led by Daniel Ortega and his brothers, was the

> ### Affiliation: Frente Sandinista de Liberación Nacional (FSLN)
>
> After graduating from secondary school, Daniel Ortega entered the Jesuit-run Central American University (Universidad Centro-Americana) in Managua to study law, but he dropped out after a few months and went underground, joining the Frente Sandinista de Liberación Nacional (FSLN) in 1963. Organized two years before by Carlos Fonseca Amador, Silvio Mayorga, and Tómas Borge Martinez (now the minister of the interior in the Sandinista government), the FSLN was a nationalist guerrilla army of students, peasants, and workers seeking to avenge Augusto César Sandino. Its immediate goals were, in the words of Amador, first, the overthrow of "the Somozaist clique" that had "reduced Nicaragua to the status of a neocolony exploited by the Yankee monopolies and the country's oligarchic groups" and, second, the establishment of "a revolutionary government based on the worker-peasant alliance and the convergence of all the patriotic, anti-imperialist, and anti-oligarchic forces in the country." Its long-term goal was "a social system that wipes out the exploitation and poverty that our people have been subjected to."

least extreme and least ideological, and it succeeded in winning a wide spectrum of support, from peasants to wealthy upper-class intellectuals.

Following Carlos Fonseca Amador's death in combat in 1976, the differences between the hardline factions and the Terceristas developed into an open rift. The chief point of contention was the participation of the Terceristas—under the cover of the Movimiento de los Doce, or the Group of Twelve, an organization of businessmen, academics, and clergy led by the Roman Catholic priest Father Ernesto Cardenal (now the minister of culture in the Sandinista government)—in the Frente Amplio de Oposicíon (FAO), a bourgeois-dominated popular alliance of anti-Somoza forces. (Even the middle and upper classes, apart from the oligarchs, had been politicized when, following the earthquakes that devastated Managua in 1972, Somoza's scandalous mismanagement of relief and reconstruction funds demoralized the country's industrial sector in addition to enraging the displaced, starving poor.) Under the leadership of the liberal bourgeoisie, the FAO sought not a radical change (which even the petit bourgeoisie wanted) but only a modification of the status quo—"Somozism without Somoza." Obstinately rejecting even that moderate demand, Anastasio Somoza Debayle set about bloodily repressing the popular movement. He succeeded only in disintegrating the FAO and discrediting its leadership, leaving in its place an insurrectional mass movement in desperate need of new guidance.

The Terceristas moved into the leadership breach. "We could not oppose this torrent-like movement," Humberto Ortega explained to an interviewer at the time. "All we could do was stand at its head . . . and give it some direction. . . . If we had not given form to this mass movement, it would have lapsed into general anarchy." With the breakup of the FAO and the discarding of a bourgeois solution to the national crisis, the major obstacle to the unification of the FSLN was removed. The three FSLN factions set up a unified command structure on December 9, 1978, and they fused into a single organization on March 26, 1979.

Numbering only in the hundreds, the FSLN was militarily vastly inferior to the 15,000-strong Somocista armed forces. To compensate, it adopted a strategy, borrowed from the Vietnamese, that forced the National Guard to disperse its technico-military capacity. That strategy combined military action with total mobilization at the social, economic, and political levels. Thus, when the Sandinista guerrillas launched their "final offensive" in the spring of 1979, they did so with the support of a dense network of mass organizations that used the frontal offensive as a prop for a general strike (widely supported by employers) and a nationwide uprising. At the same time, support for the Somoza dictatorship from abroad had crumbled: the Organization of American States almost unanimously opposed any North American intervention in the civil war in Nicaragua; the dictatorship had been condemned by the Andean Pact countries, some of which were openly aiding the Sandinistas, who also had the support of Mexico; and United States backing of the dictatorship, previously unconditional, had become ambivalent under the human rights-oriented administration of President Jimmy Carter.

Seeing that the game was up, Anastasio Somoza Debayle pursued a scorched-earth policy during his final months in power. Partly in revenge against the oppositional bourgeoisie, the National Guard systematically bombed industrial areas, destroying factories, hospitals, schools, and housing as well as people. (A total of more than 40,000 died during the civil war, and tens

of thousands more were wounded, orphaned, and left homeless.) Two-and-a-half million head of cattle from Somoza's vast ranches were slaughtered and shipped as beef to cold storage in Miami, Florida for later sale. By double-mortgaging his businesses, borrowing heavily from foreign private banks and the International Monetary Fund, and running up bills with multinational corporations, Somoza saw to it that any government succeeding his would be deluged with debt and handicapped by an abysmal international credit rating. Incredibly, the International Monetary Fund, with American approval and over the protests of respected Nicaraguan economists, gave the lame-duck dictator a loan installment of $33.2 million, which was deposited in the Central Bank of Managua in May 1979 and mysteriously disappeared after the bank closed down during the Battle of Managua the following month. In addition, Somoza looted the national treasury before fleeing to Miami with his retinue, including the National Guard high command, on July 17, 1979. He later moved to Paraguay, where he was assassinated on September 17, 1980.

The victorious Sandinista rebels marched triumphantly into Managua on July 19, 1979. To avoid the traditional Latin American pitfall of one strongman usurping the spoils, they had already decided on a collective, pluralistic Government of National Reconstruction. Pending elections (originally promised by 1985), executive power was invested in a Tercerista-dominated junta of five men (later reduced to three) coordinated by Daniel Ortega under a nine-person directorate equally representing the three FSLN factions. A range of anti-Somoza groups, including conservatives, were represented in the Cabinet and the Council of State, a vocationally diverse assembly sharing legislative power with an eleven-member consultative body, the Council of Government. Domestically, the Government of National Reconstruction promulgated a mixed economy and boasted of confiscating as few properties and enterprises as possible outside of those that had been owned or controlled by the Somoza oligarchy. Among the measures introduced were trade controls and the nationalization of local banks and insurance companies. Abolishing the death penalty, the government credited itself with relatively humane treatment of captured National Guardsmen. Internationally, it professed a policy of nonalignment. "Somoza left us in ruins," Tomás Borge Martinez recounted to Claudia Dreyfus in a group interview for *Playboy* (September 1983). "Thousands dead. Backwardness. Illiteracy. Incredible poverty. He left us old factories that could not compete in the market. He left us no money in the national treasury. . . . Everything but the debts, billions in debts, went abroad. Beyond all that, beyond many deaths, the torture, the poverty, Somoza left us bad taste—*mal gusto*. He wanted . . . to turn Nicaragua into a kind of Miami, which is not the best cultural tradition of North America."

With every sector of the economy in a state of crisis and much of the population of 2.5 million in imminent danger of starvation, Ortega sought foreign help in relief and reconstruction while remaining wary of strings that would compromise Nicaragua's international neutrality. Among the countries responding to his pleas were Mexico and Venezuela, both of which began shipping oil to Nicaragua in 1980 on a 70 percent cash-30 percent credit basis; Italy, which provided the bulk of the money for the building of a geothermic electric plant at La Paz Central; the Soviet Union, which gave economic support and help in the development of hydroelectric and other projects; Cuba, which sent teachers and technical, medical, and military experts as well as materiel; and France, which supplied economic aid and military equipment. Later, when the counterrevolutionaries began their hit-and-run forays into northern Nicaragua from havens in Honduras, Libya also offered military aid. Almost half of the economic assistance received by Nicaragua since the civil war has come from Latin America and the countries of Western Europe, including the Netherlands and Belgium; 20 percent has come from Communist countries.

Seeking United States aid, Ortega visited President Jimmy Carter in the White House in September 1979 and came away with a commitment for a $75-million loan and an additional $40 million in other forms of aid. American policy shifted abruptly when Carter was succeeded in the presidency in January 1981 by Ronald Reagan. Accusing Nicaragua of acting as a conduit of arms from Cuba to leftist guerrillas in El Salvador and "inviting alien influences and philosophies" into the hemisphere, the Reagan administration sought to "destabilize" the Sandinistas before they could "consolidate" their power. Soon after President Reagan took office, the United States government began tightening the economic screws on Nicaragua, canceling the last $15-million payment of the loan approved by the Carter administration, halting credits for the purchase of $9.6-million worth of United States wheat, and slashing by nearly 90 percent the amount of sugar Nicaragua could sell to the United States.

By September 1981 the economic crisis in Nicaragua had worsened to such a point that the Government of National Reconstruction enacted the Measures of Economic and Social Emergency. In October 1981, when the United States and Honduras held joint naval maneuvers in territorial waters of Honduras, the Sandinistas became fearful of another threat, one to Nicaragua's national security. That fear grew in November and December 1981, when the CIA's financing, training, and supplying of ex-Somocista National Guardsmen and other anti-Sandinistas on the Honduran border became public knowledge. In response to the threat of invasion, the Sandinistas began beefing up their defensive forces, and in March 1982 the Government of National Reconstruction decreed a state of national emergency, tightening censorship of the press and curtailing the civil liberties of the domestic opposition. The Reagan administration, which differentiated between "totalitarianism" (bad and unacceptable) and "authoritarianism" (bad but acceptable), interpreted the "state of siege" reflected in the September 1981 and March 1982 emergency measures in Nicaragua as a "drifting toward totalitarianism" that confirmed the rightness of Reagan's hard-line policy toward the Sandinistas.

By February 1983 several thousand American-backed Nicaraguan counterrevolutionaries were massed along the Honduran side of the Honduran-Nicaraguan border, and for the first time the contras, as they are called, were joined by Honduran military units prepared to provide artillery support. At the same time the United States increased its military presence on sea and land and in the air around Nicaragua. Early in March, cross-border raids by the contras reached a new magnitude. In the view of Robert E. White, the former American ambassador to El Salvador, the "true intent" of the incursions was "neither to overthrow the Sandinistas nor, as Mr. Reagan claimed, to interdict the negligible trickle of arms from Nicaragua to El Salvador" but rather "to provoke the Sandinistas to cross the Honduran border and attack the counterrevolutionaries' base camps." "Washington is determined to create an ill-starred, region-wide military battle," White wrote in *The New York Times* (May 2, 1983), "hoping in the end to negotiate a region-wide solution on its own terms. . . . But even the hot-headed and inexperienced Sandinistas refused to fall into so obvious a trap. They ordered their troops to stay well clear of the Honduran border and reiterated their offer to negotiate with Honduras or the United States."

While the ex-Somocistas were attacking from the north, the Sandinista defector Edén Pastora Gómez was leading incursions in the south, from Costa Rica. The raiders, north and south, failing to elicit significant popular support (except among the historically isolated Miskitu Indians, who have charged the Sandinistas with human-rights violations), took not a single town and established no permanent bases within Nicaragua, but they wreaked havoc nonetheless, destroying infrastructure (including oil facilities and bridges) and taking 1,000 lives, bringing the two-year total of Nicaraguan dead to more than 5,000. Ortega estimated the economic damage for 1983 at $128 million. The national security crisis forced the Sandinista government to raise its defense spending to 25 percent of its budget and to institute an unpopular military draft, at a time when the populace was increasingly grumbling about the prices and shortages of foods, medicine, and other basic goods and the rationing of soap, sugar, cooking oil, and gasoline.

Following the invasion of Grenada by the United States in October 1983, Ortega took steps to dispel the negative American perception of Nicaragua. That November he announced that his government was prepared to stop buying arms from abroad and to ask Cuban and other foreign military advisers to leave, and he promised the presidents of the friendly Contadora countries (Mexico, Venezuela, Colombia, and Panama) that the restraints on the domestic opposition in Nicaragua would be loosened. In overtures to that opposition as well as in response to the pressure of the Sandinistas' democratic friends in Latin America and Europe, he proclaimed an amnesty for exiles in December 1983, and announced in February 1984 the scheduling of "democratic" elections.

The amnesty, offering land or compensation to "landowners who have abandoned their property or whose property has been occupied," was directed chiefly at peasants and excluded "oligarchs" seeking restoration of "the old privileges." The elections, for president, vice-president, and a ninety-member constituent assembly, were scheduled for November 1984. At a meeting of the eighty-one-member Sandinista Assembly, Ortega was named the party's presidential candidate and Sergio Ramírez Mercado its vice-presidential candidate.

Aside from six small parties, including fragments of the traditional Liberal and Conservative parties, the chief civilian opposition was a coalition of three political parties allied with two labor federations and the organized business community. The unofficial presidential candidate of the coalition was Arturo José Cruz, an opposition leader who had been a member of the ruling junta and ambassador to the United States before resigning in protest of Sandinista policies. To encourage the participation of Cruz in the electoral campaign, the Sandinistas made some concessions, including relaxed censorship of the opposition newspaper *La Prensa,* but they refused to allow the monitoring of the elections by foreign observers. The Cruz backers let the deadline pass without registering their candidate, in the hope of discrediting the elections and forcing the Sandinistas to make more political concessions, including the release of scores of prisoners and major changes in the government. After a long period of grace, election officials announced on August 22, 1984 that no further extensions for registration could be made because such extensions would hold up the printing of ballots. In accordance with the Nicaraguan law applying to parties not participating in elections, the three coalition parties lost their legal recognition. "They did not provide conditions for a fair election," Luis Rivas Leiva, the head of the opposition coalition, told the press, "so we are staying out."

A new anti-Sandinista military offensive, begun in March 1984, reached its climax the following month in the mining of Nicaragua's ports, an operation reportedly involving American vessels offshore. The fifteen-judge International Court of Justice in the Hague condemned American involvement in the harassment of Nicaragua in May 1984. Subsequent to an agreement reached between Ortega and United States Secretary of State George P. Shultz, talks between representatives of the United States and Nicaragua finally began in June 1984 and continued through the summer. Most of the discussions, described as "substantive" by the Mexican foreign ministry, were held in Manzanillo, Mexico.

The bilateral talks had mostly to do with the regional peace plan then being mediated by the four-nation Contadora group. That plan was aimed at insuring free, internationally inspected elections, the withdrawal of foreign military forces, and the halting of support for guerrilla movements in Central America. There was disagreement among American officials on some points of the treaty that was approved by the Contadora negotiators on September 7, 1984, but, as one official explained later, "no one expected the Nicaraguans to accept it, so we didn't really worry about the treaty." Only after Nicaragua, in a surprise move on September 21, 1984, announced that it was prepared to sign the draft treaty, did nonplussed State Department and White House officials begin marshalling objections to the document. "I'm not sure what there's left to talk about at Manzanillo," one State Department official said, as quoted by Philip Taubman in *The New York Times* (September 24, 1984). "The whole point was to get the Nicaraguans to accept the Contadora proposals. Now they have, but we say we aren't satisfied. I'm not sure I would blame the Nicaraguans if they were confused."

In a speech before the United Nations General Assembly on October 2, 1984, Ortega charged that "intelligence information from various sources" indicated that the United States was planning a two-stage invasion of Nicaragua timed to force the Sandinistas to cancel the national balloting scheduled for November 4. The first-phase strategy, he said, was for contras to invade from the north "with full logistical support from the United States." The second phase was for a Grenada-style operation, in which some Central American countries would request "aid" from the United States "to eradicate the 'Sandinista threat.'" Thus, as he later told editors of *Newsweek* (October 15,1984), United States troops would take part in the invasion once the contras had made inroads. "We have been making gestures to different countries, [including] Western countries, in a search for interceptor planes. . . . Nicaragua is the only country [in the area] that doesn't possess this type of plane. And yet Nicaragua is the one country that needs it. . . . The best thing would be that the Central American countries that have this type of airplane get rid of them, so that those of us that don't have them won't be forced into seeking them."

Ortega's relationship with the United States was never very cordial, due to U.S. support for Somoza prior to the revolution. Although the U.S. supplied post-revolution Nicaragua with tens of millions of dollars in economic aid, relations broke down when the Sandinistas supplied weapons to leftist El Salvadoran rebels (something which Ortega later admitted occurred). A joint peace proposal by the Democratic Speaker of the House Jim Wright and Ronald Reagan helped precipitate a peace agreement at a meeting of five Central American chiefs of state in July 1987, which won Costa Rican President Oscar Arias the Nobel Peace Prize. The agreement led to free elections and Ortega was defeated by Violeta Chamorro in 1990. Chamorro was supported by the US and a 14-party anti-Sandinista alliance known as the National Opposition Union (Unión Nacional Oppositora, UNO). Chamorro shocked Ortega and won the election. In Ortega's concession speech he vowed to keep "ruling from below" a reference to the power that the FSLN still wielded in various sectors. He also stressed his belief that the Sandinistas had the goal of bringing "dignity" to Latin America, and not necessarily to hold on to government posts. He remained an important figure in Nicaraguan opposition politics, gradually moderating in his political position from Marxism–Leninism to democratic socialism. He was an unsuccessful candidate for president in 1996 and 2001, before winning the 2006 presidential election. During this time in office, he made alliances with fellow Latin American socialists, such as Venezuelan President Hugo Chávez, and under his leadership, Nicaragua joined the Bolivarian Alliance for the America.

In July 2009, on the 30th anniversary of the FSLN revolution, Ortega announced his intention to amend the constitution so that the president could be reelected to a second, consecutive term. In October, the Nicaraguan Supreme Court lifted the constitutional ban on consecutive reelection, allowing Ortega to run in the country's 2011 presidential election. Ortega won reelection with some 60 percent of the vote, though there were allegations of election fraud. In 2014 Nicaragua's Congress ratified a controversial constitutional amendment scrapping presidential term limits and paving the way for President Daniel Ortega to seek re-election in 2016.

PERSONAL LIFE

A short man who wears rose-tinted glasses, Daniel Ortega has the reputation of being the most intense of the Sandinista leaders. (He surprised observers with his smiling cordiality when he met with President Jimmy Carter in the White House in 1979.) While not an especially dynamic speaker or brilliant theorist, Ortega is an adroit, patient mediator and a shrewd strategist, respected by Nicaraguan conservatives as well as radical leftists. When in prison, he took to writing poetry, some of it angry and heavy with four letter words, and some on the order of "I Never Saw Managua When Miniskirts Were in Fashion." Ever flexible, he still believes, ideally, in political pluralism and a mixed economy despite some of the turns the revolutionary government has been forced to take.

Ortega married Rosario Murillo in 1979 in a secret ceremony and moved to Costa Rica with her three children from a previous marriage. Ortega remarried Murillo in 2005 to have the marriage recognized by the Roman Catholic Church. The couple has eight children, three of them together.

FURTHER READING
The New York Times p7 *Mr* 26 *'83*; *Newsweek* 101:38 Mr 21 *'83* por; *Playboy* 30:57+ S *'83* por; *Time* 121:18 Je 6 *'83* por; *U S News* 90:25+ Mr 23 *'81* por; Ridolf, James D., ed. *Nicaragua: A Country Study* (1982); Rosset, Peter and *Vandermeer,* John, eds. *The Nicaragua Reader* (1983); *Unfinished Revolution: Daniel Ortega and Nicaragua's Struggle for Liberation*, Morris, K. E. Chicago Review Press, 2010

P

VIJAYA LAKSHMI PANDIT

Indian Nationalist Leader

Born: August 18, 1900; Allahabad, British Raj
Died: December 1, 1990; Dehradun, Utter Pradash, India

INTRODUCTION

India's demand for its release from British rule "is not the result of the work of any political party or any superimposed propaganda. It is the natural result of world conditions. Gandhi did not create the desire for independence. . . . India's desire for independence is more than a matter of merely wishing to become a 'nation.' What is actually at stake is the whole question of freedom itself." So declared Vijaya Lakshmi Pandit, the Indian Nationalist leader, in an interview she gave shortly after her arrival in New York in December 1944. On more than one occasion this sister of Jawaharlal Nehru was arrested for her outspoken championship of her country's cause. Prison, in fact, has become a second home to practically every member of her family. Mrs. Pandit was the first Indian leader to come directly from her country to the United States after the beginning of World War II. During her sojourn in the United States she was an observer at the San Francisco United Nations Conference, and made an extensive lecture tour.

EARLY LIFE

Anand Bhawan, the name Motilal Nehru chose for the new home he built to accommodate his wife and children as well as the numerous relatives who lived under his roof, means "a home of joy." Here in the city of Allahabad, India, on August 18, 1900, his second child, a daughter, was born to his wife Swarup Rani (Kaul)

Nehru. At the age of five Swarup Kumari, as Mrs. Pandit was named, was taken by her parents to England. There a governess was engaged for her and taken back to the Indian home, where the girl was educated. The Nehrus, a Brahman family, had their own swimming pool, a large garden, horses, dogs, carriages, and automobiles. In this atmosphere and amidst affectionate parents and relatives, Mrs. Pandit grew to womanhood.

A "thin almost starved-looking man . . . wearing a loincloth" revolutionized the pattern of life of the Nehru family. In 1921 Motilal Nehru gave a lavish party for the marriage of his older daughter, Swarup Kumari, to a young lawyer, Ran jit Pandit. (Upon her marriage, in accordance with Hindu custom, the young girl was adopted into the clan of her in-laws and renamed by them Vijaya Lakshmi, a name derived from the given name of her husband and from the territory in which he lived.) Among the hundreds of guests at her wedding were Mohandas Gandhi, with whom her father had already become associated in the Nationalist movement, and a number of the leading members of the Congress Working Committee, then meeting in Allahabad. Two years before this occasion Gandhi had launched his *Satyagraha* ("Civil Disobedience"), a movement to obtain India's freedom by nonviolent methods, and by 1921 it had made considerable headway. In fact, wrote Jawaharlal Nehru, "1921 was an extraordinary year for us. There was a strange mixture of nationalism and politics and religion and mysticism and fanaticism. Behind all this was agrarian trouble and, in the big cities, a rising working-class movement. . . . It was remarkable how Gandhi seemed to cast a spell on all classes and groups of people and drew them into one motley crowd struggling in one direction. . . . Even more remarkable was the fact that these desires and passions were relatively free from hatred of the alien rulers against whom they were directed. . . .Undoubtedly this was due to Gandhiji's insistence on the implications of nonviolence. It was also due to the feeling of release and power that came to the whole country with the inauguration of the movement and the widespread belief in success in the near future."

One by one the Nehru family was drawn into Gandhi's movement. Both Mrs. Pandit's father and husband gave up their lucrative law practices to devote their energies to the nationalist struggle, and the latter for his efforts spent considerable time in jail, sometimes in the company of his renowned brother-in-law. (Pandit died in 1944 shortly after the British Government released him because of his ill health.) A short while before Gandhi's famous march to the sea at Dandi, the starting place for his campaign to destroy the salt tax law, Mrs. Pandit's father decided to turn over the family home to the Indian National Congress. (It was renamed Swaraj Bhawan ["Freedom House"], while the house he had built for his only son became the new "home of Joy" of the Nehrus.)

LIFE'S WORK
When she experienced her first imprisonment in 1932 Mrs. Pandit was the mother of three daughters, the youngest only three. She and her younger sister, Krishna, had been arrested for their defiance of the Crown ruling forbidding them to participate in the public observance of India Independence Day. (January 26 is the day India pays tribute to the independence it hopes to win.) To the surprise of those who were present at her trial, Mrs. Pandit received a year's sentence plus a fine for her refusal to "refrain from taking part in meetings and processions . . . for a period of one month." Repeated jailings focused national and international attention upon the Nehru family, which together with Gandhi became the symbol of India's struggle for freedom. Mrs. Pandit was chairman of the Board of Education in her native city from 1935 to 1937. In 1937 she became a member of the Legislative Assembly as well as Minister for Local Self-Government and Public Health, positions she held for the next two years. The first Congresswoman to become a provincial minister, she recorded her impressions in a collection of addresses and essays, *So I Became a Minister,* which was published in India at the end of her term of office (1939). From 1942

to 1944 she was president of the All-India Women's Conference.

After her last release from prison in 1943 Mrs. Pandit plunged into the work of relieving the famine-stricken inhabitants of Bengal. Appalled by the suffering she saw in that province, the Indian woman leader observed, "I think the Government and its 'stooges'—more interested in that they continue in power than that the conditions be cured—were responsible." Although the political activities of her husband and herself deprived her children of normal family life, they shared her sympathies and joined her in her work. Her oldest daughter, Chandralekha, spent seven months in prison before she came to the United States in the autumn of 1944 to study under the first fellowship granted by the Mayling Soong (Madame Chiang Kai-shek '40) Foundation for students from the East. The two younger daughters of Mrs. Pandit escaped imprisonment because of their youth. Nayantara accompanied her sister Chandralekha to Wellesley College as a fellow student. Later Rita, the youngest of the three children, followed her sisters to the United States for study.

During her visit to her student daughters in 1944-45 Mrs. Pandit became familiar to Americans as an unofficial ambassador of the Indian people. In January 1945 she participated in the Pacific Relations Conference at Hot Springs, Virginia. Two months later she took the affirmative side in a Town Hall radio debate, "Are Colonial Empires a Threat to World Peace?" in which she was upheld by orientalist Owen Lattimore. Despite her far from sound health, Mrs. Pandit also made an extensive lecture tour. In late October Representative Emanuel Celler, who was responsible for proposing in Congress a bill to grant American naturalization rights to Indian nationals residing in the United States and an immigration quota, introduced Mrs. Pandit to President Truman at the White House.

At the United Nations conference, in the spring, which she attended as an observer, Mrs. Pandit informed a crowded press conference that the official Indian delegates had not "the slightest representative capacity, no sanction or mandate from any responsible groups in India, and are merely the nominees of the British Government." Since world peace was the purpose for which the representatives of the United Nations had met, the sister of Nehru remarked, it was necessary to bring to their attention the fact that "India is the pivot of the whole system of imperialism and colonialism which always breeds war. India's freedom, therefore, is an acid test of the principles for which this war has been fought and the continued denial of India's freedom by Britain is a negation of those principles and of the sacrifices that have been made to win victory."

Returning to the General Assembly in the fall as chairman of the Indian delegation she asserted, in the first address by a woman to that body, "India holds that the independence of all colonial peoples is the vital concern of freedom-loving peoples everywhere." Mrs. Pandit also favored continuation of the veto, calling it "the necessary device for securing that vital decisions by the great powers rest on unanimity." Outspoken against South Africa for its racial policies, in December the Indian delegate won the two-third vote necessary to pass a General Assembly resolution calling upon both countries to work toward a reformation of the African discrimination against Indians and other minorities. In addition to serving her country in the United Nations, Mrs. Pandit, after her unopposed election to India's first Central Assembly, was named Minister of Local Government in Health on the Executive Council, which is acting as an interim Government until a constitution is drafted and approved.

PERSONAL LIFE

At the time of Mrs. Pandit's visit to the United States in the spring of 1946, she had almost completed her autobiography, "Sunlight and Shadows." Between this and her first book, *So I Became a Minister,* she had written *My Prison Days.* Both her countrymen and Americans have remarked upon her beauty and eloquence. One reporter wrote: "What a delight she is proving to be. Small, she has all the vivacity of a daring robin that dashes in and steals the tidbit right from under the beak of some bigger, more ferocious bird. It is a joy to listen to her, to watch her snatch points from her platform opponents in debate. Seeing her in action one understands better the spirit that has upheld both herself and her distinguished brother."

FURTHER READING

Christian Sci Mon p1O F 2 '45; *N Y Post Mag* p25 D 19 '44 por; *PM* p6 Ap 27 '45 por; *International Who's Who,* 1945-46; Nehru, J. *Toward Freedom* (1941); Nehru, K. *With No Regrets* (1945); Shidharani, K. *My India, My America* (1941)

GEORGE PAPADOPOULOS

Premier of Greece

Born: May 14, 1919; Elaiohori, Greece
Died: June 27, 1999; Athens, Greece
Affiliation: National Political Union

INTRODUCTION

A veteran army officer, George Papadopoulos headed a group of colonels that seized control of the Greek government on April 21, 1967. He formally succeeded Constantine Kollias as Premier on December 13, 1967. Promising to bring order to the chaotic political scene and to remove what he considered a Communist menace, Papadopoulos ruled by decree, jailed dissidents of both the right and left, and curbed traditional freedoms, but also instituted a number of reforms. He withstood an attempt by King Constantine to remove him from power and emerged as strong man of the junta after a struggle for power. Despite criticism or his methods the Premier is seen by many of his 8,800,000 countrymen as a benefactor.

EARLY LIFE

George Papadopoulos, the son of a village schoolmaster, was born in 1919 at Eleochorion, Achaea, in the northern part of the Peloponnesus. (One source gives Arahova as his birthplace.) His brothers Constantine and Haramboulos are in government service. He grew up in modest circumstances, and the family had to sacrifice to send him to high school and cadet school. In August 1940, two months before the Greek-Italian war broke out, Papadopoulos graduated from the War Academy as a sub-lieutenant in the artillery. Serving on the Albanian front throughout the six-month war, he achieved an excellent record as platoon leader in an artillery battery. He received the gold Medal of s Valor and was twice awarded the War Cross. During the German occupation Papadopoulos joined the national resistance and fought under the command of General George Grivas. He was promoted to lieutenant in 1943.

LIFE'S WORK

In November 1944, after the defeat of the Axis forces, Papadopoulos was appointed a staff officer, and from January 1945 to May 1946 he served as an intelligence officer. He graduated from the Artillery School with excellent grades in 1945 and attended Officer Training School in the Middle East in 1946. Because of the Communist guerrilla war that engulfed Greece for several years after World War II, Papadopoulos returned to the battlefield in 1946 as commander of an artillery battery that fought at Grammos Mountain, at Souli, in the Peloponnesus, in Roumeli, and at Agrafa. After serving as an artillery school training officer from October 1946 to January 1948, he was on the front lines until September 1949, commanding the 131st, and then the 144th, mountain artillery units. His decorations of that period include the Silver Cross of the Royal Order of George I, with swords. He had in the meantime attained the rank of captain in December 1946 and was promoted to major in July 1949.

In 1952-53 Papadopoulos served as commander of an artillery unit, and in 1953-54 he again was an instructor in the Artillery School, where he took courses in the American methods section for several months. He also attended the School of the Army Engineer Corps. From 1955 to 1957 he was a member of the intelligence bureau of the army general staff, and from 1957 to 1959 he was chief of staff of an artillery division. Concurrently, he took special training at the Higher War School in 1955 at the Naval Academy in 1956, and at the Armed Forces School of Special Weapons in 1959. He was promoted to lieutenant colonel in August 1956.

Papadopoulos served from August 1959 to July 1964 with the Greek Central Intelligence Service, where he is said to have been the liaison officer with the United States Central Intelligence Agency. In August 1960 he was promoted to colonel and awarded the Cross of the Commander of the Royal Order of the Phoenix. Transferred to the field in July 1964, he commanded the 117th field artillery until October 1965 and then served with the First Army force until August 1966. According to one observer who was quoted by Richard Eder in *The New York Times* (February 16, 1968) Papadopoulos had been sent from Athens to Western Thrace "because the government suspected him of intrigue." His reputation for plotting led his cob leagues to nickname him "Nasser"—a reference to Egyptian president Carnal Abdel Nasser, who had gained power through a military coup. Writing in *The New York Times* (October 10, 1969), C. L. Sulzberger linked Papadopoulos with conspiracies for military takeover dating back to 1956. From August 1966 to April 1967 Papadopoulos served with the third staff bureau of the army general staff.

Volatile even in normal times, the Greek political scene was on the verge of chaos by the mid-1960's. In July 1965 King Constantine II, fearing a leftist coup, dismissed George Papandreou, the left-of-center Premier. In the months that followed, the country was increasingly divided into hostile camps. Despite widespread fears of Communism, large masses appeared to be receptive to radical politics. In December 1966 King Constantine appointed a nonpolitical caretaker Cabinet under Panayotis Kannellopoulos with the goal of preparing for general elections scheduled for May 1967. But on April 21, 1967, while belief was widespread that the elections would result in a leftist majority, a junta of colonels seized control of the Greek government in a three-hour coup. Its leading member was George Papadopoulos. The colonels claimed the support of about one-fourth of the army's 8,000 officers, but, according to *Time* (September 15, 1967), their power base actually consisted of a few hundred junior officers intent on a total reformation of Greek life. Sydney Gruson, writing in *The New York Times* (November 14, 1967), observed that Papadopoulos and his colleagues, all of whom had been raised in rural poverty with a great sense of honor to country and family, were as embittered by the wealthy conservatives as they were by the Communists.

At a press conference six days after the coup, Papadopoulos declared that the military junta had saved Greece from anarchy and Communism and that it had acted without the knowledge of King Constantine or of any foreign power. He acknowledged that thousands had been jailed and restrictions imposed on the press, labor unions, and political activity. Comparing the curbs to the straps that bind a patient to the operating table, he explained: "If he isn't fastened to the table, he can't be cured of his disease." Although the King appointed a civilian Premier, Constantine V. Kollias, to head the new government, the real power resided in a revolutionary council and a military triumvirate headed by Papadopoulos, who assumed the post of Minister to the Premier's Office. The other two members of the triumvirate were Brigadier Stylianos Patakos and Colonel Nicholas Makerezos. In August 1967 Papadopoulos strengthened his position by placing his supporters in key military positions, establishing a general directorate of government policy under his personal control that assigns to him veto powers over laws proposed by other Cabinet members.

Although a comic opera aspect pervaded the junta's first actions, which included the banning of beards and miniskirts, the regime soon instituted a number of positive reforms. Civil servants were directed to answer mail within three days, and farmers' pensions increased by 70 percent. Since strikes were forbidden, trains and buses generally ran according to schedule. To reduce the cost of living, bus fares and bread prices were lowered. David Holden, writing in the *Saturday Evening Post* (December 2, 1967), observed that large segments of the population were grateful for the coup. Wealthy persons believed that the Communist threat had been removed and many of the poor felt more secure under a strong national leadership. On the international scene, the junta in late 1967 reached an agreement with the Turkish government for the removal of Greek troops from Cyprus. Although the agreement was seen by many as a diplomatic setback for Greece, it tended to remove the long-standing threat of war between the two nations, and it held out the promise of peace to an island long tom by civil strife.

For the first nine months of the new regime there was little overt opposition. The memory of the bloody civil war of the late 1940's was still vivid, and many hoped that the King would eventually be able to influence the junta toward more moderate actions. Some politicians felt that it was Constantine's influence that had secured the release of former Premier Papandreou and other prominent politicians from prison. But arrests were continuing, and there was little progress toward the broad reforms that Papadopoulos had announced. The draft of a new constitution, to be published in mid-December, was rumored to include provisions that would substantially reduce the King's powers and offer no timetable for a return to democratic rule.

In the face of that threat, King Constantine flew on December 13, 1967 to the Aegean port of Kavalla, in Northern Greece. Hoping to rally support from the military forces stationed in the area, the King taped a stirring speech in which he repudiated the junta and declared that he had accepted the April coup merely to avert bloodshed. The speech was broadcast from a small short-wave radio station in central Greece, and since no regular transmitter was available, it could barely be heard in Athens. Furthermore, earlier in the year, Papadopoulos had spent two months in northern Greece, installing junior officers loyal to the junta in key positions. Emboldened, those men moved toward Kavalla and arrested the generals who were the Kings

main supporters in the north. When it became apparent that there would be no popular support from Athens or die south, the King and his family, along with Premier Kollias and other supporters, fled to Rome.

Papadopoulos was sworn in as Premier on December 13, 1967, also taking on the post of Defense Minister in the new Cabinet. At a press conference the following day he explained that since the King was no longer carrying out his duties, the junta had named Lieutenant General George Zoitakis as Regent. Maintaining that Constantine had been misled by adventurers, Papadopoulos said that the King was welcome to return to his throne, but under conditions that would make him a mere figurehead. To create the impression of a civilian government, Papadopoulos retired from the army with the rank of brigadier on December 20, and the other Cabinet members also resigned their military commissions.

After granting amnesty to some opponents at Christmas, Papadopoulos took several more measures in early 1968 to make the junta more palatable to the Greeks. The bank debts of farmers were cancelled by decree; government-financed dowries were promised for working girls; and cheaper theatre tickets were made available to workers. Other promised benefits included reductions in school and university fees, free textbooks, clubs for dock workers, government-financed vacations for workers, and day nurseries for working mothers. Addressing himself to the young people of Greece, Papadopoulos appealed to them to lend their energies to the rebirth of the nation.

On March 15, 1968, the Premier presented a draft constitution to the public. He asked citizens to make suggestions for changes to the junta and announced that the government would "blend the wisdom of suggestions together with the ideas of the government and the spirit of the revolution" into a final draft to be submitted to a national referendum in September. As a further step to blunt criticism, Papadopoulos reorganized his twenty-five member Cabinet on June 20, 1968 to include nine civilian specialists. On August 13, 1968 an attempt was made to assassinate Papadopoulos with a dynamite bomb as he was being chauffeured into Athens from his home. The would-be assassin, believed to belong to the united left opposition, was soon captured and sentenced to death but, apparently giving in to international pressure, the government later commuted the death sentence.

With threats of penalties against abstainers, a national referendum on the new constitution was held on

September 29, 1968. Although only about 75 percent of the voters of Athens cast their ballots for the document, support in rural areas ran as high as 99.8 percent. Altogether 92.1 percent of the nation s 5,000,000 voters approved the draft which, according to some critics, would give Papadopoulos more power than any premier or elected president in die world. Under its provisions the King's powers were to be merely ceremonial. Communists and other groups that do not "contribute to the advancement of the national interest" were outlawed, and the authority of parliament was limited. Although the document contained provisions for individual rights, freedom of the press, and parliamentary elections, there was no immediate prospect that these would be put into effect. Clinging to his predilection for medical analogies, Papadopoulos declared after the referendum: "The country is still in a plaster cast and the fractures have not healed. The cast will be kept on even after the referendum so that it should not become necessary at a later date to suspend the constitution again."

Backed by what appeared to him to be an overwhelming vote of confidence, Papadopoulos in late 1968 instituted a purge of extreme right-wingers, who had opposed the introduction of a constitution and the addition of civilians to the Cabinet. Among those who lost their positions was Colonel Ladis, head of internal security and leader of the 'hard-liners," who was replaced by a moderate. The revolutionary council, a bastion of rightwing militarists, was officially dissolved on November 15, 1968, when the new constitution went into effect.

On his first anniversary as Premier, Papadopoulos reported to the nation that great strides had been made in education, welfare, and public affairs, and that a balanced budget had been achieved. He promised more equitable pensions and a large housing program for the next year. "The problem of those who were lured by the Communist sirens was not ideological but sociological," he said. In an interview with Wilton Wynn of *Time* (December 20, 1968) Papadopoulos affirmed a desire to eventually establish parliamentary government in Greece and outlined a five-year plan to transform Greece "from the condition of a developing country to that of a fully developed society."

In April 1969, on the second anniversary of the coup, Papadopoulos announced the restoration of some constitutional rights, including inviolability of the home and the right of assembly. At the same time he promised liberalization of press restrictions and a review of the cases of some 2,000 political prisoners still detained on Aegean islands. Nevertheless, there appeared to be little prospect for any far-reaching liberal reforms by the Greek regime, which continued to be a target of Western democratic nations, especially in view of reports—emphatically denied by Papadopoulos—that political prisoners had been subjected to torture. Although the United States government, which suspended military aid to Greece after the coup, partly removed the ban in February 1969, an American embargo on heavy equipment, such as tanks and jet planes, remained in effect for Greece. In December 1969 the Greek government, anticipating its possible expulsion from the Council of Europe, withdrew from that organization. On the other hand, the Papadopoulos regime has indicated a desire for improved relations with the Soviet Union, noting that anarchy, rather than Communism, now constitutes the main threat to Europe. With Western investors reluctant to pour money into a nation whose government lacks democratic safeguards, the Papadopoulos regime has had to borrow heavily abroad to maintain its balance of payments. In his 1969 year-end message the premier told the Greek people that in 1970 they must "work harder, spend less and invest more."

PERSONAL LIFE

George Papadopoulos was married in 1941 to Nekee Vassiliadis and has two children. He was five feet six inches tall and of medium build, and he had receding black hair, bushy eyebrows, and a small mustache. He spoke Katharevusa, the official form of modem Greek spoken by the educated classes. In August 1968 he published the book *To Pistevo Mas* (Credo), containing his thoughts on various subjects and voicing an appeal for a return to old "Hellenic-Christian values." Some 2,000,000 copies were printed of the book, which is distributed free to the Greek public. Papadopoulos liked the Greek countryside, and his interests included ancient Greek literature, book collecting, and hunting. On festive occasions he sometimes performed a traditional evzone dance.

Papadopoulos was found guilty of treason, mutiny, torture, and other crimes and sentenced to death in 1974, which was later commuted to life imprisonment. Papadopoulos remained in prison, rejecting an amnesty offer that required he acknowledge his record and express remorse, until he died of cancer on June 27, 1999.

FURTHER READING
Washington (D.C.) *Post* A pi Ap 28 '67; *International Who's Who,* 1969-70

ANDREAS (GEORGE) PAPANDREOU
Prime Minister of Greece

Born: February 5, 1919; Chios, Greece
Died: June 23, 1996; Ekáli, Greece
Group Affiliation: Pasok

INTRODUCTION

The designation of Andreas Papandreou as Prime Minister of Greece as a result of the elections of October 18, 1981 marked the coming of age of liberalism in modern Greek democracy. Papandreou's Panhellenic Socialist Movement (Pasok), which won a decisive 172-seat majority in the 300-seat Parliament, was the first leftist party to gain power in thirty-five years, and the transition from conservative to Socialist rule took place smoothly despite the fact that Greece had emerged only eight years before from a right-wing military dictatorship. The victory also marked the culmination of the extraordinary political saga of a Harvard-trained economist and scholar. The son of George Papandreou, a longtime liberal politician who served as Prime Minister from 1963 to 1965, Andreas Papandreou has been imprisoned, tortured, and exiled for his radical political views. His growing popularity was regarded as one of the reasons for the military coup in 1967, and he remained a leader of the democratic opposition during his years in exile from 1968 to 1974. When the junta fell, Papandreou returned to Greece, organized Pasok, and led the party to increasing shares of the popular vote in general elections. His foreign policy as Prime Minister is more independent of the West than that of heads of preceding Greek governments, but he remains basically pro-Western. (Pragmatically modifying his election promise to get rid of American military bases in Greece, he has agreed to let the installations remain until 1989.) In domestic affairs his major initiatives have included decentralization of governmental power, a law to give workers a voice in factory decisions, encouragement of agricultural cooperatives, and a series of highly controversial measures to separate church and state.

EARLY LIFE

Andreas George Papandreou was born on February 5, 1919 on the Aegean island of Chios, the only son of George Andreas and Sophia (Mineiko) Papandreou. His father was serving at that time as governor-general of the Aegean Islands. When Andreas was five, his parents were divorced, and he went to live with his mother in the Athens suburb of Psychiko. Although profoundly devoted to his mother, he also turned for guidance to his father, whose prominence in politics grew steadily. To please his father, who was dismayed by his early poor grades in school, he made up his mind to excel scholastically, becoming a first-rate student at the American College in Athens and then at the Athens University Law School, which he attended from 1937 to 1940. By the time he entered law school, Greece had fallen under the dictatorial rule of General Ioannis Metaxas, and George Papandreou had been exiled to the island of Andros. Andreas Papandreou, then a Trotskyist, joined a resistance group that published an anti-Metaxas underground newspaper. He was arrested in the summer of 1939, tortured for two days, and forced to sign a repentant confession that named some of his Trotskyist allies. Shaken and shamed by the ordeal, he left Greece for the United States in 1940.

In New York, Papandreou found a job to support himself and enrolled in Columbia University. Soon transferring to Harvard to concentrate on economics, he earned his M.A. degree in 1942 and his doctorate in 1943. The following year, when he became an American citizen, he entered the United States Navy for two years of military service. After World War II he pursued a flourishing teaching career, as lecturer in economics in 1946-47 at Harvard, associate professor from 1947 to 1950 at the University of Minnesota, associate professor in 1950-51 at Northwestern University, professor from 1951 to 1955 at the University of Minnesota, and professor from 1955 to 1963 at the University of California at Berkeley, where for some years he was also chairman of the department of economics. He owes his academic advancement partly to his publication of many articles in scholarly journals and several books, including *An Introduction to Social Science: Personality, Work, Community,* in collaboration with A. Naftalin, B. Nelson, M. Sibley, and D. Calhoun (Lippincott, 1953); *Competition and Its Regulation,* in collaboration with J.T. Wheeler (Prentice-Hall, 1954); and *Economics as a Science* (Lippincott, 1958).

LIFE'S WORK

During a visit to Greece in 1953 Papandreou felt estranged by the constricted political atmosphere that followed the Greek Civil War, which had raged from 1946 to 1949. However, when he returned again in 1959 on Fulbright and Guggenheim grants, his father persuaded him to stay. At the behest of Prime Minister Constantine Karamanlis, he organized and became the director of the Center of Economic Research in Athens. In 1962 the Center published two books by Papandreou: *A Strategy for Greek Economic Development* and *Fundamentals of Model Construction in Macroeconomics*. Becoming increasingly fascinated with the possibilities for political change in his homeland, Papandreou resigned his professorship at Berkeley and on January 2, 1964 renounced his American citizenship so that he could run for Parliament under the banner of his father's liberal party, the Union of the Center. In February 1964 he was elected from his father's old district near Patras, and the party won enough seats to make George Papandreou Prime Minister. He soon appointed Andreas Papandreou his chief aide, with the title of Minister to the Prime Minister. In June the son was also named Deputy Minister of Economic Coordination.

Some of the Prime Minister's old associates became indignant over the rapid rise of Andreas Papandreou, whose fiery attacks on King Constantine, the Greek military, and the United States (for interfering in Greek affairs) provided ammunition for right-wing forces opposing George Papandreou's program for social change. In November 1964 unproved charges of corruption forced Andreas Papandreou to resign his ministerial posts, but six months later he was reappointed Deputy Minister of Economic Coordination. However, on July 15, 1965 King Constantine dismissed George Papandreou and his Cabinet in a dispute over the Prime Minister's attempt to purge right-wing officers from the military. The dismissal exacerbated the polarization of Greek politics and ushered in a period of instability that lasted nearly two years. A series of caretaker governments denounced Andreas Papandreou as a Communist and an ally of a group of leftist army officers who allegedly were plotting to take over the country. Far from damaging Papandreou, the attacks helped to make him a national figure and a leader of the leftist faction of the Center Union.

On April 21, 1967—a month before national elections that the Center Union was expected to win—a group of right-wing colonels headed by George Papadopoulos seized power in a coup d'état that was motivated in no small part by their fear of the Papandreous. Both father and son were arrested, along with 6,000 other Greeks. Charged with conspiracy to commit high treason, Andreas Papandreou was kept in solitary confinement for eight months, an ordeal he considers the most painful of his life. After an international campaign that included pressure from influential Americans, the junta released Papandreou and most other political prisoners in December 1967. A month later he went into exile, so that he would be free to express his opposition to authoritarianism.

During his exile Papandreou was invited to deliver several honorary lecture series, including the Benjamin Fairless Lectures at Carnegie-Mellon University in Pittsburgh in 1969 (published as *Man's Freedom,* Carnegie-Mellon, 1969); the Edmund Burke Bicentenary Lecture at Trinity College, Dublin, 1970; and the Woodward Lectures at the University of British Columbia in 1973. He also *wrote Democracy at Gunpoint: The Greek Front* (Doubleday, 1970), an account of the events leading to the 1967 coup; and *Paternalistic Capitalism* (Univ. of Minnesota Press, 1972), a theoretical work on the failures of modern capitalism. F.E. Hirsch,

---

Affiliation: Pasok

While teaching economics at the University of Stockholm in 1968-69 and at York University in Toronto, Canada from 1969 to 1974, Papandreou led the struggle against Papadopoulos' rule as head of the Panhellenic Liberation Movement (Pasok), a coalition of antijunta groups that he organized in 1968. He traveled extensively, denouncing the Greek government for suppression of political dissent and the American government for what he charged was its complicity in the colonels' coup and its support of the junta. In an article for *The New York Times* (April 21, 1972) he outlined his view of the history of American involvement in Greek politics: "The United States approved of 'picked' premiers, interfered in elections to assure the outcome, passed on military promotions, brought officers of the Greek Army to the United States for training, controlled the Greek Intelligence Service. One million dollars a day went into Greece from 1947 through the Fifties, to assist a war-torn society and to control it. The Greek dictatorship that emerged five years ago was the final stage in a developing spiral of control." In October 1973 he refused to cooperate in elections announced by the junta on the grounds that they would be fraudulent and would simply serve to disguise the dictatorship.

commenting in *Library Journal* (April 1, 1970), called the former work "a brilliant piece of writing [that] contains some very moving passages. . . . The book is of course a partisan account, but is also by far the most impressive volume written in English on postwar Greece." David Holden disagreed in *The New York Times* Book Review (May 31, 1970): "[This] book merely confirms what [Papandreou's] political career has demonstrated: a strong disinclination to admit that there are other interests, other viewpoints, other truths than his own." Papandreou's later books include *National Planning and Socioeconomic Priorities*, written in collaboration with Uri Zohar (Praeger, 1974), and *Socialist Transformation* (Athens, 1977).

The crises precipitating the downfall of the already weakened military regime in Athens began on July 15, 1974 when a group of right-wing officers overthrew Archbishop Makarios of Cyprus in a coup inspired by the Greek junta. On July 20 Turkey, Greece's age-old enemy, invaded Cyprus and occupied most of the island. That development caused the junta to collapse. Constantine Karamanlis returned from France to head an emergency government, and on August 16 Papandreou was greeted at Athens airport by 20,000 cheering supporters. He urged moderation, saying he did not support the street demonstrations then widespread in Athens: "I am not prepared to provoke a return of the military." Since George Papandreou had died in 1968, a group of deputies from the Center Union party asked Papandreou to assume leadership. He declined and on September 3 founded the Panhellenic Socialist Movement. After an election campaign in which he advocated sweeping social change, Pasok finished third, with a disappointing 14 percent of the vote and only twelve seats in the 300-seat Parliament. Karamanlis led his New Democracy party to a huge victory, with 54 percent of the vote, and the Center Union, headed by George Mavros, took 20 percent.

Between 1974 and 1977 Papandreou built Pasok into the best-organized party in Greece, using American models to shape an efficient political machine extending to the village level. He also hammered away at the Karamanlis Administration, calling for a more independent Greek foreign policy and for extensive domestic reform. In June 1975 Parliament approved a new Constitution proposed by Karamanlis over the opposition of Papandreou, who felt that the Prime Minister would use certain provisions to strengthen himself. Again in opposition to Karamanlis, in April 1976 Papandreou bitterly denounced a new pact under which American bases would remain in Greece for the next four years in return for $700,000,000 in aid. Spurred by Papandreou's tireless campaigning and aided by popular disillusionment with Karamanlis' economic program, in the elections of November 20, 1977 Pasok increased its vote to 25.3 percent of the total, winning ninety-two seats. Mavros' party was demolished, earning only 12 percent of the vote, while Karamanlis' party retained control of Parliament with 41.9 percent of the vote and 172 seats, a loss of forty-two.

In January 1978 Papandreou called for removal of American military bases from Greece in retaliation for the appointment of Turkish generals to command NATO's southeastern forces. Just as he had predicted, in May 1980 Karamanlis used the Constitution to have himself named President. George Rallis replaced him as Prime Minister. When, in October 1980, Rallis returned Greece to the military wing of NATO after a six-year absence stemming from the Cyprus invasion, Papandreou protested that the move would cause "the cession to Turkey of Greek sovereign rights" in disputed areas of the Aegean Sea. Meanwhile, during 1979 he had argued against the treaty providing for Greece's entry into the Common Market in 1981 on the grounds that it would damage Greek industry.

Ironically, Karamanlis' rise to the Presidency may have given Pasok a crucial boost in the national elections scheduled for 1981. Rallis proved to be an uninspiring leader and campaigner, and with Karamanlis in a position to oversee the government, Greeks felt less frightened of electing the Socialists. Papandreou was aided, moreover, by the country's restlessness after seven years of New Democracy rule and by an increasingly poor economic outlook. Also basing his campaign on fervent nationalism, he attacked Turkey and charged that Greece had long been a "client state" of the West with little to show in return for its subservience. He caught the nation's mood with a one-word slogan: *allaghi* ("change").

As the campaign progressed and the chances of a Pasok victory seemed to improve, the specifics of the change that Papandreou promised became more moderate. He qualified his positions on American bases in Greece and membership in the Common Market and NATO. Among his domestic goals were decentralization of government, improved social welfare, the end of censorship and other repressive laws, and liberalization of laws regarding religion and marriage. The central problem in his campaign was to balance the fiery oratory that is one of his greatest assets with enough suggestion of moderation to draw votes from the center—while not alienating the left wing of Pasok. On October 18, 1981 Pasok won the election with a margin much larger than most observers had expected. The party took 48.06 percent of the vote and 172 seats, New Democracy took 115 seats, and the Communists won thirteen seats. In his victory speech Papandreou maintained his reassuring tone, promising that he would not "lead the country into any adventure."

At his swearing-in ceremony on October 21, 1981, Prime Minister Papandreou promised to act in accordance with the "mandate for change" that the election had given Pasok. His thirty-seven-member Cabinet was entirely made up of Pasok stalwarts, some of them old liberal allies of his father during the 1960's and some of them from the left wing of the party. Papandreou himself took the post of Defense Minister, signaling his intention to keep a close eye on the military. His first weeks in office brought a flurry of moves on various fronts: he announced that the PLO's diplomatic status would be upgraded, received Yasir Arafat in Athens, and opened an embassy in Cuba; he closed down committees that censored films and music; he granted official recognition to the Communist-led anti-Nazi resistance in World War II and speeded up procedures for the return of 40,000 Greek exiles who had fled the country after the Civil War; and he began purging rightists from the civil service and the state-run radio and TV networks.

The foreign policy that Papandreou adopted has been considerably more cautious than his campaign rhetoric. His anti-Americanism notwithstanding, he immediately responded to a telegram from President Ronald Reagan congratulating him on his election with a message promising to do everything possible "to promote the close bonds of friendship between the Greek and American peoples." Since then Papandreou has tried to steer a course independent of the superpowers while remaining basically loyal to the West. While dropping his earlier threats to withdraw from the military wing of NATO, he has kept his distance from the alliance through largely symbolic moves, such as refusing to approve NATO's call for economic sanctions against the Soviet Union in January 1982 and protesting the decision to place American cruise missiles in Europe. Papandreou's accommodations with NATO and the United States have been dictated to some extent by his hard-line posture towards Turkey in disputes over Cyprus and territorial rights in the Aegean. He has worked to win guarantees from the Western alliance that Turkey will not attack Greece, and he hopes to persuade the United States to pressure Turkey to end its partial occupation of Cyprus.

Having proclaimed after his election that private enterprise would remain the "main lever" of the economy, Papandreou announced in January 1982 a series of steps to strengthen and regulate production, among them the "socialization" of key industries by the creation of supervisory councils that would allow workers, government officials, and corporate directors to oversee long-range planning. Other steps include incentives for investment, stricter control over bank credit to ensure its productive use, special credit assistance for small- and medium-sized industries, and the encouragement of agricultural cooperatives. Papandreou's decentralization program transferred a large degree of planning and budgetary power from the bloated federal bureaucracy to local governments. And several significant and controversial social measures were enacted: the voting age was lowered from twenty to eighteen; civil marriage was legalized, adultery decriminalized, and laws were proposed legalizing abortion and divorce; and a study was begun that is expected to lead to the expropriation of the Greek Orthodox Church's vast holdings of unused land.

In October 1982 the first test of popular sentiment toward the Socialists came in the form of nationwide local elections. In the first round, on October 17, the party's share in the vote in the main urban areas dropped more than 10 percent below the 48 percent it had won in the 1981 general election. But in the second round of runoffs, aided by the Communists in districts where no Communist candidate was running, Pasok won a crushing victory, taking 173 mayoral posts out of 276, a gain of more than 100 over the last municipal elections. The results were widely seen as a vote of confidence in Papandreou's Administration. Nevertheless, as the year ended it was clear that Papandreou faced serious economic and political difficulties. Disillusionment among leftists (including the left wing of his own party) with Papandreou's cautious pace of reform contributed to a sharp increase in Communist strength in the local elections. And the international recession had hurt the Greek economy; while inflation dropped slightly, unemployment nearly doubled during 1982, and investment and production were stagnant. To deal with those problems Papandreou adopted an austere budget for

1983, offsetting increases in military and social welfare spending with a partial wage freeze, higher utility rates, and new taxes on luxury goods and fuel.

During its first year and a half in power, the Papandreou government was unequivocally pro-Arab and anti-Israel. Its absolute identification with the Palestinian Liberation Organization cause began to weaken when it became evident that the Arabs were not going to reciprocate by investing more petro-dollars in Greece and by supporting Greece *vis-a-vis* Turkey in international organizations. When Greece's turn in the presidency of the European Economic Community came around (July-December 1983), the rules of the EEC game forced the Papandreou government into more friendly relations with Israel.

Regarding American strategic airfields and military surveillance facilities in Greece, nine months of difficult negotiations ended on July 15, 1983, when Papandreou signed an accord permitting the United States to retain the twenty-four installations for another five years. The accord assured Greece that it would receive an additional $220,000,000 in American aid in fiscal 1984 (bringing the total to $500,000,000), and it removed the danger of the bases being transferred, along with increased military aid, to Greece's archenemy, Turkey.

Critics wrote off the 1980s as the "lost decade" but Papandreou did introduce some long overdue reforms. Civil marriage was introduced, changes in family law improved the status of women, and refugees who had fled to the Eastern bloc at the end of the civil war were allowed to return. Papandreou also established a national health service but, like many of his peers, he preferred to seek medical treatment abroad.

He secured a second term in 1985 with a comfortable 46 per cent share of the vote. But a price had to be paid for the excessive spending during the first Pasok administration in the form of significant belt-tightening. The government's unpopularity was further exacerbated by scandals which reached to the highest levels of government, by his own serious health problems, and by the divorce of his wife of 30 years for a stewardess, half his age. These and other factors contributed to his defeat in the election of 1989. Although he was beset by many troubles that would have destroyed other men, Papandreou's share of the vote in the three elections that ensued in 1989-90 never fell below 39 percent. Once

out of office he was indicted on charges of telephone-tapping and corruption. He was narrowly acquitted of the charges.

Perhaps the greatest testimony to Papandreou's charisma was his political resurrection in 1993 when his share of the vote, at 47 per cent, was only marginally less than at the height of his career. At this time, he had reverted to the social-democratic views that he had espoused during the mid-1960s and, once in power, he gave attempted to implement programs to bring the economy under control. He was now frail and remote, unable to work for more than few hours a day. Dimitri Liani, controlled access to the prime minister, and is said to have influenced many of the decisions. Papandreou made no serious effort to address the succession question and dissent within the ranks of Pasok came into the open as potential candidates for the leadership position began to stake out their claims.

PERSONAL LIFE

Soon after his arrival in the United States during World War II, Andreas Papandreou met Christine Rassias, a Greek-American whom he married in 1941. The marriage ended in divorce. On August 30, 1951 he married Margaret Chant, they had four American-born children: George Jeffrey, Gayle Sophia, Nicholas, and Andreas. In a controversial move, he divorced Margaret in 1989 to marry Dimitra Liani a stewardess that was half his age.

Papandreou was a tall, husky man, with bushy eyebrows and a highly expressive face, who always appeared impeccably groomed. Allies and opponents alike agree that he is a leader of extraordinary charm and power of personality, though his detractors charge that his manner concealed a streak of ruthless, opportunistic ambition and that he had autocratic tendencies. Andreas Papandreou died of a heart attack on June 23, 1996.

FURTHER READING

Chicago Tribune I p5 O 20 '81 por; *Economist* p64 D 16 '78 por; *The New York Times* Mag p42 Mr 21 '82 pors; *Newsweek* 98:46+ N 2 '81 pors; *International Yearbook and Statesmen's Who's Who,* 1982; *International Who's Who,* 1983-84; *The United States and the Making of Modern Greece: History and Power,* 1950-1974, Miller, J.E, The University of North Carolina Press; 2009

FERRUCCIO PARRI
Premier of Italy

Born: January 19, 1890; Pinerolo, Italy
Died: December 8, 1981; Rome Italy
Affiliation: Italian Republican Party; Popular Unity;
    Radical Party

INTRODUCTION
Probably the most distinguished record of anti-Fascist and anti-Nazi activity in Italy is that of Ferruccio Parri, Italy's Premier from June to November 1945. Like France's Georges Bidault, Parri was a mild-mannered history teacher who has served the cause of freedom as a writer, editor, and general of guerrillas; his underground activities continued unbroken for more than twenty years, of which nine were spent in Fascist prisons. Unlike his predecessors, Parri is from the more advanced and articulate northern section of Italy, where Fascism never attained quite the acceptance it did in the poor and semi feudal south. It was north Italy that was occupied by the Nazis after Italy's surrender to the Allies on September 1943, and it was in Milan and Turin that the patriots rose in April 1945 and drove out the invader.

EARLY LIFE
The future Premier was born in Turin about 1890. In 1915, writes Gaetano Salvemini in the *Nation,* "Parri was an instructor in history in a high school. [Other sources give his field as classical literature.] Tall, pale, with beautiful dark eyes and a great shock of black hair, as severe with himself as with others in the fulfillment of duty, Parri was adored by his pupils." He was in favor of Italy's entrance into the First World War, on the side of the Allies, which he saw as a war to obtain justice for all and to complete the unification of Italy. Entering the Army as a lieutenant, Parri participated in nine offensives, was wounded four times, and received four decorations for valor, among them the Croce per Merito di Guerra and the French Croix de Guerre. Afterward, to quote Salvemini, Major Parri "followed President Wilson's work with enthusiasm. When Leonida Bissolati resigned from the Orlando Sonnino Cabinet because he would not associate himself with its demands for Dalmatia and openly defied the Nationalists and Mussolini, Ferruccio Parri took sides with him, while Ivanoe Bonomi, who had been Bissolati's follower and friend, betrayed him by taking his place in the Cabinet."

LIFE'S WORK
An anti-Fascist from the first, after his discharge from the Army Parri became assistant editor of the liberal newspaper *Cornere della sera* ("Evening Messenger"). In 1925 he resigned because the editor in chief, Senator Albertini, had been replaced by a Fascist; and from that time on Parri devoted himself to secret counterrevolutionary activities against the Fascist dictatorship. In 1926 he was Italian correspondent for the emigre newspaper *Corriere degli Italiani,* published in France by Guiseppe Donati and other anti-Fascists. This work ended for Parri in November of that year, when he and Carlo Rosselli managed to effect the escape of seventy-year-old Filippo Turati, leader of the Socialist Party in Italy. "When ... all remnants of resistance were suppressed in Italy," Parri wrote in explanation, "I felt it my duty to make a protest which should declare my faith in a better Italy. This protest could only be made public abroad. . . . Signor Turati is well fitted to present to civilized Europe our protest against the darkness that has fallen upon our country and our faith in an Italy which will give equal liberty to all Italians."

Returning to Italy, Parri and Rosselli were stopped by customs guards at Tuscany, and admitted their complicity in "unauthorized expatriation." Under Fascist law they were entitled to be set free while awaiting trial, but the police interned them on the island of Ustica for a month. Salvemini has given in his article a graphic description of the "conditions of torture" with which the future Premier and his fellow internees were treated. At the trial Parri took the offensive, rousing the courtroom to wild applause, it is reported, by his ringing accusations that the Fascist Government itself had made the step necessary by treating Turati illegally and unjustly. This was the first real challenge anyone had dared offer the Blackshirts, and caused a sensation. The two patriots were given the minimum sentence of ten months' imprisonment, after which Rosselli was again seized and interned. Parri was freed, but the Milan police kept an eye on him, and, says Delos Lovelace, the newspapers on which he worked after that "were generally seized by Mussolini's agents as soon as an issue began to run off the presses."

In all, the future Premier spent nine years in Fascist prisons, of which three years were in detention while awaiting trial. Mrs. Parri, the former Ester Verrua, also served one term. Toward the end of 1930, when other leaders of the underground Justice and Liberty movement were seized and sent to a penal island where they remained until 1943, Parri miraculously escaped arrest, and, "amid the general hopelessness, steadfastly refused to make any compromises with the victorious Fascist regime." (The founding of the Rome-Berlin Axis added to the danger for his Jewish wife.) The coming of the Second World War and the occupation of north Italy by the Germans after the fall of Mussolini only intensified the work of the underground and Parri. "Week after week," to quote *Newsweek*, "he went to bed at 2:00 or 3:00 A.M., rose again at eight, and worked through the day without lunch. When hiding from the Germans Parri sometimes shaved off his black, gray-flecked mustache or changed his glasses." As a leader of the fighting Partisans, or guerrillas, he was best known to the Germans as "General Maurizio," and was also heard of as "Lo Zio" ("The Uncle"). Other war pseudonyms used by Parri were Milanesi, Pozzi, and Pazzolini. He always carried his own bag of secret documents, rather than entrust them to someone else whom the Nazis would be less likely to suspect, as underground leaders did. "An electrical expert and former research director of the Italian Edison Society," *Newsweek* adds, "he organized an elaborate system of radio communication with the Allies in Rome."

More than once Parri slipped across to southern Italy for conferences. Picked up by the Gestapo after one such visit, Parri identified himself frankly as "chief organizer of warfare against Nazism and Fascism." He expected to be executed, but was set free in Switzerland. In one version of the incident, a quick-thinking American major, in the name of General Mark Clark '42, ordered the release of a German general in exchange for that of the white-haired Partisan—or the General's death if Parri were killed. According to Colonel Edward J. F. Glavin of the Office of Strategic Services, the German delivered "Maurizio" and another Italian prisoner in Switzerland for return to the Allies, as proof of their good intentions in asking for surrender terms. At any rate, Parri went back to Milan and the Partisans— he was one of the highest commanders of this underground, which was said to be one of the most efficient in all of Europe. Later "Maurizio" and several of his colleagues were decorated by General Clark with the Bronze Star, which some Americans considered ridiculously inadequate for the value and difficulty of their services to the Allied cause.

The anti-monarchist and mildly socialistic Action Party, which Parri helped found in northern Italy, is not one of the largest parties, but it is one of the most influential. According to the New York *Post* correspondent Thomas Healy, "Parri's Action Party has always adopted the mediating role" between the Leftists and the parties of the Right, which include the Christian Democrats and the so-called "Liberals" and the Actionists "may be truly said to be the party without 'isms,' whose principles give homage to democracy and permit its expression. Its members—membership costs about a dime—total 120,000 in north Italy and 80,000 in the south. It raised more members of the fighting Partisan armies of the north than any other single party : seventeen divisions, or one-third of the total Partisan forces." In June 1945, when fifty days of crisis had found none of the six parties in Premier Bonomi's Government willing to succeed him, Parri was called to Rome for consultations. A few days later Prince Humbert, Lieutenant General of the Realm, designated him to form a new Cabinet. Conservatives had agreed to his selection, reportedly, as the least radical of the Leftwingers and as the most distinguished anti-Fascist.

"I would sooner have been shot by General Kappler," was Parri's reaction, .although he accepted the task. As Anne O'Hare McCormick'[40] put it, "Nobody wants a job that carries responsibility without power and depends on outside powers who don't know what they want. . . . Nearly half the territory is still under military government, and the rest is only nominally under Italian rule. The regime remains subject to the still-unpublished terms of the armistice, which restrict its political authority and give it almost no economic power. The cupboard is so bare, moreover, that economic control means very little. Italy has no ships, no material for reconstruction, no access to Lend-Lease, no assistance from UNRRA except to a limited number of children and displaced persons."

As President of the Council of Ministers, Parri abolished the title of "Excellency," and was usually addressed as "Professor." After stormy interparty sessions, he took over the important and much-disputed portfolio of the Interior, which controls elections and all local government, appointed the Socialist Pietro Nenni to make plans for a constituent assembly to vote on keeping or rejecting the monarchy, and formed a Cabinet of three members of his Action Party, the same number from each of three others, one admiral, and four of the (Roman Catholic) Christian Democrats—a compromise to reconcile the last-named to a Socialist Minister of Education.

Premier Parri broke Italian precedent by giving the people a frank and dispassionate statement of the facts: "We are still far from the status of a great nation, which our history, importance, and numbers should give us. We must merit that status. It won't be given to us as a gift." The Italians, he said, must work to gain the trust of the Allies: "their trust means bread, coal, raw materials, and credits, . . . the very possibility of our livelihood. This trust will be the base of our ability to govern ourselves." In July Italy declared war on Japan. Despite the Premier's efforts, he was unable to get the Allies to terminate or even to make public the reputedly harsh and hampering terms of the 1943 armistice, under which Italy was still technically considered an enemy nation. It was against this background of uncertainty and of unemployment and the threat of famine that the first free assembly of Italian representatives (designated by their parties) in twenty years opened, in September 1945.

The Premier labored for five months to keep his six-party coalition government united. When the Liberal party, ranked among conservatives, became alarmed at Parri's resolute purge of officials who were tainted with Fascism, two Liberals and one Independent resigned from the coalition. Thus on November 24, 1945, Italy's third national government since the liberation of Rome in June 1944 was dissolved under the weight of conservative attacks when the Premier resigned. Parri warned of a renascence of Fascism and the threat of civil war, eight large Italian cities staged protest strikes, and the United States asked all the political parties to subordinate their own aims to the national interest. Although the Rightist politicians who had forced Parri's resignation waged a high-pressure campaign to replace him with Vittorio Orlando, eighty-five-year-old former Premier, who in 1935 had published a letter praising the Fascist aggression in Ethiopia, on December 4 Alcide de Gasperi, Christian Democratic leader, was elevated to the Premiership. His government retained the coalition of liberation, six parties sharing equally in the new cabinet. It was reported on December 14 that the new government had not altered the course of the Parri regime.

PERSONAL LIFE

Ferruccio Parri was described as a tall, lean man, spectacled and weather-beaten. He had thick silvery hair, and dark eyebrows and a mustache. The Premier was soft-voiced and, unlike most of his countrymen, he made few gestures when he spoke. He enjoyed mountain climbing when he has time, and he smokes about thirty cigarettes each day. Correspondents described Parri at first as "the harassed, poorly dressed professor in politics," but several months as Premier seem to have changed his appearance and personality to that of "a perfect aristocrat." His own description of himself is "an average man—just anybody ('*uomo de strada— uomo qualunque*')" "Thomas Healy, one of his most enthusiastic American admirers, writes, "I have read everything about Parri. He is Italy's great man and will become much greater. He has the qualifications—good sense, intellect, honesty, respect for his given word— and is a true democrat." Another American, Philip Hamburger of the *New Yorker*, called Parri "a man of pure intelligence. . . . It's wonderful to hear a man . . . use words like 'morality' and 'democracy' and know that they mean something in his mouth."

Parri authored several studies on the history of the Italian resistance. He died in Rome in 1981 at the age of 91. He was buried in Genoa.

FURTHER READING

N Y Sun plO J1 11 '45; *Nation* 161:59-61 J1 21 '45; *Newsweek* 26 :40 J1 2 '45; *Scholastic* 47 :10 O 15 '45 por; *Time* 46:34-6 Jl 2 '45 por

CHRIS PATTEN

Governor of Hong Kong

Born: May 12, 1944; Cleveleys, United Kingdom
Affiliation: Conservative; Crossbench

INTRODUCTION

On June 30, 1997 Britain will end an era as it hands over the last of its major colonies, Hong Kong, to the government of China, which has agreed to honor Hong Kong's autonomy and capitalist system for fifty years. Guiding the colony through the possibly treacherous period leading up to the transfer of power is Chris Patten, a battle-tested, twenty-five-year veteran of British politics who took over as governor of Hong Kong on July 9, 1992. In that capacity, Patten must perform the precarious balancing act of overseeing the implementation of self-government in Hong Kong without jeopardizing its future (and its $64 billion economy) by going so far that the Chinese feel threatened enough to renege on the agreement and enact hard-line policies.

To accept the assignment, Patten put his political future in Britain on hold, for the posting effectively removes him from British politics until after the next general election. A moderate Conservative, Patten has never been afraid to express his disagreements with other Tory leaders, particularly former prime minister Margaret Thatcher, who kept him in out-of-the-way posts before eventually naming him to the highly controversial position of minister of the environment. Although his outspoken nature may have hindered his career at times, his free thinking has made him one of the most important intellects in the Conservative party. Many in Britain believed that he was in line for the prime ministership, but while successfully directing the 1992 campaign to retain power for the Tories and Prime Minister John Major, Patten lost his own seat in the House of Commons. After weighing several relatively safe options that would have allowed him to stay involved in British politics, Patten chose to accept the heavy responsibility of leading Hong Kong. "This job struck me as one of the most interesting and imposing in the world," Patten explained to John Newhouse for a New Yorker (March 15, 1993) profile. "Closing the last chapter of [the] British empire, and the huge challenge that was posed. ... It was quite a leap, but politics isn't the whole of life. There is a lot of life beyond Westminster."

EARLY LIFE

Christopher Francis Patten was born on May 12, 1944 in Blackpool, England, the son of Francis Joseph Patten, a music publisher, and his wife, Joan McCarthy. He attended St. Benedict's School in Ealing and won a scholarship to Balliol College, at the University of Oxford, from which he graduated with a degree in modern history. While at Balliol, Patten showed little interest in politics. Instead, his extracurricular activities included editing *Mesopotamia,* a humor magazine, and writing updated versions of Aristophanes' plays for the Balliol Players. Upon his graduation, in 1965, Patten was awarded a Coolidge Travelling Scholarship to the United States, where he whetted his appetite for politics by working on the campaign staff of John V. Lindsay, who was running for mayor of New York City. Upon his return to Great Britain in 1966, he joined the Conservative Research Department, a traditional port of entry into the political world for bright young Tories.

LIFE'S WORK

After the Conservatives came to power under Edward Heath, in 1970, Patten spent two years as a junior official in the Cabinet Office, then accepted a post in the Home Office. From 1972 to 1974 he served as the personal assistant and political secretary to Lord Carrington, then the chairman of the Conservative party. When the Tories lost control of the government in the 1974 elections, Patten became, at the age of thirty, the youngest person ever to be named director of the Conservative Research Department, where his duties included serving as secretary of the shadow cabinet. He was removed from his post as shadow cabinet secretary four years later by the new Tory leader, Margaret Thatcher, who wanted to bring the Conservative Research Department under tighter control by the party leadership. Nevertheless, he wrote much of the 1979 Tory manifesto that served as the platform on which Thatcher ran in that year's general election. As the Conservatives routed the Labour party from office, Patten, who had lost his first bid for the House of Commons when he sought to represent the Lambeth Central constituency in 1974, was elected to his first term in Parliament, representing the constituency of Bath.

During his first two years in Parliament, Patten served as parliamentary private secretary to Norman St. John-Stevas, the Conservative leader of the House of Commons and the minister for the arts. St. John-Stevas was dismissed from his leadership positions in January 1981 as part of Thatcher's first cabinet reshuffling. According to most accounts, he was sacked largely because he had criticized the prime minister at the Conservative party conference a few months earlier. Patten, however, was not intimidated. In an opinion piece for the London *Times* (June 26, 1981), he denounced Thatcher's economic policies and advocated deficit spending on infrastructure and construction projects, a measure he believed would jump-start the faltering economy. Shortly before the 1981 Tory conference, Patten and other, likeminded young wets (moderate Conservatives) renewed the attack on Thatcherism with a pamphlet entitled *Changing* Gear. Denying charges that he was betraying his party, Patten argued in another article for the London *Times* (October 10, 1981) that "no one can reasonably expect blind or unthinking loyalty" and that the wets were the true heirs to the Tory heritage of pragmatism. He continued his assault on Thatcherism in *The Tory Case* (1983), a plea for pragmatic conservatism.

The prime minister rewarded Patten for his outspokenness by shunting him into no-win, out-of-the-way bureaucratic posts for the next several years. From June 1983 until September 1985, he was parliamentary under secretary of state in the Northern Ireland Office. After a one-year stint as minister of state in the Department of Education and Science, he was named minister of state for foreign and commonwealth affairs and minister of state for overseas development. According to the *Independent* (November 28, 1987), under Thatcher that political territory had become "something of a backwater, if not a career-killer," but Patten made the most of this limited opportunity by concentrating "with ruthless logic on a Thatcherite philosophy of aid which is designed to help viable projects in nations with sound economic policies." Although he has admitted that even humanitarian aid can help oppressive governments survive, Patten has asked, "How can you watch kids starve in order to teach governments a lesson?"

Patten apparently regained favor with Prime Minister Thatcher after her election to a third term, in 1987, for he was asked to write the "compassionate bits" of her speech to the annual Tory conference. In July 1989 Thatcher appointed him secretary of state for the environment, in hopes that he could change the prevalent public perception of Conservatives as antienvironment. A popular choice for the post, Patten had lofty goals. According to Geoffrey Lean, writing in the London *Observer* (September 30, 1990), he wanted "not just to change the government's environmental policy but lay the foundations of a new society." Patten began his tenure by abandoning the plans of his immediate predecessor, Nicholas Ridley, who had wanted to privatize the government's 240 National Nature Reserves and build a 4,800-home development at Foxley Wood, in the Hampshire countryside.

The centerpiece of Patten's environmental policy was to be a white paper released in the fall of 1990. At the 1989 Tory conference, Patten declared that the white paper would "set out our environmental agenda for the rest of this century." Patten's report was eagerly anticipated by environmentalists, especially since he had prevailed upon the prime minister herself to chair the cabinet committee charged with drafting it. Thatcher's presence on the committee gave Patten some much needed clout and led to some victories, although he lost on a number of important issues to the laissez-faire ministers, particularly the ministers of agriculture, trade and industry, and transport and energy.

One of Patten's major achievements was persuading the Thatcher government to accept the decision of the sixty-eight-nation conference on climate change, which was held in Noordwijk, the Netherlands, in November 1989, to set limits for carbon dioxide emissions by the end of the century.

Patten cited more efficient energy use and a greater reliance on natural gas and, possibly, nuclear energy as ways to meet the emissions goals. Over the vigorous objections of some cabinet members, Patten also convinced the Thatcher government of the need to phase out sludge dumping in the North Sea. He was less successful in his battle to prevent the construction of the M3 highway over the Twyford Down, near Winchester. The limited nature of his influence in the cabinet became clear when the 1990 budget was unveiled. It included none of the incentives (most of them in the form of taxes and penalties) desired by Patten to conserve energy and curb pollution.

When his long-awaited white paper on the environment was issued in September 1990, Patten was lambasted by the press for delivering far less than he had promised. As Geoffrey Lean, for one, pointed out, the report turned out to be "almost entirely bereft of new concrete proposals." Of the more than 350 actions and proposals, by Patten's count, listed in the document, Lean argued, "nearly half of these merely undertake to continue or extend existing policies or to urge others to act, and almost all the rest evade a commitment to action." In the end, Patten's critics gave him credit for good intentions but faulted him for failing to persuade the Thatcher government to take bolder actions. "Probably the most environment-friendly politician ever to sit in a British cabinet, he has seen his planned program fall apart," Lean wrote.

The most explosive issue Patten faced as environment minister was the infamous Thatcher poll tax. On the heels of her 1987 election victory, the prime minister proposed replacing property taxes with a "community charge" to be paid by all adults, and it fell upon Patten to administer the tax and make it acceptable to the British public. In early 1990 Britons poured into the streets of London, Bristol, and Southampton to protest the tax, which was to go into effect on April 1. Blaming the local district councils, most of which were controlled by Labour, for the excessive level of the taxes, Patten used his authority to limit the poll-tax assessments where they rose to what he called "horrendous" levels, but that did little to stem the outcry. "If I had to do it all over again," Patten joked in an interview with Craig R. Whitney for *The New York Times* (June 19, 1990), "I'd make sure to volunteer somebody else for the job." "It's been a very radical change," he added, "and a change of excessively heroic proportions, some would argue."

In the aftermath of the poll-tax controversy, Michael Heseltine, who had served as defense minister in the mid-1980s, challenged Thatcher for the leadership of the Conservative party. After the prime minister fell short of the required majority in balloting by Tory M.P.'s, she announced her resignation. Although a number of Tory M.P.'s urged Patten to run for party leader, he supported Foreign Secretary Douglas Hurd for the job. "He refused to contemplate the race as long as Hurd was a candidate," Edward Pearce reported in the *Manchester Guardian Weekly* (December 16, 1990).

"Given the certain doom of the Hurd campaign, this betokens an odd, chivalrous pulling back improbable in any stereotyped ambitious politician." When Tories voted on November 27, 1990, Chancellor of the Exchequer John Major triumphed over Heseltine and Hurd to become Tory leader and prime minister. Despite his support of Hurd, Patten was chosen by Major to serve as chairman of the Conservative party.

Given the poll tax, a deep recession, and changes in the Labour party, which had muted its militant rhetoric, most political observers and public opinion polls predicted that the Tories would lose the next election. Nevertheless, Patten and Major led their party to a stunning victory in the April 9, 1992 election, winning 336 seats in the House of Commons to Labour's 271. "M.P.'s questioned whether the droll, intellectually fastidious Mr. Patten would prove brutal enough or relish the rough and tumble," Robin Oakley, the political editor of the London *Times*, wrote in an analysis of the election published on April 25, 1992. "But he took to the necessary brutalities of party warfare with some relish."

While helping Major and the Tories win the war, Patten lost the battle in his constituency of Bath to the Liberal Democratic candidate, Donald Foster. When Patten met with Major on the morning after the election, the prime minister offered his campaign manager three choices: wait for a by-election to the House of Commons, accept elevation to the House of Lords, or become the last British governor of the crown colony of Hong Kong, which the Thatcher administration, under the terms of a 1984 accord with China, had agreed to turn over to the Beijing government on June 30, 1997. Patten felt it would be, in his words, "unseemly and reckless" for him to shift his political base and his loyalties from Bath to another constituency, and he thought he was "too young" to join the House of Lords; consequently, he chose the most perilous option: the governorship of Hong Kong.

Patten said later that the "idea of doing a proper job," rather than serving in some honorific post, appealed to him. And as a London *Times* (April 25, 1992) editorial pointed out, the post was "no sinecure": "It is no consolation prize to a loyal lieutenant who won his party's election but lost his own. It is no imperial perk for a grandee down on his luck. It is deadly serious and had better work. . . . Patten has bitten off a tough job with as great a possibility of failing as in his last." As governor of Hong Kong, Patten is obliged to adhere to the 1984 Sino-British Joint Declaration, in which China pledged to respect Hong Kong's autonomy and its capitalist system for fifty years after assuming control. In 1990 China drew up the Basic Law, a constitution to be observed in Hong Kong after 1997, and the British assented to the terms and agreed to help gradually implement the system until 1997. The Basic Law called for a sixty-seat Legislative Council (LegCo), with some of the legislators chosen by direct election, some by an election committee, and some by functional constituencies, such as groups of businesspersons or lawyers.

His top priority as governor, Patten said shortly after accepting the appointment, as quoted by Robin Oakley, would be "safeguarding the interests of the people of Hong Kong." In a press conference just prior to taking office, on July 9, 1992, he reiterated that intention, saying he would try to make Hong Kong's return to Chinese control "a bridge rather than a precipice." The foundation for that bridge lies in balancing the demands of Hong Kong's citizens for more self-government with the need to protect Hong Kong's economic viability (billions of dollars in British, Japanese, and American investment are at stake) as well as its commercial ties to the Chinese mainland. The people of Hong Kong fear that the Beijing regime, which massacred prodemocracy demonstrators in Tiananmen Square in 1989, will impose the iron hand of repression on Hong Kong after 1997. Conversely, the Communist government in Beijing is alarmed by the possibility that the self-government movement in the colony will not only inhibit their authority in Hong Kong but also encourage those seeking democracy in mainland China. China's fears were intensified by the results of the 1991 election in Hong Kong, in which the most vocal prodemocracy party, the United Democrats, won fourteen of the eighteen directly elected seats on the Legislative Council.

In the past, Britain's policy toward Hong Kong had been directed mainly by the sinologists in the Foreign Office, most of whom saw little to be gained by angering China, and the colonial governors had generally taken a nonconfrontational stance. The appointment of Patten marked a dramatic change in Britain's administration of Hong Kong. By naming an important British politician and close friend as governor and by giving him full authority to handle the job as he saw fit, John Major was showing the Chinese that he was serious about maintaining Hong Kong's autonomy. Patten's informal style—he does not wear the official uniform, which includes a plumed helmet, and he regularly takes walks in the city and talks to the people—was immediately popular with the local citizens. The Chinese government, however, was not sure what to make of the new British governor and eagerly awaited a concrete signal of the direction in which Patten intended to take Hong Kong.

That signal came on October 7, 1992, when Patten announced his plans for Hong Kong in the waning years of British rule and, in particular, the form that he intended the 1995 election to take. Although he did not violate the letter of the Basic Law, he interpreted all its gray areas as democratically as possible. For example, he intended to make the election committee an elected body and to open the functional constituencies to all workers, not just executives, thereby ensuring that all the members of LegCo would be elected, either directly or indirectly, by the people. The United Democrats took him to task for not going far enough, but their reaction was tame compared to the Beijing government's. The Chinese objected not only to Patten's reforms but also to his failure to confer with them, as had been customary, before announcing his program to the public. In response to the new plan, which was open to negotiation and required the approval of LegCo, top-level Chinese officials snubbed Patten during his visit to Beijing in late October. Insisting that they would not discuss Hong Kong until the proposal for reform was discarded (plans to resume talks were eventually announced, in April 1993), they threatened to default on debts for a planned new airport and later went so far as to imply that they would not honor any contracts after taking control of Hong Kong in 1997.

Although Patten remained popular among the people of Hong Kong, many business leaders were worried by China's threats, and the Hong Kong stock market fell sharply. Some wondered whether Patten was looking out for Hong Kong or for his own political future in Britain, for many felt that if Hong Kong became too democratic, the Chinese would throw out the entire system when they gained control. In an interview with Alex Brummer for the *Guardian* (January 23, 1993), Patten defended his position: "I don't think I could be forgiven if I treated the Joint Declaration as a sort of curtain behind which Britain could leave its last great colony with its conscience clean. I think honor is making sure that the Joint Declaration means what it says." The governor had intended to reach an agreement with China on the reforms before presenting them to LegCo for final approval, but after months of stalemated negotiations between Britain and China, Patten announced, in a two-hour speech to legislators on October 6, 1993, that he would present the plan to LegCo without China's consent if a compromise was not reached in the next few weeks. In that speech, Patten told legislators, "I can say that we can only be as bold as you. If we are not prepared to stand up for Hong Kong's way of life today, what chance of doing so tomorrow?"

Pattep's success in politics, according to the columnist "Bagehot" of the *Economist* (March 10, 1990), owes much to "his ability to see traps ahead and avoid them." Edward Pearce described Patten's political style as "open, self-mocking, interested in ideas, leg-pullingly derisive, but acknowledging the humanity of opponents." In its profile of Patten, the *Independent* described him as an "old-fashioned Tory, interested in community and obligation. He is, further, seriously Catholic, with a peculiarly Roman sense of service and of charity. This makes it difficult to label him either progressive or reactionary." Patten has let his religion guide, but not dictate, his official actions. He opposes capital punishment and abortion, and while minister of overseas development, he enacted a policy to end British aid that promoted or paid for abortions abroad. On the other hand, although he believes promiscuity (both homosexual and heterosexual) to be a sin, during his tenure at the Department of Education and Science, he was a proponent of sex education regardless of possible objections from children's parents.

PERSONAL LIFE

Lord Patten is now Chancellor of the University of Oxford. In 2005, he published his memoirs, *Not Quite the Diplomat: Home Truths about World Affairs*. He oversaw Pope Benedict XVI's visit to the United Kingdom in September 2010, and the same year he was also named one of Britain's most influential Roman Catholics.

Chris Patten has been married to Mary Lavender St. Leger, a lawyer, since September 11, 1971. The couple have three daughters, Kate, Laura, and Alice; In his spare time, Patten enjoys playing tennis, reading, and browsing in bookshops.

FURTHER READING

Independent pl2 N 28 '87; London *Observer* pl5 O 8 '89; Manchester *Guardian* W p6 D 16 '90; *New Yorker* 69:89+ Mr 15 '93; *Dod's Parliamentary Companion*, 1992; *Who's* Who, 1993

JOSEPH PAUL-BONCOUR

Prime Minister of France

Born: August 4, 1873
Died: March 28, 1972
Affiliation: Republican-Socialist Party

INTRODUCTION

"A gentleman of the old school with an oratorical manner," Joseph Paul-Boncour was sent to San Francisco in April 1945 as a member of the French delegation to the United Nations Conference on International Organization. For more than three decades he has been a familiar figure in French politics and international affairs. An outstanding lawyer, former Socialist Deputy and Premier, in 1940 he was leader of eighty former parliamentarians who voted in Vichy against plenary powers for Marshal Henri-Philippe Petain. Shortly after his appointment to the Consultative Assembly in November 1944, Paul-Boncour was made chairman of the commission for the study for France of the Dumbarton Oaks plan, a post for which he had been well prepared by his many years at Geneva as a delegate to the League of Nations Assembly.

EARLY LIFE

Born in Saint-Aignan, in the department of Loir-et-Cher, on August 4, 1873, Joseph Paul-Boncour is the son of middle-class parents. After making a brilliant university record and receiving the degree of Doctor of Laws, young Paul-Boncour was admitted to the Paris bar. He was to become one of France's most famous lawyers—his clients included notables like Queen Marie and her son Carol. His political career began in a sense when he served as private secretary to Waldeck-Rousseau during the latter's premiership, from 1899 to 1902, and later to Rene Viviani when the Socialist was Minister of Labor (1906-9). "In an atmosphere still charged with the emotion roused by the Dreyfus case, young Paul-Boncour became an opponent of militarism, nationalism, and reaction in all its forms"; it is a fight he has waged consistently throughout his career.

LIFE'S WORK

He was thirty-six when in 1909, as an independent Socialist and a follower of Paul Painleve, he left Viviani

Joseph Paul-Boncour.

to take a seat in the Chamber His success in that turbulent assembly was instantaneous, and two years later, in 1911, he became Minister of Labor himself in the Radical Monis Cabinet. This promising political career was interrupted a few years afterward by the First World War. As commander of an infantry battalion, the French statesman won the Croix de Guerre and was made a Chevalier of the Legion of Honor. But in spite of these honors, on his discharge from the Army he renewed his fight against militarism with greater ardor.

In 1919 he had joined the Socialist Party as fulfillment of a promise he made to the Socialist leader Jean Jaures a few months before the latter's assassination in 1914. His friends had warned him that by declaring himself on the side of the Socialists Paul-Boncour was throwing to the winds his chances of ministerial promotion. (Even at this point in his career it was realized that he was a potential Premier). Their warnings were not heeded, however; for twelve years, until he was fifty-eight, he was to remain as a member of the Socialist Party, pleading its cause in his "organ-like tones" in the Chamber and the tribunals. His socialist ideas, in the words of *The Columbia Encyclopedia,* "resemble those

of Jean Jaures; he expressed belief in a gradual evolution of democracy out of the superficial realm of politics into administrative, economic, and social realities. Thus his socialism was based on faith in the ideas of the French Revolution rather than in Marxian theories."

In November 1919 Paul-Boncour was returned to the Chamber as an independent Socialist. (For some time he was to be head of the Foreign Affairs Committee of the Chamber.) He at once joined Leon Blum, then chairman of the Socialist Party's executive board and a fellow Deputy, in the Left's struggle against the conservative, anti-Communist National bloc, which had won a decisive victory in the latest elections. Under the successive premierships of Clemenceau, Millerand, Briand, and Poincare, historians point out, France instituted a policy of anti-Sovietism (despite what Sumner Welles calls "an overwhelmingly 'Marxist' working class" in France), a foreign policy which alienated Britain, and a policy of force in dealing with Germany, which meant a "cordon sanitaire" around that country and, in 1922, a nine-month occupation of the Ruhr. (Briand is described as more of a moderate in his policies.) The Left, on the other hand, demanded in part, "a reversal in foreign policy which should lead to greater cooperation with Great Britain, recognition of the Russian Soviet Government, conciliation rather than force in dealing with Germany." A Leftist bloc was formed to defeat the Nationalists, and in the elections of 1924 the National bloc lost more than one hundred seats, while the parties of the Left were returned in a majority.

Paul-Boncour had been one of those returned as a Deputy, and for the next seven year's he remained in the Chamber. In the course of his years in the Assembly, while ministries rapidly succeeded each other, France suffered and recovered from a severe fiscal crisis. Her foreign policy underwent a change: she indicated a willingness to collaborate more closely with Britain; the Russian Government was recognized; cordial relations with Germany were established and a more friendly attitude toward the League of Nations was adopted.

A stanch supporter of the League of Nations himself, Paul-Boncour was sent to Geneva soon after its founding, as a member of the French delegation. His appointment came at a time when the League was trying to carry out one of the most pressing tasks imposed by its Covenant—that of world armament reduction. It was early realized, however, that the member Powers required further guaranties of security. The temporary commission appointed by the Assembly in 1921 to make general proposals for disarmament therefore drafted a treaty which provided for mutual security to be given in exchange for the reduction of armaments. Under this treaty groups of States could enter into regional agreements to support each other if attacked. At the same time they must agree to proportional disarmament. In case of war the Council of the League was to decide which State was the aggressor. This last point was criticized because it did not define aggression, nor give a clear-cut indication of the aggressor. The regional aspect of the pacts was criticized, too, on the grounds that detailed plans for reciprocal military support not only would not encourage disarmament but would authorize the grouping of friendly States against prospective enemies—the latter result in direct conflict with the essential spirit of the League. A month after the rejection of the proposed treaty by the States, a second plan was drawn up—the so-called "Geneva Protocol," adopted by the League Assembly in October 1924.

Paul-Boncour not only gave the Geneva Protocol his vigorous support in 1924, but the spirit of its plan has governed all of his subsequent crusades to establish a potent world organization. This protocol proposed unlimited arbitration among the fifty-four member States of the League; an aggressor was defined as any State resorting to war in violation of the League Covenant or the protocol itself; and provision was made, in accordance with the Covenant, for the use against an aggressor of the economic boycott and possible military action. The defeat of the protocol, F. Lee Benns shows, was due to the fact that most of the States felt in general that it increased the international obligations of the members, a factor which was not seen as desirable in Europe after the First World War.

In 1926 Paul-Boncour proposed the adoption of a resolution which would commit to the League Council the question of defining its own duties and the means of convening for action in case of war. This measure—also defeated—further provided that the permanent consulting commission of the League should consider the means necessary to securing the peace of Europe and, in case of war, the means of placing military aid at the command of the attacked nation.

The role which Paul-Boncour had played at Geneva made him the target of attacks from many members of the Socialist Party, who reproached him with having been at Geneva as the official delegate of a bourgeois government, and who tried to force on him the choice between this role and membership in their party.

Following the withdrawal of the Radical Socialist Party's support from the Government in 1928, Paul-Boncour resigned his appointment as head of the French delegation to the League and shortly afterward, in November 1931, resigned his membership in the Socialist Party. (In September he had been elected Senator.) Although the Socialists were bitter over his resignation, many admitted later that he had broken with them chiefly because the party's rigid discipline forbade taking office. After his resignation from the Leftist group, Paul-Boncour did not join another party, but remained an independent of the Left.

After the fall of the conservative Laval and Tardieu governments in 1932, the rise and fall of ministries in the succeeding years, says Benns, was "generally connected with some phase of the Republic's perplexing budgetary, fiscal, or economic problems." In June 1932 Paul-Boncour became Minister of War in the Herriot Government, and on December 19, 1932, he was asked to form a Cabinet, which lasted until the following January 31. (He also served as Foreign Minister.) His appointment as Premier was called inevitable by the London *Spectator*, which considered that he had "every qualification that French politics require." Without great wealth, powerful connections, or social position, Paul-Boncour had risen to the premiership largely because of his League activities. The *Spectator* predicted that he would be governed by the Geneva Protocol slogan: "Arbitration, Security, Disarmament"; the British *New Statesman and Nation* declared that Paul-Boncour was incapable of international thinking because he was "essentially national and patriotic in his outlook."

During the middle 'thirties France was divided between two bitter factions, the Right and the Left. "There was no France any more," says Sumner Welles; "there were two nations." In November 1933 Paul-Boncour was again named Foreign Minister, this time in the Left Government of Camille Chautemps. When this Government resigned in the middle of the Stavisky scandal, Paul-Boncour remained as Foreign Minister in the new Daladier Government, formed in January, which lasted less than ten days. He did not return to the Government again until 1936, when he became Minister without Portfolio in the Radical Socialist Government of Albert Sarraut.

This was the period which saw the beginning of Hitler's rearmament and the triumph of the Popular Front in Spain. In France itself the Popular Front of Leftist parties had been formed against the threat of fascism within the country, and Leon Blum became Premier (June 1936 to June 1937). During his second, much briefer term in office in early 1938, Paul-Boncour served as his Foreign Minister. That spring the sixty-five-year-old statesman resigned his presidency of the Socialist-Republican union, of which he had been head since its formation in 1935, and retired from public life, not returning to the service of his country until after the De Gaulle Government re-entered liberated France in September 1944. After the liberation of Paris Paul-Boncour was made chairman of the Committee of Twenty who selected the sixty members of the Paris Parliament to be sent to the Consultative Assembly. He himself has been a member since November 7, 1944. (During that month it was reported from Paris that an attempt had been made upon his life.)

French representatives had not been present at the Dumbarton Oaks conference nor the Yalta meeting of Roosevelt, Churchill, and Stalin. Foreign Minister Georges Bidault therefore appointed Paul-Boncour as chairman of the commission for the study of the proposed world peace organization. The commission was made up of prominent jurists, experts on international affairs, members of the Consultative Assembly, and officials of the Foreign Affairs Ministry. It was the conclusions drawn from this study that prompted France to announce she would not attend the San Francisco conference as one of the sponsoring powers, a refusal reported to be based on her request that the Dumbarton Oaks plan be considered as a basis for discussion and not as a definitely settled project.

Paul-Boncour's analysis of the proposals drawn up at Dumbarton Oaks was published in *Pour la victoire*, a New York French-language newspaper, on March 18, 1945. After expressing his relief at Churchill's assurance that the new peace organization would not be founded on a big-power dictatorship, he pointed out that the small nations, "and, we must admit, not without cause," have shown anxiety over some of the plans, "which are in conflict with the Atlantic Charter and which seem to strike a blow at international democracy. . . . I might say that peace guaranties will henceforth rest exclusively on agreement among the great powers. . . . It is a fact which one may regret, but it must be acknowledged that in the present state of affairs such common action is requisite to peace and that any decision against the wishes of a great power is unlikely to be carried out." He expressed the hope that the time would come when it would be possible to restrain any power, no matter how great. He

added: "Nevertheless, evolution is determined by certain principles laid down at the start. It is these. principles which give cause for anxiety." Another salient criticism from the man who fought so many years to try to make the League of Nations a potent and effective custodian of world peace is that some of the methods proposed by the Dumbarton Oaks plan are similar to those which the Holy Alliance of 1815 used to crush democracy, "which it is now sought to maintain."

Paul-Boncour's fear in this instance was that the great powers might develop a practice of using their vetoes with a misplaced reciprocity which would paralyze the peace organization. "It may be," Paul-Boncour continued, "that, in view of the chaotic conditions in which the cataclysm will leave the world, nothing else can be done. I sincerely believe this to be the case. . . . Then, by tenacious action, in which I can assure them they will have the support of France, let the small nations endeavor to instill democracy in the somewhat arbitrary institution we are trying to build. The great nations themselves will be forced to help them. Finally. . . let us make sure that democracy will be an irresistible force; that, after preserving it within the nations themselves, it will seem contradictory not to support it throughout the world."

The ex-Premier announced himself on his arrival at the San Francisco conference as an advocate of a permanent international armed force to avoid the fatal weakness of the old League—its "lack of punch." "Peace is impossible," he said, "without a permanent big stick which the Big Five must be ready to use at the first sign of aggression." Paul-Boncour was as good as his word. Following Bidault's return to France, Paul-Boncour became head of the French delegation and drew up the report outlining a practical working program for the United Nations military arrangements for keeping the peace. His report, presented in June 1945, provided "teeth" in its significant amendments of the original Dumbarton Oaks proposals and won the unanimous approval of the conference. The spokesman for France, a land twice the victim of German aggression within a quarter of a century, insisted that the new world organization's forces have "the right of passage." Failure to have this right frustrated France's efforts from 1935 to 1939 to save the peace. Belgium, the Netherlands, and Luxembourg had stood on their rights as sovereign powers not to permit or even to consider French "right of passage" through the strategic areas of their territory which Germany would have to invade to reach France. Similarly, Poland had refused such right of passage to the Soviet Army. Because of the stand of Paul-Boncour and his equally eloquent compatriot, Leon Bourgeois, the Charter specifically mentions this "right of passage."

Two world wars taught France that promise of help is not synonymous with assistance itself. Paul-Boncour succeeded in persuading the other nations that in addition to pledging national armed forces to the Security Council their "degree of preparation and general location" must be specifically mentioned and fixed. Of the nations, Australia, Canada, and Peru principally aided France in improving the Dumbarton Oaks draft. In the most dramatic commission meeting of the conference the French delegate supported with an impassioned address the proposal of Luis Quintanilla, former Mexican Ambassador to the Soviet Union, that Spain be barred from membership in the new world organization as long as it remained under Franco's Fascist domination. James Dunn, the American Assistant Secretary of State, joined in this statement to Madrid. It was approved by acclamation by the Commission on General Principles meeting in public session on June 19.

Summing up in his speech during the final plenary session, Paul-Boncour accented the differences between the old League and the new United Nations organization: "The Covenant of the League merely provided for the recommendation of military sanctions involving air, sea, or land forces, and consequently left the nations the option of backing out. . . . In the Charter sanctioned by this plenary assembly, the obligation of all member states to help in suppressing aggression is plainly established. An international force is to be formed and placed at the disposal of the Security Council in order to insure respect for its decisions. This force will consist of national contingents arranged for in advance by special agreements negotiated on the initiative of the Security Council. . . . If called upon to do so by the Security Council, the entire force will march against a State convicted of aggression, in accordance with the provisions for enforcement as laid down for the Security Council." "The United Nations, and more especially the great nations with a permanent seat on the Council, must remain truly united," he further declared. "The whole efficacy of the Charter depends on this unity. In the hour when immense hope rises from our hearts, let us swear to remain faithful in peace to this unity which was our strength in war."

PERSONAL LIFE

Paul-Boncour was the author of several works on government and law. Pictures show him to be lion-headed and somewhat stoop-shouldered. His personality was described as likable and magnetic, and he was said to have no prejudices. He maintained a country home in his native Loir-et-Cher.

One of his favorite forms of amusement was attending the Comedie Frangaise; according to Elsa Maxwell, this theater was robbed of a star when Paul-Boncour chose the law and politics for his profession.

Paul-Boncour died in Paris in March 1972.

FURTHER READING

Free France 7:461 My 1 '45 por; *Liv Age* 343 :500-l F '33; *International Who's Who*, 1942; *Qui etes-vous?* 1924; *Who's Who*, 1945

SHIMON PERES
Israeli Politician

Born: August 2, 1923; Wiszniew, Poland
Affiliation: Mapai; Rafi; Labor; Kadima

INTRODUCTION

Shimon Peres, who has been a dominant figure in Israeli politics, has dedicated his life both to maintaining his country's national security and to upholding the ideals of its democratic socialist founders. An activist even as a youth, during the 1950s Peres served as minister of defense under Israel's first prime minister, David Ben-Gurion, a position in which he distinguished himself by developing Israel's weapons and defense industries. By the early 1970s he, along with Yitzhak Rabin, Menachem Begin, Yitzhak Shamir, and other members of the younger generation of Israeli statesmen, was at the forefront of politics, and in 1977 he was named chairman of the Labor Party, a position that made him the party's candidate for prime minister. Although he failed

Shimon Peres.

to lead Labor to a clear-cut victory in any of the elections held during his fifteen-year-long tenure as party leader, in 1984 Labor and Likud entered into a power-sharing arrangement according to which Peres served as prime minister from 1984 until 1986. In 1992, after Peres lost the party chairmanship to his long-time rival Yitzhak Rabin, Labor recaptured a majority of seats in the Knesset, the Israeli parliament, and Peres was named foreign minister.

Although at one time he was considered hawkish on defense issues, Peres has long been committed to a peaceful, negotiated settlement of Israel's long-standing conflict with its Arab neighbors and Palestinian population, and during the late 1980s he formulated a plan for implementing Israeli withdrawal from the West Bank and the Gaza Strip, territories occupied by Israel since the Six-Day War, in 1967 and for granting limited self-rule to the Palestinians. Most significant, he played a key role in the negotiations that led to the historic peace accord endorsed by Israel and the PLO in September 1993. For his efforts to forge a lasting peace in the

Middle East, Peres, together with the PLO chairman, Yasir Arafat, and the Israeli prime minister, Yitzhak Rabin, was awarded the 1994 Nobel Prize for Peace.

EARLY LIFE

Shimon Peres was born on August 16, 1923, in a small village in what was then Poland and is now Belarus. His parents, Yitzhak and Sarah Persky, were nonreligious Jews who embraced Zionist ideals, and according to one source Shimon was involved in the Zionist youth movement in Poland. In 1931 his father immigrated to Palestine, and two years later the rest of his family joined him. On settling in Palestine, Peres attended the Balfour primary school in Tel Aviv, where he was a good student. As he grew older he flourished in his studies, becoming an accomplished writer, rhetorician, and speaker. He also continued his involvement in Zionist youth organizations, including Hano'ar Ha'oved (Working Youth). He received a scholarship to the Ben Shemen Agricultural School, where he was sent by the Hano'ar Ha'oved to continue his education and to acquire the agricultural skills so highly valued by Palestine's Jewish settlers. Peres also found time to read poetry and study the works of Karl Marx.

LIFE'S WORK

While at Ben Shemen, Peres came under the influence of Berl Katznelson, an intellectual in the Jewish labor movement. In his book *From These Men: Seven Founders of the State of Israel* (1979), Peres described his relationship with his mentor and discussed his ideological development: "[Katznelson] was the cornerstone of the Labor movement; he showed the way and he was the fountain from which flowed the original and constructive spirit of the Labor movement in our country." Katznelson's lectures, Peres wrote, "left an indelible impression on many of us. They implanted in us a negative attitude toward the Communist revolution and Marxist dialectic, an attitude more interested in the values of the human race than in the study of Soviet Russian statistics." Also during high school, Peres joined the Haganah, the underground Jewish self-defense organization, which would later play a crucial role in Israel's winning the Arab-Israeli War of 1948 (also known as the Israeli War of Independence).

After leaving Ben Shemen in 1941, Peres continued his training at Kibbutz Geva and then went on to found Kibbutz Alumot, in the Jordan Valley, of which he was elected secretary. He devoted most of his energy, though, to his work with Hano'ar Ha'oved. "I traveled around the organization's farms, persuading the young people to lend their support to the unity of the movement," he recounted in *From These Men.* During this period he also joined the Mapai, the Israel Worker's Party, then the dominant political party in Palestine. According to Matti Golan, the author of *The Road to Peace: A Biography of Shimon Peres* (1989), "He was seen as a pusher in those early days, both in the field of action and in the realm of ideas. . . . He loved public affairs, felt driven to achievement, and sought positions which enabled him to implement his ideas."

In 1946 Peres attended the twenty-second World Zionist Congress in Switzerland, at which he proved himself to be a firm supporter of David Ben-Gurion, who was already a legendary figure in the Zionist movement and who was to become the first prime minister of Israel. In 1947, at the bequest of another key Israeli politician, Levi Eshkol, Peres became the director of manpower in the Haganah, in the Tel Aviv offices of the General Staff. Peres's duties included weapons procurement, which soon became his area of specialization. Not long after Ben-Gurion declared Israel a sovereign state, on May 15,1948, Peres, along with the other members of the Haganah, was sworn in as a member of the Israel Defense Forces. During the War of Independence that followed, Peres served as the head of the defense ministry's naval department. Once the war had ended, in 1949, Prime Minister Ben-Gurion asked Peres to go to the United States as the head of a mission to continue to acquire arms for Israel. Because of the United States embargo on arms sales at that time, this task was an especially difficult one. Nevertheless, Peres accomplished his assignment. During this period he also attended the New School for Social Research and New York University, both in New York City, and Harvard University, in Cambridge, Massachusetts.

In early 1952, after returning to Israel, Peres was appointed deputy director-general of the ministry of defense, and several months later he was promoted to director-general. During his seven years in that position, Peres was responsible for developing Israel's government-owned weapons industry. He devoted special attention to nuclear research and weapons procurement, and, in the process, he became known for both his formidable negotiating skills and his conviction that Israel's survival depended on its technological development. One of his most notable accomplishments in that post was his success in forging a relationship between

Israel and France at a time when Israel had few dependable allies. Israel's friendship with France, which supplied the newly independent country with much-needed weapons, was crucial to its success in capturing the Sinai Peninsula from Egypt in 1956. France remained Israel's principal supplier of arms for the next two decades. Equally significant, Peres conducted secret negotiations with West Germany on Israel's behalf in 1957, despite the fact that at that time diplomatic relations between the two countries did not exist. According to the *Toronto Globe & Mail* (September 13,1986), the German-Israeli relationship proved to be important to Israel during the Six-Day War, by which time France had greatly reduced its commitment to Israel's defense, As a result of these achievements, Peres was regarded as a member of the "Young Mapai," a group that consisted of influential members of the younger generation of Israeli politicians.

Peres entered a new phase of his career in 1959, when he ran for and was elected to a seat in the Knesset, as a member of the Mapai Party. The party itself continued its domination of Israeli politics, with the result that Ben-Gurion remained prime minister. Ben-Gurion chose as his deputy minister of defense Peres, who held the position until 1965. One of the more notable events of his tenure was his visit to the United States in 1962, when Peres helped persuade the Kennedy administration to sell Israel its Hawk antiaircraft missile system. The purchase marked the beginning of a new phase in Israel's relationship with the United States, which after 1967 became Israel's main supplier of arms.

By the mid-1960s a rift had developed between David Ben-Gurion and several other key Israeli politicians, including Levi Eshkol, who became prime minister following Ben-Gurion's resignation from that post in 1963. Two years later the conflict between Ben-Gurion and Eshkol came to a head, with Eshkol declaring that Ben-Gurion's supporters had no place in the government. As a result, Ben-Gurion resigned from the Mapai Party and formed one of his own—Rafi, or the Worker's List Party. He was joined by a number of his supporters, including Shimon Peres, who became the newly formed party's secretary general. Within a few years, though, it became clear that Rafi was unlikely to win widespread popular support, and in 1968 it merged with other pro-labor groups (including the Mapai Party) to form the Israel Labor Party, of which Peres became deputy secretary general. In 1969 Peres was appointed to the cabinet of the new prime minister, Golda Meir. Over the following four years, he held a variety of cabinet portfolios, including immigration absorption (1969), transport and communications (1970-74), and information (1974); he also served as minister without portfolio with responsibility for economic development in the occupied territories.

Labor's fortunes—as well as those of Peres—changed dramatically after the Yom Kippur War of 1973. Israel proved to be profoundly ill-prepared to defend itself against its hostile Arab neighbors, and the Israeli public placed the blame squarely on the Labor-led government. Israelis' dissatisfaction with the government was compounded by rising inflation and generally poor economic conditions. Finally, in April 1974, continued public criticism of the government prompted Golda Meir to resign from the prime ministership, a move that required new elections to be held. Peres, who was then involved in a power struggle with Yitzhak Rabin—a military hero who, although he only recently entered into domestic politics, was extremely popular among the electorate—lost the party chairmanship to Rabin, who was elected the new Israeli prime minister in the 1974 elections. In a gesture of conciliation, Rabin appointed Peres minister of defense. During his three years in that position, Peres concentrated his efforts on reinvigorating the Israeli defense forces.

The rivalry between Peres and Rabin developed into a much-publicized feud for a period during the 1970s. According to the historian Howard Sa-char, writing in his book A *History of Israel*, their inability to work together harmoniously "led to a near paralysis of executive responsibility. . . . The animus between [then-Prime Minister Rabin] and Peres became all but uncontrollable, intruding in ministerial discussions, even undermining the line of command in the defense establishment." Despite their difficulty in getting along, the two men put aside their differences and worked together on the dramatic rescue of the hijacked airline passengers in Entebbe, Uganda, in 1976. Peres was also involved in the negotiations that resulted in the 1975 disengagement agreement between Israel and Egypt.

In January 1977 Peres challenged Yitzhak Rabin for the chairmanship of the Labor Party, and for a second time he lost his bid to defeat his rival. Rabin went on to lead Labor to victory in the general elections, but several months later, following revelations that his wife had maintained a foreign bank account, a violation of Israeli law, he was forced to resign as both prime minister and party chairman. Rabin's indiscretion in turn cleared

the way for Peres's election as Labor Party chairman in June 1977. If Labor had triumphed in the elections later that year, Peres would have become prime minister. But voters, frustrated by the continued high rate of inflation and lacking confidence in Labor's ability to defend the country against its enemies, gave the right-wing Likud Party, headed by Menachem Begin, the right to lead the country. Likud went on to dominate Israeli politics for the next seven years, a period during which Peres served as leader of the opposition.

Although he lacked a portfolio, Peres remained active on the foreign-policy front during the late 1970s, and in the process he succeeded in cultivating an image as a statesman. Traveling frequently outside Israel, he met with Egyptian president Anwar Sadat and leaders of both communist and noncommunist nations. In 1978 he supported the Camp David agreement, which Begin worked out with Sadat. Whereas Peres had long been regarded as a hawk on defense issues, when compared to members of the Likud he was decidedly dovish, for he was markedly more open to the idea of reaching a negotiated settlement with Israel's Arab neighbors and its Palestinian population. Peres also worked hard to breathe new life into the party so as to increase its appeal among the Israeli electorate.

The resignation of Menachem Begin in 1983 provided Labor with an opportunity to recapture its control of the government, and in fact Peres succeeded in leading Labor to a narrow victory over Likud, with Labor winning forty-four seats in the Knesset and Likud taking forty-one. Nevertheless, Peres was unable to form a government, with the result that the two parties came up with a novel power-sharing arrangement: they agreed to form a National Unity government, in which cabinet posts would be evenly divided between them and the leader of each would serve half a term as prime minister. Under this arrangement, Peres served as prime minister of Israel from 1984 until 1986.

According to many political observers, Peres was an unusually effective prime minister. His greatest achievement was his deft handling of the economic crisis in which Israel was mired. "We have to turn first of all to ourselves, control our standard of living, reduce our expenses, and make Israel self-reliant from an economic point of view," he declared soon after taking office, as quoted in Time (October 1,1984). In addition to devaluing the shekel, he cut government spending, persuaded Israel's dominant labor federation to cut real wages, and convinced employers to freeze prices. The net result of these initiatives was that inflation dropped from an annual rate of about 445 percent (some sources give a much higher rate) in 1984 to 25 percent two years later. "Israel's success in halting inflation, with virtually no increase in unemployment, is almost unprecedented," Stanley Fischer, an economics professor at the Massachusetts Institute of Technology, told Thomas L. Friedman of *The New York Times* (October 13, 1986). "Argentina and Brazil both tried to do it at the same time as Israel, with nowhere near the same results."

Another of Peres's achievements as prime minister was his success in coordinating Israel's withdrawal from Lebanon, which the country had invaded in 1982. Its continued presence there was unpopular not only within the international community but also among Israelis. Peres also developed important diplomatic relationships. For instance, he made an official visit to Morocco, where he met with King Hassan II, an event that made him the first Israeli prime minister to be invited to an Arab country other than Egypt. He also met with President Hosni Mubarak of Egypt.

The principal disappointment of Peres's term as prime minister, according to many observers, was his failure to make any significant progress in the effort to resolve the Arab-Israeli conflict. A major stumbling block to any resolution of the conflict, though, was that Labor and Likud were fundamentally divided on how to negotiate a peace settlement. While Peres and other members of the Labor Party were willing to consider the possibility of turning over to Jordan the administration of the occupied territories in return for guarantees of Israel's security, Likud was adamantly opposed to relinquishing territory.

Despite the near impossibility of the two parties' seeing eye to eye on the issue, Peres received the most criticism for the government's failure to advance the peace process. "When it comes to changing the reality, Peres did nothing—for that you need courage," a left-wing member of parliament complained to Thomas Friedman. "I told him many times: 'With the present language of politics—the language of Golda Meir and Menachem Begin—you did the best you could. But you added nothing of your own—like recognizing the Palestinians' right to self-determination.' Peres did nothing to moderate the basic Israeli attitudes toward the West Bank or the Palestinian problems." Notwithstanding this failure, when Peres turned over the prime minister-ship to Yitzhak Shamir in October 1986 according to the previously agreed upon power-sharing arrangement, he ended what Abraham Rabinovich, writing in the Toronto *Globe & Mail* (September 13,1986), called "one of the most successful terms of office ever served by an Israeli prime minster." Also according to the two parties' agreement, Peres at the same time became vice premier and foreign minister.

In the campaign that preceded the 1988 elections, Peres and the Labor Party adopted a strategy that many observers considered to be risky: the party promised to resolve the conflict with the Palestinians—which had worsened considerably since late 1987, when the *intifada,* or uprising, erupted in the occupied territories—by trading land for peace. While the Israeli electorate was anxious to conclude a negotiated settlement with the Palestinians, in the end it was persuaded by Likud's argument that a dovish Labor-led government could not be trusted to protect Israel's security interests, and Likud scored a razor-thin victory over Labor, winning forty Knesset seats to Labor's thirty-nine. The outcome of the election left the two parties with little choice but to form another coalition government, though unlike the arrangement devised in 1984, Yitzhak Shamir was to serve as prime minister for the full four-year term. Peres, in addition to remaining leader of the opposition, served as vice-premier and finance minister.

By the early 1990s Israeli public opinion in regard to the Palestinian problem had changed dramatically. With the *intifada* continuing unabated, Israelis were growing increasingly dissatisfied with Likud's apparent unwillingness to advance the peace process. Moreover, the 1991 Persian Gulf war changed the geopolitics of the region in such a way that the United States had begun to exert considerable pressure on Israel to make peace with its Arab neighbors and the Palestinians. "We had reached one of those rare critical junctures," Peres wrote in *The New Middle East* (1993), "that enable discerning statesmen to make a quantum leap in their thinking—and perhaps turn the tide of history." Although officially out of power, during this period Peres directed a series of high-level meetings with PLO officials, meetings that were conducted in secrecy because all contact between Israelis and members of the PLO was prohibited by Israeli law.

Meanwhile, in 1992, the Labor Party elected Yitzhak Rabin as its new chairman, marking the end of Peres's fifteen-year-long leadership of the party. Rabin had emerged as a more attractive candidate for prime minister than Peres at least partly because of his reputation as a military hero: under his leadership, it was widely thought, Israel's national security would not be jeopardized. Following Rabin's election as prime minister in June of that year, Peres was named foreign minister.

According to an article in the *National Review* (March 7, 1994) that chronicled the secret PLO-Israeli negotiations that were conducted in the early 1990s, Peres spent the months following the 1992 election leading high-level discussions with the PLO. Then, in Oslo in the summer of 1993, an agreement between the two parties was reached, though it was not made public at that time. According to Mark Perry, writing in *A Fire in Zion* (1994), in August 1993 Peres secretly held an eight-hour telephone conversation with Yasir Arafat, and he later met with PLO officials to initial the "Declaration of Principles on Interim Self-Government Arrangements." This agreement was formally endorsed by both Israel and the PLO on September 13, 1993, on an occasion of state in Washington, D.C. Peres has provided his own vision of a land in which Arabs and Jews peacefully coexist in his book *The New Middle East* (1993), which he wrote with the Israeli political scientist Arye Naor and which one critic described as a "textbook lesson in how a small nation negotiates in the changed world after the Cold War, when even larger nations have given up some of their sovereignty."

On October 14, 1994 Shimon Peres, Yitzhak Rabin, and Yasir Arafat were jointly awarded the Nobel Prize for Peace. The announcement of the award was to some extent overshadowed by continuing violence in Israel, and when it was presented to the recipients, on December 10, 1994, the peace process was at a standstill. Nevertheless, each of the recipients of the prize remained committed to implementing the hard-won agreements. "There was a time," Shimon Peres declared on accepting the prize, "when war was fought for lack of choice;

today it is peace that is the 'no choice' for all of us." A little less than a year later, the tortuous negotiations between the Israeli government and the PLO, led by Peres and Arafat respectively, had resulted in an important new agreement. Initialed by the two men on September 24, 1995, the accord outlined, in a step-by-step fashion, the transfer of power to the Palestinians in the West Bank. (The two sides had earlier reached an agreement on Palestinian self-rule in Gaza and the town of Jericho.)

In 2007, Peres was elected President of the State of Israel, a ceremonial head of state position. He resigned in 2013.

PERSONAL LIFE

Shimon Peres married the former Sonia Gelman on May 1, 1945. They have a daughter, Zvia, two sons, Jonathan and Nechemia, and numerous grandchildren. Sonia died of heart failure in 2011, in their apartment in Tel Aviv.

In addition to the Nobel Prize, Peres has received a number of awards, including the French Legion of Honor. A poised, handsome man with a receding hairline and a cleft chin, Peres is not considered to be a charismatic politician. "Deep in my heart," he has said, "I'm convinced that I'm incorrigibly shy, but I must reconcile myself to the fact that many claim that I'm also a man who tried to leap forward—almost an arrogant man."

FURTHER READING

The New York Times A p2 O 13 '86 por; A pl2 S 19 '93; *Nat R* p28+ Mr 7 '94; *Toronto Globe & Mail* D p3 S 13 '86 por; Golan, Matti. *The Road to Peace: A Biography of Shimon Peres* (1989); *Political Leaders of the Contemporary Middle East and North Africa* (1990); *International Who's Who* 1994-95

MARCOS PÉREZ JIMÉNEZ
President of Venezuela

Born: April 25, 1914; Tachira, Venezuela
Died: September 20, 2001; Madrid, Spain

INTRODUCTION

The President of Venezuela, a country containing rich sources of oil and iron ore, was Colonel Marcos Pérez Jiménez, who ruled as provisional president from

December 1952 to April 1953, and as constitutional President until 1958. A career soldier, Pérez Jiménez rose to military leadership during the 1945 revolution (when President Medina Angarita was deposed), and was one of the Army officers who ousted the Accion Democratica government in 1948, establishing military rule under a three-man junta. As a member of the triumvirate, Colonel Pérez Jiménez was Minister of Defense.

Since the 1948 coup d'etat the government has spent two billion dollars on national improvements. "Dedication Week" was celebrated in December 1953, after which the new public works began operating. In March 1954 Caracas, the capital of Venezuela, was the site of the Tenth Inter-American Conference.

The city's population has grown during the past ten years (since oil was discovered within its boundaries) from 300,000 to nearly 1,000,000. The royalties from oil and iron ore have made it possible to finance many of the public works programs introduced by President Pérez Jiménez.

"The new prosperity," reports Life *(September 13, 1954) "has enabled many Venezuelan workers, whose average wages have doubled in ten years, to replace their rope-soled sandals with shoes, buy canned goods in new supermarkets and satisfy a craving for chicken and ice cream... The dictatorial rule of 'P.J.', as President Pérez Jiménez is referred to by Americans, has some definite advantages."*

EARLY LIFE

Marcos Pérez Jiménez was born on April 25, 1914 in the state of Tachira, Venezuela, the son of Juan Pérez Bustamente and the former Adela Jiménez. He was educated at the Colegio Gremios Unidos in Cucuta, Colombia; Escuela Militar de Caracas in Venezuela (comparable to West Point); and the Superior War School in Lima, Peru. He was commissioned a second lieutenant in the Venezuelan Army in 1934. The young officer served with the technical service at Maracay, and later was a member of the faculty of Escuela Militar.

LIFE'S WORK

During the presidency of General Isaias Medina Angarita (1941-1945), Captain Pérez Jiménez became section chief of the general staff, and received the rank of lieutenant colonel. Dissatisfied with the Medina Angarita regime, the Accion Democratica party and several young army officers, including Pérez Jiménez, joined in a *coup d'etat,* overthrowing the government on October 18, 1945. They installed Romulo Betancourt, a leader of Accion Democratica, as provisional president. Pérez Jiménez became Army Chief of Staff.

Professor Robert J. Alexander (New York *Herald Tribune,* December 30, 1952) wrote that one of

Latin America's most liberal constitutions was enacted in 1947. It provided for popular election of the President and legislature, as well as universal suffrage. Romulo Gallegos Freire, well-known novelist, was elected President under this constitution in December 1947. *The New York Times* (November 14, 1950) commented that this was Venezuela's first democratic election. During its 124-year history, virtually every government has taken office by military *coup* and remained in power as long as the dominant faction in the Army supported it.

The Accion Democratica government began a program of economic development. Most observers believed the new government was attempting to institute democratic rule, although *The New York Times* (December 3, 1952) commented that the Gallegos regime "proved inefficient, harsh and on the dictatorial side." *Fortune* (May 1949) noted: "The program of Accion Democratica imperiled the status of the military. It became clearer and clearer to the young officers that the government recognized for them . . . only a mundane everyday mission to support the elected government. Moreover there were intimate links between Army factions and conservative merchants and landowners who were duly horrified at the developing social revolution."

Gallegos was overthrown on November 24, 1948 in a military *coup* led by Lieutenant Colonel Carlos Delago Chalbaud, the Minister of Defense. Delago Chalbaud established a three-man junta with Lieutenant Colonel Luis Felipe Llovera Paez and Pérez Jiménez, who became the new Minister of Defense. The Accion Democratica party was outlawed on December 9, 1948. On January 21, 1949 the United States granted diplomatic recognition to the military regime but said the *de facto* recognition "does not imply any judgment whatsoever as to the domestic policy" of Venezuela.

Delgado Chalbaud was assassinated on November 13, 1950. Dr. German Suarez Flamerich, a civilian, succeeded him, but according to Herbert L. Matthews (*The New York Times,* April 28, 1951), Pérez Jiménez was "the real power in Venezuela." He was credited with sponsoring the long promised "electoral statute" that provided for a constituent assembly to determine a new form of government, and the organization of a pro-junta political party, Frente Electoral Independiente (F.E.I.). In 1951 Pérez Jiménez received the military rank of colonel.

Ex-Venezuelan Ambassador to the United States, Dr. Antonio Martin Araujo, a member of the original junta Cabinet, charged in *The New York Times* interview

November 22, 1952 that the junta conducted a "reign of terror/' assassinated army officers and others opposed to the government, and jailed "approximately 4,000 citizens, including women and children."

These charges were vigorously denied by the Venezuelan Ambassador to the United States, Cesar Gonzalez, who has said: "The present constitutional government respects human rights."

An election was held on November 30, 1952. *Time* (December 8, 1952) reported that 2,000,000 Venezuelan voters went to the polls from "jungle clearings and Caracas villas." Early returns gave the lead to a minority party Union Republicana Democratica (U.R.D.). *The New York Times* (December 3, 1952) reported that censorship obscured election news in Venezuela until December 2, when the Supreme Electoral Council said that of 1,193,240 votes counted F.E.I. had 570,123, the U.R.D., 473,880, and Copei (Christian Socialists), 138,003.

Sam Pope Brewer of *The New York Times* reported on January 28, 1953 that the opposition U.R.D. polled 1,000,000 votes to 350,000 each for the pro-government candidates and the Copei party. Pérez Jiménez and his group "issued figures that would show victory for the government's backers . . . [and] Dr. Jovito Villalba and six other U.R.D. leaders were forced to leave Venezuela."

The junta presented its resignation to the Army on December 2, 1952, and ranking Army officers named Colonel Pérez Jiménez provisional President. The national Constituent Assembly confirmed him in that position on January 9, 1953, pending the re-establishment of a "constitutional government."

The Assembly approved a new constitution which was signed by the President and promulgated on April 15, 1953. It provides for the direct election of a President and members of the lower house of Congress and contains a Bill of Rights. Eight transistory measures were appended to the main text, one of which empowered the Constituent Assembly to form a new government for the initial five-year constitutional period beginning April 19, 1953. Accordingly, the Constituent Assembly elected Pérez Jiménez as constitutional President on April 17, 1953. With the installation of the Congreso Nacional on April 19, the Constituent Assembly was dissolved.

On January 20, 1953 the Associated Press reported that Venezuela had imposed tight censorship on outgoing news. Pérez Jiménez has stated that censorship does not exist to defend the government's political actions but "to protect against any abuse of freedom of the press which incites against the interests of the nation" (*The New York Times,* December 14, 1953).

During the years of military regime, Venezuela has spent two billion dollars on government improvements. These were opened to the public during "Dedication Week" early in December 1953. *Time* (December 14, 1953) described the superhighway from Caracas to the sea as "Venezuela's most daring piece of engineering," and "more expensive per mile than any other in the world."

Other completed projects were apartment houses that replaced forty-five blocks of Caracas slums, 107 water systems, thirty-nine electric plants, sixty-three schools, thirty-two hospitals and clinics, and an underground station that houses 600 buses. In Caracas, Centro Bolivar (comparable to Rockefeller Center), Hotel Tamanaco, a 400-room hotel, and the "finest officers' club in the world" were built.

Sydney Gruson (*The New York Times,* December 18, 1953) wrote that "oil is the backbone of the booming Venezuelan economy; it supplies approximately 65 per cent of the government's annual revenues of about $700,000,000; [this is] 98 per cent of the Central Bank's foreign exchange requirements and 90 per cent of the country's total foreign exchange needs." There is a fifty-fifty split of oil profits between the government and the oil companies. About 73.6 per cent of the total oil imported to the United States comes from Venezuela. In turn, 72 percent of Venezuela's imports, all paid in cash, are from the United States.

In an effort to develop other industries, Venezuela has encouraged U.S. Steel's endeavors to mine iron ore. On January 9, 1954 U.S. Steel's first shipment of iron ore was transported through a newly constructed channel designed to let iron ore ships reach mines on the Orinoco River.

Bethlehem Steel began its operations in 1941, building rail lines and river ports. A law requires that 75% of the workers in all mines be native Venezuelans. According to *Life* (September 13, 1954), the United States now has its biggest private foreign investment ($2 billion) in Venezuela, and one of its largest overseas civilian colonies (23,000).

After it was announced that the Tenth Inter-American Conference would take place in Caracas in March 1954, President Jose Figueres Ferrer of Costa Rica declared that his country would not be represented at the conference because of the lack of civil rights in Venezuela. All of the other twenty nations, however, were represented.

At the conference, the United States sponsored a resolution which was adopted by a 17 to 1 vote (Guatemala against, Argentina and Mexico abstaining) which declared that the "control of the political institutions of any American state by the international Communist movement" was "a threat to the sovereignty and political independence of the American states" and would call for "consultation and appropriate action in accordance with existing treaties."

Following massive protests and demonstrations in support for a democratic reform to take place in the government, Perez was deposed in a coup perpetrated by disgruntled sectors within the Armed Forces of Venezuela in January 1958. Perez was exiled to Dominican Republic, then Miami, and afterward went on to settle in Spain. He died in Madrid on September 20, 2001.

PERSONAL LIFE

Pérez Jiménez married Flor Maria Chalbaud; they have three children. The President is a corresponding member of the International Institute of American Ideals, and an honorary lieutenant colonel of Ecuador. He has received the General Urdaneta Medal, Military Order of Ayacucho, Grand Cross Condor de los Andes (Bolivia),

Orden Militar de Qyacucho (Peru), Grand Cross of Order del Sol (Peru), National Honor al Merito (Haiti), Orden del Quetzal (Guatemala), Medalla Abdon Calderon (Ecuador), Grand Cross of Leon Nederlandes, Legion of Honor (France), and Grand Cross, Order of Leopold II (Belgium).

John Crosby (New York *Herald Tribune*, December 11, 1953) who visited Venezuela during "Dedication Week" described the President as "a hard working, very capable and benevolent despot" and commented that almost everything about Venezuela was "faintly incredible."

President Pérez Jiménez has stated: "Venezuela . . . suffers from a shortage of capital and . . . technical assistance, necessary factors for the development of its natural riches and for industrialization. . . . Thus, my country can do no less than look with satisfaction upon the inflow of foreign capital . . . after a short time Venezuela will be able to finance the greater part of its own development with resources derived from the national income" *(US. News & World Report,* June 26, 1953).

FURTHER READING
Life 37: 122+ S 13 '54 por; *International Who's Who,* 1953; *Who's Who in Latin America* (1951); *World Biography* (1954)

JUAN (DOMINGO) PERÓN (SOSA)
President of Argentina

Born: October 8, 1895; Lobos, Buenos Aires, Argentina
Died: July 1, 1974; Olivos, Buenos Aires, Argentina
Group Affiliation: Justicialist Party

INTRODUCTION
In one of the most remarkable political comebacks in modern history, Argentine strongman Juan Perón returned from exile in 1973 and, after a landslide election victory, reassumed the Presidency of the country from which he had been ousted nearly eighteen years earlier. During his previous tenure as President, from 1946 to 1955, Perón exercised virtually dictatorial powers, relying on demagoguery and repression as well as social reform to maintain his enormous hold over Argentina's working masses. During the years he spent in exile, Perón remained a dominant political force in Argentina. Perón exemplified the Latin American tradition of caudillos—strong, semi-dictatorial populists whose power rests more on their captivating personalities than on any clear-cut political philosophy or party.

EARLY LIFE
Juan Domingo Perón Sosa was born on October 8, 1895 in Lobos, a small country town in Buenos Aires province, to Mario Tomas Perón, who was of Italian ancestry, and Juana Sosa de Perón, whose background was Spanish Creole. Accounts differ as to whether his father was a well-to-do landowner or a small farmer. According to Arthur P. Whitaker in *Argentina* (Prentice-Hall, 1964), "both sides of the family were middle class and neither

Juan Perón.

was a newcomer to Argentina. . . . Perón's paternal grandfather had been a successful physician. . . . Whether from bad luck or bad management, however, Juan's father met with no success in a migratory life that took him from the banks of the Plata to sheep-raising Patagonia and back again to . . . the province of Buenos Aires. Young Juan thus grew up in an atmosphere of insecurity on the fringe of the rural middle class, sharing the resentment against the established order that runs through the pseudo-gaucho poem *Martin Fierro* . . . which he later... cited time and again in his public addresses."

LIFE'S WORK

Perón attended the Colegio Internacional de Olivos and the Colegio Internacional Politecnica. At fifteen he entered the Colegio Militar de la Nacion, Argentina's military academy, from which he graduated with a commission as a sub lieutenant of the infantry in 1913. In 1924 he graduated from the Sargento Cabral officers' school with the rank of captain, and from 1926 to 1930 he was a staff officer with the operations division while taking advanced training at the Escuela Superior de Guerra. In 1930 he played a minor role in the coup that toppled

the democratically elected President Hipolito Irigoyen. From 1930 to 1936 Perón was a professor of military history at the Escuela Superior de Guerra, serving concurrently as private secretary to the Minister of War and as aide-de-camp to senior officers. During that period he wrote several books on military history and strategy.

Perón was sent to Chile in 1936 as military attache in the Argentine Embassy in Santiago, but he was, according to some accounts, expelled from that country in 1938 for espionage. From 1939 to 1941 he headed a special military mission that visited European countries and spent some time in Italy, where he studied the tactics of mountain and ski warfare and became a fervent admirer of Mussolini and Hitler.

Returning from Europe in 1941, Perón, now a colonel, was placed in charge of training ski troops as commandant of a mountain detachment in Mendoza. Soon thereafter, he joined a cabal of right-wing officers known as Grupo de Oficiales Unidos (GOU), who sympathized with the fascist powers and hoped that Argentina would become predominant in Latin America. Perón's rapid rise to power began in June 1943, when he played a key role in the coup that deposed President Ramon Castillo. In the next government, headed by General Pedro Pablo Ramirez, he became undersecretary of war and chief of staff of the first army division. More important, however, was his appointment as director of the moribund National Department of Labor which he transformed into the powerful Secretariat of Welfare and Labor.

Aware that Argentina was changing from an agricultural to an industrial society and that the new working classes represented an untapped political force, Perón used his position as head of the labor secretariat to win a large and devoted following among the workers, whom he affectionately called *descamisados,* or "shirtless ones." He enacted measures bringing them such benefits as wage increases, bonuses, social security, and low-cost housing and established control over the labor unions, which he forged into powerful organizations loyal to him. As his power base grew, so did his political influence. By February 1944 he was sufficiently in control to force the resignation of Ramirez and the installation of General Edelmiro Farrell.

While Farrell was President, Perón, as Secretary of Labor and Welfare, Minister of War, and Vice-President, held the real power. But as he steered Argentina toward a corporate state, both domestic and foreign opposition grew. The Allied powers were dismayed by Argentina's pro-Axis stand and by Perón's anti-American statements. His rivals in the military resented his growing popularity, and Argentina's industrial and commercial interests assailed Perón's "social agitation."

The power struggle climaxed in October 1945, when generals opposed to Perón forced his resignation and jailed him. At that moment, Perón's strategy of courting labor produced its most dramatic result. Hearing of his imprisonment, hundreds of thousands of workers—Perón's loyal *descamisados*—staged a peaceful invasion of Buenos Aires. Frightened by the show of force, the generals released Perón. Not long after that, he married the young actress Maria Eva Duarte—popularly known as "Evita"—who had helped to rally the workers to his defense, and who soon shared his popularity.

In February 1946 Perón was formally elected to succeed Farrell as President, defeating his liberal opponent, Jose P. Tamborino, representing the Democratic Union, by a vote of 1,474,000 to 1,207,000. In the beginning, Perón—who had assumed the rank of brigadier general in 1946—was fairly successful. Argentina's coffers were filled with currency earned by exporting foodstuffs during World War II. Workers were given important benefits, such as the forty-hour week, paid vacations, and retirement pensions. Banks, railroads, and basic utilities were nationalized, and tens of thousands of public works projects were constructed. Through her government-financed Eva Perón Foundation, which had exclusive control of all charitable activities, Evita channeled some $10,000,000 a year into social benefits. An unprecedented number of small consumer industries were established to promote economic self-sufficiency. Women won the right to vote. The balance of political power in Argentina shifted, with the workers becoming an important force for the first time. Perón called his movement and his amorphous philosophy *"justicialismo"* which he defined as a "middle way" between capitalism and Communism. To ensure his continued control, in 1949 Perón persuaded his rubber-stamp Congress to rewrite the Constitution to permit presidents to succeed themselves. In the national elections of November 1951 he was handily reelected to the Presidency by a two-to-one margin.

But the first years of the Perón regime sowed the seeds of the chaos that followed. The outpouring of government spending led to inflation. Corruption flourished, the treasury was depleted, and nationalized industries stagnated. Invoking national security, Perón stepped up his dictatorial repressions, establishing control over the judiciary, imposing censorship on the press, jailing dissenters, and smothering opposition in the trade unions, the political parties, and the universities.

As Juan and Eva Perón consolidated their hold on Argentina's masses, schoolchildren were taught to venerate them as if they were saints: the countryside bristled with statues of the Peróns, and public squares and railroad stations bore their names. The Peróns did little to discourage such iconographic adulation. Evita said of her husband: "He is God for us; . . . we cannot conceive of heaven without Perón. He is our sun, our air, our water, our life." As the passionate defender of women and of the poor, Eva Perón was—and still is—revered as a saint by Perónists, and after she died of cancer in 1952 the regime seemed to lose considerable direction and force.

Although during his second term Perón belatedly tried to save the economy by introducing anti-inflationary austerity measures and encouraging greater agricultural production, by 1955 opposition to his regime had crystallized. Large segments of the population, including the powerful land-owning class, the liberal political parties, the students, and much of the military, were aligned against him. By such actions as ending religious instruction in schools and legalizing divorce, Perón alienated the Roman Catholic Church, and his excommunication in June 1955 heralded his downfall. Finally, on September 16, 1955 a military revolt erupted. Three days later he resigned the Presidency and fled the country on a Paraguayan gunboat.

For the next five years Perón lived successively in Paraguay, Nicaragua, Panama, Venezuela, and the Dominican Republic before settling in Madrid in 1960. In Argentina the military did its best to obliterate his influence. The Perónist party was outlawed, many of its leaders were jailed, and statues of Perón were toppled. Meanwhile, Perón kept in touch with his supporters in Argentina from his luxurious villa in Madrid and continued to enjoy the loyalty of a large segment of the population. About the succession of civilian and military regimes that governed Argentina in the late 1950's and the 1960's, Perón has remarked: "It was not that we were so good, but those who followed us were so bad that they made us seem better than we were."

In 1966 General Juan Carlos Ongama wrested power from a struggling civilian president and embarked on yet another attempt to bring about order and progress by means of a harsh dictatorship. He cracked down on the Peronists and other dissenters, but his main achievement was to drive the opposition underground. Ongama was ousted in 1970 and replaced by General Roberto Livingston; he, in turn, yielded a year later to General Alejandro Lanusse, who had once been imprisoned by Perón. Convinced that the only solution for Argentina lay in a return to civilian government with the full participation of the Peronists, Lanusse began long-distance negotiations with Perón, who still held sway over the single most potent political faction in Argentina. Lanusse, who hoped to gain Perdn's endorsement of ilia elections, while finding a way to keep the Peronists from gaining control, agreed to remove the obstacles that had prevented his return to Argentina and vacated a long-standing charge of treason against him. In January 1972 Perón's Justicialist party was officially recognized as a legal political party.

Perón's long-trumpeted return to Argentina, on November 17, 1972, proved an anticlimax. He met with leaders of political factions and organized a coalition, the Frente Justicialista de Liberacion, or Frejuli, around his Justicialist party, but he did not try to return to power or to overcome the residency requirement that the Lanusse government had imposed to prevent him from becoming a candidate in the coming presidential election. On December 14, 1972, four weeks after his arrival, Perón left Argentina. Two days later he sent a message to the Frejuli party congress, designating as his choice for presidential candidate Hector Campora, a colorless figure whose only claim to distinction was his total loyalty to Perón.

In a relatively dull campaign, centering on the Frejuli slogan "Campora in government, Perón in power," Campora presented the Peronists as the only effective alternative to the military government. Juan Perón directed the presidential campaign from Spain, issuing statements calculated to irritate the military and to forge unity among the various segments of the motley Peronist movement, which had expanded to include most students and much of the middle class. Peronism now encompassed groups ranging from the extreme left to the far right, and many moderates viewed Perón as the only man capable of bringing unity and peace to Argentina.

In the elections on March 11, 1973 Campora received a plurality of 49.6 percent of the vote in a field of nine candidates. Inaugurated on May 25, Campora fulfilled Peronist promises, including the establishment of diplomatic relations with Cuba and the release of political prisoners. But Campora seemed impotent to cope with the country's economic woes or with the incendiary violence of urban guerrillas of the Trotskyist People's Revolutionary Movement that had spread into the ranks of the Peronist movement itself. Young leftwing Peronists hoped for a rapid socialist revolution, which conservative labor leaders and businessmen wanted to avoid. Violent confrontations multiplied, the worst erupting on June 20, when Perón made his second return to Argentina. More than a million people gathered to greet him but gunfire broke out between rival factions, leaving many dead. Shocked by the incident, Perón retired from public view for more than three weeks.

Campora suddenly announced his resignation on July 13, 1973, clearing the way for Perón himself to run for the presidency. In a nationwide television address that same day, Perón declared: "If God gives me health . . . , I will spend the last effort of my life to complete the mission that could be entrusted to me. . . . For me this is a tremendous sacrifice . . . because the years have not passed in vain." As his vice-presidential running mate, Perón chose his present wife, Isabel, whom he had tried to groom in the image of Evita. On September 23 Perón was elected President, winning 62 percent of the vote in a four-way race, in which his nearest rival, Ricardo Balbin of the Radical party received 24.5 percent. In a simple inauguration ceremony, on October 12, 1973 Perón took over the Presidency from Raul Lastiri, who had acted as interim President since Campora's resignation.

The most serious problem facing Perón has been the continuing political violence. Within the three weeks following his election, four Peronist union leaders were assassinated, including Jose Rucci, the head of the powerful General Confederation of Labor. A wave of kidnappings of foreign businessmen culminated in the gunning down, in November, of an executive of the Ford Motor Company. Perón s attempts to purge the leftist elements in his movement not only failed to mitigate the violence but disenchanted many of his youthful followers, who felt that he had abandoned his revolutionary goals.

Nevertheless, many observers agree that Perón took power at a fairly auspicious time. By mid-1973 Argentine exports were on the upswing, and inflation had begun to decline. The powerful anti-Perón military had been eclipsed, during Campora's term. Determined to make Argentina more independent, both economically and politically, Perón planned to end what he saw as American domination by relying more on Europe for financial and technical aid, and he visualized Argentina as a leader of non-aligned nations. In December 1973 Perón announced a far-reaching three-year economic program aimed at nearly doubling the economic growth rate and "recovering economic independence by demolishing foreign financial, technological, and commercial control" over the Argentine economy.

Perón's health declined in his final year in office due to heart disease and an enlarged prostate, and his wife often took over as Acting President.

PERSONAL LIFE

Juan Perón was first married in 1925 to Aurelia Tizon, who died of cancer in 1938. His third wife, the former Maria Isabel Martinez, has failed to rival the popularity of Evita. A former cabaret dancer, thirty-five years his junior, "Isabelita" met Perón during his exile in Panama, and they were married in Madrid in 1961. Perón stood slightly over six feet tall, weighed about 200 pounds,

and had black hair that he touches up with dye. The power and charm that marked his rise to prominence remained with him over the years. Even in poor health before he died, he was, according to *The New York Times* (July 14, 1973) "still a commanding figure of a man. His smile is still dazzling. His physique is that of a retired athlete. ... He looks the part of a leader."

Perón was buried in La Chacarita Cemetery in Buenos Aires, and in 2006 his body was moved to a mausoleum at his former summer residence, now a museum. The Peronist movement remains the central political struggle of Argentina.

FURTHER READING

Ferns, H. S. *Argentina* (1969); Luna, Felix. *De Peron a Lanusse* (1973) Seobie, *James R. Argentina* (1971); Whitaker, *Arthur P. Argentina* (1964)

FREDERICK WILLIAM PETHICK-LAWRENCE

British Government Official

Born: December 28, 1871; London, United Kingdom
Died: September 10, 1961; London, United Kingdom
Party Affiliation: Labour Party (UK)

INTRODUCTION

The man largely responsible for the proposals in Britain's widely praised May 1946 White Paper on Indian independence was Lord Frederick William Pethick-Lawrence, Secretary of State for India in Prime Minister Attlee's Cabinet. Seventy-four years old when assigned the difficult Indian question, Pethick-Lawrence had a long career as crusader, first in the fight for women's suffrage in England in the 1900's, and then for many years as a Labor Party member of Parliament. He has stated his credo at the end of his autobiography Fate Has Been Kind, *which was published in 1943: "I venture to assert that, unless an individual can transcend the limits of sex, class, age and creed, his personality remains of necessity to that extent incomplete."*

EARLY LIFE

Frederick William Lawrence, the son of Alfred Lawrence, became Pethick-Lawrence at his marriage in 1901: he added his wife's name to his own to indicate

that they were to be equal. His grandfather William Lawrence was a Cornish carpenter from Plymouth who founded a successful firm of contractors in London, two of his uncles were Lord Mayors of London, and others in his family were members of the House of Commons. Frederick William was born December 28, 1871. Because Alfred Lawrence died in his son's infancy, an uncle "of notable mind and character" directed the child's care in a cultured home environment. "This uncle," the British author Mary Agnes Hamilton tells, "was, like all his clan, an ardent Unitarian; he may have developed the boy's conscience to excess; but he saw to it that he had an excellent schooling. Moreover, he had ample means, and his nephew, while remaining simple to austerity in his personal tastes, has always had enough money to travel widely, to map his course as he chose."

LIFE'S WORK

Although an Etonian (one of the two in Prime Minister Attlee's Labor Cabinet), Pethick-Lawrence is "by no means a typical product" of the famous public school. A hard worker by nature, in a school which in the 1880's was "inhospitable to work," he considered Eton "mainly absurd," and was something of a misfit there.

Frederick Pethick-Lawrence.

He came into his own, however, at Trinity College, Cambridge, where he made many close friends, played tennis, billiards and football, and became president of the Union Debating Society. His academic work gained him a "double first" (first class honors in mathematics in 1894, and in natural science in 1895), and the Adam Smith prize in economics for a paper on local variations in wages. On the basis of the economics paper, he was made a Fellow of Trinity in 1897. After Cambridge he traveled for a year in India, the Far East, Australia, and the United States, and then came back to London to read law. Interested in social reform from the beginning, he went to live in London's East End, became the treasurer of Mansfield House, a nonconformist settlement house in Canning Town, and as a young barrister took the cases of the poor.

At the settlement house Lawrence met an evangelist "Sister," Emmeline Pethick, the belle of an exclusive social circle who had offered her services to the West London Mission. According to Miss Hamilton, "When he fell in love with her—on sight he was a

Conservative. An impassioned social reformer, she told him this was an insuperable bar. Her stand and the Boer War [his sympathy was with the Boers] . . . awoke all his deep latent idealism and swept inherited prepossessions aside; it was not long before he was in the Labor Party." The two were married in 1901 in a public hall; the guests included David Lloyd George, and fifty workhouse women, who were friends of the bride's. He was now swept "heart and soul" into the movement for women's suffrage. The Pethick-Lawrences became the "hero and heroine" of the suffragettes.

At the time Lawrence was married he owned a controlling interest in *The Echo,* a pioneer halfpenny evening paper in London. He edited the paper from 1902 to 1905, and when it failed paid staff and creditors out of his own pocket. From 1905 to 1907 he was editor of the *Labour Record and Review.* Meanwhile, the suffragettes were becoming increasingly militant. In 1905 Mrs. Emmeline Pankhurst organized the Women's Social and Political Union, with Pethick-Lawrence as the union's financial guarantor. From 1907 to 1914 he owned and jointly with his wife edited the weekly *Votes For Women.* The offices of the paper were a headquarters of "insurgent women," who smashed post-office windows, chained themselves to iron fence palings, went on hunger strikes in England's jails, and otherwise caused "disturbances," in a campaign for suffrage which lasted until the outbreak of World I. Pethick-Lawrence stood bail for at least a thousand women. Both he and his wife were sentenced to prison in 1912, and endured forcible feeding, the Government's method of dealing with hunger-strikers. When the Prime Minister "capitulated," Pethick-Lawrence's nine-month sentence was cut to one month, his wife was released, and forcible feeding was abolished. "From beginning to end," reported the London *Observer,* "he displayed a fidelity to principle, a quiet and unfailing courage, which have ensured for him an honored place in the annals of women's enfranchisement."

When World War I broke out Pethick-Lawrence was forty-two, "again a rebel, though, as usual, a constructive one," writes Miss Hamilton—he was Treasurer of the Union of Democratic Control, which was pledged to fight for "open covenants openly arrived at." In 1917, standing; for Parliament as a "peace-by-negotiation" candidate in South Aberdeen, he received only a few votes, but made numerous loyal friends. He was an unsuccessful Labor candidate in 1918 and in 1922. Then, in 1923, defeating Winston Churchill, who was making his last stand as a Liberal, Pethick-Lawrence entered Parliament as the Labor member for West Leicester, the seat he held until the Labor crash in 1931. One of the few Labor members who could handle questions of finance and currency, he was Financial Secretary to the Treasury in the 1929-31 Government. In 1931 he was not re-elected, but East Edinburgh returned him to Parliament four years later, in 1935. The post of leader of the Labor Party in the House was his from 1940 until 1942, when he yielded it to Arthur Greenwood (who had at that time ceased to hold office in the national Government), and himself became vice-chairman of the party. In August 1945 Prime Minister Attlee, in choosing nineteen ministers from among the most experienced men in the Labor Party, named him Secretary of State for India. The seventy-three-year-old Secretary the same day was created a Baron to sit in the House of Lords.

The new Secretary's interest in India had begun several decades earlier. In 1926 Pethick-Lawrence, in India with his wife on a "silver honeymoon," was permitted to attend the Indian National Congress; he talked with Indian leaders of all factions, renewed old associations, and made new ones. "These relationships were kept open," Miss Hamilton reports. "Indians coming to London were always made welcome at the Pethick-Lawrences'." Returning to London after the 1926 tour, he advised a "clear declaration of principle and aim," and the calling of a Round Table Conference. In 1931 he was a member of the second Indian Round Table Conference.

In early 1946 a special mission of three senior Cabinet members (Secretary of State for India Lord Pethick-Lawrence, First Lord of the Admiralty A. V. Alexander, and president of the Board of Trade Sir Stafford Cripps) left for India intending, in the words of Attlee, to use "their utmost endeavors to help India to obtain freedom as fully and speedily as possible." The mission had sufficient power to negotiate an agreement with Indian leaders. Leaving England "without any specific proposal or plan," Lord Pethick-Lawrence "refused to envisage failure." For six weeks the mission attempted to bring to agreement on a constitution the leaders of India's two strongest groups, the Hindus and the Moslems, but were not successful. Determined to "push through a solution," they prepared a White Paper which proposed a Federated Union of India, with complete independence or dominion status. Its constitution would include provisions to safeguard the interests of the Moslems, but the Moslem League's demand for a separate Moslem

state (Pakistan) in India was rejected. This White Paper was adopted as the official Labor Government policy on India, Attlee reading the proposals in the House of Commons on May 16, 1946.

World reaction to the plan was favorable, with praise for the British Government for presenting "not a weasel-worded promise nor a string-tied offer, but a concrete plan—for the government of an independent, unified India." Indian leader Gandhi considered the plan "the best document the British Government could have produced in the circumstances" and advised his countrymen to accept it. But from Winston Churchill, leader of the opposition in Parliament, came the comment that the paper was "an able but melancholy document"; that the "sincerity" and "zeal" of the ministers "would be natural were it to gain an empire, not to cast it away." Indian leaders began discussing the proposals. Meanwhile, Pethick-Lawrence told reporters : "What will happen if one person . . . or groups of people in some way tried to put spanners [monkey wrenches] in the wheels, I am not prepared at this stage precisely to say; but the intention is to get on with the job." On June 5 came the announcement that the Moslem League Council had accepted the British proposals, and on June 25, 1946, although it had rejected the British plan for an interim government, the Working Committee of the All-India Congress Party accepted the long-range plan. This agreement by both the major Indian parties was considered a "triumph of British statesmanship" by newspaper commentators. On July 29 the Moslem League reconsidered its decision, and, objecting to the way the Congress Party interpreted the proposals, rejected the British plan.

In Parliament it was held that the main task of the mission—the task of removing doubts in Indian thought of Britain's sincerity in wishing for a free India at the earliest possible moment—had been successful. Indian independence was not yet in sight, however, as religious and political factions continued to disagree over how the proposed new Government was to be constituted. After four days of conferences in London, the Hindus and the Moslems reached no agreement and the Constituent Assembly began in India without the Moslems, although the British Government stated that no constitution would be "forced" on any part of India unless both sides approved it. In the House of Lords, Pethick-Lawrence announced that the Constitution must follow the basic form recommended by the Cabinet mission, unless a departure "is agreed upon with the approval of the representatives of each major party."

PERSONAL LIFE

In his early career as editor and crusader, as well as in his later years with the Government, Pethick-Lawrence wrote and published articles, pamphlets, and books on mathematics, free trade, women's suffrage, finance and economics. His early writings include: *Women's Fight For the Vote, The Man's Share, A Levy on Capital, Why Prices Rise and Fall, Unemployment, The National Debt,* and *The Heart of the Empire.* His book *This Gold Crisis* appeared in 1931. He also wrote the finance chapter for *Twelve Studies in U.S.S.R.* (1932), and *The Money Muddle and the Way Out* (1933).

The British peer and statesman, called Pethick by his friends, was described by Miss Hamilton: "Though he is very thin, and rather dried, and what little hair remains on his high domed head is, like his bristling eyebrows, absolutely white, his dark eyes are as bright as ever; he still plays a good game of tennis, walks tirelessly, with a curiously short, springy step, and plays almost as good a game of billiards as when he used to encounter professionals on their own ground." Pethick-Lawrence died in London at the age of 89.

FURTHER READING

Cur Lit 53:162-4 Ag T2 por; *Who's Who,* 1946

AUGUSTO PINOCHET UGARTE
President of Chile; Army Commander

Born: November, 25, 1915; Valparaíso, Chile
Died: December 10, 2006; Santiago, Chile
Affiliation: Independent

INTRODUCTION

On September 11, 1973, General Augusto Pinochet Ugarte, Commander in Chief of the Chilean Army, led a four-man military junta in a bloody coup that resulted in the death of Marxist President Salvador Allende, ending his experimental attempt to lead Chile down "the democratic road to socialism." A career army officer, Pinochet, who assumed full power as chief of state in June 1974, emerged as a strict authoritarian, determined to rid the country of all vestiges of Marxism. Although Chile's military government, during its first year in power, made some headway toward ending the political strife and economic chaos that had bedeviled the country during the Allende government, the atmosphere remained shrouded in repression and austerity. Under Pinochet, Chileans had little hope that they could return to their traditional democratic constitutionalism, until his arrest under an international warrant on a visit to London, October 10, 1998, in connection with human rights violations.

EARLY LIFE

Augusto Pinochet Ugarte, whose ancestors came from Brittany, was born on November 25, 1915, in Valparaiso, Chile, the son of Augusto and Avelina Pinochet. Like most members of Chile's officer corps, he came from the upper-middle class. Educated in local schools, he entered the Escuela Militar, Chile's military academy, in Santiago, at 18 and graduated with the rank of *alferez,* or second lieutenant, in the infantry in 1936. According to one authoritative source, he also spent two years at the University of Chile in Santiago, studying law and the social sciences.

LIFE'S WORK

Early in his military career, Pinochet served as an instructor at the Escuela Militar. In 1942, he attained the rank of *teniente,* or first lieutenant and, in 1946, he advanced to captain. The following year, he was assigned to the garrison in Iquique in the desolate north of Chile. He returned to Santiago, in 1949, to attend the Academia de Guerra, or War College, and completed his course of study there, in 1952. Promoted to major in 1953, he was then assigned to the Rancagua Regiment in Arica. In 1954, he joined the staff of the Academia de Guerra as a professor, teaching geography and artillery courses, and the next year he served as adjutant at the Undersecretariat of War. During 1956, Pinochet spent some time in Washington, D.C., as a military attaché to the Chilean Embassy, and also served in Quito, Ecuador, as a member of his country's military mission. In 1961, he was appointed commander of the Seventh Infantry ("Esmerelda") Regiment in Antofagasta. He returned to the Academia de Guerra, in 1964, as Assistant Director and

Professor of Geopolitics and Military Geography. Fellow officers who knew him during the 1950s and 1960s remember him as a relatively colorless, conservative officer who, in keeping with the tradition of the Chilean military, remained aloof from politics. According to *The New York Times* (September 15, 1973), they also respected him as "intelligent, ambitious, and professionally competent."

Under the reformist government of Christian Democratic President Eduardo Frei Montalva, who took office in 1964, Pinochet continued to scale the military ladder. He was promoted to colonel in 1966 and became a brigadier general in 1968, the year he was appointed Interim Commander in Chief of the First Army Division at Iquique. In 1965, 1968, and 1972, Pinochet visited the schools of the United States Southern Command in the Panama Canal Zone, where, among other subjects, counter-insurgency tactics were taught. During 1968, he also made an official tour of the United States.

By 1970, Frei's reforms had raised expectations and sharpened political consciousness, but had failed to satisfy most Chileans. In the Presidential elections in September of that year, the Christian Democrats and the rightist National Party lost to the Popular Unity movement, a five-party leftist coalition. Its candidate, Dr. Salvador Allende Gossens, a Socialist, who proclaimed his intention to bring socialism to Chile, won a narrow plurality, with 36.3 percent of the vote, and became the hemisphere's first freely-elected Marxist President. He was inaugurated on November 4, 1970.

Within a year after Allende's election, the Chilean government had nationalized most mining operations, which included the mammoth American-owned copper mines that provided the country with most of its foreign exchange, as well as many other industries, banks, and large farms. In many cases, farms and factories were taken over by workers or peasants. Whether as a result of government blunders or the implacable opposition of the anti-Allende interests and the United States, inflation skyrocketed, industrial and agricultural production dropped, and critical food shortages developed.

During the Allende years, Pinochet served in various key army command posts in the Santiago area, including that of Commanding General of the Santiago Army Garrison. It was in the latter post that he first won public attention. When rioting between pro-and anti-Allende groups in December 1971 caused the President to declare a state of emergency in the capital, Pinochet instituted a curfew, ordered more than 100 arrests, and

announced: "I hope the army will not have to come out, because if it does, it will be to kill." A few days later he temporarily closed the right-wing paper *Tribuna* for "insulting the military." He insisted at the time that "coups do not occur in Chile."

By mid-1972, Chile's economic and political situation was desperate. A middle-class strike in October and November, begun by truck drivers and ultimately embracing nearly the entire professional and mercantile sectors, almost sparked a civil war. To resolve the crisis, Allende brought several military men into his Cabinet in November, including General Carlos Prats Gonzalez, who became Minister of the Interior. Pinochet temporarily replaced Prats as Commander in Chief of the Army. The move polarized the Chilean military into pro-and anti-Allende factions, ending its long-standing policy of noninvolvement in politics.

Opposition leaders hoped to win the two-thirds parliamentary majority that would enable them to impeach Allende, but, in the March 1973 congressional elections, Popular Unity received 43.4 percent of the vote. That result reinforced the widely held view that only a coup could remove Allende from the scene. In late June, part of the military, sponsored by extreme right-wing forces, attempted an anti-Allende revolt. It was, however, suppressed by troops loyal to the government.

In July 1973, the truckers capped a series of debilitating work stoppages by resuming their strike and effectively throttling commerce. On August 9, in a last-ditch effort to placate the opposition, Allende again brought military men into the government and named Prats Defense Minister. But anti-Allende factions in the military forced Prats to resign his command and his Cabinet post two weeks later. Pinochet, who had been serving as Chief of Staff (or second in command) of the Army since 1972, was appointed Commander in Chief by Allende on August 24, 1973. Prats had reportedly assured Allende that he could depend on Pinochet, and although in the days preceding the coup some of the President's supporters tried to warn him that the general stood with the opposition, they apparently failed to convince him.

The stage was thus set for the military coup which, as Pinochet later revealed, had been in preparation since mid-1972. "I don't think even my wife knew of the planned coup," he later told reporters. On September 5, Pinochet held secret talks with the other members of the junta: Air Force Chief General Gustavo Leigh; Admiral Jose Toribio Merino of the Navy; and, National

Police Chief General Cesar Mendoza. Four days later, the commanders made the irrevocable decision to overthrow Allende.

Even by Latin American standards, the coup d'état was an extremely violent one. It began in the early morning hours of September 11, 1973, when navy units seized the Port of Valparaiso. At La Moneda, the Presidential palace in Santiago, Pinochet gave Allende the ultimatum to surrender or face attack. After Allende refused, the palace was bombed, strafed, and shelled by tanks. In the afternoon, infantrymen entered La Moneda and found Allende dead. According to the junta, the President committed suicide to avoid surrender. Others, including Allende's widow, had claimed that he was killed by the military insurgents.

To their own surprise, the military were in control of Chile by the end of the day, although bitter resistance by Allende supporters continued for some time. A 24-hour curfew was imposed, and soldiers warned that violators would be shot on sight. On September 13, General Pinochet was named President of the junta, an office that was to rotate among its four members, according to the original plan. He swore in a fifteen-man Cabinet that included ten military men.

One of the junta's first acts was to break off relations with Cuba, and to announce that some 14,000 leftist exiles in Chile would be tried or expelled from the country. In the days that followed, Allende supporters were rounded up and jailed or executed. A new constitution, giving a major role to the military, was promulgated by decree. The junta suspended civil rights, imposed heavy censorship, purged the universities, outlawed the Marxist political parties, placed all other parties in "indefinite recess," and abolished the country's largest labor confederation. Xenophobia was encouraged by the junta, and rightists blamed "foreign subversives" and Jews for Chile's plight.

Claiming to have found evidence of an Allende-supported "Plan Zeta" to assassinate military commanders and opposition leaders, members of the junta asserted that their takeover had been intended "to restore institutional normality" in Chile and to "stop a disastrous dictatorship from installing itself." Lashing out at "mentally deranged" Chileans who continued to resist the new government, Pinochet declared, a few days after the coup: "I am not a murderer, but if people insist on fighting, we will act as we do in time of war." He described his government as "a junta of old generals without ambitions" and "men without a future who can bring a future," and he pledged that "democratic normality" would eventually return to the country.

Pinochet had emphatically denied that the United States had intervened to bring the junta to power, declaring that "the armed forces. . . . of Chile, with a pure tradition of respect for legitimate authority, will never accept foreign intrusion." (It was later revealed that, in addition to imposing economic sanctions, such as an "invisible blockade" that virtually isolated Chile's socialist government from the world money market, the United States government had authorized its Central Intelligence Agency to spend millions of dollars to "destabilize" the Allende regime.) On September 24, 1973, the United States granted full recognition to the Chilean junta.

In the months that followed, the junta moved to de-socialize the economy and restore the "free market." Although some legally expropriated businesses remained under government control and parts of Allende's land reform program were continued, some 300 companies, including 40 that had been under American ownership, were returned to their former owners. Compensation was promised to United States companies for the copper mines that had been expropriated by the Allende government. Prices were allowed to rise to their natural levels, while wages were held down, a move that eased shortages, but placed a severe burden on the working class. Foreign investments were encouraged by the junta, and credit from abroad was again made available to Chile.

Whatever stability had been achieved by the junta during its early months in power was obtained at an enormous human cost. Estimates of the number of persons who died in the coup and its aftermath ranged from several hundred to as many as 20,000. Roman Catholic sources placed the number of political prisoners that were still being held by the junta, at the end of 1973, at 10,000. According to various respected sources, including Amnesty International, the International Commission of Jurists, and the Human Rights Commission of the Organization of American States, the torture of leftist prisoners was widespread, although Pinochet reportedly repudiated its use. Many people simply "disappeared," including Charles Horman, a U.S. journalist.

At first, most members of Chile's powerful middle class backed the junta. As it became clear, however, that long-term repression was in store, and that the generals envisioned a corporate, technocratic, apolitical state resembling those in Spain or Brazil, opposition surfaced. In February 1974, the Christian Democratic leaders criticized the junta for "deeds that amount to a denial of justice and a grave violation of human rights." As reported by *The New York Times* (April 25, 1974), the Roman Catholic Bishops of Chile accused the junta of "the use of torture, arbitrary and lengthy detentions, of causing large scale unemployment, of making job dismissals for political reasons, and of establishing an economic policy that . . . shifted the burden to the poor."

The first major shakeup in Chile's military government came on June 26, 1974, when Pinochet assumed sole power as "Supreme Chief of the Nation," while the other junta members were relegated to subordinate roles as "a sort of legislative body." Explaining the move, a government spokesman said: "History has shown that collective leaderships simply do not work. We need one-man rule." The editors of *The New York Times*, who had observed earlier that Pinochet seemed to favor a Gaullist type of government, rather than more extreme forms of authoritarianism, greeted the change in the Chilean government with guarded optimism in their editorial of June 27, 1974. They noted that Pinochet, alone among the junta leaders, had promised to preserve gains made by workers under Allende, that he showed some sensitivity to world opinion, and that he had established a dialogue with church leaders.

Addressing a crowd of several thousand Chileans in Santiago on September 11, 1974, the first anniversary of the coup, Pinochet offered to free most political prisoners, provided they agreed to leave the country, and challenged Cuba and the Soviet Union to free an equal number of prisoners. To alleviate the burdens of the working class, he promised that wages would be adjusted quarterly to increased living costs. He asserted that continued police surveillance of farms, factories, and schools was necessary "to provide tranquility to the citizenry." Ruling out any early return to democratic government, Pinochet declared: "The recess for political parties must continue for several more years, and can only be responsibly lifted when a new generation of Chileans, with healthy civic and patriotic habits, can take over the leadership in public life."

General Pinochet and his government continued total suppression of his opponents, which included tracking down and assassinating members of his government's opposition beyond Chile's boundaries. The passage of a constitutional referendum, in 1980, brought in a new national constitution with provisions that Pinochet would remain as President for another eight years, with increased powers, and then face another re-election referendum with a "yes," or "no vote" to decide if he should remain as President. In the meantime, he was under increased pressure to decrease his suppression and human rights violations, which included a visit by Pope John Paul II.

In 1988, the Chilean national plebiscite was held to vote on the referendum of Pinochet's Presidency with a "yes" or "no vote." The vote was 44.01 percent "for" and 55.99 percent "against." The Pinochet continued in office until free elections installed a new President, the Christian Democrat Patricio Aylwin, on March 11, 1990. Pinochet then remained in the government as "senator for life" (as provided in the 1980 constitution for Presidents who had been in office for at least six years), and held the post of Commander-in-Chief of the Army, until March 1998. He frequently thwarted human rights prosecutions against members of the security forces. In 1998, he was detained by British authorities after Spain requested his extradition in connection with the torture of Spanish citizens in Chile. It was eventually determined that his health was too frail for him to stand trial, so he was sent home to Chile and placed under house arrest. In 2002, he was stripped of his immunity and charged with human rights violations, but Chile's Supreme Court upheld a ruling that he was mentally incapable of defending himself in court. In 2005, however, after more human rights violations turned up, the Supreme Court voted to remove his immunity for illegal financial dealings, as well as for a case involving the disappearance and execution of at least 119 political dissidents, whose bodies were found in 1975 in Argentina. Although found to be fit to stand for trial for those alleged crimes, Pinochet died on December 10, 2006, before ever being tried for any of his human rights abuses.

PERSONAL LIFE

General Augusto Pinochet Ugarte and his wife, the former Lucia Hiriart (or Hieriarte) Rodriguez, were married on January 30, 1943; they had two sons (Augusto Osvaldo and Marco Antonio) and three daughters (Inés Lucía, María Verónica, and Jacqueline Marie). In 2005, his wife was sued by the Chilean Internal Revenue Service and later arrested over tax evasion, along with son Marco Antonio. In October 2007, she was arrested again, along with their five children and other people, on charges of embezzlement, using false passports, and illegally transferring $27 million to foreign bank accounts during Pinochet's dictatorship.

Pinochet was the author of several books, including a standard text on the geography of Chile, a study of Latin American geopolitics, and a history of the War of the Pacific of 1879. His decorations included Colombia's Order of Merit and Chile's Star of Military Merit. He was a practicing Roman Catholic.

FURTHER READING
The New York Times pl3 S 15 73 por; *Time* 102:38 S 24 73 por; *Diccionario biografico de Chile,* 1968-1970.

POL POT

Cambodian Political Leader

Born: May 19, 1928 (or 1925); Kampong Thom, French Indochina
Died: April 15, 1998; Oddar Meanchey, Cambodia
Affiliation: Communist Party

INTRODUCTION

Once a peaceful and prosperous nation, Cambodia, since 1975, fell victim to what United Nations Secretary General Kurt Waldheim has called "a national tragedy that may have no parallel in history." The man believed responsible for the country's disastrous plight was Pol Pot, whose efforts, as Prime Minister of "Democratic Kampuchea," to create a "pure agrarian society" resulted in the deaths of millions and turned Cambodia into a wasteland rampant with starvation and disease. Driven from power in January 1979 by insurgents supported militarily by pro-Soviet Vietnamese forces, the Chinese-backed Pol Pot regime nevertheless was still being recognized, as of late 1980, by the U.N. and a majority of its members, including the United States. Meanwhile, as commander of the formidable Khmer Rouge guerrilla force, Pol Pot has continued to offer steady resistance to Cambodia's present rulers from his mountain retreat.

EARLY LIFE

Although some question remains as to the true identity of Pol Pot, reliable sources identify him as Saloth (or Salot) Sar, who emerged as a key Cambodian Communist leader in the 1960's and adopted his present name as a nom *de guerre* in 1976. (He has also been identified as Pol Porth or Tol Saut.) A native of the Cambodian province of Kompong Thom in what was then French Indochina, Pol Pot was probably born on May 19, 1928, but some sources give the year as 1925. "I am the son of a peasant," Pol Pot said in an interview with the Vietnam News Agency in July 1976. "When I was young I

helped my parents in their labor. Later on I stayed in a [Buddhist] monastery ... for six years, two ... of which I spent as a monk."

After attending primary and secondary school, Pol Pot studied for a year at the College Technique (Technical School) in Phnom Penh, where he concentrated on carpentry and obtained an industrial education diploma. During the 1940's he took part in the anti-French resistance under Ho Chi Minh, and in 1946 he became a member of Indochina's clandestine Communist party. For a time he reportedly worked on a rubber plantation.

In August 1949 Pol Pot went to Paris on a scholarship to study radio electronics at the Ecole Franpaise de Radio-Electricite, and while there he joined the Marxist-Leninist Khmer Students' Association. Acquaintances remember him as intelligent, gregarious and decidedly militant. His European sojourn also included a trip to Yugoslavia, where he spent a month during the summer of 1950 working on the construction of the Belgrade-Zagreb highway project.

At least one observer has attributed Pol Pot's later anti-intellectualism to his failure to pass examinations at his Paris school for three years in succession. Pol Pot himself maintains that his academic failure resulted from his revolutionary activities. "The first year ... I became a fairly good student," he recalled in the 1976 interview. "Later I joined the progressive student movement. As I spent most of my time in radical activities, I did not attend many classes." He went on to relate, "The state cut short my scholarship, and I was forced to return home."

LIFE'S WORK

Returning to Phnom Penh in January 1953, Pol Pot joined the anti-French underground as a member of the People's Revolutionary party of Kampuchea (Pracheachon). He continued his opposition during the rule

Affiliation: Communist Party

At the founding congress of Cambodia's Communist party in September 1960, Pol Pot was elected a standing member of its central committee. The following year he became deputy secretary, and in 1962, after the assassination of the party's secretary, he was named acting secretary. The second party congress, in 1963, elected Pol Pot secretary, and he was later reelected to that post in 1971 and 1976. Meanwhile, in 1963, Sihanouk included him among thirty-four political leaders of various persuasions, whom he invited to help form a new government. But Pol Pot, along with other Communist leaders, feared that the move foreshadowed repression of the left. Rejecting the offer, he fled to the jungles, where he helped to organize the Communist guerrilla force known as the Khmer Rouge.

of Prince Norodom Sihanouk following the Withdrawal of the French under the 1954 Geneva agreement. At the same time he taught history and geography from 1954 to 1963 at a private school in Phnom Penh and engaged in left-wing journalism.

After the overthrow of the neutralist Sihanouk regime by the United States-supported Khmer Republic under General Lon Nol in March 1970, the Khmer Rouge waged relentless warfare against the new government from the jungles and mountains. According to William Shawcross, author of *Sideshow: Kissinger, Nixon, and the Destruction of Cambodia* (Simon & Schuster, 1979), the 1970 bombings and invasion of Cambodia by American and South Vietnamese forces were mainly responsible for the strength of the Khmer Rouge, which grew over a five-year period from a 4,000-man force into a "callow and very brutal army" of some 70,000.

Virtually nothing was heard of Pol Pot during his years underground. "My name was not well-known," he said in his 1976 interview. "Even Lon Nol's secret service, which kept following me . . ., had no idea of my position." In 1971 Saloth Sar (Pol Pot) was one of the signers of an appeal by intellectuals to support the Peking-based National United Front of Kampuchea, nominally headed by Sihanouk from his exile in China. In March 1972 he was designated by Sihanouk as one of three vice-chairmen of the People's National Liberation Armed Forces of Kampuchea, with responsibility for the military directorate.

The bloody five-year old Cambodian civil war ended on April 16, 1975, when Khmer Rouge forces captured Phnom Penh and overthrew the last remnants of the Lon Nol regime. On the following day Khmer Rouge soldiers, invoking the name of Angka Loeu (Organization on High)—later identified as the Cambodian Communist party, headed by Pol Pot—began to drive Phnom Penh's population of 2,000,000 or more, including some 20,000 sick and wounded hospital patients, on a forced march to the countryside, using as a pretext an alleged threat of imminent American bombing raids. "Darkness cloaked the machine-like maneuvers of the Khmer Rouge," Nayan Chanda wrote in the *Far Eastern* Economic Review (October 21, 1977). "The black pyjama-clad figures marched into Phnom Penh . . ., drove the population out of the city . . ., and closed the country's borders. As far as the outside world was concerned, Cambodia became a non-country."

The evacuation of the capital was later explained by government spokesmen as motivated by the shortage of food in the cities resulting from war damage to transportation facilities; the need to control epidemics of malaria, cholera, and typhoid; and, as confirmed by Pol Pot, the necessity of "smashing all sorts of enemy spy organizations," notably the United States Central Intelligence Agency. Another explanation was given by an Angka Loeu commissar: "From now on, if people want to eat, they should go out and work in the rice paddies. . . . Cities are evil. . . . That is why we shall do away with cities."

According to John Barron and Anthony Paul, whose Murder *of a Gentle Land* (Reader's Digest Press, 1977) is based on interviews with refugees, "Angka Loeu had resolved to annul the past and obliterate the present so as to fashion a future uncontaminated by . . . either. . . . The emptying of the cities; the burning of books, markets and houses; the looting of stores and homes, not to acquire but to destroy valuables; the demolition of buildings; the desecration of temples; the smashing of automobiles, medical equipment, and other products of foreign technology—all seemed like madness. Yet, given the resolve of Angka Loeu, all it did was purposeful, consistent and logical."

The entire Cambodian population was mobilized on a semi-military basis with the aim of reconstructing the economy and making the country self-sufficient in food production. Hundreds of thousands of people were shifted from place to place to harvest the rice crop, clear land, build dikes, and dig irrigation canals. Radio broadcasts—virtually the sole remaining means of communication—issued daily reports on economic progress and exhorted the people to work harder.

Although in the first year Cambodia was still formally ruled by the wartime National United Front of Kampuchea, headed by Sihanouk, the real power was apparently vested in a five-man committee headed by Pol Pot, who maintained a "faceless" leadership, evidently for reasons of security. To cement ties with China, in June 1975 Pol Pot secretly visited Peking, where he was received by Mao Tse-tung and Chou En-lai, and in the same month he went to Hanoi to settle a border dispute.

On December 14, 1975 a congress of the National United Front approved a new constitution that became effective on January 5, 1976. It described "Democratic Kampuchea" in utopian terms, as "an independent, united, peaceful, and nonaligned democratic state" and a "nation of workers and peasants" where "unemployment does not exist and the standard of living of the people is guaranteed." In the elections to the new 250-member People's Representative Assembly on March 30, 1976, Pol Pot was reportedly chosen as a representative of rubber plantation workers. On April 11, a week after Sihanouk resigned as chief of state, the Assembly elected a new government, with Khieu Samphan in the honorary post of President of the State Presidium. The formal governing power was vested in a nine-member Cabinet headed by Prime Minister Pol Pot, who was for the first time referred to by his *nom de guerre* and identified as Secretary General of the Kampuchean Communist party.

In his July 1976 interview Pol Pot conceded that because of adverse postwar conditions his government had "made no great achievements," but he expressed satisfaction with the "revolutionary movement of the masses." Reports from refugees fleeing to Thailand during that period indicated that many thousands of Cambodians had died as a result of executions, disease, malnutrition, and overwork. There were also revelations of resistance to the regime, attempted coups, and purges in government ranks. Pol Pot himself was believed to have fallen victim to a purge in September 1976, when he took a leave of absence for reasons of health and was succeeded by acting Prime Minister Nuon Chea. But although nothing was heard directly from Pol Pot for a year, important government communications continued to bear his signature.

Pol Pot resurfaced as Prime Minister in September 1977, when on the eve of his departure on state visits to China and North Korea he made a five-hour speech. Taking a nationalist position, he asserted that Cambodia's revolution was the product of the spontaneous struggle of its people and that aid from foreign allies was "only supplementary." While conceding that "spy rings working for imperialism" continued to exist, he said that only "the smallest possible number" of opponents to the revolution had been eradicated. The Prime Minister maintained that the "collective cooperative of the peasants," in which the money economy had been supplanted by a "communal support system," had transformed Cambodia into a prospering society, where "people are basically assured of all needs." He called special attention to progress in the building of factories, in social welfare and public health, and in the effort to eradicate illiteracy, and he maintained that in a decade Cambodia could support a population more than double its present 8,000,000.

But the Prime Minister's glowing accounts were refuted by reports from refugees and other sources during 1977 and 1978. Cambodia was said to resemble one huge work camp from which family life had virtually vanished. Children were instructed to eavesdrop and inform on their elders, and, from the age of five on, were forced to work in factories and fields. Those deemed the offspring of "undesirables" were reportedly buried alive. Aside from political indoctrination institutions, most schools remained closed. People were compelled to work as many as sixteen hours a day, and those who failed to meet production quotas or complained about conditions were executed. Of the country's 500 physicians only a handful survived, and medical services were limited to the distribution of herbs and roots. In their efforts to root out the educated classes, Khmer Rouge troops went so far as to kill persons who wore eyeglasses or spoke French.

Sihanouk, who was under virtual house arrest during the Pol Pot regime, told an interviewer for Time (January 22, 1979): "The temples and pagodas were burned or turned into pigsties or granaries or schools of politics, where the young were taught to work hard and love the heart and soul of Pol Pot. ... I was the only practicing Buddhist in all Cambodia for three years." As many as 4,000,000 Cambodians were said to have died at the hands of the Pol Pot regime. Of those who survived, many were turned into mute, apathetic creatures devoid of will or human feeling, as the result of brutal brainwashing combined with severe physical hardship. The U.N. Human Rights Commission and Amnesty International launched investigations into Cambodian conditions in 1978, but were hindered in their efforts to gain firsthand information. But although some Western commentators, including Manchester *Guardian* correspondent Richard Gott and the American scholar Douglas Pike, suggested that accounts of the excesses of the Pol Pot regime were exaggerated, enough documentation was available to indicate that they were substantially true. Reports of atrocities prompted President Jimmy Carter in 1978 to condemn the Cambodian regime as "the worst violator of human rights in the world today." Even Pol Pot's Chinese mentors privately expressed dismay over Cambodian excesses but insisted that they could not interfere in the country's internal affairs.

The traditional hostility between Cambodians and Vietnamese escalated into a bitter conflict during 1977 and led to a break in diplomatic relations in December of that year. As border fighting erupted in 1978, the Pol Pot regime rejected Vietnamese peace overtures, accusing the Hanoi regime of trying to destroy the government and of seeking to dominate all of Indochina through a proposed federation in which Cambodia would hold a weak minority position.

In December 1978 Hanoi Radio announced the creation of the rebel Kampuchean United Front for National Salvation, headed by the former Pol Pot lieutenant Heng Samrin, that aimed at overthrowing the "dictatorial, militarist, and fascist regime" of Pol Pot and Deputy Prime Minister Ieng Sary. Acting in the name of the United Front, Vietnamese armed forces overthrew the Pol Pot regime on January 7, 1979 and established the Hanoi-backed People's Republic of Kampuchea, with Heng Samrin as chairman of its People's Revolutionary Council. Pol Pot fled with his Khmer Rouge supporters to the mountains of southwestern Cambodia and vowed to fight "for eternity if necessary." Meanwhile, although the Heng Samrin government restored many of the liberties abolished by the Pol Pot regime, it was reluctant to implement international relief efforts to aid the more than 2,000,000 Cambodians reported to be facing imminent starvation, for fear that food and supplies might fall into the hands of Pol Pot's Khmer Rouge.

A special tribunal of the Heng Samrin government in August 1979 sentenced Pol Pot and Ieng Sary to death in absentia for "genocidal crimes." Nevertheless, when in September the Soviet delegate to the U.N. General Assembly moved for recognition of the Heng Samrin government, maintaining that the Pol Pot regime had been "thrown out on the garbage heap of history," the assembly voted seventy-one to thirty-five to retain the Pol Pot representative. The United States delegate, who voted with the majority, explained that although the excesses of the Pol Pot government were to be condemned, the Heng Samrin regime had no superior claim to the seat, since it had been imposed by Vietnamese military force. In October 1980 the Assembly reaffirmed its verdict of the preceding year by a vote of seventy-four to thirty-five, as guerrillas supporting Pol Pot continued to struggle with forces of the Heng Samrin regime along the Thai-Cambodian border.

Meanwhile, it had been reported in December 1979 that Pol Pot, who retained the title of Prime Minister after his overthrow by the Heng Samrin regime, had been replaced in that post by the more moderate Khieu Samphan, apparently to improve the rebel regime's national and international image. Nevertheless, as commander in chief of his Khmer Rouge guerrilla army, estimated to number some 30,000 to 40,000, Pol Pot remained the regime's most powerful man.

PERSONAL LIFE

Although scant information is available about Pol Pot's personal life, he is known to have married Khieu Ponnary, a former schoolteacher, whom he met as a student in Paris, and who headed the Association of Democratic Women of Kampuchea. Richard Dudman of the St. Louis *Post-Dispatch,* who along with *Washington Post* correspondent Elizabeth Becker was granted a ninety-minute audience with him in late 1978, reported that Pol Pot, dressed in a gray Mao jacket and speaking in Khmer, received the American journalists "as if he were king." Dudman, quoted in the Christian *Science* Monitor (December 4, 1979), described Pol Pot as having "very bright eyes," a "touch of gray in his black hair," a "very youthful-looking face," and "tiny, very delicate, almost spidery hands." Miss Becker found him to be "pleasant-looking," "very composed," and "a little larger than most Cambodians."

The former Cambodian Prime Minister, who is credited with having "an acute sense of history," was characterized by Douglas Pike as "something of a genius, in the same sense that Hitler was." Pol Pot died in 1998 while under house arrest.

FURTHER READING
Christian Sci Mon B pl-f D 4 *79* por; *Far Eastern Economic Review p20 + O 21 '77* pors; *Journal of Contemporary Asia 7:418 + no 3 77; The New York Times* pl5 *Mr 19 *78; New York 11:33 Ja 16 *78* por; *International Who's Who, 1979-80*; Ponchaud, Francois. *Cambodia: Year* Zero *(1978)*

KOCA POPOVIC

Yugoslav Government Official

Born: March 14, 1908; Belgrade, Kingdom of Serbia
Died: October 20, 1992; Belgrade, Former Yugoslavia
Affiliation: League of Communists of Yugoslavia

INTRODUCTION

Since the beginning of World War II one of the important figures in Yugoslavia's stormy history has been Koca Popovic. He fought with the Yugoslav Partisans to drive out the Axis invaders, served as chief of staff of the Yugoslav Army from 1945 to 1953 in the Communist government established by Marshal Tito (see C.B., March 1955), and after 1953 he was been Secretary of State for Foreign Affairs and a member of the Federal Executive Council of the country. He became a deputy to the Yugoslav Federal People's Assembly, the parliament, in 1943 and since 1952 has also been a member of the Central Committee of the League of Communists of Yugoslavia.

Partly under his guidance, the international position of Yugoslavia became, as described by the Manchester Guardian *(May 8, 1956), the "half-way house for East and West," in the ideological clash between Communist and democratic countries. Some of Popovic's speeches before the United Nations General Assembly, whose meetings he has attended since 1953, have been published in the* United Nations Bulletin *(since July 1954 the* United Nations Review*).*

EARLY LIFE

Koca Popovic (other spellings include Kocha Popovich, Kotsa Popovitch, and Konstantin Popovitch) was born on March 14, 1908 in Belgrade in Serbia, then an independent monarchy. He was the son of Aleksandar and Ruza (Zdravkovic) Popovic. His father was a wealthy businessman and his family was in the banking business in Belgrade. In a discussion once with Tito, Popovic remarked, "After the war, in 1919, my father bought a Daimler [automobile]. It was white, and every Sunday afternoon the whole family, my father and mother, and the sons and daughters, would pile into the long, open car and drive proudly through the streets of Belgrade, our noses in the air. People would say, 'There goes Popovic's bathtub' " (quoted by Vladimir Dedijer in *Tito Speaks; His Self-Portrait and Struggle zvith Stalin,* 1953).

Young Popovic studied at the University of Belgrade and in Switzerland and was graduated from the Sorbonne in Paris in 1932. Interested in literature, he became a journalist and a member of a group of progressive Yugoslav writers. "After failing to make a name for himself as a surrealist poet in Paris," according to Leigh White in *Balkan Caesar, Tito versus Stalin* (1951), Popovic joined the Communist Party of Yugoslavia in 1933. (The independent Kingdom of the Serbs, Croats and Slovenes had been formed after World War I in 1919; since 1929 it has been called Yugoslavia.)

LIFE'S WORK

In *Tito's Yugoslavia* (1955) Eric L. Pridonoff wrote that when the Russians under General Fedor I. Tolbukhin moved into Yugoslavia against the Germans in the fall of 1944, "Tito followed with his Partisans and reorganized civilian control. It was during this march . . . that he substituted Koca Popovic in place of Arsa Jovanovich as his chief of general staff. It was advantageous for Tito to impress the Serbian population with Koca Popovic, a Serb." This displeased the Soviets, but Popovic retained command and headed the Second Army in the general offensive for the final liberation of the country, which began on March 20, 1945 and ended on May 15. Yugoslavia lost about 1,700,000 persons during the war.

Tito, having emerged supreme in the struggle against the monarchists, set up a Communist-dominated government which was recognized by Great Britain and the United States on December 22, 1945. Several Yugoslav veterans of the Spanish Civil War were given

Affiliation: League of Communists of Yugoslavia

As one of a number of Yugoslav Communists, Popovic fought in the Spanish Civil War in the late 1930's with the international artillery unit in the Republican Army. Those Yugoslavs who survived this war provided Tito with his original cadres in World War II. When the country was occupied by the Axis, active resistance was offered by the Partisans under Tito and by the Chetniks under the monarchist Draza Mihailovic, who also fought against each other for the future control of Yugoslavia.

Popovic was an early organizer of the Yugoslavian Liberation Army during the war. In December 1941 Tito created the First Proletarian Brigade and made Popovic its commander. He later became a divisional, corps, and Army commander. Dedijer observed that at the first meeting of the partisan commanders, most wore fierce moustaches, "but the fiercest adorned the commander of a detachment from Serbia, Koca Popovic" (*Tito Speaks*).

leading positions in his regime and their group became known as the "Spanish nobility." Popovic was again made chief of the general staff with the rank of colonel general and served actively in that capacity until 1953.

In the spring of 1945 Tito had signed a treaty of friendship and mutual assistance with the Soviet Union. The following spring Popovic accompanied Tito to Moscow for a discussion on economic affairs and took notes on the meetings and talks, reprinted by Dedijer in *Tito Speaks*. Popovic describes how, at a supper party, Stalin invited him to drink *Bruderschaft* (brotherhood).

Early in 1948 Popovic accompanied Milovan Djilas, Secretary of the Politburo of the Yugoslav Communist party, on a trip to the Soviet Union. It was then that the first indication of a Soviet-Yugoslav rift appeared. Thomas Taylor Hammond in *Yugoslavia—Between East and West* (1954) noted: "Stalin tried to subordinate the Yugoslav economy to Soviet control, recruited secret agents in the Yugoslav army and police, and even worked to undermine Tito's power. When Tito refused to tolerate these activities he was publicly denounced in Moscow as a traitor to world communism, and the Yugoslav Communist party was ejected from membership in the Communist Information Bureau (Cominform)." At about this time, Popovic published his pamphlet,

Revision of Marxism-Leninism on the Question of the Liberation War in Yugoslavia (Belgrade, 1949).

Looking to the West for help in maintaining his independent path, in the spring of 1951 Tito sent Popovic to the United States to discuss the procurement of a large quantity of modern weapons and other military supplies. He received permission and aid from the United States for purchasing the arms. In the fall of 1951 a formal military aid agreement was signed by the two countries.

When the new Yugoslav Constitution went into effect in January 1953, Popovic became Secretary of State for Foreign Affairs and a member of the Federal Executive Council. In line with the country's growing interest in Western-allied nations, the Yugoslavs concluded a treaty of friendship and cooperation with Turkey and Greece on February 28, 1953. The signing had been delayed a few days because "General Popovic, a gifted French scholar, had contested the phraseology in some paragraphs of the French text, and when corrections were made to his satisfaction, the draft was retyped" (*The New York Times,* February 25, 1953). The three countries joined in August 1954 in a military alliance for collective action against aggression, thus linking Yugoslavia indirectly with the North Atlantic Treaty Organization (NATO), of which both Greece and Turkey are members.

Popovic played a large role in the discussions and final settlement of the Trieste problem. In May 1953 he stated that Yugoslavia was willing to deal directly with Italy on the dispute at any time. He protested against the decision of Great Britain and the United States to give Zone A to Italy and noted that the only solution should be to internationalize the city itself and to give Yugoslavia both zones, A and B. This problem was solved by an agreement between the two powers in October 1954 whereby Italy received most of Zone A, Yugoslavia kept Zone B, and the city of Trieste was internationalized.

At the 1953, 1954 and 1955 meetings of the United Nations General Assembly in New York Popovic headed his country's delegation. Speaking at the tenth anniversary session of the United Nations in June 1955 in San Francisco, he called for "new ways of strengthening international peace and cooperation" and stated that his country pursues a policy of "active coexistence, fully independent but not evading any international responsibility."

In his capacity as Foreign Secretary, Popovic has accompanied Tito on a number of state visits: to Great

Britain in March 1953, to India and Burma in early 1955, to Egypt in December 1955, and to France in May 1956. He took part in the discussions during the summer of 1956 when Egyptian President Gamal Abdel Nasser and Prime Minister Jawaharlal Nehru of India visited Yugoslavia.

With the softening of the Soviet position after the death of Joseph Stalin, relations between the two countries were bettered. In June 1956 Popovic accompanied Tito on a state visit to the Soviet Union and he attended the meetings during the visits to Yugoslavia of the Soviet First Deputy Premier Anastas I. Mikoyan in July and of the First Secretary of the Soviet Communist party, Nikita S. Khrushchev, in September.

Later in the fall of 1956 at the meeting in New York of the UN Security Council on the Suez Canal crisis, Popovic spoke in favor of the Indian proposals, for the establishment of an international organ with advisory, consultative and liaison functions and offered a Yugoslav resolution. In the final voting he favored the six British-French general principles, but, in support of the Soviet and Egyptian position, decided against international control of the canal.

While in New York, Popovic gave the American Secretary of State John Foster Dulles assurances that Yugoslav relations with Russia had not been altered by Tito's secret talks with Soviet leaders.

PERSONAL LIFE
Koca Popovic was awarded the Order of Freedom, Spomenica, in 1941 and has received other decorations. He married Lepa Ponovic in 1947. He has laughingly referred to an instance when a Soviet general once jeeringly called him a "general, millionaire, poet." For recreation he enjoyed swimming and fishing with an underwater harpoon. He was described as a "slender" and "dapper" man.

FURTHER READING
Dedijer, V. *Tito Speaks; His Self-Portrait and Struggle with Stalin* (1953); *International Who's Who*, 1955; *Who's Who in America*, 1956-57

VLADIMIR PUTIN
President and Prime Minister of Russia

Born: October 7, 1952; Leningrad (now Saint Petersburg), Russia
Party Affiliation: United Russia

INTRODUCTION
After December 31, 1999, when he became acting president of Russia, Vladimir Putin saw his public image undergo a slight transformation. Initially, the poker-faced official was best known for how little was known about him, other than the fact that he had spent nearly 17 years as a member of the KGB—the Soviet Union's elite intelligence organization—followed by less than 10 years in politics, which had led to his appointment as prime minister in August 1999. But when he emerged as President Boris Yeltsin's heir apparent, his public-relations team saw the need to demystify him for the voting public, in time for the 2000 presidential election. Putin thus began to reveal himself as "a man of simple tastes," as Bernard Gwertzman described him in The New York Times Book Review *(May 14, 2000)—a*

family man who had been inspired to join the KGB by a movie he saw as a teenager.

What has not changed is Putin's reputation as a capable leader. Since he was elected president, by an overwhelming margin, in March 2000, he has taken steps to increase Russia's control over its many provinces, to strengthen its military, to fight corruption, and to ensure the continued improvement of its once-ailing economy. He has also made strides in developing stronger ties to the West, including gaining a role in NATO discussions and supporting the United States and its war on terrorism. While some have worried that Putin's firm hold on power comes at the cost of liberty within the country, many perceive him as the strong figure Russia needs at its helm.

EARLY LIFE
The only child of a factory foreman and his wife, Vladimir Vladimirovich Putin was born on October 7, 1952 in Leningrad (renamed St. Petersburg after the collapse

Vladimir Putin.

of the Soviet Union, in the early 1990s). Putin grew up in a communal apartment shared by three families, but he enjoyed a comfortable upbringing. His parents enrolled him in martial-arts classes, and by the age of 16, he ranked as an expert in sambo, a combination of wrestling and judo. He became Leningrad's judo champion in 1974, while he was attending university, and he instructed students in karate while he was with the KGB.

Putin has often been described as driven and ambitious, traits that he exhibited even as a teenager. At age 16 he entered a college-preparatory secondary school that had a reputation for academic rigor. The school emphasized debate-oriented classes over traditional lectures, and it accepted only the brightest students, who were thereby guaranteed spots at St. Petersburg's most prestigious technical university. Although Putin intended to study chemistry, he soon switched his focus to the humanities and such "soft" sciences as biology, letting his grades in math and chemistry slip. "I spoke to

his father about this," his biology teacher told Michael Wines. "He said his son was so goal-oriented that he already knows what he wants—and between us, why should he be expending so much energy on chemistry and math when he is going to do something else?" Putin also played handball and was a deejay for the school radio station, playing Western rock music for his fellow students.

Putin has revealed that the 1968 movie *The Sword and the Shield*, whose main character is a Soviet double agent in Nazi Germany, led to his desire to join the KGB. According to *Komsomolskaya Pravda* (February 17, 2000, as reprinted on-line by *Russia Today*), Russia's largest newspaper in terms of circulation, Putin approached the KGB when he graduated from high school and asked to be admitted into the service; KGB officials advised him to get a degree in law. In 1970 Putin enrolled at Leningrad State University, considered to be one of Russia's top schools, to study civil law. By all accounts, he conducted himself quietly and seriously. He graduated five years later, with honors, and was recruited by the extremely selective KGB.

LIFE'S WORK

Reports about Putin's time with the intelligence organization are sketchy and contain half-statements and misinformation. It appears that the KGB trained him in Moscow and that he then spent some time in St. Petersburg. Igor Antonov, a former KGB co-worker of Putin's, told Michael Wines that the KGB would not station an unmarried agent outside the country; in the early 1980s Putin married, and in 1985 he was sent to East Germany, considered one of the most important foreign posts. The nature of his work abroad remains unknown. Some reports claim that he did nothing more than push papers. The Stratfor Intelligence Service, a private think tank based in Austin, Texas, suggested that he acted as an "economic spy," stealing Western technology. Still other sources maintained that he kept tabs on East Germans and recruited agents for the KGB. In 1989 the Berlin Wall, which separated Communist East Germany from democratic West Germany, fell, and the two nations united under democratic rule. Putin returned to Russia, which was undergoing major reforms instituted by President Mikhail Gorbachev with the goal of pushing the Soviet Union toward democracy, economic privatization, and rapprochement with the West. According to some sources, Putin's stint with the KGB ended at this point, but most observers agree that he continued to work as a KGB mole at his new job in the international relations department at Leningrad State University, where he monitored reaction to Gorbachev's new policies.

In the early 1990s Putin accepted a position in the St. Petersburg government. The mayor, Anatoly Sobchak, had taught Putin law at the university, and they had become reacquainted when Putin returned to Russia. "[Putin] worked under the cover of the University International Department and participated in meetings of the external economic politics," Antonov told a reporter for Komsomolskaya Pravda. "Sobchak noticed him because Putin gave him advice several times. If Sobchak hadn't needed him badly, how could he take a person from the KGB to work as his closest aide at a time when all special services were marred with criticism?" Putin worked behind-the-scenes for Sobchak's administration, earning the sobriquet "gray cardinal" because of his colorless yet powerful presence. Under Sobchak, Putin oversaw St. Petersburg's businesses and exports and persuaded foreign financiers to invest in the city. "In outside appearance, he is a calm, inconspicuous, quiet man," Sergei Stepashin, a former prime minister of Russia, told Michael Wines for *The New York Times* (January 1, 2000). "But his grip, which was felt by all the financiers in St. Petersburg, was amazing." In 1994 Putin became the first deputy mayor of St. Petersburg. His stint in city administration ended two years later, when Sobchak failed to win reelection and fled the city amid charges of corruption.

Shortly after Sobchak's departure Putin was invited to Moscow to work for the Kremlin. He started in the office of the property manager, which oversees the Kremlin and all its outlying properties, including government buildings and homes for officials. In March 1997 he became the head of the Main Control (or Oversight) Department, responsible for carrying out President Boris Yeltsin's decrees, and a year later he was appointed to oversee the Kremlin's relations with Russia's many regions. (The Stratfor Intelligence Service maintained that he was awarded the title of first deputy chief of staff at this juncture.) In July 1998 Putin became the head of the Federal Security Service (FSB), one of the two sections into which the KGB had been divided after the Soviet Union disbanded. In March 1999 he took on the duties of secretary of the presidential Security Council. Then, on August 9, 1999, Yeltsin sacked his fourth prime minister in 17 months, Sergei Stepashin, and appointed Putin to the post.

Putin's incredibly quick succession of promotions has been attributed to his unswerving loyalty to Yeltsin, who was known for firing prime ministers when their public approval ratings rose to a point that he considered unacceptably high. Reporters and political analysts speculated that the upcoming presidential elections, scheduled to be held less than a year later, spurred Yeltsin to appoint a successor who would follow his decrees and protect his interests—someone who would be, in effect, a puppet. (Yeltsin was finishing his second term in office and was thus disqualified from running again.) Putin had always remained faithful to his bosses; in 1996, for example, when Sobchak lost the election for mayor of St. Petersburg, Putin was the only top aide to resign, saying, "Better to be hanged for loyalty than rewarded for treason." He had proven his loyalty to Yeltsin in 1999, when chief prosecutor Yuri Skuratov ran a corruption-finding campaign against a close Yeltsin associate. Videotapes depicting Skuratov cavorting with two prostitutes aired on Russian television, and Putin, as head of the FSB, verified their authenticity. Rumors circulated that Stepashin had failed the loyalty test because he did not stop Yuri Luzhkov, the mayor of Moscow and a strong opponent of Yeltsin's, from forming a coalition with other competitors for the presidency. One of Putin's first actions as prime minister was to weaken Luzhkov's regional and Moscow-based support, which he accomplished, many claimed, with the help of knowledge he had acquired through the FSB.

When Yeltsin appointed Putin prime minister, he also declared that his new right-hand man was his choice for the next president of Russia, despite Putin's lack of experience in any elective office. Neither reporters nor citizens knew anything about the new prime minister, and Putin began his new job with an approval rating of just 2 percent. By November, however, his rating had climbed to 29 percent, an unprecedented level in Russia, where a rating of 18 percent is considered extremely favorable. The turnaround came as a result of the renewed war against Chechnya, an independent, primarily Muslim region within Russia. Chechnya's declaration of independence in 1994 had precipitated a war with Russia, which did not want the region to secede. The war continued into 1996, until Chechen guerrillas routed the Russian soldiers, some of whom had already captured Chechnya's capital. After the ignominious Russian defeat, Chechnya secured an agreement that granted the region the right to govern itself independently and the chance to discuss its official status at meetings to be held in 2001. In August 1999, however, Chechen militants launched several incursions into the neighboring Russian region of Dagestan, which has a substantial Muslim population. Under Putin's leadership, the Russian army rebuffed the rebels and set up watch posts along the Chechnya border. The majority of Russian citizens, still feeling the sting of the humiliating loss of three years before, approved Putin's actions, and the prime minister promised to eradicate the rebels. Then, in September, several bombs tore through apartment buildings in Volgodonsk and Moscow, killing approximately 300 civilians. The Russian government claimed that the bombs were set by Chechen terrorists, and though the charges were never proven, the Russian army once again entered Chechnya. Its advances and victories buoyed Putin's reputation, and the Russian press hailed him as a strong leader, one strikingly different from the ailing and sometimes incoherent Yeltsin. Reactions outside Russia, however, were not favorable: the brutality of the second Chechen campaign provoked criticism from the U.S. and other Western powers dismayed about the killing of Chechen civilians trapped in the conflict.

In December 1999 elections were held for the Duma, the lower house of the legislature, which was dominated by the Communist Party. Although the Communists held onto their majority, the Unity Party, which had formed only a couple of months prior to the election and had made its support of Putin the sole item on its platform, won a significant number of seats, thus diminishing the Communists' base. Two weeks later, assured of Putin's loyalty as well as of his popular support, Yeltsin resigned as president of Russia. On December 31, 1999 Putin became both prime minister and acting president of Russia.

As one of his first acts as president, Putin granted Yeltsin and his family lifetime immunity from prosecution for corruption (charges of which were already being aired) and allotted them a salary and secret-service protection. For his part Yeltsin had done his best to ensure Putin's succession to the presidency by moving the election up from June to March 2000, thereby reducing the preparation time of any rivals.

Before the election, under Putin's guidance, First Deputy Prime Minister Mikhail Kasyanov negotiated with London-based investors a new repayment schedule for Soviet debts. Putin expressed the hope that the West, with renewed confidence in Russia's ability to control its finances, would invest more money in the economy,

which had been boosted by recent increases in the price of oil, one of Russia's major exports. Putin also started investigations into the rampant political corruption that, more than anything else, has been responsible for weakening Russia's economy and government. Charges of corruption had been leveled against Putin himself in the past, particularly during his St. Petersburg years and during his tenure as FSB chief, but none has ever stuck.

In elections held on March 26, 2000, in a field of 11 candidates, Putin commanded just over 50 percent of the vote; he was sworn in as president on May 7. In the months following the election, he maintained his high level of popularity, by taking steps that bolstered his image as a strong leader. While he stressed the need to modernize the country's nuclear arsenal, he won the Russian Parliament's approval for the Start II nuclear arms reduction agreement with the United States, which proposed that both nations cut the number of such weapons by half. Over the summer, he succeeded in pushing through parliament his plan to organize Russia into seven large districts—each to be headed by a figure in the Kremlin—with the aim of stripping provincial governors of much of their power and increasing central control over the country. Along with Putin's high approval ratings came concern from some corners that his firm hand was maintained at the expense of freedoms within Russia. Fueling these worries was an incident in May 2000, in which federal agents raided the offices of Media-Most, the country's largest independent media conglomerate, whose television network had been critical of Putin; Media-Most's head, Vladimir A. Gusinsky, was arrested and charged with financial wrongdoing. Gusinsky was released after four days, and Putin himself publicly criticized the arrest. Gusinsky, however, accused the president of having been behind the agents' actions. Gusinksy, still under investigation, fled Russia in June 2000, and the government issued a demand for his extradition.

More damaging to Putin's reputation were missteps in the wake of a military disaster. Shortly before midnight on August 12, 2000, the Russian nuclear submarine Kursk sank in the Barents Sea after explosions on board instantly killed most of the 118 crew members. (23 men left alive after the blasts later perished.) In the days that followed, the government was slow to request foreign help in rescuing the surviving crew members and seemed reluctant to share details with the public; Putin himself remained for days at the Black Sea resort where he had been vacationing. Later, however—in what some viewed as a sign of a new openness on the part of the Russian government—Putin admitted to feelings of "responsibility and guilt" over the tragedy, and he promised that over the next 10 years, each of the families of the dead crew members would receive payments equal to an officer's salary.

By the end of 2000 Putin appeared to have accomplished few of his political aims. The economic and military reforms he promised had failed to materialize, and a resolution of the conflict in Chechnya—his signature policy initiative—had not been achieved. Yet his approval ratings remained high and a biography of his life became a best-seller in Russia. To account for Putin's popularity, observers have cited the strength and authority which he brought to the presidency. Putin fostered a feeling of optimism about Russia's future, and his belief in the primacy of a respected and powerful statehood helped mend the weakened Russian self-esteem that had been the result of the Soviet Union's untidy dissolution and economic collapse. "He has given Russians hope," Yuri Levada, one of the country's leading sociologists, remarked, as quoted by Paul Quinn-Judge for Time (January 22, 2001). One notable aspect of Putin's attempts to restore Russian prestige was his tendency to revive certain elements of the past, such as the Soviet national anthem and the State Council—the appointed consultative body that replaced the legislature's upper chamber in September 2000. (The original State Council was an important governing body in the 19th and early 20th century, during the rule of Czar Nicholas II, the last czar of Russia. In contrast to its predecessor, which comprised some elected members, Putin's State Council is wholly appointed.)

Putin's international reputation deteriorated in 2001 amid reports that his government was behind the growing internal assault on independent media. With Gusinsky out of the country (a Spanish court ruled not to extradite him), state-controlled conglomerate Gazprom liquidated the remaining properties of the Media-Most empire, including the nationwide TV network NTV, the daily newspaper Segodnya, and the weekly magazine Itogi. Additionally, TNT, a small Media-Most TV network, was investigated by the government and charged with tax evasion. The media crackdown continued well into 2002, when TV6—a revamped NTV that employed many of NTV's former workers—was pulled off the air in February. Government officials, however, continued to insist that such moves were not politically motivated

but simply part of a larger effort to stamp out corruption and illegal business practices.

Meanwhile, Putin worked to build his image as a world leader, traveling widely and meeting with several heads of state. Although he enjoyed an amicable first meeting with U.S. President George W. Bush in Slovenia in June 2001, Putin's foreign policy tended to focus on strengthening relations with countries that had traditionally been on good terms with the former Soviet Union, including Iraq, Libya, Vietnam, and North Korea. He visited China, reportedly hoping to forge some kind of alliance to counter President Bush's decision to break away from the 1972 U.S.-Soviet Antiballistic Missile Treaty. He also irked the U.S. administration by contributing aid to Iran's plan to develop a civilian nuclear reactor.

At the same time Putin showed an interest in strengthening Russia's ties to the West. He met with Britain's prime minister, Tony Blair, and Germany's chancellor, Gerhard Schroder, and publicized Russia's hopes of one day belonging to the World Trade Organization and gaining full membership in NATO (North Atlantic Treaty Organization). In what appeared to many as a symbol of Putin's turn toward "Westernization," he was one of the first world leaders to offer sympathy and support to President Bush following the terrorist attacks against the U.S. on September 11, 2001. Putin telephoned Bush, flying on board Air Force One immediately after the attacks, and informed the president that although he knew the U.S. military would be placed on full alert, Russia would keep its forces on standby—thereby breaking the Cold War cycle in which an escalation of activity on one side would trigger a defensive escalation on the other. In the ensuing months Putin aligned Russia with the U.S. in the fight against terrorism, agreeing to allow American troops to use locations in the former Soviet Republics of central Asia (such as Uzbekistan) as staging areas for offensive military strikes against Afghanistan. The diplomatic move had the effect of dampening international criticism of Russia's approach to dealing with the Chechen rebels, which it had long referred to as a war on terrorism.

In December 2001 Putin appeared on an unprecedented call-in show fielding questions from concerned citizens regarding poverty, the proliferation of drugs, and increasing numbers of homeless children. Putin responded to 47 of about 500,000 questions submitted for the show, which aired live on Russian TV and radio. "Despite many problems and living standards remaining very low, the dynamics are very positive," Putin reported, as quoted by Andrei Zolotov Jr. in the Moscow Times (December 25, 2001). "One can say today that the departing year 2001 was a good year for Russia." Putin also expressed confidence in the country's future, explaining that the economy had grown by 5.2 percent in 2001 and that the average salary, adjusted for inflation, had increased by more than 20 percent in the same period. In addition, he noted that the government had been working on paying back 1990s wage arrears, which were now down to 1.5 billion rubles from 3.5 billion rubles.

Complementing these achievements, in May 2002 Putin and Bush signed a historic bilateral arms control agreement, committing both nations to reduce their strategic nuclear arsenals from about 6,000 to between 1,700 and 2,200. Putin also succeeded in gaining Russian participation in NATO, the military alliance created in 1949 to counter the threat of Soviet expansion. Although Russia was not granted full membership in the 19-member organization, it was granted a role in NATO discussions concerning such issues as crisis management, missile defense, and counterterrorism—replacing a 1997 agreement reached under U.S. President Bill Clinton that allowed Russia into NATO discussions only after the committee had reached a consensus. In another overture directed toward the U.S. and Europe, Putin began allowing foreign access to Russia's extensive petroleum reserves, and encouraged trade and foreign investment in other sectors as well. "For decades we had voluntarily created walls and barriers around ourselves and decided to live within our walls," Putin remarked to an audience at St. Petersburg University the day after signing the arms treaty with Bush, as quoted by Agence France Presse (May 25, 2002). "Now, both in terms of NATO and in economic relations, we are starting to blend into the family of civilized countries."

In July 2002 Putin won support from an unlikely source, French President Jacques Chirac, who criticized the European Union's proposal to require that citizens of Kaliningrad, a Russian republic on the Baltic Sea, obtain a visa when passing through Lithuania and Poland (which surround Kaliningrad) after 2004, when those countries are slated to join the E.U. The informal summit between Putin and Chirac also resulted in France's tempering its criticism—which had been particularly strong—of Russian military operations in Chechnya. Nevertheless, as objections to Russia's conduct of the war continued to mount—including accusations from

human rights organizations that Russian attacks in the area had killed an estimated 10,000 civilians—Putin indicated that the campaign was nearing an end.

Hopes for a resolution to the conflict were dashed in late August 2002, when a Russian transport aircraft crashed near an army base in Chechnya, killing 119. The Russian government claimed Chechen rebels were responsible. A few weeks later, on September 11, Putin delivered an ultimatum to the ex-Soviet state of Georgia, accusing it of harboring the rebels. He threatened military strikes unless Georgian President Eduard Shevardnadze made an effort to curb the activity of terrorists within Georgian territory. In a letter sent to the United Nations, Putin wrote, as quoted by CNN. com (September 12, 2002): "If the Georgian leadership doesn't take concrete actions to destroy the terrorists, and bandit incursions continue from its territory, Russia will take adequate measures to counteract the terrorist threat, in strict accordance with international law."

Although there has been little public or political debate in Russia about the war in Chechnya, internal support appeared to flag prior to October 2002. On the evening of October 23, 2002, however, more than 40 Chechen separatists infiltrated a Moscow theater during a production of the popular musical Nord-Ost, holding more than 600 audience members and players hostage to force the Russian government to withdraw from Chechnya and end the war there. The hostage-takers, who were fully armed and had planted female rebels in the audience, threatened to blow up the building if their demands were not met. The siege lasted for three days, ending when Russian counterterrorist forces stormed the theater in an early morning raid that began with the release of a narcotic gas to quiet the rebels. The gas killed more than 100 of the hostages and hospitalized about 400 others. Though Russian officials deflected questions about the success of the raid, Putin was granted overwhelming support from the Russian public in the weeks afterward; many questioned in an All-Russia Public Opinion Center poll believed that a worse outcome had been averted with the use of the narcotic gas, and 85 percent supported Putin's actions, with only 10 percent opposed.

In 2004, Putin was elected as president for a second term with over 70 percent of the vote. Barred for a third term in 2012, he became Prime Minister of Russia when Dmitry Medvedev was elected president. In 2012, he again ran for president and won, amid accusations of vote rigging.

In 2014, Putin ordered Russian troops to seize Crimea from Ukraine, stating that this decision would not reversed because Crimea was Russia's "spiritual ground." Several countries sanctioned Russia, and as a result there has been economic instability in the region. Putin has said that he will not allow a defeat of the Pro-Russia side of the conflict.

Putin's approval rating in Russia climbed to an all-time high of 89 percent in 2015, likely as a consequence of significant improvements in living standards and Russia's prominence on the world scene during Putin's presidency. Based on polling in Russia, he has also been viewed as the world's most popular politician.

PERSONAL LIFE

Putin married Lyudmila Shkrebneva, a specialist in foreign languages, in 1983 (they divorced in 2014); they have two teenage daughters, Katya and Masha. Putin has boasted that his children's knowledge of German surpasses his own facility with that language, which is good enough to enable him to imitate regional dialects. He is fond of literature and music, and he has acknowledged that he is a practicing Orthodox Christian. "When I was a few months old," he recalled to a Reuters reporter, as quoted in *Russia Today* (February 13, 2000, on-line), "my mum and her neighbor in the communal apartment where we lived took me to church without telling my father, he was a Communist Party member, and baptized me." Early on in his presidency, Putin appeared somber and serious in public, but he has since revealed himself as a master of witty one-liners, even making humorous asides at high-profile diplomatic events. Opening a congress of European audit institutions, he made a joke about the once-revered fathers of communism, Friedrich Engels and Karl Marx. "I see the name of a Mr. Engels from Germany on the list," he remarked, referring to one of the conference attendees. "Thank God he came without Marx."

FURTHER READING

Agence France Presse May 25, 2002; CNN.com Sep. 12, 2002; *Maclean's* p46+ Jan. 17, 2000, with photo; *Moscow Times* Dec. 25, 2001, Sep, 17, 2002; *Nation* p3+ Jan. 24, 2000; *The New York Times* A p11 Jan. 1, 2000, with photo, A p4 Jan. 10, 2000, with photo, p1+ Feb. 20, 2000, with photos, IV p1 May 19, 2002; *Russia Today* Web site; Stratfor Intelligence Service Web site; *Time* p90+ Jan. 1, 2000, p24 Jan. 22, 2001, p26 Apr. 30, 2001, p42 May 27, 2002; Putin, Vladimir, with Nataliya Gevorkyan, Natalya Timakova, and Andrei Kolesnikov, *First Person: An Astonishingly Frank Self-Portrait by Russia's President Vladimir Putin,* 2000

Q

MUAMMAR AL QADDAFI

Prime Minister of Libya

Born: 1940–1943 (?); Qasr Abu Hadi, Italian Libya
Died: October 20, 2011; Sirte, Libya
Affiliation: Arab Socialist Union (1971–1977); Independent (1977–2011)

INTRODUCTION

Muammar al Qaddafi, the dictator of Libya for more than 42 years before his death, in 2011, had the reputation of being mercurial, oppressive, and eccentric. His allies and enemies seldom could predict his next political move; he was reputed to think of himself as "the king of Africa," and when he traveled, he preferred to stay in his Bedouin tent.

El-Gamaty, a Libyan academic and politician, has stated in a February 17, 2016, article on Aljazeera. com that, "The end of his brutal era left a huge political and security vacuum in the country which was then filled by armed groups that were formed during and after the revolution," explaining that after Qaddifi's death, "[a policy was put into place by] the first transitional government in post-revolution Libya to pay salaries to those who took part in the uprising and belonged to armed groups that were acting as the new security bodies.

"These generous salaries encouraged unemployed Libyan young men to take up arms and set up their own militias or join existing ones. The proliferation of armed militias turned out to be one of the biggest problems after the revolution."

He then stated, "It has become clear that Qaddafi has left behind a long, damaging legacy caused by his deliberate decimation of any forms of state institutions. . . .

[His] legacy also included having no formal constitution or an independent judiciary system as well as the prohibition of political parties, civil society organizations and free press throughout his 42-year rule."

Today, Libya is a country with instability and insecurity for its citizens and is facing the terrorist threat of the Islamic State gaining footholds in cities such as Derna, Benghazi and, mainly, Sirte. The New Government of National Accord (GNA), headed by Fayez Serraj, "will have to face the mammoth challenge of ending the civil war and reuniting the country and its main institutions, as well as providing safety and security and restoring better socioeconomic conditions," El-Gamaty stated.

Qaddafi, a devoted follower of Egypt's strongman, Gamal Abdel Nasser, was described by the late President of Egypt as "naïve." His successor, Anwar Sadat, the Egyptian president from 1970 to 1981, on a number of occasions publicly accused Qaddafi of being "100 percent sick and possessed of the demon." The former Sudanese leader Gaafar Nimeiri once asserted that Qaddafi had "a split personality and both of them are evil."

Yet, Qaddafi never gave up his goal of uniting the Arabs of Africa into one Pan-Arab, Pan-Africa unit: "I believe that the Arab nation can become a paradise," Muammar Qaddafi, Libya's self-styled "Leader of the Revolution," declared in a 1985 interview. The paradisiacal "Arab nation" that Qaddafi long envisaged was a utopian state whose inhabitants are governed according to the tenets of Islam and that stretches from the Persian Gulf to the Atlantic Ocean on the North African coast. *For most Arab leaders, that somewhat quaint be-lief in the existence of a mythical Pan-Arabia had re-mained just that, but for Qaddafi it had been the driving force behind his relentlessly adventurist foreign policy and his sponsorship of the activities of some of the most widely feared terrorist organizations in the world. Con-ceiving himself as a latter-day Saladin or, as more than one scholar has noted, a "Bismarck of the Arab world," Qaddafi had willingly gone to battle with, or financed acts of terrorism against any country—Muslim or infi-del—whose government he perceived as a threat to the realization of his dream of "Arab unity."*

As a result of his refusal, despite repeated failures, to abandon his quixotic crusade to unify the Arab lands, Qaddafi had become possibly the most reviled, hated, ridiculed, and (by some) feared head of state of the mod-ern era. He was the target of at least 19 coup attempts since coming to power in 1969 and, since 1982, of as many as half a dozen would-be assassins, Qaddafi was regarded as the enemy not only of the United States and many European countries, but also, at one time or an-other, of virtually every government in the Middle East and North Africa. His rhetoric, however, gave Libyans a strong sense of identity and a greater sense of their importance in world affairs.

EARLY LIFE

The only son and youngest of the four children of Mo-hammed Abdul Salam bin Hamed bin Mohammed, an illiterate Bedouin herder of camels and goats, and his wife, Aisha, Muammar Abu Meniar al-Qaddafi was born in a tent in the Libyan desert about 20 miles in-land, according to one source, from the coastal town of Sirte. (As transliterated from the Arabic, the family name also appears in such forms as Gaddafi, Qhadafi, and Khadafi.) Qaddafi's middle name, Abu Meniar, means "the father of the knife" and is the name by which his father was commonly known. Qaddafi be-lieved he was born in 1942 in the Islamic month of Mu-harram, the month of peace, which corresponded at the time to March in the Gregorian calendar. (The Islamic calendar is lunar.) The family belonged to the Qaddad-fa, one of the lowlier tribes of North Africa, whose tra-ditional homeland is in the Sirte Desert in present-day northwestern Libya. Like the overwhelming majority of North Africa's nomadic inhabitants, Qaddafi's fam-ily enjoyed few, if any, of the modern conveniences of Western civilization, living much as their forebears had lived for centuries before them.

Notwithstanding what many Westerners would call the Bedouins' "primitive" existence, the peoples of North Africa were nonetheless eager to take advantage of the opportunity to attend school, a luxury that became increasingly available after Libya, which was colonized by Italy, achieved independence in 1951. Muammar Qaddafi, who by most accounts was an exceptionally bright boy, was the first member of his family to avail himself of that opportunity. At ten, he entered the el-ementary school at Sirte, and for the next four years he made his home-away-from-home in a neighborhood mosque, returning to his family's tent only on weekends and holidays. Although his father recognized the value of education, reportedly scrimping and saving to pay for his son's school fees, he, like his fellow tribesmen, deeply resented the privileged status of foreigners in his land, a state of affairs that went virtually unchallenged during the tenure of King Idris I, independent Libya's first head of state.

Already opposed to the pro-Western policies of King Idris, Muammar Qaddafi, as a youth, was thus ripe for conversion to the philosophy of Egypt's Gamal Ab-del Nasser, a Pan-Arabist to his very core and the preem-inent leader of the independence movement in the Arab world. Possibly Nasser's most devoted disciple, Qad-dafi listened regularly to Radio Cairo, which broadcast his hero's impassioned speeches calling for Arab unity and self-determination. He also committed to memory Nasser's *Philosophy of the Revolution*, which included, among other things, a discussion of the events leading up to his overthrow of the corrupt regime of King Farouk I. Qaddafi immediately identified the Egyptian monarch with King Idris and vowed to depose him.

By the time Qaddafi entered secondary school at Sebha in 1956, a town in what was then the Fezzan Province in the southwestern part of the country, where he and his family were then living, he had become so convinced of the truth of Nasserism that he spent much of his time proselytizing his classmates. Charismat-ic and fearless even in those days, Qaddafi gradually emerged as the leader of a small group of like-minded youths who staged demonstrations against the European presence in Africa and the Middle East. In about 1961, as a result of his participation in one such protest, Qad-dafi was expelled from school. It was only through the intercession of his father, who pleaded with an influen-tial man in Sebha to find a place for his son in another institution, that Qaddafi gained admission to a second-ary school in Misurata. During the following two years,

Qaddafi renewed contact with several of his friends from his elementary school days at Sirte, whom he also converted to the Nasserist camp. After graduating in 1963, he persuaded several of his followers to join him in enrolling at the Royal Libyan Military Academy in Benghazi, believing that he could realize his ambition of overthrowing King Idris more easily once he gained a following within the ranks of the army.

Although Qaddafi and his equally militant cohorts were to become Libya's most infamous revolutionaries, they were not alone in their opposition to the rule of King Idris. Plagued by corruption and gross mismanagement of resources—especially of the wealth derived from the nation's vast, newly discovered oil reserves—the government had unwittingly contributed to the formation of a number of clandestine groups that, by the mid-1960s, were actively plotting its overthrow. Compared to the wealthy Shahli family and other potentially powerful political groupings, Qaddafi's band of youthful zealots (most of who, like Qaddafi, were from the country's poorer tribes) was scarcely thought to pose a significant threat to the regime. As a result, the Free Officers' Movement, which Qaddafi founded in 1964—and which he so named after Nasser's cabal of the same name that had overthrown King Farouk I a decade before—was able to carry on its subversive activities without interference from the government. Qaddafi's machinations against King Idris continued after he graduated from the Academy in 1965 and after he was commissioned as an officer in the Libyan army in the following year.

LIFE'S WORK

On September 1, 1969, while King Idris was out of the country receiving medical treatment, a group of young army officers took control of key government offices, including radio stations and military facilities, in Benghazi and Tripoli, the capital, in a bloodless coup d'état. The leaders of the coup immediately identified themselves as the Revolutionary Command Council (another throwback to Nasser's revolution), although, fearing a reprisal from other factions of the army, they remained anonymous for the first several days of their rule. Before long, however, Muammar Qaddafi, who was promoted to colonel, the highest rank in the Libyan army, revealed himself to be the leader of the coup, and declared himself the Commander in Chief of the Armed Forces, a position that made him the de facto head of state. At age 27, he was also among the youngest leaders in the Middle East and North Africa. Ironically, by the time Qaddafi launched his coup, Nasser, having witnessed the dissolution of his country's union with Syria and Yemen in the early 1960s and preoccupied with the bitter reality of Israel's victory over the Arab world during the Six-Day War of 1967, had abandoned the goal of Arab unity as impracticable.

Seemingly oblivious to those realities, Muammar Qaddafi forged ahead with his crusade to tear down the artificial borders created, in his words, by "the colonial powers to partition the single Arab people." Soon after coming to power, for instance, he played a key role in the creation of the Federation of Arab Republics, comprising Libya, Egypt, and Syria, which formally came into existence in January 1972, but like the scores of other mergers that Qaddafi had proposed over the years, few practical benefits were derived from the union. Apparently emboldened by his early, albeit dubious, success, Qaddafi spent the following two years trying to engineer an even closer union with Egypt, which by then was ruled by Nasser's successor, Anwar Sadat. In September 1973, a potentially far-reaching political and economic union between the two countries came into existence, but the sequence of events that preceded its collapse just three months later revealed Qaddafi to be more dangerous and unpredictable as an ally than as an adversary. Particularly disconcerting was Qaddafi's sponsorship of the so-called "people's march" on Cairo during the summer of 1973. After rallying some 30,000 Libyans to his cause, Qaddafi directed the "marchers" to drive en masse to the Egyptian capital, where, he apparently hoped, they would incite the Egyptian masses to launch a popular revolution in support of Arab unity. When faced with the horde of revolutionary enthusiasts at the border, however, the Egyptian authorities had little choice but to send them home.

Notwithstanding the Egyptian government's understandable uneasiness over Qaddafi's erratic behavior, the reasons for the collapse of the 1973 union between Egypt and Libya—and, ultimately, for the deterioration of the two countries' relations in general—had more to do with the profound differences between their leaders with regard to the Arab-Israeli conflict and, specifically, with Qaddafi's disgust over his reluctant ally's willingness to negotiate with the Israelis, the legitimacy of whose "occupation" of Palestine he refused to acknowledge. In fact, so intense was Qaddafi's hatred for the Israelis ("You forced these Jews on us and you must take them back," he once told two Western journalists, as quoted in *Life* [February 1980]. "Why punish Arabs for a German mistake?"), that he maintained equally uneasy relations with those Arab leaders whom he perceived as too moderate with respect to Israel, Egypt, or both. Among those leaders who had, in Qaddafi's view, betrayed the Palestinian cause were the Sudan's Gaafar Nimeiri, whose government he tried to overthrow at least twice; Palestinian Liberation Organization chairman Yasir Arafat (also spelt "Yasser" or "Yassir,"), whom he accused, in 1979, of committing "treason" for having indicated a willingness to negotiate with the Israelis, and whom he continued to attack verbally in the years that followed; and Jordan's King Hussein, for whose assassination he had regularly called since 1970. As might be expected, Qaddafi had long been even more vehemently opposed to the generally pro-Western governments of Kuwait and Saudi Arabia, once referring to the Saudis as the "pigs of the Arab peninsula."

At the same time that Muammar Qaddafi found himself battling Egypt and the other moderate countries of the Mashreq, or the Arab East, he was also pursuing his "Bismarckian" ambitions in the Maghreb, or the predominantly Muslim countries of northwest Africa, although with equally disastrous results. He began with Tunisia, a tiny country wedged in between northern Libya and Algeria on the Mediterranean. In much the same fashion that he would try to reach the Egyptian masses through his aborted "people's march" in 1973, Qaddafi tried to take his message of Arab unity directly to the Tunisian people, calling for the union of the two countries during a speech in Tunis in 1972. He neglected to inform Tunisian President Bourguiba of the contents of the speech, however, forcing the latter to hurriedly and diplomatically disavow the proposal. Understandably piqued by Qaddafi's presumption, Bourguiba later described the young leader as "considerably lacking in experience." Relations between the two countries remained rocky throughout much of the following 13 years, taking a sharp turn for the worse in 1980, when the Tunisian government expelled the Libyan ambassador in protest against Qaddafi's attempt to set up a revolutionary government (presumably in the hope of overthrowing Bourguiba) in Gafsa, in western Tunisia, and coming to an ignominious end in 1985, when the Tunisian government caught nearly 300 Libyan spies operating in the country. Qaddafi's relations with the governments of Algeria and Morocco were similarly marked by discord.

Possibly as a result of his growing isolation, Qaddafi concluded a "strategic alliance" with Iran in 1985 and agreed to support the non-Arab Muslim nation in its war with Iraq. Other than Iran, only Syria—the intensity of whose hatred for Israel and whose support for terrorist organizations alone may have exceeded Libya's—maintained relatively cordial relations with the Qaddafi regime during the 1980s.

If measured according to his own standards, it appeared for a time that Muammar Qaddafi's greatest foreign policy achievement was his success in imposing his will on Chad, an impoverished and little-understood nation to the south of Libya that had been wracked by civil war throughout most of its 50 years of independence. In 1973, Libyan troops occupied the Aouzou Strip, a swath of territory in northern Chad thought to be rich in uranium and other minerals, and until recently Libya's claim to the region was not seriously disputed. Moreover, in the 1970s and early 1980s, the Libyan government succeeded in concluding several treaties of "friendship" with Chad. But Qaddafi's ability to influence events in Chad became increasingly tenuous after 1983, when the Libyan-backed government there fell to rebel forces. Although Libyan troops managed at that time to retain control of the northern half of Chad (or most of the territory above the sixteenth parallel), in 1987, they suffered a humiliating defeat. Crushed by the French-supported government forces, they were forced to retreat into the Aouzou Strip.

The loss of Chad has, for the time being, at least, shattered what appeared to have been Qaddafi's dream of uniting the Muslim populations of black Africa into a "Greater Saharan" Islamic Republic. The notion that he harbored such ambitions is supported by evidence that he had been involved in plots, some of which were successful, to topple the governments of Niger, Upper Volta (now called Burkina Faso), Ghana, Senegal, Mali, the Gambia, and Somalia. Moreover, as Martin Sicker pointed out in *The Making of a Pariah State* (1987), "unofficial maps" published in Tripoli in 1976 delineated "an expanded Libya that included 96,200 square kilometers of Chad, 19,500 of Niger, and a similar [amount] of Algeria."

Although Muammar Qaddafi had been implicated in political assassinations, coup attempts, and other subversive activities from Beirut to Casablanca, it had been as a result of his alleged sponsorship of terrorist organizations whose targets include Europeans and Americans that he has gained notoriety in the West. Although experts have admitted that conclusive evidence linking the Qaddafi regime to specific acts of terror had been difficult to come by, his government had been repeatedly implicated in the activities of a number of radical Palestinian organizations, including Black September and Abu Nidal's Fatah Revolutionary Council, and, to a lesser extent, of the Irish Republican Army, the Black Panthers in the United States, and the Shining Path in Peru.

Among the most widely publicized terrorist acts to which he had been linked was the April 5, 1986, bombing of a discotheque in what was then West Berlin, in which one American soldier was killed. Alleged Libyan complicity in the bombing led then United States President Ronald Reagan, who had identified Muammar Qaddafi as a paymaster of international terror several years before (and who referred to him as "the mad dog of the Middle East,"), to retaliate by sending warplanes to Libya with orders to bomb not only suspected terrorist training camps but also Qaddafi's residential compound in Tripoli. United States-Libyan relations remained tense throughout the late 1980s and 1990 (Libya supported Iraq in the 1990-1991 Persian Gulf crisis), and took a turn for the worse in 1992; largely as a result of Qaddafi's reluctance to cooperate in the investigation into the December 1988 bombing of Pan Am Flight 103, in which 270 individuals perished. British police investigations identified two Libyans–Abdelbaset al-Megrahi and Lamin Khalifah Fhimah–as the chief suspects, and in November 1991 issued a declaration demanding that Libya hand them over. Qaddafi refused; the U.N. imposed Resolution 748, in March 1992, initiating economic sanctions against Libya that had deep repercussions for the country's economy. Many African states opposed the U.N .sanctions, with Nelson Mandela criticizing them on a visit to Qaddafi, in October 1997. The sanctions were lifted in1998, when Libya agreed to allow the extradition of the suspects to the Scottish Court in the Netherlands, in a process overseen by Mandela. (The extradition agreement stipulated that the two suspects were to be tried in a "neutral" country. Great Britain asked the Netherlands to host a "Scottish Court" for the suspects' trial under Scottish law.)

Just as Qaddafi's utopian vision of society had influenced his foreign policy, so too had it shaped his economic and social policies at home. Arab nationalism, for example, was the inspiration for his decision in the 1970s to unilaterally declare the government a majority shareholder in the major oil companies operating in Libya and to nationalize banks and insurance companies. In keeping with his reverence for Islam, he called in 1973 for the "Islamicization" of Libyan society, declaring the sharia, or Quranic law, the supreme law of the land. Believing capitalism to be inherently evil, in 1978, he banned all private retail trade and mandated that all such enterprises be replaced by monolithic government cooperatives. Although Qaddafi had always been vehemently opposed to the "exploitative" economic policies that predominate in the West, he had been equally opposed to communist ideology, notwithstanding his alliance with the Soviet Union in the 1970s and 1980s, which he considered strategic. Qaddafi's Islamic fundamentalist and quasi-socialistic conception of society eventually became known as the "Third Universal Theory," aspects of which he discussed in the *Green Book*, a three-volume work published between 1975 and 1978.

If the subtleties of Qaddafi's political philosophy were beyond the understanding of ordinary Libyans, they immediately grasped the implications of his stated commitment to improving the quality of their lives. Unlike his predecessor, whose policies tended to benefit Western businessmen and Libya's political elite at the expense of the Libyan masses, Qaddafi poured a significant portion of government revenues (earned primarily from the sale of petroleum products) into agricultural development and the construction of new housing, educational, and health care facilities. His efforts to provide for a more equitable distribution of the nation's natural wealth contributed to the widespread popularity of his regime during the 1970s.

Qaddafi's critics long maintained that his domestic accomplishments were overshadowed by the problems created by inefficiency and chronically low productivity in the agricultural and industrial sectors, but as long as the price of oil remained high on world markets, Qaddafi was able to buy his way out of his problems, and thus retain the support of the people. Beginning in the early 1980s, however, when the proverbial bottom fell out of the world petroleum market, causing a precipitous decline in state revenues, the charge that his economic policies had failed became increasingly difficult to shake off. Exacerbating popular dissatisfaction with his rule were Libya's defeat in its war with Chad in 1987, as well as its isolation from the rest of the world, which was made all too clear by its Arab neighbors' perfunctory denunciation of the United States raid in 1986.

Realizing that his political survival was at stake, Qaddafi had in recent years begun to take steps, albeit small ones, to reform the economy. In 1987, for example, he lifted the ban on private trade, though only for certain segments of the population. (Incongruously, Qaddafi forbade former businessmen to engage in free trade.) But the most significant change in Qaddafi's thinking had been in the realm of foreign policy. Since 1987, the imperious Libyan leader had either restored or strengthened his country's relations with a number of Arab nations, including Jordan, Tunisia, Iraq, Chad, and Egypt (Qaddafi's historic visit to Cairo, in 1989, was his first since 1973) and, in February 1989, Libya joined Algeria, Morocco, Mauritania, and Tunisia in forming the Arab Maghreb Union. The year 1987 also saw the reconciliation between Qaddafi and Yasir Arafat, the Chairman of the Palestine Liberation Organization. According to Mary-Jane Deeb, Qaddafi's decision to enter into negotiations with Egyptian president Hosni Mubarak "may have been the most important foreign policy decision that [he] has made in a decade," as she wrote in *Current History* (April 1990). "Having long criticized Egypt for its peace treaty with Israel, Libya seems finally to have accepted the fact of Israel's existence, and has undertaken to ignore it."

The Arab Spring Revolts broke out first in Tunisia in 2010, and escalated when Mohamed Bouazizi, a Tunisian who was unable to find work, was selling fruit at a roadside stand. A municipal inspector confiscated his wares on December 17, 2010. An hour later Bouazizi doused himself with gasoline and set himself on fire. After his death, various groups dissatisfied with the existing system, began the Tunisian Revolution. By the end of February 2012, rulers had been forced from power in Tunisia, Egypt, Libya, and Yemen; there were protests and political unrest in most of the other Arab nations in the region.

Qaddafi was one of the victims of the Arab Spring. The National Transitional Council (NTC) overthrew the government on August 23, 2011, when it took over Bab al-Azizia, a military compound in Tripoli. Qaddafi went into hiding. He was killed on October 20, 2011, in his hometown of Sirte after the NTC took control of the city. Video footage showed his capture and beating. Later, he had either been caught in crossfire or shot in the stomach. Reports indicate that the doctor who performed the autopsy stated Qaddafi died from a gunshot wound to the head, but the results of the autopsy were never made public. Qaddifi was put into a freezer with son Mutassim, and his Minister of Defense Abu-Bakr Yunis Jabr, who were also killed. All three bodies were put on display for Libyans to view for four days, and then buried at an unidentified place in the Libyan Dessert.

PERSONAL LIFE

In private, Qaddifi reportedly came across as a soft-spoken, pious family man with an appreciation for Western culture, particularly classical music. Notwithstanding his abhorrence for the "imperialist" policies of the United States government, Qaddafi professed to be an admirer of George Washington and Abraham Lincoln, about whose lives he presumably learned while enrolled at the University of Libya at Benghazi, before being commissioned as an army officer. "I used to read a lot about Abraham Lincoln, how he became a famous lawyer without attending college, how he used to pocket orders to his commanders, if he decided he couldn't carry them out himself," he said, according to the *Life* article. "Gandhi is another person I admire because he lived for others. He was humble."

Although he formally shared a large, two-story home in Bab al-Aziziya barracks with his second wife, Safiya (whom he married in 1970), and their ten children (one of whom was born to him and his first wife, Fatiha al-Nuri [whom he married in 1969 and divorced in 1970]; two are adopted), he preferred to live alone in a Bedouin tent, which was pitched near the family home on a mound of sand specially imported from the Libyan Desert. Further contributing to the ambiance of the desert was the continual champing of a pair of camels tethered to one side of the tent. Its interior was colorful, with lots of pillows and mats, and its "walls" were made out of quilt-like fabric onto which a collection of Qaddafi's philosophical pronouncements, taken mainly from the Green Book, were embroidered. In keeping with his image of himself as a devout Muslim, Qaddafi appeared to enjoy being photographed while praying in the Libyan Desert, and when posing for Western audiences, he often wore a gandourah, the traditional dress of his people. Other sartorial quirks included his penchant for wearing Italian suits and for pairing his extravagantly embroidered, Napoleonic military uniforms with darkly tinted sunglasses.

After his death, his second wife and the rest of his children were reported to have escaped to Algeria, and were later granted political asylum in Oman.

FURTHER READING

Chicago Tribune IV pl5+ fa 5 '86 por; Christian Sci Mon p9+ fa 7 '86 por; Cur Hist 86:65+ F '87, 89:149+ Ap '90; The New York Times A p4 fa 11 '86 por, A p2 fe 14 '86 por; Sunday Times p!5 Ag 14 '83 pors; Blundy, David and Lycett, Andrew. Qaddafi and the Libyan

Revolution (1987); Cooley, John K. Libyan Sandstorm (1982); International Who's Who, 1991-92; Reich, Bernard. Political Leaders of the Contemporary Middle East and North Africa: A Biographical Dictionary

(1990); Sicker, Martin. The Making of a Pariah State: The Adventurist Politics of Muammar Qaddafi (1987); St. John, Ronald Bruce. Historical Dictionary of Libya (1991)

MANUEL L(UIS) QUEZON
President of the Philippine Islands

Born: August 19, 1878; Philippines
Died: August 1, 1944; New York
Group Affiliation: Nacionalista Party

INTRODUCTION

On December 19, 1941 in an address broadcast from Manila, President Quezon announced: "We are fully prepared to defend the cause of liberty and democracy to the last drop of our blood." A week later Manila was formally declared an open city by General MacArthur (see sketch this issue) and Quezon fled with the armed forces and other heads of the Philippine Government. The capital was murderously bombed by the Japanese 30 hours later.

"We owe our loyalty to America and we are bound to her by bonds of everlasting gratitude," said President Manuel L. Quezon on Loyalty Day (late in June 1941), a new holiday in the Philippine Islands. To the 100,000 demonstrating in Manila and to a curious world, he placed himself on record for the first time about where he stands on the Second World War. "Should the United States enter the War, she will find all of the people of this country, to the last man, on her side. Our stake in this War is our own future independence, and assurance that independence may endure."

This statement marked a radical and realistic change from an earlier attitude on the part of the Filipinos, inclined to appease Japan so as to avoid affronting a powerful neighbor whom they might one day be forced to face alone. In 1940 Quezon was openly expressing doubts about the country's ability to defend itself, and a slackening in the Philippine defense effort appeared in subsequent cuts in appropriations for munitions and equipment. But in April 1941, $50,000,000 was appropriated from funds owed to the Island Government, to be spent by the War, Navy and Interior Departments for defense of the Philippine Islands.

Now the 7,083 islands of the Philippine Archipelago, whose armed forces were incorporated into those of the United States by President Roosevelt's order of July 26, 1941, are rapidly being transformed into the United States' first line of defense in the Orient. Key cities are being fortified and preparations have been made to evacuate the civilian populations of cities most exposed to attack. In a message to the National Assembly on February 1, President Quezon had maintained that it was up to the United States to provide air shelters and other civilian defense measures for the Islands until their independence became effective—in opposition to High Commissioner Francis B. Sayre, who held that the extent of the autonomy of the Philippine Government made it necessary for Philippine authorities to assume civilian defense responsibilities. However, on March 22, after the issue had been tossed back and forth, Quezon appointed a Civilian Emergency Administration.

Until 1941, President Quezon's most important problem was his attitude on the independence promised for July 4, 1946. Some people believe that he would like to see independence postponed indefinitely, perhaps in the form of a Dominion government. But reversing the political doctrine upon which he has based his whole meteoric career is no easy task, even for the supple President. He once told a graduating class at the normal school that he "prefers a government run like hell by Filipinos to one run like heaven by Americans." Strong factions in Manila, it is reported, particularly rich sugar men, have started a movement to request the United States to maintain some sort of tie with the Islands. Prime factors in this movement are the realization that the United States' withdrawal will smash up the Islands economically, open them wide to Japanese domination. The Philippine Government has offered to shut down exports of strategic materials—copra, iron ore, hemp—to all countries except the United States in the interest of American armament.

EARLY LIFE

This political leader who has "more power than Franklin D. Roosevelt has yet dreamed of" was born Manuel Luis Quezon Antonio y Molina, in Baler, a desolate village on the eastern coast of the Island of Luzon, on August 19, 1878. His father, Lucio Quezon, was a Filipino and his mother, Maria (Molina) Quezon, was partly Spanish. Both schoolteachers, they taught Manuel his ABC's. The parish priest then carried on his education until he was 11. At school in Manila he was "bright but lazy" and nicknamed gulerato—"bluffer"—by his classmates. After having finished his work at the junior college at San Juan de Letran, he was appointed a lecturer at the University of Santo Tomas so that he could receive free board, lodging and tuition while studying law. His law studies were interrupted by the Spanish-American War.

"A fearless, quick-tempered, obstinate fighter," Manuel, who enlisted as Manuel Kison, was rapidly promoted from private to major, fighting first against the Spanish rulers and later against the American invaders. After the insurrection collapsed in 1899 he surrendered his sword, spent six months in jail, then returned to Manila. There he studied theology at the University until the Catholic fathers advised him to give up any idea of the priesthood and sent him to oversee one of their farms. Pie did not stay long: he returned to Manila to work in a Catholic savings bank. At the same time he resumed the study of law at the University of Santo Tomas and in 1903 passed the Bar examination. Sergio Osmena, who was alternately to be his political ally and rival and who is now regarded as likely to succeed Quezon, was graduated at the same time.

LIFE'S WORK

At the death of his father Manuel Quezon returned to Baler and set up a law practice in Tayabas Province. In a few months he had more clients than he could handle. In answer to a call to public service, however, he gave up a lucrative private practice to take the post of provincial fiscal—prosecuting attorney—of Mindoro and later of Tayabas. He earned a national reputation almost at once for his prosecution of an American lawyer for fraud. In 1906 he resigned to start his political career. He was elected provincial Governor. "Demonstrating in the early elections characteristics of jumping from one side of an issue to another [he considers consistency a weakness], always picking the popular one," he showed that "he was obviously the potential Nationalist leader of the Islands." The following year he resigned from the

Governorship to become a candidate for the Philippine Assembly on the Nacionalista Party platform. In the Assembly, Osmena was elected Speaker of the House and Quezon floor leader.

As a reward for his ability to win over malcontents by his persuasive powers, in 1908 Quezon was sent as Philippine representative to an International Navigation Congress in St. Petersburg. The appointment was not made in time for him to attend the conference, but he visited and enjoyed Paris. Returning to the Islands, he decided that Washington, D.C., would be the best place to work for Philippine independence and next had himself appointed to the post of Resident Commissioner (with a voice in Congress, but no vote), a post which he held from 1909 to 1916. A Beau Brummell in Washington, "one of the world's best ballroom dancers" (among the best pupils Arthur Murray ever had, one night he took out 16 Murray instructresses all at once), he was rapidly becoming also one of the "world's supplest and hardest-boiled politicians." An effective lobbyist, he had the law revised so that Filipinos would form a majority on the Philippine Commission; in 1913 he helped arrange the appointment of pro-Filipino Francis Burton Harrison as Governor General; in 1916 he was the spiritual author of the Jones Bill.

In 1916 Quezon returned to the Islands, "the hero of his country," bringing with him the Jones Act, which gave the Filipinos power to legislate for themselves subject to a veto by the American Governor General, and which abolished the Philippine Commission. He was promptly elected to the Senate. At that time Osmena and Quezon were almost of equal strength; but in the elections Quezon attacked Osmena on the strength of the Wood-Forbes investigation and became President of the Nacionalista Party. In the Senate he was elected President.

There followed years of passionate struggle with General Wood, the Governor who had succeeded Harrison and reversed his pro-Filipino policy. Once, feeling slighted when he was made to wait in the Governor's office for an interview, Quezon stormed out, shouting: 'Tell General Wood to go to hell!" As Senate President, Quezon fought to reduce the Governor Generalship position to a mere figurehead, "because we want a government of Filipinos, by the Filipinos and for the Filipinos." With other Governors "he ingratiated himself, cajoling, bluffing, threatening." He dodged back and forth to Washington; he had the 1925 Fairfield Law (for independence) shelved by insisting on instant, not eventual, complete independence for the Islands. In 1927, when

---

Affiliation: Nacionalista Party

The Nacionalista Party is the oldest political party in the Philippines. It was responsible for leading the country through the majority of the twentieth century. The party began as the country's voice for independence through the building of a modern nation-state and through advocating efficient self-rule and peaceful leadership.

By the second half of the century the party was one of the main political contenders for leadership in the country, in competition with the Liberals and the Progressives, during the decades between the devastation of World War II and the violent suppression of partisan politics of the Marcos dictatorship. The party was revived during the late 1980s and early 1990s by the Laurel family, which has dominated the Party since the 1950s.

The Nacionalista Party is now being led by party president Manuel Villar, former Senator, and has fielded three in the upcoming 2016 Philippine Elections. Two of the other present parties, the Liberal Party and the Nationalist People's Coalition are breakaways from the Nacionalista Party.

Throughout their careers, many of the country's greatest politicians, statesmen, and leaders were Nacionalistas in whole or part, including Manuel Quezon. Today, the continuing struggle for independence in the Philippines center on freeing its people from the oppressive poverty by encouraging fresh ideas, courage, and self-sacrifice.

---

he returned again to Washington to resume the struggle, he became ill. In his absence he was nevertheless elected Senator (1928) and re-elected President of the Senate. In 1931, after the Hawes-Cutting-Hare Law had been passed by the United States Senate, vetoed by President Hoover, and the veto overridden, Quezon opposed it. In Quezon's words, "America would still hold military and naval bases in the Philippines even after the latter's independence, and, moreover, export duties regulated in the law would destroy both industry and trade." Some say his opposition was based on a fear that Osmena, who had accompanied him to Washington, might return to the Islands a national hero. In any case, the legislature supported Quezon and voted against the bill.

Quezon returned to the United States to lobby for a better law. In 1934 he secured the passage of the Tydings-McDuffie Bill, which, tentatively at least, won the fight. Complete independence was promised for 1946, and the bill also provided for duty-free importation of the principal Philippine products, sugar, coconut oil and cordage (Manila hemp) to the United States.

With the passage of this bill, Quezon's leadership was assured. In the election of 1935 he formed a Coalition Party (he believes in a one-party system, since "political parties are good only for evil things") reuniting the Nacionalistas, who had split over the Hawes Act, and with Osmena as Vice-Presidential candidate he defeated General Aguinaldo for President by an overwhelming majority. His first act as chief executive, alarmed by aggressions in the Far East and in Europe, was to railroad a national defense bill through the rubber-stamp unicameral legislature. This made him chairman of the Council for National Defense, with the chief of staff directly subordinate to the President.

Some observers see in this national defense plan, which makes it almost impossible for any military clique to overthrow or dominate the President, "a strong Quezon personal defense plan." When he divested the speaker of the Philippine Assembly of his most important prerogative—the leadership of his party in that body—Quezon said: "The speaker of the legislative assembly presides over the deliberations of that body. That is his main and most important function. That is his only function." As for the President's functions: the purse strings of the nation are in his hands; he approves all bills before they are introduced into the legislature; and in 1940 the Constitution was amended so that he could run for re-election.

Another important step in the assumption of what his opponents call dictatorial powers was taken on August 10, 1940, when Quezon won "one of the hardest fights" of his colorful political career by jamming through the National Assembly the Emergency Powers Bill, which may change the social and economic structure of his country drastically. By a vote of 62 to 1 he was given authority to require civilians to give service to the Government, to outlaw strikes, to commandeer shipping and other transportation, to control food resources and to revise the educational system. President Quezon insisted that the measures, particularly the anti-spy restrictions, were necessary for the safety of the Islands, which contain large Japanese colonies and are almost surrounded by the expanding Japanese Empire. He also requested the extension of these powers until the new Assembly was elected in November. At that time he was re-elected President, for on August 16, 1941 his Nacionalista Party, taking advantage of the 1940 ruling although Quezon's health was reportedly "impaired from overwork," had nominated him as its candidate. At the time of nomination he said: "If the people elect me, I will serve."

Quezon can ordinarily count on about 75 or 85 per cent of the vote on any issue he puts up to the Filipinos. "By masterly handling of the patronage (he even appoints the village schoolteachers), by a passionate love of all things Filipino (except the opposition), and by a colorful personality that keeps him bounding into the limelight, he has kept first place among Island politicians." Perhaps John Gunther (see sketch this issue) revealed the secret of Quezon's phenomenal rise and his hold over his people when he wrote: "He is indisputably the best orator in the Islands, in any of the three languages, English [which he learned in six months], Spanish or Tagalog. His considerable charm, his patriotism, his executive capacity, his curious combination of American characteristics, like aggressive practicality, with a Latin heritage of suppleness and adroit facility in negotiation, all contributed to his career. But his knack of getting along well with both rich and poor, with the miserably fed peasants of the countryside as well as the Spanish millionaires in Manila, is probably his single most valuable characteristic. The masses adore him, because he gives them something. The rich eat out of his hand—when he isn't eating out of theirs—because he guarantees their survival. By using both he has built up an irresistible machine." Though according to Quezon any such report is "nonsensical," a movement is reported to be afoot to change the name of the Islands to Quezon; already there is a Quezon City; and students of the state-supported University of the Philippines have supposedly organized a "Quezon for King" Club.

In 1941, Quezon was re-elected with nearly 82 percent of the vote. After the Japanese invasion of the Philippines during World War II, he evacuated to Cooregidor, then Australia and finally the United States, where he established the Commonwealth government in exile with headquarters in Washington, D.C. He served as a member of the Pacific War Council, signed the declaration of the United Nations against the Axis powers, and wrote an autobiography, *The Good Fight*, in 1946.

In a humanitarian act, Quezon helped facilitate entry into the Philippines of Jewish refugees fleeing

Europe, and he was instrumental in promoting projects to help resettle them in the Philippines.

PERSONAL LIFE

On his way to the United States in 1918, when he was 40 years old, Quezon married his cousin, Aurora Aragon, then 29. They had four children: Maria Aurora "Baby" Quezon; Maria Zeneida "Nini" Quezon-Avancena; Luisa Corazón Paz "Nenita" Quezon; and Manuel L. "Nonong" Quezon, Jr. Quezon's flair for living was both proverbial and prodigious. His Malacanan Palace outclassed the White House. His private office was large and richly furnished, and as he talked to visitors he teetered back and forth in a brocaded swivel chair. He made frequent trips through the Islands on his swank white yacht, the Castanet; he liked to dance and had lost none of his love for gaiety; his clothes were the wonder of the Islands.

Short, slim, swarthy Don Manuel, as he was affectionately called by his people, looked much younger than he was. Above his handsome face his hair was graying; bushy black eyebrows top penetrating eyes that even with pince-nez are sharp and bright.

During his exile in the United States he died of tuberculosis at Saranac Lake, New York. Until the end of World War II he was buried in Arlington National Cemetery. His remains were then moved to Manila. His final resting place is the Quezon City Memorial Circle, a national park and a national shrine in Quezon City, which was the capital of the Philippines from 1948 to 1976.

FURTHER READING

Atlan 163:59-70 Ja '39 (Same abr. Read Digest 34:10-13 F '39); *Cristian Sci Mon Mag* pl-2+ My 11 '38 il por; *Commonweal* 24:259-60 J1 3 '36; *Life* 8:14+ Ap 1 '40 por; *Nation* 144 ;320-2 Mr 20 '37; *Philippines-Japan* 4:4-5+ D '39; 5:11-12+ Ja '40; 5:11-12+ F '40; 5:7-8+ Mr '40; 5:27-35 Ap '40; 5:23-34 My '40; 5:27-31 Je '40; *Time* 30:11-12 S 20 '37 por; 36:16 S 2 '40 por; *American Catholic Who's Who;* Gunther, J. Inside *Asia* p287-304 1939; Nolasco, T. D. *de Filipino Case for American Retention* 1940; Quezon, C. Manuel, *The Good Fight* 1946; Quirino, C. Quezon, *Man of Destiny* 1935; Rodriguez, E. B. *President Quezon, his Biographical Sketch, Messages and Speeches* 1940; *Who's Who in America 1916-17; Who's Who in the Philippines*; Wise, J. H. and others, eds. *Essays for Better Reading* pl29-43 1940

R

YITZHAK RABIN (YITS-AHK RAH-BEAN)

Prime Minister of Israel

Born: March 1, 1922; Jerusalem
Died: November 4, 1995; Tel Aviv, Israel
Affiliation: Alignment; Labor Party

INTRODUCTION

"The sight you see before you at this moment was impossible, was unthinkable just two years ago," Yitzhak Rabin, the prime minister of Israel, declared at the signing of the peace accord between Israel and the Palestine Liberation Organization in September 1995. "Only poets dreamed of it, and to our great pain, soldiers and civilians went to their death to make this moment possible." The agreement—which expanded Palestinian self-rule in the Israel-occupied territories of the West Bank (land Israel had captured in the 1967 Six-Day War)—has been hailed as a significant milestone on the road to peace in the Middle East. For Rabin, the hard-won accord with the Palestinians and the peace treaty Israel signed with Jordan in October 1994 are the crowning achievements in his long career as a soldier, diplomat, politician, and international statesman. A veteran of the 1948 Israeli War of Independence, Rabin played a key role in building up Israel's military might during the 1950s and 1960s, a period that culminated in Israel's victory in the Six-Day War, while he was army chief of staff. He gave up his uniform to serve as his country's ambassador to the United States from 1968 until 1973, and in 1974, as leader of the Labor Party, he became prime minister. A political scandal forced him to resign in 1977; for the next several years, Rabin, although he remained a member of the Israeli parliament, was relegated to the back benches. During the 1980s, when the

right-wing Likud Party dominated Israeli politics, he served as defense minister, developing a reputation as a hard-liner in his efforts to quell the violence that had begun to spread among the increasingly discontented Palestinian population in the West Bank and Gaza Strip.

A frustrated Israeli electorate, discouraged by the lack of progress toward peace, voted the Likud out of power in 1992 and reinstated the more liberal Labor Party, and Rabin once again became the country's prime minister. Israelis seemed willing to trust Rabin to be a peace broker, confident that the man who had spent so much of his career defending the country against its enemies would be a reliable protector of its security. By 1992 Rabin had become convinced that it was time for Israel to conclude a political settlement with both its Palestinian population and its Arab neighbors. Among the reasons for Rabin's change in perspective were the end of the Cold War, which transformed the geopolitics of the Middle East, and Israel's failure to quell the intifada, the sustained uprising that had been raging in Israel's occupied territories since 1987. For his efforts to create a lasting peace in the Middle East, Rabin, along with Yasir Arafat, the chairman of the PLO, and Shimon Peres, Israel's secretary, won the Nobel Prize for Peace, on October 14, 1994.

EARLY LIFE

The older of the two children of Nehemiah Rabin and Rosa (Cohen) Rabin, Yitzhak Rabin was born on March 1, 1922 in Jerusalem, in what was then Palestine. (Four months later the League of Nations adopted the British mandate for Palestine, which affirmed Great Britain's

Yitzhak Rabin.

established by Jewish settlers with the aim not only of educating students but also of providing them with the practical skills needed to settle what was then a largely undeveloped land. At the age of thirteen, Rabin entered Givat Hashlosha, an intermediate school organized by Rosa Cohen and modeled after Bet Hinuch. His mother's death in 1937 affected Rabin deeply. Following a period of mourning, he returned to Kadoorie Agricultural High School, which he had just entered, "with the feeling that [he] had crossed over the threshold of manhood," as he wrote in *The Rabin Memoirs* (1979). "Part of my home no longer existed," he continued, "and I had to strike out on my own path." Although on entering Kadoorie he had had no interest in pursuing a military career—"My purpose in life was to serve my country, and I believed that the best way to do it was to prepare myself to be a farmer," Rabin has said—that prospect became increasingly more likely as his years there passed.

After graduating from Kadoorie, with honors, in 1940, Rabin applied to the University of California to study hydraulic engineering. The idea appealed to him because an expertise in that field would serve the Yishuv well in the coming years, water being a scarce resource in the region. But the exigencies of World War II soon compelled him to abandon those plans. (Rabin's academic education thus ended when he left Kadoorie.) He instead joined the Hagana, the underground military arm of the Jewish Agency, and was assigned to the Palmach, the Hagana's secret commando force, soon after it was formed in May 1941. As part of the Pal-mach's campaign to prevent the Nazis from taking over the Middle East, in June of that year Rabin participated in sabotage operations conducted against the Vichy French government in Lebanon and Syria. He also attended a special military training course offered by the British, with whom the Hagana were allied.

LIFE'S WORK

Later in the war Rabin worked part-time on a kibbutz; all the while he remained in the Palmach, of which he was named platoon commander in 1943 and deputy battalion commander in 1944. According to Robert Slater, the author of the biography *Rabin of Israel* (1993), Rabin "acquired a reputation as one of the leading thinkers of the strike force. Other commanders, even his seniors, often sought his advice or opinion. He was not only a willing and persevering soldier, he had a special understanding of the unique role of the Palmach." With the conclusion of World War II, Rabin considered

commitment to supporting the establishment of a Jewish homeland in Palestine.) Rabin has a sister, Rahel. His father, who emigrated from his native Russia to the United States as a boy and who later settled in Palestine, was a worker, intellectual, and member of the Jewish Legion. His mother, also a Russia-born Jew who immigrated to Palestine, became well known in the Yishuv, the Jewish community in Palestine, because of her work as a leader in the labor movement and as a member of the high command of the Hagana, the Jewish underground army. Both parents were nonreligious, Socialist Jews. Rosa Cohen, as she preferred to be called even after she got married, Was the dominant figure in the family. Rabin has described her as "a very austere, extreme person, who stuck to what she believed in; there were no compromises with her."

Rabin began his education at the age of six, when he entered the Bet Hinuch, in Tel Aviv, where the family had moved several years before. The school had been

Affiliation: Labor Party

On his return to Israel in 1973, Rabin decided to run for a seat in the Knesset, Israel's parliament, as a member of the Labor Party. (Until 1971, when he joined Labor, he had not belonged to a political party.) The elections had been scheduled for October 31, 1973, but they were put on hold after Israel was attacked by Egypt and Syria on October 6, marking the beginning of the Yom Kippur War. While Israeli forces ultimately succeeded in driving back the enemy, the war was costly both in human and economic terms, and the government was blamed for having been poorly prepared to defend the country against attack. In the elections, held in December, Labor won a plurality of the vote, an outcome that enabled Prime Minister Golda Meir to form a government, but in April 1974 she resigned her post as a result of mounting public criticism of her government's lack of defense preparedness.

Rabin, who had won a seat in the Knesset in the elections, was a political beneficiary of those events. Thanks to his popularity among Israelis and his lingering reputation as the hero of the Six-Day War—and despite his lack of a solid political base within the Labor Party itself—he emerged as a candidate for prime minister. (The Labor Party's central committee was to choose the new prime minister, who would then form a new government.) His rival in the ensuing battle for the leadership of the party was Shimon Peres, with whom Rabin had never been on the friendliest of terms. In winning the contest, Rabin became Israel's youngest prime minister and the first sabra, or native-born Israeli, to hold that post.

---

reapplying to the University of California, but he decided to remain in Palestine to take part in the creation of a Jewish state.

Following World War II the already unstable alliance between Jewish settlers in Palestine and the British deteriorated further. (The settlers and the British had been united in their opposition to the Axis powers, but were deeply divided politically; in 1939 Great Britain greatly reduced its commitment to the establishment of a Jewish homeland, when the fate of European Jewry was at its most precarious.) A major point of contention was Britain's policy on Jewish immigration; Britain not only opposed the immigration of Holocaust survivors to Palestine but sought to return those immigrants who had entered Palestine "illegally." A confrontation occurred in the summer of 1945, when the Palmach, in an attempt to thwart Britain's plans to evict illegal Jewish immigrants who were being held at the Atlit detention camp, set out to rescue the detainees. Still with the Palmach, Rabin was a key participant in the daring raid on the camp. (The raid was fictionalized by Leon Uris in his novel *Exodus;* Rabin was said to be the basis for the character Ari Ben-Canaan.) As a result of that and similar exploits, Rabin became a wanted man, and in June 1946 he was among the many Jewish settlers who were arrested and imprisoned by the British.

Soon after Rabin's release from prison, in November 1946, the British decided to relinquish their responsibilities under the mandate. A year later the United Nations voted to partition Palestine into two states—one Palestinian, the other Jewish. Rabin joined in the general celebration in Tel Aviv, but, as he wrote in his memoirs, he "harbored few illusions." "The irony of it all was that the success of our political struggle left us more vulnerable than ever to destruction," he continued. "We would now have to protect our political gains by force of arms." Indeed, the partition plan was rejected by the neighboring Arab states, which invaded Israel as soon as it declared itself a sovereign state in May 1948.

During the Arab-Israeli War of 1948 (also known as the first Arab-Israeli War and the Israeli War of Independence), Rabin played an important role as commander of the Palmach's Harel Brigade. Early in the war he was given "the extremely difficult task," as Avishai Margalit described it in the *New York Review of Books* (June 11, 1992), of securing the route linking Jerusalem and Tel Aviv, but he was unable to do so. He was also placed in charge of carrying out Israeli prime minister David Ben-Gurion's controversial order to sink the *Altalena,* which was defying government orders by transporting arms to the Irgun, a militia whose politics were at odds with those of the government. In the final phase of the war, Rabin helped to push back Egyptian forces into the Negev desert, and he took part in the negotiations for the 1949 armistice.

In late 1948 David Ben-Gurion, feeling that the Palmach constituted a threat to his authority, had dissolved the organization and integrated it into the new Israel Defense Forces (IDF). Ben-Gurion was also distrustful of some of the former Palmach members and saw to it that they had no place in the IDF. Rabin's loyalty was thus divided between the Palmach veterans and the government, and when the ousted Palmach members held a gathering to demonstrate both their solidarity and their opposition to the government's action, Rabin attended it despite government orders not to do so. According to some observers, Ben-Gurion delayed promoting Rabin to a top leadership position because of the act of disloyalty. Some insiders have claimed that Rabin would have been promoted to chief of staff by 1953 but for that blemish on his record; as it turned out, he did not receive that promotion until 1964.

Following the war Rabin was named commander of the brigade that patrolled the Negev and was recruited to help in the overall organization of the Israeli military. Although he had grown comfortable with the methods employed by the Palmach, which has been likened to a guerrilla organization, he nevertheless successfully adapted his skills to the needs of the regular army. In 1954, after spending a year at the British Staff College in Camberley, England, which offered a nine-month course in military education, he was promoted to the rank of major general and was asked to head the training branch of the IDF.

Rabin was appointed commander in chief of the Northern Front, on Israel's border with Syria, in 1956; he thus played no direct part in the Sinai Campaign, waged that year. At one point he considered leaving the military to enter Harvard University's Graduate School of Business Administration, but he decided to remain with the service when changes in command made it clear that he could advance to a top leadership position. Rabin's most significant promotion—to chief of staff, in 1964—not only placed him in charge of the army but also brought him into a leadership role with respect to the government.

Following his promotion, Rabin flexed Israel's military muscle against the Syrians and ordered reprisals against terrorist operations encouraged by the formation of the Palestine Liberation Organization in the same year. According to some Israeli political leaders, including David Ben-Gurion, Rabin's aggressive stance contributed to the escalation of tensions between Israel and its Arab neighbors in the spring of 1967. Shaken by the view of Ben-Gurion and others that he was leading Israel to the brink of war, in May of that year Rabin experienced a nervous breakdown that rendered him unable to perform his duties for a twenty-four hour period. "There can be no doubt that I was suffering from a combination of tension, exhaustion, and the enormous amounts of cigarette smoke I had inhaled in

recent days . . .," he wrote, as quoted by Robert Slater. "But it was more than nicotine that brought me down. The heavy sense of guilt that had been dogging me of late became unbearably strong on 23 May . . . Perhaps I had failed in my duty as the prime minister's chief military adviser. Maybe that was why Israel now found itself in such difficult straits. Never before had even I come close to feeling so depressed."

The heightened tensions between Israel and its neighbors culminated in the outbreak of the Six-Day War, on June 5, 1967, with Israel launching preemptive strikes against Egypt, Jordan, Iraq, and Syria. Whatever his role in provoking Israel's neighbors, Rabin prosecuted the war with great efficiency, to the extent that Israel succeeded in taking control of the Sinai peninsula, the western bank of the Jordan River, the Gaza Strip, and the Golan Heights—and thus in growing to three and a half times its prewar size. While the international media, enamored of the charismatic Israeli defense minister Moshe Dayan, gave most of the credit for Israel's victory to Dayan, among Israelis Rabin was the hero of the war. "No event shaped the image of Yitzhak Rabin in the pubic's mind as much as the Six-Day War . . .," Robert Slater wrote. "When people asked themselves in later years whether Yitzhak Rabin would make a worthy prime minister or defense minister, his intimate involvement in the 1967 war was all the credentials he required. The Six-Day War . . . became Yitzhak Rabin's calling card for political leadership."

Before the war Rabin had lobbied to be appointed ambassador to the United States, which was proving to be Israel's most dependable ally, and in early 1968 he was posted to Washington, D.C. His assignment was to strengthen the relationship between the two countries, obtain economic and military aid, and gain support for Israel both within and outside government circles. Although he lacked the usual credentials of a diplomat, he made a highly creditable showing, and he succeeded in persuading the Americans to continue to supply Israel with arms and other forms of aid.

During his three years as prime minister, Rabin's challenges included contending with a new wave of immigration, reviving the economy, which was plagued by high inflation as a result of the 1973 war, and accommodating the heightened domestic concerns for security, also a result of the war. By most accounts, he had some success in the economic sphere, and he made rebuilding the IDF one of his top priorities. In 1976 Rabin won considerable praise for authorizing what turned out to be the successful military operation at Entebbe, Uganda, in which Israeli soldiers rescued 103 airline passengers who had been held hostage by the PLO. Another of his successes was the conclusion, through the mediation of United States secretary of state Henry Kissinger, of Sinai II, one of several Israeli-Egyptian disengagement agreements, in 1975.

In late 1976, hoping to receive a mandate to continue leading the country, Rabin resigned in favor of new elections. His reelection campaign was soon beset by a variety of problems, among them the revelation that his wife had an active bank account in Washington, D.C., which constituted a violation of Israel's unusually strict rules governing such matters. Although initially a minor issue, it eventually developed into a full-blown political scandal that, in May 1977, prompted Rabin to abandon the race for the prime ministership. His rival Shimon Peres took his place as the leader of the party. In the elections the right-wing Likud Party gained control of the Knesset, beginning what was to become its fifteen-year-long domination of Israeli politics.

For the first half of that period, Rabin, who remained a member of the Knesset, was relegated to the party's back benches. With the publication of his memoirs in 1979, Rabin's rivalry with Shimon Peres became a much-talked-about news item, for in it he accused Peres of "subversion" and of undermining Rabin's premiership. In spite of the criticism he received for airing his grievances, by 1980 Rabin's popularity among the electorate had rebounded, to the extent that he was again considered a leading candidate for prime minister. But as it turned out, Peres received the party's nomination, and the Likud was returned to power in the June 1981 vote.

The surprise resignation of Menachem Begin in 1984 was followed by a closely contested election in which Labor captured forty-four seats in the Knesset, just three more than Likud. Neither party, however, could muster enough support from Israel's minor parties to form a government, with the unprecedented result that the two agreed to form a National Unity Government in which Shimon Peres and then Yitzhak Shamir would each serve a two-year term as prime minister. Also as part of this arrangement, Rabin was to serve as defense minister during the government's entire four-year term. The appointment reflected not only his return to a position of leadership within Israeli politics but also

the confidence that both the left and the right had in his ability to head Israel's military establishment.

One of Rabin's major initiatives as defense minister was to withdraw Israeli forces from Lebanon, which it had invaded in 1982. Rabin had apparently supported the invasion initially but had later come to oppose it on the grounds that Israel's war aims, which included removing Syrian troops from Lebanon and trying to arrange the installation of a government friendly to Israel, were unattainable. The withdrawal was completed in 1985. Rabin was confronted with an even more serious problem when, in December 1987, impoverished and oppressed Palestinians living in the Gaza Strip and the West Bank launched a spontaneous revolt, which came to be known as the *intifada*. The revolt, which was characterized by mass demonstrations and random acts of violence, took Rabin, along with most Israeli and Arab leaders, by surprise, and he at first downplayed its significance. Viewing it as the work of a few extremists, he took a hard line against the rioters. Indeed, he is said to have commanded his soldiers not to shoot the demonstrators but to break their limbs—an order that many in the West found to be appalling. A. M. Rosenthal of *The New York Times,* for example, went so far as to call for his resignation.

Within several months, however, the failure of his policy convinced Rabin that the Palestinians could not be ignored indefinitely. "I've learned something in the past two and a half months—among other things that you can't rule by force over 1.5 million Palestinians," he said in early 1988, as quoted in *Time* (January 3, 1994). An alternative, he concluded, was to devise a political solution to the conflict. While he still opposed the creation of a Palestinian state, he came to believe that such a solution might involve ceding Israel's authority over territory inhabited by Palestinians to Jordan. He also expressed a willingness to negotiate with PLO officials, provided they adhered to certain conditions, including a recognition of Israel's right to exist. Rabin thus set himself apart from Yitzhak Shamir, who remained staunchly opposed to compromise of any kind.

Following the 1988 elections Labor and Likud again agreed to form a National Unity Government. Rabin retained the post of defense minister until 1990, when Yitzhak Shamir formed a new, more conservative government. Although in his public utterances Shamir expressed an interest in working toward peace, he failed to advance the peace process substantively. As a result, he not only alienated Israel's closest ally, the

United States, but also taxed the patience of both the Israeli public and Israeli political leaders—factors that contributed to the fall of the Likud-led government in January 1992.

Notwithstanding popular dissatisfaction with Shamir and Likud, a Labor victory was far from assured, for the Israeli electorate, while fed up with Shamir, could at least trust that he would not jeopardize Israel's security. Labor's electoral prospects were therefore enhanced after Rabin succeeded in wresting control of the party from Shimon Peres, in February, for while Rabin appeared to be more willing than Shamir to negotiate a peace settlement—he went so far as to say that he would be willing to trade land for peace—he was, unlike Peres, someone who could be trusted not to jeopardize the country's security. As predicted by the polls, Rabin led his party to victory in the June 23, 1992 elections.

Once in office, Rabin set out to make good on his promise to make significant progress in negotiating a peace settlement. A breakthrough occurred in August 1993, following secret talks between the Israeli government and the PLO in Norway, when the two parties concluded a preliminary accord on Palestinian self-rule in the occupied territories. In another dramatic development, in September Rabin wrote a sober note to Yasir Arafat that stated, "Israel has decided to recognize the PLO as the representative of the Palestinian people and commence negotiations with the PLO within the Middle East peace process." According to the agreement on Palestinian self-rule, an interim Palestinian government was to be established in the Gaza Strip, the West Bank town of Jericho, and, later on, in the rest of the West Bank. At the historic signing of the accord, on September 13, 1993, in Washington, D.C., Rabin shook hands, albeit somewhat tentatively, with his former enemy Yasir Arafat. The signing of the accord was followed by a torturous but ultimately fruitful series of negotiations with other of Israel's neighbors. A peace treaty between Israel and Jordan was signed on October 26, 1994; it was the second peace treaty Israel signed with an Arab country, coming fifteen years after its accord with Egypt. At the historic signing ceremony, held at Arava Grossing, a desert outpost on the Israeli-Jordanian border, Rabin said: "For nearly two generations, desolation pervaded the heart of our two peoples. The time has now come not merely to dream of a better future but to realize it." By early 1995 Israel and Jordan had established full diplomatic relations and had also committed themselves to cooperate in such areas as agriculture, water, tourism, economic development, and environmental protection.

Eleven months after signing Israel's peace treaty with Jordan, Rabin put his pen to another historic document that expanded Palestinian self-rule in the West Bank and authorized the withdrawal of Israeli troops from cities where nearly half the West Bank population lives. The treaty with the Palestinians did not settle the final borders between Israel and the West Bank entity, which is not as yet—and may or may not become—a state. The pact with the PLO has aroused considerable controversy in Israel, where it is opposed by many in the Likud and other right-wing parties who see the West Bank as land to which Israel has a historical right. It has also generated opposition among radical elements of the Palestinians, who views peace with Israel as capitulation. Recognizing the fragility of the Israel-PLO accord, Rabin said at the signing ceremony, "If all the partners to the peace do not unite against the evil angels of death by terrorism, all that will remain of this ceremony are color snapshots, empty mementos."

PERSONAL LIFE

Yitzhak Rabin was married to Leah Schlossberg, a German-born teacher he met in Tel Aviv, since August 28, 1948. They have a son, Yuval, and a daughter, Dalia. Rabin was known as a poor public speaker and was said to be uncomfortable in social situations. In addition to the Nobel Prize, he received many honors, including honorary doctorates from Jerusalem University, Brandeis University, and Yeshiva University, among other institutions. When he received the Nobel Prize, Rabin claimed it was "for the whole nation, for the citizens of the State of Israel, for the bereaved families and the disabled, for the hundreds of thousands who have fought in Israel's war." "Today," he said, "the Palestinians face the moment of truth. If they do not defeat the enemies of peace, the enemies of peace will defeat them."

Yitzhak Rabin was assassinated on November 4, 1995, as he left a peace rally in Tel Aviv, by Yigal Amir, an Israeli right-wing extremist opposed to the Israeli government's self-rule agreement with the Palestine Liberation Organization.

FURTHER READING

London Observer p25 fe 28 '92; *N Y R of Bks* pl7+ Je 11 '92; *Time* 143:40+ fa 3 '94 por; *International Who's Who,* 1994-95; Rabin, Yitzhak The Rabin Memoirs (1979); Slater, Robert. Rabin of Israel (1993)

RONALD (WILSON) REAGAN
44th President of the United States

Born: Feb. 6, 1911; Tampico, Illinois, U.S.
Died: June 5, 2004; Bel Air, California, U.S.
Affiliation: Republican Party

INTRODUCTION

Ronald Reagan, the personable former motion picture actor and Governor of California and, for 16 years the Republican Party's great conservative Presidential hope, finally reached the White House in January 1981, with what he regarded as a mandate for radical change. During his "honeymoon" with Congress, President Reagan signed into law budget and tax reduction legislation marking, what he called, "an end to excessive growth in government bureaucracy and government spending and government taxing." Later in his Administration the economic realities of a recession and mounting government deficits forced the President to modify his supply side tax policy.

While closing what he viewed as the military "window of vulnerability" vis-à-vis the Soviet Union, domestically Reagan accomplished only a fraction of what he set out to do. He had been excoriated not only by some Democrats as the destroyer of the social gains of half a century, but also by right-wing fundamentalists in his own party as a traitor to the purity of their cause. For all that, he had redefined the perimeters of political discourse in the United States, so that the wiser and more adaptable among the liberal critics of his policies now acknowledge the desirability of economic freedom and incentive, and of some decentralization of the functions accumulated by the federal government. As Lou Cannon observed in the epilogue to his candid, conscientious biography Reagan *(1982), "He has set the agenda and, on most issues, outlined the priorities. . . . Whatever the judgment of historians, Reagan has made a difference."*

President Reagan passed away of pneumonia, a complication of Alzheimer's disease, at the age of 93, on June 5, 2004. According to a Washington Post *article of February 16, 2015, Reagan was ranked by 162 members of the American Political Science Association's Presidents & Executive Politics section as the 11th greatest President of the United States, just one tier below the top ten.*

EARLY LIFE

Ronald Wilson Reagan, at the time the ninth chief executive of the United States of Irish ancestry, was

Ronald Reagan.

descended paternally from Michael and Catherine (Mulcahy) Reagan (originally O'Regan), Roman Catholic natives of County Tipperary, Ireland, who settled on a farm in Illinois, in 1858. Their grandson John Edward ("Jack") Reagan, an itinerant shoe salesman, married Nelle Wilson, a Protestant of Scots-English descent, in 1904. The first of Jack and Nelle Reagan's two sons, (John) Neil Reagan, born in 1909, was baptized a Catholic. The second, Ronald Wilson Reagan, born on February 6, 1911 in a flat above the general store where his father was working on Main Street in Tampico, Illinois, was raised in his mother's faith, the Christian Church, better known as the Disciples of Christ. Although Nelle Reagan displayed no favoritism in her treatment of her sons, she influenced Ronald more than Neil, giving him her happy outlook and encouraging his reading, memorizing abilities, and his caricature drawing, all before he became of school age.

Jack Reagan was as strong in his unfulfilled business ambitions, his antipathy to religious ethnic, and racial bigotry, and his Democratic political partisanship as he was weak in his tolerance of alcohol. As Ronald Reagan recounted in his autobiography, *Where's the Rest of Me?* (Duell, Sloan and Pearce, 1965), written with Richard G. Hubler, "the sharp odor of the speakeasy" on his father's breath left him with an aversion to hard liquor. Nelle Reagan, a theater-lover and a do-gooder, gave dramatic readings in prisons and hospitals and never turned a mendicant [beggar] away empty-handed. "My father's cynicism never made the slightest impression on her," Reagan recalled, "while I suspect her sweetness often undermined his practical view of the world. Neither she nor my father had [any schooling] but the elementary grades. No diploma was needed for kindness, in her opinion, just as my father believed energy and hard work were the only ingredients needed for success." The bedrock of Reagan's world view was the ruggedly individualistic, optimistic ethic of his parents, along with the general values ambient in his small-town Midwest boyhood, centered in home, family, and patriotism.

Reagan grew up in the succession of towns in northern rural Illinois where his father pursued his never-to-be-realized dream of striking it rich as an elegant shoe emporium proprietor. When Reagan was nine, the family settled in Dixon, Ill. At Dixon High School, he played football and basketball, ran track, was president of the student body, and did his first acting. Summers, he worked as a lifeguard, and he continued doing so after matriculating at Eureka (Illinois) College, a small liberal arts college affiliated with the Christian Church. He supplemented his partial scholarship at Eureka with his earnings as a lifeguard, as a dishwasher at his fraternity house, Tau Kappa Epsilon, and as a college swimming coach.

LIFE'S WORK

The future President first ventured into politics when, as a freshman at Eureka, he was the spokesman for a strike committee that successfully protested an administration plan to reduce the curriculum for budgetary reasons. As he wrote in his autobiography, it was on that occasion that he discovered "that an audience has a feel to it and, in the parlance of the theatre that audience and I were together." Joining the student dramatic society, he won an award at Northwestern University's annual one-act play festival for his role in the Eureka troupe's production of Edna St. Vincent Millay's *Aria de Capo,* an antiwar drama congenial at the time to Reagan. He was, briefly, a pacifist of the isolationist variety then common in the Midwest. As in high school, at Eureka he played guard on the football team, was president of the student body, and, academically, his photographic memory enabled him to breeze through his classes with minimal last-minute cracking of books.

With the coming of the Depression, Jack Reagan lost, first, his partnership in a shoe store he had opened

with borrowed money, and then, on Christmas Eve 1931, his job as a traveling salesman. Without his father's knowledge, Ronald tided the family over financially from his own frugal pocket until his mother found work as a seamstress in a dress shop, and his father took on odd jobs. In 1932, Jack Reagan went to work full time in the Presidential campaign of Democratic Presidential candidate Franklin Delano Roosevelt. The Depression was the most important influence in Reagan's young adult life. President Roosevelt, who took office in the darkest hour of the economic crisis, in March 1933, became his political hero, and the influence of Roosevelt's heroic populist rhetoric, memorized as Reagan sat listening to FDR's "Fireside Chats" on the radio, still marked his own speaking style.

Encouraged by his former high school drama teacher, B. J. Frazier, to "have a shot at . . . the field in which [he had] so much talent," Reagan decided to go into communications when he graduated from Eureka College with a B.A. degree in economics and sociology, in June 1932. The following autumn, he landed a temporary job broadcasting University of Iowa home football games over WOC, a small radio station in Davenport, Iowa, and, early in 1933, he was hired as a staff sports announcer at WOC. Reagan's easy, warm conversational voice, his outstanding gift, was a natural for play-by-play ad-libbing, but his reading of a script, as required for commercials, was, in his own words, "just plain awful." He overcame that weakness by memorizing scripts and reciting them aloud until the delivery was spontaneous, a practice that would serve him in good stead as a political speechmaker. A few months after Reagan's arrival at WOC, the station was consolidated with its powerful big-sister station, WHO in Des Moines, which made "Dutch" Reagan's voice, announcing Chicago Cubs baseball games, familiar to Cub fans throughout the Midwest. Dutch, the name he used as an announcer, was the nickname his father had given him when he was a baby.

The dream of Dutch Reagan the sportscaster was to become a Hollywood actor. That dream became a reality, in 1937, when Reagan, covering the Cubs' spring training on Catalina Island, near Los Angeles, was discovered by an agent for Warner Brothers and signed to play the lead, a crusading radio announcer, in *Love Is On the Air* (1937). Under contract to Warner Brothers, he became, in his own assessment, "the Errol Flynn of the B's," a persona who, contrary to a popular canard that Reagan resented, often *did* "get the girl." Standing out among his numerous early screen credits were *Brother Rat* (1938) and *Dark Victory* (1939). The first role that he fought for, and got, was that of George Gipp, the Notre Dame University football player who died young, in *Knute Rockne—All American* (1940), the film that established him as a serious actor. That reputation was reinforced by his portrayal of the small-town playboy Drake McHugh, whose legs are needlessly amputated by a vengeful surgeon in. *Kings Row* (1941). The title of Reagan's autobiography is the line uttered by McHugh when he awakens from surgery.

As a sportscaster in Des Moines, Reagan had, out of his love of horseback riding, enlisted as an officer in the United States Army's Cavalry Reserve. Called to active duty in the army in 1942, during World War II, he was disqualified from combat duty because of his nearsightedness and assigned to make air force training films. After the war, he returned to Hollywood, where his Warner Brothers credits included *The Voice of the Turtle* (1948) and *The Winning Team* (1952). For other studios he starred in, among other films, *Bedtime for Bonzo* (Universal, 1951) and *Hellcats of the Navy* (Columbia, 1957), in which Nancy Davis, who became his second wife (died, March 6, 2016), was his co-star. In all, he accumulated 52 credits during his motion picture career, not counting the made-for-television feature *The Killers* (Universal, 1964), the only film in which he played a villain.

What Reagan had referred to as his "hemophiliac" liberalism began to coagulate during his tenure as the President of the Screen Actors' Guild, from 1947 to 1952 (and again in 1959 and 1960), when he became disillusioned through his firsthand experience of the rule-or-ruin tactics of Communists in Hollywood unionism. While cooperating with the Hollywood blacklist of Communists, and with the investigation by the United States House of Representatives' Committee on Un-American Activities into Communist influence in the motion picture industry, he came to view Representative J. Parnell Thomas and his committee as "a pretty venal bunch," and was wary in his testimony, not naming names.

Reagan's movement to the right, from enmity toward big business to championing American free enterprise, progressed during his employment by the General Electric Company from 1952 to 1962. Between appearances as host and occasional performer on the weekly network television dramatic series *General Electric Theater,* he toured the United States for

General Electric's personnel relations program, giving speeches with such titles as "Encroaching Controls" and "Our Eroding Freedoms." His increasing opposition to the progressive income tax may have been motivated in part by his own increasing income from speaking, but there was another reason for his general political evolution, as he has pointed out: The broad majority of Americans represented by the audiences at his speeches "were very different people than the people Hollywood was talking about;" seeing "the same people he grew up with in Dixon, Ill.," he realized he "was living in a tinsel factory," and "the exposure brought him back." After *General Electric Theater* went off the air, in 1962, Reagan hosted and performed in the network television Western series *Death Valley Days* for three years.

Reagan turned Republican in 1962. The leadership of political conservatism in the United States passed from Senator Barry Goldwater to Reagan in 1964, when Republican Goldwater lost by a landslide to Democrat Lyndon B. Johnson in the Presidential election. Conservative Republicans regarded Reagan's pre-taped nationally televised speech for Goldwater, "A Time For Choosing," as the one shining moment in the bleak campaign. Whereas Goldwater's blunt rhetoric terrified the electorate with its "extremism," Reagan's Rooseveltian language ("You and I have a rendezvous with destiny . . .") and friendly, low-keyed delivery were reassuring, suggesting plain patriotic concern and continuity with the past.

On October 28, 1964, the day after Reagan's television address, a group of conservatives formed the national "Republicans for Ronald Reagan" organization. In California, two months later, a group of millionaires headed by Holmes P. Tuttle formed "Friends of Ronald Reagan" for the purpose of running Reagan for governor. After trouncing moderate George Christopher in the Republican primary, in June 1966, Reagan campaigned against incumbent Democratic Governor Edmund G. ("Pat") Brown, stumping in California with his basic speech, essentially unchanged since his G.E. days, calling on "ordinary citizens" to bring "the fresh air of common sense to bear" on the problems created or exacerbated by big government. In November 1966, he swept to victory over Brown by almost a million votes, and he handily won re-election as Governor four years later, defeating Democratic State Assembly speaker Jesse Unruh by 3,439,664 votes to 2,938,607.

As Governor of the State of California, Reagan learned how to compromise with legislators and turned out to be much more pragmatic and restrained than his simplistic conservative campaign rhetoric would have suggested. Fulfilling his campaign promise to "clean up the mess in Berkeley," he took a hard-line toward dissident students and "permissive" administrators in the state education system. By freezing state hiring, he succeeded in restraining the growth of California's government bureaucracy. Inheriting a state treasury that was in deficit, he successfully sought from the legislature multibillion-dollar tax increases in his first term. At the same time, however, he began reducing expenditures in social services, education, and other areas, and those initiatives, combined with the prospering of the state's economy, later resulted in substantial budget surpluses, so that in 1973 Reagan was able to institute generous programs of income tax rebates and credits, and property tax relief. Also on the positive side, the major tax law enacted under his Governorship introduced into the previously regressive state revenue-raising system progressive features, taking into account the ability to pay. The major achievement of Reagan's second term as Governor was the California Welfare Reform Act of 1971, which reduced the welfare rolls while boosting payments to the "truly needy," notably recipients of Aid for Families with Dependent Children. As Governor, he also signed into law some measures that were frankly liberal, including an abortion statute that he later regretted because of abuse of its loopholes.

Reagan's run for the Presidency began tentatively in 1968, when he waited until the opening of the Republican National Convention to announce his candidacy, too late to stop the nomination of Richard Nixon, whose candidacy he asked the convention to make unanimous.

President Nixon's incumbency ruled out a Presidential bid by Reagan in 1972, but Reagan was looking forward to 1976, when Nixon, after two terms, would be required to retire from the Presidency. His plans were dampened by the Watergate scandal, which, in 1974, forced Nixon's resignation and moved Vice-President Gerald R. Ford into the Oval Office. Reagan campaigned anyway, beginning with the New Hampshire primary in February 1976. While Ford won the nomination, it was only by a handful of votes, and Reagan laid the groundwork for 1980 by his strong showing generally, especially in the South; by the response to his no-holds-barred conservative speeches in North Carolina; and, by forcing Ford to accept the approval of a conservative platform by the Republican National Convention.

Overcoming questions about his age by the vigor and stamina he displayed in the 1980 primaries, Reagan arrived unopposed at the Republican National Convention, in July 1980. In his acceptance speech, he pledged to support a conservative platform calling for voluntary prayer in public schools, tuition credits for private schooling, and opposition to school busing, abortion, and the Equal Rights Amendment. Reagan called on Republicans "to build a new consensus with all those across the land who share a community of values embodied in these words: Family, work, neighborhood, peace, and freedom." In the general election campaign against the Democratic incumbent, President Jimmy Carter, charges that Reagan was a trigger-happy extremist were dissolved by his disarming performance in a nationally televised debate with Carter on October 27, 1980. Reagan swamped Carter at the polls on November 4, 1980, taking 51 percent of the vote to Carter's 41, and the Electoral College gave him 489 votes to Carter's forty-nine.

In his inaugural address on January 20, 1981, President Reagan announced the beginning of "an era of national renewal." Domestically, he said, it was time "to reawaken this industrial giant and get government back within its means and lighten our punitive tax burden." In foreign affairs, he pledged to "match loyalty for loyalty" with allies and neighbors; to "the enemies of freedom, those who are potential aggressors," he addressed the warning that "when action is necessary to preserve our national security, we will act" and "we will maintain sufficient strength to prevail if need be." As he concluded his address, at precisely 12:33 P.M., the revolutionary government in Iran released the 52 Americans it had held hostage for 444 days. Reagan sent outgoing President Jimmy Carter to greet the returning hostages when they landed in Wiesbaden, West Germany.

Assuming the Presidency at a time of double-digit inflation and rising interest rates, Reagan made the economy his first order of business, as he had promised. At the top of his agenda was a reduction in government expenditures, except for defense. His first act in office was to freeze government hiring, and his major request to Congress was to slash the budgets of federal domestic programs. At the same time, he asked Congress to cut taxes, in keeping with his supply side belief that while tax reductions may diminish government revenues in the short run, they stimulate savings, investments, and entrepreneurship in the private sector that will, in the long run, increase those revenues. His aim was a balanced federal budget by 1984.

Only quick and expert medical attention saved the President from death when John W. Hinckley, Jr., fired a bullet into his chest on a Washington sidewalk, on March 30, 1981. The good humor, grace, and remarkable resiliency with which Reagan recovered from the wound in his left lung swelled his already sizeable popularity, as was evident in the thunderous ovation he received when he went before a joint session of Congress with his economic message on April 28, 1981.

After much wrangling, Congress in 1981 gave President Reagan pretty much what he asked for—the largest tax cut in history, amounting to $335 billion over the three years, beginning fiscal 1982, and a budget for fiscal 1982 that was $35,200,000 less than President Carter had proposed, even with a $28 billion defense increment. The budget provided for outlays of $769.82 billion and revenues of $665.9 billion, leaving a deficit of $103.9 billion, somewhat higher than Reagan wanted.

The Reagan Administration was embarrassed by a candid interview in the December 1981 issue of *Atlantic Monthly,* in which David Stockman, who, as Director of the Office of Management and Budget, was the Administration's chief supply side strategist, expressed misgivings about its programs. But the gist of Stockman's self-criticism was already evident in the behavior of the economy. While inflation was dropping, from 13.5 percent in 1980 to 5.1 percent in 1982, a recession had set in. By October 1982, unemployment had exceeded 10 percent for the first time in some 40 years, and bankruptcy figures were the highest in 50 years. These were in part symptoms of an internal contradiction in the Reagan Administration's economic policy, whose supply side tax stimuli were uncongenially combined with the Federal Reserve Board's tight money policy, a policy supported by the Administration.

Faced with the prospect of federal deficits soaring to $500 billion over the next three years, and keeping interest rates aloft with them, Reagan reversed field and asked Congress for a tax increase, as well as further budget cuts, in 1982. In August 1982, Congress passed a tax increase calculated to raise $98.3 billion over three years, an unprecedented boost, but one representing only a 20 percent retreat from the tax decrease of the year before. During the same month, Congress also cut $30 billion in Medicare, CETA (Comprehensive Employment and Training Act), and other domestic programs, and Treasury Secretary Donald Regan predicted the Administration would wrest another $60 billion in cuts from Congress in the fiscal 1983 budget. The Administration also was pressing for an amendment to the Constitution that would require a balanced federal budget within three or four years. On other domestic front, the President appointed the first woman, Sandra Day O'Connor, to the Supreme Court; refused to negotiate with the illegally striking members of the Professional Air Traffic Controllers Organization; and announced plans for a "New Federalism," which would ultimately place under the control of cities, counties, and the several states many programs now operated from Washington.

Taking a breather from his preoccupation with the domestic economy, President Reagan traveled to Europe for a series of meetings with Western leaders, in June 1982. Although the President kept his campaign promise to American farmers that he would lift the embargo on wheat to the Soviet Union that President Carter had imposed in response to the Soviet invasion of Afghanistan, and although he continued the amicable relations with China initiated by President Nixon, the salient motif of his Administration's foreign policy was a hardened line toward Communism. That line was exemplified in a prohibition against sale of American equipment for use in the construction of the U.S.S.R.'s Siberian-European natural gas pipeline (a sanction invoked after the imposition of martial law in Poland) and "drawing the line" against Communist interference in Central America. The line was drawn in El Salvador, where the United States sent arms and military advisers to a "centrist" junta mortally threatened by leftist guerrillas. In the Mideast, a bold Reagan peace plan involving a homeland for the displaced Palestinians was rejected by Israel, on September 1, 1982. Later that month Reagan made the most daring foreign policy gamble of his Presidency in redeploying 1,200 United States Marines in Lebanon after the massacre of Palestinian refugees there by Christian Lebanese allies of the Israeli occupation force.

Although President Reagan remained true to the extreme right faction of his constituency in his advocacy of voluntary school prayer and anti-abortion legislation, and his opposition to the Equal Rights Amendment, that faction felt betrayed by what it considered the shiftiness of "Reaganomics" and the influence in the White House of two "liberal internationalist" think tanks, the Council on Foreign Relations and the Trilateral Commission, through Vice-President George H. Bush and Treasury Secretary Donald T. Regan. Liberals on the other hand ,were apprehensive about the fact that two members of the Cabinet, Defense Secretary Caspar Weinberger and Secretary of State George Shultz (who had replaced Trilateralist Alexander Haig) were from the Bechtel Corporation, a California-based engineering firm chiefly involved in the construction of energy facilities, including nuclear power, breeder, and fuel reprocessing plants. The sniping from left and right occasionally brought a choleric retort from the President, but the only accusation that bothered him profoundly was the charge that his programs were unfair to poor people and minorities.

He won his second term in office, winning with a landslide, in 1984, with the largest Electoral College victory in history. His second term was dominated by foreign affairs, including ending of the Cold War, the bombing of Libya, and the Iran–Contra Affair. Reagan publically called the Soviet Union the "evil empire," and he successfully transitioned Cold War policy from détente to rollback, by escalating an arms race with the U.S.S.R. while engaging in talks with Soviet General Secretary Mikhail Gorbachev, the outcome of which culminated in the INF Treaty, shrinking both countries' nuclear arsenals. In 1987, Reagan stood in front of the Brandenburg Gate, calling for the leader of the Soviet Union, Mikhail Gorbachev, "to tear down this wall." Five months after Reagan left office, in 1991, the Berlin Wall fell, ushered in the reunification of Germany and, later, the fall of Communism in Europe.

When Libya's dictator Qaddafi was implicated in the April 5, 1986, bombing of a discotheque in what was then West Berlin, where one American soldier was killed, Reagan responded by bombing suspected terrorist training camps, and also Qaddafi's residential compound in Tripoli.

Reagan was called the "Teflon President," due to his ability to let allegations roll off of him, when the major scandal of his Administration broke open: The Iran-Contra Affair. In October and November of 1986, it was discovered that for several years, agents of the United States government had been running an illegal operation to sell weapons to Iran and funnel the profits to the Contras, a military organization dedicated to overthrowing the leftist government of Nicaragua. In December, 1986, Lawrence E. Walsh was appointed independent counsel by the U.S. Court of Appeals for the District of Columbia Circuit. According to the *Encyclopedia of Espionage, Intelligence and Security* web site, "the Iran-Contra investigation lasted from 1986 to 1994. During this period, Walsh charged 14 Reagan Administration officials with criminal acts. He obtained convictions and guilty pleas in 11 cases. Two

convictions were overturned on a technicality, and several officials, including Secretary of Defense Caspar Weinberger, were issued pre-trial pardons by President George H. W. Bush during the 'lame duck' period following his electoral defeat in 1992. Walsh's investigation concluded that 'the sales of arms to Iran contravened United States Government policy and may have violated the Arms Export Control Act,' that 'the provision and coordination of support to the Contras violated the Boland Amendment ban on aid to military activities in Nicaragua' (passed by Congress in 1984), and that 'the Iran operations were carried out with the knowledge of, among others, President Ronald Reagan, Vice-President George H. W. Bush, Secretary of State George P. Schultz, Secretary of Defense Caspar W. Weinberg, and Director of Central Intelligence William J. Casey.' Walsh did not have legal power to bring charges against President Reagan or Vice-President . . . Bush, as the Boland Amendment was not a criminal statute containing specific enforcement provisions. Congress did not . . . impeach."

In August 1994, during his retirement at his California ranch, Reagan was diagnosed with Alzheimer's disease at the age of 83. He announced it publicly, in November, in a letter to the American people. As the years went on, the disease slowly destroyed Reagan's mental capacity, but he remained active, taking walks and visiting his office in Century City. He suffered from a broken hip in January 13, 2001. On the afternoon of June 5, 2004, Nancy Reagan released a statement that the President had died. President George W. Bush declared June 11 a National Day of Mourning. On June 7, where a brief family funeral was held at the Ronald Reagan Presidential Library, conducted by Pastor Michael Wenning, a viewing was held in the Library lobby until June 9. Then his body was flown to Washington, D.C., where he lay in state. At the U.S. Capitol, 104,684 people filed past the coffin. On June 11, President George W. Bush presided over a state funeral, which was conducted in the Washington National Cathedral. The Reagan entourage was flown back, after the funeral, to the Ronald W. Reagan Presidential Library in Simi Valley, Calif., where another service was held, and President Reagan was interred. He is now the second longest-lived President, just 45 days fewer than Gerald Ford.

PERSONAL LIFE

As soon as Reagan entered the White House, the portrait of Harry S. Truman in the Cabinet room was replaced with that of Calvin Coolidge, the first supply-sider. The President (who had doodled caricatures during Cabinet sessions) delegated the details of administrative work to the Cabinet and to his chief White House lieutenants, James A. Baker 3rd, Edward Meese 3rd, and Michael Deaver. (Meese and Deaver were carryovers from Sacramento.) He did so not because he was weary with age (he was the oldest President ever inaugurated), but because it had always been his practice, in Sacramento as well as Washington, not to fall victim to executive fatigue. Jealous of his solitude and leisure, he retreated often to his ranch, "Rancho del Cielo," near Santa Barbara, Calif., where he spent much of his time riding on horseback with his wife and chopping wood. His other recreations included watching television and privately screened motion pictures, and his favorite reading was the *Reader's Digest* and the conservative periodicals *National Review* (edited by his friend William F. Buckley, Jr.), *Current Events, Conservative Digest,* and *Commentary.*

As viewers of his frequent television appeals to the nation and listeners to his weekly radio chats may surmise, the 40th President of the United States was a man of imposing physique (large-framed, six-foot-one, 185 pounds) and beguiling voice who flaunted neither his physical presence nor his vocal gift, emphasizing his most urgent points with shrugs and whispers. Less well known than his nearsightedness (for which he wore contact lenses) was an auditory problem.

A man of simple tastes, noted for his appetite for jelly beans, President Reagan owed much of the opulence of his White House to his wife Nancy, whom he married on March 4, 1952, four years after his divorce from the actress Jane Wyman. By his first marriage, Reagan had a daughter, Maureen (died August 8, 2001), and an adopted son, Michael, a business executive. A daughter, Christine, died in infancy in 1947. By his second marriage, he had a daughter Patricia, an actress whose professional name is Patti Davis, and a son, Ron, a ballet dancer.

FURTHER READING
Boyarsky, Bill. Ronald Reagan (1981); Cannon, Lou. Reagan (1982); Edwards, Lee. Ronald Reagan: A Political Biography (1981); Reagan, Ronald, with Hubler, Richard G. Where's the Rest of Me? (1965); Smith, Hedrick, et al. Reagan the Man, the President (1981); Van der Linden, Frank. The Real Reagan (1981)

KARL RENNER
President of Austria

Born: December 14, 1870; Dolni Dunajovice, Austria-Hungary
Died: December 31, 1950; Vienna, Austria
Affiliation: Socialist Party

INTRODUCTION
Karl Renner, President of the liberated Austrian state, was a leading figure at the several key points of his country's history. Born three years after the Ausgleich *which established the Dual Monarchy, he was the first Chancellor of the Austrian Republic and signer for defeated Austria of the treaty of 1919 which made her a small, powerless state. Later he was one of the Socialist leaders jailed in early 1934, when events foreshadowed Austria's annexation by Nazi Germany; he became the first Chancellor of the Provisional Government set up after her liberation, and in December 1945 was elected President of Austria.*

EARLY LIFE
The son of peasants, Matthias and Marie (Habiger) Renner, Karl Renner was born in Dolni Dunajovice, Moravia, on December 14, 1870. He studied law at the University of Vienna, where he was introduced to Neo-Marxist thought, and before his graduation with an LL.D. he became a Social Democrat and leader of the Neo-Marxist movement. (The Neo-Marxists sought to make Marxian socialism evolutionary rather than revolutionary.) In 1907 he was elected a deputy to the National Assembly, and, as a leader of the Social Democrats, he was in the vanguard of the opposition to the Hapsburg monarchy. The Government was notorious for suppression of its heterogeneous minority groups, and in the years leading up to the outbreak of the First World War the spirit of nationalism within the empire became very strong. Renner himself is the author of *Das Selbstbestimmungrsrecht der Nationen*

("The Nations' Right to Self-determination"), published in 1918.

This rising and disruptive nationalism in Austria-Hungary was an expression of the feeling prevalent throughout the whole of Europe on the eve of the war. It was particularly strong among the Serbs, Croats and Slovenes—known collectively as the Yugoslavs—within and without the empire. Consequently, when the Dual Monarchy acquired the predominantly Croatian and Serbian provinces of Bosnia and Herzegovina in 1908, the nationalistic fervor of the Serbian Yugoslavs exploded, setting off a series of events that eventually led to the assassination in 1914 of the Archduke Francis Ferdinand, the heir to the Hapsburg throne. In a tense Europe, where the "engrained competitive nationalism [of the great powers] proved to be stronger than the more recently awakened ideal of international conciliation," this event was only the last of the crises that plunged the world into war, and ended in the dissolution of the Austro-Hungarian empire.

LIFE'S WORK

The end of Austria-Hungary as a unit came on November 12, 1918, when German Austria was proclaimed a republic and a temporary Cabinet formed with Renner as its head. Attempts were made by Communists to bring Austria into the ranks of the Soviet republics, but Renner thwarted all demands of the Communists made with the object of overthrowing the Provincial Government. In the first republican elections, in February 1919, the Social Democrats won the largest representation in the new National Constitutional Assembly, and Renner, the moderate Socialist, became the first State Chancellor of the Austrian Republic, in a coalition Government composed predominantly of Social Democrats and the conservative Christian Socialists. That summer the Chancellor went to Paris to accept Allied peace terms, and when Foreign Minister Otto Bauer resigned rather than accept certain provisions of the treaty, Renner took over his portfolio. In September, as head of the Austrian delegation, he therefore signed the Treaty of St. Germain with the victorious Allied powers. A second coalition Government was formed the next month, in which Renner retained both the Chancellorship and the Foreign Affairs portfolio. When the coalition was dissolved the following June he remained as Foreign Minister, until his resignation that October.

The establishment of a republic was, however, not to be the solution to Austria's postwar economic and social problems. Under the terms of the Treaty of St. Germain she had been forced to recognize Czechoslovakia, Yugoslavia, and Poland as independent states, and to cede to them and to other states large portions of her land. As a result, she was deprived of three-fourths of her territory and people, and reduced to a small landlocked state. This left the country without sufficient food and raw materials, and trade was cut off by the tariff barriers erected at the end of the war by the succession states of central Europe. To many Austrians at this time, including the Social Democrats, the only way out of this situation was *Anschluss* or union with Germany, a move forbidden by the terms of the treaty and vigorously opposed by the Allies and by the monarchists and clericals within Austria itself. Renner, a member of the National Assembly in 1922 (president from 1931 to 1933), was one of those who supported the union. "Of course we all know," he said, "that as things are now, Austria has no future. We can keep ourselves alive just until the hour of liberation strikes, that is, until we as Germans can decide in favor of the state to which we belong by the nature of things."

The League of Nations, by arranging for loans and supplying financial supervision, came to the aid of the young Republic in the early twenties, and again at the time of the world depression; notwithstanding, a desire for union with Germany remained. With the rise of Hitler [42], however, the *Anschluss* question developed complications, for *Anschluss* now meant union with a Nazified Germany. A subdivision of Hitler's National Socialist Party was established in Austria, and a concerted effort was made by the Nazis to bring about annexation by Germany. Nazism spread rapidly among the conservatives in Austria, and Dollfuss decided to rule by decree in order to maintain the country's independence.

Meanwhile, Austria was disturbed as well by the antagonism between the radical urban proletariat and the conservative rural classes, rep resented, respectively, by Renner's Social Democrats and the Christian Socialists. (In Vienna, where the Social Democrats were strong—after 1919 they never again gained a majority in the National Government—the city passed legislation providing for social welfare, public health, housing, education, recreation, and city improvements.) The result of this hostility was the formation of two militant organizations, the Schutzbund of the Socialist workers, now opponents of the *Anschluss* movement, and the Heimwehr of the peasants, described as "a type of Fascist organization, strongly anti-Socialist." In February 1934 Dollfuss, seeking the aid of these Austrian Fascists and Mussolini against Germany, began raiding Social Democratic headquarters—the price of Fascist support. When leaders of the party (among them Julius Deutsch) declared a strike, it was put down with accompanying bloodshed by the Army. In the end the party was outlawed and Renner and other leaders jailed. Renner was released the following June, however, there being insufficient evidence to hold him.

Shortly after the suppression of the liberal elements in the country, Austria, by a new constitution, became an authoritarian corporate state like Italy, and universal suffrage was abolished. In July the Nazis made an abortive attempt at a coup d'etat that ended with the assassination of Dollfuss. During the next four years Austria, under Chancellor Schuschnigg, became merely an appendage of Germany. On March 13, 1938, this relationship was made official; Austria no longer existed as a nation. Earlier in the month, when there was a faint chance that there might be a plebiscite on the question of *Anschluss,* Renner made this statement : "As a Socialist and as an adherent to the principle of self-determination of nations. . . . I will vote 'Yes.' " Whether this was delivered under pressure is not known.

After Austria's extinction as a state, those democratic forces who did not leave the country went underground. Renner, too, it is reported by Selwyn James in *PM,* is believed to have worked in the underground movement during the war. Shortly after the Red Army reached Vienna in April 1945 Moscow announced the formation of a Provisional Government headed by the seventy-four-year-old Renner, and consisting of Social Democrats, Communists, and People's Party and non-party representatives. This government, wrote Ernst Karl Winter, an Austrian political refugee, for the *Nation,* is the kind of government political realists have wanted for Austria since 1930. Renner's Government (Renner himself is anti-Communistic and anti-Soviet) has been recognized by the Soviet Government, but has still to be officially authorized by the British and American governments through their representatives on the Allied Control Council for Austria. In the meantime, it is faced with the problem of feeding a starving population and providing fuel for the winter.

In September the issue of Allied recognition of the Austrian and other provisional governments in Europe was placed before the meeting of the Big Five Foreign Ministers in London. The question seemed to be one of "British-American anxiety over the spread of Communism and Russia's insistence that governments of neighboring states must be friendly to her for security reasons if nothing else." In the case of Austria, it was felt that Renner's Government was more representative of radical Vienna than of the whole of Austria, a condition, according to the Chancellor, that was due to the fact that all of the country had not been liberated when the Government was formed. (Of fourteen Ministers, three were Communists.) In a letter to the *Times* of London, Renner pointed out that Austria had turned for guidance to the League of Nations in 1920, to Rome in 1934, and to Berlin in 1938. Now, he concluded, Austria was turning, not to Moscow, but to the United Nations organization and nothing else. "I hope," he wrote, "to have succeeded in having at least explained that the guaranty for Austria's existence and her future does not rest solely, nor even in the first instance, with the people of her soil, but that it rests, to a higher degree, with the world outside."

Delegates from Austria's nine provinces met in Vienna on September 24, 1945, for the first time since the Anschluss of 1938 to construct a representative Government acceptable to the Allies. The new broadened and strengthened provisional Government, headed by Rentier, which came into being as an outgrowth of the three-day conference, was formally recognized by the United States, Great Britain, Russia, and France on October 20. Action was taken in behalf of the four occupying powers by the Allied Control Council, on orders from the members' respective capitals; one of the principal conditions enumerated was that free elections were to be held "as early as possible and no later than December 31."

The first national elections in fifteen years were thus held on November 25. Leopold Figl's Rightist Volkspartei (Catholic People's Party) won more than 51 per cent of the seats. Upon resigning, Renner was designated as acting chancellor of the interim provisional government, pending the meeting of the new National Assembly on December 12. In a joint meeting on December 20, 1945, both chambers unanimously elected Renner Austria's President, to serve six years. Future Presidential elections are expected to be by popular ballot. According to the Constitution of 1929, which has been restored with slight modifications, Renner will have limited powers; he can dissolve Parliament but has no power to veto bills passed by the Lower House.

Personal Life

The elderly Renner was once General State Librarian of the National Assembly. He has been president of the International Association for Social Progress in Basle, and a member of the International Cooperative Alliance in London. Since 1901, when his first publication appeared, *Staat und Parlament,* he was a prolific writer, chiefly in the fields of economics, government, law, and socialism. Some writings were published under the pseudonyms of Rudolf Springer and Synopticus. As head of the Austrian Government he was believed to be the lowest paid chief of state in Europe.

With his wife Luise, he lived in an old house in the American zone in Vienna, with which his Government provided him. Renner died in 1950 in Vienna. He was buried in Vienna in the Presidential Tomb at the Zentralfriedhof, one of the largest cemeteries of the world.

Further Reading

Encyclopaedia Britannica (1929); *International Who's Who,* 1942; *Who's Who in Central and East-Europe,* 1935-36

Franklin D(elano) Roosevelt
President of the United States

Born: January 30, 1882; Hyde Park, New York
Died: April 12, 1945; Warm Springs, Georgia
Affiliation: Democratic Party

Introduction

When President Roosevelt's mother, the late Sara Delano Roosevelt, was informed that her son had won the Presidential election of 1932, she responded with less than the expected enthusiasm. "The Presidency," she said, "I have always felt to be a most taxing and trying occupation." And yet her son, through years of economic depression, through disaster, change, domestic turmoil, and foreign war, through years of "the crudest job in the world," kept "his ebullient gaiety, an excellent digestion, and the ability to sleep like a child."

The thirty-second President of the United States is the descendant of fairly prosperous Dutch ancestors. His father, James Roosevelt, was president of the Louisville and Albany Railroad and vice-president of the Delaware and Hudson Canal Company, "a sober and severe gentleman who might have felt a few pangs of surprise had he lived to hear that his son was a champion of stringent governmental regulation of public utilities." He was fifty years old, a widower with one son, James Roosevelt, Jr., when he married twenty-six-year-old Sara Delano, the daughter of Warren Delano, a wealthy importing merchant.

Early Life

James Roosevelt was more country squire than business executive and spent most of his time on the family

Franklin Delano Roosevelt.

estate at Hyde Park, New York. It was there that Franklin Delano was born. "At the very outset," according to his mother, "Franklin was plump, pink, and nice." Though he lost his plumpness and pinkness, he continued nice, she said, through all the years in which he was growing up in Hyde Park. He lived at home, taught by governesses and tutors, spending long vacations at Campobello, an island off the coast of Maine, taking occasional trips abroad. It was a quiet and full life of study, play, and sailing that he lived until at fourteen he was sent to Groton. There he was manager of the baseball team, a member of the debating team, and a generally successful student. He intended to give up school life, though, at the time of the Spanish-American War, and laid thorough plans for running away and enlisting. Only an unexpected case of the measles brought them to an ignominious end.

Roosevelt left Groton for Harvard, and there established for himself a reputation for sociability and energy. He was a member of eight clubs; he went out for crew, though he didn't make varsity; he wrote for the *Crimson* and in his last year edited it. There were editorial crusades against everything from lack of sportsmanship to "listless hockey practice," and a campaign against the campus authorities' neglect of safety regulations in case of fire. He graduated in 1904 more or less in the middle of his class (his Phi Beta Kappa key was awarded to him after he became eminent) but with the honor of being its permanent chairman.

Roosevelt's father had died while he was at Harvard, and his mother took a house in Boston in order to be near her son. When he left Harvard for Columbia's Law School she didn't come with him. Roosevelt wasn't without female companionship long, however. On March 17, 1905 he married his distant cousin, Anna Eleanor Roosevelt, daughter of Theodore Roosevelt's brother, Elliott. The President himself came to the wedding of his niece and his fifth cousin, and the Franklin Roosevelts still remember how nobody noticed them in the flurry of excitement over Theodore Roosevelt.

After a honeymoon, the couple took a tiny house on 36th Street in New York. At that time Franklin was attending Law School. Before the end of his second year a daughter, Anna Eleanor, was born to them, and not very long after came a son, James. Roosevelt wasn't graduated from Columbia Law School, but left in 1907. He passed his Bar examination that same year and started practice with Carter, Ledyard, and Milburn, one of New York's prominent law firms. He remained with the firm until 1910, promoted to managing clerk and busy with municipal court cases and admiralty cases.

LIFE'S WORK

While practicing law in New York City, Roosevelt spent much time in Hyde Park, managing the 600-acre estate,

entering into community activities. It was suggested to him by local Democrats that he run for State Senator. Despite the fact that it seemed a futile gesture in a solid Republican district, Roosevelt agreed, embracing politics, as one historian put it, "with a mixture of *noblesse oblige,* good sportsmanship, and solemn dedication." The issue then was "bossism," and Roosevelt played it for all it was worth as he campaigned up and down his district. To the amazement of everyone, including his own Party, he was elected by the substantial majority of 1,140 votes.

Shortly after he went to Albany to take up his post, Roosevelt had his first run-in with Tammany. Tammany had selected "Blue-Eyed Billy Sheehan" for United States Senator and took his election for granted. But Roosevelt and some others objected. There was a fight, and finally Sheehan's candidacy was withdrawn and a candidate acceptable to both camps selected. During this first term Roosevelt caused comment, too, by refusing an appropriation for Dutchess County. It wasn't needed, he said. At least three other politicians hastened to tell him: "You ought to have your head examined."

Roosevelt had decided not to run for a second term in 1912, but was informed that Tammany would be delighted to have him get out. With out hesitation he campaigned again and was sent back with a larger majority than he had received in 1910. He was working at this time, too, for Wilson's nomination, and he went to the 1912 Democratic Convention determined to get Wilson in. His success at organization and his loyalty put him clearly in line for something handsome from the new Administration, once Wilson was elected. He was offered the Collectorship of the Port of New York or the position of Assistant Secretary of the Treasury, both jobs that would lead to splendid business connections. He turned them down. Then Josephus Daniels, Secretary of the Navy, asked him whether he would like the position of Assistant Secretary of the Navy. Roosevelt, whose interest had long been the sea, who already had a large collection of books on naval affairs, replied without hesitation: "Would I like? I'd rather have that place than any other in public life."

In March 1913 Roosevelt left the State Assembly and his positions there as chairman of the Forest, Fish, and Game Committee and as member of the Canals, Railways, and Agricultural Committees and settled down in Washington, probably the handsomest young man there. He had, according to Hugh Johnson, "a cameo face, broad shoulders, narrow hips, straight legs—a musical voice and a Hahvahd accent." Immediately he got to work. Believing in "preparedness," he estimated even before the First World War the supplies needed; he placed contracts; he gathered statistics on American industrial plants. Civilian personnel, Navy yards, docks, and the purchasing of supplies were under his immediate direction, and, with an almost complete disregard for red tape, he attacked the problems they entailed. He converted Navy yards into productive, self-supporting plants, each with its own specialty; he instituted novel reforms, like requiring that middies learn how to swim; he did away with middlemen in buying supplies and quashed profiteering. According to one story, he did so well that Wilson called him in one day to confer with the Army chief of staff. "I'm very sorry," Wilson is reported to have said. "But you've cornered the market for supplies. You'll have to divide up with the Army."

When the United States entered the First World War, Roosevelt built housing projects, waged a fight for the construction of 110-foot submarine chasers, helped establish the North Sea barrage, and generally did much to break the back of submarine warfare. In July 1918 he went to Europe, where he talked with King Albert of Belgium, Lloyd George, Foch, Clemenceau, and other leaders. But on his return he was stricken with pneumonia, and by the time he was well the War was almost over. There was a job for him to do even then, however. On January 2, 1919 he and Mrs. Roosevelt set sail for Europe, where Roosevelt had the job of liquidating the huge Navy stores in warehouses and Naval stations there.

It was in 1920 that Roosevelt returned to politics. He had already tried for a major position in 1914 when he ran for the Democratic nomination for United States Senator from New York and lost. Now he aimed at a still higher position, and he was nominated for the Vice-Presidency of the United States on the same ticket with James M. Cox. Roosevelt resigned from the Navy and campaigned vigorously. Far and wide over the country he traveled, making more speeches than any other Vice-Presidential candidate in history. But despite his campaigning, despite the campaigning of Mrs. Roosevelt, who frequently accompanied him and often addressed organizations and women's groups, Roosevelt and Cox were defeated by the biggest margin in the history of the Republic, even losing Hyde Park, Roosevelt's home town.

Roosevelt accepted defeat and decided to devote himself to making money. He had five children (Elliott,

Franklin Delano, Jr., and John had been born since his Law School days), and the interest on the $100,000 estate left him by his father didn't go very far. On January 24, 1921 he became vice-president of the Fidelity and Deposit Company of Maryland, with offices in New York and a salary of $25,000 a year. He kept this position until 1928 and also was associated with other commercial firms. He was active in other ways, too: in the Boy Scout movement, in the affairs of Harvard, which made him an overseer in 1917, as chairman of a committee to raise funds for the Woodrow Wilson Foundation.

But all these activities were suspended when Roosevelt was stricken with infantile paralysis in the summer of 1921. He refused to bow to the prospect of long crippled years and with the encouragement of his wife, of Margaret Le Eland, still his friend and personal secretary, and of the late Louis Howe, his long-time friend and aide, fought for recovery. It was a hard period in his life, but one which, according to Max Lerner, developed in him "a sense of mastery over himself and others." By 1924 he was well enough to get about on crutches, to take an active part in Democratic politics, to place Al Smith's name before the Democratic Convention of that year.

As soon as the convention was over, Roosevelt went to Warm Springs, Georgia, then an abandoned summer resort and now a foundation for crippled children, to practice strengthening his muscles in the water. After several months of this he was able to ride a horse, drive a specially designed car, and by 1928 he was walking with braces and two canes. Long before that, though, he had ceased to lead the life of an invalid. He was a member (1924-33) of the law firm of Roosevelt and O'Connor; he kept up his business connections; he took an interest in politics. Al Smith wanted him to run for the Governorship of New York State. Smith, whose candidacy for President had been supported by Roosevelt, felt him the right man for his ticket.

Roosevelt demurred. Smith insisted, making a personal matter of it, and after insurance examiners and other doctors had pronounced him "a splendid physical specimen," Roosevelt consented to be "drafted." He undertook a vigorous campaign and was elected Governor of New York State by a majority of 25,564 in an election in which Smith lost the state by more than 100,000. But it wasn't easy going, once he was in. There was a Republican Legislature. As a result Roosevelt gained, in the words of John T. Flynn, "an excellent record in his support of those policies of social justice for the workers and poor that had been initiated by Smith, but he did not have much success in passing the laws he supported."

Roosevelt, throughout his two terms as Governor, pressed for the public development, operation, and transmission of the hydro-electric resources of the St. Lawrence River. He urged old age pensions, state unemployment insurance, prison reform, a forty-eight hour work week for women and children, labor legislation, rural land utilization, the modernization of local governments. Some of these he got, though in modified form; many of them he did not get. His supporters wholeheartedly blamed the political opposition, but *The Nation* commented on his tenure: "His weakness and readiness to compromise have been as evident as have his personal charm and his absolute integrity."

To *The Nation* this was most evident in Roosevelt's handling of the Walker-Tammany scandal, which demanded most of his political astuteness after he was re-elected in 1930 with the largest plurality ever given any New York Governor. The government of New York City had been discovered to be most unsavory. Roosevelt signed the bill appropriating money for the Seabury investigation and also gave Seabury a free hand. He himself, however, refused to interfere in the fight, despite strong pressure for him to take over the affairs of the city and remove corrupt officials. His policy was to delay action, to let hearings go on, until facts mounted and Walker resigned. For this policy people like John Chamberlain'[40] have praised him. "He simply let Walker and Tammany kill themselves," Chamberlain wrote. But the New York *Evening World* told its readers that "he has lost a respect for which no victory can compensate." Actually, the consensus seems to be that the situation was such that "he was certain to be damned whatever he did."

It was a particularly delicate situation because Roosevelt was being mentioned frequently for the Presidency. He had the necessary qualifications: good family, the name of Roosevelt, practice in politics, practice in Washington affairs, practice running for national office. And despite the lack of backing from the delegation from his own state (he had already lost the support of Al Smith, who was to come out for Landon in 1936), Roosevelt was nominated in Chicago by the Democratic Party. He flew there to accept the nomination. Then he started campaigning,

Roosevelt gathered around him a number of economists, professors, and experts on various problems, whom journalists soon dubbed the "Brain Trust," and stumped the country "if for no other reason than because I want to get acquainted with the People." There weren't many concrete issues in the campaign—Some called his platform speeches "platitudes and generalizations"—but Roosevelt did commit himself to the repeal of Prohibition, and he did introduce one telling figure: "the forgotten man." While he campaigned he was praised for his liberal viewpoint, though Bruce Bliven countered: "To me he seems rather the good fellow who talks in terms of restitution to the poor, but would not do anything which would seriously hurt the rich." And there were people like Walter Lippmann to call him "a pleasant man who, without any important qualifications for the office, would very much like to be President." Nevertheless, Roosevelt was elected over Hoover by a plurality of 413 electoral votes. Farley, chairman of the Democratic National Committee, partly explained it after the elections were over when he said that the country was in such a state of economic disease in 1932 that it would have been almost impossible for a Democrat not to be elected. "Roosevelt could have spent the entire fall and summer in Bermuda and been elected just the same," he said.

Roosevelt came to the Presidency at a time when business was stagnant, millions unemployed; when ships were moored to their docks and cars tied up on sidings; when banks were failing and thousands starving. Unperturbed by an attempted assassination in February 1933, he rose to the emergency. Two days after his inauguration he closed every bank in the country and set up an examining committee in the Treasury Department which arranged to open only those that were "sound." Then he called Congress and presented to it one immensely important bill after another. "Our task now," he reminded it, "is . . . adapting existing economic organizations to the service of the people."

Congress was in session for 104 days in the spring of 1933, and in those 104 days Roosevelt sponsored fifteen pieces of major legislation, "a record of sheer effort . . . that has no parallel in the history of American Presidents." From this session of Congress came the Agricultural Adjustment Act, the Civilian Conservation Corps, the Securities Act of 1933, the Home Owners' Loan Corporation, the Farm Relief Act, the Tennessee Valley Authority, the Federal Emergency Relief Administration, the Emergency Railroad Transportation Act, the Public Works Administration, the Civil Works Administration, The Commodity Credit Corporation, the Federal Surplus Relief Corporation, the National Industrial Recovery Act. From this session came an enlargement of the powers of the Reconstruction Finance Corporation, the abandonment of the gold standard. Then, in the summer of 1933, the National Emergency Council was established to coordinate the many new departments set up.

It was the NRA, probably, that had the greatest and most immediate effect on the people of this country. Called by Roosevelt "the most important and far-reaching legislation ever enacted by the American Congress" and "a supreme effort to stabilize for all time the many factors which make for the prosperity of the nation and the preservation of American standards," its central feature provided for the drawing up of codes of fair competition by which trades and industries were regulated. There were other features: a Federal bond issue to finance public works, a blanket code setting national minimums for workers, a guarantee of labor's rights to collective bargaining—all intended to regulate competition, improve wages, shorten hours, increase the workers' purchasing power. In every store window the blue eagle was placed. But almost from the beginning, there were complaints as to its running under General Hugh Johnson and later under Donald Richberg and S. Clay Williams. The workers complained that certain clauses weren't being enforced; the consumers complained that retail prices had not been controlled; the retailers complained of a trend toward Big Business in the choice of deputy administrators. And there were some, like John Chamberlain, who called Roosevelt's "great liberal revolution" a "movement toward slavery, toward a type of Chamber of Commerce Guild Fascism." There was criticism, too, of Roosevelt's "sciittling" of the World Economic Conference which met in London in July 1933, with Raymond Moley, the President's close adviser at that time, representing his country. After the darkest days of 1933 had passed a minority even began to say that reform should cease. They were unable to realize, wrote Roosevelt later, that "permanent recovery was impossible without the eradication of the economic and social maladjustments which permitted wealth and prosperity to concentrate in the control of a few. . ."

By the time of the 1934 elections there was a lining up of those for and against what had become known as the "New Deal," with muttered talk of "usurpation of power by the Executive", "unconstitutional legislation", "imminent Federal bankruptcy," counterposed against a belief that the New Deal was actually establishing a fairer order that would give, in Roosevelt's words, "every man, woman, and child the right to stand erect in

pride and self respect." Roosevelt's supporters won, and the Democratic majority in both houses of Congress was increased.

With the aid of his Cabinet, which included Secretaries Hull, Roper, Farley, Perkins, and the aid of "a soviet of brilliant thinkers," the personnel of which changed from time to time but consistently included young lawyers recommended by Felix Frankfurter and economics professors, Roosevelt continued to devise and press through Congress major legislation. In 1934 he reduced the gold content of the dollar; he obtained Federal supervision and regulation for securities and commodities exchanges; he urged through Congress measures making use of natural resources, reciprocal trade agreements, improvements of Federal judicial procedure; he obtained gold and silver legislation; he got the Federal Housing Administration set up. In 1935 Congress passed measures giving more aid to agriculture; it voted for the National Labor Relations Act which gave labor the right to organize and bargain collectively, for the Utility Holding Company Act, for the Guffey Bituminous Coal Act, for the Social Security Act. Billions were voted for housing projects, rural rehabilitation, rural electrification, the conservation of natural resources, public works, relief. Pensions for railway employees were authorized, the banking business was more closely controlled, special taxes were imposed on large incomes and estates.

Complaints grew, especially of the taxes, and in 1935 Roy Howard wrote Roosevelt: "You fathered a tax bill that aims at revenge rather than revenue—revenge on business." But complaints were less important to Roosevelt than a series of decisions in 1935 and 1936 by the Supreme Court which limited the Government's ability to achieve New Deal objectives. In January 1935 section 9(c) of the NIRA was declared unconstitutional; in February the Gold Clause was upheld in private obligations but not in Government ones; in May the Railroad Retirement Act was declared unconstitutional, and in that same month the court found the code-making provisions of the NIRA unconstitutional (a decision which is said to have more or less relieved many New Dealers who were finding the NIRA "an old man of the sea"). In 1936, in January, the AAA was declared unconstitutional; in May the Bituminous Coal Conservation Act of 1935 (the first Guffey Coal Act) was discovered to be the same; in June the New York State Minimum Wage Law was invalidated. With these decisions, Roosevelt says, "we were stopped and thrown back in our efforts to stabilize national agriculture, to improve conditions of labor, to safeguard business ... to protect disorganized interstate industries . . . and in other ways to serve obvious national needs."

Many of these decisions offered fuel for the fierce fires of discussion about Roosevelt and the New Deal which flamed through the country. Newspapers, financial, industrial, and business leaders attacked "That Man." As Roosevelt summed it up later: "Every effort was made by the opposition to magnify minor errors of administration, to misrepresent actual facts, and at the same time to give lip service to the cause of social betterment." The specific charges were many. Roosevelt aimed to "tax the few, spend for the many and win elections through that process" (yet radicals complained that his chief mission had been to save the fortunes of the very rich) ; he had burdened the country under crushing debt, inculcated the doctrine that the State owes all its citizens a living and so converted many into loafers and beggars; he had raised taxes so that there was no profit in business, played wildly with the country's monetary policy, sustained the economy "largely by artificial braces." He was trying to alter the fundamentals of the Constitution and, worst of all, was bringing socialism to this country.

At this last charge, even *Fortune* demurred. "He has had the preservation of capitalism at all times in view," the editors wrote. Roosevelt himself wrote later that the task of reconstruction "did not call for the creation of strange values. It was rather finding the way again to old, but somewhat forgotten ideals and values." The Left found this not enough. If the new Deal is compared "with measures necessary for a thorough renovation of our society, it is sadly deficient and even, in some aspects, reactionary," commented the *New Republic*.

Both sides commented on Roosevelt's inconsistency, at his approving an act to regulate the stock exchanges and at the same time appointing Joseph Kennedy, a Wall Street speculator, to its head; at his sponsorship of both the conservative Banking Act of 1935 and the stringent undistributed profits tax; of the RFC on the one hand and the Public Utility Act on the other. Yet supporters claimed for Roosevelt not consistency in immediate action but in his objectives. The London *Economist* probably summed up the reaction of many people to the whole controversy when it wrote: "Mr. Roosevelt may have given the wrong answers to many of his problems. But he is at least the first President of modern America who has asked the right questions."

Sixty per cent of the people agreed at the 1936 election, and Roosevelt defeated Alfred M. Landon by 523 electoral votes out of a possible total of 531 and an impressive Congressional majority. Grave problems still confronted him then—strikes, unemployment, unrest in Europe. In his inaugural address Roosevelt conceded this. "I see one-third of a nation ill-housed, ill-clad, ill-nourished," he said. But he said, too: "Our progress out of the depression is obvious." And he emphasized and dramatized the forward steps made in the Good Neighbor Policy, always a major consideration of his Administration, when shortly after the inauguration he made a trip to South America.

Only the very beginning of this term seemed auspicious, however. Shortly after he took office Roosevelt announced his plan to enlarge, or, as some said, "pack," the Supreme Court. To him the reasons f or this step were clear: during the first four years of his Administration, he said, the Court had laid "a dead hand" upon the whole program of progress and hadn't permitted the Federal Government to function as the people had voted for it to function. Much of the public was aghast; much of his Party was upset by what seemed to them tendencies toward dictatorship, for Roosevelt hadn't consulted Party leaders before presenting his proposal. Albert Jay Nock said the Court issue gave disaffected members of the Party a chance to pour forth the anger of years. The fight was lost, though eventually Roosevelt was to achieve his objective through the appointment of seven liberal Justices.

The Court fight wasn't Roosevelt's only problem. As a result of his belief, stated in 1933, that "no business which depends for its existence on paying less than living wages to its workers has any right to continue in this country," and subsequent labor legislation, Labor had organized. The number of strikes yearly had risen from 1,695 in 1933 to the all-time high of 4,740 in 1937. Labor, too, had devised a new technique, that of the sit-down strike. It was mainly on this issue that Roosevelt and Vice-President Garner split, though other differences on public spending, business conciliation and other policies had appeared from time to time. On this issue, too, Roosevelt alienated a good deal of the conservative section of the country. At the same time he was able to shock Left-wing liberals when during the Little Steel strike he announced to John L. Lewis and the companies: "A plague on both your houses."

To add to the storm of controversy, in 1937 a severe "recession" set in: business indexes dropped from 110 to 85; there was unemployment; retail sales dropped off; steel operations were down to about thirty per cent of capacity. Even the usually loyal *New Republic* printed T. R. B.'s lament for "the wreckage of Mr. Roosevelt's second term." And yet some things were accomplished. The Farm Security Administration was created as a successor to the Resettlement Administration, and the ever-normal granary plan for agriculture advanced. The United States Housing Authority was set up under the United States Housing Act of 1937. And large sums, though not so large as in Roosevelt's first term, were devoted to relief.

The controversy became even greater in 1938, when according to Max Lerner, the President experienced "a fierce lynching bee." There was even criticism of his family, criticism which to some extent continued to be spoken in the years to come. Mrs. Roosevelt was condemned for "running around all over the country" and for supporting radical causes instead of staying in the White House and entertaining in the ladylike way of Mrs. Hoover, for instance. There had been divorces in the family: Elliott was divorced in 1933, a year after his marriage to Elizabeth Donner, and he married Ruth Googins in that same year; Anna and Curtis Dall were divorced in 1934, and she, too, was remarried later, to John Boettiger. In 1940 James was divorced from Betsy Cushing and a year later he married Romelle Schneider. Roosevelt's children's careers, too, were material for criticism. James went into the insurance business, and talk of the advantages of being Roosevelt's son were rife. There was even more talk when he was made a White House secretary by his father. Elliott entered the advertising business, and then became president and general manager of a Hearst chain of radio stations. Franklin Delano, Jr., married Ethel Du Pont, and his alliance, together with Elliott's, became the source for a frequently repeated ditty about Roosevelt:

He'll never have to hunger, he'll never have to thirst,
He has one son with Du Pont and another one with Hearst.

Later, people were to acclaim the patriotism of the Roosevelt sons (after strong objection to Elliott's appointment as a captain in the Army Air Corps), for all four of them, including John the youngest (married to Anne Clarke), had left their wives and positions to enter the armed services of their country.

More significant to the country as a whole in 1938, however, were statements like those of *Business Week*, which complained of the country's need for "encouragement for private enterprise rather than Government largesse" and of Roosevelt's public appeal, which was "frequently directed to suspicion, fear, and class hatred." The article concluded: "Whatever his intentions may have been, his method was to destroy our economy and substitute for it one more to his liking, one which he would conjure up as he went along." Roosevelt countered attacks of this sort with the assertion that the basis for the depression and disaffection rested squarely upon "certain highly undesirable practices" on the part of business. And yet, at the same time that businessmen and industrialists were casting doubts on Roosevelt's interest in their survival and progress, the liberals and the Communists were presenting evidences of a switch by Roosevelt to the Right.

Roosevelt's party in Congress had never returned to the semblance of unity it had had before the Supreme Court fight. He tried to remedy this in the 1938 elections by speaking against the re-election of his Democratic opponents. His detractors called this a "purge," spoke of Roosevelt's desire to punish the boys who hadn't stayed in line, of his desire for a rubber-stamp Congress. His supporters insisted that Roosevelt's only desire was to achieve the program in which he believed, much of which was being made unattainable. In any case, the "purge" was unsuccessful, and all the "purged" Congressmen except one returned triumphantly to office.

Nevertheless, despite criticism and a certain lack of support in Congress, important social legislation was passed during 1938. The Fair Labor Standards Act, setting a minimum on wages and a maximum on hours and establishing basic working conditions, and an Agricultural Adjustment Act went through Congress. The Temporary National Economic Committee also was set up to investigate monopolies. The next year, though, Roosevelt was less successful in obtaining his desires. The Relief Deficiency Bill had 150 million lopped off by Congress; the Reorganization Bill, intended to modernize and reorganize the machinery of the Federal Government, was greeted by cries of "dictatorship" and passed only after much controversy and some, changes. Things looked bad, according to the *New Republic*, which editorialized: "The New Deal and the hope of building a more prosperous and secure America were never in greater danger." *Fortune*, in August 1939, stated this fact another way when it said: "Just about the last vestige of Roosevelt domination is gone." And to underline the problem, there were still millions of unemployed, tremendous Government debts, idle plants.

There was, too, a War in Europe. Back in the 1920's Roosevelt believed in a collective world order for peace. There were modifications and changes in his foreign policy during his first years as President, but one aspect of it was consistently present in his advocation of low tariffs and reciprocal trade agreements, expressed through the successful negotiations of his Secretary of State, Cordell Hull; another, in his building up of the Good Neighbor policy. Perhaps even stronger was Roosevelt's belief in preparedness—even in 1936 the budget for military and naval purposes was about $1,200,000,000.

More than once between 1935 and 1938 Roosevelt had authorized the State Department to ask Congress for the right to discriminate between nations engaged in a foreign war on the basis of a judgment as to the rightness or wrongness of the quarrel. In 1935, for instance, he went beyond the terms of the Neutrality Act to discourage the shipment of raw materials to Italy during the Ethiopian War, and in the fall of 1937 he refused to invoke the Act in relation to the Sino-Japanese struggle, on the ground that it would hurt China more than Japan. By this last act, however, he laid himself open to charges of inconsistency and of aiding Japan, as he had laid himself open to charges of aiding the Fascists by his refusal to sell arms and ammunition to the Spanish during their civil war.

Even after the amending of the Neutrality Act in April 1937 and after his speech in Chicago in October of that same year in which he insisted that this country must "quarantine" the aggressors, Roosevelt's policy did not seem clear to everyone. Some called his Chicago speech an invitation to war; others hailed it as an effort to preserve peace; still others found it ambiguous. In 1938 there continued to be many who found his foreign policy difficult to follow: one commentator said he had handled it according "to his favorite quarterback tactics." Another analyzed his policy as one of active though unacknowledged cooperation with England in opposing "those violations of treaties and those ignorings of humane instincts which today are creating a state of international . . . instability from which there is no escape through mere isolationism or neutrality." To this last commentator, at least, the President's personal appeal for justice and peace to Hitler at the time of Munich and his recalling of the American Ambassador

to Berlin were evidence of such a policy, as were the United States' taking over of two islands in the Pacific near Australia, his reception of the King and Queen of England in 1939, and loans to China that started in 1938 and continued. More significant in most minds, however, was Roosevelt's speech to the nation in January 1939 telling Americans: "There are methods short of war, but stronger and more effective than mere words, of bringing home to aggressor, governments the aggregate sentiments of our own people." One method was by changing the existing neutrality legislation, and in September 1939, after the outbreak of the Second World War, Roosevelt was successful in getting Congress to pass a new Neutrality Act permitting belligerents to purchase war materials from the United States on a "cash and carry" basis. He had failed in a similar attempt a few months before.

When Germany marched into the Low Countries in 1940 Roosevelt responded by asking Congress for a billion dollar emergency arms program. By May 1940 the National Defense Commission of seven men had been set up. By June, Roosevelt had asked Congress for a "two ocean Navy" and summoned a Latin American parley. In September he exchanged fifty over-age destroyers for bases with Great Britain. In October the Selective Service Act was passed. In December the Office of Production Management was created, replacing the National Defense Advisory Board. By this time Roosevelt had announced that plans for extending the New Deal were shelved. When old projects were referred to, he replied: "It's there on the shelf. It will have to wait."

By the time Roosevelt's third term began in January 1941 there were many who felt that the United States was not at war and not at peace. But there were more who supported what Roosevelt was doing, for his election, with Henry Wallace, former Secretary of Agriculture as Vice-President, by a majority of 451 electoral votes (the popular vote, however, was close) was achieved in the face of a strong "no third term" tradition in the United States, a sharply vocal isolationist group, and an able opponent, Wendell Willkie. After the campaign Roosevelt set to work stiffening his foreign policy, trying to bring about more aid to Britain, trying to achieve hemispheric solidarity, rearmament in the United States, national unity.

In March 1941 the Lend-Lease Act was passed, by which those fighting the Axis could get supplies far more freely from the United States and by which, some felt, the country was projected into "an undeclared war."

Certainly it committed the United States, now "an arsenal of democracy" to a British victory. And Roosevelt emphasized this when he stated that we would "deliver the goods" to the British. He denied in April, however, charges that convoys were being used, and said there were only patrol ships operating out from our shores. To add to their number and the number of ships needed for other purposes, Roosevelt asked Congress for legislation empowering him to requisition and pay for foreign vessels immobilized in United States waters.

In May 1941 the President proclaimed an unlimited national emergency and particularly demanded the end of work stoppages in defense industries (the National Defense Mediation Board had been set up in March to solve labor differences). In June he ordered the freezing of the assets in the United States of Germany, Italy, and all invaded and occupied European countries. In July he asked Congress to enact legislation permitting him to hold selectees, national guardsmen, and reservists in the Army longer than the statutory period of one year. He asked for aid to Russia. In August he met at sea with Winston Churchill to draw up eight peace aims, "the Atlantic Charter." In October he recommended the arming of ships and the removal of the prohibition against sending American flagships into belligerent ports.

These actions weren't made without criticism. There were many who disliked the virtually unlimited powers Roosevelt had been given. There were many who attacked the alleged inefficiency (later brought out by the report of the Truman Committee) of the National Defense Advisory Commission and its successor, the Office of Production Management, to which was added in September the Supply, Priorities, and Allocation Board. It was felt by some that New Dealers were getting too much power from these boards; by others that the OPM was fostering a "business as usual" attitude which led in some instances to "war for profits" activities and insufficient speed in production for defense. It was claimed that Roosevelt's frequent reluctance to fire anyone led to inefficiencies in the defense effort, as did his interest in handling himself details of problems and situations. In fact, *Fortune* pointed out: "It has become a truism that the worst bottleneck in the United States defense program is the President's desk."

Most criticism, however, was launched by those opposed to the United States' intervention in the European War. Men in Congress like Senator Robert Taft, Senator Burton Wheeler, and Senator Gerald Nye, as well as members of the America First Committee like Charles Lindbergh and John T. Flynn, charged that his methods were "secretive and dictatorial," that his real war policies weren't clear, that steps like the destroyer deal, aid to Russia, the occupation of Iceland, and the meeting with Churchill had been taken without due regard for the democratic processes. Most important, they averred, was the fact that, without doubt and without hesitation, Roosevelt was inevitably plunging his country into a foreign war. And at the same time there were individuals and organizations who complained that he was gambling with the nation's safety by his reluctant delays and the ambiguous policies of his State Department toward countries like Vichy France and Japan.

The storm of isolationist attack was at least temporarily silenced when on December 7, 1941 Japanese bombs fell on Pearl Harbor. The next day Congress declared war on Japan, and on December 11 Roosevelt asked Congress for a declaration of war against Germany and Italy. Congress voted it unanimously, as it later voted requests for tremendous appropriations. And in January the Senate passed the Second War Powers Bill which expanded the Government's authority to expedite production and the movement of supplies. A normally anti-Administration Congress was apparently doing its best to implement Roosevelt's words after Pearl Harbor: "No matter how long it may take us to overcome this unpremeditated invasion, the American people in their righteous might will win through to absolute victory."

Roosevelt himself did much to keep them. In January 1942 he appointed the War Production Board, under Donald M. Nelson, to have full power over the defense and victory effort; he issued a new draft proclamation; he held conferences with Anglo-American military leaders; he urged on unwilling Congressmen the passage of the Price Control Bill, aimed against inflation; he presented an acceptable plan for current labor peace to the C. I. O. and A. F. of L. and announced the conversion of the National Defense Mediation Board into the National War Labor Board; he encouraged the Rio Conference at which most South American countries voted to break their Axis ties. President Roosevelt worked energetically to prepare for the "hard war . . . long war, bloody war, costly war" he saw ahead. And on his sixtieth birthday the Gallup poll reported eighty-four per cent of the country satisfied with his policies, although by then the Administration was having many bitter battles with Congress.

In the following months Roosevelt continued to work energetically. He created the War Shipping Board, at the same time placing all Federal employees on a War footing, with some agencies merged and others abolished; he participated in the formation of the new Pacific War Council; he created the War Manpower Commission of nine members "to bring about the most effective mobilization and the maximum use of the nation's manpower in the prosecution of the War"; he spoke for the curbing of high salaries. In June, his busiest month since the beginning of the War, he secured Congress' declaration of war against Bulgaria, Hungary, and Romania, welcomed Mexico as an ally, created the Office of War Information, and met Churchill for the third time. During the conference between the two leaders they came to what was described as "hearty and detailed agreement on plans for winning the War." It was understood that commitments were made to Russia to "divert German strength from the attack on the Soviet Union," and "vague promises of aid to China" were also made. During the summer of 1942 Roosevelt met with labor leaders to confer on inflation and rebuked the farm bloc on several occasions for standing in the way of effective anti-inflationary measures. In September he asked Congress to pass legislation to stabilize the cost of living by October 1, and threatened to regulate farm prices under his War Powers if this were not done. The following month he made a two weeks' "coast to coast and border to Gulf" tour of the United States, covering 8,754 miles in twenty-four states, and stopping to inspect war industries and defense centers in eleven of them.

By this time Congress was frankly on the warpath against the Administration again. The third "War Powers Bill" in which the President on November 2 requested power to suspend laws pertaining chiefly to tariff and immigration was dropped on December 10 and left for the new Congress to consider. The November elections increased the President's problems still more by reducing the Democratic majority in both Houses. Many commentators believed that if the successful American invasion of North Africa had come before, instead of a few days after, the elections, the results would have been quite different. Roosevelt revealed that he and Churchill had planned the African campaign in June as more feasible than a European invasion, but Churchill gave Roosevelt all the credit as "the author of this mighty undertaking," and the American public seemed inclined to agree. At the same time, however, critics of the New Deal, flushed with a different kind of victory, seemed to be preparing a legislative Blitzkrieg on the domestic front.

There are some who believe that Roosevelt has consistently retained the support of a majority of the American people, despite depression, change, war, and the opposition of important pressure groups, not only because of his real efforts to improve the condition of his country's economy and especially of its lowest "one-third of a nation" but also because of his ability as a politician. Throughout his three terms he has had to deal with groups in his Party as different and dissident as Southern Right-wing Democrats like Carter Glass, liberals like Senator Wagner, machine-men like Mayor Kelly of Chicago. He has been able to do so, according to John Chamberlain, because he "loves politics as a game," and "from his love of the game as a game comes the power of refreshment and renewal." In fact, there are some, like Max Lerner, who believe that Roosevelt might never have emerged as more than merely a skillful politician "if history had not conscripted him to its wars."

There are others who attribute his achievements to his ability to choose well-informed advisers: men like those of the first Brain Trust, most of them dispersed by 1936, or Harry Hopkins, or Felix Frankfurter or the men in his Cabinet and in the inner White House Circle, though Hugh Johnson denies this, calling Roosevelt a "congenital prima donna" who "thrives on adulation and submission." There are still others who feel the answer lies in Roosevelt's own innate qualities of mind, appearance, and personality: in his "marvelous ability to grasp details and his extraordinary memory"; in his thorough understanding of complicated situations; in his real concern for the welfare of the lowest "one-third of a nation"; in his "expansive, witty" handling of the press conferences which he, unlike other Presidents, has held regularly twice a week since 1933; in his friendly "fireside chats" to the people. *Fortune* summed up some of the reactions to this personality when it wrote: "Surrounded by the glamorous aura of the Presidency, his statuesque head set on tremendous shoulders and chest, vibrant voice and flashing smile, aristocratic ease, complete self-mastery and utterly confident sense of command produce an electric effect on public and private audiences. His magnificent voice and skill in delivery can make even second-flight oratory inspiring, and for all his literary limitations he does have a gift of conversational lucidity." (At the December 1942 conference of the National Association of Teachers of Speech the President was named "the greatest public speaker of all contemporary American orators" and "the most effective in estimating audience reaction."

PERSONAL LIFE

A "remarkable resiliency" persisted through years in which Roosevelt spent "longer hours on the job than any President in living memory." His face became heavier and more deeply lined; his hair was grayer and thinner. But his mannerisms of tossing his head before answering a question, of fitting one cigaret after another into a reedlike holder, of gesturing vividly, still persisted. He was still "serene under fire," still "marvelously able to throw off his cares when the time comes to relax . . . famous for the belly laughs he sends booming through the White House corridors." And his living habits changed little through the years.

In the somewhat less hectic days before the Second World War the pattern was slightly different. Then Roosevelt liked to spend an evening reading or working on his large stamp collection or going over his collection of ship pictures and models, or seeing motion pictures. Sometimes he would spend the evening chatting with his friends like Harry Hopkins, delivering impromptu lectures on a variety of subjects. He liked to spend weekends at Hyde Park, driving along the dirt roads, inspecting trees and fences.

Accompanied by his mother until her death in 1941, he liked to attend the village Episcopal Church there on Sunday mornings, carrying out his duties as senior warden. He would take fishing trips and go sailing.

In April 1945, Roosevelt was resting before an appearance at the United Nations, when he had a pain in the back of his head. His cardiologist diagnosed a cerebral hemorrhage, and he died in the afternoon of April 12, 1945. His death was met with shock and grief. *The New York Times* declared "Men will thank God on their knees a hundred years from now that Franklin D. Roosevelt was in the White House."

FDR was buried in the Rose Garden of the family's home in Hyde Park. Eleanor died in 1962, and she was interred next to him. A few weeks after Roosevelt's death, the war in Europe ended.

FURTHER READING

Am Mag 133 :24-5 F '42 por; *Collier's* 98 :7-9+ D 26 '36 por; *Cur Hist* 36:513-20 Ag '32; *Fortune* 20:70-7+ O '39; 25:36-40+ Ja '42 il pors; *Harper* 166 :257-64 F '33; *Ladies' H J* 55:11 Mr '38 por ;(Same abr. *Read Digest* 32 :41-5 Ap '38); *Life* 9:68-7 S 9 '40 il pors; 9:105+ O 14 '40 il por; 10:66-73 Ja 20 '41 il pors; 11:22-3 Ag 4 '41 il R of Rs 86:24-7 Ag '32 il por; *Read Digest* 40:85-94 Mr '42; *Sat Eve Post* 209:5-7+ Ag 15 '36; 209:12-13+ O 31 '36 *Survey G* 29:283-5 My '40; (Same abr. *Read Digest* 36:1-6 My '40); *Time* 39:11-12 F 9 '42 Babson, R. W. *Washington and the Revolutionists* p26-66 1934; Beard, C. A. *Presidents in American History* pl43-6 1935; Flynn, J. T. *Country Squire in the White House* 1940; Johnson, G. W. *Roosevelt: Dictator or Democrat?* 1941; Lindley, E. K. *Franklin D. Roosevelt* 1931; Looker, E. *This Man Roosevelt* 1932; Ludwig, E. *Roosevelt: A Study in Fortune and Power* 1938; Moley, R. *After Seven Years* 1939; Roosevelt, F. D. *The Public Papers and Addresses of President Franklin D. Roosevelt* [1937-40] 1941; Roosevelt, S. D. *My Boy Franklin* 1933; Wharton, D. ed. *Roosevelt Omnibus* 1934; *Who's Who in America* 1942-43

DILMA ROUSSEFF

President of Brazil

Born: December 14, 1947; Belo Horizonte, Brazil
Affiliation: Democratic Labor Party; Workers' Party

INTRODUCTION

When Dilma Rousseff assumed the presidency of Brazil on January 1, 2011, she became the first female head of state in the country's history. "It's not easy being the first woman to govern your country," Michelle Bachelet, who led Chile from 2006 to 2010, wrote for Time *magazine (21 Apr. 2011, online). "Beyond the honor it signifies, there are still prejudices and stereotypes to confront. Nor is it easy to govern an emerging nation: when societies begin to see the light of development at the end of the tunnel, there is a surge of optimism and enthusiasm, but the challenges become more complex and the citizenry more demanding. It's harder still to govern a country as large and globally relevant as Brazil. Bachelet continued, "Brazil is living a unique moment in its history, one of great opportunity, which requires a leader with solid experience and firm ideals.*

Dilma offers precisely that virtuous combination of wisdom and conviction that her country needs." In addition to her readily apparent wisdom and conviction, Rousseff is an ex-guerrilla who fought against Brazils once-powerful military dictatorship and was imprisoned and tortured in the 1970s. As a presidential candidate, she offered another exceptionally important quality to Brazilian voters: she received an enthusiastic endorsement from her predecessor, President Luiz Inacio Lula da Silva. Known as "Lula," he is the most popular leader in Brazils modern history. "In an age when 'change' is a common political battle cry," Bradley Brooks wrote for the Associated Press (20 Sep. 2010), "in Brazil the majority just want more of the same."

EARLY LIFE

Rousseff was born on December 14, 1947 in Belo Horizonte, the capital of the Brazilian state of Minas Gerais. Pier mother, Dilma Jane da Silva, hailed from a family of ranchers, and worked as a teacher. Rousseff's father, Pedro Rousseff, was born in Bulgaria as Petar Russav. He was a lawyer, contractor, and real estate developer. Russav left Bulgaria in the late 1920s, leaving behind a pregnant first wife, Evdokiya Yankova. (Dilma Rousseff had a half-brother, Lyuben-Ka-men, from that union.) Some sources speculate that he was forced to leave because his involvement with the Bulgarian Communist Party made him susceptible to political persecution; others state that he left because his business interests were doing poorly.

Whatever the reason for emigrating from his native land, Russav settled in France for several years before moving on to Argentina and then Brazil, where he changed his surname to Rousseff. There he met Dilma Jane da Silva, and they married in 1946. The couple had three children—Igor (born in January 1947), Dilma, and Zana (born in 1951). Their son Pedro died in 1962, and their daughter Zana died at the age of twenty-six. Lyuben-Kamen, reportedly always longed to go to Brazil to visit his half-siblings, but he died in 2007, never having done so.

Rousseff's father provided a comfortable life for the family in Belo Horizonte, with a large home, membership in a tennis club, and a staff of household help. Rousseff has said that she had no political aspirations in her youth. She attended Nossa Senhora de Sion, an all-girls school, before transferring as a teenager to the Colegio Estadual Central do Brasil, a co-ed public school that, at the time, was a hotbed of student activism.

LIFE'S WORK

In March 1964, Brazil's president, Joao Goulart, was deposed in a bloodless coup. The event ushered in two decades of authoritarian military rule. Coup leaders enjoyed the backing of the US government, which feared the spread of communism in South America. Still a student, Rousseff joined the *Organizagao Revoluciondria Marxista-PolMca Ofenria* (Revolutionary Marxist Political Worker's Organization, or POLOP), one of many leftist groups that opposed Brazil's military rulers.

In 1967, Rousseff married her first husband, Claudio Galeno Linhares, a journalist and fellow leftist. Soon after, amid dissension in POLOP's ranks about engaging in armed struggle, Rousseff joined the militant Comando de Libertagao Nacional (National Liberation Command, or COLINA).

Rousseff s exact role in COLINA has been debated in the media. While some assert that her duties were largely clerical and organizational, others have claimed that she developed a deep familiarity with weapons and was an influential leader with the group. Rousseff has admitted only to transporting weapons on occasion, and she claims never to have engaged in actual shooting, in part because of her poor vision. Nonetheless, COLINAs activities in Minas Gerais were limited. The group undertook some small bank robberies, car thefts, and organized two bombings that resulted in no casualties.

Following one of the organizations robberies, several members of the COLINA guerillas were arrested. As COLINA members gathered to discuss the arrests, police raided their meeting place. In the melee that ensued, two officers were killed by machine-gun fire. Following the incident, COLINA found itself the target of an intense police investigation. Linhares and Rousseff, who had just finished her fourth semester as an economics student at the Universidade Federal de Minas Gerais (Federal University of Minas Gerais), began sleeping in separate, hidden locations. Soon, they travelled to Rio de Janeiro, and took shelter with one of Rousseff's aunts, who believed that the fugitive couple was on vacation.

When Linhares was ordered by COLINAs leadership to travel to Porto Alegre, the capital of Rio Grande do Sul, Rousseff remained in *Rio de Janeiro, where she continued working for the organization and where she met a leftist lawyer named Carlos Franklin Paixao de Araujo, with whom she fell in love. Rousseff and* Linhares split amicably, and she and Araujo, ten years her senior, embarked on a relationship that, although rocky, lasted some thirty years.

Araujo, the son of a prominent Brazilian defense attorney, was head of a dissident offshoot of the Partido Comunista Brasileiro (Brazilian Communist Party), and was chosen as one of the leaders of the Vanguarda Armada Revolucionaria Palmares (Palmares Armed Revolutionary Vanguard). The VAR Palmares, as the group was commonly known, was formed when COLINA merged with another leftist group, the Vanguarda Popular Revolucionaria. Rousseff also played a role in VAR Palmares. A military prosecutor once referred to her as the groups "Joan of Arc," referring to the fifteenth-century French peasant girl who led the French army to several victories during the LIundred Years' War.

VAR Palmares funded their activities partly by robberies. Among their most notorious exploits was the theft of more than $2 million in cash from a safe in the home of Anna Gimel Benchimol Capriglione, the secretary and mistress of Adhemar de Barros, a former governor of Sao Paulo known for his corruption. Rousseff has always steadfastly denied involvement in the storied caper, and her exact role remains a matter of debate.

In January 1970, Brazilian authorities captured and imprisoned Rousseff. She remained jailed in a facility on the outskirts of Sao Paulo for almost three years, during which time she was subjected to repeated beatings and torture by electrical shocks. Some forty years later, charges were filed against Mauricio Lopes Lima, a former army captain whom Rousseff was able to name as one of her tormentors. She was released from custody in 1972, and went to live in Porto Alegre, where Araujo, who had also been arrested, was finishing his jail sentence. She resided during that time with his parents, and was able to visit him often, bringing along books and newspapers.

Unable to re-enter the Federal University of Minas Gerais because she had been branded a subversive, Rousseff entered a university in Rio Grande do Sul. In 1975, she earned an undergraduate degree in economics, completing an internship at the Foundation of Economics and Statistics, which was affiliated with the Rio Grande do Sul state government. The following year, she gave birth to her only child, a daughter she named Paula. Rousseff entered a graduate economics program at the state university in Campinas in 1978, but she never completed her thesis. Despite her academic work and obligations to her children, Rousseff remained

politically active, participating in a movement to win amnesty for expelled or persecuted dissidents.

In the early 1980s, Rousseff worked with politician Leonel Brizola to establish the Partido Democratico Trabalhista (Democratic Labour Party, or PDT). Brizola, the former governor of the state of Rio Grande do Sul, was the brother-in-law of former President Goulart. Rousseff and Araujo threw themselves into party politics; she served as an economic adviser to PDT members of the Rio Grande do Sul Legislative Assembly, and he won a post as a state deputy for the party.

In 1985, following mass protests related to Brazils economic recession, the country's military rulers peacefully ceded power. A new era of democracy in Brazil began. Rousseff and Araujo worked for the successful campaign of Alceu Collares for mayor of Porto Alegre. After Collares took office in 1986, he appointed Rousseff as the municipal secretary of the treasury. She remained in that post until 1988, when she stepped down to aid Araujos mayoral bid. Araujos mayoral campaign was unsuccessful.

In 1989, Brazil held its first direct presidential election in decades. President Tancredo Neves had won the presidency indirectly in 1985 via electoral college. When Neves died one day before being inaugurated, his vice president, Jose Sarney, had assumed power. Rousseff initially supported her political colleague Brizola in the 1989 election. When Brizola lost the first round of voting, she transferred her allegiance to Luiz Indcio Lula da Silva, who represented the Partido dos Trabalhadores (Workers' Party or PT). The election was ultimately won by Fernando Collor de Mello, a former governor of Alagoasa.

In 1990, Collares was elected governor of Rio Grande do Sul. Fie appointed Rousseff as president of the Foundation of Economics and Statistics, where she had served as an intern more than a decade earlier. In 1993, she was named State Secretary of Mines, Energy and Communications under Collares.

Rousseff left public service in 1994 after she learned that Araujo had fathered a child with another woman. She served briefly as the editor of the magazine *Indicadores Economicos (Economic Indicators)* in 1995, and also enrolled in a doctoral program. Flowever, she did not complete her PhD. Rousseff was reappointed as State Secretary of Mines, Energy and Communications for Rio Grande do Sul following Olivio Dutra's election as governor in 1998. As secretary, she handled one of the largest blackouts in the region's history.

Rousseff and Araujo divorced in 2000. In 2002, Lula da Silva was elected president of Brazil. He appointed Rousseff Minister of Energy and Mines. Shortly before taking office, at a time when Brazil was facing a severe energy crisis, Lula had called a meeting of economic experts, which included Rousseff. "She arrived with a laptop and would press the little buttons all the time while telling me, 'No, Mr. President, it's not like that, it's like this,'" he later recalled in a speech, as quoted by Alexei Barrionuevo for *The New York Times* (31 Oct. 2010).

As energy minister, Rousseff launched a program dubbed Luz para Todos (Light for All), which made electricity available to more than ten million Brazilians living in rural areas, She also oversaw an increase in research into the development of alternative fuel sources in Brazil. During Rous self's tenure as energy minister, Brazil's energy company, Petrobas, added thousands of new jobs.

In 2005, Rousseff was appointed Lula's chief of Staff and minister of the Civil Flouse. She became the first Brazilian woman named as minister of the Civil Flouse, which includes management of all domestic functions of the national government, and oversight of all other cabinet ministers. Rousseff was instrumental in launching the Programa de Aceleragao do Crescimento (Growth Acceleration Program, or PAG), an ambitious effort to improve Brazil's infrastructure through an unprecedented increase in economic investment and the undertaking of numerous social initiatives. She also helped establish the public housing program known as Minha Casa, Minha Vida (My House, My Life), which provides homes to tens of thousands of disadvantaged Brazilians. Minha Casa, Minha Vida precipitated a boom in construction jobs throughout Brazil.

Rousseff underwent treatment for lymphatic cancer in 2009, Despite speculation in the media regarding her health, her name was widely circulated as a potential replacement for President Lula as he approached the end of his term-limited tenure in office. In June 2010, Rousseff officially announced her candidacy in Brazil's 2011 presidential election. Fler opponents in the race included Marina Silva, an environmental activist with whom Rousseff had clashed in the past as a director of Petrobras, and Jose Serra, a social democrat and former governor of Sao Paulo. Rousseff's campaign had the advantage of President Lula's unequivocal support.

Critics protested that Rousseff was merely riding Lula's coattails, that she had never before held elected office, and that she lacked her mentor's charisma. Some

suggested that Lula was using her until the constitution could be changed, allowing him to run again. In the first round of voting, in early October 2010, Rousseff received almost 40 percent of the vote to Serra's 32.5 percent. Political observers speculated that her refusal to denounce abortion caused her to fall short of the decisive 50 percent mark in the first round of voting. Silva's presence on the ballot also contributed; representing Brazil's Green party, she garnered a respectable 19.3 percent of the total vote. In the run-off election held later in the month, Rousseff emerged the victor, earning 56 percent of the vote.

Rousseff was sworn in on January 1, 2011, becoming Brazil's first woman president. In her inauguration speech, she stated, "I didn't come here to extol my [own] biography, but to glorify the life of each Brazilian woman. My supreme commitment is to honor women, protect the [weak] and govern for all." Political analysts wondered whether as president she would manage to step out of Lula's shadow.

Soon after she took office, Rousseff's cabinet underwent a significant period of political controversy. Antonio Palocci, her chief of staff, resigned in the wake of accusations that he had used his political connections to earn lucrative consulting contacts. Alfredo Nascimento, Rousseff's Minister of Transportation, resigned over allegations of corruption in his department, as did the Minister of Agriculture, Minister of Tourism, and Minister of Sports. Nelson Jobim, the Minister of Defense, was forced to step down after publicly insulting two fellow cabinet members. While some political observers complained that Rousseff was tainted by her association with these cabinet members, others saw the fact that she had called for their resignations as proof that she would be tougher on corruption than Lula had been.

Despite the doubts of her detractors, Rousseff has differentiated herself in other ways as well. "Less than three months into the job, Ms. Rousseff, once thought to be a potential puppet of Mr. da Silva, has swiftly moved out of [his] shadow," Alexei Barrionuevo wrote for the *International Herald Tribune* (19 Mar. 2011), praising the fact that she "is more likely to pursue foreign policy driven by economic goals than by a desire for the kind of global grandeur that Mr. da Silva often sought/' Similarly, Mac Margolis asserted for *Newsweek* (26 Sep. 2011), "Barely nine months in office, Rousseff has stamped her understated style on a country Lula had owned." Brazil's economic growth, which began under Lula, has continued during Rousseff's tenure. Brazil is readying for two important moments on the world stage as it prepares to play host to the 2014 FIFA World Cup and the 2016 Olympics. "[A]mong the world's major economic powers, [Brazil] has achieved a rare trifecta: high growth (unlike the United States and Europe), political freedom (unlike China), and falling inequality (unlike practically everywhere)," Nicholas Lemann wrote for the *New Yorker* (5 Dec. 2011). "Brazilians usually rank at the very top in international measures of how optimistic the citizens of a nation are about its future."

In December 2015, impeachment proceedings against Rousseff began in the Chamber of Deputies, and in May 2016 her powers as President were suspended for six months or until a verdict is reached. Vice President Michel Temer is serving as Acting President during the suspension.

PERSONAL LIFE
Rousseff lives with her mother and aunt in the Palacio da Alvorado, Brazil's official presidential residence. Rousseff enjoys the opera and has a pet Labrador retriever.

FURTHER READING
Bachelet, Michele. "The 2011 *Time* 100." *Time*. Time, 21 Apr. 2011. Web. 10 Apr. 2012. Barrionuevo, Alexei. "Poised to Lead Brazil, an Ally of the Current President Faces Unfinished Tasks." *The New York Times* 31 Oct. 2010: A06; Lemann, Nicholas. "The Anointed." *New Yorker* 05 Dec. 2011: 50; Margolis, Mac. "Don't Mess with Dilma." *Newsweek 26* Sep. 2011: 36.

S

ANWAR (EL-) SADAT
President of the United Arab (Egypt) Republic

Born: Dec. 25, 1918; Mit Abu al-Kum, Egypt
Died: October 6, 1981; Cairo, Egypt
Affiliation: Arab Socialist Union

INTRODUCTION

On September 28, 1970, Egyptians were thrust into a frenzy of grief by the death of Gamal Abdel Nasser, Egypt's leader for almost two decades and the most powerful figure in the Arab world in generations. Yet with an impressive show of political stability, the reins of government passed smoothly to Anwar Sadat, who was sworn into office on October 17, 1970, for a six-year term as President of the United Arab Republic (Egypt's official name until 1971, when it resumed the name "Egypt"). Sadat, a close personal friend and loyal supporter of Nasser, was a member of the original group of Egyptian army officers who began plotting with Nasser in the late 1930s for the overthrow of the feudal monarchy that finally took place in 1952. (Most of the other dozen plotters are dead or have lapsed into obscurity.) Sadat's role in Nasser's Egypt was primarily that of a publicist for the regime; he served as editor of the semiofficial newspaper Al Gomhuriya *for a time and as Nasser's representative on visits to many nations. He also held posts in the government and was Vice-President when Nasser died.*

When Sadat was elected to the Presidency many observers prophesied that he would exert little real power, but within a year he had aborted a coup, purged the government of his rivals, and emerged as a strong and popular leader. Later, he was the first leader of an Arab nation to negotiate peace with Israel, sharing the 1978 Nobel Peace Award with Israel's Prime Minister Begin.

Anwar Sadat.

Sadat, who was assassinated in 1981, now is considered in Egypt and in the West as one of the most

645

influential Egyptian and Middle Eastern figures in modern history.

EARLY LIFE

Anwar el-Sadat was born on December 25, 1918, in Talah Monufiya, a village in the Nile Delta, to a military hospital clerk and his Sudanese wife. The Sadats were poor but devout Moslems, and they saw to it that Anwar attended a local religious primary school, where he studied the Quran. He received his secondary education at a school in Cairo.

As a youth, Sadat longed to become an army officer and to oust the British, who continued to hold considerable power in Egypt, even after their protectorate was formally abolished in 1936. When the Abbassia Military Academy was opened to members of the lower and middle classes in 1936, Sadat was admitted, and it was there that he met Gamal Abdel Nasser, who was just 11 months his senior. The two soon became close friends. In the winter of 1938, after graduating from the military academy, Sadat, Nasser, and ten other officers stationed at the garrison town of Mankabad in Upper Egypt formed what Sadat has described as a "secret revolutionary society dedicated to the task of liberation." Their group became the nucleus of the Free Officers Committee that seized power from the Farouk regime some 14 years later.

To weaken the hold of the British over neutral Egypt in World War II, Sadat collaborated clandestinely with the Germans, but his efforts met with little success. His assignment of smuggling a cashiered Egyptian general into German hands was bungled when first, a getaway car broke down, and then an airplane crashed on takeoff. The general was captured and imprisoned by Egyptian authorities. Then Sadat began working with two inept Nazi spies in Cairo who, it became apparent, were more interested in drinking and women than in spying. One of their escapades led to their arrest along with Sadat, and in October 1942, following a court-martial, the Egyptian army officer was dismissed from the service and imprisoned.

Sadat remained in a detention camp for two years while his fellow conspirators paid his family $200 a month, which he described as "a balm to my soul," in his book on the Egyptian revolution entitled *Revolt on the Nile* (Day, 1957). He continued, "All those who have fought for an ideal know that it is not the fear of death or torture that causes a man to weaken, but the thought of what may happen to his wife and children who are weak and defenseless." In November 1944, he escaped from the camp and went into hiding in Egypt, continually changing disguises and residences and working at a variety of odd jobs, including selling used tires and driving a cab.

As he related in *Revolt on the Nile*, Sadat was an impetuous and romantic revolutionary in those early days. "I was always eager to step up the pace, but Gamal [Nasser], a man of deliberation, acted as a restraining influence. . . . My idea was to blow up the British Embassy and everybody in it. . . . Gamal listened attentively and then . . . said, 'No.'" Sadat was again imprisoned, in 1946, after a series of terrorist attacks against pro-British officials. Although he stoutly maintained his innocence, he served almost three years in prison on charges of involvement in the assassination of Finance Minister Amin Osman Pasha, whom he called "a die-hard Anglophile." While in prison, Sadat missed out on the fighting between Israel and the Arab nations after Israel proclaimed independence in 1948. Sadat described that period of imprisonment as "the most terrible years of my life." Released from prison in 1949, Sadat worked as a newspaper reporter, until some of his influential friends were able to get his army commission restored in 1950. He was then stationed as a captain at Rafah in the Sinai Desert, where his main revolutionary duty was to maintain liaison between Nasser's Free Officers Committee and civilian terrorist groups.

The conspirators' plans to overthrow Farouk came to fruition on the night of July 22, 1952, when the Free Officers Committee led by Nasser staged a swift and bloodless coup d'état. Sadat, who had been summoned back from Rafah to Cairo by Nasser, on July 21, almost missed the event. Finding no further message from Nasser upon his return to Cairo on July 22, Sadat decided to take his children to the movies. When he returned home, Sadat discovered that he had missed Nasser and that the revolution had started without him. By the time he arrived at Cairo military headquarters, it had already surrendered, but Nasser gave him the job of announcing the news of the coup on the morning of July 23. On Egyptian radio, Sadat reported to the world that the Free Officers Committee had seized power and demanded the abdication of King Farouk I. He then was given the task of flying to Alexandria to oversee the departure of Farouk on July 26. "From the bridge of the destroyer, I watched Farouk pass into the twilight of history," Sadat recalled in his book. "The sailors round me were jubilant. Suddenly I felt faint. For three days I had not slept. I had lived on my nerves. Now I was feeling the effect of those long hours of tension. I had to be helped down the gangway."

Affiliation: Arab Socialist Union

At first, the new government was nominally headed by General Mohammed Naguib, but, by 1956, Nasser, the real power behind the revolt, had seized control as Premier and President of the Egyptian Republic. Although Sadat served as a member of the military junta's Revolutionary Command Council and in a number of other posts, Nasser did not give his friend a truly leading role in the new government. According to Edward R. F. Sheehan (*The New York Times Magazine*, November 29, 1970), "Nasser never entrusted [Sadat] with important jobs because he did not consider him efficient." At first, Sadat was appointed Director of Army Public Relations, and then he became Editor of *Al Gomhuriya*, the semi-government newspaper, for which he wrote scathing anti-Western editorials during the Suez crisis. From 1954 to 1956, Sadat was a Minister of State and, in 1957, he was appointed Secretary General of the National Union, the forerunner of the present Arab Socialist Union, Egypt's only political organization. In 1961, he exchanged that job for the Presidency of the National Assembly, where he remained until 1968. During the mid-1950s, he served as Secretary General of the Islamic Congress, a short-lived body established by Nasser to promote Moslem unity, and, in 1958, he was Chairman of the Afro-Asian Solidarity Conference. During the 1960s, Sadat represented his government on a number of ceremonial visits to the Soviet Union, Czechoslovakia, Mongolia, North Korea, and the United States, and he served as one of Nasser's troubleshooters in Yemen, where the United Arab Republic supported the Republicans in a civil war.

Nasser was wary of letting anyone get too much power in his government, but he seemed to have trusted Sadat more than anyone else. Therefore, while others fell from favor, Sadat maintained his prominence. From 1962 to 1964, he was a member of the Presidential Council and, from 1964 to 1967, he was one of four Vice-Presidents, until Nasser abolished the post in the aftermath of the June 1967 Six-Day War with Israel.

Following a lengthy illness, President Nasser reestablished the Vice-Presidency, in December 1969, and named Sadat to the post, reportedly because he was the only man he trusted not to take advantage of the position. When Nasser suffered a fatal heart attack on September 29, 1970, Sadat became President, under the terms of the nation's constitution, for up to sixty days, in which time the National Assembly was to choose a successor. On October 7, 1970, the legislative body unanimously nominated Sadat, apparently because he was uncontroversial and had agreed to share the nation's leadership with his rivals. Speaking before the National Assembly after his nomination, Sadat pledged to work toward Nasser's goals: The recovery of Arab lands occupied by Israel; the unification of the Arab nations; the definition of "the enemies of our nation"; the maintenance of a non-aligned posture between the major world powers; the support of national liberation movements in other countries; and, the defense of Egypt's socialist goals. In a national Presidential referendum on October 15, 1970, Sadat received a 90.4 percent "yes" vote from the seven million Egyptians casting their ballots, and he was sworn into office for a six-year term, two days later.

LIFE'S WORK

Sadat took office in the midst of an uneasy truce with Israel. In March of 1968, Nasser had launched a "War of Attrition" against Israel, vowing to continue until his country regained its territory occupied by Israel in 1967. During the summer of 1970, however, Nasser had agreed to a 90-day ceasefire, beginning in August, and to negotiations with Israel through United Nations mediator Gunnar V. Jarring. A bitter foe of Israel, Sadat had reportedly been strongly opposed to the ceasefire, and some observers doubted, at the time he took over the government, that he would continue Nasser's policy of cautious receptivity to negotiations. Yet, once in office, Sadat agreed to a 90-day extension of the truce, beginning in November and, in late December, Israel agreed to rejoin the peace talks that it had boycotted since August, in protest against the Egyptian buildup of missiles in the Suez Canal zone.

In an interview with James Reston for *The New York Times* (December 28, 1970), Sadat stated that his nation's primary demand for peace in the Middle East was that Israel give up "every inch" of territory she had captured from the U.A.R. in June 1967. If she did, said Sadat, the U.A.R. would recognize the rights of Israel as an independent state and was prepared to negotiate Israel's "rights of passage" through the Gulf of Aqaba and the Strait of Tiran. However, he stipulated that Israel's "rights of passage" through the Suez Canal would depend on settlement of the "[Palestinian] refugee problem." Sadat agreed to one more extension of the ceasefire, until March 8, 1971, but he had refused further extensions until progress had been made in peace negotiations with Israel.

In January 1971, Sadat dedicated the Aswan Dam, Nasser's largest domestic project, which had been under construction for ten years. Another of Nasser's dreams, for Arab unity, moved closer to realization under Sadat's aegis when a loose confederation of Arab states, called the Federation of Arab Republics, was agreed upon in September 1971 by Egypt, Libya, and Syria. (In 1957, Egypt and Syria had merged to form the United Arab Republic; however, three years later, Syria withdrew from the union.)

In conjunction with Hafez al-Assad of Syria, Sadat launched the October War, on October 6, 1973, also known as the Yom Kippur War, a surprise attack against the Israeli forces occupying the Egyptian Sinai Peninsula, and the Syrian Golan Heights. It was an attempt to retake these Egyptian and Syrian territories that had been occupied by Israel since the Six-Day War, six years earlier. In the initial stages of the war, the Egyptian and Syrian performances astonished Israel and the Arab World. As the war progressed, three divisions of the Israeli army led by General Ariel Sharon had crossed the Suez Canal, and tried to encircle the Egyptian Second Army; when this tactic failed, the Israeli army tried to encircle the Egyptian Third Army. The United Nations Security Council passed Resolution 338, on October 22, 1973, calling for an immediate ceasefire. Although agreed upon, the ceasefire was immediately broken, with the Israeli military continuing the drive to encircle the Egyptian army. The encirclement was completed on October 24, three days after the ceasefire was broken. A second ceasefire was imposed cooperatively, on October 25, to end the war. Israel recognized Egypt as a formidable foe, and Egypt s renewed political significance eventually led to regaining and reopening the Suez Canal through the peace process.

He negotiated two agreements on disengagement of forces with the Israeli government. The first was signed on January 18, 1974; the second on September 4, 1975. On November 19, 1977, Sadat became the first Arab leader to visit Israel officially. He met with Israeli

Prime Minister Menachem Begin, and spoke before the Knesset in Jerusalem about his views on how to achieve a comprehensive peace to the Arab–Israeli conflict. On March 26, 1979, following the Camp David Accords (1978), a series of meetings between Egypt and Israel, which were facilitated by U.S. President Jimmy Carter, the Peace treaty was finally signed by Anwar Sadat and Israeli Prime Minister Menachem Begin in Washington, D.C. Sadat and Begin were awarded the Nobel Peace Prize for creating the treaty. Egypt officially recognized the state of Israel; Israel withdrew its armed forces and civilians from the Sinai Peninsula; Egypt granted free passage of Israeli ships through the Suez Canal; and, the Strait of Tiran, and the Gulf of Aqaba were recognized as international waterways.

In response to the treaty, which was extremely unpopular with the rest of the Arab world, the Arab League suspended Egypt in 1979 and moved its headquarters from Cairo to Tunis. Egypt was not re-admitted until 1989. Egypt's relations with the Western bloc improved, spurring economic growth, but its strained relations with the rest of the Arab world resulted in rapidly rising inflation.

Because Sadat renewed ties with Iran and the Shah of Iran after Nasser's death, Iran assumed a leading role in cleaning up and reactivating the blocked Suez Canal, after the Yom Kipper War. Iran also facilitated the withdrawal of Israel from the Sinai Peninsula by promising to substitute free Iranian oil for the loss of Egyptian oil wells in western Sinai, if the Israelis withdrew. After he was overthrown in Iran, the Shaw spent the last years of his life in Egypt, was given a state funeral, and interred at the Al-Rifa'i Mosque.

After years of unrest and government crackdowns, on October 6, 1981, Sadat was assassinated during the annual victory parade held in Cairo to celebrate Egypt's crossing of the Suez Canal. Eleven others were killed and 28 were wounded, including Vice-President Hosni Mubarak. The assassination squad was led by Lieutenant Khalid Islambouli after a *fatwā* approving the assassination had been obtained from Sheik Omar Abdel-Rahman, a terrorist now serving a life sentence at the Butner Medical Center, which is part of the Butner Federal Correctional Institution in Butner, North Carolina, U.S., due to his involvement with the 1993 bombing of New York City's World Trade Center. Islambouli was executed by firing squad after being tried and convicted. Three hundred Islamic radicals were indicted in the trial of assassin Khalid

Islambouli, including future al-Qaeda leader Ayman al-Zawahiri.

Sadat was succeeded by his Vice-President, Hosni Mubarak, and his funeral was attended by a record number of dignitaries from around the world, including three former US presidents: Gerald Ford, Jimmy Carter, and Richard Nixon. Representatives of most of the Arab World did not attend the funeral. Menachem Begin, the Prime Minister of Israel, considered Sadat a personal friend and insisted on attending the funeral, walking in the funeral procession so as not to desecrate the Sabbath. Sadat was buried across the street from the stand where he was assassinated. His nephew, Talaat Sadat, was imprisoned in October 2006 for accusing the Egyptian military with complicity in his uncle's assassination.

PERSONAL LIFE

Sadat was married twice. He divorced Ehsan Madi to marry half-Egyptian/half-British Jehan (also spelt "Gehan") Raouf on May 29, 1949. They had three daughters and a son named Gamal. By a previous marriage, Sadat had three daughters, all married, and several grandchildren. His wife, a published author, is now a senior fellow at the University of Maryland, College Park (where The Anwar Sadat Chair for Peace and Development has also been endowed).

FURTHER READING

N Y Post p24 O 3 70 por The New York Times p16 Sep 30 70; p47 O 21 70 por; The New York Times Mag p30 + N 29 70 por; p6 + Jl 18 71 pors; Time 97:23+ My 17 71 pors International Who's Who, 1970-71 Sadat, Anwar. Revolt on the Nile (1957)

HELMUT SCHMIDT

Chancellor of Germany

Born: December 23, 1918; Hamburg, Germany
Died: November 10, 2015; Hamburg, Germany
Affiliation: Social Democratic Party

INTRODUCTION

On May 16, 1974 Helmut Schmidt became the fifth Chancellor of the Federal Republic of Germany, following the dramatic resignation of his predecessor, Willy Brandt, in the wake of a top-level spy scandal. Although Brandt's broad, statesman-like vision helped to bring about detente between East and West in the late 1960's and early 1970's, it is Schmidt's tough-minded pragmatism—which he put into practice as Defense Minister in Brandt's first Cabinet and as Finance Minister since 1972—that seems best suited to the resolution of the immediate day-to-day problems of Germany and Western Europe. "No government can work miracles, but it must do everything in its power to achieve what is possible," Schmidt declared in his first policy speech as Chancellor. "In this respect we are making a new approach in that we are concentrating our energies on what is essential today."

EARLY LIFE

Helmut Heinrich Waldemar Schmidt was a native of Barmbek, a tough working-class district of the traditionally Social Democratic city of Hamburg. He was born on December 23, 1918 to Gustav Schmidt, a secondary-school teacher, and Ludovioa (Koch) Schmidt. His boyhood ambition was to become an architect. Although Barmbek was largely dominated by Communist dockworkers during the early years of the Weimar Republic, Schmidt's upbringing was anti-Communist. After Hitler came to power in 1933, Schmidt joined the Hitler Youth, eventually becoming a group leader in its maritime division. On the other hand, Nazi influences on him were minimal at the progressive Lichtwark-Schule in his native city, where he received his secondary education.

LIFE'S WORK

After a stint with the Reichsarbeitsdienst, the national labor service, Schmidt was drafted into the Wehrmacht in 1937. During World War II he served on both the Russian and Western fronts. As a member of the anti-aircraft artillery he became a battery commander with the rank of Oberleutnant (first lieutenant) and was decorated with the Iron Cross. During the Battle of the Bulge, in the final stages of the war, he was taken prisoner by the British. In the prisoner of war camp Schmidt was converted to the Social Democratic cause by his fellow captives.

Helmut Schmidt.

Returning to his war-ravaged native city in 1945, Schmidt enrolled in the University of Hamburg, where he studied political science and economics while his wife worked as a schoolteacher and dressmaker to make ends meet. Among his professors at the university was Karl Schiller, who later became West Germany's first Social Democratic Minister of Finance. In 1946 Schmidt joined the Social Democratic party, and in the following year he became the first national chairman of the Socialist Student League, then a moderate organization that bore little resemblance to the revolutionary group it became in the 1960's. In 1949, after completing a thesis comparing German and Japanese currency reforms after World War II, he obtained his diploma in political economy from the university.

In 1948, while still a student, Schmidt joined the Social Democratic municipal government of Hamburg on Schiller's recommendation, becoming an adviser in its division of economic affairs and commerce. By 1949 he was head of the division, where he acquired a reputation as an authority on municipal transportation

problems. In the national elections of 1953 Schmidt was elected to the federal Bundestag in Bonn, where his audacity and gift of gab soon earned him the nickname "Schmidt-Schnauze" ("Schmidt the Lip").

Within Social Democratic ranks, Schmidt became known as something of a maverick of the right. In 1957, when most Social Democrats still opposed German rearmament, he supported it, and he became one of the" first Bundestag deputies to accept a reserve commission in the Federal Republic's newly organized Bundeswehr. In 1959 he stormed out of a student congress meeting in Berlin in protest against a resolution calling on the Bonn government to consider interim confederation with Communist East Germany. On the other hand, when in 1960 the West German government considered acquiring military facilities in Spain for the Bundeswehr, Schmidt joined with other Social Democrats in protest, declaring that he had "about the same degree of sympathy" for Spanish chief of state Francisco Franco as he had for East German Communist leader Walter Ulbrioht.

In 1961 Schmidt, who did not relish the prospect of being perennially in the opposition, decided to forego his candidacy for reelection to the Bundestag. Returning to Hamburg, he entered the state government as Senator (the equivalent of Minister) of the Interior. In that role he attained national prominence in February 1962 when, following a disastrous North Sea flood that took some 300 lives, he singlehandedly took control of rescue and salvage operations, relegating Hamburg's mayor and other officials to the sidelines.

Following his reelection to the Bundestag, Schmidt returned to Bonn in 1965. As the party's expert on defense matters, he criticized the defense establishment under Christian Democratic Chancellor Ludwig Erhard and Defense Minister Kai-Uwe von Hassel, and what he saw as the demoralization of the armed forces. Modifying his earlier anti-Communism, Schmidt proposed, after visiting the Soviet Union and Eastern Europe in the summer of 1966, that the Federal Republic abandon the Hallstein Doctrine, which had prevented it from recognizing governments that had established formal ties with Communist East Germany, and he called for diplomatic relations with Romania and Czechoslovakia. In early 1967 he outlined a "step by step" process to normalize relations between East and West Germany. His views accorded with the Ostpolitik of Willy Brandt, who had become Vice-Chancellor and Foreign Minister in a "grand coalition" government of Christian Democrats and Social Democrats under Chancellor Kurt Kiesinger in December 1966.

Elected in March 1967 to succeed the late Fritz Erler as floor leader of the Social Democratic parliamentary group, Schmidt consolidated his reputation as one of the Bundestag's most skilled and incisive speakers, especially on defense and foreign policy. Called by some observers the "John F. Kennedy of Germany," Schmidt was regarded as a potential candidate for the Chancellorship. He became second in command to party Chairman Willy Brandt in March 1968, when the Nurnberg Social Democratic congress elected him vice-chairman.

The national elections of September 1969 placed the Social Democrats in the catbird seat for the first time, enabling them to form a coalition government with the small, old-fine liberal Free Democratic party. In the new Cabinet, headed by Chancellor Willy Brandt, Schmidt agreed to head the Defense Ministry, a thankless job, but one for which he was eminently qualified.

On October 22, 1969 Schmidt was sworn into office, along with the other Cabinet members. His mission as Defense Minister, as he saw it, was to effect reconciliation between the armed forces and the traditionally antimilitarist Social Democratic party, and to revitalize West Germany's moribund defense establishment. He modernized its arsenal of weapons, rejuvenated its antiquated officer corps, and improved military morale by making his Bundeswehr more democratic, improving barracks conditions, and allowing recruits greater freedom, including the privilege to sport long hair and beards. As a step toward making the Bundeswehr an all-professional force, he planned to establish armed forces universities.

In discussions with American officials in Washington, D.C., Schmidt stressed the importance of a continued United States military presence in Europe. He accepted Brandts Ostpofitik of detente with the Communist bloc, but he considered the continued strength of the North Atlantic Treaty Organization of equal importance. "The balance between the two military pact systems in Europe . . . has been the vital condition for the preservation of peace . . . during the past twenty years," he asserted in a speech at Georgetown University in Washington in February 1971. "And I do not have the slightest doubt that it needs to remain that way."

On July 7, 1972, shortly after Karl Schiller resigned from his dual post as Minister of Economics and Finance in protest against a Cabinet decision to impose foreign-exchange controls, Chancellor Brandt appointed Schmidt as his temporary successor. Brandt indicated that the functions of Economics and Finance Minister, united into a single "super-ministry" under Schiller in May 1971, would again be separated following national elections later in the year, with Schmidt retaining one of the two portfolios.

As Economics and Finance Minister during the last half of 1972, Schmidt concentrated on combating inflation, West Germany's most urgent economic problem. An advocate, like Schiller, of a free-market economy, he favored tight-money policies rather than price and wage controls, thereby drawing criticism from some of the left-wing elements of the party. During the campaign that preceded the November 1972 elections, he defended the Brandt government's record on inflation against attacks by the Christian Democratic opposition, thereby helping the Social Democratic-Free Democratic coalition to return to power with increased strength. In Brandt's new Cabinet, sworn in on December 15, 1972, Schmidt retained the portfolio of Finance, and he reorganized the Finance Ministry into a smoothly functioning machine.

To cope with the international monetary crisis of early 1973, partly brought on by what Schmidt termed the "worldwide frailty" of the United States dollar, six of the nine member countries of the European Economic Community, including West Germany, agreed in March to fink their currencies in a common float against the dollar. The move was seen as a step toward the ultimate establishment of a Western European economic and currency union, long advocated by Schmidt as essential for the prevention of future crises. Also Schmidt announced a 3 percent upward valuation of the mark, aimed at curbing an anticipated inflationary boom. An additional 5.5 percent increase in the value of the mark, intended to safeguard European monetary unity and "restore calm to the currency markets," was announced by Schmidt in June.

In May 1973 Schmidt announced a stringent anti-inflation program, including an 11 percent tax on new investments and imported capital goods, a 10 percent tax surcharge on high personal and business incomes, and major reductions in public expenditures. In his budget message to the Bundestag in September, Schmidt revealed that the rate of inflation had dropped to 6.4 percent after having increased to nearly 8 percent in mid-1973, but he asserted that despite "indications of a price slow-down and a cooling-off of the economic climate" the anti-inflation measures would remain in effect for the time being.

During the height of the energy crisis, brought on by the embargo on crude oil shipments by Arab nations to the West in late 1973, Schmidt took the initiative in lining up all the Common Market nations except France solidly behind the United States for a united front to deal with the oil-producing countries of the Middle East. He emerged with heightened prestige from the thirteen-nation conference on the energy crisis held in February 1974 in Washington, D.C., where he joined with United States spokesmen in demanding a cutback in Middle Eastern oil prices and rebuking the French government for its independent dealings with the Arabs. In March 1974 Schmidt concluded a $2.28 billion agreement with United States officials in Washington for West German payments to cover the cost of the continued stationing of American troops in the Federal Republic.

By the early spring of 1974 the Brandt government seemed to be suffering from a malaise. The Social Democrats lost in one local election after another, and public opinion polls indicated that the party now had the support of no more than 30 percent of the population. The press abounded with rumors of Brandt's impending resignation. Schmidt, who according to a profile in *Newsweek* (May 20, 1974) had been waging "a shrewd behind-the-scenes campaign to displace Brandt," became increasingly critical of some of the Chancellor's policies. In February, for example, he publicly described a 12.5 percent pay increase that Brandt had awarded, against his advice, to 3,500,000 striking public service and utility workers, as "a financial and economic calamity." Despite the opposition of the militantly leftist Young Socialists (Jusos), who made up about 25 percent of the party's ranks, Schmidt was now rated in opinion polls as the most popular Social Democrat in the Brandt government.

What occasioned Willy Brandt's resignation from the Chancellorship on May 6, 1974 was the discovery, a few days earlier, that Gunter Guillaume, a top member of his staff, was an East German Communist spy. Taking full responsibility for negligence in the affair, Brandt handed over the reins of government to Vice-Chancellor Walter Scheel, who became interim Chancellor of a caretaker government on May 7. On the same date the Social Democratic party, with the assent of the Free Democrats, nominated Schmidt to the Chancellorship. Brandt continued, however, to serve as party chairman, with Schmidt remaining as vice-chairman.

On May 16, 1974, after negotiations between the Social Democrats and Free Democrats, Schmidt was elected the fifth Chancellor of the Federal Republic of Germany by a Bundestag vote of 267 to 255. Sworn into office on the same day, Schmidt declared that he would carry on the foreign policy begun by Brandt, but that for the time being he would "concentrate more strongly on domestic political problems, in the broadest sense." In his Cabinet of eleven Social Democrats and four Free Democrats, Schmidt retained most of Brandt's appointees. The most significant change was the appointment of former Minister of the Interior Hans-Dieter Genscher, a Free Democrat, as Vice-Chancellor and Foreign Minister, replacing Scheel, who had been elected to succeed Gustav Heinemann as President of the Federal Republic.

In his policy speech to the Bundestag on May 17, Schmidt stressed the goal of "political unification of Europe in partnership with the United States" but warned Common Market partners that they must make "resolute efforts" to help themselves. With reference to the recent spy scandal, he asserted that political radicals had no place in public service. His domestic policies, he said, would be marked by austerity in public spending "to ward off all excessive demands," and he would seek to guarantee continued full employment and to safeguard West Germany's position as the country with the lowest rate of inflation and the largest volume of trade in Western Europe.

About two weeks after taking office, Chancellor Schmidt visited Paris to meet with newly elected French President Valery Giscard d'Estaing, an old friend. The Schmidt government survived its first vote test on June 9, 1974, when in a state election in Lower Saxony the Social Democratic-Free Democratic coalition managed to retain control of the legislature by a narrow margin. It was also during his early weeks in office that a treaty, described by Schmidt as "the final stone" in the structure of Brandt's Eastern policy, was approved by the Bundestag. The treaty provided for the normalization of relations between West Germany and Czechoslovakia and nullification of the infamous Munich pact of 1938.

Schmidt has written two important books on Western defense strategy: *Verteidigung oder Vergeltung; Ein deutscher Beitrag zum strategischen Problem der NATO* (1961), translated as *Defense or Retaliation; A German View* (Praeger, 1962); and *Strategie des Gleichgewichts; Deutsche Frie-denspolitik und die Weltmdchte* (1969), translated as *The Balance of Power; Germany's Peace*

Policy and the Superpowers (Kimber, 1971). His other writings include *Beitrdge* (1967), a collection of his essays, lectures, and addresses. He has contributed to European and American periodicals, including *Foreign Affairs*. In 1972 he received the United States Medal for Distinguished Service. Newberry College in South Carolina conferred an honorary LL.D. degree on him in 1973.

PERSONAL LIFE

Helmut Schmidt was married in 1942 to Hannelore Glaser (nicknamed Loki), whom he met at the Lichtwark school. They have a daughter, Susanne. A handsome, strong-featured man, Schmidt had thick, graying hair that he keeps neatly parted. Standing at five feet six inches, he wore thick-soled shoes in order to appear taller, and he watches his diet because of a tendency to be overweight. He has been suffering from a chronic thyroid condition that caused him to be hospitalized several times during 1972 and 1973. A former chainsmoker of cigarettes, he usually smoked a pipe in his later years.

A pragmatist who has little patience with philosophizing, Schmidt was noted for his efficiency and organizing ability, and for his boundless energy that often kept him working eighteen hours a day. Although he was described as arrogant, with a roughhouse style, an occasionally volatile temper, and a lack of warmth and compassion, he was also known for his sense of humor, his informality, and his knack for teamwork. When his busy schedule allowed, he enjoyed reading, painting, playing chess with his wife, listening to baroque organ and harpsichord music (he occasionally plays the organ himself), and sailing on the lake near his weekend home in Schleswig-Holstein that he built with the help of a local carpenter. He was a member of the synod of the Evangelical church of Hamburg.

Schmidt's wife of 68 years, Loki, died on October 21, 2010 at the age of 91. In 2012 at the age of 93, Schmidt had fallen in love again with Ruth Loah. Schmidt died on November 10, 2015, at the age of 96. He was buried alongside the remains of his parents and his wife Loki.

FURTHER READING

London Observer pl5 My 19 '74 por; *The New York Times* pl6 My 8 '74; p3 My 17 74 por; *Newsweek* 84:53 O 21 74 por; *Time* 103:39+ My 20 74 por; 104:55 + O 2 74 por; *Wirtschaftswoche* pl8+ My 17 74 pors; *International Who's Who*, 1973-74 Wer ist Wer? (1973); *Who's Who in Germany* (1964)

GERHARD SCHRÖDER

Chancellor of Germany

Born: April 7, 1944; Mossenberg, Germany
Affiliation: Social Democratic Party

INTRODUCTION

"Learning is the essence of politics. You should never trust politicians who think they have nothing left to learn." Gerhard Schröder made that remark to R. W. Apple Jr. for The New York Times *(September 4, 1998) less than one month before the national elections in which Schröder decisively defeated the incumbent, Helmut Kohl, in the race for the chancellorship of Germany. A member of Germany's liberal Social Democratic Party (SPD), Schröder has often been compared to U.S. president Bill Clinton and British prime minister Tony Blair, because he is neither a hard-line liberal nor a conservative, but a pragmatist who seems to adopt prevailing popular opinion regarding any given issue.*

"To put it kindly," Peter Schneider wrote for The New York Times Magazine *(September 13, 1998), "he isn't fond of specific policy proposals. 'Schröder,' goes the constant refrain, 'is ready to say anything and everything—as well as the exact opposite.'"*

While many people have criticized Schröder for being ambiguous, many others have applauded his flexibility. Schröder himself calls his political position "die neue mitte *("the new middle"). Being on middle ground, he has explained, will enable him to remain more closely in touch with the needs of his country than did Helmut Kohl, and will prevent his politics from becoming stale or biased, as has happened with so many politicians who adhere strictly to their party lines. "I've had to give up the old Hegelian idea that when theory and reality clash, reality is wrong," Schröder explained to Apple. "Reality is often right."*

As chancellor of Germany, the largest and most prosperous nation in Europe, Schröder's expressed goals will be to shrink unemployment by encouraging the growth of private enterprise and to maintain Germany's social-welfare system while, simultaneously, improving the country's economy. "The main question is balance," Schröder told Jordan Bonfante for Time *(July 20, 1998). "How to modernize the society and modernize the economy and have social security—how to keep that balance." Most political analysts believe that Schröder's goals are contradictory and that the "balance" he speaks of will elude him. High taxes and tough labor laws, they say, both of which have helped to support Germany's social-welfare system—perhaps the most comprehensive one in the world—do hot foster economic expansion.*

Under Helmut Kohl, who was elected chancellor of West Germany in 1982 and then of a united Germany in 1990, the public payroll mushroomed even as the country's economic situation worsened. A member of the Christian Democratic Union, Kohl oversaw the reunification of East and West Germany and was one of the key figures in the formation of the European Community and the European Monetary Union. As chancellor, Schröder will play a prominent role in the activities of the European Community and the development of the European Monetary Union, the latter of which his party has never wholeheartedly endorsed. His policies will thus directly affect not only Germany but all the nations in the European Community.

EARLY LIFE

Gerhard Schröder was born on April 7, 1944, in the small town of Mossenberg, in the German state of Lower Saxony. His father, a conscript in the German army, was killed in Romania in World War II, during the retreat of German forces from Russia. Afterward, his mother supported her five children by working as a housekeeper. When he was 14, his family's dismal financial situation forced Schröder to drop out of school and take a job in a shop that Sold china ware. He also worked part-time in construction. For years, he attended classes in the evening, and he did not complete high school until he was in his early 20s. In the late 1960s, he enrolled at the law school at Gottingen University, in Lower Saxony. "I wasn't a kid from a privileged home who wanted to rebel," he told Peter Schneider. "The chance to study at the university was a dream come true for me." In *The New York Times* (September 29, 1998), Edmund L.

Andrews reported that Schröder earned a law degree in 1976, when he was 32.

In 1978, Schröder set up his own law practice in Hannover, the capital of Lower Saxony. By this time, he had also become active in the local branch of Germany's Social Democratic Party, and he was elected president of the Jusos, a group of young Social Democrats who called themselves Marxists and who were known for their strong anti-American and anti-nuclear-arms stances. When R. W. Apple Jr. asked Schröder if he thought his membership in the Jusos would affect his chances in the forthcoming election, Schröder responded, "I don't think so. As you see, the revolution I planned didn't take place, so there's no point in bringing up what I said then."

LIFE'S WORK

In 1980, Schröder was elected to the Bundestag (the lower house of the West German legislature). Soon after, he made heads turn by becoming the first man ever to speak in the Bundestag without wearing a necktie. One evening in 1982, according to an anecdote often repeated during his campaign for the chancellorship, after drinking a considerable amount of beer in the company of friends, he walked up to the gates of the chancellery, shook them vigorously, and shouted, "I want to be in there!"

In 1984, Schröder ran unsuccessfully as the SPD's candidate for premier (the German equivalent of governor) of Lower Saxony, Germany's second-largest state. Four years later, he won election to that office, and, having won reelection in 1992 and 1996, has served as premier ever since. The premier of Lower Saxony automatically sits on the board of directors of Volkswagen, Europe's leading car manufacturer; Volkswagen's main plant is in the Lower Saxony city of Wolfsburg, and the state is the main shareholder in the Volkswagen corporation. As a board member, and also through his friendship with Volkswagen's chairperson, Ferdinand Piech, Schröder learned firsthand what must be done to keep large corporations from moving to countries where labor is cheaper. One of Schröder's key themes in his recent election campaign was that he will use his intimate knowledge of the business world to create jobs and thereby lower Germany's high rate of unemployment, which recently rose to over 10 percent. (In what was formerly East Germany, unemployment is twice as great.)

As premier of Lower Saxony, Schröder has attempted to accommodate simultaneously the demands of the business community and those of both the socially oriented SPD and the Green Party, the latter of which was formed in the 1970s and concentrates on environmental issues. Early on, he did so with the help of his third wife, Hiltrud Schröder. "Hiltrud raised consciousness for Chernobyl, while [Gerhard] Schröder negotiated nuclear waste disposal at home," Jane Kramer reported in the *New Yorker*, (September 14, 1998). "Her causes were vegetarianism and gay and lesbian rights; his causes had to do with keeping Volkswagen and its 80,000 workers happy to be making their cars in Lower Saxony." According to Kramer, Schröder may have lost some support among the Greens by allowing Mercedes-Benz to build a plant of questionable ecological safety in Lower Saxony and by giving the go-ahead to a shipbuilder's plan to deepen the Ems River. After Hiltrud and Gerhard divorced, in 1995, Hiltrud wrote a book, *On My Feet,* in which she disparaged Schröder and cast his political intentions in a negative light. "No one in Germany paid much attention" to the book, Kramer reported.

Schröder's political career has suffered several setbacks, however. One occurred in 1993, after Bjoern Engholm was ousted from the presidency of the SPD after being charged with perjury. Schröder made a bid to succeed him, but the SPD, harshly criticizing his blatant ambitiousness, rejected him. Then, in the 1994 national primary, Schröder ran for the chancellorship, but he lost to Rudolf Scharping. Schafping lost to Kohl in the national election, but he gained the presidency of the SPD, and he named Schröder the party's economic spokesperson. In 1995, Schröder was dismissed from that job, after making comments that were considered critical of the SPD's economic and social policies. (According to Judy Dempsey in the London *Financial Times* [September 1, 1995], Schröder had remarked to a reporter for a respected German political journal that "it was no longer the question whether a party had social, democratic, or conservative economic policies, but whether it was modern or not.")

Meanwhile, the SPD was gearing up for the 1998 national elections, but there was no consensus as to who could best challenge Kohl. Scharping's defeat by Kohl in 1994 made him an unlikely candidate. While some SPD members looked to Schröder as the best alternative, most favored the far-left candidate Oskar Lafontaine. Lafontaine, however, like most Social Democrats, opposed the development of a single European currency. Schröder said very little about the introduction of the euro (as the currency is called), other than agreeing with his party that it would probably worsen Germany's unemployment problem in the near future. According to David Marsh in the *New Statesman* (March 6, 1998), Schröder also expressed his belief that the continued existence of the European Monetary Union would ensure Germany's "economic dominance over Europe." Schröder's stance appealed to the SPD because it differed from that of Kohl, who predicted that the use of the euro would "cut unemployment and lead to a fairer distribution of economic power in Europe."

In Schröder's most recent years as the premier of Lower Saxony, both unemployment and the deficit have risen in the state. According to Kramer, no new industries have been created there, and many cuts have been made in education; the University of Hannover, for example, has dropped most of its programs and staff. Schröder did manage to salvage almost 30,000 jobs in 1997 by arranging a state takeover of a steel company that was about to be moved to Austria, but his maneuver triggered the fear that the cost would include a significant tax increase in Lower Saxony.

Those problems notwithstanding, in the March 1998 state elections, Schröder defeated the Christian Democratic Union's candidate, Christian Wulff, by a landslide. "Never in my wildest dreams did I expect such a beautiful result," Schröder said after the election, as reported by William Drozdiak for the *Washington Post* (March 2,1998). "The voters in Lower Saxony have sent a clear signal to Bonn—that the Kohl era is finally coming to an end." In a conversation with Kramer, Wulff attributed Schröder's victory to his ability to "reduce the complex to the simple, to second-guess the majority, and to play the media to his advantage." Schröder's victory made the SPD confident that he was the right candidate to run against Kohl, and led Oskar Lafontaine to withdraw his bid for the chancellorship. Less than one month later, Schröder was 10 points ahead of Kohl in public-opinion polls.

On September 27, 1998, in what Roger Cohen, writing for *The New York Times* (September 28, 1998), described as "a clear expression of the weariness of Germans with Mr. Kohl's 16-year-rule," Schröder resoundingly defeated Kohl. His victory marked the first time in post-World War II German history that an incumbent chancellor was swept out of office. "The voters have chosen a change of generation," Schröder asserted to cheering supporters outside the headquarters of the

Social Democratic Party in Bonn after the results of the election became clear.

Schröder has said that as chancellor, he would create jobs, by making Germany more industry-friendly, while simultaneously maintaining all of Germany's existing social programs and lowering taxes. When asked how he planned to accomplish that, Schröder said, as quoted by Drozdiak, "We'll sort things out in practice. I want to encourage people to speak their minds so I get the broadest possible range of advice. At the proper time, we will decide what is the right policy to apply when we form the next government." Schröder's platform has struck most political observers as remarkably vague. "You can't quite get hold of him," Josef Joffe, the editor of the editorial page of *Suddeutsche Zeitung*, one of Germany's major newspapers, explained to Apple. "He was given the nod very grudgingly by the party bosses, who stand well to his left, because they were convinced he was the only one with a chance to win. So he tries to placate the left wing of his party and to win over the swing voters at the same time. He . . . says as little as possible." Poking fun at Schröder's habitual equivocation, a current advertisement for a popular German car shows two people who look just like Schröder driving in opposite directions. The caption reads, "Cars for people who don't know where they want to go." Schröder himself has described his strategy as "an American campaign."

Schröder has acknowledged the truth of the charge that he is not an expert on international issues that affect Germany. But he has maintained, as he put it in a speech he gave at Georgetown University, in Washington, D.C., that "the true challenge to our transatlantic partnership today is how we can help to make the world more peaceful. For me as a German, this means Europe first and foremost. Now that communism is no longer an obstacle, we can begin to create a stable peace for all of Europe.... Whatever we can do to expand the zone of stable peace in Europe should be done, and the U.S. and Europe should do it together. This protects our values and interests." Schröder has also said that he supports the inclusion of Russia in NATO, because "without the Russian determination to continue on the path of reform, there will be no stability for all of Europe. The closer our cooperation with Russia, the more Russia

will consider NATO expansion not as a threat, but as a contribution to its own stability." Whether Schröder, as chancellor, would be able to act independently of his party is an open question. Lafontaine, the chairman of the SPD, has said, according to R. W. Apple Jr., "Yes, Schröder can be chancellor . . . but under me."

Gerhard Schröder was sworn in as chancellor of Germany on October 27,1998. As was anticipated, his party has formed a coalition with the Greens, with whom the Social Democrats currently share a 21-seat majority in the 656-member German Parliament. The first item on Schröder's agenda is the problem of unemployment, which he will tackle with the help of his appointee for economics minister, Werner Muller, a former executive of Veba, an industrial corporation. Other problems that Schröder and his newly former Cabinet will address include the compensation of Holocaust victims and other people who were forced to labor without pay during the Hitler regime; the end of Germany's longstanding blood-based citizenship laws; a curb on the production of nuclear energy; and the broader recognition of gay rights.

After Schröder's party lost the 2005 election, he stepped down as Chancellor in favor of Angela Merkel. He is presently chairman of Nord Stream AG, after being fired by bank Rothschild.

PERSONAL LIFE

Apple described Schröder as "handsome, telegenic, [and] a ferocious worker." His most distinguishing features are his large build, his icy blue eyes, and his dark hair, which he dyes. Known to his friends as Gerd, Schröder married his fourth wife, the journalist Doris Kopf, in 1995. He lives in Hannover with his wife, who now goes by the name Doris Schröder-Kopf, and her daughter.

FURTHER READING

International Herald Tribune Aug. 4, 1998 (on-line); (London) *Guardian* Apr. 18, 1998 (on-line); *New Statesman* pl4+ Mar. 6, 1998; *The New York Times* A pi, Sept. 4, 1998, with photos; *The New York Times Magazine* p8Q+ Sep. 13, 1998, with photos; *New Yorker* p58+ Sept 13, 1998; *Time* July 20, 1998 (on-line); *Washington Post* A p5 Apr. 18, 1998

HAILE SELASSIE I

Emperor of Ethiopia

Born: July 23, 1892; Ejersa Goro, Ethiopian Empire
Died: August 27, 1975; Addis Ababa, Ethiopia

INTRODUCTION

Among the royal visitors to the United States, few have so stirred the imagination of the American people as His Imperial Majesty Haile Selassie I of Ethiopia, who began his first tour of North America in May 1954. The Emperor is remembered for his eloquent although fruitless appeal to the League of Nations in 1936, calling for collective security against the Italian invaders of his kingdom.

Haile Selassie was the temporal and spiritual ruler of one of the oldest Christian domains, Ethiopia (generally known as Abyssinia prior to World War I) in eastern Afried. Ethiopia is a charter member of the United Nations Organization, and several battalions of the Swedish-trained Ethiopian Imperial Guard fought with U.N. forces in Korea. In September 1953 Ethiopia ratified a new treaty of "friendship and commerce" with the United States. Later, in May, 1954 it was announced that he had signed an agreement granting the United States ninety-nine-year military base rights in Ethiopia (The New York Times, May 15, 1954).

EARLY LIFE

Tafari Makonnen assumed the name of Haile Selassie in 1928 when he was crowned Negus (King). He was born at Harar on July 17, 1891, the son of Ras Makonnen, governor of Harar and trusted adviser of Emperor Menelik II. Tafari is believed to be descended from Menelik I, the son of King Solomon and the Queen of Sheba.

Reared in the Coptic Christian faith, the boy commenced his secular education at the age of seven under private European tutors. Tafari was appointed governor of Gara Muleta in Harar province when he was fourteen years old. He was governor of Salale when his father died in 1906.

Tafari studied for a year at a French mission school in Addis Ababa. At this time he was considered in line for the throne. However, in 1909, Emperor Menelik, redesignated the succession, naming Lij Yasu, his grandson, as heir presumptive.

LIFE'S WORK

Menelik II died in 1913 and Lij Yasu assumed the reins of government although he was never crowned. Handsome and athletic, Yasu was at first popular, but soon alienated the Christians among his subjects by encouraging Mohammedanism and polygamy. In 1916 he was excommunicated by the Ethiopian church, and the Rases proclaimed Zauditu, the daughter of Menelik, as Empress, and Tafari as heir presumptive and regent. (He had meanwhile become governor of Sidamo and later governor of Harar.) Tafari was given the title of Ras (prince), and was invested with the insignia of the Cordon of the Order of the Crown of Solomon.

Almost all visitors to Ethiopia during Ras Tafari's regency paid tribute to his ability, patriotism and progressive views. He obtained a seat for Ethiopia in the League of Nations in 1923. (Admission was at first opposed because of the institution of slavery in the country, whereupon Tafari promised to abolish the slave trade, which he did in the following year, and provided for the gradual emancipation of the slave population.)

In 1924 Ras Tafari paid his first visit to Europe, and after returning to his own country he introduced many reforms. Four years later he was crowned Negus, decreasing considerably the authority of Empress Zauditu. He sought to counterbalance Anglo-French influence by concluding with Italy a treaty of "perpetual amity." In March 1930, Tafari defeated an armed revolt against him organized by Empress Zauditu's consort. The latter was killed, and the Empress herself died shortly afterwards.

On November 2, 1930 Tafari became His Imperial Majesty Haile Selassie I, King of Kings of Ethiopia, Lion of Judah, and Elect of God. The monarch proclaimed a new constitution in July 1931.

Four years later an armed clash occurred on the border of Haile Selassie's empire and the Italian colony of Eritrea. The Italians used the incident as an excuse to invade Ethiopia in October 1935. Pressing inland, they captured Addis Ababa on May 5, 1936. Haile Selassie escaped to Palestine, and then proceeded to England.

Having failed to enlist British support for his cause, he addressed the League of Nations in a speech on June 30, 1936. He pleaded for military sanctions against Italy, declared that international morality was "at stake," and predicted that if the League failed to enforce the conditions of its Covenant it would be "digging its grave." However, only mild economic sanctions were voted and were never seriously enforced. On November 18, 1938 Great Britain formally recognized King Victor Emmanuel III of Italy as the Emperor of Ethiopia, and the union of Ethiopia, Eritrea and Italian Somaliland under the name of Italian East Africa. Selassie retired to a temporary home at Bath in England.

After Italy entered World War II on the side of Germany, Haile Selassie was recognized by Britain as an ally. Later an Allied-supported invasion of Ethiopia was launched. The Italian troops, cut off from help from home, were routed, and on May 5, 1941, Haile Selassie was able to re-enter Addis Ababa, although the final Italian surrender did not occur until November.

By the terms of an Anglo-Ethiopian agreement concluded on January 31, 1942, the autonomy of Ethiopia and the authority of Haile Selassie as Emperor were formally recognized by Great Britain. Nevertheless, the status of Ethiopia until after the end of World War II was that of a virtual dependency of Britain. On May 17, 1943 *Time* noted that "the actual chores of government are handled (through agreement) by British civilian and military commissioners."

The Anglo-Ethiopian agreement was renewed, in December 1944, for an additional two years. However, the aid and advice of other powers have gradually supplanted that of the British. An agreement ratified in December 1944 permitting U.S. aircraft to use American-built airfields in Ethiopia, and a meeting between Haile Selassie and President Franklin D. Roosevelt after the Yalta conference aboard the U.S.S. *Quincy* paved the way for an extension of American interests in Ethiopia.

By 1947 the Sinclair Oil Company had been granted a fifty-year oil-prospecting concession, and the American Trans-World Airlines had reorganized the air services. Swedish officers undertook the training of the Ethiopian air force, and operation of the railway was returned to the French.

In the summer of 1946 Ethiopia began to press claims for the former Italian colony of Eritrea. The monarch appointed in August 1947 a New York University law professor, Albert H. Garretson, as adviser on "all legal questions to come before the Ethiopian foreign office" including "the problem of the peace settlements and . . . certain territorial questions."

On April 1, 1950, in a speech broadcast from Addis Ababa while a U.N. Commission of Inquiry for Eritrea was making its survey, the Emperor stressed the "identity of dress and manners" and "virtual identity of language" in Ethiopia and Eritrea as well as "Ethiopia's vital need for access to the sea and return to her control of her ancient port of Massaua." (Eritrea had been part of the Ethiopian empire prior to the 1890's.)

The U.N. General Assembly voted on December 2, 1950 to federate an "autonomous Eritrea" with Ethiopia "under the sovereignty of the Ethiopian crown." Under the terms of federation, which became effective September 15, 1952, Eritrea (with a population of about 1,000,000) has its own constitution, an elected legislature and chief executive, and controls most of its internal matters. Ethiopia is responsible for defense, foreign relations, trade, and finance.

Despite the Emperor's efforts Ethiopia remains a backward nation. It is true that slave-holding was made illegal in 1942, and a strong central administration now functions. Nevertheless, because of the continued illiteracy of the vast majority of its estimated 10,000,000 inhabitants, Ethiopia has not instituted universal suffrage.

"I have three priorities in my country," Haile Selassie told Francis Ofner *(Christian Science Monitor,* August 19, 1950). "I first want to expand education. My second ambition is to develop communications. And the third—I want to secure employment for all Ethiopians." In the field of education, progress has been made; Ethiopia in 1954 has nearly 600 schools with about 60,000 pupils. Haile Selassie I University, now under construction, will include a College of Liberal Arts, College of Law, College of Medicine, and a College of Science.

Nevertheless (as *Time* noted October 13, 1952), "the country does not have a single native graduate engineer, architect, chemist, or agricultural expert," and Haile Selassie "must rely on foreign help to bolster his ministries," such help being at the present time mainly American.

"The claim that Ethiopia is now a democratic government," according to *Christian Century* (June 9, 1954), "under a constitutional monarch, is farcical. Actual power continues to be held firmly by feudal lords and landlords . . . who see to it that very little reliable information as to what is actually going on in the country ever reaches the well-meaning Emperor."

Haile Selassie paid a visit to the United States, Canada and Mexico from May to July of 1954. This was his first trip to the United States. In Washington,

D.C., he was an overnight guest of President Dwight D. Eisenhower at the White House. Addressing a joint session of Congress on May 28, the monarch referred to the principle of his 1936 plea which he said had been "vindicated" in Korea. "We felt that nowhere can the call for aid against aggression be refused," he declared. "It is either a universal principle or it is no principle at all" (*Washington Post,* May 29, 1954).

From Washington, he visited New York, Boston, Ottawa, and other cities, and received cordial welcomes. He inspected an American agricultural college and the Grand Coulee Dam, and received honorary degrees from Howard, Columbia and Montreal universities. The Emperor was accompanied by his third and youngest son, a granddaughter, and consultants, including three Cabinet ministers.

In the 1970s, famine in Ethiopia killed thousands of people. By some estimates 200,000 Ethiopians died of starvation. A group of army officers around this time instigated a coup against the emperor's regime. Selassie was placed under house arrest in 1974.

PERSONAL LIFE

The imperial couple were married in 1912 and had six children, Crown Prince Asfa Wusen Haile Selassie; Prince Makonnen Haile Selassie, Duke of Harar; Prince Sahle Haile Selassie; Princesses Lilt Kaluma Work and Tsahai (both are deceased) ; and Princess Tenegn Work.

The Emperor was deeply religious, strictly adhering to the fasts of the Coptic Christian faith. He was five feet four inches in height and weighed about 100 pounds. He has "an olive complexion, a thin hooked nose, tiny fluttering hands . . . and thin, sensitive lips." His black hair and beard showed little sign of graying.

His Majesty was insistent on the deference due to royalty. However, he quickly puts his visitor at ease, and his smile was infectious and expansive, even though his "characteristic expression" is said to be "a singular mixture of melancholic sadness and cold determination" (Curtis Lubinski, *Washington Post,* May 23, 1954). One of his favorite relaxations was viewing American motion pictures. Another was listening to the music of Beethoven.

Shortly after his house arrest, Selassie died on August 28, 1975, due to respiratory failure. His doctor insisted that this wasn't true, and to this day some believe that he was assassinated.

FURTHER READING

Christian Sci Mon Mag p5 Ag 19 '50 por; *Life* 23:57 N 10 '47 por; 34:103+ My 4 '53 pors; N Y *World-Telegram* p4 My 22 '54 pors Scholastic 64:9+ Ap 21 '54 por *Time* 41:35+ My 17 '43 por; 54:32 N 21 '49 por; U N Bui 8 :397 My 1 '50 *U S News* 36:16 My 28 '54 por Washington (D.C.) Post pip+ My 23 '54 por; *International Who's Who,* 1953 Powell, E. A. *Beyond the Utmost Purple Rim* (1925); Rogers, J. A. *World's Great Men of Color* (1946-1947); Sandford, C. *Ethiopia Under Haile Selassie* (1946); *Ten Eventful Years* (1947); *Who's Who in America,* 1954-55; *World Biography* (1954)

YITZHAK SHAMIR (YITS-HAHK SHA-MEER)

Israeli Prime Minister

Born: October 22, 1915; Ruzhinoy, Russian Empire
Died: June 30, 2012; Tel Aviv, Israel
Party Affiliation: Likud

INTRODUCTION

By the time Yitzhak Shamir stepped down as Israeli prime minister in 1992, he had held the job longer than anyone other than David Ben-Gurion. For a man who did not become a full-time politician until he was 58 years old, and who was initially considered only an interim replacement for his predecessor, Menachem Begin, this was a remarkable accomplishment. Shamir's rise to the prime ministership crowned a career that spanned over 60 years of service and ideological devotion to the Jewish state. Born in Poland, he immigrated to Palestine in 1935 and soon became involved in a splinter group of the Jewish underground that, unlike the mainstream Zionist group, targeted officers of the British mandatory government for assassination. Arrested twice for his activities, Shamir escaped both times from the internment camps where he was held. After Israel became a state in 1948, he had a hard time adjusting to the "normal life" of a businessman. He therefore jumped at the chance, in 1955, to join the Mossad, Israel's secret intelligence service, for which he worked for 10 years.

Shamir was elected in 1973 to the Knesset (parliament) as a member of the right-wing Herut Party, and he subsequently served as the Knesset's Speaker. In 1980 Prime Minister Begin tapped him to be foreign minister—a controversial choice, because Shamir had opposed the peace treaty between Israel and Egypt, on the grounds that it called for the dismantling of Jewish settlements in the Sinai peninsula. After Begin resigned in 1983, Shamir was selected by Herut to serve as his successor. He was considered, at first, to be only a caretaker, but he proved to be an astute politician. One of his primary goals was to solidify Israel's hold on the West Bank and Gaza Strip, which had been captured in the Six-Day War of 1967. In his view, the territories were an integral part of the Jewish state and therefore should never be "traded" to the Palestinian inhabitants for the sake of peace. His approval of the large-scale construction of Jewish settlements in the occupied areas strained Israel's relationship with the United States during the administration of George Bush. Shamir won Bush's gratitude, however, during the Persian Gulf war in 1991, when he chose not to retaliate against Iraq for launching Scud missiles at Israel. That decision, he wrote in his autobiography, Summing Up (1994), was "one of the hardest" decisions of his life. After the Likud was defeated by the Labor Party in 1992, Shamir took a seat in the Knesset as a member of the opposition. In June 1996 he retired from public life, hoping to be remembered, in his words, "as a man who loved the land of Israel and watched over it in every way he could, all of his life."

Early Life

Yitzhak Shamir was born in 1915 in the small town of Rujenoy, Poland to Shlomo Yerzernitzky, who owned a small leather factory, and Perla Yerzernitzky. (Shamir, meaning "thistle" or "sharp point," is the Hebraized surname that he adopted after immigrating to Palestine.) The family, which included his older sisters, Miriam and Rivka, often discussed the Zionist dream of the establishment of a Jewish state in the biblical land of Israel. Shamir received his early education at a Hebrew elementary school, and he later graduated from a Hebrew high school in Bialystok, Poland. He enrolled at the University of Warsaw to study law but left in 1935 to go to Palestine. (His relatives, all of whom stayed behind in Poland, were later killed during the Holocaust.)

Life's Work

Soon after Shamir arrived in Palestine, he got a job as a construction worker and then as a bookkeeper. At that time the country, which was under British rule, was embroiled in conflict between the Jews, who wished to establish a state there, and the indigenous Arabs, who opposed them. In the late 1930s Shamir joined the Irgun Zvai Leumi (National Military Organization), a small, splinter group that had left the Haganah, the Jewish defense organization led by David Ben-Gurion. Rejecting the self-restraint practiced by Ben-Gurion's followers, the Irgunists launched revenge attacks against Arab raids. The group's mission changed in May 1939, however, after the British government issued a document (known in Israeli history as the "White Paper"), which severely restricted Jewish immigration into Palestine at a time when European Jews were in grave danger. Incensed by that decision, the Irgun decided to target British officials for assassination. "I am not, by nature, a hater: I have never felt hatred toward the Arabs," Shamir wrote in his memoir. "Not all wars require hating. But in that autumn of 1939, my thoughts, my very being, centered on the need for the Jews of Palestine to be rid of the British so that we could establish Jewish sovereignty—before it was too late."

With the outbreak of World War II, the Irgun, led by Menachem Begin, suspended its operations against the British and cooperated with them in the common struggle against the Nazis. But a small group, including Shamir, insisted that British imperialism was no less an enemy of the Jewish people than was Nazism. In the summer of 1940, the dissenters left Begin's group to form Lehi (an acronym of the Hebrew for Fighters for the Freedom of Israel), but they were more popularly known as the "Stern Gang," after their charismatic founder, Abraham Stern. Hunted as a terrorist, Shamir was arrested by the British during the winter of 1941-42 and sent to a detention camp near Acre. While there, he learned that Stern had been killed in Tel Aviv by British police. In August 1942 Shamir and another Lehi fighter, Eliahu Giladi, escaped and fled to Haifa, where other Lehi members spirited them away to the organization's base of operations in Tel Aviv.

Along with two other underground veterans, Shamir reorganized Lehi and became its operations chief. Disguised in the long, black clothing worn by Hasidic Jews, he ventured outside only after dusk. Using the code name of "Michael" (after the Irish revolutionary Michael Collins), he communicated with his followers principally through letters carried by Shulamit Levy, a young Bulgarian who had come to Palestine in 1941 as an "illegal" immigrant and who became Shamir's wife in 1944. Lehi's modus operandi of gunning down British police and military officers in the street was roundly denounced at the time by the mainstream Zionist establishment. Years later, Shamir defended the attacks, asserting that it was more humane to assassinate certain prominent figures rather than target military installations and possibly kill innocent bystanders, as the other underground groups did. "A man who goes forth to take the life of another whom he does not know must believe only one thing—that by his act he will change the course of history," he was quoted as saying by Joel Brinkley in *The New York Times Magazine* (August 21, 1988),

Despite Lehi's bitter dispute with the other Jewish underground organizations, the rivalry had not escalated to bloodshed. Therefore when Eliahu Giladi, the Lehi guerrilla with whom Shamir had escaped from prison, proposed killing David Ben-Gurion, among other deadly schemes, Shamir grew increasingly concerned about the young man's mental stability. In his autobiography, the former prime minister admitted for the first time that, in 1943, after conferring with two or three colleagues, he ordered that Giladi be killed. "I have often asked myself, over the years, had there really been a choice?" Shamir wrote. "Could I have acted differently? I tried to find out what happened in other underground groups, other resistance movements, but never found a parallel. It is my belief that I had no alternative—though it took its toll of me and cost me no small anguish."

In November 1944, in Cairo, two members of Lehi assassinated Lord Moyne, Britain's resident minister in the Middle East, whom the group had accused of going out of his way to block Jewish immigration to Palestine. Moyne's death provoked considerable indignation in Great Britain and elicited expressions of outrage from Zionist leaders, who were determined to punish, in Shamir's words, "the criminals who dared disobey Ben-Gurion and who, by their recklessness and extremism, had placed the Jewish community in such jeopardy." The Haganah, Irgun, and Lehi groups managed to put their differences aside after World War II, however, when the newly installed Labor government in Great Britain refused—despite international pleas—to open the gates of Palestine to the thousands of displaced European Jews who had survived the Holocaust. United in their outrage, in late 1945 the rival organizations began to undertake joint attacks on British army camps,

military airfields, and arms depots in Palestine. The cooperative movement fell apart in the wake of the Irgun's July 1946 bombing of the British military offices at the King David Hotel in Jerusalem, which killed nearly 100 people despite advance warnings to vacate the building. Afterward, the Haganah disassociated itself from the two other groups, and decided to commit its energies to smuggling immigrants into the country.

In response to the King David bombing, the British initiated a massive dragnet, in an attempt to arrest every underground fighter on their "wanted" list. Shamir was confident that his Hasidic garb would deceive the police, but a British detective recognized him from his bushy eyebrows. Deported to an internment camp in Eritrea (which became part of Ethiopia in 1962), Shamir was one of five prisoners who escaped in January 1947 through a crudely dug tunnel. After hiding out in the homes of sympathizers in nearby Asmara for several weeks, he made his way to Addis Ababa, Ethiopia and then to Djibouti, French Somaliland, where he was imprisoned for four months. Meanwhile, on November 29, 1947, the United Nations had voted to partition Palestine into two states—one Jewish, one Palestinian. The Jews accepted the plan; the Arabs did not, insisting that the whole country was theirs. On May 14, 1948, after the last British officer had left Palestine, Ben-Gurion announced the creation of the independent state of Israel. The next day, the new nation was invaded by five Arab armies. On May 20 Shamir returned to the besieged Jewish state where he, along with most of his colleagues, accepted Ben-Gurion's order that all "private armies" join the war effort under the auspices of the Israeli Defense Force (IDF). Against all odds, the ragtag IDF soldiers managed to repel their Arab foes.

After a cease-fire was reached in 1949, Shamir helped organize Lehi veterans into the Fighters Party, which won one seat in Israel's first Knesset, but the party was disbanded in 1951. The predominant political force in the country was the Labor Party, headed by Ben-Gurion, who had become the first prime minister. Turning next to business, Shamir tried his hand at a variety of ventures that failed, and he eventually became a manager for two small companies. Unhappy that he had become, in his words, "a bystander rather than a participant" in national affairs, Shamir was grateful when the opportunity arose, in 1955, to join the Mossad, the Israeli secret intelligence agency. Hired by the legendary spymaster Isser Harrel, he became a senior staff member, serving primarily in France, where he reportedly trained several top Israeli agents. Apparently suited to the Mossad's clandestine lifestyle, which he has declined to describe in detail, Shamir left the agency in 1965 because he disagreed with the policies of Harrel's successor.

Faced with the challenge of finding an "above ground" job, Shamir became a business manager. In the late 1960s he also got involved in the effort to help Soviet Jews immigrate to Israel, using his experience as an underground operative to aid that cause. Turning to politics in 1970, Shamir joined Herut and worked as a volunteer at the party's Tel Aviv headquarters at night. Elected in December 1973 on the Herut slate as a member of the eighth Knesset, he became, at the age of 58, a full-time politician. He served on the foreign affairs and defense committees and in 1975 became chairman of Herut's executive committee.

The Israeli election of June 1977 was historic, for the Labor Party was voted out of office for the first time, and a political bloc consisting of Herut and other right-wing parties came into power. The new entity, called the Likud, was led by Menachem Begin, who became prime minister. Shamir was elected the Speaker of the Knesset, a position he held for two and a half years. During the momentous visit of Egyptian president Anwar Sadat to Jerusalem in November 1977, Shamir was instrumental in organizing the warm reception Sadat received at the Knesset. But when the Camp David accord spelling out the terms of peace between Israel and Egypt was presented to the Knesset for ratification in September 1978, Shamir abstained. "I had no other alternative . . .," he wrote in Summing Up, "though I knew it would anger Begin—not because I was opposed to peace (how stupid such allegations are), nor because I was intrinsically against the frameworks (or later the treaty itself), but because to abstain from voting in favor of the enforced removal of Jewish settlements [in the Sinai desert] was the least I could do and remain at peace with myself." When the final peace treaty was put before the Knesset in March 1979, he abstained again.

The following October Moshe Dayan resigned as minister of foreign affairs, and Begin named Shamir as Dayan's successor. Politicians from across the political spectrum denounced the choice, citing Shamir's lack of diplomatic experience and his objection to the peace treaty with Egypt. As a result of the criticisms, the prime minister withdrew the nomination and took on the foreign-affairs portfolio himself. In March 1980, after it had become clear that he could no longer perform two

jobs, Begin persuaded his cabinet to endorse Shamir's appointment. Working diligently to win over his critics, Shamir pored over foreign-ministry documents, so that he could represent the country in a knowledgeable manner, and he forced himself to put aside his natural reserve in order to chat amiably with dignitaries in the world's capitals.

In June 1982 the IDF invaded southern Lebanon to destroy the military bases of the Palestine Liberation Organization, which had been used to launch missile attacks against Israel's settlements in northern Galilee. What was supposed to be a limited strike with a clearly defined goal, however, bogged down into a two-year campaign with a large number of casualties. For the first time in the country's history, Israeli citizens staged public protests against an ongoing military action. Israel also faced strong opposition from governments abroad, especially after its military allies, the Lebanese Christian Phalangists, massacred hundreds of civilians in two Palestinian refugee camps in Beirut in mid-September 1982, apparently with the knowledge of Israeli troops stationed nearby. An Israeli commission of inquiry cleared the country's military and political establishment of direct complicity in the killings but harshly rebuked several leaders, particularly the defense minister, Ariel Sharon, for serious errors in judgment. The commission's February 1983 report also chided Shamir for "not taking any measures" after receiving a phone call on September 16 from Mordechai Zippori, the communications minister, who said that he had heard that the Phalangists were "running wild" in the camps. "The foreign minister should have at least called the defense minister's attention to the information that he had received," the commissioners wrote. In his memoir, Shamir defended himself by saying, 'Running wild' at that point described almost everything done by almost everyone in Lebanon, so it didn't occur to me that any special significance lay in what [Zippori] said."

In August 1983 Menachem Begin, who was reportedly suffering from a deep depression, announced his intention to resign from office. Shortly afterward, on September 2, the Herut Party elected Shamir its new leader over the deputy prime minister, David Levy, by a vote of 436 to 302. After weeks of tough negotiations with the small parties in the Likud bloc, Shamir presented his 64-member coalition to the 120-member Knesset on October 10th, and thus became Israel's seventh prime minister. "Many saw the low-key, colorless man as an interim leader," Joel Brinkley wrote in *The New York Times Magazine*, "especially since he was inevitably compared with his charismatic predecessor. . . . Nevertheless, Shamir did grow in his new job."

The new government's first action was to authorize a substantial devaluation of the Israeli shekel in an attempt to rein in an annual inflation rate that had skyrocketed to 400 percent. Cuts in government subsidies for some basic commodities and services were also ordered. Shamir made it clear, however, that the costly construction of Jewish settlements in the West Bank, which he called "sacred work," would not stop. In his view, as expressed in *Summing Up,* "Judea and Samara [the Biblical names of the territories] are an integral part of the land of Israel, neither 'captured' in 1967 nor 'returnable' to anyone." Shamir's shaky political coalition collapsed less than a year after it was established. A new election was called, and on July 23, 1984, the voters awarded 44 Knesset seats to the Labor Party, led by Shimon Peres, three more than they accorded to the Likud. For weeks both Peres and Shamir tried without success to establish a coalition with the marginal, religious parties. In the end, a national unity government made up primarily of representatives from Labor and Likud was established, and Shamir and Peres agreed to a unique arrangement whereby the jobs of prime minister and foreign minister would be rotated during the four-year term of the government, with Peres taking the prime ministership for the first two years.

In 1986, when Shamir took over the top job, tensions were high in the Gaza Strip and West Bank, and in December 1987, the Palestinians who lived there launched a spontaneous revolt, which came to be known as the *intifada* [Arabic for uprising), to protest 20 years of Israeli military rule. In Shamir's view, the *intifada* was not a form of civil disobedience or an expression of frustration but a "form of warfare," whose purpose was to force Israel out of the disputed areas and establish a Palestinian state. The Israeli army, under the direction of Defense Minister Yitzhak Rabin, tried for several months to stop the demonstrations with brute force. When that failed, Rabin came to the conclusion that a political solution was the only answer to the problem.

Shamir, however, adamantly refused to consider a compromise that involved a "land for peace" formula, or Israeli recognition of the PLO. Because of his reluctance to initiate change, he was often labeled the "defender of the status quo" by his critics. "The main thing about this guy is he's so suspicious," Yossi Beilin, a Labor member of the Knesset, told Brinkley. "He doesn't believe the Arabs. He doesn't believe there can be peace with them." In the opinion of Avi Pazner, Shamir's media adviser, however, the prime minister's cautiousness was based on pragmatism and security concerns. "Everything he does he weighs slowly, carefully," Pazner told Jackson Diehl of the Washington *Post* (October 26, 1991). "His first concern is always not making a mistake that will put Israel in danger."

As one of the most outspoken critics of Arab terrorist attacks against Israelis, Shamir was often asked to explain why he believed political assassination, as practiced by Irgun and Lehi members in the 1930s and 1940s, had been justified but was no longer a viable option. During his 1988 conversation with Brinkley, he said, "There are two big differences between what I did, I and my friends did, and what the Arabs are doing now. First of all, our aim was to establish a Jewish state where there was no state, not to destroy an existing state. The main aim of the Palestinians is to destroy the state of Israel. They have Arab countries, more than 20 of them. They have enough. This is the only Jewish state. And second, our methods were different. We fought against the armed forces and the leaders of the British government. But we never attacked civilians, women, and children."

In November 1988 Israeli voters went to the polls again, and the result was a virtual dead heat, with the Likud winning 40 seats, and Labor, 39. Each of the two parties once again attempted to set up a coalition without the other, but the demands of the various religious parties proved to be unacceptable to either side. Finally, a national unity government was established once again, with Shamir as prime minister for the full term. Meanwhile, in the United States, George Bush had been elected president. Bush took a dim view of the construction of Jewish settlements in the occupied territories, seeing them as an obstacle to peace. During several meetings with Bush and his secretary of state, James Baker, Shamir lobbied for endorsement of his "autonomy" peace plan, whereby West Bank and Gaza Palestinians would be responsible for their daily affairs, while military control of the territories would remain in Israeli hands. That proposal, however, was unacceptable to the United States, because, as Baker once said, it advanced the "unrealistic vision of a Greater Israel." In March 1990 a showdown between Shamir and Peres, who had been odds over the direction of the peace process for years, brought down the nearly paralyzed unity government. Three months later, Shamir presented a narrow, right-wing coalition to the Knesset, and the Labor Party returned to the opposition.

After the Iraqi invasion of Kuwait in August 1990, Iraqi president Saddam Hussein threatened to launch chemically laced Scud missiles into Israel if allied forces, led by the United States, tried to dislodge his troops. The Shamir government ordered the distribution of gas masks to every Israeli citizen and made the necessary military preparations for war. In the early morning hours of January 17,1991 (local time), the allied mission against Iraq began with an air raid on Baghdad. The next night, the Iraqi army lobbed eight Scuds (without chemical warheads) at Tel Aviv, beginning a weeks-long bombardment. Shamir had three options: do nothing and let allied forces handle the problem (as Bush strongly advocated); send the Israeli air force to Iraq to locate and destroy the missile launchers; or coordinate a joint Israeli-American attack. The prime minister favored the third choice but was informed by Bush that Jordan would not permit Israeli jets to fly over its airspace, and to do so might irrevocably harm the unity of the allied coalition, which included a number of Arab countries. After consultations with his cabinet, Shamir opted to keep his country's military on the sidelines and let the allies punish Iraq, at least partly to foil Hussein's strategy of trying to draw Israel into the war. "I can think of nothing that went more against my grain as a Jew and a Zionist, nothing more opposed to the ideology on which my life has been based," he wrote in his memoir. The decision, he added, "was one of the hardest tasks I ever imposed on myself." By the time the war ended, on February 28, 1991, with an allied victory, Israel had withstood a total of 18 attacks by 39 Scud missiles. Two Israelis had been killed and another 13 had died during the raids of heart failure, or other causes relating to the improper use of gas masks. Less than two weeks after the war's conclusion, Baker traveled to Jerusalem and personally thanked Shamir for his restraint.

Meanwhile, Israel had been struggling to absorb the hundreds of thousands of Soviet Jews who had been flocking to the country since the late 1980s. In the summer of 1990 and again in the fall of 1991, the Shamir government asked the United States to guarantee $10 billion in commercial loans over a five-year period, to help provide the new arrivals with housing and jobs. Bush resisted, linking his approval to a promise from Israel to put a halt to the construction of settlements in the territories. The United States had never before attached a political condition to a request by Israel for aid, and Shamir refused to accept the terms. The rancor that the disagreement engendered complicated Secretary Baker's diplomatic efforts to persuade the Israelis to attend a peace conference in Madrid with representatives of Syria, Lebanon, and a joint delegation of Jordanians and Palestinians. The sticking point for Shamir was the composition of the Palestinian group; he would not agree to speak directly to members of the PLO. Eventually, Baker was able to work out a compromise that appeased all the parties, and on October 30, 1991 the historic summit began. In his opening remarks, Shamir reiterated the biblical links of the Jewish people to their homeland. Appealing to the Arab leaders to show that they accepted Israel's right to exist, he called for an end "to war, to belligerency, and to hostility." The conference marked the first time that representatives of Israel and her Arab neighbors publicly sat across a table from each other and engaged in prolonged discussions.

Back in Jerusalem, a festering disagreement between Shamir and the leaders of three right-wing coalition partners, who accused him of being too "moderate" in his dealings with the Arabs, led to the dissolution of the government in January 1992. Labor's prospects for victory in the national election, scheduled for the following June, were greatly enhanced when Yitzhak Rabin, who was widely respected as an experienced military leader, succeeded in wrestling control of the party from the less popular Shimon Peres. Weary of the *intifada* and frustrated by the Likud's failure to make peace, many Israelis voted for Labor largely because they trusted Rabin to negotiate a deal with the Arabs that would not endanger the country's security. The final tally was 32 seats for the Likud, and 45 for Labor, enabling Rabin to establish a left-of-center coalition.

After more than nine years in the government, Shamir took his seat in the Knesset as a member of the opposition. He stepped down as the leader of the Likud, and Benjamin Netanyahu, the former deputy foreign minster, was elected to succeed him. Shamir was bitterly opposed to Rabin's decision, in 1993, to negotiate with the PLO and to the subsequent, interim peace accord worked out by Israeli and PLO leaders in Oslo, Norway. "For the first time ever, an Israeli government had consented to give away parts of the land of Israel, thus helping the way to the virtually inevitable establishment of a Palestinian state," he wrote in his autobiography. Such an eventuality, he argued, would only be a prelude to Arab demands "for other parts" of Israel, including Jerusalem. In May 1996, seven months after Rabin's assassination, Netanyahu led the Likud to an electoral victory; about a week later Shamir announced that he would step down as a member of the Knesset and retire from politics.

PERSONAL LIFE

Yitzhak Shamir lived in Tel Aviv with his wife, Shulamit. The couple's son, Yair, was born in August 1945 while Shamir was in hiding, and a daughter, Gilada, was born in 1949. A short, stocky man with a taciturn, almost secretive manner, the former prime minister struck David Makovsky, who profiled him for *U.S. News & World Report* (June 22, 1992), as someone who "has yet to emerge from the underground." In an interview upon his retirement with John Lancaster for the *Washington*

Post (June 8, 1996), Shamir said, "I was in this struggle for more than 60 years, and I think we got something. We made progress, and I hope we will again, but never by concessions . . . never by submission. This is the lesson of our life, of our history."

In 2004, Shamir's health declined from Alzheimer's disease, and he died on June 30, 2012. He was given a state funeral and buried alongside his wife, who had died the year prior. He has been remembered as a brave warrior for Israel.

FURTHER READING

The New York Times mag p27+ Ag 21 '88 pors; *Washington Post* A pl3 O 26, '91 por; *U S News & World Report* p56+ Je 22 '92 pors; *International Who's Who*, 1996-97; Shamir, Yitzhak. *Summing Up* (1994)

MOHAMMAD NAWAZ SHARIF (MUH-HAH-MUHD NUH-WAHZ SHAH-REEF)

Prime Minister of Pakistan

Born: December 25, 1949; Lahore, Punjab, Pakistan
Affiliation: Pakistan Mustlim League-Nawaz

INTRODUCTION

On February 3, 1997, the Pakistan Muslim League (PML), led by Mohammad Nawaz Sharif, captured a majority of the vote in a nationwide general election and thereby won the opportunity to form a new government. Sharif had served as Pakistan's prime minister once before, from 1990 until 1993, and had been ousted by the president on charges of corruption and other misdeeds. In becoming prime minister for the second time, Sharif beat out Benazir Bhutto, the incumbent, whose family has been a fixture of Pakistani politics for decades. For Sharif, who has a business background, the victory signaled a mandate from Pakistan's growing middle and entrepreneurial class to implement reform-oriented economic policies in hopes of rescuing Pakistan from a severe fiscal crisis. "Though the economy is a mess and his coalition shaky, he is Pakistan's strongest leader in a decade," Asiaweek (May 30, 1997, on-line) declared.

One year later, in a show of strength sparked by India's underground testing of five nuclear devices, Sharif ordered the underground detonation of as many as six nuclear devices in a remote desert region of

southwestern Pakistan. He did so despite the threat that the United States and other countries would impose severe economic sanctions on Pakistan and despite several personal pleas from President Clinton not to respond in kind to the Indian tests. According to the U.S. secretary of state, Madeleine K. Albright, Sharif had acted in response to "overwhelming domestic pressures and regional dynamics." That interpretation was shared by Senator Tom Harkin of Iowa, who said, as paraphrased by Tim Weiner of The New York Times *(May 29, 1998), "The pressures were so intense that Mr. Sharif's government might have fallen" had he not proceeded with the tests. The sanctions were duly imposed, seriously worsening the precarious economic condition of Pakistan, which is among the world's 10 poorest nations.*

EARLY LIFE

Little has been revealed in public about the early years of Mohammad Nawaz Sharif, who was born in Lahore, Pakistan, on December 25, 1949, into a prominent industrialist family. (His family controls Ittefaq Industries, one of Pakistan's wealthiest conglomerates; its holdings include the country's largest private steel mill, a sugar mill, and several textile factories.) After attending the Government College at Lahore, he studied law at Punjab University, and then entered business and politics. In 1981, Sharif was appointed finance minister of Punjab, Pakistan's most populous province. This appointment was attributed in part to Sharif s association with influential Pakistanis, most prominent among them General Mohammad Zia ul-Haq, who had headed the military junta that had overthrown Prime Minister Zulfikar Ali Bhutto in 1977 and who had become president 14 months later. (Zulfikar Ali Bhutto, Benazir Bhutto's father, was later executed.) General Zia ruled Pakistan as a military dictator until his death in a plane crash, in 1988.

LIFE'S WORK

Meanwhile, in 1985, at the age of 35, Sharif was elected chief minister of Punjab, and in 1988, he won reelection to that post. He entered national politics in 1990, when, in that year's general election, he headed a group of nine parties under the banner of the Islamic Democratic Alliance (IDA), which pitted him against Benazir Bhutto and her Pakistan People's Party (PPP). Sharifs alliance emerged victorious, with 41 percent of the vote, and Sharif became Pakistan's prime minister. He was the first Pakistani prime minister from the province of Punjab and the first who did not come from the feudal landlord class.

As prime minister, Sharif led his country toward economic reform, in part by instigating the privatization of some of its state-controlled industries and other entities, among them two nationalized banks. But, in his efforts to spur the development of private industry and to encourage entrepreneurship, he became best known for implementing an unsuccessful economic initiative dubbed the Yellow Cab Scheme, in which the government subsidized the sale of more than 100,000 imported cars that were to be used as taxis. The idea was to create jobs for thousands of Pakistani drivers, but the supply of taxis proved to be far greater than the demand. The cost to the government amounted to approximately $700 million.

In April 1993, President Ghulam Ishaq Khan, using powers granted to the president by the eighth amendment to Pakistan's constitution, dissolved the government and ousted Sharif, on the grounds that he and his allies had not governed "according to the constitution." (The eighth amendment, which had been adopted in the mid-1980s, was a vestige of the military dictatorship of General Zia.) According to many observers, Sharifs dismissal was supported by Pakistan's military

establishment, which remained highly influential in setting national policy.

In the ensuing election, held in October 1993, Benazir Bhutto (whose government had been similarly dissolved in 1990) and the PPP came out on top. Before long, her government became embroiled in charges of corruption and various irregularities, including allegations that Bhutto had ordered wiretaps on the telephones of chief justices, and in December 1996, her tenure in office came to an abrupt end, when President Farooq Leghari dissolved the government. (It was the fourth consecutive government to be sacked by the Pakistani president before the end of the legislators' five-year terms.) Within a month or so, President Leghari appointed an acting prime minister and established a Council for Defense and National Security, whose 10 members included the acting prime minister and the chairman of the joint chiefs of staff; the chiefs of the army, navy, and air force; and the ministers for defense, foreign affairs, and finance.

In the general election of February 1997, Sharif, who had led the opposition during Bhutto's stint as prime minister, headed a coalition known as the Pakistan Muslim League (PML) and ran against Bhutto and her PPP. The turnout on election day was abysmally low; according to various sources, less than 35 percent of Pakistan's 56.5 million registered voters cast ballots. (Some observers attributed the voter apathy to widespread disenchantment with the nation's politicians as a group and unhappiness about the prospect of having to choose new legislators for the fourth time in nine years.) Among those who did vote, a decisive majority opted for the PML and Sharif: The PML, which in the previous government had held just 72 seats of the 217 in the National Assembly, wound up with 135. Bhutto's PPP won only 18 seats.

When Sharif took the reins of leadership again, both the president and the Council for National Defense and Security (the latter of which routinely deferred to Pakistan's military establishment) remained an ever-present threat to his authority, thanks to the terms of the notorious eighth amendment. Taking the bull by the horns, on April 1, 1997 Sharif pressed Parliament to pass a constitutional amendment that would eliminate the power of the president to dismiss elected governments, call for new elections, or appoint chiefs of the armed services. "We have decided to scrap some parts of the eighth amendment which have clouded the democratic scene," Sharif explained, as quoted by the *Electronic Telegraph* (April 2, 1997). In what was dubbed "a lightning constitutional coup," the new amendment was passed by Parliament less than 12 hours after he had proposed it. Sharif thus gained the power to appoint provincial governors and the armed services chiefs, previously prerogatives of the president. The amendment seemed to signal a new era, one in which the Parliament would hold the ultimate power in the country and in which there would no longer exist an informal power-sharing arrangement among the president, the military, and the prime minister.

Another challenge Sharif faced was the precarious economic condition of Pakistan, which was suffering from both high unemployment and high inflation. The federal budget deficit for 1997 was projected to be more than 5.5 percent of Pakistan's GDP. Much of Pakistan's fiscal difficulties stemmed from its large foreign-debt obligations. Furthermore, according to Richard N. Murphy in the *New Leader* (March 10, 1997), roughly two-thirds of the nation's budget was being swallowed up by the military and by interest payments on the national debt. (Two months later, in an op-ed piece for *The New York Times* [May 30,1998], Robert C. McFarlane, who, from 1983 to 1985, served as President Ronald Reagan's national security adviser, wrote that that figure was 70 percent.) Sharif claimed that the policies of his predecessor were responsible for Pakistan's economic woes. "Benazir Bhutto has totally destroyed our economy, so we'll have to bring in very bold reforms," he said soon after the election, as quoted in the *Manchester Guardian Weekly* (February 9, 1997). In March 1997, Sharif initiated an economic-revival effort by banning the import of luxury items and by opening a bank account to receive donations from Pakistanis living abroad, to help pay off the country's national debt. He also met with business executives to solicit suggestions on cutting government bureaucracy.

In August 1997, Sharif, along with his nation's 130 million citizens, celebrated the 50th anniversary of Pakistan's independence from Great Britain (and separation from India). The festivities were dampened by growing ethnic and sectarian violence. An ethnic conflict in the capital, Karachi, between the Muhajir Qaumi Movement, a party of Urdu-speaking migrants from India, and government forces had been escalating for over a decade. And in Punjab, animosities between Shi'a Muslims and Sunni Muslims exploded in assassinations and street violence.

That same month, Sharif's government passed a law giving the police sweeping powers over suspected terrorists, including the power to arrest suspects without a warrant and to shoot at suspected terrorists. Not surprisingly, the law provoked censure from human-rights watchdog groups. Salim Asmi, a human-rights activist in Karachi, was quoted by Anthony Spaeth for *Time* (September 1, 1997, on-line) as saying, "Even during the worst days of martial law, the law enforcement agencies were not given so much power." For his part, Sharif insisted that the added powers were necessary. In a speech honoring Pakistan's 50th anniversary, he said, as reported by Anthony Spaeth, "A few hundred terrorists have held 140 million people hostage, and I will not allow them to destroy the country."

Another of Sharif's most pressing concerns was Pakistan's troubled relations with India. Since 1947, the two countries had fought each other in three wars. Contributing to the thorniness of their relationship was the issue of Kashmir, a predominantly Muslim region that borders both countries and is not recognized by the United Nations as belonging to either. Kashmir was divided between Pakistan and India in 1949, and for years the region's Muslims had crusaded for its autonomy. In May 1997, Sharif met with Prime Minister Inder K. Gujral of India in the Maldives, a neutral island republic in the Indian Ocean, for the highest-level talks between their nations in nearly a decade. The two leaders failed to reach an accord about Kashmir and other long-held disputes, but each agreed to free jailed nationals of the other's country and to create a telephone hotline between the two leaders. They also agreed to hold future meetings and to create working groups to address pressing issues.

A month later, the International Monetary Fund (IMF) approved a three-year, $1.6 billion loan to Pakistan. In announcing the loan, the IMF praised the Pakistani government for lowering inflation, taking steps to reform the tax system, and improving the quality of government. The IMF acted after Pakistan's central bank, acquiescing to an IMF requirement, devalued Pakistan's rupee by 8 percent against the U.S. dollar. At that time, Pakistan's foreign-exchange reserves amounted to only $1.6 billion, while its foreign debt totaled $30 billion.

Earlier, in June 1997, Sharif had engineered the Parliament's passage of a constitutional amendment that prohibited legislators from casting votes against their own party—in other words, party disloyalty was outlawed. The following October, the Pakistani Supreme Court ruled that the amendment was invalid. Since the Parliament had banned precisely such actions by the

Supreme Court, the justices' decision was viewed as a "blatant attack" on Sharif. In November, a dispute between the Supreme Court and Sharif involving the appointments of five judges led the court to formally charge him with contempt of court. Some of the members of his party and the state-controlled Pakistani television, among others, were also charged with contempt. "This crisis is more than just another set of democratic growing pains for Pakistan," Phil Goodwin declared on *BBC News* (November 19, 1997). "It has got to the stage where many people are questioning if the country's politicians can be trusted to make democracy work. . . . [Sharif's] party openly admits that this second term of office by Nawaz Sharif is something of a last chance for democracy in Pakistan. " In December, in another round of what has been described as an "ongoing power struggle" between Sharif, the president, and the judiciary, President Leghari, who had threatened to dismiss Sharif, resigned, and the chief justice of the Supreme Court, Sajjad Ali Shah, was demoted. The resignation and demotion followed the army's declaration of support for Sharif. "The army behaved responsibly by insuring the continuation of an elected government," an editorial writer for *The New York Times* (December 6, 1997) declared. "Still, it is discouraging to see the army remain such a powerful arbiter." Leghari was succeeded by Mohammad Rafiq Tarar, Sharif s nominee, after a presidential election on December 31, 1997. Tarar won 374 votes in the 476-member electoral college, which is made up of members of both chambers of the national Parliament and four provincial assemblies.

Relations between Pakistan and India worsened significantly in mid-May 1998, after India conducted a series of five underground nuclear tests. It was the first time that India had tested a nuclear device since 1974. In Pakistan, which in 1992 had announced that it had "the components and knowhow to make at least one nuclear explosive device," as John F. Burns reported in *The New York Times* (May 29,1998), reaction to India's tests was swift and intense: Members of the Muslim clergy, politicians (prominent among them Benazir Bhutto and other members of the opposition party), editorial writers, and Pakistani citizens, countless numbers of whom participated in public demonstrations, demanded that Pakistan carry out nuclear tests of its own. Meanwhile, in four personal telephone conversations with Sharif, President Bill Clinton "all but begged him not to detonate a weapon," according to *The New York Times* correspondent Tim Weiner, and promised that if Sharif acquiesced to that request, Clinton would do all he could to forge a "changed relationship" between the U.S. and Pakistan that would benefit Pakistan both economically and militarily.

Apparently, the specifics of Clinton's promises were insufficient to outweigh the pressures on Sharif, and on May 28 and 30, Pakistan carried out several underground nuclear tests—a total of six, according to Pakistan. (Seismic recordings made by the U.S. and other countries indicated that the number of tests was actually less than six.) "Today, we have settled the score with India," Sharif said in a televised address on May 28, as reported by John F. Burns. He also said, "Today, we have made history. Today, God has given us the opportunity to take critical steps for the country's defense. We have become a nuclear power." After describing India as an "expansionist power" that had "started" the wars with Pakistan in 1947, 1965, and 1971, Sharif asserted that the tests "must be seen as a natural reaction on our part" to India's detonations two weeks before.

Commenting on the threatened imposition of severe economic sanctions on Pakistan by the U.S. and other nations, Sharif declared that "by imposing sanctions, the Western powers will have done us a favor. They will have given us a chance to effect a revolution in our way of life, to learn to live within our means, and to stop this cynical wastage of our national resources. . . . We will have to be disciplined, at all times, in all places." Speaking in Urdu, Pakistan's national language, he announced that the official residences of the prime minister and other government ministers would be turned into schools, welfare centers, and clinics. He also announced steps to "conserve every penny of foreign exchange" and, as Burns reported, "a crackdown on rampant tax evasion and a drive against smuggling, which has cut into the customs duties that are the government's largest revenue source." The escalating arms race between India and Pakistan triggered fears internationally of an actual nuclear confrontation in that part of the world. "I cannot believe that we are about to start the 21st century by having the Indian subcontinent repeat the worst mistakes of the 20th century, when we know it is not necessary to peace, to security, to prosperity, to national greatness, or to personal fulfillment," President Clinton declared, as quoted by Bums. Clinton immediately announced the suspension of American economic aid to Pakistan. Other sanctions include a ban on U.S. bank loans to Pakistani government institutions. Moreover, the foreign ministers of the U.S., Japan, Canada, and five other industrialized nations decided in June 1998 that they would act together to postpone the payment of loans to Pakistan and India by major international financial institutions, including the IMF, the World Bank, and the Asian Development Bank. In the absence of such loans, Pakistan's economy reeled even more dangerously than it had under the weight of its large foreign debt obligations and depleting government revenue. International sanctions will not affect most Pakistanis, however, as John Burns pointed out; and "for many Pakistanis, belt-tightening [by the Pakistani government] is likely to be superfluous, since tens of millions live in conditions of extreme deprivation, with menial jobs or none at all, no access to safe drinking water, and little in the way of education or medical care." According to figures obtained by Barry Bearak for *The New York Times* (August 30, 1998), less than 1 percent of the population in Pakistan pays income tax.

Under the strain of Pakistan's economic difficulty, the groundswell of popularity and support that Sharif had enjoyed immediately after the nuclear-arms tests soon dissipated. "If this is an economic meltdown, as many say, Pakistanis who have stashed money away overseas—or who have relatives living overseas—are likely to leave," Abida Hussain, a former ambassador to the United States and a member of Sharif's Cabinet, was quoted as saying by Bearak. "The institutional framework of government, already so stressed out, might come under unbearable pressure."

During a visit to the United States in September 1998, Sharif spoke before the United Nations General Assembly. He announced that he would sign the Comprehensive Test Ban Treaty (which bans nuclear testing) within the next year if economic sanctions on Pakistan were lifted. He also met with President Bill Clinton and his counterpart from India, Prime Minister Atal Behari Vajpayee, who made a similar offer in an address the General Assembly. Although many U.S. and international officials had hoped that India and Pakistan would agree unconditionally to sign the treaty, they welcomed the announcements by Sharif and Vajpayee as steps in the right direction. The two prime ministers also agreed to resume their talks on the dispute over Kashmir.

In 2013, Nawaz Sharif was sworn in for an unprecedented third term as Prime Minister. He has been faced with challenges, including U.S. drone strikes and attacks by the Taliban, as well as a poor economy. In 2014, his administration unveiled an ambitious vision to transform the country into an economically strong and prosperous nation by 2025. He is also a strong believer in constructing nuclear power for energy.

PERSONAL LIFE
Mohammad Nawaz Sharif is said to hold interests in several companies and has often been reported to be a multi-millionaire. His mentor and brother, Shahbaz Sharif, aided him during his 1997 election campaign. According to *Asiaweek*, he is married and the father of two sons and two daughters.

FURTHER READING
Asiaweek May 30, 1997 (online); *Electronic Telegraph* Feb. 4, 1997, Apr. 1, 1997, Apr. 2, 1997 (on-line); *Manchester Guardian Weekly* pi Feb. 9, 1997, with photo; *New Leader* p7+ Mar. 10, 1997; *New Statesman* p 14 Feb. 7, 1997; *The New York Times* A pl8 Dec. 6, 1997, A pi + May 29, 1998, with photos; *Time* Sept. 1, 1997; June 8, 1998 (on-line); *International Who's Who, 1996-1997*; *International Year Book and Statesmen's Who's Who, 1995-96*

ARIEL SHARON (AH-REE-EHL SHAH-ROHN)
11th Prime Minister of Israel

Born: February 26, 1928; Kfar Malal, Israel
Died: January 11, 2014; Tel HaShomer, Ramat Gan
Affiliation: Gahal Party; Likud Party; Kadima Party

INTRODUCTION
One of Israel's most colorful and controversial figures, Ariel ("Arik") Sharon capped a life-long career in the service of his country as the 11th Prime Minister of Israel. Elected in February 2001, his Prime Ministership followed a long political and military career, including his appointment, in August 1981, as Minister of Defense in former Prime Minister Menahem Begin's Cabinet. A bold and flamboyant battlefield commander in the tradition of General George S. Patton, Sharon planned and

669

Ariel Sharon.

Jim Wallace (Smithsonian Institution)

carried out decisive military operations in all of Israel's wars, earning from his inspired troops the appellation "Lion of the Desert." In the early 1970s, he took that same unwavering determination and dedication to the political arena, when he helped to found the right-wing coalition Likud Party, which, in 1977, unseated the governing Labor Party for the first time in the history of the Jewish state. A hard-line Zionist, Sharon was the most outspoken advocate of his government's aggressive program of Jewish settlement in occupied Arab territories as a precondition to Palestinian autonomy talks. As The New York Times correspondent David K. Shipler observed, Sharon acted as "a kind of militant conscience, adamant and relentless in the face of any move that strikes him as a betrayal of either the past or the future of the Jewish people." In the eyes of many Israeli political observers, he was Begin's most trusted adviser.

As Prime Minister, in 2004 to 2005, Sharon took a different tact and orchestrated Israel's unilateral disengagement from the Gaza Strip. Facing stiff opposition to this policy within the Likud, in November 2005, he left Likud to form a new party, Kadima. He had been

expected to win and planned on "clearing Israel out of most of the West Bank," in a series of unilateral withdrawals. He suffered a stroke, however, on January 4, 2006, which left him incapacitated until his death in January 2014.

EARLY LIFE

Ariel Sharon, the son of Shmuel and Devorah Sharon, was born in 1928 at Kfar Maalal in the Sharon Valley, one of the first cooperative Jewish farming settlements in Palestine. (The family's original European surname was Scheinermann). His parents, ardent Zionists who had emigrated from Russia after the end of World War I, frequently had to defend their property from attacks by marauding Bedouin tribes or raiding parties from neighboring Arab villages. When anti-Jewish rioting spread throughout Palestine in the early 1930s, the Sharons joined other settlers to form defensive units, and Shmuel Sharon taught his young son armed combat and survival techniques. By the time he was 14, Ariel Sharon was a full-fledged member of GADNA, a paramilitary youth battalion.

After completing his elementary education at a regional school not far from his home, Sharon attended high school in nearby Tel Aviv, where he studied agriculture, politics, and military affairs. During those years, he joined the Hagganah, the underground Jewish defense force. Upon his graduation from high school in 1945, Sharon enrolled in an officers' training course. Two years later he became an instructor of the Hagganah police units assigned to protect the farming settlements. Promoted to platoon commander of the Alexandroni Brigade at the beginning of Israel's War for Independence, in 1948, he was badly wounded in the stomach during one especially fierce battle in his native Sharon Valley. It was while he was hospitalized that he came to believe that victory depended, in a large part, on esprit de corps and on the example an officer set for his men. Idolized by his troops, Sharon always went into battle at the head of his unit, often in an armored car stocked with caviar and vodka. "I believe to control a battle you must be with the forward units," he explained to Charles Mohr in an interview for *The New York Times* (November 12, 1973). "One minute you are a general and another minute a soldier shooting a machine gun at Arabs and throwing grenades and climbing on bulldozers to convince men they can work under shellfire."

After an armistice was signed between Israel and her Arab neighbors in 1949, Sharon enlisted as a military intelligence officer in the Israeli army. Assigned to the Northern Command, he gathered information on Arab guerrillas in Syria and Lebanon and performed various administrative functions. In 1952, he took a leave of absence from the army to study Middle Eastern history at the Hebrew University of Jerusalem. The following year, the district commander in Jerusalem recruited him to lead commando raids into Jordanian territory, in retaliation for attacks against Israeli settlements.

When his first raid on a Jordanian village was repulsed rather easily by well-armed townspeople and Jordanian soldiers, Sharon proposed the formation of a small mobile unit of "crack soldiers" that were specifically trained to launch surprise attacks. Mordechai Makleff, the Chief of Staff, and Kloshe Dayan, then the Head of Operations, approved the project and appointed Sharon to head the elite group, known as Commando Unit 101. In his zeal, Sharon sometimes overstepped his orders. For example, in 1953, he was instructed to blow up ten homes in the Jordanian border village of Quibya in retaliation for a raid on an Israeli settlement that had resulted in three deaths. Instead, his men demolished 39 houses and a school, and killed 69 Jordanians. The incident, now known as the "Quibya Massacre," earned Sharon a worldwide reputation for ruthlessness and provoked such an outcry in the international diplomatic community that Prime Minister David Ben-Gurion was forced to apologize publicly.

Border disputes and bloody reprisals continued throughout the 1950s. Provoked by repeated Arab threats of invasion, Israel mounted a preemptive strike on Egyptian territory, in October 1956. Sharon's troops captured the strategic Mitla Pass in the Sinai Peninsula in a gory battle. Some of his superior officers, including Army Chief of Staff Dayan, thought it was unnecessary. Sharon had always insisted that the solution to Israel's persistent security problem was a stronger, more self-confident army. "We have to prove that we can strike hardest and best," he explained to Matti Shavitt in an interview for Shavitt's book *On the Wings of Eagles; the Story of Arik Sharon* (Olive Books, 1972). "To do this, we must be trained and able. And if we can strike secretly and efficiently, without employing large forces, we'll . . . have taught the Arabs a thing or two about our power. ... If we succeed, our own mood will change for the better, and we will have reinstated the self-confidence that is so necessary to an army like ours."

After the war, Sharon studied military theory at Staff College in Camberley, England. Advanced to the rank of Colonel on his return to Israel in 1958, he spent the next three years as a senior administrative officer in the training division of the General Staff, where he headed the Infantry School. He was named Brigade Commander of the Armored Corps in 1962 and, two years later, Chief of Staff of the Southern Command headquarters on the Egyptian front. During that period, he also studied law at Tel Aviv University, but, although he received his law degree in 1966, he had never practiced that profession. He was appointed head of the training division of the General Staff that same year, and eventually promoted to the rank of Major General in February 1967.

In June 1967, in response to Egyptian President Gamal Abdel Nasser's blockade of the Israeli port of Eilat, Israel attacked Egypt, Jordan, and Syria. As commander of the Egyptian front, Sharon directed a battle that has since become a classic in military textbooks. In a lightning assault conducted at night, his division overran the strongly fortified Egyptian encampment at Abu-Ageila, and then went on to recapture the Mitla Pass and the vital corridor to the Suez Canal. According to some reports from the scene, Sharon and his men deliberately slaughtered Egyptian prisoners of war, but, although Sharon admitted, as quoted in the *London Observer* (November 4, 1973), that he had made "no special effort to take prisoners," the charges were never confirmed.

In the late 1960s, Israeli occupation of Arab territory—the Gaza Strip, the Sinai Desert, the West Bank of the Jordan, and the Golan Heights—taken during the Six-Day War removed heavily populated Jewish areas from the range of Arab artillery, but sporadic border skirmishes continued, and Arab guerrillas stepped up their incursions. During that so-called "War of Attrition," Sharon traded his desk job with the General Staff for a field position as Brigadier General of the Southern Command at the Suez Canal. While supervising internal security in the Gaza Strip, he was once again accused of brutality for his alleged mistreatment of suspected Arab terrorists, but he was exonerated after a government investigation.

At about the same time, Sharon became embroiled in a dispute with other members of the high command over the proposed construction of extensive fortifications along the banks of the Suez Canal to protect Israeli positions there from possible Egyptian attacks. Contending that a permanent garrison would be little more than a stationary target for Egyptian artillery, he suggested the creation of a mobile defense force, spearheaded by

Affiliation: Gahal Party

Apparently because of his impulsiveness, dogmatism, and fierce independence, Sharon failed to win the expected promotion to Chief of Staff. Frustrated by the rebuff, he resigned from the army to seek a seat in the Knesset, Israel's Parliament, as a member of Gahal, a right-wing coalition party led by Menahem Begirt. Gahal advocated the annexation of the Arab lands taken in the Six-Day War to ensure Israel's continuing security, and rejected the ruling Labor government's willingness to make territorial compromises, in the event of a peace settlement. To broaden Gahal's political base and provide a viable alternative to the Labor party in the upcoming national election, Sharon helped negotiate, in September 1973, a right-center alliance known as Likud (Unity), which included Gahal, the Independent Liberals, and the Free Center. The parties kept their independent organizational structures, but agreed to nominate a joint slate of candidates.

The Egyptian-Syrian surprise attack on Israel, October 6, 1973, the Jewish High Holy Day of Yom Kippur, interrupted Sharon's promising political career. Taking over as leader of the Southern Command, at the head of an army reserve division composed of three armored brigades, he smashed through the Egyptian lines and established an Israeli bridgehead at Ismailia on the western side of the Suez Canal. To secure that advantageous behind-the-lines position, he called for immediate reinforcements, but before committing additional troops, the high command ordered him to construct and defend bridges across the Canal. In Sharon's opinion, the delay cost Israel a decisive victory in strategic territory before the United Nations-sponsored ceasefire went into effect, in late October. A few months later, largely through the mediation efforts of United States Secretary of State Henry A. Kissinger, formal disengagement agreements were signed.

Outraged by the hesitation that resulted in an "undecided war," to use his term, Sharon turned Israel's lack of military preparedness into a political issue. "We defeated the Egyptians, but we didn't finish the war," he told Joseph Kraft in an interview for the *New Yorker* (February 11, 1974). "I know we have a strong country and a lot of energetic and ingenious people . . . , but for twenty-five years, we had a posture of deterrence—a posture that deterred the Arabs from attacking us. Now we've lost it." Sharon's candid public criticism of Israeli strategy was disputed by other senior army officers, some of whom deplored his statements as self-serving and "biased."

tanks, but he was overruled, and the earthwork, the so-called "Bar-Lev Line," was built. Sharon's outspoken opposition to the project further alienated the high command and the Labor government.

LIFE'S WORK

In the 1977 election, the Likud Party scored a historic victory over the Labor Party, winning 44 seats in the Knesset to Labor's 33. The new coalition government, under the leadership of Prime Minister Menachem Begin, included Ariel Sharon, who had been appointed Minister of Agriculture. Sharon greatly expanded the role of the Ministry, which had previously restricted itself to such purely agricultural problems as land distribution, to include programs for establishing permanent Jewish colonies in the occupied territories. Shortly after taking office, he announced his own "master plan" to settle two million Jews in the West Bank and Gaza Strip, during the next two decades, to prevent the establishment of a Palestinian state, which, he fervently believed, would threaten the security of Israel. "You're wrong if you think that peace will come if Israel remains a nation of three million Jews," Sharon explained to Milan J. Kubic in an interview for *Newsweek* (September 19, 1977). "Peace will come, but our first problem is to [ensure] that Israel will exist forever. To that end, we have to have a population of six million to eight million Jews within the next 20 to 50 years, and we have to settle them. I don't believe that my plan blocks any diplomatic solutions, because we've made it perfectly clear that we'll never leave the West Bank," he continued. "I believe that if we establish these settlements, we will feel sufficiently secure to accept risks for the sake of peace."

Sharon opposed his government's acceptance of the Camp David Peace Accords hammered out in 1978 by President Jimmy Carter, Anwar Sadat, the President of Egypt, and Prime Minister Begin because, in his opinion, the guidelines for future talks on Palestinian autonomy were not clearly defined. As a member

Affiliation: Likud Party

In December 1973, Sharon was elected to the Knesset on the Likud ticket. Taking his fight to the floor of the Knesset, he demanded the resignation of the Labor government on the grounds that its mismanagement of the Yom Kippur War and its early acceptance of a ceasefire had deprived the Israeli army of an imminent victory over the Egyptians. A commission of inquiry, appointed by Prime Minister Golda Meir, absolved her government of any wrongdoing, but, in April 1974, under continuing pressure from the Likud bloc, Mrs. Meir stepped down and was succeeded by Yitzhak Rabin. Because he was fearful that Israel might become involved in another war, Sharon resigned from the Knesset, in December 1974, to accept a senior emergency position in the reserves, where he could "contribute to the security effort," as he put it. Six months later, Prime Minister Rabin chose Sharon to be his defense adviser, even though they frequently disagreed on defense policy. Sharon was totally committed to continued Israeli occupation of Arab territory taken in the Six-Day War and believed that Rabin might make too many territorial concessions in exchange for secure borders.

In 1976, Sharon left the government to form the Shlomzion (Peace-Zion) party, which was founded on the premise that lasting peace would come only if Israel permanently annexed and settled the lands captured in 1967. Despite its obvious appeal to the more nationalistic segments of the population, the party won just two seats in the Knesset in the June 1977 election. It was eventually absorbed by the larger, more powerful Likud group. "People trusted [Ariel Sharon] as a soldier," an Israeli poll taker explained, as quoted in *Newsweek* (September 19, 1977), "but as a politician, he sounded too reckless."

of the six-man Israeli negotiation team that met with Egyptian and American officials, in May 1979, to discuss that question, Sharon ruled out any concessions and reaffirmed his commitment to an intensive Jewish settlement effort. Without additional settlements, he said, as quoted in *The New York Times* (May 31, 1979), "we might as well proclaim a Palestinian State and withdraw to the coastal plains, permitting the breakup of everything we have created in 30 years of wars and 100 years of constructive efforts." To underscore his determination, he openly supported the attempts of Gush Emunim, a right-wing nationalist group that had set up several settlements in the Biblical lands of Judea and Samaria, the modern-day West Bank. He also approved a controversial government plan to build seven settlements on state-owned land in the West Bank.

When he took over as Minister of Defense, in August 1981, Sharon issued revised liberal guidelines for the administration of the occupied Arab territories. The new policy, which was confirmed by the Defense Ministry on September 23, 1981, was formulated to create the political and social conditions conductive to limited autonomy under civilian authority. Under Sharon's plan, the civilian government would be headed by Israelis but would also include Palestinians in a number of "senior positions."

Sharon was the principal architect of Israel's invasion of Lebanon in June 1982, a war that led to the removal from Lebanon of the Palestine Liberation Organization and its armed offshoots. In September 1982, militia members of the Phalange (a right-wing Maronite Lebanese group then allied with Israel), which was acting under an Israeli military umbrella, committed massacres at the Sabra and Shatila Palestinian refugee camps in Israeli-occupied Beirut. Widespread public outcry, including demonstrations in Tel Aviv, forced the government to launch an investigation. The Kahan Commission (1982) found that the Israeli Defense Forces (IDF) were indirectly responsible for the autocracies because they took place in land held by the IDF. The commission also took Sharon to task and recommended that he resign as Minister of Defense, which he did after a grenade was thrown into a dispersing crowd at an Israeli Peace Now march, killing Emil Grunzweig, an Israeli teacher and peace activist, and injuring ten others. Sharon agreed to step down from the post of Defense Minister, but stayed in the cabinet as a Minister Without Portfolio.

Before his successful run as Prime Minister, Sharon was involved in an incident that, although did not start the Second *Intifada* (also known as the Al-Aqsa Intifada), exacerbated it. Sharon, on September 28, 2000, and an escort of over 1,000 Israeli police officers visited the Temple Mount complex, site of the Dome of the Rock and al-Aqsa Mosque, the holiest place in the world to Jews, and the third holiest site in Islam. The next day, Palestinian demonstrators, which threw stones at the police, and an Israeli police contingent, using rubber bullets, confronted each other at the site. Four demonstrators were killed, 200 more injured, and 14 Israeli police also were injured. Sharon's visit to the site was because of allegations of the destruction of antiquities; his supporters said that the Intifada was a Palestinian Liberation Organization (PLO) plot. After an investigation, it was determined that Sharon's visit, although "ill-timed," did not start the Intifada, nor was there any evidence of a PLO plot. Most of the fault finding was against the Israeli police force for possibly using excessive force for controlling "mobs," and for being unprepared for incidents.

Due to violent Palestinian resistance to Israeli occupation in the Gaza Strip, in December 2003, Sharon announced the "Disengagement Plan," the withdrawal of 8,500 Jewish settlers. The reasons were to increase security of residents of Israel, relieve pressure on the Israeli Defense Forces (IDF), and reduce friction between Israelis and Palestinians. (*Washington Post*, August 10, 2005, web site.) Israel's right-wing and religious parties were most opposed to the withdrawal. Finance Minister Binyamin Netanyahu, a member of Sharon's Likud Party, resigned in early August in protest. He stated that the concession did not ask Palestinians for reciprocal concessions by the Palestinians. After the Israeli withdrawal, settlements would be destroyed and the Gaza Strip governed by the Palestinian National Authority.

Before Sharon could run for office as leader of the Kadima Party in 2006, he suffered a minor stroke, later followed by a hemorrhagic stroke, on January 4. Sharon endured two surgeries, which stopped the bleeding in his brain, but he slipped into a coma. Ehud Olmert became

Acting Prime Minister and, later, was named Interim Prime Minister. He became Prime Minister on May 4.

Meanwhile, Sharon spent almost eight years in a coma and suffered from renal failure, on January 1, 2014. He died January 11, 2014; his body lay in state, January 12, at the Knesset Plaza, and was followed by a state funeral on January 13. Sharon was laid to rest next to his second wife, Lili, after a funeral held at the family's ranch in the Negev desert.

PERSONAL LIFE

Sharon married Margalit Zimmermann in 1953; she died in a car accident in 1962, and their only child, their son, Gur, died in 1967 in a fatal shooting accident. Sharon married his second wife, Lili, the younger sister of Margalit, in 1963. She died of lung cancer in 2000. They had two sons, Omri (who was convicted of corruption and served a prison term) and Gilad (a journalist), and six grandchildren.

FURTHER READING

Guardian p5 N 17 '73 por; London Observer pl3 N 4 '73 por; The New York Times pl + N 9 '73 por, A p6 Ag 5 '81 por; The New York Times Mag p41 + O 18 '81 por; Nat Observer pl+ F 2 '74 pors; New Yorker 49:102+ F 11 '74; Newsday pl7 N 11 '73 por; Newsweek 40:65 S 19 '77 por; Time 102:40 N 26 '73 por, 118:22+ S 7 '81 por; Washington Post A p22 N 6 '73 por; International Who's Who, 1980-81; Schiff, Zeev. A History of the Israeli Army (1974); Shavitt, Matti. On the Wings of Eagles (1972); Who's Who in Israel, 1978.

SIR HARTLEY (WILLIAM) SHAWCROSS

British Government Official

Born: February 4, 1902
Died: July 10, 2003; Cowbeech, East Sussex

INTRODUCTION

Late in the year 1945 international attention was focused on the long-awaited war-crimes trials in Nuremburg, Germany, conducted by the United States, the United Kingdom, the Soviet Union, and France. The chief United Kingdom prosecutor is Sir Hartley Shawcross, K.C., M.P., appointed to the post on August 13, 1945. Shortly before that the relatively young barrister

had become Britain's Attorney General, following the Labor Party victory.

EARLY LIFE

Hartley William Shawcross was born on February 4, 1902 to John and Hilda Shawcross. Educated at Dulwich College near London, he also attended the London School of Economics for a brief period. The Englishman then went abroad, spending some time in Geneva, where he studied at the University. Shawcross had become interested in politics at an early age and at sixteen

Walter Stoneman

Sir Hartley Shawcross.

had joined the Labor Party. While he was in Geneva, where the second Socialist International Conference was in session, he assisted in the secretariat and also met many delegates from various countries. Back in England, Shawcross served as election agent for Lewis Silkin during the 1922 General Election when the latter waged an unsuccessful battle for a Conservative district. (Silkin is the present Minister of Town and Country Planning.) As Shawcross gained experience in the Labor movement, he became determined to remain active in its work.

LIFE'S WORK

At about this time Shawcross began his legal studies, in which he won first class honors in all examinations, and came out highest in the Bar Final. Called to the Bar at Gray's Inn in 1925, he then practiced law in London for two years. In 1927 he moved from the capital to Liverpool where, until 1934, he was senior law lecturer at Liverpool University. (He received an honorary LL.M.

degree from that institution in 1932.) During these years he also practiced law on the Northern Circuit. At a trial at Manchester, Shawcross was junior counsel for the prosecution of a Lancaster murderer. At one time, the barrister led an inquiry into the Gresford Colliery disaster. Conducting the investigation on behalf of the coal owners, he was matched with his friend, Sir Stafford Cripps, on the miners' side. It is believed that his conduct of this inquiry considerably aided his career. In 1939 Shawcross became a bencher (one of the senior and governing members who control calling to the bar) of Gray's Inn, and that year "took silk"—received letters patent as a King's Counsel. In 1940 he left his private practice to accept a Government assignment, arid a year later, while engaged in important government work as independent chairman of the Kew District Board on coal mining, he was appointed recorder of Salford, in Lancashire. About that time he was also appointed deputy regional commissioner for the South Eastern Region, one of the many zones into which the country had been divided for purposes of defense, and he was a Justice of the Peace for Sussex and assistant chairman of the East Sussex Quarter Sessions. The following year Shawcross was promoted to the post of commissioner of the North Western Region. Charged with the responsibility of the region's entire defense organization, he traveled constantly in his district. In public speeches he repeatedly warned of the probable resumption of large-scale air attacks and urged mutual aid plans among small traders, to become operative during raids, which would benefit storekeepers and the community alike.

The lawyer's work as regional commissioner was a valuable prelude to his duties as chairman of the Catering Wages Commission, established in July 1943 by the Ministry of Labor and National Service. This Commission was set up to investigate wages and to suggest methods of developing the catering, restaurant, and hotel industry in the postwar period in order to meet the needs of the domestic public and foreign visitors. Shawcross served on the commission until July 1945, at which time he resigned to run for Parliament. However, at the time of his resignation most of the Commission's investigations had been completed and its report was published in September. It has been said that this report, when implemented, will "stabilize wages and conditions throughout the previously unorganized industry, and pave the way for an improved standard of hotel accommodation."

Active for many years in Labor Party work, Shawcross had been asked to stand for election in 1924 but at that time had declined. In July 1945 he was a successful candidate for Parliament in the General Election which swept the Labor Party into power. Shawcross won a majority of about 17,000 over his Conservative opponent, quadrupling the former Labor majority in his constituency. Under Prime Minister Clement R. Attlee's new Labor Government, the new M.P. was appointed Attorney General and shortly thereafter was named chief prosecutor of the war crimes trials for Britain. A few days later, on August 15, Shawcross was knighted. His appointment to these vital offices was welcomed in both legal and non-legal circles, with the press describing him as one of the country's "most highly-regarded young attorneys." The new Attorney General was in the headline news barely a month later as prosecutor of William Joyce in the treason trial at Old Bailey. Joyce's defense, based on the contention that he was an American citizen, was shattered when the judge accepted the prosecutor's view that "A person who enjoys the effective protection of the British Crown is under duty of allegiance so long as the protection continues." (The defendant had a British passport, issued in 1939). Found guilty by the jury, Joyce was sentenced to be hanged for his broadcasts as "Lord Haw-Haw."

Less than a week after he became chief prosecutor Shawcross flew to Nuremberg with his American, French, and Russian colleagues to inspect the facilities for the trial. The basis for the case against the major war criminals had been established by the four Powers in the formal agreement made in London on August 8, 1945. At that time an historic new code of international law was adopted, defining aggressive warfare as a crime against the world. The agreement established a four-Power international military tribunal and three classifications of war crimes: 1) crimes against peace, involving the planning, preparation, initiation, or waging of aggressive war; 2) war crimes, defined as violations of the laws or customs of war; 3) crimes against humanity. Pursuant to this agreement, the four United Nations representatives prepared a lengthy indictment against the twenty-four major Nazi war criminals, which was released in October, bearing the signatures of Robert H. Jackson for the United States, Shawcross for the United Kingdom, Frangois de Menthon for France, and R. A. Rudenko for the Soviet Union. Proceedings began on November 20, 1945. Each person in the courtroom was supplied with earphones which could be tuned to the verbatim proceedings or to any of four translations, and twelve interpreters were also in attendance. Two hundred and fifty newsmen had arranged to cover the trials, and Justice Jackson had announced that there would be no censorship. Sir Hartley's deputy in the prosecution, incidentally, is Sir David Maxwell Fyfe, who was Attorney General in the coalition Government of Winston Churchill.

In his thirty-thousand-word address which opened the British presentation of the case against the twenty Nazi defendants on December 4, 1945, in Nuremberg, Sir Hartley reviewed the international treaties and agreements since the 1899 Hague Convention to prove that the world had outlawed aggressive war. Thus, it is not correct, he declared, to regard punishment for aggressive war as retroactive justice. As to the individual responsibility each defendant bore, he contended: "There comes a point when a man must refuse to answer to his leader if he is also to answer to his own conscience." The British prosecutor was one of the four delegates the House of Commons chose later in December to accompany Prime Minister Attlee to the United Nations General Assembly scheduled to convene early in January 1946.

Both in his legal and political activities Shawcross has expressed his convictions strongly. An ardent Socialist, he made his first political speech as a youth at a public meeting in Birmingham. The Attorney General has expressed himself forcibly against some British prison and punishment methods. In discussing the Penal Reform Bill in 1939, he condemned flogging: "A punishment which makes strong men sick cannot be a good thing," he said. "If flogging is a good thing, why not go back to the thumb-screw, the rack, and other systems of medieval torture?" Known as a hard worker, Shawcross is said to study every brief himself, never passing on his work to juniors.

In 1957, Shawcross helped form JUSTICE, a human rights and law reform organization, and he was chairman until 1972. He helped found the University of Sussex, and served as chancellor from 1965-1985. In 1974, Lord Shawcross was appointed a Knight of the British Empire.

PERSONAL LIFE

The Chief Prosecutor was described by Margaret Armour as "a tall, spare, at once dignified and athletic-looking man, with high cheekbones and the healthily weather-tanned complexion of the sportsman." He had dark eyes and hair and a quiet voice. After the death of his first wife, who was Rosita Alberta Shyvers, he married Joan Winifred Mather whom he met while serving as regional commissioner when she was assigned to drive him through the area. They lived in a small old country house near Uckfield in Sussex. When he had time for recreation Shawcross liked reading, golfing, or riding. A yachting enthusiast, he belonged to four yacht clubs, Royal Thames, Royal Cornwall, Royal Mersey, and Royal Motor. Sir Hartley was a member also of the Reform Club.

Shawcross died at his home in East Sussex at the age of 101.

FURTHER READING
Who's Who, 1945

ANATOLY SHCHARANSKY
Jewish Activist; Dissident

Born: January 20, 1948; Donetsk, Soviet Union
Group Affiliation: Jewish Dissident Movement

INTRODUCTION
On February 11, 1986, the internationally renowned Soviet-Jewish dissident Anatoly Shcharansky walked across a bridge to West Berlin and freedom, following years of imprisonment. A founding member of the Moscow Helsinki Watch, a group devoted to monitoring Soviet violations of human rights, Shcharansky was jailed by Soviet authorities in 1977 for his outspoken criticisms of his country's repressive policies on Jewish emigration and political dissent. Combining liberal political convictions with a strong Jewish identity, Shcharansky provided a link between the two previously separate strands of dissent in the Soviet Union—the Jewish emigration movement and the broader human rights movement.

Thanks to the tireless efforts of his wife, Avital, and his brother Leonid, Shcharansky's fate became an international cause célèbre. Finally, in February 1986, apparently as part of an effort to improve relations with the United States, the regime of Mikhail Gorbachev released Shcharansky in an East-West prisoner exchange, and he was allowed to join his wife in Israel. Since gaining his freedom, he has visited the United States to press the cause of Soviet Jews and political prisoners. For many, Shcharansky's great courage and strong convictions have made him a "hero of our time."

EARLY LIFE
Anatoly Shcharansky was born on January 20, 1948, in Donetsk, a Ukrainian coal mining town near the Black Sea. He was the second of two sons born to Boris Shcharansky, a filmwriter and journalist, and his wife, Ida Milgrom, an economist. Anatoly received a gold medal for scholarship when he graduated from high school and, having played chess since he was eight, became his city's chess champion when he was just fourteen. Growing up in an assimilated Jewish family, he learned little about Judaism and, because of his parents' protectiveness, remained unaware of the widespread anti-Semitism of post-Stalinist Russia.

Shcharansky's awareness of his Jewish identity began to grow during his student years in Moscow, where he went in 1966 to attend a special mathematics school. His first brush with anti-Semitism came on a hiking trip with his best friend, who during an argument called him a "Yid." He later told an American reporter, "I think it was then that I decided [the Soviet Union] was no place for me."

LIFE'S WORK
But it was the dramatic Six-Day War of 1967, in which tiny Israel defeated a strong coalition of Arab enemies, that brought Shcharansky, along with many Soviet Jews, to a new consciousness of his Jewish heritage. In the late 1960s and early 1970s, the "Jews of Silence," as Elie Wiesel once termed them, began to find their voice: to organize classes in Hebrew language and Jewish culture, to memorialize the victims of the Holocaust, and above all, to dream of going to Israel.

In April 1973, a year after graduating from the prestigious Moscow Physical-Technical Institute with a specialty in cybernetics and taking a job as a computer specialist with the Moscow Research Institute for Oil and Gas, Shcharansky applied for an exit visa to go to Israel. His request was rejected, on the grounds that

Affiliation: Jewish Dissident Movement

Now branded as a "refusenik"—a Jew denied an exit visa—Shcharansky was subject to special harassment by the authorities. Angered by that state of affairs, he joined the Jewish dissident movement which, starting in the late 1960s, had begun to challenge the government's restrictive emigration policy. Those who protested too openly or tried to escape were given harsh prison sentences. As the numbers of the imprisoned grew, other Jews, among them the twenty-five-year-old Shcharansky, began to organize public protests in their behalf.

It was at one such public protest in October 1973, that the young activist met Natalia Shtiglits (or Stieglitz), an ardent Zionist, whose "refusenik" brother was serving a brief prison term for his political activities. The young couple began to live together soon after and, having decided to marry the following spring, both applied for exit visas to go to Israel. In June 1974, while Shcharansky was serving his first prison term as part of the "suspicious and subversive element" that was hidden from view during President Richard Nixon's second visit to the Soviet Union, Natalia learned that her visa had been granted. Believing that Anatoly's visa would soon follow, they were married the day he was released from prison, on July 4, 1974, and on the following day Natalia, now using her Hebrew name, Avital, left for Israel.

his work had given him "access to classified materials," though none of the work he had done at the Moscow Physical-Technical Institute had been of a military nature. His thesis was on programming computers to play chess, and the institute where he worked was classified as an "open" institution, not involved in secret work.

But Shcharansky's visa never came. That second refusal, coupled with separation from his wife, redoubled his commitment to the dissident movement. He became part of a team, closely watched by the KGB, that traveled to outlying towns and provinces during October and November 1974, collecting information on the experiences of the "refuseniks" and was one of nine signatories to a letter to President Gerald Ford that detailed many cases of abuse and harassment that they had discovered on their journeys. The letter was dated November 18, 1974, five days before Ford flew to Vladivostok to meet with Soviet leader Leonid I. Brezhnev.

As a result of a compromise negotiated by Henry A. Kissinger during those talks, the United States Senate in 1974 passed the Jackson Amendment to the Trade Reform Act of 1972, linking East-West trade to the easing of Soviet emigration restrictions. A further amendment to the act, introduced by Senator Adlai Stevenson 3d, set a $300 million limit on United States banking credits to the Soviet Union, making Soviet-Jewish emigration one of the conditions for any increase in those credits. The amended Trade Reform Act was signed by President Ford on January 3, 1975, but Soviet authorities, irate over the amendment, canceled the agreement seven days later. With others who had pinned their hopes on the Jackson Amendment, Shcharansky now took part in new letter-writing campaigns and protest demonstrations, including a rally on the steps of Moscow's Lenin Library on February 24, 1975. Two of the organizers were arrested, tried, and sentenced to five years of exile in Siberia.

In August 1975, even as reprisals against the "refuseniks" increased, the Soviet government signed the Helsinki accords, which recognized Soviet hegemony over Eastern Europe in exchange for a guarantee of human rights, including the right of emigration. Shcharansky later observed in an interview in the Washington *Post* (May 4, 1986) that the agreement was meaningless: "The moment they signed it, they started to take steps to discourage people from using it." Nevertheless, the Helsinki accords gave Soviet dissidents a new platform around which to organize. In May 1976, led by the physicist Yuri Orlov, a small group of activists, among them Anatoly Shcharansky, founded the Moscow Helsinki Watch to monitor Soviet compliance with its human rights provisions. In the following months, the group collected information on a wide range of abuses and published regular reports that were distributed to the embassies of the nations that had signed the Helsinki accords, as well as to the press.

Because of his central role in the Helsinki group, Shcharansky lost his job and was subjected to constant surveillance and threats. Then he was accused in *Izvestia* of spying for the CIA, and on March 15, 1977, he was arrested and charged under the Soviet penal code with "treasonable espionage" and with anti-Soviet agitation and propaganda.

Despite the fact that his former roommate, Sanya Lipavsky, named him as a CIA agent, Shcharansky insisted that he was not a spy. Even President Jimmy Carter came to his defense by issuing a statement that the Jewish activist had no links with the United States intelligence agency. Western observers agreed that the spy charge was a trumped-up cover for Shcharansky's real "crime," his prominent role in the dissident movement. The authorities intended to make an example of him, to frighten other dissidents.

Shcharansky's trial began on July 10, 1978, two days before the start of United States-Soviet Strategic Arms Limitation Talks (SALT) in Geneva. Western observers and supporters of Shcharansky were barred from the courtroom, but his brother Leonid was allowed to attend (except for a secret session on July 11 and 12, which met to consider classified material that Shcharansky was alleged to have passed to foreign agents) and he conveyed information about the proceedings to about 150 supporters and journalists outside the courtroom. The prosecution charged Shcharansky with passing classified documents to agents posing as journalists, in particular to Robert Toth, a reporter for the Los *Angeles* Times, who was accused by Soviet authorities of working for the CIA. Conducting his own defense, Shcharansky rejected the charges as "absurd." Denied permission to call witnesses for his defense and restricted by the judge in his questioning of prosecution witnesses, Shcharansky was convicted on July 14 and sentenced to three years in prison, to be followed by ten years in a labor camp.

Then began almost a decade of nightmarish imprisonment. Shcharansky spent the first three years at Chistopol prison in solitary confinement. To keep his sanity, he did mental exercises: playing imaginary chess games with himself (which he always won, as he once jokingly told a reporter), outlining a book that he wanted to write, and singing Hebrew songs as loudly as he could, "I was sure that my people and my friends hadn't forgotten me," Shcharansky recalled, as quoted in the *Washington Post* (May 4, 1986), and that gave him the strength to resist the KGB's continued efforts to break his will.

Indeed, his family and friends had not forgotten him, and after the immediate protests over his imprisonment died down, they worked ceaselessly to keep his memory alive. His mother and his brother Leonid kept petitioning the Soviet authorities in his behalf and met regularly with Western journalists in Moscow. Those activities cost Leonid his job. Because he was considered a security risk; he was fired in 1982 from his position as a computer programmer for a Moscow industrial firm. Meanwhile, in Jerusalem, Avital founded the Association for the Release of Anatoly Shcharansky.

With the support of international Jewish organizations, she took his case to Western heads of state, embarrassing the Kremlin with her outspoken condemnation of her husband's treatment.

Shcharansky remained optimistic and good-humored in his imprisonment. Moved to Perm 35, a labor camp for political prisoners, where he was assigned to work as a welder, he had more access to the outside world. His reading was heavily censored, but occasionally the camp authorities slipped up; an anti-Zionist magazine that they once gave him to read included a facsimile of a letter from Ronald Reagan to his wife, Avital. Shcharansky's spirit of resistance remained strong. Since he refused to work unless he was allowed to keep prayer books and candles, he was often sent to the "punishment cells." Accused of being a "bad influence" on other prisoners, he was sent back in January 1981 to Chistopol prison to serve a three-year sentence. In February 1982 he began a four-month hunger strike to protest the confiscation of his mail, during which he was forcibly fed.

Although his emotional stamina was exceptional, Shcharansky's physical health was poor. As a result of his severely restricted diet, his weight dropped at one point to less than 110 pounds. He suffered from chronic heart and blood pressure problems, and lack of medical attention for his eyes left him nearly blind. Fearing for her husband's life, Avital became increasingly outspoken in her public appeals in his behalf. Ignoring hints from the Soviet leader Yuri Andropov that Shcharansky might be released if she stopped her "noisy campaign," she went to the United States in 1984 for a White House ceremony on human rights and unexpectedly asked for a private interview with President Ronald Reagan. His administration later used every opportunity to tell Soviet authorities that the United States would regard the release of Shcharansky and his fellow "prisoner of conscience," Andrei Sakharov, as an important sign of their willingness to work for better East-West relations.

With Mikhail Gorbachev's accession to power, the Soviet Union became more receptive to the idea of freeing Shcharansky as a way to help thaw Soviet-American negotiations. Although the precise details were never revealed, Reagan and Gorbachev evidently reached an agreement on his release at the Geneva summit conference in November 1985. After some unexplained delays on the Soviet side, final plans were made to include the activist in an East-West exchange of captured intelligence operatives. To underline their insistence that

Shcharansky had never been a spy, the United States authorities insisted that he be released before the other prisoners. As hundreds of journalists watched, along with the United States ambassador to Bonn and West German officials, Anatoly Shcharansky walked across the Glienicke Bridge from Potsdam into West Berlin on February 11, 1986, and at long last became a free man. Shcharansky immediately flew to Frankfurt, where he met Avital and, demonstrating his usual wit, greeted her with the words, "I'm sorry I'm late." That same day, nine years after their wedding, husband and wife finally realized their dream to go to Israel together. At Jerusalem airport, where they were met by Prime Minister Shimon Peres and a joyful crowd, Shcharansky said that it was the "happiest day of our life" and added, "I am not going to forget those whom I left in the camps, in prisons, who are still in exile or who still continue their struggle for the right to emigrate and for their human rights."

Physically and emotionally exhausted, Shcharansky went into seclusion for a few months to prepare for a trip to the United States, which he planned and financed himself, to thank his American supporters. He arrived in New York City on May 7, 1986, to a hero's welcome. Four days later he was the guest of honor at the annual Solidarity Parade in behalf of Soviet Jews, which culminated in a rally at Dag Hammarskjöld Plaza that drew an estimated 300,000 people. The following day, in the office of Random House publisher Robert Bernstein, who is chairman of the United States Helsinki Watch Committee, Shcharansky met for the first time in a decade with Yelena Bonner, another founder of the Moscow Helsinki Watch, who had been sentenced, along with her husband, the Nobel Prize-winning Soviet physicist Andrei D. Sakharov, to internal exile in Gorky for "anti-Soviet slander," but was in the United States on medical leave. Shcharansky then flew to Washington, D.C., where on May 13 he received the key to the city from the mayor and was awarded the Congressional Gold Medal, at a reception in the Capitol Rotunda. On the same day, he met with President Reagan, Vice-President George Bush, Secretary of State George P. Shultz, national security affairs adviser John M. Poindexter, and White House chief of staff Donald T. Regan, in a closed forty-minute conference in the Oval office, but the details of that conference were not released because of the administration's emphasis on "quiet diplomacy." During the next two days he met individually with leaders of the Senate and the House of Representatives and testified at hearings before the congressional committee that monitors compliance with the Helsinki accords.

During his visit, Shcharansky repeated the same message at every opportunity. While acknowledging that "quiet diplomacy" had helped to gain his release, he urged the United States to continue putting public pressure on the Soviet Union to release the estimated 400,000 Jews still awaiting exit visas and to moderate its policies on human rights in general. He told reporters that the United States "must leave no doubt with the Soviet authorities that the human rights problem is not a propaganda issue but a question of principle on which all the structure of the relationships between East and West can be built." Describing his release as a "cosmetic" gesture, Shcharansky expressed the view that the Soviet regime would not change markedly under Gorbachev unless it was subject to relentless pressure, including economic sanctions. "Just the fact that Gorbachev understands things better than his predecessors gives some reason for optimism," Shcharansky told Francis X. Clines in an interview for *The New York Times* (February 8, 1987). He added, however: "The West must not be deceived by his campaign of gestures and must be firm. ..."

Shcharansky, who now uses his Hebrew given name "Natan" and has changed the spelling of his surname to Sharansky, continued to face some difficult challenges in his new homeland. Although he tried to steer clear of Israel's bitter factional politics, he has on occasion become embroiled in controversy. In the late summer of 1986 he came under fire for insisting that arms controls talks with the Soviet Union be tied to human rights issues and for opposing a meeting between Israeli and Soviet negotiators to reopen diplomatic relations between their two countries. Asked how he felt about the criticism, Shcharansky replied, "That's the beauty of democracy."

But in November 1986 the activist became embroiled in a more embarrassing controversy by meeting with two Palestinians, who asked him to investigate alleged human rights violations by Israeli authorities on the West Bank—in particular, the expulsion of a Palestinian newspaper editor. Rightist spokesmen maintained that the two men had connections with the Palestine Liberation Organization and bitterly attacked Shcharansky for listening to them. He issued an apology, explaining that he had been ignorant of their PLO ties and affirming that Israeli efforts to suppress the PLO "birds of prey" could never be considered a violation of human rights.

PERSONAL LIFE

In the midst of his turbulent new life, Shcharansky's family has been a special source of joy. Honoring a commitment made at the time of his release, the Soviet Union allowed his brother Leonid, along with his wife and their two sons, and his mother, to immigrate to Israel in August 1986. Then, in November, Shcharansky's wife presented him with their first child, a girl. Asked how he and his wife were getting along after their long separation, Shcharansky replied that he had always felt spiritually close to her in their years apart. "But I was surprised," he admitted, "how we started understanding one another from the very first moment" after his release, and added that he was very proud of the political prominence she had acquired in his absence. Avital Shcharansky, a convert to Orthodox Judaism, is religiously more observant than her husband and has been identified with the religious right.

Described by Richard Grenier in *Insight* (March 17, 1986) as an "awesomely cheerful little man" who is "amiable, intelligent, even amusing," Anatoly Shcharansky is five feet two inches tall, stocky, and bald. After reading his moving letters from prison, which are quoted at length in Martin Gilbert's biography *Shcharansky: Hero of Our Time* (Viking, 1986), reviewers were eagerly awaiting his memoirs, scheduled to be published by Random House. On November 1, 1981 a flight of steps opposite the United Nations building in New York City was named the "Shcharansky Steps" at a ceremony sponsored by the Greater New York Conference on Soviet Jewry, the Student Struggle for Soviet Jewry, and Mayor Edward Koch of New York City. An honorary degree, conferred by Yeshiva University, was accepted for him by his wife in 1984.

FURTHER READING

Insight 2:32+ F 2 '86 por; *N Y Rev of Bks* 33:13+ S 25 '86 por; *Newsday* II 4+ My 19 '86 por; *Washington Post* C pl+ My 17 '86 por; Gilbert, Martin. *Shcharansky: Hero of Our Time* (1986). *International Who's Who*, 1986-87

NORODOM SIHANOUK

King of Cambodia

Born: October 31, 1922; Phnom Penh, Cambodia
Died: October 15, 2012; Beijing, China
Affiliation: FUNCINPEC

INTRODUCTION

King Norodom Sihanouk has spent virtually his entire adult life shifting political alliances in an effort to achieve an independent and peaceful future for Cambodia under his own rule. In September 1993, fifty-two years after he was crowned king of what was then e French-colonial monarchy, the charismatic Sihanouk was for a second time coronated king of Cambodia, which, by accident of geography, has long been a battleground for the deep-seated enmity between China and Vietnam as well as for the East-West struggle joined in the Vietnam War. During his early years in power, Sihanouk managed to exploit Cold War tensions by extracting aid from both camps to sustain the sovereignty of Cambodia, but by 1965 he had decided to cast his fate with China. When Sihanouk's government was overthrown five years later, he retreated into exile in China, where he joined forces with Pol Pot's Communist Khmer Rouge, which restored him to power in 1975. His role as an international apologist for the Khmer Rouge ended in 1976, when the Communist regime placed him under virtual house arrest for the following three years, during which the Khmer Rouge undertook the wholesale slaughter of as many as a million Cambodians.

In January 1979 Vietnamese-backed forces overthrew the Khmer Rouge and sent Sihanouk into exile for twelve years. Upon his return to Cambodia in 1991, he froze the Khmer Rouge out of a planned power-sharing arrangement and demanded that its leaders be tried for murder. Such ephemeral allegiances have often been cited by Sihanouk's critics as proof that he cannot be trusted. Sihanouk, however, has steadfastly insisted that his only purpose has been to maintain the integrity of Cambodia. "My foreign policy . , , ," he once explained, as quoted in Look *(October 20, 1970), "was conceived solely to keep my country from being a satellite of the great powers or being dragged into the horrors of war."*

EARLY LIFE

Norodom Sihanouk has claimed to be a descendant of no fewer than eighty Cambodian kings. The eldest son of King Norodom Suramarit and Queen Kossamak, he was born in Cambodia on October 31, 1922. A pampered child, Sihanouk was educated at French schools in what was then Saigon, Vietnam, in Cochin China, and in Paris. He underwent military training in Saumur, France. On April 26, 1941 the Nazi-controlled Vichy government of France crowned Sihanouk king of Cambodia, bypassing his father, on the assumption that an unformed eighteen-year-old monarch would be less likely to cause trouble. That supposition proved to be correct, for Sihanouk offered no resistance to the Japanese occupation of his country during World War II. After the war Sihanouk began to take his political responsibilities more seriously. Among other things, he launched a royal crusade for independence, traveling around the world to enlist support for his cause. He even went into voluntary exile in Thailand to pressure France to grant complete sovereignty to Cambodia.

LIFE'S WORK

During that time, while on his first official visit to Washington, D.C., in 1953, Sihanouk became disenchanted with the United States government. As he later explained in an interview with Oriana Fallaci for *The New York Times Magazine* (August 12, 1973), he presented his case for independence to Secretary of State John Foster Dulles, who dismissed him with the words, "Go home, your Majesty, and thank God that you have the French." Still seething twenty years after the rebuff, Sihanouk told Fallaci, "From that day on I have detested [the Americans], them and their fake democracy, their fake freedom, their imperialism put through in the name of Christian civilization." Later in 1953 he met with Vice-President Richard Nixon, who came away from their discussion with a decidedly negative impression of the Cambodian ruler. "He was an intelligent man, but vain and flighty," Nixon recalled in his *RN: The Memoirs of Richard Nixon* (1978). "He seemed prouder of his musical talents than of his political leadership, and he appeared to me totally unrealistic about the problems he faced." Nevertheless, by the end of 1953, Sihanouk had won independence for Cambodia without bloodshed, after nearly a century of French rule, an achievement for which he became known among his people as the Hero King.

On March 2, 1955 Sihanouk unexpectedly abdicated the throne in favor of his father (thereafter he affixed the honorific "prince" to his name) in order to form the Popular Socialist Community (some sources translate the name as People's Socialist Community), a political party that he led to victory in national elections later in the same year. As prime minister and foreign minister in the new government, Sihanouk established diplomatic relations with China, the Soviet Union, and the West, and in 1956 he served as Cambodia's representative to the United Nations. Upon the death of his father four years later, he amended the constitution to provide for the direct election of the head of state. Sihanouk himself won the first such election, in 1960, handily. During the early 1960s, Sihanouk strove to improve the lives of his people with financial aid from governments on both sides of the Cold War, including $30 million annually from the United States. "He got the United States to build a four-lane highway to the port of Kompong Som [Sihanoukville]," James Wilde, a longtime observer of Sihanouk, noted in *Time* (January 22, 1979), "and when the monsoons washed parts of it away, he got the Russians to repair it. He delighted in inviting the diplomatic corps to help build irrigation projects. Every time he dug up a bit of earth at one of those ceremonies, the peasants would catch it, for he was sacred, and so was everything he touched." in addition to roads, he oversaw the construction of schools, hospitals, factories, and airports.

Sihanouk seemed determined to maintain strict neutrality during the Cold War. "When two elephants are fighting," he was fond of saying, "an ant should step aside." Gradually, he came to believe that China would inevitably dominate Southeast Asia, and on May 3, 1965, he severed diplomatic relations with the United States after the American-supported South Vietnamese air force attacked two Cambodian villages. Except for a brief period in November 1967, when Prince Sihanouk escorted Jacqueline Kennedy, the former first lady, on a much photographed tour of the ruins of the great temple at Angkor Wat—a reception that was widely regarded as a diplomatic overture to the United States at a time when relations between Phnom Penh and Beijing were strained—Cambodia remained beyond the influence of Washington and was a source of growing concern to the United States. As the Vietnam War escalated, Cambodia's tactical and strategic significance increased because Communist guerrillas began establishing sanctuaries in eastern Cambodia, from which they staged raids into South Vietnam.

In 1968 Sihanouk condemned the United States' military involvement in the war as not only immoral but also counterproductive to American objectives. "America is most afraid of Chinese communism," he explained to Hal Wingo in an interview for *Life* (February 16, 1968). "America is trying to fight Chinese communism and is destroying Vietnamese communism. Vietnam is as different from China as Cambodia is different from China. You are working for China by stamping out the only barrier to Communist China's aggression—Vietnamese nationalism. You should let these people develop themselves, and it would be an excellent barrier to Chinese expansionism."

On March 18, 1970, while Sihanouk was on a diplomatic mission to the Soviet Union, General Lon Nol, who was then the premier of Cambodia, seized control of the government in Phnqm Penh. Unlike Sihanouk, who had tolerated the presence of North Vietnamese arid Viet Cong troops on Cambodian soil, General Lon demanded the withdrawal of all Vietnamese troops from Cambodian territory and tacitly permitted the United States to attack Communist sanctuaries inside Cambodia. In his book My *War with the CIA* (1973), which he wrote in collaboration with the veteran war correspondent Wilfred Burchptt, Sihanouk asserted that the Nixon administration had been behind the coup and that Lon Nol \vas a tool of the United States Central Intelligence Agency, a charge Nixon has denied. On May 5, 1970 Sihanouk, from exile in China, established the Royal Government of National Union and threw his support behind the Communist Khmer Rouge guerrillas in their struggle to topple Lon Nol.

Five years later, on April 17, 1975, the Khmer Rouge captured Phnom Penh and overthrew the tottering Lon Nol regime. Within eight days Sihanouk returned to the capital as head of state. From 1975 to 1976 he served as the Khmer Rouge's figurehead and chief apologist to the international community, The real power, however, rested in Pol Pot, a brutal dictator who forced millions of Cambodians to abandon their homes in the cities for resettlement in government-supervised "cooperatives" in the countryside. During this time an estimated one million Cambodians, more than 10 percent of the population, either were killed or died from starvation or disease. Among those who perished in what came to be known as the Killing Fields were members of Sihanouk's own family, including two

sons, three daughters, two sons-in-law, and at least fifteen (some sources say nineteen) grandchildren. "I did not see the killing," Sihanouk told Christopher Wren of *The New York Times* (September 22, 1982), "but I saw the forced labor of my people." Sihanouk was shielded from the worst excesses of the government because he was under virtual house arrest, from 1976 to 1979, in the royal palace.

Released just in time to flee yet again into exile, Sihanouk left Cambodia in January 1979, just ahead of a Vietnamese invasion that led to the establishment of the Hanoi-backed People's Republic of Kampuchea. At a six-hour news conference soon after his arrival in China, Sihanouk denounced the Vietnamese invasion while both praising and criticizing the Khmer Rouge regime. "The people were hot unhappy under Pol Pot," he said. "But 1 would like to see my government . . . give the people the right to practice their religion . . . the right to each other's company without restraint. I could not write to my children and grandchildren who were sent off to a cooperative. I was never aware of their whereabouts. I still do not know. . . . When Pol Pot organized the working people, it was good. The progress in agriculture was tremendous, and in industry it was good."

For much of the next decade, Sihanouk worked from his bases in China and North Korea to expel the Vietnamese from Cambodia. He was willing to overlook, for the time being at least, the holocaust wrought by the Khmer Rouge, because he needed its battle-tested army to lend credibility to the anti-Vietnamese resistance. In 1981 he founded the National United Front for an Independent, Neutral, Peaceful, and Cooperative Cambodia, which, in alliance with the Khmer Rouge under the leadership of Pol Pot, and the Khmer People's National Liberation Front, the remnants of the rightist faction that had brought Lon Nol to power and was now led by former prime minister Son Sann, constituted a government in exile known as the Coalition Government of Democratic Kampuchea. Under the terms of the agreement, Sihanouk served as president of the coalition government, Khieu Samphan as vice-president in charge of foreign affairs, and Son Sann as prime minister. "This coalition is not my dream," Sihanouk conceded in ail interview with Jacques Bekaert of the *Nation* (January 15,1983), "I have always favored an alliance between the nationalists, between Son Sann and myself. But nowhere could we find real support for such an idea. We have been forced into this coalition.

It is for us to make the best of it. . . . Our people are increasingly worried about the Vietnamese presence in our country. And by now we know the Khmer Rouge. They will always be isolated, with no real support among the people. For the time being, we have no choice but to include them."

After traveling around the world to enlist backers, Sihanouk won for his coalition the Cambodian seat at the UN arid the international recognition that came with it. He argued that the new partnership was not a government in exile per se but the legitimate ruler of Cambodia, whose current regime, he asserted, was nothing more than a contrivance of the Vietnamese occupiers. By 1984 Sihanouk had seized the attention of Hun Sen, whom the Vietnamese had installed as prime minister of the People's Republic of Kampuchea. The main stumbling block to serious negotiation between Sihanouk and Hun Sen seemed to be Sihanouk's unwillingness to break with the Khmer Rouge. In an interview with reporters from Newsweek (April 8, 1985), Hun Sen said, "We have only one condition [for a political settlement]. If the people want to join us they have to abandon Pol Pot. We can talk to Sihanouk, If he abandons Pol Pot today, I can talk to him tomorrow. But if he is still with Pol Pot, and I talk to him, then it seems as if I am talking to Hitler." Despite his personal feelings, Sihanouk consistently refused to cut himself off from Pol Pot's military might. "If I can forgive the Khmer Rouge and bury the hatchet, then everyone else in Cambodia can bury it, too, " he argued in response to written questions from Uli Schmetzer of the *Chicago Tribune* (March 23, 1989). Although Sihanouk angrily resigned as head of the coalition on a few occasions, once charging that the Khmer Rouge had been murdering his loyalists, he never stayed away for long.

In 1987 Hun Sen dropped his demand that Sihanouk purge the Khmer Rouge from his coalition as a precondition for talks. But during their first face-to-face meeting, outside Paris in December of that year, the two sides made little progress. In their second encounter, in Jakarta, Indonesia in May 1989, Hun Sen and Sihanouk broke new ground when they agreed on the establishment of a free-market economy, private-property rights, and Buddhism as the official religion. Moreover, Sihanouk held out the prospect of eventually breaking with the Khmer Rouge, whom he now denounced as "criminals." In July and August of the same year, when the coalition members attended a nineteen-nation conference in Paris charged with working out a comprehensive

settlement among the principals and their major backers, the delegates disagreed over whether the Khmer Rouge should be included in a provisional government. In an odd coupling of convenience, Vietnam and the United States stood together in opposition to the Khmer Rouge, while China and the Sihanouk coalition argued that the Khmer Rouge, whose army had occupied large parts of the countryside, could not be ignored. On February 23, 1990, after the Vietnamese had withdrawn completely from Cambodia, Sihanouk returned to his homeland and established a military base in the mountains in northwestern Cambodia.

Despite increasing international pressure to break his alliance with the Khmer Rouge, Sihanouk bowed to its will in reneging on an agreement that he had reached with Hun Sen in June 1990, in which Hun Sen and Sihanouk were to have divided evenly between them the seats on a provisional ruling council. Nevertheless, Sihanouk managed to keep the peace process alive, paving the way for an accord concluded in June 1991, in which all sides agreed to an unconditional ceasefire and an end to accepting outside sources of arms. According to some sources, Sihanouk had pressured the Khmer Rouge into agreeing to the cease-fire by threatening to exclude them from any political settlement. "The war is over," Sihanouk proudly declared on August 27, 1991.

The formal peace treaty, which was signed on October 23, 1991, called for the creation of a national reconciliation council, led by Sihanouk, which in consultation with the UN was to administer the country pending UN-supervised elections scheduled for 1993. At Sihanouk's insistence, the Khmer Rouge was promised a full share in the new government. As Philip Shenon reported in *The New York Times* (October 25, 1991), it was at least partly Sihanouk's "tireless coaxing and impish charm" (as Shenon noted, the prince occasionally brought his poodle to the negotiations) that made the agreement possible. "Prince Sihanouk is responsible for [the treaty,]" an unidentified senior Western diplomat told Shenon. "His performance in these negotiations has been utterly brilliant."

On November 14, 1991 Sihanouk returned to Phnom Penh under the protection of North Korean bodyguards and 100 of his most trustworthy followers to end nearly thirteen years in exile. Within two days, he had broken his pledge to the Khmer Rouge, giving full vent to the rage he had suppressed while the Khmer Rouge army was vital to his plans for Cambodian renewal. At a news conference on November 16, he endorsed the prosecution of the Khmer Rouge leadership for inhumane acts, declaring, "I support 100 percent the idea of setting up a tribunal to judge, to condemn, the Khmer Rouge leaders, the ones who are responsible for the deaths of so many innocent people. I don't trust them. I don't believe them. We have to control them very tightly." In a surprise announcement on November 20, 1991, Hun Sen appointed Sihanouk president of Cambodia, pending the 1993 elections. Three days later Sihanouk delegated the position of party leader of the National United Front for an Independent, Neutral, Peaceful, and Cooperative Cambodia to his son Prince Norodom Ranariddh, who planned to form a bipartite government with Hun Sen, with no slots reserved for the Khmer Rouge.

Although Sihanouk had claimed to be a neutral figure in the election, which ended in victory for Prince Norodom Ranariddh's party in May 1993, he announced, and hours later retracted, a plan to control Cambodia's coalition government as its prime minister, head of state, and military leader. By most accounts, Sihanouk's plan fell through because he failed to win over his son's royalist opposition party. The coalition's collapse "left people angry and confused at a time when Cambodians should have been allowed to celebrate the success of their elections," a senior UN official told Philip Shenon, as quoted in *The New York Times* (June 6, 1993). "The image we're left with is of this old autocrat who will not share power with anyone, not even with his own son." Nonetheless, Sihanouk has remained, in Shenon's words, "the most beloved figure in the country."

Many Cambodians, however, have expressed concern about Sihanouk's frequent—and occasionally prolonged—absences from the country, for medical treatment or on private visits to his homes in China and North Korea. It was only after intense pressure from world leaders, among them the UN secretary general, Boutros Boutros-Ghali, and President Frangois Mitterrand of France, that Sihanouk returned from a trip to Beijing in time for the May 1993 elections. "His absences may seem a minor issue, but the fact that he will not remain in Phnom Penh for any extended period is very worrying to the public," an Asian diplomat told Philip Shenon, explaining that they fear their leader may abandon them altogether.

After the May 1993 elections, an interim government with Prince Ranariddh and Hun Sen sharing power was put in place until a constitution could be enacted by the new 120-member National Assembly. The new constitution called for the return of Sihanouk to the throne as king and put Ranariddh and Hun Sen in place as first and second prime minister, respectively, and on September 24, 1993, Sihanouk was crowned for the second time. His government immediately received formal diplomatic recognition from the United States. The major challenge facing King Sihanouk is negotiating an accord with the Khmer Rouge, who were left out of the coalition government and are still fighting in parts of Cambodia.

King Norodom Sihanouk stands about five and a half feet tall and has brown eyes and gray hair. His chubby frame, moonish face, and ready smile have always given him a pixieish appearance. He typically delivers his frequently long-winded addresses in a monotonous, high-pitched voice. Sihanouk has been described as volatile, irrepressible, ebullient, and unpredictable. Resentful of what he believes is the Western sense of superiority, Sihanouk complained to William Attwood, the editor in chief of *Look* (April 2, 1968), "[The American reporters] always talk about 'tiny' Cambodia—'the pocket kingdom.' They never say 'tiny' Belgium, which is smaller, and what about that so-called country of Grace Kelly's? It's racism. Those little European countries are white, and we are yellow and 'backward.'" In Newsweek (September 12, 1966), an unidentified analyst described the prince's attitude this way: "Sihanouk's concern for what the press says about him may seem obsessive, but he does accept criticism. What he can't stand is writers treating Cambodia like a joke."

An accomplished musician and composer, Sihanouk plays the piano, accordion, and saxophone, and he has written a number of songs and military marches. He also enjoys playing badminton and preparing French cuisine. He wrote, scored, produced, directed, and/or starred in numerous motion pictures, including *Preah Vihear* (1967), a romantic wartime melodrama co-starring his wife, the former Monique Izzi, and featuring his then-defense minister, Nkiek Tioulong, as the villain. *Shadow over Angkor* (1968) was based loosely on the true story of an abortive coup in Cambodia in 1959; in the film, Sihanouk's character thwarts an American plot to divide the country.

On July 6, 2004, Sihanouk announced his plans to abdicate as King, citing a recent political stalemate as the reason. A coalition government was then formed.

PERSONAL LIFE

As a young man Sihanouk took advantage of the Cambodian royal custom of maintaining many wives and concubines. While in exile in China in the early 1970s, he claimed that he had settled down. "Before, I spent too much time playing with music, with moviemaking, and with mistresses," he told John Burns of the *Toronto Globe and Mail* (August 18, 1973), "but now I am like a Buddha—I am faithful to my wife, I have no love adventures, no sports cars, and no dancing parties." He and Princess Monique have two children; he also has more than a dozen children by his previous wives. Sihanouk was the author of several books, among them *Chronicles of War and Hope* (1979), about the Khmer Rouge regime. His religion is Buddhism. Sihanouk died of a heart attack on October 15, 2012.

FURTHER READING

London Observer p!2 Ap 20 '75 por; *Newsweek 118:29;N 25 '91 pors; New Yorker 40:150+ Ap 18 '64, 43:66+ Ja 13 '68; N Y Post p28 N 11 '67 por, p39 Mr 19 '70 por; The New York Times p5 Mr 19 '64, p4 D 11 '67 por, A plO fa 9 '79, A p6 O 25 '91 por; Parade p4+ Jl 8 '73 por; International Who's Who, 1993-94; International Yearbook and Statesmen's Who's Who, 1992; Lacouture, Jean. The Demigods: Charismatic Leadership in the Third World (1970)*

SIR BEN SMITH

British Government Official

Born: January 29, 1879
Died: May 5, 1964

INTRODUCTION

The important post of the Minister of Food in the Attlee Labor Government of the United Kingdom was given in July 1945 to one of the most colorful Members of Parliament, Sir Ben Smith, A former sailor, merchant seaman, cab driver, dockyard worker, and union organizer, "Big Ben" Smith had been knighted in June for his work during the wartime coalition Government of Winston Churchill.

EARLY LIFE

Born in 1879 to Mr. and Mrs. Richard Smith, the future M.P. was named simply Ben. Like many boys of working-class families, he left home at an early age, in his case eleven, to enter the Royal Navy. While serving as ship's boy on the training ship H.M.S. *Warspite* for fifteen shillings (less than four dollars) a month, the tall young boy was for a year middle-weight champion of the Royal Navy lower-deck. Soon afterward he turned to the Merchant Navy, becoming cook on a topsail schooner, in the days when, as he recalls, "We had to float our biscuits on top of the hot tea so as to frighten off the weevils."

LIFE'S WORK

At twenty, Smith was married to Mildred Ellen Edison of Peckham and left the sea. (The Smiths now have two sons.) "Necessity rather than choice" forced him to become a cabby. In 1906 Smith gave up his horse for an automobile, which was one of the first taxis in London. "In those days," says George Darling of the BBC, "the taxi-men were not only exploited by hard hire-purchase [installment buying] terms and low fares, but they made the exploitation worse by cutting each other's livelihood. Altogether the conditions were such an offense to Ben Smith's practical common sense that he started organizing his fellow cabbies to cooperate for standard fares and agreements and the promise of a decent living." He became an official of the new union, and in 1920, when it was merged with several others to form the huge Transport and General Workers' Union, he continued as an organizer.

To quote Darling again, "Ben Smith worked among the dock workers on London's riverside and the men who run London's ubiquitous bus services, for dockers and road transport operators are the backbone of the union. He did more organizing than negotiating. His job was to make the union strong and make the members aware of its strength. He suited London's transport workers."

"He looked like a union organizer, tough, bluff, and strong, but the men he worked with learned also to respect his mind. He has a surprising grasp of industrial technique and organization and like most of Britain's trade union officials he is keenly interested in local government. The dockers elected him to the Bermondsey Borough Council. Bermondsey is a poor district on the south side of the Thames, stretching from London Bridge down below the network of the Surrey Commercial Docks. Waterside workers, mechanics, railwaymen, workers in London's markets, warehouses, and back street factories live there, and Ben Smith has served them well. He is still an alderman of the borough."

In 1923 Alderman Smith was elected to Parliament from the Rotherhithe Division of Bermondsey, and continued to serve there for eight years. In 1925 he was chosen Labor Party whip, thus making him responsible for party discipline and attendance; the party whip is also responsible, usually, for obtaining pairs for members who cannot be present when a vote is taken. In 1924 he led a procession of hired vehicles through Hyde Park, which had been reserved for private carriages for three hundred years. Later he became general manager of his union, which has been described as probably the largest in the world. In the Ramsay MacDonald Labor Government of 1929-31, the unionist was Treasurer of the Royal Household—a post in which he, like two fellow Laborites, wore a resplendent uniform, complete with ceremonial sword and wand of office. King George V allowed Smith and the others to keep the wands for souvenirs when the Government resigned, and also presented them with photographs of himself and Queen Mary. During a vacation, incidentally, the Smiths toured Egypt and Palestine, in company with another Labor M.P., traveling both ways by tanker.

Smith lost his seat in the Conservative landslide of 1931, after Prime Minister MacDonald left his party. While out of office Smith contested the Clay Cross, Derbyshire, by-election, but without success. In 1935 he won back his seat for Rotherhithe, defeating Nora Runge. Back in Parliament, he entered vigorously into debate on his subjects of shipping, railways, and road haulage. (Smith is vice-chairman for roads of the Safety First Association, an executive member of the Roads Improvement Association, a member of the London Traffic Advisory Committee, and an associate of the Institute of Transport.) In. 1937 the Laborite was in the news as he led an unsuccessful deputation of protest to the Home Secretary, Sir Samuel Hoare '40, asking him

not to permit the British Fascists to march through South London. Later that year the M.P. charged that he had been enrolled as a constable of West Hartlepool, without his consent, in an attempt to curb his trade union activities, a charge denied by the mayor and town council.

When the Second World War broke out Smith, then sixty, took an active part in recruiting drives. After Lord Beaverbrook M0 became Minister of Aircraft Production in the all-party War Cabinet headed by Winston Churchill '42, he "looked round for the toughest trade union leader he could find to . . . smooth out all the appalling labor difficulties," and chose Ben Smith. In July 1940, when, Smith entered on his unpaid duties as honorary labor adviser to the Aircraft Ministry, the Germans had smashed through Belgium, the Netherlands, and France, had driven the Allied armies into the Dunkerque retreat, and only the ill-equipped RAF and the English Channel stood between Britain and an enemy astride the Continent. When Beaverbrook undertook to speed up the production of Spitfires and Hurricanes, "the speed and urgency of the job created a welter of labor problems. Green labor, mostly conscripted women and girls, had to be trained, billeted, settled into jobs, put on a ten-hour day, seven-day week schedule. New wage rates had to be fixed somehow, and canteens provided in the factories; shop committees had to be set up, and a thousand other jobs done." In the Cabinet shuffle of March 1942 Smith's two years of work on these problems were recognized, and he was elevated to the junior ministry as Parliamentary secretary to the Ministry of Aircraft Production. "Since then," says Darling, "he has repeatedly surprised everybody with his clear understanding of the complex technical organization of the aircraft industry. He became a big-business executive, helping to direct at the top an industry which now [1944] produces thirty-five hundred aircraft a month." Smith also did some work in Civil Defense, and in 1941 he obtained from the Ministry of Health redress for the captured British seamen who had been freed from the prison ship *Altmark* by Captain Philip Vian, only to find that they were asked to make up the insurance payments they had missed or lose their pension rights.

In 1943 Smith was made a member of the Privy Council, and in November of that year was appointed Minister Resident for Supply in Washington, D.C., to succeed Colonel John Llewellin. After he had been in the United States for eleven weeks, working hard at four jobs (chairman of the British Supply Council in North America and of the Principal Commonwealth Supply

Committee, British member of the UNRRA Committee on Supply, and senior alternate member on the UNRRA council), a London *Daily Express* correspondent asked Americans what they thought of Smith. Said the columnist Marquis Childs '43: "He speaks straight from the shoulder, more than any other man you have sent here. He is tremendously shrewd. He has worked very quietly, but effectively." Smith had impressed a group of editors of industrial publications with his knowledge of technical trade matters; and an unidentified official was quoted as saying, "Ben Smith is the finest shipment of reverse Lend-Lease ever sent here from the Old Country." After Smith resigned in May 1945 in order to campaign for re-election, and was knighted (K.B.E.) in June for his services, he was mentioned as the most likely choice to succeed Lord Halifax as Ambassador to the United States, should the Attlee Government be unable to resist pressure to remove the Conservative appointee. Sir Ben was, however, chosen for the difficult and important post of Food Minister, again succeeding Colonel Llewellin.

"In his first press conference," to quote an American reporter, "Sir Ben was faced with the task of telling the British that, although the war is over, the sacrifices are not." Postwar rationing in Britain became even more severe after V-J Day. There was less meat, fats, and cheese; and the supply of dried eggs, which had largely replaced shell eggs in the British menu, was cut after the termination of Lend-Lease. Serious as Britain's economic position was, it was better than most of the rest of Europe, and her leaders felt the need of dipping into their own depleted rations to help maintain life on the Continent. One of the Food Minister's first announcements was that Britain would lend France fifty thousand tons of refined sugar and ten thousand tons of margarine, to be repaid later in raw sugar and ground nuts.

PERSONAL LIFE

Sir Ben Smith's most obvious quality was said to be his toughness. "He stands well over six feet and in spite of his years his back is straight and broad, like a Guardsman's. He looks aggressive, although he is really a mild-mannered good fellow, one of the most popular members of the House of Commons, ever ready to entertain his friends with a never-ending flow of good stories and personal anecdotes." He was described as looking much younger than his years, and as being one of the best boxers and jujitsu artists among men of his age. Smith was a member of the City Livery and Royal Automobile clubs, and was a Liveryman of the City of London: he belonged to the Bakers' and Carmens' companies, two of the medieval guilds, which in these days carry on charitable work and elect certain officials, including the Lord Mayor. The Food Minister was given to wearing somber clothes and a wide-brimmed black hat, and had what the British call "a distinctive taste in stickpins."

FURTHER READING

N Y Herald Tribune II p3 D 19 '43 por; *The New York Times* pl4 N 12 '43; *International Who's Who*, 1942; *Who's Who*, 1945

ALI SOHEILI

Iranian Statesman

Born: 1896; Tabriz, Iran
Died: 1958; London, United Kingdom
Affiliation: Party for Progress

INTRODUCTION

The Middle Eastern state of Iran, the ancient kingdom known as Persia, was the scene of a "diplomatic tug of war" between Germany and the Allies until late in 1941 when Allied pressure forced out the Axis interests. Although the culture of Iran antedates the culture of the Western world, the twentieth century country is primitive by Occidental standards, with a low literacy rate, poor transportation, undeveloped natural resources (except for those, such as the Iranian Oil Company, which have been developed by foreign capital under foreign supervision), and with a largely nomadic population. The capital, Teheran, however, is a modern city on the surface, at least, and it is there that Ali Soheili as Prime Minister directed Iranian cooperation with the Allies. It was there, too, that the famed Teheran conference took place in late 1943.

EARLY LIFE

Ali Soheili was born in Iran in 1897 and educated at Tehran University. He entered public life early and rose to head the Iran-Soviet Fisheries Department and then to act as secretary to the Minister of the Interior. From 1931 to 1936 he was Under-Secretary of State for Foreign Affairs, and in 1936 he went to London as Iranian Minister to Great Britain. In 1938 he returned to Iran to take his place in the Cabinet as Minister of Foreign Affairs; two years later he added the portfolio of the Minister of the Interior.

Soheili is a statesman of the new Iranian regime dating from 1925, when the old Sultan was deposed and the insurgent faction chose as their king (Shah) the Prime Minister, Riza Shah Pahlavi. Although the Shah was made supreme ruler to be succeeded by his son, by virtue of having placed him in office his Parliament had more power than the Majlis (the Iranian legislative body elected for two years) had hitherto enjoyed. Under the new system, like the old, the Shah chose the Prime Minister, but only if he were acceptable-to the Majlis could he form a Cabinet.

The new Shah proceeded to modernize Teheran, build railroads, and encourage education. He drove a sharp bargain with the British, abrogating previous agreements with the Anglo-Iranian Oil Company, and he secured an annual revenue of from ten to twelve million dollars from the development, although it still remained in British control. British-Iranian amity, however, subsequently declined (despite Soheili's efforts to maintain amity during his 1936 to 1938 tenure in London). The Trans-Iranian railway completed in 1938 was regarded by many to indicate Iranian fear of British invasion because it avoided all cities, with the exception of Teheran, and did not run near the oil fields or the fertile farming districts. It could have, therefore, little other purpose than to serve as a military line.

When Soheili returned to Iran in 1938 he found Anglo-Iranian unfriendliness stronger than ever. The Iranian Government had granted a commercial aviation concession to the German-owned Lufthansa instead of to the British Imperial Airways and had given its order for sloops and gunboats for the small Iranian Navy to Italian shipyards. The money for these projects all came from the royalties on the British oil developments, and when the Second World War broke out the British had to face the possibility that they would be opposed by an Iranian army of 150,000 to 190,000 men, all equipped and trained with money received from the British in royalties.

The struggle for control of Iran and her resources started out as a three-cornered one, with Russia reportedly on Germany's side at first, and then pulling with British interests. In May 1941 it was reported that Russia and Germany were arranging some "joint action in the Middle East," and the Soviet Army began spring maneuvers with a considerable concentration of troops at Tashkent, near the Iranian frontier. Early in June hundreds of German "fifth columnists" were reported to have visited Iran with Russia's consent, so that the two countries could share the benefits of the Iranian oil fields. By June 7, however, the "Russo-German negotiations" had broken down. As Minister of the Interior and Foreign Affairs, Ali Soheili met frequently with representatives of the British, Russian, and German interests, although the decision as to the fate of Iran did not seem really to be in his government's hands.

After the invasion of Russia by Germany, on June 22, 1941 the Russians and the British coordinated their pressure on Iran to drive out the Germans. In August the Iranian Government replied to an Anglo-Soviet ultimatum demanding the expulsion of some 5,000 German "tourists and technicians" with a "belligerent" note indicating that they would be turned out only when the Iranian Government convinced itself they were a menace, and not before. Later the same month British and Russian troops made simultaneous advances into Iran. The Iranian Minister to the United States, Mohammed Schayesteh, called upon the State Department to say that the invasion was based on a pretext and that Iran was a remote country, not dangerous to either side, and entitled to neutrality. The Premier, Ali Khan Mansur, told an extraordinary session of the Majlis that all necessary precautions had been taken and that Iran would resist the British and Russian attack by land, sea, and air.

In less than twenty-four hours the British forces had taken control of the world's largest oil refinery plant at Abadan and had captured the entire Iranian Navy.; they had seized the strategic wireless station at Muhammereh, and had trapped several Axis merchant ships in the harbor at Bandar Shahpur. After a futile attempt to stop the war by guaranteeing that all Germans except a few at indispensable technical posts would be ousted within a week, the Cabinet of Prime Minister Mansur resigned and a reorganized Iranian Government was formed by Ali Furanghi. The new Prime Minister, a famous Iranian philosopher and once president of the League of Nation's Assembly, announced to the Majlis that the troops had been ordered to cease firing. In his Cabinet Furanghi retained Soheili as Minister of Foreign Affairs. (According to Andre Visson, Soheili belongs to the "'old gang' of self-interested politicians.")

Although actual fighting had ceased, the Russians and the British continued their advance until they met at Sinneh in Western Iran, cutting off Iran from Turkey. Furanghi had accepted the armistice terms of August 30, 1941 but he balked at a stiffer note of September 8 which provided for mass expulsion of Axis nationals, closing of Axis legations, and the occupation of strategic points by the Russian and English forces. The agreement was signed, but Riza Shah delayed in carrying out the terms. When a series of tribal uprisings threatened the stability of his Government, and when Persian-language broadcasts from Great Britain urged the Iranian people to turn against their cruel and autocratic leader, Riza Shah abdicated in favor of his son, who is married to a sister of the King of Egypt and who is considered friendly to the English. The former Shah retired first to the island of Mauritius and later received permission to settle in Canada. The Allies considered his abdication their first major gain in safeguarding "the Indian frontier and the back door to the Middle East." The Russians, who isolated the three northern provinces of Azerbaijan, Guilan, and Khorassan, think of Iran as their Burma Road, on which moves the flood of American-British supplies. The British occupied the southern provinces "to help the Russians, but partly also to assure themselves that the presence of the Russian forces will not endanger British post-War interests on the Persian Gulf shores. American troops are stationed there to guarantee the protection of American supplies moved to Russia."

Upon the Shah's abdication the Majlis seized the opportunity to demand the establishment of a constitutional government, recognition of civil rights, reform of the nation's finances, release of political prisoners, and the return to their owners of illegally seized property. The new Shah acceded and on September 21 Furanghi formed a new Cabinet which had seven new members. Ali Soheili, however, remained as Minister of Foreign Affairs. The new Shah made a radio broadcast praising the democratic form of government. In January 1942 the Iranian Government signed an Anglo-Soviet pact binding the fortunes of Iran with those of Britain and the Soviet Union "for not longer than six months after the end of the War." Opinion in London was that although the people of Iran were unenthusiastic over the treaty provisions, it was a useful document for the United Nations and would "in the long run" secure good will in the Near East. The sincerity of the Soviet pledge to respect the independence and Integrity of Iran was unofficially questioned in Britain and America, however, especially since the economic situation in the Soviet-occupied north ("superior to what it was in the days of Riza Shah," according to Visson) contrasted so favorably with the "economic chaos" of the areas under British control as to contribute to the rise of Russian credit with the Iranian peasants.

In February 1942 the British changed "Iran" (which the Irani call themselves) to "Persia" in official documents. Ali Furanghi's Government proved itself increasingly unstable. Furanghi had formed several Cabinets by the summer of 1942, when Ali Soheili became Prime Minister with a Cabinet which lasted for a few months. During this time Soheili announced that Iran would welcome a post-War Polish refugee colony if the colonists would apply for Persian citizenship. In August the Soheili Cabinet fell, and Ahmed Qavam Sultaneh tried to form a government, but without lasting success.

Premier Sultaneh appointed Ali Soheili as Ambassador to Afghanistan, but before Soheili finished the preparations for leaving for his new post the Sultaneh Cabinet resigned, and the Shah asked Soheili to try his hand again at forming a Cabinet. Much of the difficulty was said to have been purely because of internal questions, chiefly differences over constitutional procedure.

In the middle of February 1943 Soheili succeeded in forming a Cabinet. When he opened the Majlis he received a strong vote of' confidence following a speech in which he said that there was "no reason to be alarmed because the Americans came to execute works to help their Allies." He continued: "The United States Government and people belong to those unselfish and liberal people and government which never refused to give all assistance to others in trouble." Soheili received eighty-nine of the ninety-five votes and was expected to maintain a firm government. In April 1943 a reciprocal trade agreement was signed by Secretary of State Hull and Mohammed Shayesteh, the Iranian Minister; and in September Soheili, now Prime Minister of Iran, declared war on Germany. This move assured his country Lend-Lease aid and a seat at the peace table.

The Teheran conference late in November 1943 brought forth an Anglo-American-Rus-sian statement concerning Iran that banished worries about Russia's intentions in that country. Iran's independence and territorial integrity was guaranteed. Next, in December, it was reported that Soheili had presented his resignation to the Shah. "The move was believed designed to permit reanimation of the Cabinet in accordance with new political conditions in Iran resulting from the recent tri-power conference there. Iran Cabinet members also submitted their resignations, and political circles said the Shah was expected to ask Premier Soheili to form a new government that would show few changes."

PERSONAL LIFE

Little is known, but it is written that Soheili was well versed in fine arts, specifically music and painting. He died of cancer in London at the age of 62.

FURTHER READING

N Y Herald Tribune II p4 J1 4 '43; p4 D 12 '43; *The New York Times* p8 F 36 '43; *International Who's Who* 1942

PAUL-HENRI SPAAK

Belgian Government Official

Born: January 25, 1899; Schaerbeek, Belgium
Died: July 31, 1972; Belgium
Affiliation: Belgian Workers' Party; Belgian Socialist Party

INTRODUCTION

Paul-Henri Spaak was an influential Belgian politician and statesman. He was considered one of the founding fathers of the European Union. Spaak served in World War I and after the war became a lawyer, famous for his high-profile cases. He served as Belgium's foreign minister for 18 years, among other titles.

EARLY LIFE

The Belgian Foreign Minister, Paul-Henri Spaak, was born in Brussels on January 25, 1899. His father Paul Spaak, a well known poet, was director of the Brussels opera, the Theatre Royale de la Monnaie; his mother, an active Socialist, was Belgium's first woman Senator. Former Prime Minister Paul Emile Janson is his uncle. Paul-Henri was only fifteen when the Germans invaded Belgium in August 1914. Two years later, at seventeen, he was caught trying to cross the Dutch border in order to rejoin the Belgian Army on the Yser, and was therefore interned until the end of the war. After the war young Spaak studied law at the Universite Libre de Bruxelles, a liberal-minded institution which became important when the Belgian Relief Commission under Herbert Hoover presented it with their thirty-million-dollar surplus. The gift was made to the non-sectarian University of Brussels, rather than to one of the more prominent universities, because of political considerations. To this day, it is reported, there are annual street fights between students of Brussels and those of the Catholic University of Louvain.

Spaak received his LL.D. and was called to the bar at Brussels, where he practiced "brilliantly." He was an outstanding tennis player, too, and in 1922 was a member of the Belgian team in international competition. A Socialist like his mother, an eloquent speaker, and "a bit of a firebrand," in 1932 the thirty-three-year-old lawyer was elected Socialist Deputy for Brussels to the Chamber of Representatives of the Belgian Parliament, in which he has served ever since. Two years later he joined the staff of a revolutionary weekly, *l'Action civique*; he became co-editor. In March 1935 he accepted the post of Minister of Transportation, Posts and Telegraph in the Cabinet of progressive Paul van Zeeland—a coalition government, like most Belgian cabinets, which lasted until June. When Van Zeeland again became Prime Minister in 1936 Spaak was chosen Minister of Foreign Affairs. At thirty-seven he was one of the youngest foreign ministers in Belgian history.

The year 1936 was one of universal rearmament, the year of the founding of the Rome-Berlin-Tokyo Axis. "As in the hectic prewar days," to quote the historian F. L. Benns, "the vicious cycle of national fear and resultant increased armaments was once more present to undermine the peace of the world." In October Belgium announced her determination to resume a policy of neutrality, while at the same time increasing her military establishment to protect her neutrality. Both Britain and France promised Belgium their military support in case of unprovoked aggression. Foreign Minister Spaak and King Leopold conducted the negotiations which resulted, in April 1937, in those two powers releasing

Paul-Henri Spaak.

Belgium from her obligations under the Locarno Pact of 1925 and the Anglo-Franco-Belgian Agreement of 1936, while reaffirming their protection of her neutrality.

In 1937 Spaak was chairman of the Nine-Power Conference in Brussels on Far Eastern Questions. In November 1937 the Van Zeeland Government was succeeded by that of Spaak's uncle, the Liberal Paul Emile Janson, described as "something of an isolationist in foreign policy and a reformer in internal affairs." When this Government fell Paul-Henri Spaak became Premier; his Government lasted from May 1938 to February 1939, when he was succeeded by the Catholic Conservative Plubert Pier lot.

According to Lemuel F. Parton in the New York *Sun,* "as Spaak rose in politics, he moved more to middle ground, admitting the need for organization and discipline and pioneering authoritarian democracy," what Spaak himself termed "adapting democratic institutions to modern realities." Says Parton, "He has been effective against both the Communists and Fascists [Leon Degrelle's Rexists], although his political enemies insisted that his allegiance was shifting to the latter when he aided in severing Belgium's old alliance with Britain, as he urged a defensive alliance of small neutral countries. This, it would appear, has been elaborately disproved."

On September 3, 1939, the day Britain and France declared war on Germany, Deputy Spaak was again appointed Minister of Foreign Affairs. Eight months later, on May 10, 1940, German troops marched into Belgium, Luxembourg, and the Netherlands, "in defiance of solemn engagements which Germany had renewed a few days before the invasion"; four hours later German Ambassador Biilow-Schwante called on Foreign Minister Spaak to notify him of the fact. At the end of the eighteen-day battle of Belgium, Spaak and the other Cabinet ministers went to France, where they were interned. After France was attacked Spaak and Prime Minister Pierlot escaped across the Spanish border on their second try. In Spain they were again kept in "enforced residence," reportedly on the demand of Nazi agents. After two months Spaak and Pierlot made their escape, and dodged the Gestapo for the five days it took them to reach Lisbon. On October 22, 1940, the two reached London, where Spaak took up the duties of Foreign Minister and Minister of Labor in the Belgian Government-in-Exile.

In June 1942 Paul-Henri Spaak and British Foreign Secretary Anthony Eden signed two treaties, formalizing the agreements by which Belgian forces in Africa were to operate under the Supreme Command of the United Nations, and by which the British were to purchase all the gold, copper, and rubber produced in the Belgian Congo. At this time the Belgians had one squadron in the air and another forming. "They have contributed an extraordinarily large percentage to the fight against Germany," cabled *The New York Times* reporter. "The Germans would love to know the number of Belgians who are fighting against them in proportion to the number of Belgians at home; the Germans would love to know this because they would base their atrocities accordingly." Later, in February 1943, Spaak broadcast to the Belgian people the news that the Government "would continue her economic understanding with Luxembourg and would be ready to join in new and closer ties with the Netherlands and France, as well as endeavoring both in Europe and Africa to tie up her interests with Britain." That November Spaak headed the Belgian delegation to the United Nations

Relief and Rehabilitation Administration Conference at Atlantic City, New Jersey, where he presided over the first meeting of the Committee on Organization and Administration.

In September 1944 Belgium was liberated, and later Spaak returned to London to "talk Western power bloc" with Anthony Eden, as *Time* put it. "The benefits of such a West European power bloc were chiefly political, but there were others: (1) Belgium and Holland have planned a trade agreement which is virtually a customs union, specifically designed with collaboration of France and Britain in mind; (2) Belgium hopes to coordinate her military policy with Britain's, pool her air force with the RAF." At this time Spaak was described by *Newsweek* as "the most popular and respected member of the Government." In London, in November 1944, he told newsmen that he had discussed "immediately equipping a Belgian Army so that it can participate in the occupation of Germany next spring." According to reports of the projected "Western bloc" (a term Spaak deprecates), France would maintain a strong army, Britain a powerful fleet and air force, while "Belgium and Holland would waive their former [prewar] attitude of neutrality to provide air bases near Germany's borders. After the Allied forces have been withdrawn entirely from Germany, this arrangement would give the Western alliance a combination able to act quickly in concert by sea, land, and air." Belgium made known, too, her reservation of the right to demand portions of former German territory. Wrote Homer Metz, "A coterie of extreme Belgian nationalists has agitated for a frontier on the Rhine for generations. Yet very few Belgians now believe that this would provide more than a tissue-paper bulwark against the renascent German militarism. If certain reports coming out of Europe are to be credited, Belgium is talking about extending its hegemony eastward chiefly because it wants a diplomatic weapon to counter what it fancies are threats to its independence in the collective security envisaged by the United Nations." This writer cites a dispatch from Brussels to the effect that "the Belgians also are somewhat apprehensive over what they believe may be imperialistic ambitions on the part of France. . . .The Belgians still remember Napoleon . . . and the spread of communism in France also worries them."

Like other swiftly liberated countries, Belgium was suffering from a completely disorganized economy after the fighting had moved on past her borders, which led to a four-day uprising at the end of November.

Andre Visson, describing Premier Pierlot as "honest, tired, and weak," stated that the two strongest men of the Cabinet were Spaak, who had the confidence of the trade unions, and Camille Gutt, the Conservative Minister of Finance. Alexander H. Uhl wrote in *PM*: "This crisis has all the characteristics of the late nineteen-thirties—the demonstrations in the streets, the placards denouncing the Government, the gendarmes too handy with their rifles, and the scared little men in Parliament seeing the revolution around the corner. Actually what you have is a Parliament whose mandate expired more than a year ago coming back to power as though the war and the occupation hadn't happened, and a Communist and working-class resistance group beating its head in frustration against what it feels is a stone wall of Belgian reaction."

A *PM* editorial by Blair Bolles headed "The People Can't Win Without Some Help" complained that "Belgian Socialists, represented in the Government chiefly by Foreign Minister Paul-Henri Spaak, have the name but not the inclination of radicals. It is a watered-down party, and Spaak dispenses reactionary dogma out of a book with a Socialist cover." Uhl pointed out, however, in a later article that the Socialists were in an intolerable position, forced to support a Government whose policies they could not approve, because no other was available. As Spaak retorted to Uhl, it was true that the Pierlot Government did not reflect accurately the true feelings of the Belgian people—but neither did the Communists. At the same time, however, Spaak was reportedly working to create a Leftist bloc. And in February 1945 the Pierlot Cabinet was finally replaced by that of the Socialist Labor Minister, Achilles van Acker. Spaak, who was on the way to Paris at that moment, was retained as Minister of Foreign Affairs.

It was expected that a stronger Government would "help to clarify the Belgian international position," and later that month announcement was made of four international agreements Spaak had negotiated with General de Gaulle and French Foreign Minister Georges Bidault. Belgium announced also that she would support the French proposals for separation of the Ruhr Valley and the Rhineland from Germany; France had offered to let the Belgian Army take over part of the territory which, it was thought, might be the French zone of postwar occupation of the Rhineland. And in April Spaak headed the nine-man Belgian delegation to the United Nations Conference on International Organization at San Francisco, which included a "former political enemy and now fast friend," the Communist, Albert Marteaux. On his departure Spaak defined the role of the small nations at the conference as "to do nothing to make more difficult an agreement between the great powers and to defend at the same time the essential interests, moral and material, which they represent." At the conference Spaak was chairman of one of the four commissions, that on general provisions. "M. Spaak is becoming one of the important voices in the conference," reported Anne O'Hare McCormick. "He is eloquent, active, and conciliatory. He was one of the half-dozen who voted with Russia on [refusing to admit] Argentina, and in the Steering Committee he supports the view of one of the Big Four on this issue and another on that. M. Spaak will be worth watching."

Back in Brussels Spaak addressed the Socialist Party Congress in June, pointing out that the formula of a government of national unity was no longer sufficient. To this he added, "We must find a government in which all members are agreed on structural reforms. I believe that at the present time only socialism is possible. Thousands of people are unconsciously tending toward the socialist solution." The Minister also said that Belgium's food situation was better than that of other liberated countries and that his country would enter an extraordinary period of prosperity if it could solve the coal problem.

On the question of what King Leopold's position in his homeland should be following his liberation from German detention, Spaak spoke in no uncertain terms. He told the Belgian Parliament in July that the King, his former friend, leaned in Hitler's direction as early as 1940 when the monarch pronounced the Allied cause lost, differing radically with the Government. "If Belgium survives today it is because we disobeyed the King at that time," said Spaak. "All those who carried out sabotage during the occupation or worked against the Germans likewise disobeyed the king. Leopold can no longer be accepted as a symbol of unity."

Spaak went to London as Belgian delegate to the Preparatory Commission of the United Nations Organization which opened its sessions on November 25, 1945. Contrary to the opinion of many delegations he was elected second vice-chairman—not chairman of the commission. It was understood, however, that the British delegation headed by Philip J. Noel-Baker was pressing behind the scenes to achieve the election of Spaak as chairman of the General Assembly of the United Nations and that this was an important factor in the election of Dr. Zuleta-Angel of Colombia as chairman. Spaak favored a European site for the United Nations' headquarters, his main argument against choosing the United States for its future home being that the equality of the Big Five would thus be upset. Pleading against the concentration of international life in one country, since most of the other big international organizations had American headquarters, the Belgian Foreign Minister continued: "The placing of the headquarters in Europe would be an act of faith and confidence in the old Continent, which has been stricken by war. It would be a way of bringing her back to life and of showing that you believe in her resurrection to become the balance between the Old World and the New."

PERSONAL LIFE
Photographs show Paul-Henri Spaak to be a chubby, cherub-faced man, partly bald. He was described as "a brilliant lawyer, an excellent organizer and campaigner, and an eloquent orator," who "considers Marxism obsolete."

Spaak retired from Belgian politics in 1966, and he died in 1972. He remains an influential figure in European politics, with his name carried by a charitable foundation, a building of the European Parliament, and a method of negotiation.

FURTHER READING
N Y Sun p22 O 24 '40; Who's Who of the Allied Governments, 1943

JOSEPH STALIN

Secretary of the Central Committee of the Communist Party of the U.S.S.R.; Former Premier

Born: Dec. 21, 1879
Died: March 5, 1953; Kuntsevo Dacha, Kuntsevo, Russian SFSR, Soviet Union
Affiliation: Bolshevik Party; Communist Party of the U.S.S.R.

INTRODUCTION

Joseph Stalin, "The Man of Steel," who ruled The U.S.S.R. with an iron fist for decades until his death in 1953, left a legacy of death and terror as he turned a backward Russia into a world superpower. It has been estimated that more than 20 million people died during his brutal, dictatorial, rule. He often has been compared to Adolf Hitler, the Führer of The Third Reich.

EARLY LIFE

Born Iosif Vissarionovitch Dzhugashvili, Joseph "Stalin" was originally one of many *nom de guerre* of the revolutionary who became the longest ruling dictator of the U.S.S.R. He was born December 21, 1879, in the village of Gori, Georgia, the son of Ekaterina Georgievna (Geladze) and Vissarion Ivanovitch Dzhugashvili, a worker in a shoe factory in Tiflis (now Tbilisi), the capital of a now independent Georgia. Georgia, which forms the district of Transcaucasia (also known as "South Caucasus," a geopolitical region located on the border of Eastern Europe and Western Asia with Armenia and Azerbaijan), had long ago been independent, but under the rule of Czarist Russia at the time of Stalin's birth, it "had no right save that of being tried." It was a hotbed of separatist as well as socialist movements, and the government was anxious to educate priests to fight revolutionary ideas. In 1893, therefore, Joseph's mother, a pious member of the Orthodox Church and by this time a widow, entered her son, then known as "Sosso," in the Seminary at Tiflis. (Of his earlier years she told an American interviewer, years later: "He was always a good boy. . . I never had to punish him. He worked hard, was always reading and talking, and tried to understand everything. He went to school when he was eight.") In 1894, on the birthday of Alexander III, he sang a solo in the Orthodox Church in Tiflis—a strange beginning for a career of revolutionary activity.

Joseph Stalin.

Soon, though, the restrictions of the seminary and the system of priestly espionage made the young Georgian a rebel. He joined the revolutionary movement at the age of 15, and, by 1897, was secretly leading a Marxist circle at the seminary. Official Communist literature says that he was finally expelled from the seminary on grounds that he displayed a lack of "political balance." His mother told one interviewer that this was untrue, that she took him out on account of his health (as a young man he was tubercular), but another interviewer has quoted her differently: "I know my son rules in the Kremlin, but if he had not been naughty and turned away from God, and, been forced to leave his school, he might by now be a bishop."

From the Seminary, according to some accounts, "Sosso" went back to his job in a shoe factory;

Affiliation: Bolshevik Party

During the tumultuous years that followed, Stalin was to be arrested and exiled six times, usually for crimes far more minor than his actual offenses, and to change his name almost as frequently as his shirt. ("David" and "Koba" are the best known of the early Party aliases.) But he was to escape from exile several times, and much could happen between escapes and arrests. When the Russian Social-Democratic Party split into two factions—the Mensheviks, who believed in compromise and gradual reform, and the Bolsheviks, the extremists, led by Lenin—he became the leader of the Transcaucasian Bolsheviks. He organized demonstrations and strikes, disseminated illegal tracts, edited numerous papers, the first of them *The Fight of the Proletariat*. At the close of 1905, during the Russo-Japanese War, he traveled across European Russia as Caucasian delegate to the secret Bolshevik conference in Tammerfors (also known as "Tampere"), Finland, and established personal connections with Lenin. In St. Petersburg, that same year, he assisted in planning the unsuccessful revolution, and after its failure, when most of the other leading conspirators were forced to flee to France, England, and Switzerland, he remained in Russia.

According to Walter Duranty, who was once the Moscow Bureau Chief for *The New York Times*: "It is not too much to say that Stalin held together the Bolshevik Party in Russia during the bitter years, which followed 1906." "One of Lenin's most trusted lieutenants," in 1906, Stalin saw Lenin again as a delegate to the Russian Social-Democratic Congress in Stockholm and, in 1907, in London; and over a period of years he carried out Lenin's orders within Russia. According to many sources, he was particularly gifted at raising money for the Party by an unconventional method known as "expropriation," and, in June 1907, was supposed to have led—or, at least, organized—a successful street attack on a Tiflis bank convoy. Stalin neither confirmed nor denied this.

In January 1912, Lenin called a Social-Democratic conference at Prague, and Trotsky called a rival conference elsewhere. Stalin was elected in absentia a member of the Central Committee or governing body of the former. That same year, he worked on the newspapers *Zvesda* ("The Star") and *Pravda* ("The Truth"), and, back in St. Petersburg after another arrest, exile, and escape, he organized the small Bolshevik group in the first *Duma* (Parliament), and acted as its chief. It was during this period that he framed the policy of autonomy for racial groups and the preservation of local languages and cultures, which was published as *Marxism and the National Question*. Some say that this was the first time he signed himself "Stalin," a name which means "Man of Steel."

In March 1913, Stalin was for the sixth time arrested, and this time deported to the faraway Turukhansk region. He did not escape, but, for four years he managed to keep himself in good physical condition. After the First Revolution in 1917, when the Czarist government was overthrown, the non-Marxist Alexander Kerensky, then Minister of Justice in the newly formed Russian Provisional Government, freed all political prisoners in March 1917. Stalin returned to Petrograd [St. Petersburg], where he helped direct the destiny of the Bolsheviks before Lenin returned from Switzerland via Germany, in April. There are conflicting reports as to the position he took regarding collaboration with the new government before Lenin took an uncompromisingly revolutionary line, but in any case Stalin defended Lenin's line at the Pan-Russian Bolshevik Conference, was elected a member of the Central Committee, and in May became a member of its Politburo. When, after the events of July 3 to 5 in Petrograd (an uprising of the workers against the provisional government and the shooting of the demonstrators), Lenin and other leaders were forced to live temporarily underground; Stalin was able to remain in Petrograd. There he delivered the political report at the Sixth (illegal) Congress of the Party, which he helped to direct, and he served as a member of the Committees of Five and of Seven, which provided the political and organizational leadership of the successful insurrection that took place on October 25. The returned exiles then united with them to form the Central Executive Committee of the new Soviet Government, and it was not long afterward that peace was concluded at Brest Litovsk between Russia and Germany.

After the October Revolution, from 1917 to 1923, Stalin was People's Commissar of Nationalities, from 1919 to 1922, People's Commissar of the Workers' and Peasants' Inspection, and, from 1920 to 1923, a member of the Revolutionary War Council of the Republic. "Dispatched repeatedly to take personal charge of the

WORLD POLITICAL INNOVATORS

most critical and dangerous sectors of the far-flung battlefronts during the civil war and intervention by some 14 foreign nations," he referred to himself during this period as "a specialist for cleaning the stables of the war department." Lenin, according to Albert Carr, "used Stalin's tactical skill and supreme organizing ability to get the best results from Trotsky's strategy."

Stalin, however, remembered Trotsky's Menshevik past (he had not been admitted to the Bolshevik Party until the summer of 1917), regarded him as an undependable and self-willed intellectual. Trotsky, in turn, thought of Stalin as "the most eminent mediocrity of our Party," dull and crude. There was continual dissension between them. Late in 1918, for instance, Stalin, who had been rebuilding the shattered army at Tsaritsin (Volgograd), ruthlessly purging it of disloyal elements, was recalled after quarrels with Trotsky over his

methods, and it was not until Tsaritsin fell into General Pyotr Nikolayevich Wrangel's hands that Stalin was given an independent command (Wrangel was the commanding general of the anti-Bolshevik White Army in Southern Russia in the later stages of the civil war). General Anton Denikin's troops in the White Army, as a result, were finally driven back to the Black Sea, and Stalin received the Order of the Red Banner, highest military distinction in Soviet Russia. Some of the other military successes with which he had been credited are the defeat of General Yudenitch's forces near Petrograd, in the spring of 1919, the working out of the strategy of the First Cavalry Army against the Polish invasion of the Ukraine in 1920, and the crushing of the mutiny of the Kronstadt sailors in 1921. But it was the more spectacularly active Trotsky who was the military idol of the day.

Affiliation: Communist Party of the U.S.S.R.

In 1922, on Zinoviev's proposal, Stalin was made Secretary of the Central Committee of the Communist Party, a position to which he had been re-elected ever since until close to his death, in 1953. Up to that time the position of Party Secretary had not been extremely important, but, once in control, he had "the enormous advantage of running the Party mechanism, and to some extent of controlling patronage." His methods of solidifying his position were likened by many commentators to those of a political boss in the United States.

A current saying in Moscow, in 1922, was: "Lenin trusts Stalin; Stalin trusts no one." In 1923, when Lenin's possible successor was being discussed, *The New York Times* correspondent predicted that it would be "the must trusted of all . . . the present Commissar of Nationalities, Stalin. . . Of all the Soviet notables, he is the least visible to outsiders. Trotsky . . . and many other Commissars have been close enough to Lenin, but his real intimate is Stalin." Walter Duranty, too, wrote: "During the last year, Stalin has shown judgment and analytical power not unworthy of Lenin. . . Suppose today Stalin outlines a policy that he thinks should be adopted; others criticize it—Stalin answers."

They proved better prophets than most, whatever the truth of the story of "Lenin's last testament" may be. Of this document, which was supposed to have

been placed in the safekeeping of Lenin's wife in December 1922, to have been read by Stalin himself at a gathering of 19 members of the Central Committee after Lenin's death, and to have later been suppressed, there are at least six slightly different versions outside the Soviet Union. One reads: "Comrade Stalin, having become General Secretary of the Party, has concentrated tremendous power in his hands, and I am not sure he always knows how to use that power with sufficient caution. . . Stalin is too rude. . . I propose to the comrades to find a way of removing Stalin. . . From the point of view of preventing a split in the Party, and from the point of view of the relations between Stalin and Trotsky . . . it is not a trifle, or it is a trifle that may acquire decisive significance." Stalin, it was said, offered to resign, but there was a unanimous vote in favor of his remaining at his post, particularly in view of the fact that Trotsky was also criticized for his "non-Bolshevik past," and no alternative recommendation made.

During the next years, with the country devastated and impoverished and opposition to the Soviet power, particularly among the peasants, by no means at an end, it was necessary to construct the new economic system and to industrialize at one and the same time. Lenin had already initiated the New Economic Policy

---

Affiliation: Communist Party of the U.S.S.R. *(Continued)*

(N.E.P.), under which private capital and the new State and cooperative industries temporarily competed with one another. The policy of the government was to continue this policy and to behave leniently toward the *kulaks* (the rich peasants) until the State industries and agricultural collectives were in a position to take care of the great part of the population's needs by themselves. Trotsky and others (the "Ultra-Left" minority within the Communist Party) believed in greater speed in socialization, questioned the possibility of "building socialism in a single State," and attempted to organize opposition outside the Party, as well as within its councils. In November 1927, Trotsky, who in January 1925, had been forced to resign as Commissar of War

(though Stalin had refused to let him be expelled from the Politburo), attempted to convert the annual celebration of the anniversary of the Revolution into a mass demonstration against Stalin. The attempt failed; the next month he and 70-odd leading members of the opposition were expelled from the Communist Party, and, in January 1928, they were exiled. (Trotsky, during his Mexican exile, until his death in 1940, made pronouncements and wrote articles and books defending himself as a true follower of Lenin, and accused Stalin of having "betrayed the Revolution." His followers, though split into many quarreling factions, were united on one thing: Uncompromising opposition to the Stalinists.)

---

according to others, to work as a bookkeeper. He also earned money as a tutor both during his student days and afterward. He had joined the Tiflis branch of the newly-organized Russian Social-Democratic Workers' Party, in 1898, and it was not long before he was a professional paid agitator. In 1900 and 1901, he led mass strikes and demonstrations in Tiflis and Batum, and had his first experience as an underground worker. Imprisoned for his activities and deported to Eastern Siberia, he escaped and returned to Tiflis to assume membership in the Transcaucasian District Committee of the Party and to work on various illegal periodicals.

LIFE'S WORK

By now, Stalin himself had decided the time was ripe to launch a vast program of industrialization and collectivization, and, in 1928, the First Five-Year Plan was projected. It went ahead in spite of the vast hardships that it wrought on the population, in spite of a famine brought about by peasant resistance, in spite of a new opposition from the Right, led by Nikolai Ivanovich Bukharin, which pleaded that the kulak should be allowed to "grow peacefully into socialism." It went ahead in spite of the almost unanimous assurances of the foreign press (which during the N.E.P. period had been sure that the hated theory of socialism had been abandoned in Russia) that nothing but catastrophe could result. "It is sometimes asked," Stalin said in February 1931, "whether it is not possible to slow down a bit in tempo, to retard the movement. No, comrades . . . it is necessary as far as possible

to accelerate it. . . The backward are always beaten. . . We are 50 to 100 years behind the advanced countries. We must cover this distance in ten years. Either we do this or they will crush us." In 1932, the First Five-Year Plan ended one year early with the achievement of 93 percent of its objects, according to Soviet figures, and the Second Five-Year Plan was even more ambitious. Still, however, the emphasis was on heavy industry, on the materials of further production and of war, rather than consumers' goods. The average Soviet citizen was getting education and security, but his standard of living, while continually rising, was still very low.

In 1934, Stalin became one of the 37 members of the Presidium of the All-Union Central Executive Committee of the U.S.S.R., his first government (rather than Communist Party) post. In 1936, the new Soviet Constitution was launched. It was as democratic as that of any of the democracies, even in American eyes, but the elections that followed were not. It was said that the growing Nazi threat was making Stalin uncertain as to the wisdom of instituting complete political democracy at that particular moment. He was also accused of encouraging a new Russian "nationalism" in order to meet it. His accomplishments were still receiving praise in the columns of liberal weeklies, however, until the shock of the "purges"—first of "traitors" in the Red Army, then of "Trotskyites" (who were supposed to have conspired with Germany) in the high councils of the Communist Party, and all over the nation. Many of Stalin's admirers were alienated, and the conservative press was uniformly skeptical. The Red Army had been irretrievably weakened, one read; "old Bolsheviks" were being liquidated purely for reasons of Stalin's personal prestige, which was slipping; during the trials the amazing confessions had been obtained by the use of drugs, by false promises of leniency, and even by the use of actors from the Moscow Art Theatre. Joseph Davies, American Ambassador to the Soviet Union at that time, wrote: "Practically every device of German Fifth Column activity, as we now know it, was disclosed and laid bare by the confessions and testimony elicited at these trials of self-confessed 'Quislings' [synonym for "collaborator" or "traitor," derived from the name of Vidkun Abraham Lauritz Jonssøn Quisling, executed Norwegian leader who was executed for collaborating with the Nazis] in Russia," but his was not a popular opinion at the time.

It was still possible for Stalin's unpopularity abroad, however, to increase, and it did just that in August 1939, when the Governments of Soviet Russia and Nazi Germany suddenly signed The Molotov–Ribbentrop Pact, or officially the Treaty of Non-aggression. Little had heralded the move except Stalin's reference, earlier that year, to "warmongers who are accustomed to have others pull the chestnuts out of the fire for them" and the resignation of People's Commissar for Foreign Affairs, Maxim Maximovich Litvinov, from his post. Soon after the rise of Hitler, Stalin had begun calling for "collective security" in the interests of world peace, had entered into a pact of mutual assistance with France, and had warned the European democracies that appeasement of the Fascist dictators would lead to their own downfall. In the Soviet Union itself, expenditures for armament had increased forty-fold and, when in 1938 Czechoslovakia had been threatened by Hitler, the Russians had been ready and willing to march against Germany. Even after Munich nullified the Franco-Soviet pact, made Germany's military position far stronger, and seemed to lay grounds for the suspicion that Hitler was being fattened to march eastward, Stalin had continued his appeals to England and France. In June 1939, with Hitler threatening Poland, he had made his "premature" proposal of a united military plan.

Heretofore the willingness of Chamberlain to negotiate an effectual alliance with Russia had been suspect. But now liberals, even liberals who had been warning that a nonaggression pact would be the logical fruit of Chamberlain's dilatoriness, were stricken: The Soviet Union had been party to a "super-Munich." Conservatives were also stricken: Hitler had betrayed them. Only those who for years had professed themselves opposed

to cooperation with the Soviet Union on the grounds that a Nazi-Soviet alliance was a possibility were triumphant: If this was not overtly an alliance, it could easily be interpreted as one. When Nazi bombers appeared over Poland in September, it was a common saying that Stalin had made World War II possible.

When the Red Army marched into Eastern Poland later that same month, there were some (including Winston Churchill) to defend the move on the grounds that it was necessary for the safety of the U.S.S.R. George Bernard Shaw actually crowed: "Stalin has taken Hitler by the scruff of the neck." But when, on November 30, the Red Army invaded Finland after negotiations for leasing bases on Finnish territory near Leningrad [St. Petersburg] had suddenly broken down, Stalin found few defenders in the democracies. France, Britain, and the United States were prompt to send aid to Finland; there were suggestions from some quarters that the ultimate result might be a general anti-Soviet war; French generals made plans for bombing the Baku oil fields; stories of Finnish military exploits and Red inefficiency crowded the Western *Sitzkrieg* (also known as the "Sitting" or "Phony War") off the front pages; French and British expeditionary forces were almost ready by the time Finland sued for peace, in March 1940. By this time, the expression "Communazi," invented by *Time*, was in common circulation, and writers for liberal weeklies who had formerly been friends of the Soviet Union were speaking as confidently as anyone else of the utter misery of the people under Stalin. It was generally agreed that the Soviet-Nazi pact had been concluded because Stalin's regime could not possibly survive a major war, nor the Red Army (made up of "sub-normal Russians," according to *Life*) possibly fight one successfully.

After the Nazi victories in Denmark and Norway, the conquest of the Low Countries and of France, along came the Battle of England and the Battle of the Balkans. This obviously involved behind-the-scenes friction between Hitler and Stalin. In June 1940, two months after the Baltic Republics had already become Soviet Republics, the Red Army marched into Northern Bukovina and Bessarabia, territory, which had belonged to Russia before the Treaty of Versailles gave it to Romania. Hitler promptly gave a "guarantee" to Romania. And the next victories were his. Early in1941, he "coordinated" not only Romania but also Bulgaria, where the Communists had been agitating against King Boris' pro-Axis policy. A few weeks later, he defeated the armies of Yugoslavia's General Simovitch, who, encouraged both by Britain and the

Soviet Union had staged a coup against the government that had submitted to the Nazis. Greece came next on the Nazi schedule, and Turkey apparently awaited her turn.

Still nothing happened but troop movements, rumors, and diplomatic feints. The great part of Hitler's troops had for some time been concentrated in the East, and on April 13, four days after *Red Star* had warned that with the invasion of England off, the burden of the War would be transferred from West to East, the Soviet Union and Japan signed a neutrality pact. Some commentators hopefully pointed out that this gave Russia a freer hand against Germany; others saw it as leaving Japan freer to concentrate her forces elsewhere, even though Soviet aid to China continued. There also was disagreement over the meaning of Stalin's appointment as Chairman of the Council of the Peoples' Commissars of the U.S.S.R. on May 6, 1941, succeeding Molotov as Premier. Alexander Kerensky [then in exile], for instance, was sure that this presaged the Soviet Union's active participation in the War on the side of Germany. In June, when rumors of extensive Nazi troop movements filled the press, most commentators still believed that Stalin would make any concessions to Germany rather than risk war.

On June 22, however, the unheralded attack came. The next day, Hitler declared war on the Soviet Union, claiming, among other things, that Stalin had prevented an attack on England, in the fall of 1940, and had set the Balkans in motion against Germany. Churchill immediately promised all possible aid to Russia, probably surprising Stalin by his promptness, for Communists had been warning of a "second Munich." Later, British and American missions to Moscow and concrete aid from both countries were to arrive.

In the beginning, however, the Anglo-American press was far from hopeful of Russian chances. With rare exceptions, American military critics promised Moscow to the Nazis in six weeks or less. Those same critics were amazed by the quality of Russian resistance and Russian morale, but remained pessimistic long after the six weeks were up. By November 1941, the Nazis and their allies had overrun the Ukraine, were besieging Leningrad [St. Petersburg], and were within a few miles of Moscow. But another surprise was to come. Stalin was, by this time, in supreme command of the Russian defense, having been appointed Chairman of the State Committee of Defense, on June 30, and People's Commissar of Defense, on July 20. On December 6, he gave the signal for a Russian counteroffensive. Less than three months later, on the 24th anniversary of the Red

Army, he was announcing that "the Moscow and Tula armies have been cleared of the enemy. Tens of towns and hundreds of villages have been liberated." He also asserted that "the initiative is now in our hands—firmly." The American hero of the day, General MacArthur, was among those who sent a cable of congratulations. "The hopes of the civilized world are placed in the glorious banner of the Russian Army," were his words.

Again, in 1942, the situation in Russia looked dark indeed. A British-Soviet pact, in which both countries pledged themselves to mutual assistance for the duration of the War and in the making of a just peace, had been signed in May 1942, and it was understood that Britain, the United States, and Russia had agreed on the "urgent task" of creating a Second Front in 1942. Nevertheless, as the Nazis pressed forward in the Russian Caucasus in their great summer offensive, the expected assistance did not come. The Russians were excluded from the London military conference, in July, when American and British military men met to discuss future operations in Europe, and Stalin was not satisfied with Churchill's explanations for lack of action when the British Prime Minister visited Moscow in August. By September, as the Battle for Stalingrad (now Volgograd) raged and military prophets shook their heads hopelessly, the suggestion that the Russians had been let down by their Allies was beginning to creep into Soviet propaganda. In a statement to the foreign press, on October 4, Stalin informed the world that the possibility of a Second Front occupied a place of first-rate importance in Soviet estimates of the present war situation. Allied aid to Russia, he declared, compared to Soviet aid to the Allies, "has so far been little effective," and it was necessary for the Allies to "fulfill their obligations fully and on time." To his own desperately fighting people he was saying at about this time: "Hold firm."

They held. And Stalin's address to the Moscow Soviet on November 6, the 25th anniversary of the Bolshevik Revolution, was less bitter. German Field Marshal Erwin Johannes Eugen Rommel, also known as the "Dessert Fox," had already been routed by the British in Egypt, and although Stalin compared the 240 Axis divisions the Russians had had to hold with the few divisions held by the other Allies, he also pointed to "a progressive rapprochement between the members of the Anglo-Soviet American Coalition and their uniting into a single fighting coalition." On November 14, following the American offensive in North Africa, he went even further. The American and British campaign in Africa, even if not the Second Front for which he had been calling was a prerequisite for that Second Front and had turned the military and political position in Europe radically in favor of the Allies, he said. He was prompt to take advantage of the situation by a series of spectacular Russian offensives, which, by the end of 1942, seemed about to succeed in isolating not only the Germans fighting in and around Stalingrad, but also those in the Caucasus. Another winter found the Nazis in retreat.

American opinion of Stalin's domestic and foreign policies had changed markedly since Russia's entrance into World War II. It was obvious, for instance, that Russia was far better prepared than people had thought, the Red Army far better trained, the system of transportation far more efficient, and the population notable not for its hatred of Soviet leaders but for its unity and confidence in time of danger. On the other issues there was more controversy. Emil Ludwig said of the Nazi-Soviet Pact: "In reality it was a treaty of defense against Hitler. . . It gave Stalin two years in which to complete his preparedness, and to push Russia's frontiers a considerable distance westward." Those of similar mind pointed out also that if Britain could not create a military diversion in the West against Hitler by 1942, it is extremely unlikely that Russia would have received any help at all in 1939; that, furthermore, during the period of the pact fear of a Russian stab in the back was all that prevented Hitler from attempting an invasion of England. The Finnish entrance into the War on the side of Germany has also brought about general recognition of the position in which the Soviet Union would have been placed, if the Finnish borders had remained as near Leningrad as "White Plains is from New York, or Evanston from Chicago." There were many, however, who, while wishing the Russians well against Hitler, still called the Nazi-Soviet Pact an "alliance" or, at best, a mistaken form of appeasement, with tragic consequences. There were still others who, like the *American Mercury's* Eugene Lyons, warned against strengthening Communism in the United States by aiding Russia and predicted a "sell-out" by Stalin at the earliest possible moment. In any case, "only political morons could contemplate without goose-pimples the possibility of the Red forces actually licking Hitler's hordes," Lyons wrote in November 1941.

Russia's war aims were stated by Stalin in his speech of November 6, 1942: "Abolition of racial exclusiveness; equality of nations and integrity of their territories; liberation of enslaved nations and restoration of their sovereign rights; the right of every nation to arrange its affairs as it wishes; economic aid to nations that have suffered and assistance to them in attaining their material welfare; restoration of democratic liberties; the destruction of the Hitlerite regime."

In 1944, Stalin, whom Churchill called, "Uncle Joe," and his troops made significant advances across Eastern Europe toward Germany. By April 1945, Nazi Germany faced its last days. German soldiers in the East, estimated at fewer than two million, fought more than six million Red Army soldiers. In the West, one million German soldiers in the West battled four million Western Allied soldiers V.E. Day (Victory in Europe) came on May 8, 1945. The U.S.S.R. led by Stalin during the postwar period, maintained its troops in the territory it had occupied during the Eastern drive, including Eastern Europe, East Berlin and East Germany. At the Potsdam Conference from July to August 1945, Stalin still maintained that he would refrain from "Sovietizing" the areas it occupied and pressed for war reparations. Stalin also pushed for "war booty," which would permit the seizure of property from the conquered nations, and a clause was added permitting this to occur with some limitations.

Meanwhile, refugees fled the Soviet-occupied territories, fearing a Communist takeover. Stalin, on April 8, 1945, declared war on Japan, helping to end World War II in the Pacific Theater by invading Japanese-occupied Manchuria and quickly defeating the Kwantung Army. His troops also occupied Korea above the 38th north parallel. Later, after Soviet forces left Manchuria, and the Chinese continued its civil war between the Communist and Nationalist factions, with the Communists winning. Stalin and Mao Zedong, the leader of the Communists, signed the 1950 Sino-Soviet Treaty of Friendship and Alliance. Later, Stalin gave the "go-ahead" for North Korean troops to attack South Korea in 1950, thinking that the United States would not come to the aid of South Korea.

Back in Europe, Stalin moved to ensure that the U.S.S.R. had a "buffer zone" to protect it in case another European War occurred. (The U.S.S.R. had suffered the most casualties during World War II of any European nation.) Communist governments, called "puppet regimes," were set up in the areas the U.S.S.R. occupied, resulting in Churchill's famous Iron Curtain Speech of March 5, 1946, referring to the military fortifications the Soviets had erected. The "Cold War" between the Western and Eastern blocs had begun, not ending until after the fall of the Berlin Wall on November 9, 1989.

In 1947, the President of the U.S., Harry S. Truman, responded with the Truman Doctrine, an American foreign policy created to counter Soviet geopolitical spread during the Cold War.

In 1948, Berlin rejected Communist Party candidates in an election, and the Soviet Union blockaded West Berlin (the portion of Berlin not under Soviet control), cutting off all supply of food and other items. The Western governments responded with supplying the city with a massive aerial resupply campaign, known as the Berlin Airlift. East Germany, officially The German Democratic Republic, came into being on October 7, 1949, and gave the Soviet-controlled Socialist Unity Party (SED) control.

The Soviet Union annexed Estonia, Latavia, Lithuania, Eastern Poland (including the Ukraine), Eastern Finland, Northern Romania, and the Kaliningrad Oblast, which was part of Northern Prussia. Besides setting up East Germany as a satellite state, the U.S.S.R. also set up Bulgaria, Romania, Hungary, Czechoslovakia, and Poland as satellite states. Albania became aligned with the Soviet Union; Yugoslavia, under Josip Broz Tito, went its own way in 1948, but had a Communist government.

All of these developments were planned and executed with the approval of Stalin. Before his death in 1953, he had proposed the 1952 Stalin Note for German reunification and Superpower disengagement from Central Europe, but the Western bloc was skeptical of his intentions and rejected the offer.

Tales of human rights violations and other autocracies during the postwar period abounded. In the U.S.S.R., there was the "Doctor's Plot," which Stalin alleged was a plot by Jewish doctors planning to kill Soviet officials. There was the Leningrad [St. Petersburg] case, where Stalin purged several Party officials in Leningrad because of another alleged plot to kill him. Most of Stalin's autocracies did not come to light until after his death, when Premier Nikita S. Khrushchev came in possession of Lavrentiy Pavlovich Beria's secret files. (Beria had become the First Deputy Premier upon Joseph Stalin's death, but was overthrown in a coup and executed. Beria had been chief of the Soviet security and secret police during Stalin's reign. He had even joked to one of his rivals, Vyacheslav Molotov, that he had "taken Stalin out" by poisoning him.)

Stalin died on March 5, 1953, at the age of 74, from a stroke resulting from high blood pressure. An autopsy revealed that he also had suffered from a cardiac and gastrointestinal hemorrhage. Yuri Borisovich Levitan, the primary Soviet radio announcer during and after World War II, announced Stalin's death to the public. After a visitation of more than one million people, Stalin's embalmed body was laid to rest on March 9, 1953, in Lenin's Mausoleum. Later, during Premier Khrushchev's "de-Stalinization" campaign, Stalin's body was re-interred in the Kremlin Wall Necropolis next to the Kremlin walls.

PERSONAL LIFE

Stalin lived in great simplicity, in a small apartment in the Kremlin. He married his first wife, Catherine [Ekaterina Svanidze], in 1906. They had one son, Chapaev (also known as "Yakov"). After his first wife died, in 1917; Stalin married Nadezhda Alliluyeva, in 1919, whom died in 1932. They had a son, Vassily (died, 1962), and a daughter, Svetlana. (In 1942, Vassily, a member of the Red Air Force, was decorated for valor. Chapaev, a captain of Artillery [who died in a German concentration camp], received the Order of Lenin. His daughter, Svetlana, later lived in the U.S., where she died in 2011.) Stalin's best known essays and speeches are collected in *October Revolution* and *Marxism and the National and Colonial Question*. He also was the author of several treatises, including *Leninism, Foundations of Leninism,* and *Problems of Leninism.*

FURTHER READING

Am Mag 132:14-15+ D '41 il por; 132: 80-1+ D '41; Am Mercury 32:315-22 Jl '34; 53 :583-9 N '41;Cur Hist 29:961-8 Mr '29 por (Same cond. R of Rs 80 :94-6 J1 '29) ; 34:73-7 Ap '31; 36:673-8 S '32; 51:17-20+ F '40; ns 1:6-11 S '41; Harper 172:19-32 D '35; Life 11:25-7 S 8 '41 pors; Liv Age 334:585-8 Ap 1 '28; 349:48-52 S '35 ; 358:128-32 Ap '40; Look 6:13-15 Ap 7 '42 pors ; New Repub 63:275-7 Jl 23 '30; 86:271-3 Ap 15 '36; 90:267-70 Ap 7 '37; The New York Times VII p3+ Je 29 '41 por; VII pl2-13+ D 14 '41 il; VII p7+ Ag 23 '42 il pors; Time 27:26 Mr 16 '36; 35:14-17 Ja 1 '40 il pors; 38:22-3 Jl 14 '41; 38:18 S 22 '41; Barbusse, H. Stalin, 1935; Davies, J. E. Mission to Moscow, 1941; Fernsworth, L. A. ed. Dictators and Democrats p201~ll, 1941; Forbes, Mrs. R. T. These Men I Knew p61-77, 1940; International Who's Who, 1942; Ludwig, E. Nine Etched from Life P345-83, 1934; Ludwig, E. Stalin, 1942; Men of Turmoil, by various authors pl2-23, 1935; Sforza, C. Makers of Modern Europe p381-5, 1930; Simone, A. Men of Europe, 1941; Souvarine, B. Stalin, 1939.

JESSICA STERN

Terrorism Expert; Writer; Educator

Born: February 11, 1958; New Rochelle, NY

INTRODUCTION

When Jessica Stern entered the fledgling field of nuclear weaponry and terrorism, nearly two decades ago, few understood the significance of her work, through which she addresses the possibility that nuclear weapons will fall into the hands of terrorists and seeks ways to prevent such an occurrence. Many who knew Stern called her profession "bizarre." "I was used to people thinking I was very weird," she told Laura Shin for Barnard Magazine *(Summer 2005). But after the terrorist attacks of September 11, 2001, terrorism and national security became ubiquitous topics for discussion, and news organizations have repeatedly published or broadcast statements obtained from terrorism experts. Few of those experts can boast of anything like the credentials, experiences, and accomplishments that have brought Stern renown. Having earned a bachelor's degree in chemistry, a master's degree in chemical engineering and technology policy, and a doctorate in public policy, she has worked in scientific laboratories, at the National Security Council (NSC), and, since 1999, as a lecturer at the Belfer Center for Science and International Affairs at Harvard University's John F. Kennedy School of Government. At the NSC she headed the Nuclear Smuggling Group, whose work inspired the film* The Peacemaker *(1997), which features a character based on Stern. Among her most unusual characteristics is her willingness, and even eagerness, to step beyond the safe boundaries of academia in conducting her research. For her critically acclaimed book* Terror in the Name of God: Why Religious Militants Kill *(2003), the diminutive Stern, who is of Jewish descent, interviewed some 75 terrorists around the world, many of them radical Muslims. While she has sought to understand the impulses that lead to hatred and violence, she hopes that her work will help to "make people feel better," as she told* Current Biography. *Her first book,* The Ultimate Terrorists, *was published in 1999.*

EARLY LIFE

Jessica Eve Stern was born on February 11, 1958 in New Rochelle, New York, to Ernest Stern, a solid-state physicist who had come to the U.S. as a refugee from Nazi Germany, and Shola Stern, a labor organizer. Her mother died three years after Jessica's birth. When Jessica Stern was about five, her father remarried and moved the family to Concord, Massachusetts, where Jessica was raised with her sister, four stepsiblings, and two half-sisters. As a child Stern had a keen interest in an elementary form of chemistry. "I wanted to play around with stuff in the kitchen. I made my own [mixtures], what I decided was herbicide, but it really wasn't that at all," she told *Current Biography.* "I guess I was on the nerdy end of the spectrum." Nevertheless, she had no desire to attend college after her high-school graduation. Instead, for almost five years she worked in cafes, took dance classes, and read Russian novels. Then she enrolled at Barnard College (which is affiliated with Columbia University], in New York City. She considered herself the "arty" type and intended to focus on creative writing or Russian literature (she was fluent in the language), but she ended up majoring in chemistry, studying under the eminent organic chemist Jacqueline Barton. "Much to my surprise, it turned out that chemistry was the most fun for me and it turned out I was a bad writer. It was a lot easier on my ego to stick with science courses," she wrote for the Women of NASA Web site (1998).

LIFE'S WORK

For a time in the early 1980s, during her undergraduate years, Stern worked as an assistant to the commercial attache (a specialist who worked for the U.S. State Department) in Moscow, in what was then the Soviet Union. She also took classes in technical Russian, went horseback riding in the Caucasus Mountains, studied ballet with a grand master, and attended performances at the Bolshoi Theater. The Cold War was raging then, and Stern was "very aware of what felt like the danger of war," as she told Lev Grossman for *Time* (December 17, 2001). "I became interested in national security living in Russia, and at that time, it was hard not to become interested in international security," she told *Current Biography.* "I still felt interested in chemistry, but I wanted to combine my interests, and so I was looking into nuclear weaponry to do that—something that people thought was a bizarre plan." Stern graduated from Barnard in 1985. At the suggestion of a friend, she abandoned her plan to pursue a Ph.D. in chemistry at

Columbia and instead enrolled in an innovative master's-degree program in technology policy at the Massachusetts Institute of Technology (MIT), in Cambridge. "The program changed my life and allowed me to combine my interests in chemistry, Russia, and war," she wrote for Women of NASA. Stern gained expertise in such areas as science policy, engineering systems analysis, and economics. The subject of her master's thesis was chemical-weapons disarmament. She received an M.S. degree in chemical engineering and technology policy from MIT in 1988. She then entered the Kennedy School of Government, at Harvard University, also in Cambridge, to pursue a doctorate in public policy. For one year (1989-90) she was a Harvard MacArthur Fellow. Her dissertation was entitled "The Control of Chemical Weapons: A Strategic Analysis." She earned a Ph.D. from Harvard in 1992.

Stern next went to work as a postdoctoral fellow at Lawrence Livermore National Laboratory, in Livermore, California. She spent the next two years analyzing the potential for smuggling, or the unauthorized use of, nuclear weapons in Russia. In 1994 she was awarded an International Affairs Fellowship by the Council on Foreign Relations. That year, at the NSC, she helped to develop national policy aimed at preventing nuclear smuggling. "Normally [fellows] coming in for a year can't decide what they want to work on, and there are all these turf battles," Stern told Shin for *Barnard Magazine*. "But as it happened, nobody at the NSC was really working on the aspect of nuclear materials or weapons and the threat of nuclear terrorism." Thanks to her specialty, Stern was appointed the NSC's director of Russian, Ukrainian and Eurasian Affairs, in which her main task was the fashioning of national-security policy with regard to Russia and the former Soviet states. She also headed several other entities, among them the Nuclear Smuggling Group, which she had co-founded and which analyzed reports of nuclear theft and developed policies to reduce the threat of nuclear smuggling and terrorism. In addition, she helped oversee the final stages of Project Sapphire, a secret operation in which a large cache of highly enriched uranium was brought from Kazakhstan to a storage site in the U.S.

One day the NSC press office asked Stern to meet with the award-winning journalist Leslie Cockburn, who was known as something of a muckraker. A specialist in foreign affairs who had spent time in Russia, Cockburn knew that the smuggling of nuclear weapons was a real danger, and she asked Stern what the White House was doing to prevent it. Stern told Cockburn about the Nuclear Smuggling Group and the completed Project Sapphire and, afterward, gave their conversation no more thought. But Cockburn used the information Stern had provided as the basis for her nonfiction book *One Point Safe* (1997), which discusses the efforts of the administration of President Bill Clinton to deal with the problem of unguarded nuclear weapons. Without Stern's knowledge, Cockburn adapted the book for a screenplay with Stern as the heroine and pitched the script to DreamWorks. Months later Stern received a telephone call from Michael Schiffer of DreamWorks and, at his request, met with him to discuss a filmscript about nuclear terrorism. To her surprise, she discovered that the reporter she had met earlier in the year for a seemingly routine interview had written the script. At the insistence of Stern, who served as a consultant for the movie, the studio renamed the character who was meant to be her and made that character less recognizable in other ways as well. "I thought [the movie] would be fun, but I also thought it could ruin my career," Stern told *Current Biography. The Peacemaker* centers on the frantic efforts of the main characters (played by Nicole Kidman and George Clooney) to prevent the detonation of a nuclear weapon in Manhattan; it drew mixed reviews and enjoyed moderate box-office success.

Stern left the NSC in 1995. In 1995-96 she held a fellowship at the Hoover Institution on War, Revolution and Peace, at Stanford University, in California. In 1998 and 1999 she worked at the Council on Foreign Relations, in Washington, D.C., as a so-called next-generation fellow; she was also known as a "superterrorism" fellow. Earlier, with the help of a MacArthur Foundation research and writing fellowship (1995-97), she had written *The Ultimate Terrorists,* which was published in 1999. The book offers a scholarly overview of the history of weapons of mass destruction, assesses the threat of chemical, biological, and nuclear terrorism (which, according to Stern, had been exaggerated in the media and by government spokesmen), and provides possible defenses against that threat. In a review of the book for *Salon* (March 23, 1999, online), Tim Cavanaugh wrote, "The ominous-sounding title . . . can't outweigh the balanced and blessedly concise arguments that Jessica Stern presents in the book itself." James T. Dunne wrote for *Security Management* (August 1, 2000), "The *Ultimate Terrorists* provides one of the better models of how such menaces might be approached, analyzed, and perhaps even countered. It's not the only book one should read on the topic, but it is one of the most incisive and refined."

For four years beginning in March 1998, while still working with the Council on Foreign Relations, Stern embarked on a project in which she ultimately interviewed 75 known terrorists of various religious affiliations, and family members of known terrorists, in the U.S. and widely scattered other parts of the world. She visited prisons and the homes of men who had killed ostensibly for reasons connected with their religious devotion.

Her decision to undertake the project, she admitted to *Current Biography,* was not particularly rational. "Usually, when you're in academia you do what you're trained to do, not what you're curious about. My whole career is on weapons of mass destruction and national security. I didn't get any training at all that would prepare me to talk to the perpetrators, but I was curious." Stern told a reporter for *BuzzFlash* (May 12, 2004, on-line), "It was only after Sept. 11 that I realized the nature of the real threat I had taken. For example, I did talk at length to the leader of a Pakistani jihadi group who is personal friends with bin Laden, and his group is very closely aligned with al-Qaeda. I knew that I didn't want to present myself to bin Laden. I thought that was not a very good idea, given my government experience. . . . But I didn't realize just how close I was getting. And of course, I did exactly what Daniel Pearl did"—a reference to a *Wall Street Journal* reporter who, after entering Pakistan in early 2002 in an attempt to meet and interview militants, was abducted and murdered. "I was scared on a number of occasions," Stern told Ron Hogan for *Publishers Weekly* (June 30, 2003), "but once I was in the presence of the militants, I didn't feel they were going to hurt me. My vulnerability as a woman alone also made me safer, ironically. I felt that I was entering a psychological compact: by making myself vulnerable to them, they would agree to take care of me and not kill me." But given the kidnappings and killings that have become everyday events in some areas, Stern told Buzzflash in 2004, "I would not, myself, repeat what I did in the post-Sept. 11 environment." While growing up, as a member of a secular household, Stern had thought that "faith made people better—more generous, more capable of love," as she wrote in the introduction to *Terror in the Name of God: Why Religious Militants Kill* (2003), which is based on her 75 interviews. But after her first talk with Kerry Noble, the former second-in-command of Covenant, Sword and the Arm of the Lord (CSA), a violent apocalyptic cult active in the 1980s, she began asking herself, as she told Buzzflash.com, "How is

it that people who profess strong moral values, who, in some cases, seem truly to be motivated by those values, can be brought to do evil things?" She tried to answer that question in the first part of *Terror in the Name of God.* In many cases, according to Stern, humiliation and fear of one thing or another lead people to join violent groups whose leaders persuade them that killing is a moral and religious duty and is not only looked on with favor by God, but commanded by Him. As is evident in the book, Stern questioned her subjects in a detached and nonjudgmental manner and seemed to empathize with them. "My colleagues have told me that they can't believe—they say they couldn't do it—that I am capable of sitting down and talking to someone whose views I reject completely, and, during the conversation, try to enter that person's head," she told Buzz-flash.com. "Try to really almost be that person for the period of the conversation, in terms of their thought process—to follow along with how they see the world. It's not just a matter of not expressing disapproval, but not allowing myself to think of disapproval." In the second part of her book, Stern described the structures of an array of terrorist organizations.

In one of the many enthusiastic reviews of the book, the neurologist and author Oliver Sacks wrote, as quoted on the book jacket, "Stern's extensive interviews with terrorists, and the empathetic (though never sympathetic) rapport she is able to establish, illuminates these states of mind which most of us can only regard with bewilderment and incomprehension. This is a psychological and moral achievement of a very rare order." In the *Boston Globe* (August 27, 2003), Scott Bernard Nelson wrote that *Terror in the Name of God* is "one of the most interesting books you'll ever read on terrorists and terrorism. . . . Stern opens an incredibly intriguing window into the minds of those who use God to justify violence against others." The London *Guardian* international-affairs columnist Isabel Hilton heralded Stern's work in *The New York Times Book Review* (November 16, 2003) as an "odyssey into the hearts and minds of religious terrorists. ... On a subject that tends to be richer in rhetoric than in detail, a writer able and willing to get this close [to such extremists] is hard to find." Jonathan Schanzer, writing for the *Middle East Quarterly* (March 22, 2004), was similarly impressed: "Stern's work deserves praise. Most terror experts spend hours reading the tracts and communiques of terrorists as a means to understand the radical mindset but never talk to terrorists directly. Stern has taken that next step; her interviews bring the reader one step closer to getting inside the radical mind."

PERSONAL LIFE

Stern currently works as a Research Professor at Boston University. Her most recent book is *ISIS: The State of Terror*, which she co-authored with J.M. Berger. Many op-ed pieces by Stern have been published in such major newspapers as *The New York Times*, the *Washington Post*, the *Boston Globe*, and *USA Today*. She has also written many articles for scholarly journals, among them *International Security*, the *Bulletin of Atomic Scientists*, the *Journal of the Centers for Disease Control and Prevention*, and the *Brookings Review*.

Stern lives in Cambridge, Massachusetts, with her son, Evan.

FURTHER READING

Barnard Magazine pi7 Summer 2005; *BuzzFlash* (online) May 12, 2004; International Speakers Bureau Web site; ksgfaculty.harvard.edu; *Newsweek* p42 Oct. 1997; NPR.org; *Publishers Weekly* p71 June 2003; *Terror in the Name of God: Why Religious Militants Kill*, 2003; *Time* p62 Dec. 17, 2001; *The Ultimate Terrorists*, 1999; *Washington Post* B pi Sep. 27, 1997; Women of NASA Web site, 1998

T

MARGARET (HILDA) THATCHER
Prime Minister of Great Britain

Born: October 13, 1925; Lincolnshire, United Kingdom
Died: April 8, 2013; Westminster, London, United
  Kingdom
Affiliation: Conservative

INTRODUCTION

"I am not a consensus politician, I am a conviction politician," Margaret Thatcher announced in February 1975, when she assumed leadership of the Conservative party. To Mrs. Thatcher, a Tory member of Parliament since 1959, the consensus that she rejected stood for the socialist policies pursued by the Labour party and acquiesced to by the Conservatives in postwar Britain. Following the establishment of a comprehensive welfare state, nationalized industries, and strong unions, Britain experienced decades of declining economic competitiveness and a corresponding loss of international stature. Convinced that nothing short of the eradication of socialism could restore economic prosperity and greatness to the nation, Mrs. Thatcher was prepared to ignore key assumptions taken for granted by her predecessors—that unions had to be appeased and that high levels of unemployment were politically intolerable. The strength of the unions vis-à-vis the government had become so formidable during the 1970s that, by the end of the decade, many Britons were receptive to Mrs. Thatcher's message. In May 1979 she became the first woman in British history to serve as prime minister. Reelected in 1983 and again in 1987, she is the twentieth century's longest-serving British prime minister, the senior statesman of the Western alliance, and the most powerful woman in the world.*

Margaret Thatcher.

One of Britain's few prime ministers to lend her name to an era and a political philosophy, Margaret Thatcher has left an indelible mark on virtually all areas of British life. Under her forceful, if sometimes strident, leadership, the Conservatives accomplished what no previous British government in the postwar period had done: they emasculated the unions, denationalized important industries, curbed inflation, and swelled the ranks of the middle class. But under Mrs. Thatcher's regime (as she herself refers to her long tenure), unemployment skyrocketed—especially in the impoverished northern industrial cities. Critics charged that the gap between the haves and the have-nots—what Disraeli once referred to as the "Two Nations"—was widened by Thatcherism to a degree not seen since the mid-Victorian days of Charles Dickens. But for voters in the service industries in London and southern England, Mrs. Thatcher's policies were, credited not only with economic recovery, but also with restoring a sense of pride in being British, which reached new heights in the aftermath of her victory over Argentina in the Falklands War of 1982.

Thatcherism denotes the prime minister's style no less than her policies. Her unbending will, self-righteousness, and love of argument earned her the sobriquet Iron Lady, which was applied to her by the Soviet press after she harshly denounced communism in 1976 and which she has worn as a badge of honor ever since. Her extraordinary political vision and self-confidence, as well as her profoundly nationalistic approach to foreign policy, have prompted comparisons with Winston Churchill, Charles de Gaulle, Elizabeth I, and Victoria. Leaders with whom she has been compared less charitably include Genghis Khan and "Attila the Hen," the latter for her tendency to wear out her opponents in Parliament with her "sometimes hectoring, sometimes condescending" style of debating, in the words of one reporter. R. C. Longworth described her in the Chicago Tribune (April 30, 1989) as "perhaps the most admired, hated, fascinating, boring, radical, and conservative leader in the Western world."

EARLY LIFE

Mrs. Thatcher's unparalleled trajectory in British politics is all the more remarkable considering her differences from previous Tory leaders. Unlike them, she is a woman and hails from the lower-middle class in a highly class-conscious society. She was born in Grantham, England on October 13, 1925, the second daughter of Alfred Roberts, a lay Methodist minister and local politician, and Beatrice Roberts, a dressmaker. In a flat over Alfred Roberts's grocery store (he eventually owned two of them), Margaret and her sister Muriel, who was born four years earlier, grew up without indoor plumbing or hot water. Beatrice Roberts was a stolid woman who saw to it that her pretty daughters were always

well dressed and well groomed. Citizens of Grantham remember Margaret as "a studious, determined little girl with the cherubic looks of a cupid on a Victorian valentine," according to Time (May 14, 1979) magazine.

Alfred Roberts was by far the more influential parent in his daughter's life. On the day that Margaret Thatcher ascended to the nation's highest office, she said, "Well, of course I just owe almost everything to my father. He brought me up to believe almost all the things that I do believe. ... It's passionately interesting for me that the things that I learned in a small town, in a very modest home, are just the things that I believe have won the election." The values thus imparted were summarized by the British journalist Peter Jenkins in his recent book Mrs. Thatcher's Revolution (1988): "The individual owed responsibility to self, family, firm, community, country, God." Independence was another value esteemed by her father, who told her, "You don't follow the crowd, you make up your own mind, " she recalled in an interview with Gail Sheehy for Vanity Fair (June 1989).

Growing up in Grantham, Margaret acquired more than a set of moral precepts from her father; she learned invaluable political skills while accompanying him to meetings of the local Rotary Club, which he founded. Successively a councilman, an alderman, arid mayor of Grantham, Alfred Roberts took Margaret on many a political outing. His expectations for her were high, but no higher than her own ambitions. He sent her to a reputable local grammar school and paid for coaching in the classics and Latin so that she could meet the admissions requirements of Oxford University. Margaret also took elocution lessons to improve her accent. At the age of seventeen she enrolled in Somerville College, the best women's college at Oxford, where she majored in chemistry with a view toward combining her scientific expertise with legal training in order to practice patent law. The only extracurricular activity in which she indulged was political debating. Barred from the all-male Oxford Union, the debating society, she joined the Oxford University Conservative Association, which in 1946 elected her its first female president. From there she made a smooth transition into local Tory politics, in which she was actively involved from then on.

LIFE'S WORK

After graduating with a B.S. degree in 1947, she worked for four years as a research chemist. (She also holds an M.A. degree from Oxford.) In 1950 she stood for a seat considered almost impossible to win in the solidly Labour district of Dartford, Kent; at the age of twenty-four she was the youngest person running for Parliament. Although she lost with 36 percent of the vote, she tried again the following year and increased her support to 40 percent. Meanwhile, in 1949, she met Denis Thatcher, a wealthy divorced businessman ten years her senior. Their marriage in December 1951 afforded her both financial and emotional security but in no way dampened her political ambitions or hindered her upward progress. On the contrary; by all accounts, Denis Thatcher has been his wife's staunchest supporter during their thirty-eight-year partnership. Around the time of her marriage, Mrs. Thatcher switched her allegiance from the Methodist church to the Church of England.

In August 1953 Mrs. Thatcher gave birth to twins, Carol and Mark. Four months later she passed her bar exam, having squeezed part-time legal study into an already overflowing schedule filled with her job, party politics, and motherhood. She practiced as a barrister specializing first in patent law, then in the more elite area of tax law, until 1961. By then she had served for two years as a member of Parliament from Finchley, a wealthy suburb of London. She has represented that district, which became Barnet, Finchley in 1974, ever since.

Lacking the advantages enjoyed by those who had access to the upper-class old-boy network that still pervades the 650-member House of Commons, Mrs. Thatcher excelled by dint of hard work, intelligence, and a forceful personality. In 1961 the Conservative prime minister, Harold Macmillan, appointed her joint parliamentary secretary to the Ministry of Pensions and National Insurance. From 1964 to 1970 the Conservatives, led by Edward Heath, were out of power. In opposition to the Labour government of Harold Wilson, Mrs. Thatcher served in Heath's shadow cabinet as minister for gas, coal, electricity, and nuclear energy, then for transportation, and finally for education and science.

When Edward Heath was elected prime minister in 1970, Mrs. Thatcher became the only woman in his cabinet. As Secretary for education and science, she made a name for herself by abolishing the free-milk program for schoolchildren. Labour MPs shouted her down in Parliament with cries of "Thatcher the milk snatcher" and "Ditch the bitch!" That was a turning point for Mrs. Thatcher. "I thought, I'm not going to be beaten by this," she told Gail Sheehy. From that point on, taunts and resistance to Mrs. Thatcher's agenda would only make her more resolute in pursuing her goals.

As the Heath government repeatedly capitulated to the demands of striking miners, confidence eroded in both the Conservative party and its leader. In March 1974 Heath resigned as prime minister; eleven months later he was deposed as leader of the Conservatives. When none of Heath's loyal deputies stepped forward to succeed him, Mrs. Thatcher seized the initiative, declared her candidacy, and in February 1975 became the first woman to assume the party leadership. During the following four years of Labour government—first under Harold Wilson, then under James Callaghan, beginning in 1976—Mrs. Thatcher called for a returned free-market principles and the dismantling of the welfare state. The message that had earlier fallen on deaf ears began to reach an increasing number of voters as it became clear that the policies pursued by both parties in the past were no longer tenable in the face of growing labor unrest.

The public's patience with powerful unions—and with governmental impotence—was tested more severely than ever before during the so-called winter of discontent in early 1979. Six weeks of strikes by everyone from garbage collectors and gravediggers to hospital workers and teachers culminated in a vote of no confidence for the Callaghan government in March 1979. Mrs. Thatcher proclaimed her willingness to confront the unions during the election campaign that followed, promising also to revive the economy, reduce welfare spending, and improve national defense capabilities. In May 1979 she was elected to a five-year term as prime minister with 43.9 percent of the vote and a parliamentary majority of forty-three seats. Her manifesto had not changed since she became party leader four years earlier. At that time, according to Gail Sheehy, her newly hired speech-writer inadvertently incorporated a quotation from the very same speech of Abraham Lincoln's that Mrs. Thatcher had been carrying with her in her wallet: "You cannot strengthen the weak by weakening the strong. . . . You cannot help the poor by destroying the rich. . . . You cannot help men permanently by doing for them what they could and should do for themselves."

One month after taking office, Mrs. Thatcher revealed her first budget. She slashed the top tax rate on earned income from 83 percent to 60 percent and reduced the highest tax rate on unearned income from 90 percent to 75 percent; raised value-added taxes; and removed restrictive foreign-exchange controls. She took steps to do away with wage-and-price guidelines, reduced government subsidies to inefficient industries, and began selling off state-owned enterprises and public housing to encourage more people to become stock-holders and homeowners. Many of those who did also became loyal Tories. But there was no paucity of people who found themselves worse off under Mrs. Thatcher. The number of unemployed doubled between 1979 and 1980, when it surpassed two million. A poll taken in late March 1982 revealed that the Tories trailed both Labour and the Alliance of Liberals and Social Democrats with a 22 percent approval rating. Many Britons were convinced that Mrs. Thatcher would go down in history as England's worst prime minister.

Less than one month later, imminent war provided the embattled leader with an opportunity to win the loyalty of those not persuaded by her economic policies by appealing to their redblooded patriotic instincts. The Argentine attack on the British Falkland Islands in April 1982 was repelled by a British naval task force in ten weeks at a cost of 255 British lives. The military campaign's success, against the odds, was widely credited to Mrs. Thatcher's fierce determination to achieve victory, and her approval rating jumped to 59 percent as a result. Proclaiming that "Great Britain is great again," she called for an early election the following spring. In June 1983 she won a second term with 42.7 percent of the vote and a 144-seat majority, despite the plight of three million unemployed. Most of the economic hardship was borne by the North, which experienced a 20 percent reduction in manufacturing from 1979 to 1981 alone. The Tories obtained most of their support from the more prosperous South.

In her second term Mrs. Thatcher forged ahead with the program she called "popular capitalism" by selling off $30 billion worth of shares in British Telecom, British Airways, Rolls-Royce, and other nationalized concerns to private citizens. By 1987 the proportion of the British electorate who owned stock was 20 percent, triple the number in 1979. Similarly, over one million municipally owned council houses were sold to their occupants during the same period, raising the percentage of home-owners from 52 percent to 66 percent (only 63.9 percent of Americans owned homes in 1988). According to *Fortune* (June 8, 1987) magazine, Britain's economic indicators illustrated that declining competitiveness had been halted, if riot reversed, for those who had jobs in 1987, real disposable income was up by 15 percent over 1979 levels. Inflation had dropped from 22 percent in 1980 to 3.4 percent in 1986; the budget deficit decreased from 6 percent of gross domestic product in 1981 to 1 percent in 1987; the economy had maintained an annual growth rate

of 3 percent since the recovery began in 1981, ranking second only to Japan among industrialized nations.

The most important achievement of eight years of Thatcherism was indisputably the prime minister's success in probing the power of the unions. Even David Owen, the leader of the Social Democratic party, said Mrs. Thatcher deserved credit for that, according to John Newhouse, writing in the *New Yorker* (February 10, 1986). New laws required union leaders to poll members before calling a strike, rendered national unions responsible for the actions of members, and banned Sympathy strikes and the closed shop. In March 1984 she took on Arthur Scargill, the Marxist leader of the National Union of h4ineWorkers, in a violent and acrimonious coal strike that lasted nearly a year, and she won. The successful outcome of her refusal to give in to union demands owed as much to the high level of unemployment, which reduced the leverage of union bosses, as to her intransigence. The number of unionized workers fell by 25 percent to nine, million by 1987, depriving the Labour party of much of its constituency.

In international affairs no less than in domestic policy, Mrs. Thatcher convinced Britons—despite dramatic swings in her popularity over the course bf her second term—that she provided leadership superior to that of any candidate fielded by the opposition. In contrast to Labour's disastrous (for their electoral prospects) policy of unilateral nuclear disarmament, Mrs. Thatcher inspired confidence with her determination to modernize the nation's nuclear weapons. In meetings with Mikhail Gorbachev in Moscow in April 1987, she spoke out forcefully in favor of linking arms control negotiations to Soviet progress in human rights and defended the need to maintain Britain's independent nuclear deterrent. Her relationship with the Soviet leader is a curiously close one that is based on mutual respect for each other's ability to argue at length without being stumped by the facts. She also sees many parallels between his efforts to reform the Soviet economy and her own battle to reverse Britain's economic decline.

Mrs. Thatcher enjoyed a clubby relationship with President Ronald Reagan as Well, though their rapport was based more on shared anticommunism than on the quality of intellectual discourse. In April 1986 Mrs. Thatcher reciprocated the logistical support she had received from Reagan during the Falklands War by allowing him the use of British air bases from which to launch his attack on Libya, and in so doing she withstood a storm of criticism. The argument that her decision was taken in a spirit of international solidarity against terrorism did not prevent her popularity from plummeting, nor did it seem consistent with her confining refusal to join the forty-eight other Commonwealth nations in placing sanctions ort South Africa's apartheid regime.

Mrs. Thatcher reiterated her concern regarding deterrence of terrorism at European forums on the political and economic unification of Europe that is slated for 1992. She objected to the abolishment of national border controls, fearing that such measures would facilitate the travel of drug traffickers, illegal immigrants, and international terrorists no less than that of tourists. Closer to home, she condemned the terrorist activity of the Irish Republican Army, which placed a bomb in her hotel in Brighton in 1984. The explosion destroyed her bathroom, which she had left just two minutes before the blast occurred. "All attempts to destroy democracy by terrorism will fail," she vowed. In 1985 she showed similar fortitude in overriding Protestant objections to an agreement giving the Irish Republic a role in Northern Ireland's affairs.

The combination of a vigorous foreign policy and ambitious domestic policies created a seemingly impregnable bastion of Tory support in the 1987 election campaign. Mrs. Thatcher had called an early election once again, this time hoping to reap the political dividends of her recent trip to Moscow—the first in twelve years by a British prime minister. The Labour party put up a much stronger fight under Neil Kinnock in 1987 than it had under Michael Foot in 1983. Kinnock hammered away at the prime minister's inflexible and arrogant style of leadership, and he castigated her for lacking compassion for the poor. Mrs. Thatcher rallied with charges that the Labour party was all talk and no action, reminding the electorate that social services could be paid for only in an expanding economy under Conservative direction.

Elected to an unprecedented third term in June 1987 with 42.8 percent of the vote and a 102-seat majority, Mrs. Thatcher planned to apply her free-market principles to previously tiptoed areas such as health care, education, utilities, and professional services. That latest round of proposals has encountered stiff resistance. Her agenda includes encouraging greater efficiency in the National Health Service; which serves 90 percent of the British public, by introducing competition for government funding; allowing public schools to develop competitive fees; privatizing the water and electrical utilities, which is opposed by environmentalists and consumers; and ending the historic separation of barristers and solicitors in the legal profession.

Mrs. Thatcher has been censured by journalists and intellectuals for invoking the 1911 Official Secrets Act to harass the British Broadcasting Corporation (which presents issues with a leftist slant, in her view). Her unsuccessful attempt to suppress publication of Peter Wright's Spy catcher; *The Candid Autobiography of a Senior Intelligence Officer* (1987) likewise provoked a public outcry over the erosion of freedom of the press and civil liberties in Britain.

Compounding the difficulties faced by the seemingly indefatigable prime minister, who in 1987 had hinted broadly that she planned to run for a fourth and even a fifth term, was bad news on the economic front in the fall of 1989. Inflation had risen to 7.6 percent, the rate of growth had slowed, interest rates had jumped from 7 percent to 15 percent in just sixteen months, and the trade deficit was estimated at $32 billion. Unemployment was down to two million, or 6.9 percent, but that rate was high enough to attract much of the blame for Britain's rising levels of drug and alcohol abuse and violent crime. Public opinion polls showed the Conservative party trailing the Labour party by ten percentage points.

But it was Mrs. Thatcher's attitude toward British participation in the European Monetary System (EMS)—rather than her domestic economic policies—that precipitated the gravest political crisis her government had thus far experienced. In July 1989 she demoted Sir Geoffrey Howe from the post of foreign secretary to that of deputy prime minister following his vocal support for the economic policies of Nigel Lawson, the chancellor of the exchequer. A staunch advocate of sooner-rather-than-later British membership in the ten-year-old EMS, Lawson resigned on October 26, 1989 in protest over the prime minister's refusal to dismiss Sir Alan Walters, her economic adviser, whose anti-EMS views had been recently published. Hours later, Sir Alan also resigned, causing British journalists to call the situation a crisis and the country's ministers to speculate that a challenge to Mrs. Thatcher's leadership was imminent. Although the prime minister remained confident of her staying power, she was reportedly quoted as saying that she would be likely to run for only one more term, in 1991 or 1992, rather than go "on and on," as she had previously indicated.

PERSONAL LIFE

In her later years, Margaret Thatcher was often described as looking younger and prettier than she did when she first took office ten years ago. The French president Frangois Mitterrand once quipped, "She has the eyes of Caligula and the mouth of Marilyn Monroe." She reportedly enjoyed male admiration as much as a good argument, and she was always prepared for either.

Mrs. Thatcher spent long hours poring over briefing papers, recharging herself with only three to five hours of sleep a night, coffee, and vitamin tablets. Her husband, Denis, who retired from business in 1975, was an avid golfer. He died of cancer in 2003. Their daughter, Carol, earned a law degree in 1975 and is a freelance journalist in London. Their son, Mark, is a former race-car driver who is currently an auto executive in Dallas, Texas.

Mrs. Thatcher was appointed a Lady Companion of the Order of the Garter (LG), the UK's highest order of chivalry, in 1995. Mrs. Thatcher had several small strokes in 2002. She died of a stroke in London in 2013 at the age of 87.

FURTHER READING

The New York Times Mag pl6 My 31 '87 por; *New Yorker* 61:68+ F 10 '86 por; *Time* 113:30+ My 14 '79 pors; Vanity Fair 52:102+ Je '89 pors; Gardiner, George. *Margaret Thatcher* (1975); *International Who's Who*, 1989-90; *International Year Book and Statesmen's Who's Who*, 1989; Jenkins, Peter. *Mrs. Thatcher's Revolution; The Ending of the Socialist Era* (1988); Minogue, Kenneth and Biddiss, eds. *Thatcherism, Personality and Politics* (1987); Riddell, Peter. *The Thatcher Government* (1983); Thatcher, Margaret. *In Defence of Freedom* (1986); Young, Hugo. *The Iron Lady* (1990)

PIERRE ELLIOTT TRUDEAU (TROO-DO')

15th Prime Minister of Canada

Born: Oct. 18, 1919; Montreal, Quebec, Canada
Died: September 28, 2000; Montreal, Quebec, Canada
Affiliation: Liberal Party of Canada

INTRODUCTION

At the time of Pierre Elliott Trudeau's first election, in 1968, as Liberal Party Leader and Prime Minister of Canada, much was made of the dashing cosmopolite who was called "Canada s most eligible bachelor." (Trudeau was known for dating high-profile women, including the entertainer Barbra Streisand, until his marriage.) A bilingual Québécois, born in wealth and educated internationally in law and political science, Trudeau, early in his career, dedicated himself to the pursuit of what he has called a "just society" for his country. A maverick and a pragmatist, he worked outside of regular political structures at first, as a labor lawyer, intellectual, and university don. After considering and rejecting affiliation with, the Socialist New Democratic Party, he turned to the Liberal Party in the early 1960s. His opposition to Prime Minister Lester B. Pearson's nuclear arms policy—which accepted United States warheads on Canadian soil—deterred him for a

time, but, in 1965, he successfully ran for Parliament as a "New Wave" Liberal. A year later, Pearson named him Minister of Justice, and when Pearson resigned, early in 1968, Trudeau was elected to succeed him as Party leader and Prime Minister. To obtain a clear mandate from the people, the new Prime Minister called a general election, in June 1968, and won for himself a stunning popular endorsement and for the Liberals an overwhelming majority in the House of Commons.

When he retired in 1984, Pierre Trudeau was Canada's third-longest serving Prime Minister at 15 years, 164 days, non-consecutively. His greatest legacy was passage of The Canada Act 1982, an Act of the Parliament of the United Kingdom that was passed at the request of the Canadian federal government to "patriate" Canada's Constitution, ending the necessity for the country to request certain types of amendments to the Constitution of Canada to be made by the British Parliament. The Act also formally ended the "request and consent" provisions of the Statute of Westminster 1931 in relation to Canada, whereby the British Parliament had a general power to pass laws extending to Canada at its own request. The Canada Act was the last request

Pierre Trudeau.

Rob Mieremet / Anefo

of the Canadian government to the British Parliament to amend the country's constitution. The Constitution Act of 1982, the Canadian equivalent, was signed into law by Elizabeth II, as Queen of Canada, on April 17, 1982, on Parliament Hill in Ottawa. Canada, although independent as a self-governing entity from the United Kingdom since the passage of the British North America Act, on July 1, 1867, was not truly a sovereign nation until the passage of these two acts in 1982.

Another "legacy" Trudeau gave to Canada was his son, Justin Pierre James Trudeau, the 23rd Prime Minister of Canada, and the leader of the Liberal Party, as well as the first child of a previous Prime Minister to hold the post.

EARLY LIFE

Joseph Philippe Pierre Ives Elliott Trudeau was born in Montreal, Canada, on October 18, 1919, to Charles-Emile Trudeau, a French-Canadian, and Grace (Elliott) Trudeau, a Canadian of mixed Scots and French descent. He had a brother, Charles Trudeau, Jr., who was an architect, and a sister, Suzette Trudeau Rouleau. His

father, a lawyer who made a fortune in the 1920s from a chain of service stations, died in 1935, leaving an estate of five million dollars.

Trudeau was raised in Outremont, an affluent Montreal suburb, in a household where the prevailing political bias was conservative. Trudeau himself took little interest in politics in his formative years. He attended Jean-de-Brebeuf, an elite French-Canadian Jesuit prep school in Montreal, where he established a brilliant academic record, despite several suspensions for disciplinary reasons. Keith Spicer in the *Toronto Globe and Mail* (April 23, 1968) traced Trudeau's "opposition to accepted opinions" and "his theory, or non-theory, of creating counterweights" to his days as a schoolboy. "At Jean de Brebeuf . . . Trudeau shone in every revolt against established authority," Spicer wrote. "By temperament, then design, he seemed to oppose all official orthodoxies. One day he would be suspected of burning a Union Jack; the next he would applaud, alone in an outraged class, the British victory on the Plains of Abraham."

Trudeau's chief interests at the time he graduated from prep school were psychology and law, in that order. Because the Université de Montréal did not then have a psychology department, he chose law. In 1943, he took his law degree with honors at the Université de Montréal (University of Montreal) Law School and was admitted to the Quebec bar. During World War II, he joined with other young French-Canadian activists in campaigning against military conscription.

Trudeau dated his real political awakening to his matriculation as a student of political economy at Harvard University, in the United States. After taking a Master's degree at Harvard, he did further study at the Ècole des Sciences Politiques of the University of Paris and at the London School of Economics, where he studied under Harold J. Laski. Tired of academic work, he abandoned his pursuit of a Ph.D. degree and toured the world, traveling where possible by motorbike, with a knapsack on his back. He illegally entered Hungary, Poland, and Yugoslavia, and was expelled from the latter; he was mistakenly arrested as an Israeli spy in Arab-held Jerusalem during the 1948 Arab-Israeli War; was in China during the 1949 revolution; witnessed street fighting in Rangoon, Burma (now, Yangon, Myanmar), during the civil war there; hitched a ride across war-torn Indo-China (Cambodia and Vietnam) in a military convoy; and, he was arrested crossing the border between India and Pakistan shortly after the partition of those countries. Later, he attended an international conference

Affiliation: Liberal Party of Canada

On April 4, 1967, Prime Minister Pearson appointed Trudeau his Minister of Justice and Attorney General of Canada. In the Ministry of Justice, as in the House of Commons, Trudeau worked effectively for the expansion of social welfare programs, the tightening of gun control laws, and the liberalization of laws relating to gambling, divorce, abortion, and homosexuality. Regarding sex laws, he once said: "The state has no business in the bedrooms of the nation."

When, in December 1967, Prime Minister Pearson announced that he planned to retire, Trudeau and 19 others entered into competition for the Liberal Party leadership and with it the Prime Ministership. (In Canada, the leader of the largest party in the House of Commons becomes Prime Minister.) In a tireless cross-country campaign, Trudeau's charisma became immediately apparent in the huge admiring crowds he drew and, particularly, in the rapport that he struck up with young people. Canadian newspapers coined the term "Trudeaumania" to describe the phenomenon. On April 6, 1968, Trudeau was elected Party Leader on the fourth ballot at the Liberal Party Convention, in Ottawa, with 1,203 votes to his nearest opponent's 954. "In all our history," one seasoned Canadian political observer noted, "probably no man has entered the Prime Ministry so untried, so unfamiliar, so formless in his policies, yet so capable of capturing the imagination of so many Canadians."

of economists in Moscow, an act that apparently landed him on some (Joe) McCarthyite blacklists. For a brief period in the 1950s, immigration authorities were instructed to deny him admission to the United States and, throughout the 1950s, he found it impossible to obtain a teaching post at the Université de Montréal.

During his studies and travels abroad, Trudeau became aware of the crying need for political and social reform in Canada, particularly in the province of Quebec, which was, in his view, stagnating under an unholy alliance of the entrenched authoritarian regime of Quebec's Premier Maurice Duplessis and the local ecclesiastical establishment. He returned home, in 1949, determined to work for a "democratic revolution" that would effect "separation of church and state, electoral reform, [and] a re-evaluation of our educational system."

At the time of Trudeau's return to Canada, the miners of Asbestos, a town in the province of Quebec named for its essential industry, were engaged in a bitter strike against the American company that owned and operated the asbestos mines. Premier Duplessis threw his police into the fray on the side of the company, and Trudeau, dubbed an "outside agitator" by clergy as well as police, entered the dispute as a legal aide to the miners. Later, he edited a book about the strike and the principles involved in it, *La Grève de L'Amiante* ("The Asbestos Strike"), published, in 1956, under the imprint of Les Editions Cité Libre. *Cité Libre* was a left-of-center intellectual quarterly, founded by Trudeau and others, in 1950, which gradually developed into a formidable adversary of the Duplessis regime, and which contributed significantly to its downfall in the late 1950s.

After two years as a junior economist on the staff of the Privy Council in Ottawa, Trudeau set up in Montreal a law office that someone described as "a free clinic for anyone with an interesting case." In 1956, he and others founded Rassemblement, a short-lived political movement dedicated to a "new and broadened left in Quebec." In a landmark article entitled *Un Manifesto Democratique* in *Cité Libre,* in October 1958, Trudeau called for a coalition of democratic forces. The main thesis of the article, as summarized by Peter Gzowski in *Maclean's* (February 24, 1962) was this: "It is still too soon for the socialist revolution in Quebec, but the need for a democratic one has never been more evident. . . . We must find a basis for fighting Duplessis on a democratic platform and whether the means is a union of the provincial CCF [a democratic socialist forerunner of what is now known as the New Democratic Party] and Liberals, or an agreement to stay out of one another's constituencies and form a coalition later, we must agree to work on the principles we have in common."

Trudeau joined the faculty of the Université de Montréal as an associate professor of law in 1961, and he remained at the university for four years, teaching classes in constitutional law and civil liberties and doing research as a member of the university's Institute of Public Law. In 1965, he joined the Liberal Party and won election to the House of Commons as a Liberal candidate from the prosperous Montreal suburb of Mount Royal. In Parliament, Trudeau was a leading spokesman for a "one Canada" policy and an opponent of separatists, who sought a special status for French-speaking Quebec. He served on several legislative bodies, including the Justice and Legal Affairs Committee, the External Affairs Committee, the Broadcasting and Assistance to the Arts Committee, and the Divorce Committee. Appointed Parliamentary Secretary to the Prime Minister, in January 1966, he was re-appointed to that post in January 1967.

In April 1966, Trudeau was a delegate to the Canada-France Interparliamentary Association meetings in Paris, and he served as a Canadian delegate to the 21st session of the United Nations General Assembly from September to December 1966. In February 1967, he toured French-speaking African nations on behalf of Prime Minister Pearson to determine the role that Canada should play in forming a French-speaking cultural association.

LIFE'S WORK

Trudeau was sworn in as Canada's 15th Prime Minister—the third of French-Canadian descent—on April 20, 1968. At a news conference marking the occasion, he promised to seek a "just society" at home and a foreign policy based on a realistic assessment of Canada's means and best interests. He indicated that his government would be more frugal and more cautious than its predecessor about putting Canadian resources into international military alliances and peace-keeping commitments; that it would try to improve Franco-Canadian relations; and that it would move toward diplomatic recognition of Communist China "on suitable terms." On the subject of China he said: "The present situation in which a government which represents a quarter of the world's population is diplomatically isolated, even from countries with which it is actively trading, is obviously unsatisfactory."

The House of Commons that Trudeau inherited from Pearson had a plurality, but, not a majority, of Liberal party members. Not wanting to depend upon minority support to achieve his legislative goals, Trudeau dissolved Parliament three days after taking office and called for general elections on June 25.

In a colorful campaign during which he danced the frug, exhibited his diving ability, and kissed the pretty girls who flocked to meet him, he urged the voters to give him a mandate for his "just society." His campaign oratory had a ring of honesty rare in politics. In promising to work for a stable economy, for example, he warned that people could not demand expanded government services and programs without expecting the imposition of higher taxes to pay for them. "If you want pie in the sky, you'll have to vote for another party," he

said. He repeatedly expressed his view that the richer provinces of Canada must, in effect, contribute to the support of the poorer provinces.

Almost 8,300,000 Canadians—about 75 percent of the eligible voters—went to the polls on June 25 and gave Trudeau the mandate for which he asked. The Liberal party won a clear majority of 154 seats—out of 264—in the House of Commons, and Trudeau himself was re-elected to a five-year term from his home district in Montreal.

As a French Canadian, Trudeau was naturally sympathetic to the grievances of French-speaking Canadians *vis-a-vis* the English-speaking majority, but he also was a staunch federalist who believed that separatism was inexpedient both for the minority group and for Canada as a whole. "French Canadians must refuse to be enclosed within Quebec . . . he wrote in *Federalism and the French Canadians*, published, in 1968, by Macmillan in Canada and by St. Martin's Press in the United States. "Even more than technology, a culture makes progress through the exchange of ideas, through challenge. The federal system obliges Quebec's political culture to stand the test of competition." Elsewhere in the same book he wrote: "The die is cast in Canada: there are two main ethnic and linguistic groups; each is too strong and too deeply rooted in the past, too firmly bound to a mother culture, to be able to engulf the other. But if the two will collaborate at the hub of a truly pluralistic state, Canada could become the envied seat of a form of federalism that belongs to tomorrow's world." He urged the adoption of a Pan-Canadian bill of rights that would guarantee not only the civil but also the cultural rights of all Canadians, including the right to choice of language.

The first step toward Prime Minister Trudeau's just society was, as he saw it, governmental reform. In July 1968, within a week after naming his Cabinet, he began a sweeping reorganization of the federal government, creating new departments, merging old ones, and changing the size; and scope of others. The Department of Consumer and Corporate Affairs, for example, was strengthened, for greater consumer protection, and a Department of Communications was set up. On September 3, 1968, Trudeau called upon the ten Canadian provinces to assist the federal government in reviewing the century-old federal Constitution, particularly as it applies to Parliament. He pointed out, for example, that a reform of the Senate was one of the prerequisites to the establishment of bilingual equality in Canada.

In 1970, Trudeau faced his first serious test as the head of state of Canada. Called the October Crisis, on October 6, a Marxist group, the *Front de libération du Québec* (FLQ) kidnapped British Trade Consul James Cross at his residence. Five days later, Quebec Labor Minister Pierre Laporte was also kidnapped. Trudeau, with the reluctant acceptance of the Premier of Quebec, Robert Bourassa, responded by invoking the War Measures Act, which gave the government additional powers of arrest and detention without trial. Trudeau exhibited a determined stance to the public, answering, when asked how far he would go to stop the violence, "Just watch me." Laporte was found dead on October 17 in the trunk of a car and the cause of his death is still under debate. Five of the terrorists were flown to Cuba in exchange for the life of, and release of, British Trade Consul James Cross. (Eventually they returned to Canada, years later, and served prison terms.)

Trudeau's Administration announced a "Multiculturalism Policy" on October 8, 1971. This statement recognized that while Canada was a country of two official languages, it recognized a plurality of cultures. Trudeau also pushed for passage of The Official Languages Act (French: *Loi sur les langues officielles*) on September 11, 1972, which gave the English and French languages equal status in the government of Canada. He also called for an expanded social welfare system, including universal health care.

During his first government, the Prime Minister kept Canada in NATO (the North Atlantic Treaty Organization), but exercised independence in foreign relations, such as establishing diplomatic relations with The People's Republic of China before the United States.

At the federal election of October 30, 1972, Trudeau's government and the Liberal Party were returned to power with a slim victory; The Liberal Party won 109 seats, compared to 107 seats for the opposition Progressive Conservatives. A further 48 seats were won by other parties and independents, of which 31 seats were won by the New Democratic Party led by David Lewis, which leaned further to the left and socialism. The new government created Petro-Canada, a state owned enterprise and a symbol of Canadian nationalism.

In May 1974, the House of Commons passed a motion of no confidence in the Trudeau government, defeating its budget bill. The 1974 election focused on the then economic recession. The Liberals were re-elected with a majority government with 141 of the 264 seats.

Trudeau's moderate reforms did little to lower rising inflation. In October 1975, Trudeau and Finance Minister Donald Macdonald introduced wage and price controls by passing the Anti-Inflation Act. Because it introduced measures considered to be in the domain of the provinces, it prompted a Canadian Supreme Court reference, asking the Court's opinion of the constitutionality of the Anti-Inflation Act. The Court upheld the legislation as an emergency that required intervention by the federal government under the British North America Act.

Trudeau and the national Liberal Party began to face growing opposition in his home province of Quebec. The 22nd Premier of Quebec, Robert Bourassa, and Quebec Liberals became more confrontational with the federal government over the Constitution, French language laws, and the language of air traffic control in Quebec. Bourassa called a "surprise election," in 1976, that resulted in René Lévesque and the Parti Québécois (PQ) winning a majority government in Quebec. The PQ advocated for national sovereignty for Quebec, involving independence of Quebec from Canada and establishing a sovereign state. PQ had chiefly campaigned on a "good government" platform, but promised a referendum on independence to be held within their first mandate. Trudeau's poll numbers fell, and he and the Liberal Party suffered defeats in by-elections in 1978. He called for the 31st Canadian general election the spring of 1979. The Progressive Conservatives, led by Joe Clark, focused on "pocketbook" issues and they were elected to power, but with only a minority of seats in the House of Commons. Trudeau announced that he was resigning as head of the Liberal Party, but, before he could do so, the Liberals voted against Clark's government on a Motion of Non-Confidence, which along with NDP votes and abstention of the Social Credit Party, led a collapse of the government and a new election. Trudeau kept a lower profile for the February 1980 election, declining media appearances and refusing a televised debate. Trudeau and the Liberal Party defeated Clark and returned to power.

The first challenge Trudeau faced was the referendum on Quebec sovereignty, called by the Parti Québécois government of René Lévesque, on May 20, 1980. Trudeau appointed Jean Chrétien, a fellow "Quebecer" to represent the federal government as "spokesman," helping to push the "*Non*" (No) cause to working-class voters who tuned out the intellectuals like Trudeau. Jean Chrétien refused to acknowledge the legitimacy of the referendum, noting that the "association," as he called Quebec's quest for sovereignty, required consent of the other provinces. As the referendum was vigorously debated in the Quebec legislature, Trudeau and Lévesque became heavily involved, with Lévesque mocking Trudeau's English middle name and aristocratic upbringing. Trudeau responded by extolling the virtues of federalism, mocking the unclear nature of the referendum, and stated that his name was neither French nor English, but Canadian. He also noted that English Canada would have to listen to the issues that prompted the referendum and promised a new constitutional agreement if Quebec decided to stay in Canada. The "No" to sovereignty won 60 percent of the vote, and Quebec remained with Canada.

After a reference to the Canadian Supreme Court and considerable negotiations with the premiers of the Canadian provinces, Trudeau was able to get all of the provinces except Quebec to agree to the "patriating" of the Constitution and implementing the Canadian Charter of Rights and Freedoms, with the stipulation that provincial legislatures would have the ability to use a "notwithstanding clause" to protect some laws from judicial oversight. Finally, the Canada Act, which included the Constitution Act, 1982, and the Charter of Rights and Freedoms, was proclaimed by Queen Elizabeth II, as Queen of Canada, on April 17, 1982.

During Trudeau's last term in office, the government saw an expansion of support for Canada's poorest citizens and the introduction of the National Energy Program (NEP) in 1980, which, according to Minister of Finance, Allan J. MacEachen, "limits the rise in prices of oil and gas to domestic consumers and thus continues to protect us from the violent shocks of OPEC [Organization of the Petroleum Exporting Countries] prices."

The federal government planned to rely on the oil produced by the Western provinces to remove dependence on foreign imports of the Eastern provinces. Also, the NEP's Petroleum Gas Revenue Tax (PGRT) instituted a double-taxation mechanism that did not apply to other commodities, which would ". . . redistribute revenue from the [oil] industry and lessen the cost of oil for Eastern Canada . . .," in an attempt to insulate the Canadian economy from the shock of rising global oil prices. This legislation created a firestorm of protest in the Western provinces and increased what many termed "Western alienation."

By the beginning of 1982, polls showed that the Liberal Party was headed for defeat if Trudeau continued as its leader. After what he called, "a long walk in the snow," Trudeau announced to his party that he would not lead it into the next election. He retired on June 30, joined the Montreal law firm Heenan Blaikie as counsel, and settled in Montreal. He continued to voice his political opinions: He spoke out against both the Meech Lake Accord and Charlottetown Accord proposals to amend the Canadian Constitution; and, he continued to speak against the Parti Québécois and the sovereignty movement. In 1985, he met with Soviet leader Mikhail Gorbachev and other leaders in 1985, to discuss easing world tensions. Trudeau also published his memoirs in 1993.

Trudeau was afflicted with Parkinson's disease and prostate cancer in later years. He died on September 28, 2000, from prostate cancer and was buried in the Trudeau family crypt, St-Rémi-de-Napierville Cemetery, Saint-Rémi, Quebec. His body lay in state to allow people to pay their last respects. Several world politicians attended the funeral.

PERSONAL LIFE

The Prime Minister was a founding member of the Montreal Civil Liberties Union and a member of the Royal Society of Canada. Of the Roman Catholic faith, he rarely missed Mass on Sunday. He married Margaret Sinclair on March 4, 1971, at St. Stephen's Catholic Church in North Vancouver. After three children, Justin, Alexandre (Sacha), and Michel (died, 1978), the couple divorced in 1984. In 1991, Trudeau fathered a daughter, Sarah, with Deborah Coyne, a politician.

FURTHER READING

Life 64:87+ Ap 19 '68 pors; Macleans Mag 75:23+ F 24 '62 por; The New York Times p8 Ap 8 '68 por; The New York Times Mag pio+ Je 16 '68 pors; Toronto Globe and Mail p7 Ap 23 '68 por; Wall St. Journal pi8 Ap 17 '68; Washington (D.C.) Post K pn Ap 28 '68 por.

FRANJO TUDJMAN (FRON-YO TOOJ-MON)

President of Croatia

Born: May 14, 1922; Veliko Trgovisce, Kingdom of
Serbs, Croats and Slovenes (now Croatia)
Died: December 10, 1999; Zagreb, Croatia
Affiliation: Croatian Democratic Union

INTRODUCTION

*On June 15, 1997, Franjo Tudjman won his third term
as president of Croatia, capturing more than 60 percent
of the vote. For many observers, his victory came as
little surprise: Tudjman has been Croatia's most popular political leader since 1990, when he was elected
president of the Croatian Republic (which was then still
part of Yugoslavia). His popularity was not surprising
either, for his determination to attain and preserve Croatian independence—the issue upon which he staked his
reputation—has had broad support among the Croatian
people. To many people living in the West, however, his
popularity seemed peculiar. For if judged by Western
standards, Tudjman could be described as an anti-
Semite, an ultranationalist who has no qualms about
discriminating against non-Croats, and an authoritarian leader whose commitment to democratic ideals is
dubious at best. On the positive side, he has been remembered for winning the first presidential election in
Croatia in which all citizens—not only Croats but Serbs
as well—had the right to vote. And he will undoubtedly
be remembered as the founding father of an independent Croatia, and as the one who, for good or ill, led his
boomerang-shaped country on the northwestern part
of the Balkan Peninsula from its birth, in June 1991,
through a costly civil war, to a time of peace and hope
for the future.*

EARLY LIFE

Franjo Tudjman, who was born on May 14, 1922, in Veliko TrgoviSde, a municipality in the region of the Croatian Zagorje, in Yugoslavia, was not always an ardent
nationalist. As a young man, he was inspired more by
Marxism than by nationalism, and as a result, after Nazi
Germany invaded Yugoslavia, in 1941, the 19-year-
old Tudjman refused to support the Croatian nationalist extremists, or Ustashe, who ran the puppet state
set up in Croatia by the Nazis and who, in their drive
to rid Croatia of Serbs, Jews, gypsies, and anti-fascist
Croats, committed horrific atrocities. Instead, Tudjman

Franjo Tudjman.

joined the partisan resistance against the Nazis and the
Ustashe, which was led by the Croatian Marxist revolutionary Josip Broz Tito. Tudjman's father, Stjepan, was
a prominent member of the Croatian Peasant Party, and
under the influence of Franjo, the middle of his three
sons, he, too, opposed the Ustashe.

LIFE'S WORK

After World War II, Yugoslavia—the Yugoslavia that
existed until 1992, consisting of six loosely federated
republics—was born under the leadership of Josip Broz
Tito. At first, Tudjman thrived under the Communists.
He worked in the personnel office of the Ministry of
National Defense; completed his studies at the Higher
Military Academy in Belgrade, Yugoslavia's capital, located in the republic of Serbia; and then rose rapidly
through the ranks of the Yugoslav army, becoming, in
1960, at 38, its youngest general. A year later, Tudjman
retired from the army to become an historian. In Zagreb,

the capital of the republic of Croatia, he founded the Institute of the History of the Worker's Movement, and he remained its director until 1967. Meanwhile, in 1963, Tudjman became a tenured professor of political science at the University of Zagreb, where he taught courses on the socialist revolution and contemporary national history. In 1965, after defending his dissertation, entitled "Causes of the Crisis in Monarchist Yugoslavia from the Time of Its Unification in 1918 until its Disintegration in 1941," he earned a doctorate in political science.

Over the next few years, Tudjman delved more deeply into Croatian history, and in time became convinced that the Communists and the Serbs, who dominated the Communist leadership, were perpetuating a terrible untruth—the idea that Croats, because of their collaboration with the Nazis during World War II, were fascistic and genocidal. In 1967, Tudjman published a work called *Declaration on the Croatian Literary Language,* and then continued to disseminate his pro-Croatian views. Soon, he was expelled from the Communist Party, and was forced to leave not only the institute he founded but the university as well. Then, after the "Croatian spring," in 1971, when Communists attempted to liberalize the economy and gain greater autonomy for their republic, Tudjman, along with many Croatian dissidents, was jailed. In 1972, he was sentenced to two years in prison, but his sentence was later reduced to nine months.

One of Tudjman's most controversial theses dating from this period concerns the atrocities committed during World War II at Jasenovac, the infamous concentration camp in Croatia where Jews, gypsies, and Serbs were slaughtered by the Ustashe. At some point—sources are unclear as to when—Tudjman examined documents relating to those events, and as a result of his investigation, he became convinced that the Serb death toll had been lower than previously believed and that the number of Croats killed by Serb Chetniks had been higher than the official version. His claims were, and are, alarming to Serbs and people of other ethnic groups who were victims of the Jasenovac crimes. His claims were also surprising, given that as a young man he had fought against the Ustashe and that his younger brother had been killed by the Nazi-Ustashe forces. At the same time, Tudjman was not alone in his nationalist sentiments; many Croats felt that Croatia's history had been distorted by the Serb-dominated Yugoslav government, and they resented this deeply. As Tudjman told *Le Monde* (October 14, 1990), "I joined the Marxist Communist Party as a youth convinced I was going to build paradise on earth and a free Croatia. Tito won in World War II precisely because he announced he was fighting for Croatian equality and the people's right to self-determination. Everybody now knows what happened afterwards."

Throughout the 1970s, Tudjman continued to work toward an independent Croatia. In 1982, he gave interviews on Swedish and German TV and French radio in which he spoke out in support of democracy and against communism. Soon afterward, he was sentenced to three years in prison and was banned from taking part in any kind of public activity for an additional five years. He was imprisoned from January 1982 until February 1983, when he was released so that he could undergo medical treatment. He was returned to prison in May 1984 to complete his sentence, and then was conditionally released in September of the same year due to his poor health.

In 1986, Tudjman learned what he considers to be the truth about the death of his father and stepmother, Olga, in 1946—a truth that made him all the more committed to his version of Croatian history. Back in 1946, while Tudjman was stationed in Belgrade, his father and stepmother were found dead in their apartment, lying in a pool of blood near a pistol. The deaths were written off as suicides, but four decades later, Tudjman was told, by a former officer in the Belgrade secret police, that they were murdered by two Croat hard-line Communists on orders from the regional secret police. (This account has been disputed by, among others, the aforementioned Belgrade secret police officer.) Presumably, the alleged killings were done as part of the Communists' drive to liquidate all Croatian nationalists. (Stjepan Tudjman, though a member of Tito's partisan movement, retained his affiliation with local Croatian nationalist groups.) Tudjman told the *Washington Post* (March 1, 1993) that on the day he learned his father had been murdered, he wrote in his diary, "My father, forgive me. ... It has taken me 40 years to discover the truth."

Tudjman's political life was given a boost in 1987, when his passport, which had been confiscated for 17 years, was returned to him. He traveled abroad and lectured in Canada, the U.S., and Europe, stirring up nationalist sentiments among Croatian emigres, who later helped fund Tudjman's political campaign. By the very end of the decade—with pro-democracy movements toppling Communist governments throughout Eastern Europe and, ultimately, the Soviet Union, and without the strong-willed Tito (who died in 1980) to help keep in check tensions among Yugoslavia's many ethnic groups—calls for self-determination were being made throughout the various Yugoslav republics, Croatia included. Thus, when Tudjman founded the Croatian Democratic Union, or Hrvatska Demokratska Zajednica (HDZ), and became its president, his message—that Croatian self-determination was in reach—was one that resonated with his fellow Croats. Tudjman realized that goal not long after his election to the presidency of the Croatian republic, on May 30, 1990, in the first democratic elections in Croatia since World War II. On December 22 of that year, Croatia implemented a new constitution, which declared Croatia "the national state of the Croatian nation," and on June 25, 1991, Croatia declared its independence from Yugoslavia.

But Croatia's independence came at a great price: a bitter civil war between Croatian government forces and Serbs living in Croatia. Thanks to the strong military support they received from the Serb-dominated Yugoslav National Army, the Croatian Serbs quickly outgunned the Croats. Indeed, within seven months, Croatia lost a region called Krajina, which represented nearly a quarter of Croatian territory, to rebel Serbs. In addition, 6,000 Croats had been killed or had died of war-related causes. Thousands more were wounded. Four hundred thousand were homeless. One-third of Croatia's industry was severely damaged. And its once-lucrative tourist industry was shattered. Though the United Nations intervened, and ceasefires were declared, fighting would continue sporadically for the next three and a half years.

According to most Western observers, Tudjman was largely responsible for the Serb insurgency. As has been extensively reported, after he became president, Tudjman undertook what might be described as a systematic campaign of anti-Serb discrimination. That campaign entailed, among other things, the absence in the 1990 constitution of any reference to Serbs, despite the fact that they made up 12 percent of the population and had previously had equal status with Croats. Also, after his election, Tudjman set about correcting what he claimed was the former bias in favor of Serbs in state employment. The result: Thousands of Serbs were purged from their jobs in the Croatian government, police, security forces, media, and factories. Tudjman further fed Serb fears by having his government adopt a new flag that featured a red-and-black checkerboard emblem, the same emblem that the Ustashe had used during their five-year regime. Rather than acknowledge

the Serbs' concerns, Tudjman instead defended the design by saying that the checkerboard pattern dated back to Croatia's medieval past and ought not be associated solely with the Ustashe. What finally spurred the Serbs to take military action was Croatia's declaration of its independence.

After the war ended, Tudjman chose to honor the United Nations-mediated cease-fire, concluded in early 1992, a decision that proved to be popular among war-weary Croats. In fact, some observers speculated that it was as a result of that decision that Croats returned Tudjman to the presidency in November 1992, in Croatia's first direct presidential elections. In honoring the cease-fire, Tudjman also won the favor of the Western powers, which were already somewhat more sympathetic toward Croatia, the vanquished party, than they were toward the Serbs, who were regarded as the principal aggressors in the Balkan conflict. Tudjman's nominal support at that time for the Muslim-led government in Bosnia and Herzegovina (in contrast to the position taken by the Bosnian Serbs, who wanted a significant portion of Bosnia and Herzegovina for themselves, or for the Bosnian Croats), further consolidated his good standing within the international community.

By 1993, though, Tudjman had reversed his policy vis-à-vis Bosnia's Muslim-led government. In hopes of expanding Croatian borders, he began to lend assistance to Bosnian Croat hard-liners in the Bosnian government who wanted to create a state of their own that would then become part of Croatia proper. (In this Tudjman was in collusion with the Serb-dominated Yugoslav government, which, through its alliance with the Bosnian Serbs, hoped to annex a chunk of Bosnian territory for itself.) Tudjman's territorial ambitions were not well received by the West. His reputation was further damaged when his Bosnian Croat allies committed atrocities against Bosnian Muslims—crimes that were every bit as grisly as those perpetrated by Bosnian Serbs—and further still when Tudjman denied responsibility. "We have drawn our lessons from this, and some of the responsible people were removed from both political and military life," he was quoted as saying in the *Christian Science Monitor* (April 1, 1994), in a reference to the massacre of an estimated 55,000 Bosnian Muslims at Mostar. "It is not only the Croats who are to be blamed for the developments at Mostar."

It has been said that Tudjman is a shrewd politician, and by any measure, over the next two years he proved himself to be just that. In 1994, Tudjman reversed his Bosnia policy yet again. Under pressure from the international community, and especially the United States, he persuaded his Bosnian Croat allies to conclude a peace with Bosnia's Muslim-led government, and he agreed to support the creation of a Muslim-Croatian federation in Bosnia that would have loose ties to Croatia. In return, his government won, in essence, the West's acquiescence to his desire to win back, by force, Croatian territory lost to rebel Serbs during the 1991 civil war. Tudjman achieved his goal in August 1995, when his government's army mounted an all-out assault on Krajina. In a 60-hour blitzkrieg, the Croatian army recaptured Krajina and drove out of the country more than 100,000 Serbs. It was the largest forced movement of people since the beginning of the Yugoslav conflict. Many had cautioned against the Krajina attack, on the grounds that Tudjman was overestimating Croatia's military strength, but in one stroke, Tudjman turned the tide of the conflict. The Serbs no longer had the military advantage, their troops were demoralized by the defeat, and the number of Serbs left in Croatia had been reduced to less than 3 percent of the entire population.

It was Croatia's Krajina victory that forced the Serbian leader, Slobodan Milosevic, to come to the bargaining table to end the war. On November 1, 1995, Tudjman convened with Milosevic and Alija Izetbegovic, the president of Bosnia, at Patterson Air Force Base in Dayton, Ohio, for U.S.-sponsored peace talks. After weeks of negotiations mediated by the U.S. secretary of state, Warren M. Christopher, and others, they reached an accord that ended the four-year war. The treaty stipulated that 51 percent of the territory within Bosnia and Herzegovina's original borders would go to a Moslem-Croat federation, and that 49 percent would belong to the Bosnian Serbs. The official peace treaty was signed on December 14, 1995, in Paris. In all, the war in the former Yugoslavia had lasted four years, and had resulted in the loss of a quarter of a million lives, the creation of three million refugees, and the destruction of the Yugoslav state.

Since becoming president, Tudjman has been controversial not only because of his foreign policy but also because of his domestic policies. His refusal to permit a free press has received much criticism, for example, both inside and outside Croatia. On May 7,1996, Tudjman's one-party government indicted two members of the *Feral Tribune*, an independent weekly published in the Adriatic port city of Split, under a controversial law prohibiting the media from insulting

the president. In another incident, in November 1996, 100,000 demonstrators took to the streets when the government withdrew the license of Radio 101, Croatia's last free radio station. Radio 101 was eventually allowed to resume broadcasting, but the episode damaged Tudjman's reputation in the eyes of the world. Indeed, on May 14, 1996, the Council of Europe decided to postpone indefinitely Croatia's entrance to that body, citing concerns about civil rights. It was the first time in the history of the 39-nation organization, created in 1949 to promote democracy and human rights in Europe, that member states did not promptly endorse a favorable entry vote by the council's Parliamentary Assembly, which had already approved Croatia's application.

Another troubling feature of Tudjman's government, according to human rights advocates, has been its unwillingness to live up to a provision of the Dayton Peace Accords requiring Croatia to allow refugees to return to their homes. Croatia's repatriation procedure for refugees is complex and arranged so that only a few can return. For those who do make it back, there are few safeguards ensuring that they will not be harassed or intimidated. Tudjman has also been criticized for the authoritarian nature of his rule. He once unilaterally made the highly unpopular decision to change the name of Zagreb's soccer team from Dinamo to Football Club Croatia. And in 1995, he overrode the results of local elections that gave control of Zagreb's City Council to opposition parties. Zagreb went without a mayor for over a year and a half because Tudjman refused to recognize the council's nominees.

Yet another criticism often lodged against Tudjman is his inclusion in his government of former members of the Ustashe. He nominated as ambassador to Argentina Ivo Rojnica, an ex-Ustashe commander; Rojnica later asked Tudjman to withdraw his nomination. And Tudjman appointed as a member of parliament Vinko Nikolic, who was an official of the Ustashe Education Ministry. Stillmore controversial was his plan, announced ill 1996, to disinter the bones of Ustashe soldiers from various cemeteries in Croatia and rebury them in the largest Ustashe death camp, Jasenovac. The site of the camp, now a memorial, contains the remains of the thousands who were killed there by Ustashe forces. Critics have said this plan is part of Tudjman's effort to rehabilitate the Ustashe regime.

What incites Tudjman's critics most, perhaps, have been his statements regarding Jews and the Holocaust. In his book *Wastelands: Historical Truths,* published in 1988, Tudjman wrote that the number of Jews who died in the Holocaust was 900,000, not 6 million. Claims such as these prompted the Nobel laureate Elie Wiesel to harshly condemn the invitation extended to Tudjman to attend the dedication of the U.S. Holocaust Memorial Museum in Washington, D.C., in April 1993. Wiesel told Diana Hean Schemo of *The New York Times* (April 22, 1993), "[Tudjman's] presence in the midst of survivors is a disgrace." For his part, Tudjman has apologized directly to Jews for their suffering under Croatia's fascist regime. At a 1994 ceremony honoring Branko Lustig, a Croatian-born Jew who was a producer of Steven Spielberg's Oscar-winning film about the Holocaust, *Schindler's List,* Tudjman said, as quoted in the *Guardian* (May 29, 1994), "I take this opportunity to apologize to you and to all the members of the Jewish community for those who, in the Independent State of Croatia, took part in the implementation of the Holocaust and Nazi-Fascist laws."

PERSONAL LIFE

Tudjman, like the late Tito, had a penchant for wearing regal military garb, and often appears in public in flashy white military uniforms. His office was in a former Tito mansion outside Zagreb, and he had adopted Tito's villa on the island of Brioni as his own. Tudjman was the author of numerous books and other publications and had been a member of the Society of Croatian Writers since 1970.

Ill with stomach cancer since 1993, he died in 1999. Tudjman was married to the former Ankica Zumbar, with whom he had two sons and one daughter.

FURTHER READING

Christian Science Monitor p6 Apr. 1,1994, with photo; *Economist* p63+ Dec. 21, 1996, with photo; *Financial Times* p8 Aug. 5-6, 1995, p8 Sept. 23, 1995, with photos; *Guardian* p18 Oct. 14, 1990, p1O Mar. 1, 1994, with photos; *London Observer* p23 Nov. 10, 1991; *The New York Times A* p1+ Apr. 22, 1993, A p1O Aug. 5, 1993, with photo, A p1+ Nov. 1, 1995, with photos; *Wall Street Journal* A pi July 25, 1996; *Washington Post* B p1+ Mar. 1, 1993, with photo; *War Against War,* 1957; *Wastelands: Historical Truths,* 1988; *Horrors of War,* 1996

V

HUBERTUS J(OHANNES) VAN MOOK
Minister of Colonies; Governor General of the Netherlands East Indies

Born: May 30, 1894; Semarang, Dutch East Indies
Died: May 10, 1965; L'Isle-sur-la-Sorgue, France
Affiliation: Netherlands Indies Civil Administration

INTRODUCTION

The Japanese advance into the Netherlands East Indies was accomplished despite the efforts of Dr. Hubertus J. Van Mook, Lieutenant Governor General, "strong man", "watch-dog," and "shrewdest trader of them all." By conferences with the Japanese, by urgent pleas to the United Nations, Van Mook tried day and night throughout the troubled months of 1940, 1941, and 1942 to avert the inevitable Japanese attack on his rich islands and to defeat the attack, once it had come.

Come it did, on January 17, 1942, when the Japanese began attacks against Borneo. Van Mook escaped to Australia to govern in exile before the Japanese occupation. When Van Mook returned, it was as the last Governor-General of the Dutch East Indies, now known as The Republic of Indonesia. Although two representatives of the Dutch government followed "Huib," his resignation signaled the end of his hope for an Indonesian Federation with ties to the Netherlands, similar to that of the former colonies of Great Britain's association in the Commonwealth of Nations. There was only one problem with "Huib's" vision, however; the people of Java, the most populous island of Indonesia, and people in the surrounding islands, had learned self-government from the Japanese during their occupation in World War II, and they wanted to sever all ties with the Netherlands, including the pro-Dutch residents in the East Indies and the Dutch born there, such as Van

Mook. A Dutch web site (Huygens Institute-The Hague) states that Van Mook could not give up the old colonial way of thinking and "he could not finally realize his conception [was] opposite dynamic Indonesian nationalism in the era of global decolonization." Despite their Proclamation of Independence on August 17, 1945, the Netherlands did not recognize their independence until 1949, after the diplomatic and armed resistance of the Indonesian National Revolution.

EARLY LIFE

Van Mook was a self-made man. He was born in Semarang, Java, on May 30, 1894, the son of Amsterdam schoolteachers who had come to the Indies shortly after their marriage, in 1893. He attended elementary school at Semarang and then, like most colonials, went to The Netherlands for his university training. At Amsterdam and Delft he studied chemistry until the outbreak of World War I interrupted his studies. He joined a cyclist company in South Holland, but, after a year and one-half of service, was dismissed because of his poor eyesight. In 1918, after studying Indonesian affairs at Leyden, he returned to the Indies.

In 1919, Van Mook entered the Civil Service. For two years, he was Food Commissioner of his native city and then became Agricultural Adviser to the Sultan of Jodjakarta (now officially known as "Yogyakarta"), in which position he instituted some needed agrarian reforms and came to know the people of his islands. In 1925, Van Mook went back to Leyden (also spelt "Leiden") to study Indies law and stayed there for three years. Back in Batavia (now known as "Jakarta"), he was made Assistant Resident, a minor but promising administration post.

By 1931, when he decided to enter politics and was elected to the *Volksraad* or People's Council, Van Mook had become a man of very liberal ideas, "for a Dutch colonial." He was editing the radical biweekly, *De Stuw,* as well as the more conservative *Koloniale Studien.* As a member of the *Volksraad* he advocated more influence for the Indies in Empire affairs, and even talked of the day when the "natives" must be given more power in the colonies. He studied economics and began thinking in broad terms of Pacific, rather than simply East Indian, economics.

In 1934, Van Mook's interests and abilities were recognized in his appointment to the Department of Economic Affairs, and, in 1937, he was made head of this department. It was as a member of the Economic Affairs Department that he went to the United States, in 1936, to attend the Yosemite Conference of the Institute of Pacific Affairs as Chief Netherlands East Indies Delegate. At this conference, he first met Kenkichi Yoshizawa, whom he was later to meet again in the momentous Dutch-Japanese trade talks in Batavia, during the first years of the World War II.

These talks started in September 1940, but, even before that, Van Mook had won worldwide attention through his preparations for the defense of the Netherlands East Indies. These islands paid little attention to the Axis before the fall of France, but shortly after the disaster they "woke up with a bang. Their alarm clock was Van Mook." He realized that the United States hadn't enough tin and rubber; he realized that the Netherlands East Indies hadn't enough guns and airplanes. Van Mook arranged a trade. The United States got needed materials, and the Netherlands East Indies were being armed.

Japan, too, needed Netherlands East Indies' tin and rubber, and, especially, Netherlands East Indies' oil. In September 1940, an economic mission, headed by the Japanese Minister of Commerce and Industry, Ichizō Kobayashi, therefore arrived in Batavia to review Japanese economic relations with the Indies. Kobayashi was accompanied by Army and Navy officers, who, he politely explained, were experts on supply. Van Mook gave them a guard of high, wide, handsome Dutchmen who towered over the Japanese, and, when Kobayashi asked Van Mook for Netherlands East Indies' oil, the latter replied, in the course of lengthy conferences, that the government wasn't a merchant; the Japanese

Minister would do better to negotiate with the oil companies. From them Kobayashi did get some crude and refined oil, but no aviation gas—the British had contracted for the entire high-octane output. Finally, after some admirable entertainment, Kobayashi discovered it was necessary for him to return home to celebrate the 2,600th anniversary of the founding of the Japanese Empire. He shortly afterward ceased to be Minister for Trade and Industry.

The Japanese tried again. This time Kenkichi Yoshizawa came to discover whether the Dutch colonials couldn't be made more amenable. He suggested a share in Dutch mines, Japanese colonists, artisans, farmers, items of fishing concessions; Japanese surveys of the lands between Java, the Celebes, New Guinea, and Australia; the establishment of an airline from Tokyo to Batavia. "In brief, Japan proposed to share the 'white man's' burden in these difficult parts," and she wanted the Indies to share in her "co-prosperity" sphere. The response was blunt, for Indies' defenses were being built up. As the Netherlands Ambassador to Tokyo said: "The Netherlands Government rejects any and every suggestion for the inclusion of her territory in a New Order in East Asia." With his country's basic position thus clarified, Van Mook was ready to renew the economic chats.

Yoshizawa, finding the situation all too difficult, on May 14 presented a final memorandum, "and if it was not an ultimatum, it was what you might consider the opening remarks, preamble, and prelude." Van Mook and other Netherlands officials considered it carefully and, on June 6, replied that raw materials supplied to Japan must not go to Germany; that the Indies were committed to priorities for the United States and Britain; that the purchases of the last five years were a reasonable basis for further business; that the Indies could not make extraordinary concessions to Japan. Yoshizawa found the reply "disappointing." The Indies had won, and meanwhile, through Van Mook's skillful delays, American war industries had been getting rubber and tungsten while the Indies had been getting American bombers.

LIFE'S WORK

Shortly after the conferences, just before the outbreak of the Pacific War, Van Mook was appointed Minister of Colonies by Queen Wilhemina. Though he knew the appointment meant leaving behind much important work, Van Mook accepted. "Realizing that the general welfare of my country will be served by inclusion of men from this important free part of the Netherlands Kingdom in the Cabinet, I could not refuse the offer," he said. But he accepted it only under the conditions that if war broke out in the Pacific he would be allowed to return to his homeland—"in what capacity did not matter." Accordingly, on December 29, after Pearl Harbor, the appointment was canceled, and Queen Wilhemina made him, instead, Lieutenant Governor General of the Netherlands East Indies.

In this capacity Van Mook set out for the United States. He arrived, on January 12, 1942, to set forth the Dutch case. Speaking with an American accent and puffing an American cigarette, he said: "We will fight but we need help and need it badly." He minced no words in summarizing the increasingly desperate situation in the Far East. "Unless America gets immense reinforcements of equipment to us immediately, we cannot hold out more than another two months." And he added, in conferences with President Roosevelt and Secretary of State Hull, in speeches from the platform and over the radio: "We want nothing except what we have bought and paid for and that which has been agreed upon by the Allies, but we want it now." He warned too: "Don't say, 'You'll keep the Japanese off.' Say, 'We'll keep them off.'"

After talking with Princess Juliana in Canada, with the Netherlands Foreign Minister, Dr. Van Kleffans, in Washington (from whom he learned that the Netherlands Government had tentatively decided to give the Netherlands East Indies independence in all matters except foreign relations and military affairs after the War), and with all important American officials who could give his country help, Van Mook returned to Batavia by way of Australia. From Australia, on February 18, he appealed to the United Nations to take the offensive, search out the enemy, and fight. The policy of constantly retiring to prepared positions, he said, could lead to a position in which the Allies might lose the War.

Back in Batavia, Van Mook continued to plead for strong efforts from the United States and Britain. "The loss of Java," he warned, "would mean that the Western nations would be virtually expelled from the Far East." He pleaded that tremendous forces weren't needed; "only comparatively small reinforcements of men and materials would make all the difference." Despite his pleas and his warnings, the Japanese advanced slowly but surely on the Netherlands East Indies, and, on March 3, Van Mook was quoted as "bitterly criticizing" the United Nations command in the Pacific and as saying: "This has been a War of lost chances." "Certainly

we Dutch deserve some blame," he added, "but the Americans also are partly responsible, because repeated suggestions that Japan should be struck even with meager forces five weeks ago when six unprotected lines of communication had been opened southward resulted only in inaction. The British likewise share a responsibility because following Singapore's fall the emphasis shifted sharply from British Malaya to British Burma."

The Japanese continued to advance, until the last stronghold of the Netherlands East Indies seemed certain to fall into their hands. At the command of Starkenborgh Stachouwer, Van Mook left Bandung in the very teeth of the Japanese advance, his plane taking off, he said, "from the last strip of runway available." He went to Australia, reportedly to reconstruct a new Netherlands East Indies Government there and to mold a new army from the Netherlands forces that had escaped from the Japanese. From Australia he continued to criticize. "There should be an end of the retreating and destroying that has been the general policy among the Allies," he stated firmly. "It has not been very effective. If you keep on retreating and losing fights, I don't see how it is going to rally the enthusiasm of the Indians and Chinese. They were expecting something different."

In the middle of April, Van Mook and a party of 120 arrived in the United States on their way to London. In Washington, he conferred with President Roosevelt; he expressed belief to the press that United Nations' operations in the Southwest Pacific had stopped the Japanese march toward Australia; and, reported that the Australian people were "much more confident than they were a month ago."

A short time later, Van Mook was in London, working with the Netherlands Government there. On May 21, he was appointed Netherlands Minister of Colonies and resigned as the Lieutenant Governorship of The Netherlands Indies to take over the post. His first task, he said, would be to use all Dutch resources at his disposal to help "regain a foothold in the East Indies."

The Netherlands had been weakened by the ordeal of the German occupation in Europe; so much of the task of retaking the East Indies following the Japanese surrender in August 1945 was carried out by Australian and British forces. They occupied the Outer Islands with minimal resistance, but British forces in Java and Sumatra were challenged by an emerging Indonesian Republic led by Sukarno and Hatta.

On October 1, 1945, Van Mook arrived back in Java, along with elements of the Netherlands Indies

Civil Administration. However, their presence generated much outrage from most of the Indonesian populace, who were opposed to the restoration of Dutch colonial rule. Van Mook had planned to grant Dutch East Indies independence, but on his terms: He advocated a Federal Republic of the United States of Indonesia with strong political and economic ties to the Netherlands. Van Mook regarded Sukarno's Republic as economically inept and unable to ward off the Indonesian Chinese, Indonesian Indians, and the rising Indonesian Communist Party.

Van Mook tried to negotiate with the Prime Minister of the Sukarno government, Sutan Sjahrir. Although negotiations had begun in October, the official negotiations took place November 11 to 12, 1946, in Linggadjati (now Linggajati) on the slopes of Mt. Ceremay (now Mount Ciremai) around 16 miles towards the south of the West Java city of Cirebon. The Netherlands, represented by Van Mook, agreed to recognize Republican rule over Java, Sumatra and Madura. The Republic would become a constituent state of the United States of Indonesia, which would be established by January 1, 1949, at the latest, and form a Netherlands-Indonesian Union together with the Netherlands, Suriname, and the Netherlands Antilles. The Dutch Queen would remain official head of this Union. The Dutch House of Representatives, on March 25, 1947, ratified a 'stripped down' version of the treaty, which was not accepted by the Indonesians. Further disagreements rose over the implementation of the agreement. On July 20, 1947, the Dutch government cancelled the accord and proceeded to commence military intervention in form of the *Operatie Product,* the first "police action." Diplomatic disputes and open conflict in Indonesia continued for much of 1947 between the Dutch and Indonesian factions. The Dutch military held large areas of Java and Sumatra, with the Republican army offering only weak resistance. U.N. and American pressure, however, kept the Dutch from conquering all Republican areas. The U.N. Security Council established a Committee of Good Offices (consisting of three members, one from Australia [chosen by the Republic], one from Belgium [chosen by the Dutch], and one from the United States [chosen by both]) to mediate. This mediation led to the signing of the Renville Agreement in January 1948 on the *U.S.S. Renville,* anchored off Jakarta. The Renville Agreement stipulated the withdrawal of Indonesian forces from Dutch-occupied territory and the establishment of a ceasefire boundary known as the Van Mook

Line. The Dutch continue to move ahead in the creation of Indonesian states. Meanwhile, the leadership of the Republican government splintered and began infighting, with resignations, kidnappings, and murders. Moscow trained Munawar Musso returned to Indonesia to infiltrate a faction of the Republican government and subvert the Indonesian National Revolution into a Communist Revolution. (His efforts ended with his death on October 30.) Van Mook announced creation of a provisional government for a federal Indonesia with himself as President. However, the Republican government secretly began guerilla operations against the Dutch, and the conflict escalated again. Van Mook was pressured to resign his post by the man who succeeded him, Louis Beel, which he did on October 29, never to return to the land of his birth.

The violence continued in the Dutch East Indies, with another Dutch military police action and arrest of the Republican government leaders, led by Beel, High Commissioner of the Crown in the Dutch East Indies. However, Beel clearly saw that the Indonesians did not want the Dutch remaining in the East Indies. Eventually, upon his recommendation, the Netherlands transferred total sovereignty to The Republic of the United States of Indonesia, abbreviated as R.U.S.I., on December 27, 1949, following the Dutch-Indonesian Round Table Conference.

Meanwhile, Van Mook eventually ended up in Berkeley, Calif., in 1949, where he taught. After briefly serving with the United Nations in 1950, he taught at the Institute of Social Studies in The Hague. In 1960, he moved to France, where he died in 1965 of a brief illness.

PERSONAL LIFE

Van Mook married Alberta Diederika Maureau on June 7, 1918, who was born in Yogyakarta and was the daughter of a teacher. They had a son, Cornelius, and daughter, also named Alberta. Mook's former home in Batavia, on Kebonsirih Street, was unpretentious and comfortable, with a large veranda and a pleasant back garden. His country house, in the mountains not far away, where he, his wife, and their children used to spend weekends and vacations, was designed by Van Mook himself of brown wood with red trimming.

Van Mook's wife and children remained behind when he escaped from the East Indies prior to the Japanese occupation. They ended up in Tjideng Camp, a Japanese concentration camp set up in a poorer neighborhood of Batavia (now Jakarta), with poor conditions, such as overcrowding. Miraculously, they survived their internment. Many Dutch, Eurasians, and Chinese were brutally tortured and killed by the Japanese and Indonesians during the occupation. Cornelius ended up in the United States and studied engineering at Massachusetts Institute of Technology (died, 1993). According to genealogy records online, his daughter, Alberta, returned to the Netherlands, married in the 1960s, had two children, and still is living in Groningen, a province in the Netherlands. Van Mook's wife, Alberta, also returned to the Netherlands, where she passed away on September 23, 1987, at the age of 92, in Leusden.

FURTHER READING

Christian Sci Mon pS F 21 '42 por; *Nation* 154:111-14 Ja 31 '42; *N Y Herald Tribune* II p3 F 22 '42 por; *The New York Times* IV p2 Mr 15 '42 por PM pll F 24 '42 por; *Time* 37:35-6 Je 16 '41 por; 38:20-3 Ag 18 '41 por (cover); 39:18 Ja 26 '42; *U S News* 12:39 Ja 23 '42; McGuire, P. *Westward the Course,* 1942.

W

KURT WALDHEIM

UN Secretary General; Austria President

Born: December 21, 1918; Sankt Andrä-Wördern, Austria
Died: June 14, 2007; Vienna, Austria
Group Affiliation: The People's Party

INTRODUCTION

On June 8,1986, Kurt Waldheim, a career diplomat who had served as secretary general of the United Nations from 1972 to 1982, won election as president of Austria after a bitter controversy over his World War II service in the German army. During the election campaign, evidence surfaced that, contrary to his two books of memoirs and his official UN biography, Waldheim had served in the Balkans with a German army unit that had committed brutal reprisals against Yugoslav partisans and arranged mass deportations of Greek Jews to death camps. After the war, the Yugoslav war crimes commission listed Waldheim as a war criminal, but, for reasons unknown, never prosecuted him. Confronted with that evidence, the former secretary general admitted that he had served with the German army in the Balkans, but not in any decision-making capacity. After combing archives for evidence, the World Jewish Congress and other groups revealed that Waldheim had in fact been an intelligence and ordnance officer and alleged that he had a direct role in the Nazi atrocities. Far from hurting Waldheim, the accusations apparently helped him to defeat his Socialist opponent in a runoff contest for the largely ceremonial presidency being vacated by the retiring Rudolf Kirchschlager. But the bitter controversy over their new president revived a "half-buried national past" that many Austrians would prefer to forget.

EARLY LIFE

Like most Austrians of his generation, Kurt Waldheim grew up in an era that forced uncommonly hard choices on its young people. He was born on December 21,1918, in Sankt Andrä-Wördern, a village near Vienna, the oldest child of Walther and Josefine (Petrasch) Waldheim. A conservative Roman Catholic school inspector of modest means, Walther Waldheim sacrificed to educate his three children for more promising careers. But his ambitions for them were soon disarranged by political upheaval.

Struggling to overcome the economic depression resulting from the devastating loss of its empire in World War I, Austria succumbed to civil war and the growing domination of the Nazi regime to the north. In March 1938 a German army marched into Austria and declared an *Anschluss*, or union of the two nations, Because of his openly anti-Nazi views, Walther Waldheim was jailed briefly and forced to resign his post.

At the time of the *Anschluss*, Kurt Waldheim was a student at the University of Vienna, pursuing legal and diplomatic training. Although in his later career he denied having belonged to any Nazi-affiliated organizations, the recent investigations indicated that on April 1, 1938, three weeks after the *Anschluss*, he joined the Nazi student union, and on November 18, 1938, shortly after the *Kristallnacht*, when anti-Semitic violence reached its height, he joined the mounted unit of the Nazis' paramilitary *Sturm-Abteilung*, or S.A., also known as the "brownshirts."

LIFE'S WORK

When war broke out in 1939, Waldheim was drafted into the German army with the rank of lieutenant. In the spring of 1941 he was sent to the Eastern Front, and he was wounded in the ankle the following December. According to his autobiographies, *The Challenge of Peace* (Rawson, 1980) and *In the Eye of the Storm* (Adler & Adler, 1986), that wound ended his active service. On his return to Vienna, he was allowed to resume his studies toward his law doctorate, which he received in 1944, after completing a dissertation on the nineteenth-century political theorist Konstantin Frantz, who proposed the creation of a central European federation that would dominate the continent. But photographs and documents show that concurrently Waldheim remained an officer in the German army from 1942 to 1945, a fact he had concealed for over forty years. According to the historian Gordon A. Craig, who analyzed Waldheim's doctoral dissertation in the *New York Review of Books* (October 9,1986), the work was "a summary rather than an analysis of Frantz's thought" and was "largely accomplished, in all probability, during the three months of leave that followed Waldheim's service in Bosnia."

It was Waldheim's military service in the Balkans that became the focus of the recent controversy. In March 1942 he returned to active duty, assigned as an intelligence officer to the staff of General Alexander Löhr, an Austrian who was executed as a war criminal in 1947. Under Löhr's command, the German Army Group E engaged in brutal campaigns against the Yugoslav partisans led by Marshal Tito, burning whole villages and slaughtering their inhabitants. Löhr's forces also helped arrange the deportation of some 40,000 Greek Jews from Salonika to Auschwitz.

The extent of Waldheim's knowledge of and participation in these atrocities has remained unclear. Researchers have uncovered army daybooks written by Waldheim and intelligence reports apparently initialed by him that strongly suggest that he had detailed knowledge of the partisan campaigns and the deportations of Jews. Moreover, in July 1942, he received the Order of the Grown of King Zvonimir from the Nazi puppet state of Croatia, honoring him for his service "under fire" and "heroic bravery in the battle against the insurgents in the spring and summer of 1942."

Waldheim told reporters in 1986 that his duties on Löhr's staff were primarily those of an interpreter and clerk. He admitted to having known of the partisan campaigns but swore he had no part in the interrogation of suspects or military actions against the guerrillas. While at first he categorically denied receiving the Zvonimir medal, he later told the Associated Press that the decoration was routinely handed out "like chocolates" to all staff officers, regardless of their service. He denied having any awareness of the Jewish deportations although, as Gordon Craig and others pointed out, all Jews had to wear yellow stars, and it would have been difficult not to notice the disappearance of one-fifth of the population of Salonika.

Whatever his own recollections, evidence of Waldheim's complicity in the brutal work of Army Group E was strong enough to warrant his inclusion on lists of Nazi war criminals compiled after the war. In December 1947 the Yugoslav war crimes commission forwarded a four-page report on Waldheim to the Allied war crimes commission, seeking extradition rights to try him for the murder of Yugoslav partisans. The charges were based on the testimony of three witnesses who said that Waldheim had supervised the destruction of three partisan villages in October 1944.

Reviewing the evidence, the Allied war crimes commission gave Waldheim an "A" ranking, denoting a suspect who should be subject to trial as a war criminal. But the Yugoslavs never followed up on the charges, and Waldheim's file, along with those of some 40,000 other suspects who were never tried, was sealed and given to the United Nations for safekeeping. Waldheim has refuted the testimony of the three witnesses, whom he described on the GBS-TV program *60 Minutes* in 1986 as desperate men trying to "save their skins" by naming others. "I was never involved in anything that would justify a feeling of guilt," he said as quoted in *U.S. News & World Report* (April 28, 1986).

In the turbulent aftermath of World War II, Waldheim's wartime service never became a public issue. Because Austria had been "invaded" by Germany in 1938, the Allies declared it the "first victim" of Hitler's regime and excused it from the reparations imposed on Germany. Despite the enthusiasm many Austrians had shown for Nazism, including its anti-Semitic excesses, the nation never went through the kind of collective self-examination and public remorse experienced by the Germans. Like Kurt Waldheim, many Austrians were eager simply to forget their wartime complicity with the Nazis.

In postwar Austria, the talented and ambitious Waldheim advanced rapidly. He entered the Austrian foreign service as soon as the war ended. After clearance by the Office of Strategic Services he became the personal secretary of Karl Gruber, the Austrian foreign minister, and quickly rose through the diplomatic ranks. When Austria regained its sovereignty in 1955, Waldheim went as its delegate to the United Nations, and he then served from 1956 to 1960 as Austria's ambassador to Canada. In 1960 he returned to the ministry of foreign affairs, where he was head of the Western political department from 1960 to 1962 and director general for political affairs from 1962 to 1964. In 1964 Waldheim returned to the UN for a four-year term as Austria's permanent representative, serving also as chairman of the Committee on Peaceful Uses of Outer Space from 1965 to 1968 and as chairman of the Special Committee on the Definition of Aggression in 1967.

In a cabinet reshuffle in 1968, Austria's chancellor and leader of the ruling People's party, Josef Klaus, named Waldheim as his minister of foreign affairs. One of the first crises that Waldheim had to deal with in that post was the Soviet invasion of Austria's neighbor, Czechoslovakia. In *Eye of the Storm* he wrote, "The Austrian media were practically unanimous in condemning the Soviet attitude, and Moscow became very concerned about this reaction. The Austrian government had to tread something of a tightrope in order. . . to respect its commitment to neutrality." A document made public by the World Jewish Congress in October 1986 alleged that Waldheim was responsible for ordering his country's embassy in Prague to turn away Czech citizens seeking asylum. But the Austrian ambassador in Prague, according to the document, ignored the directive and issued more than 5,000 visas a day, enabling Czechs to leave the country.

When the Klaus party lost the elections in 1970, Waldheim resumed his post as ambassador to the UN. He then took leave to stand for election as president of Austria but lost to the incumbent Socialist, Franz Jonas, and returned to the UN, where he became chairman of the safeguards committee of the International Atomic Energy Agency. When, in the fall of 1971, UN Secretary General U Thant of Burma announced his intention not to run for

Affiliation: The People's Party

After losing his bid for a third term as secretary general to Javier Pérez de Cuéllar of Peru, Waldheim was a visiting professor of diplomacy at Georgetown University in Washington, D.C., from May 1982 to July 1984. In 1985 he announced his intention to run as the conservative People's party candidate for president of Austria, a post that the Socialists had held for sixteen years, The People's party hoped to capitalize on growing concern about nuclear power, scandals involving the adulteration of wine, and government corruption, to break the Socialists' long monopoly on high office.

In the course of what had been a quiet, almost lackluster campaign, the revelations about Waldheim's war record came as a bombshell in early March 1986. The Austrian news magazine *Profil* and the World Jewish Congress produced documents revealing his membership in the Nazi organizations and his military service in the Balkans. In an interview with *The New York Times* reporter John Tagliabue (March 4,1986), Waldheim admitted the authenticity of the documents but denied that he had committed any war crimes. Asked to explain his affiliation with the Nazi organizations, he insisted that he had no political sympathies with the Nazis but joined the groups only so that he and his family would be spared persecution. He told the interviewer that he regarded the youth groups as "harmless" and justified his membership by saying, "If I ever had the idea of finishing my studies, I had to have some protection."

a third term, Waldheim emerged as his likely successor, His polished, nonideological style was acceptable to both superpowers, but the People's Republic of China, newly admitted to the UN in Taiwan's place, at first blocked his appointment. After three closed sessions of the Security Council, Waldheim finally won the nomination and took office in January 1972. He won a second term in 1976, and only narrowly missed taking an unprecedented third term in 1981 because the Chinese insisted on a Third World candidate. In none of those elections did Waldheim's war record arise as an issue.

During Waldheim's tenure at the UN, the organization's political character changed dramatically. The admission of the People's Republic of China and the addition of many former colonies to membership increased the power of the Third World or "nonaligned" nations. The old East-West divisions of the 1960s gave way to much more complex political alignments, in which the Western nations were often outvoted. As secretary general, Waldheim faced the almost impossible task of reconciling American, Soviet, and Third World interests. Aware that several of his predecessors had lost their effectiveness by pursuing their own political visions too vigorously, Waldheim sought to lead by consensus. Despite the many obstacles he faced, Waldheim was generally recognized as a dedicated and active secretary general. One of his first goals was to put the UN back on a sound financial basis by reducing operating costs and persuading recalcitrant members to pay their assessments. He then turned his energies to peacekeeping efforts in Cyprus, Vietnam, and the Middle East,

Perhaps Waldheim's finest hour as secretary general came during the 1973 Middle Eastern war when he helped to bring Israel and Egypt to the negotiating table. But he soon drew upon himself the ire of Israel and the American Jewish community, In 1975 the UN General Assembly passed a resolution condemning Zionism as a form of racism, an action for which many Israelis blamed Waldheim, even though the secretary general had no power to influence the assembly vote, Then, in 1976, the secretary general condemned Israel's raid to rescue hostages held on a hijacked plane at the Entebbe airfield in Uganda as "a serious violation of the national sovereignty of a United Nations member state."

In his second term as secretary general, Waldheim faced other serious challenges to world peace: Israel's occupation of southern Lebanon; the war in Afghanistan; the Iran-Iraq conflict; and the Iranian hostage crisis, "Waldheim was not lucky in what was tossed his way, during his ten years as secretary general," the Irish diplomat and former UN official Conor Cruise O'Brien wrote in the *Times Literary Supplement* (January 17,1986), "He got pretty hopeless stuff . . . where there was nothing much the UN could do, . . , " O'Brien, who had the opportunity to work closely with Waldheim, described his *modus operandi:* "the discreet and effaced style; the accurate assessment of restricted possibilities; the setting of modest objectives; and the patient and even crafty pursuit of the same."

According to some sources, Communist bloc officials who had known of Waldheim's war record allegedly used it to blackmail him. A report in the *Washington Post* in late October 1986, quoted Anton Kolendic, a former Yugoslav intelligence officer, as saying that he was "absolutely certain" that Soviet officials had approached Waldheim in the early postwar years and tried to pressure him to become an agent for them, using their knowledge of his activities in the Balkans as a threat, His statement was corroborated by another, unidentified, Yugoslav intelligence officer. An editorial in the *New Republic* (June 30,1986), evaluating those reports, listed Waldheim's pro-Soviet actions during the postwar

years and noted, "In 1971, when he first ran for secretary general of the UN, Waldheim was stoutly supported by the Soviet Union, and that support never wavered throughout his tenure. . . ." But interviews conducted in June 1986 by *The New York Times* reporter Elaine Sciolino with both Western and Eastern-bloc UN officials, seemed to reveal no pattern favoring either East or West. Some pointed to times when on issues involving Vietnam and Cambodia he appeared to bow to American pressure. Officials on both sides expressed the view that his extraordinary ambition made him susceptible to pressure by various missions at different times.

The documents and Waldheim's admission of their authenticity touched off an international uproar. As the World Jewish Congress continued to dredge up material on Waldheim's wartime service, authorities in Israel, Austria, and the United States asked to see the confidential file on Waldheim compiled by the Allied war crimes commission contained in the UN archives.

Within Austria, however, the charges created sympathy for Waldheim, who before the controversy started had been having difficulty in establishing rapport with the average voter. Angry at what they perceived to be foreign interference in their domestic politics, many Austrian voters accepted Waldheim's portrayal of himself as the unfortunate victim of a smear campaign. Affixing a sticker that read "Now More than Ever" to his original campaign poster, which said "The Man the World Trusts," Waldheim lashed out against his accusers. "We were not doing anything but our duty as decent soldiers. We were not criminals but decent men who faced a terrible fate," he said in one campaign speech reported in *The New York Times* (May 1, 1986).

The voters apparently responded to his argument, because Waldheim's standing in the opinion polls steadily rose. But the campaign unleashed an ugly wave of anti-Semitism. Austria's small Jewish population was deluged with hate mail, and there were angry street demonstrations. Despite warnings from Socialist leaders that Waldheim's election would cause dissension, voters gave him 49.6 percent of the vote in the election of May 4, 1986, as compared to 43.7 received by his Socialist opponent, the former health minister Kurt Steyrer. Having failed to win a clear majority, Waldheim faced Steyrer in a runoff election on June 8, 1986, which he won with 53.9 percent of the vote. Waldheim was inaugurated for a six-year term as President of Austria on July 8, 1986 in what United States Senator Daniel P. Moynihan of New York termed "a symbolic amnesty for the Holocaust."

Waldheim's election did not end the controversy, however. Israel boycotted the inauguration and immediately recalled its ambassador to Austria. In London, a senior government official said that it was unlikely that Waldheim would be invited to make an official visit, and there were indications that the new president would not be welcome in other countries such as Yugoslavia, Greece, and Holland. In the United States, after reviewing the evidence, Neal Sher, the director of the Justice Department's office of special investigations, recommended to Attorney General Edwin Meese 3d in late April 1986 that Waldheim be barred from the country as a suspected war criminal. The State Department, according to an article in *The New York Times* (May 16, 1986), informed Edgar M. Bronfman, the president of the World Jewish Congress, that it was launching its own investigation. But in December 1986, amid objections, Waldheim was invited by the UN office in Vienna to be a guest of honor at a ceremony scheduled for January 1987, commemorating the first UN secretary general, Trygve Lie.

The United States Justice Department for the first time branded the head of state of a friendly country an undesirable alien when in April 1987 it formally placed Kurt Waldheim on a list of persons barred from entering the United States, citing evidence that established a "prima facie" case that Waldheim had "assisted or otherwise participated in" activities that amounted to persecution of Jews and others in Greece and Yugoslavia during World War II. The Austrian president called the American decision "incomprehensible" and insisted that he had a clear conscience.

Meanwhile, Waldheim remained under fire both at home and abroad. Invitations from other European countries were not forthcoming, and Austria's ruling Socialist party went so far as to ask him to resign the presidency. Waldheim's audience with Pope John Paul II in June 1987, his first official trip abroad since his election as president, provoked anger among Jewish spokesmen which was only partially mitigated by a pastoral letter written by the Pope in August that addressed Jewish suffering in the Holocaust and by a meeting of the Pontiff and American Jewish leaders in Miami, Florida in September 1987.

PERSONAL LIFE

Kurt Waldheim was described, in retrospect, by some former aides at the UN as a tyrant to his subordinates and obsequious to higher-ups. Such organizations as the World Jewish Congress have continued to hold to the belief that Waldheim was a war criminal, but many commentators seemed to concur with the view of Simon Wiesenthal, the veteran hunter of Nazi war criminals, who considered him "an opportunist" but not a war criminal. Similarly, according to Linda-Marie Deloff, writing in *Christian Century* (August 27-September 3, 1986), Professor Fritz Fellner, a distinguished political scientist at the University of Salzburg, regarded Waldheim as "an inveterate opportunist who has always known how to advance himself in any given situation," but who "was at too low a level of responsibility to know automatically what was going on around him. . . . "

The debate over his past took its toll on the tall, angular, gray-haired Waldheim whose smile, during the election campaign seemed forced and who often appeared drawn and anxious throughout the controversy. His mainstay was his wife, the former Elisabeth Ritschel, known as "Cissy," whom he married in 1944, and who has admitted to having once been a member of the Nazi party. The Waldheims have two daughters, Liselotte and Christa, and a son, Gerhard, a lawyer, who has traveled to the United States to present the legal case for his father's innocence to the Justice Department. Waldheim's published books, in English, include The *Austrian Example* (Macmillan, 1971), *Building the Future Order* (Macmillan, 1980), and his now partly discredited two volumes of memoirs.

Kurt Waldheim died on June 14, 2007, from heart failure. He was survived by his wife, Elisabeth, and their three children. His funeral was held June 23 in St. Stephen's Cathedral, Vienna, and he was buried at the Presidential Vault in the Zentralfriedhof ("central cemetery"). In his speech at the Cathedral, Federal President Heinz Fischer called Waldheim "a great Austrian" who had been wrongfully accused of having committed war crimes. Fischer also praised Waldheim for his efforts to solve international crises and for his contributions to world peace. At Waldheim's own request, no foreign heads of states or governments were invited to attend his funeral except Hans-Adam II, the Prince of Liechtenstein.

FURTHER READING

Christian Sci Mon p1+Ap 9 '86 por; *The New York Times Mag* p38+ S 13 '81 pors; *Newsweek* 107:30+ Je 9 '86 por; *U S News* 100:37+Ap 28 '86 por; *Contemporary Authors* vols 89-92 (1980); *International Who's Who*, 1986-87; *Worldmark Encyclopedia of the Nations* vol 1 (1984)

LECH WAŁĘSA

Polish Political Leader

Born: September 29, 1943
Party Affiliation: Nonpartisan Bloc for Support of
Reforms; Christian Democracy of the 3rd Polish
Republic; Civic Platform

INTRODUCTION

*Lech Wałęsa is known the world over for his valiant, and
ultimately successful, efforts to deliver his native Poland
from Communist rule. He burst onto the political scene
in 1980, during a historic strike in the Lenin Shipyard in
the port city Gdansk, over the course of which he proved
himself not only willing to stand up to the Communist
authorities but also capable of persuading them to address the needs of the working class. As leader of Solidarity, the labor union he helped to found, Wałęsa came
to embody the spirit of revolt in Polish society. In this
role he was supported by a broad cross section of Polish society, from workers and farmers to intellectuals.
He reached the height of his popularity in 1989, when,
as the standard-bearer of the prodemocracy movement
in Poland, he forced the Communist-led government to
hold free elections, thus bringing an end to Communist
rule in Poland.*

*Yet even then, when he seemed invincible, Polish
support for Wałęsa was not as monolithic as it seemed
at first glance. Many intellectuals, in fact, were put off
by his rough manners and comparative lack of education; while they had been willing to support Wałęsa in
spite of what they considered to be his failings for the
sake of unity during the Communist era, they considered
him to be more of an embarrassment once freedom had
been won. The rift between members of the intelligentsia on the one hand and Wałęsa and his working-class
and peasant supporters on the other deepened during
the 1990 presidential campaign, and although Wałęsa
emerged victorious, he never regained the popularity he
had previously enjoyed. Five years later he lost his bid
for reelection to the presidency to a former Communist,
Alexander Kwasniewski.*

EARLY LIFE

Lech Wałęsa was born on September 29, 1943 in Popowo, a village in the Dobrzyn region of Poland. His father, Boleslaw Wałęsa, was a landowner who had gone
into the construction business after his marriage to the
former Feliksa Kaminska. At the time of Wałęsa's birth,
during World War II, when Poland was under German
occupation, his father was captured and imprisoned in a
Nazi prison camp. He returned home at the end of the
war, but within 18 months, his health ruined, he died.
In about 1946 Wałęsa's mother married Boleslaw's
brother, Stanislaw, whom Lech and his two brothers and
sister never fully accepted as their father. Eventually,
Wałęsa's mother and stepfather left Poland in search of
a better life in the United States; Feliksa Wałęsa died
there, in an automobile accident.

As a youth Wałęsa did well in such subjects as
mathematics and physics, and the headmaster at his
school suggested that he pursue his education at a technical university. Lack of funds prevented this, though,
and so, because he wanted to do something other than
make a career as a farmer, at 16 he entered a vocational
school in the nearby town of Lipno. He matriculated in
the school's agricultural mechanization division, where
he earned good marks—as well as a reputation among
the teachers for being a "troublemaker and smoker." After receiving his certificate, in 1961, Wałęsa was hired
as a technician in a town near Popowo with the state
agriculture department. Two years later he was drafted
into the army. By the end of his two years of obligatory
military service, he had risen to the rank of corporal.

LIFE'S WORK

Wałęsa then returned to the state agricultural department. Frustrated and deriving little satisfaction from his
work, in 1967 he made a sudden decision to leave the
countryside for a new life in the city and boarded a train
heading to Poland's Baltic coast. Although he originally
intended to settle in the port city of Gdynia, he disem-
barked at Gdansk, another city on the coast, where he
ran into a friend who worked at the Lenin Shipyard,
a huge industrial complex that employed more than
15,000 people. Wałęsa never made it to Gdynia; he instead took a job at the shipyard as a naval electrician.

In early 1968, several months after Wałęsa's arrival in Gdansk, student protests rocked Poland, with
the demonstrators demanding greater freedom of expression. Polish workers also had grievances for which
they blamed the government, though they were of an
economic, rather than political, nature. Specifically, the

workers were distressed by appalling working conditions, chronic food shortages, and low pay. The authorities, wanting to ensure that the groups did not unite in their opposition to Communist rule, exploited the divisions that already existed between them, telling the workers, for example, that the students were spoiled. For his part, Wałęsa seems to have seen through the government's manipulations. Although he had been familiar with such treachery on a small scale at his earlier jobs, "at the shipyard the stakes were much higher," he has contended, "and the contemptible behavior of the authorities automatically took on a political dimension."

In December 1970 the Polish government, acknowledging the economic crisis in which the country was mired, announced its plan to raise the prices of basic commodities. Poles, who were entering one of the most festive times of the year, were outraged as much at the government's decision as at the poor timing. Within two days, workers in several cities, including about a thousand at the Lenin Shipyard, went on strike to protest the price increases. On December 15 Wałęsa joined the strike, and Gdansk erupted in violence, with workers battling the police and militia all over the city. Despite his best efforts, Wałęsa, who was chosen as a delegate to a strike committee that was then being formed, was unable to control the workers. "I hadn't the slightest notion of how to manage a strike," he admitted in his book *A Way of Hope* (1987). "I was out of my depth." Nevertheless, he later came to feel that the strike "provided an incomparable experience, enabling us to understand what makes them behave the way they do in a crisis. And it convinced us that we would have to find other solutions."

The 1970 riots precipitated the fall from power of the Communist Party's secretary, Wladyslaw Gomulka. He was succeeded by Edward Gierek, who, taking his cue from the fate of his predecessor, adopted an economic program that entailed borrowing heavily from the Soviet Union and Western countries. The idea was that the loans would be repaid with hard currency earned from a prospective increase in Polish exports. The plan backfired. Within a few years, the country had indeed incurred new debts, and it was exporting such high-quality products as Polish ham (which native Poles were thus unable to buy), but its earnings did not cover its debts and interest payments. Wałęsa voiced the discontent of his fellow workers during the elections for representatives to the state-run trade union in 1976. Speaking out publicly for the first time, he delivered a

passionate speech in which he criticized the shipyard's management and declared that the workers needed a trade union to protect their rights. Soon after, Wałęsa was dismissed.

Wałęsa next took a job with ZREMB, a repair company in Gdansk, at which he overhauled old vehicles. During this period he also became associated with the Committee for the Defense of Workers Rights and the Free Trade Unions. Through his involvement with these groups, Wałęsa both gained experience as an activist and began to earn a reputation within the growing, though still loose, coalition of workers, students, and intellectuals who opposed Communist rule. At ZREMB, Wałęsa's activism did not help his reputation, and in 1979 (or in late 1978, according to one source) he was fired. A few months later he got a job at an engineering firm, one writer reported. During the same period, he was arrested several times and briefly detained by authorities.

In December 1979, nine years after the infamous strike in Gdansk, Wałęsa and other dissidents made plans to commemorate the workers slain in the rioting. At the celebration he declared to his fellow workers, "Only an organized and independent society can make itself heard. I beg you to organize yourselves in independent groups for your own self-defense. Help each other." Not only did the speech make Wałęsa a local hero but the ceremony itself marked the beginning of what he has called "a period of creativity and growth for our movement." Indeed, dissident students, intellectuals, and workers, who had formerly been disunited, began to work together in their opposition to a common foe. Wałęsa and his cohorts also steeled themselves to harsh treatment by the authorities. "We were no longer concerned about the searches, the arrests, and the spells in prison," he wrote in *A Way of Hope*. "We took them in our stride as occupational hazards, disturbing, yes, but by now commonplace." Soon after the commemoration, Wałęsa was fired from his new job along with several other workers, one of whom was later found murdered.

Wałęsa's emergence as the de facto spokesperson of the Polish working class and leader of the opposition occurred in 1980. Tensions reached a new high that summer, following the government's announcement of an austerity program calling for drastic price increases for meat and other goods. The wave of protests that ensued compelled the government to increase wages to compensate for the price rises, but this failed to placate workers, who were demanding not only economic reforms but political ones as well, the principal one being the right to organize free and independent trade unions. A turning point came on August 14, when Wałęsa, harassed by the police, showed up at the Lenin Shipyard, where 16,000 striking workers (according to one estimate) were occupying the grounds. In a dramatic move, Wałęsa scaled the shipyard walls—the entrance was closely guarded—upstaged the director, and delivered a riveting speech from atop a bulldozer. Over the next two days, negotiations yielded a limited agreement that Wałęsa, who had become the leader of the strike, himself was ready to accept. But when more radical workers insisted on continuing the walkout until the right to strike had been won, Wałęsa supported them. At this juncture, the strike became transformed into a social revolution.

On August 22, 1980 the strike committee presented a historic manifesto of 21 demands, among them an eight-hour workday, free-speech guarantees, and, most important, the right to strike. "The workers are not fighting merely for a pittance for themselves," the document stated, "but for justice for the entire nation." Over the next week Wałęsa led negotiations with Poland's deputy prime minister, Mieczyslaw Jagielski, and in doing so he became the "hero of the hour," as Mary Craig wrote in *Lech Wałęsa and His Poland* (1987). "It was a collective leadership, not a one-man show; but it was his finger that felt the pulse of the strikers."

During the talks, the government made several major concessions: in addition to granting workers the right to form independent unions and to strike, it pledged to give strikers and their supporters immunity from reprisal, to increase wages, and to improve social services and distribution of consumer goods. These and other points were spelled out in the Gdansk Agreement, which Wałęsa and Jagielski signed on August 31, 1980. The document marked the first time that workers in any country of the Soviet bloc had been granted such freedoms. Before long, the original Gdansk strike committee had evolved into the National Committee of Solidarity, with Wałęsa as its chairman. By 1981 the union included some 10,000,000 of the nation's 17,300,000 workers.

In the months that followed the conclusion of the Gdansk agreement, Wałęsa, seeming to sense how far he could push the authorities without triggering a backlash, pressed them to make good on their promises as spelled out in the accord. For instance, there were rumors that the Soviet Union might invade Poland to crush the opposition, and Wałęsa, in an attempt to stave off Soviet intervention, worked to contain strikes that broke out in the fall of 1980. But in spite of his prestige, he was unable to control the more radical members of the movement, and relations between Solidarity and the government worsened throughout 1981. By the end of the year, after he was reelected chairman of Solidarity, Wałęsa has written, it had become "obvious that we were in a state of civil war."

On December 13, 1981 the Polish government, led by General Wojciech Jaruzelski, declared martial law. It suspended the activities of all unions, arrested thousands of Solidarity members, including Wałęsa, announced that publications would be censored, and declared public gatherings (except religious services) illegal. Following his arrest Wałęsa was held in detention, first alone at a villa near Warsaw and later in reasonably comfortable circumstances in a more isolated town where, using a smuggled transistor radio, he kept abreast of developments in the nation. In the end, martial law failed to accomplish one of its main aims—that of neutralizing Solidarity—for the union successfully reorganized itself as an underground organization. In the fall of 1982 the government officially outlawed Solidarity, which had formerly merely been "under suspension," and released Wałęsa from prison.

During Solidarity's years as an illegal organization, Wałęsa found himself under the watchful eye of the government, though he nevertheless managed to meet with the leaders of the union and could not be kept from the political spotlight. Indeed, by the time he was awarded the Nobel Prize for peace, in 1983, he had become an international symbol of the hope for political freedom.

In 1986 the government declared a limited amnesty under which it released many political prisoners. It also proposed political reforms as well as an austerity budget that required it to raise prices. The program, which was opposed by Solidarity, was put to a referendum in 1987; because a large segment of the Polish electorate boycotted the vote, the government could not claim that it had the support of the people, forcing it to proceed more cautiously. Still, the price increases that were ultimately put in place were devastating to Poles, who had seen their real wages decline over the previous several years. The spring of 1988 was thus marked by more labor unrest, the worst since that which preceded the imposition of martial law. To forestall still more chaos, the government felt it had little choice but to appeal to Solidarity's leadership to help it restore order to the country. Representatives from the two camps then entered into negotiations on how to govern Poland and reform its economy.

The Polish government's acknowledgment that it lacked the ability to rule the country effectively was followed by something even more extraordinary: in 1989 it both relegalized Solidarity and invited the union to join the Communist Party in forming a coalition government. During the campaign for the nationwide parliamentary elections, set for June 1989, Wałęsa promoted the candidacies of the Solidarity contenders (as a result of these events Solidarity had been transformed into a political party), though he himself decided not to run for a seat, feeling that he should remain above the fray. As expected, Solidarity candidates trounced their opponents: the new party won 99 of the 100 seats (all of which were contested) in the newly established Senate and all of the 161 contested seats in the 460-seat Sejm, the lower house of the Polish parliament. (During their negotiations Solidarity acceded to the Communists' demand that 299, or 65 percent, of the seats in the Sejm be reserved for members of the party.) The election results signaled the death knell of Communism in Poland, and Wojciech Jaruzelski (who was then serving as first secretary of the Communist Party and president of Poland) was compelled to ask a Wałęsa aide, Tadeusz Mazowiecki, to form a government.

In April 1990 Wałęsa was reelected chairman of Solidarity. By then he had already begun to hint at his interest in serving as president of Poland, and a few months later he expressed his intentions explicitly. His prominence notwithstanding, Wałęsa's candidacy was not enthusiastically welcomed by many of the country's new leaders. Voytek Zubek, writing in *Problems of Communism* (January-April 1991), suggested that the intellectuals' cool response to Wałęsa's intentions derived from inborn class prejudices that had been suppressed during the Communist era, when the need for a united opposition was paramount, and their longing for a Polish leader cast in the mold of the Czech dissident-turned-president Vaclav Havel: "The Western mass media's portrayal of Czechoslovakia's Velvet revolution' inundated the world with depictions of a stylish, sophisticated politics: the president-writer, who was the scion of an old aristocratic family, clad in jeans and a sweater, filling palatial governmental offices with the Bohemian figures of dissidents-turned-officials. Poland's intelligentsia felt outdone and embarrassed with their presidential office occupied by Jaruzelski, an unappealing figure who carried highly damaging historical baggage, and with the prospect of Wałęsa, who could hardly have been a more un-Havelian figure, knocking at the door of the office." Such sentiments, Zubek further contended, were what lay behind statements such as those expressed by Senator Andrzej Szczypiorski in an open letter to Wałęsa; among other admonitions, the senator suggested that Wałęsa "hit the books and start learning, because it is never too late for that." Another criticism of Wałęsa was that he was only interested in acquiring power for its own sake.

Nevertheless, Wałęsa ultimately won the support of Solidarity and became the leader on a slate of 14 candidates. On election day, November 25, 1990, dark-horse candidate Stanislaw Tyminski captured 23 percent of the popular vote, against Wałęsa's 39 percent, which necessitated a runoff election, held on December 9. In that vote, Wałęsa was swept into the presidency with more than 74 percent of the ballots cast, thus becoming Poland's first popularly elected president. In The *Struggle and the Triumph* (1992), his second volume of autobiography, Wałęsa expressed his ambivalence over the way many Poles' perception of him had changed, writing that his critics "found it impossible to admit that a mere worker had become president. The nation should have chosen a businessman, a professor, an intellectual, somebody who embodied learning and deft manners. Instead, the nation had chosen me."

Poland's new leaders inherited a host of economic problems, not least among them high inflation—which reached 600 percent in 1991—growing unemployment, and the task of transforming a moribund state-run economy into one that operates according to free-market principles. Yet another challenge was simply governing—while they had a wealth of experience in opposing Poland's government, they had none in ruling a nation. In 1991 Wałęsa's own difficulties were compounded when, following general elections, he was compelled to support one of his critics, Jan Olszewski, as prime minister. Olszewski's government lasted only a year before it was succeeded by one led by Hanna Suchocka, with whom Wałęsa established a good working relationship. Still, Wałęsa remained under fire from many quarters; among other things, he was accused of high-handedness, of forging ties with military figures he had long despised, and of seeking unchecked power for himself.

When the austerity policies of prime minister Hanna Suchocka earned her government a vote of no confidence in May 1993, Wałęsa called for parliamentary elections, to be held that September. He hoped that a new election law designed to limit the number of parties that could win seats in parliament would produce a more solid coalition that would be able to enact important measures on privatization, but instead the major beneficiaries of the new law were the Democratic Left Alliance and the Polish Peasant Party, both of whose memberships comprised former Communists. The subsequent coalition government, led by Waldemar Pawlak, was still more critical of Wałęsa. By mid-1994 the president was being blamed for a host of ills plaguing Poland, including its high unemployment and inflation rates. Wałęsa counterpunched, accusing the parliamentary coalition of corruption and threatening to dissolve it, which he did in February 1995. As a result, his approval ratings, which had hovered around 5 percent the previous summer, improved somewhat. (Pawlak's government was succeeded by one led by Jozef Oleksy, of the Democratic Left Alliance.)

In 1995, with his first presidential term nearing its end, Wałęsa announced his intention to run for reelection. In a development that surprised many observers, Aleksander Kwasniewski, the young and telegenic leader of the Democratic Left Alliance, who had held several posts in the former Communist regime, emerged as Wałęsa's principal rival. At times, Wałęsa was less than diplomatic in his treatment of Kwasniewski, so disgusted was he with the rising popularity of the former Communists; for instance, he referred to Kwasniewski's association with "a gang of thugs" and refused to shake his hand during debates. Although Wałęsa made a strong comeback in the polls and won 33 percent of the vote, just 2 percentage points less than his opponent, in the November 5 elections, he lost the runoff, on November 19, to Kwasniewski. While the ballots cast during the runoff were still being tallied, Wałęsa told reporters that he planned to remain active in Polish politics. He suggested that he would not do so in an official capacity but that he would resume his role as an opponent of the government, telling one journalist that he intended to put so much pressure on the new government that Kwasniewski would be compelled to call early elections.

PERSONAL LIFE

For his efforts to free Poland from Communist rule, Wałęsa has won many honors. Besides the Nobel Peace Prize, he has received 16 honorary doctorates, Norway's Free World Prize (1982), the Social Justice Award (1983), and the White Eagle Order (1989). He was named man of the year in 1980 by the *Financial Times*, the London Observer, and *Die Welt*, and in 1981 by *Die Zeit, UExpress, Le Soir,* and *Time*. Since November 8, 1969 he has been married to Miroslawa Golos, whom he calls Danuta, with whom he has eight children. He is a devout Roman Catholic. As of 2016, Wałęsa continues to speak and lecture on history and politics in Poland and abroad.

FURTHER READING

Problems of Communism p69+ Ja-Ap '91; *Washington Post A* pi fl 5 '94; *Wałęsa, Lech. A Way of Hope* (1987), *The Struggle and the Triumph* (1992); *International Who's Who,* 1995-96

CHING-WEI WANG

Born: May 4, 1883; Sanshui, China
Died: November 10, 1944; Nagoya, Japan
Primary Field: Chinese Politician
Group Affiliation: Reorganized National Government of the Republic of China

INTRODUCTION

Wang Ching-wei was considered a great Chinese revolutionist and patriot until he declared himself at peace with Japan, and was chosen the puppet ruler of Japanese-occupied China in 1940. Then he was berated as a traitor to his country. Chinese patriots in Chungking, provisional capital of the fighting part of China, cir-culated chain letters asking for money to be used for Wang's assassination.

The chain letters asked receivers to contribute a dollar to a "kill Wang Ching-wei Fund," and to send 11 copies of the letter to friends. Funds would be collected by the Kuomintang, or Nationalist Party, according to the letters, and would go to a successful assassin. Men who attempted to kill Mr. Wang but failed and fell into Japanese hands would have the satisfaction of knowing that one percent of the fund would go to members of their families.

What gauge of popular opinion the letters were, it would be hard to make out in the complex situations arising from China's long war with Japan. But certainly they reflected the general opinion, shared strongly in America and Britain, that Wang Ching-wei had sold his country down the river when he made secret terms with Japan and became head of Japanese-occupied China. In November 1940 he was formally recognized by Japan as China's ruler, and made a "last" plea for peace in China.

EARLY LIFE

As a young law student, Wang had joined the forces of China's George Washington, Sun Yat-sen, founder of the Chinese Republic. Wang and Chiang Kai-shek were Dr. Sun's foremost disciples. Wang was a favorite student of Dr. Sun, wrote many of his manifestoes, and even took down the famous will the great revolutionist delivered on his deathbed.

LIFE'S WORK

On Dr. Sun's death in 1925 his party split, and Wang and Chiang Kai-shek fought for the mantle of their leader. Wang joined the Cantonese and led several revolts. Chiang Kai-shek, with the aid of Communist advisers, won in the vicious, bloody civil war. Politics eventually brought the two men together again. After Canton made peace with Nanking, Wang became Premier of China.

Wang resigned as Premier in 1932, and ironically enough it was with loud charges that Chinese generals should fight Japan more aggressively. The following year he again took the post of Premier, and again resigned in 1935, giving ill health as his reason.

When the war with Japan started Generalissimo Chiang Kai-shek and Wang continued together. As deputy leader of the Nationalist (Kuomintang) Party, Wang followed the Chinese government from Nanking to Hankow and to Chungking, as the Japanese made inroads into China. But in 1938, in the mountain fastness of Western China's provisional capital, Wang addressed peace pleas to Chiang Kai-shek and members of the embattled Kuomintang. Chiang refused to consider cessation of hostilities as Wang advised. Wang then took his two sons out of school, sent them out of the country, packed his own belongings and one night left Chungking secretly for Hanoi, French Indo-China. Chiang Kai-shek read him out of the party, branded him as a traitor and arrested his followers. Wang was found in Indo-China and several attempts on his life were made.

But the erstwhile Chinese patriot had declared himself at peace with the Japanese. From Indo-China he went to Hong Kong, then Shanghai, and later to the Japanese-conquered Kankow. The Japanese recognized him as a good catch for their puppet regimes in China. And since he was the only Chinese leader they could win over, they entered into negotiations with him to set up a central Chinese government in those parts of China which they had occupied.

The "all China" Japanese-sponsored regime headed by the former Chinese Premier Wang Ching-wei was proclaimed March 30, 1940 in brief ceremonies at Nanking. The purpose of the new regime was to establish peace between China and Japan and to put an end to the 33 months of war. It was a strange installation of what Wang and the Japanese declared was a new Chinese government. With the exception of Japan, no foreign nation sent diplomatic representatives to the ceremony. The American, French, British and Soviet Ambassadors were in Chungking, where Generalissimo Chiang Kai-shek's government was recognized by their countries as the sole legal government of China, although the British Ambassador had made a speech conciliatory to Japan two days before.

The installation was not without its incidents. Wang's home in Shanghai for months had been ringed with pill boxes in which Japanese soldiers stood guard. Five Japanese boats escorted the steamer bringing Wang from Shanghai to Nanking. And a Japanese-operated train bringing Japanese officials and foreign correspondents to the Japanese-guarded walls of Nanking was derailed by unidentified persons, believed to have been Chinese guerrillas. Chungking held a huge outdoor demonstration, burning wooden effigies of Wang and his wife.

In a broadcast from Chungking, President Lin Sen of China bitterly denounced Wang as a traitor, and declared that he (Lin) and Chiang Kai-shek would lead China to fight "to the end for her liberty, sovereignty and territorial integrity." He appealed to the world to continue to support China, which he declared would live despite the Japanese and their puppets.

President Lin Sen pointed out that Wang was already under death sentence as a traitor, and ordered all responsible government organizations to arrest him. Wang was carrying on a large scale rebellion under cover of a peace campaign, he declared.

A peculiar phase of the Wang situation was that Lin had been elected as President in the Japanese conference with Wang in Nanking, and Wang merely named as acting President until such time as Lin might decide to "play

Affiliation: Reorganized National Government of the Republic of China

In late 1938, Wang left Chongqing for Hanoi, French Indochina, where he stayed for three months and announced his support for a settlement with the Japanese. During this time, he was wounded in an assassination attempt by KMT agents. Wang then flew to Shanghai, where he entered negotiations with Japanese authorities. The Japanese invasion had given him the opportunity to establish a new government outside of Chiang Kai-shek's control.

In March 1940, Wang became the head of state of what came to be known as the Reorganized National Government of China. He served as the President of the Executive Yuan and Chairman of the National Government. In November 1940, Wang's government signed the "Sino-Japanese Treaty" with the Japanese, a document known for its political, military, and economic concessions. In June 1941, Wang gave a public radio address from Tokyo in which he praised Japan and affirmed China's submission to it. He pledged to work with the Empire of Japan to resist communism and Western imperialism.

The Government of National Salvation of the collaborationist "Republic of China," which Wang headed, was established on the Three Principles of Pan-Asianism, anti-communism, and opposition to Chiang Kai-shek.

ball" with the Japanese. Lin's speech was his first personal answer to the Nanking election. Wang, despite all this, at his inauguration as the puppet premier blandly acted as if he represented all China. While Japanese armed soldiers guarded the city, he spoke of cooperation with "our Japanese neighbors so that our sovereign independence and territorial integrity may be safeguarded." He suavely proclaimed the new Chinese government at Nanking the only legal government of the country. Hereafter, he announced, any decree issued to the nation and any treaty or agreement entered into by the Chungking regime with foreign powers will be automatically invalid. "Chungking," he said, "has now been reduced to the status of a regional refugee regime." He formally ordered the cessation of the 33 months' hostilities with Japan.

The domestic political strategy Wang sought to use to win over the Chinese was revealed when he called on all civil servants still serving Chungking and various local governments to report for duty at the capital within the shortest possible time. He added that on proper identification they would be appointed to the same rank they now held and at the same salary.

But although Wang set himself up as the successor to the Chiang Kai-shek government, his authority

actually extended only to the areas occupied by the Japanese Army, the seaports and principal cities of North and Central China. In those areas he contemplates a system of stringent passport control in order to raise revenue and to refuse to return to China persons considered anti-Japanese.

In his 50's, the new puppet ruler looks about 20 years younger. He is handsome, a dapper dresser, witty, and an eloquent speaker. Japanese-educated, a graduate of the law college at Tokyo, he has traveled often in Europe. He learned to speak French fluently and several times took diabetes cures in Germany.

He has gone a long way since his early days as a young revolutionist seeking to overthrow the Manchu dynasty. As a young man he was imprisoned in 1910 for plotting the assassination of the Prince regent of Imperial China. Meanwhile the revolution of 1911 led by Dr. Sun Yat-sen broke out, and he was released. The chains which he wore in prison were displayed in a Peking museum.

By 1940 the "Chinese patriot" was proclaiming peace with Japan. He did not make public his terms with Japan, however. His inauguration had been put off for months. The terms which Wang's followers gave out sought to prove that Wang stubbornly refused to head a Central Chinese government unless the Japanese lived up Jo certain pledges to respect China's territorial integrity and independence.

He was said to have, held out against Japanese political and military advisers for his government, accepting only economic advisers. His agreement also is said to have called for the eventual withdrawal of Japanese troops in China. And he was said to have insisted on the use of the Chinese flag, with pennants attached to distinguish it from the old Chinese Nationalist flag. Rumors were current in November 1940 that fighting had broken out between Wang's troops and Japanese troops and that rather than accede to harsh Japanese demands Wang has twice tried to give up his regime and leave for Hong Kong.

But in Chungking they are still sure of what Japan meant when she spoke of "the new order in East Asia." No one can change Japan's traditional policy of conquest any more than the leopard can change his spots, Chiang Kai-shek declares.

PERSONAL LIFE

Wang was married to Chen Bijun and had six children, five of whom survived into adulthood.

In March 1944, Want went to Japan to receive medical treatment for a wound left by an assassination attempt in 1939. He died in Japan in November 1944.

Wang was buried in an elaborate tomb in Nanjing near the Sun Yat-sen Masoleum. The tomb was destroyed soon after Japan's defeat and Wang's body was burned. The site is commemorated with a small pavilion noting Wang as a traitor.

FURTHER READING

Amerasia 3:542-8 F '40; *Asia* 40:151-3 Mr '40; *Christian Sci Mon* p4 Mr 30 '40 por; *Cur Hist* 50:11 Ag '39; *Life* 8:16 Ja 29 '40 por; 9:58+ S 30 '40 por; *Liv Age* 358:260-6 My '40; *Newsweek* 6:14 Ag 17 '35 por; 15:27 Ja 15 '40; 15:26 Ap 8 '40; *Time* 34:23 Jl 10 '39 por; 35:39 Mr 25 '40; 35:28-9 Ap I '40 *International Who's Who; Who's Who in China*

SIR ROBERT ALDERSON WRIGHT

Chairman of the United Nations War Crimes Commission

Born: October 15, 1869; South Shields, County Durham
Died: June 27, 1964; Burbage, Wiltshire

INTRODUCTION

In January 1945 the sixteen-nation United Nations War Crimes Commission, which acts as a sort of international grand jury, elected the Right Honorable Lord Wright as its chairman. Lord Wright, more formally Baron Wright of Durley, is a distinguished lawyer, a member of the highest British tribunal, who is entitled to place after his name the initials K.C. (King's Counsel), P.C. (Privy Councilor), J.P. (Justice of the Peace), and F.B.A. (Fellow of the British Academy). Knighted in 1925 as Sir Robert Alderson Wright, the jurist became in 1932 one of England's law lords, a life peer.

EARLY LIFE

Lord Wright was born Robert Alderson Wright, the son of John and Elizabeth Middleton (Carr) Wright of South Shields, in England's North Country. The date was October 15, 1869. He was educated privately, and started his professional life, according to the British *Illustrated,* as a schoolmaster. Wright entered Trinity College of Cambridge University, receiving his B.A. in 1896, at the age of twenty-seven. In 1899 he was made a Fellow of the College, which he remained until 1905, meanwhile acquiring his M.A. in 1900. Wright had been studying law at the Inner Temple, perhaps the most famous of England's four inns of court (the combination law schools and bar associations to one of which all barristers must

Sir Robert Alderson Wright.

belong, and which alone possess the power of calling to the bar and disbarment). In 1900, when he was thirty-one, the future peer was called to the bar and entered the practice of law.

"There is no aspect of the law," to quote a British magazine, "in which Lord Wright's penetrating and analytical mind is not well versed." In 1917 he "took silk"—applied for and received letters patent from the Lord Chancellor as a King's Counsel, "one of His Majesty's counsel learned in the law," which made official his position as a leading barrister. Six years later he became a bencher of the Inner Temple; the benchers pass on the applicants for admission, and for sufficient cause, subject to appeal to the judiciary, may refuse to call offenders to the bar or may disbar or disbench them. In 1925 Wright was knighted and appointed a judge of the High Court of Justice, King's Bench Division. While in this post, Sir Robert was married to Margery Avis Bullows of Sutton Coldfield; this was in 1928, when he was fifty-nine.

LIFE'S WORK

In 1932 Sir Robert Wright was made a Lord of Appeal in Ordinary—a member of the highest judicial tribunal of the United Kingdom, and, as such, of the Judicial Committee of the Privy Council, which is the highest court of the British Commonwealth of Nations. The Lords of Appeal are made life peers (non-hereditary), with seats in the House of Lords, and Sir Robert was created Baron Wright of Durley in the county of Wiltshire. He continued to serve as a Lord of Appeal until 1935: then he became Master of the Rolls, a position ranking next after the Lord Chancellor and Lord Chief Justice, and also became chairman of a Royal Commission on Historical Monuments. Since 1937 Lord Wright has again been a Lord of Appeal. His *Legal Essays and Addresses* were published in 1939, and in 1940 he was elected a Fellow of the British Academy.

In July 1944 the High Commissioner appointed Lord Wright to represent Australia on the sixteen-member United Nations War Crimes Commission, a fact-gathering agency with *no* official authority to conduct trials or determine policy. In January 1945 the commission chairman, Sir Cecil Hurst, resigned, "partly for ill-health," in the words of John MacCormac in *The New York Times,* "and partly because he could get no cooperation from the Foreign Office"; the American member, Herbert C. Pell, was released by his Government; and Lord Wright was elected chairman. (Pell declared that he had been dropped because certain State Department officials opposed his proposal to hold the Nazis criminally responsible for offenses against their own nationals on the grounds of race, creed, or political

opinion, and he stated that Sir Cecil Hurst had a similar complaint.)

In Lord Wright's words: "When the United Nations War Crimes Commission was charged with investigating crimes . . . what it had to do was to 'investigate' the statements sent in to it in order to report whether a prima facie case of war crime was shown, and report it to the governments accordingly. . . .It was thus necessary to have some body or bodies to conduct the detailed detective inquiries in the appropriate localities. That duty was imposed on the National Offices . . . established and maintained by each of the United Nations. . . .The whole idea of the system was that the United Nations should each do its own work in bringing to justice those enemies who had committed offenses against its nationals. . . . The primary function of the military [in this connection] was to apprehend the criminals named in lists issued by the Commission. . . . The Commission has [also] power to act on its own initiative in listing offenders and has done so in its Seventh and Ninth Lists of Key Criminals. . . . It is also a central clearinghouse for the records and is thus able to classify and compare the cases and frame general charges of conspiracy in crime. . . . The Commission stands as the public embodiment of justice and of international law in the particular sphere of war crimes.

"The special feature of the Nazi or Fascist crimes is that they are not merely done on an unprecedented scale over the whole range of military operations and enemy occupation, but that they exhibit every trace of a general scheme; they all clearly emanated from a master criminal and his entourage and were carried out according to plan by elaborate organized agencies and instrumentalities—that is, by individuals acting under common direction and in common concert. This mass criminality has been forced on the attention of the Commission and has caused them to consider special methods of dealing with it. In particular, experience has made the Commission realize that membership in a particular organization which has systematically organized and effected the perpetration of atrocities is prima facie evidence of guilty complicity. I say prima facie, because it might be possible for an accused member to show that he was in no way implicated. ... The Commission is acquiring the material to compare and classify, to point to common features, and to trace the crime from the actual perpetrators to the central mind or authority, such as Hitler or Goering, right through the intermediate agencies, often by a chain of orders or directives passing down the line,

741

and to analyze the element of common purpose or conspiracy. . . . They are all manifestly part of a systematic plan to crush and degrade and dehumanize the spirit of the peoples who are attacked, if not to exterminate them. . . . The Commission has positively declared its view that obedience to superior orders is not a defense and that heads of states are not immune. This last is a curious revival of the old bad idea of the divine right of kings."

Lord Wright also expressed his hope that the Commission would coordinate its work with that of the equivalent Soviet group, and in May 1945 the Commission submitted a proposal for an international tribunal to try the "arch-criminals" whose crimes affected nationals of many different countries. On August 8 the War Crimes Commission in London announced a pact, the Jackson agreement, establishing an International Military Tribunal to try the major European Axis war criminals. The Tribunal will consist of four members— one each from Britain, the United States, Russia, and France. Lord Wright published an article in *The New York Times Magazine* of October 28, 1945, in which he discussed the legal basis for bringing war criminals to justice.

PERSONAL LIFE

The white-haired, beetle-browed judge was described as "a tower of strength in our [British] supreme legal tribunal." He had been awarded honorary LL.D.'s by the universities of London and Birmingham as well as Cambridge, of which he is Deputy High Steward; he also was an honorary Fellow of Trinity College. Since 1934 he was a member of the Universities Committee of the Privy Council, and he was on the Visiting Committee of Harvard Law School in the United States, where he has often lectured on jurisprudence. Wright is a member of four clubs. "To his mental powers," it is said, "he can add physical prowess of which any man many years his junior might well be proud ... is still a fine sportsman," and "performs without difficulty the acrobatics necessary when he has to search ceiling-high shelves for works on international jurisprudence." The Wrights, whose household included eight assorted live dogs as well as many animal statuettes, were fond of horseback riding. (Lady Wright has won competitions in the United States and Canada.) The Baron was a believer in the public's right to information: "Secrecy," he has said, "is always undesirable if it can be avoided." He retired in 1947 and was appointed Order of St. Michael and St. George, the British order of chivalry, in 1948.

FURTHER READING
Burke's Peerage (1936); *Who's Who,* 1945

Y

AHMED YASSIN
Spiritual Leader of Hamas

Born: January 1, 1937; Mandatory Palestine
Died: March 22, 2004; Gaza Strip
Affiliation: Hamas

INTRODUCTION

When Sheikh Ahmed Yassin returned to the Gaza Strip in 1997, after having spent eight years in an Israeli prison, he was greeted as a hero by throngs of jubilant Palestinians. Yassin is considered to be the spiritual leader of Hamas, which he founded in 1987 as an offshoot to his work promoting social and economic advancement for Palestinians. Since then, Hamas has evolved into a militant Islamic movement dedicated to establishing a Palestinian homeland. Hamas opposed the 1993 Oslo peace accord between Israel and the Palestine Liberation Organization, and it has been responsible for a series of suicide-bombing attacks that have killed scores of people in Israel. Before his release from prison, Yassin had been serving a life sentence after pleading guilty to manslaughter for planning the murders of four Palestinians who were suspected of collaborating with Israel. He won his freedom not long after two Israeli secret service agents were caught in Jordan after a botched assassination attempt on a senior Hamas political official. Israeli prime minister Benjamin Netanyahu ordered Yassin's release, as well as that of about 50 other jailed Palestinians, at the request of King Hussein of Jordan, who had been infuriated by the Israeli action. At about the same time that the Palestinians were freed, Hussein allowed the Israeli agents to go home.

Yassin's return to Gaza was seen by some political analysts in the region as a threat to Yasir Arafat, the chairman of the Palestinian Authority.

Hamas and Arafat have had a long-running feud over how to wage the struggle for Palestinian independence from Israel, as well as over what terms would be acceptable for a final resolution. "Knowing Mr. Arafat, of course he doesn't like to have another symbol sitting here in Gaza," Ziad Abu Amr, a Palestinian legislator and political scientist, told Barton Gellman of the Washington Post *(October 7, 1997). "That's his monopoly. To have someone contesting his leadership, his influence, his charisma—I wonder if Gaza has room for the two of them." But at the rally at a soccer stadium in Gaza celebrating his freedom, Yassin made conciliatory comments about Arafat. "We are all one people, and we will remain one people," he said. "I send my regards to Yasir Arafat and hope he will gain the freedom of the homeland." Considered to be a relative moderate within the Hamas hierarchy, Yassin could play a key role in any future settlement in the region.*

EARLY LIFE

One of nine children, Sheikh Ahmed Yassin was born in 1938 in what is now southern Israel. His father, a local dignitary who had four wives, died shortly after his birth. Like thousands of other Palestinians, the Yassins fled their home following the 1948 Israeli War of Independence. They ended up in the Egyptian-controlled Gaza Strip, where they lived in the squalid Shati refugee camp, near the Mediterranean Sea. As a boy, Yassin often dove into the sea from rocks along the shore. On one such occasion, in 1952, he dove into shallow water and severely damaged his spinal column. As a result, all four of his limbs became paralyzed, and he has been confined to a wheelchair ever since.

After the accident, Yassin concentrated on the study of language and religion, areas in which he excelled. Lacking the money to attend college after graduating from high school, he got a job as a teacher. He became involved in the Muslim Brotherhood, which was outlawed by the Egyptian government. Because of his association with the group, he was jailed for 45 days.

LIFE'S WORK

After the Six-Day War, in 1967, in which Israel won control of the Gaza Strip, the West Bank, and several other territories, Yassin devoted himself to strengthening the Muslim Brotherhood in Gaza. At the time, he was more interested in the religious and economic advancement of his people than in the political and military struggle against Israel. In 1973, he established the Islamic Center, which he used to coordinate the social-welfare programs sponsored by brotherhood-affiliated organizations. The center, which was funded by the OPEC nations of the Persian Gulf, was tacitly endorsed by the Israeli authorities, who apparently hoped that Yassin's movement would counterbalance the influence of the Palestine Liberation Organization (PLO) among Arabs living within Israel.

During the first 15 years of Israel's occupation of Gaza and the West Bank, the brotherhood did not participate in the PLO's armed struggle against Israel, which included terrorist attacks against civilians. Some members of Fatah, the powerful guerrilla faction of the PLO, which was run by Yasir Arafat, accused Yassin and his followers of cooperating with the "Zionist entity." Because of this, the brotherhood lost many members to Fatah and other militant groups.

In response, Yassin and his followers decided that to remain a viable force among the Palestinian people, the Muslim Brotherhood would have to become actively involved in the political and guerrilla battle against Israel. In 1984, Yassin was arrested by the Israeli authorities on charges of sedition and sentenced to 13 years in jail, but he was freed a year later in a prisoner-exchange program. During 1985 and 1986, the brotherhood began issuing pamphlets urging Palestinians to use civil disobedience to resist the Israeli occupation. In 1987, when the Palestinian uprising known as the *intifada* erupted in Gaza

and the West Bank, Yassin decided to set up a separate faction, called the Islamic Resistance Movement, to deal with the situation. The faction became known by its acronym, Hamas, which means "zeal."

In May 1989, Yassin was arrested and sentenced to life in prison. With his imprisonment, along with that of several other relatively moderate political directors, "Hamas lost a vital component of its leadership, creating a void filled by more militant cadres," Ahmad Rashad wrote in *Middle East Affairs Journal* (Summer/Fall 1996). During the early 1990s, Hamas mushroomed into a large-scale operation with separate administrative, charitable, political, and military elements. The military wing, the Qassam Brigades, was divided into a series of small cells consisting of about four or five hardcore fighters and supported by group sympathizers. Members of the Qassam cells opposed the 1993 Oslo peace accord between the PLO and Israel, and since then, have been responsible for a wave of suicide attacks directed against Israeli citizens. Ironically, now that Arafat and his former Fatah followers—who once openly supported and/or participated in terrorist acts—have established the Palestinian Authority in Gaza and Jericho, they are responsible for suppressing terrorism. As a result, they have arrested some members of Hamas who, in turn, have accused them of collaboration with Israel.

Meanwhile, for several years, the Israelis had been considering releasing Yassin from prison, principally because he is in fragile health. He reportedly has had trouble breathing, and has an assortment of other ailments. Some sources have speculated that the Israelis were concerned that if Yassin were to die in jail, he would become a martyr for the Palestinians. In addition, the Israelis were only all too aware that several Hamas-sponsored terrorist attacks had been carried out in demand for Yassin's freedom, along with that of other Palestinian prisoners.

Although both Israeli and Jordanian authorities later insisted that there had been no quid pro quo prisoner swap after Israel reportedly tried, unsuccessfully, to assassinate Khaled Meshal, a Hamas political leader in Jordan, that is what happened, in effect. Upon Yassin's release from prison, on October 1, 1997, he was flown to Jordan, where he received medical attention. Mahmoud Zakhar, a Hamas leader in Gaza, denounced the move as a "deportation" and demanded the return of Yassin to "his homeland." In fact, plans for Yassin's return to Gaza were already in the works, and on October

6, he made a triumphant appearance before a crowd of thousands at Yarmuk Stadium, a soccer field in Gaza.

In interviews with reporters soon after his release, Yassin made what observers called "moderate" remarks about Palestinian relations with Israel. He said that Hamas would agree to a "truce" with Israel if the Israelis withdrew from the entire West Bank, including East Jerusalem, and from the Gaza Strip, and dismantled all Jewish settlements in those territories. He also said that Hamas would cease its suicide-bombing attacks in Israel if the Israeli government stopped taking punitive measures against Palestinians, such as shutting businesses, demolishing houses, and seizing land. Israel has never accepted the terms he spelled out, but David Bar-Ilan, the communications director for Netanyahu, said Yassin's remarks were "worth watching" and "a positive development if it means something, [and is] not just part of the usual rhetoric." (Other Hamas leaders, including Khaled Meshal, have taken a harder line, saying that Hamas would never recognize Israel, even if it withdrew to its pre-1967 borders.)

In other statements since his release, however, Yassin has spoken out in more militant terms. "A nation that does not wage *jihad* [holy war] cannot exist," he proclaimed to students at Islamic University in Gaza City, as quoted by *The New York Times* (October 23, 1997). "God is with us and Satan with them. We will fight and fight until we regain our rights and our homeland, God willing."

In several interviews, Yassin has been asked to justify the Hamas tactic of sending young men with explosives strapped to their bodies to blow themselves up in crowded Israeli shopping centers and buses. "Islamic tenets prohibit us from attacking civilians, but the Israelis were the first to violate these regulations—they've killed women, the elderly, children," Yassin asserted to Roger Gaess in an interview for *Middle East Affairs Journal* (Summer/Fall 1997). "They've demolished our homes and confiscated our land; they've arrested thousands of Palestinians and embargoed our nation, preventing many, many people from supporting their families. We feel sorrow and pain when Jewish women and children and other civilians are injured. But the Israelis initiated these kind of attacks, and we are defending ourselves. We are the victims."

PERSONAL LIFE

Sheikh Ahmed Yassin lived in a two-room cinder-block shack in Gaza City, where aides and admirers took turns caring for him. Palestinian men would come by the hundreds to pay him homage and seek his advice. Although he was a sickly man who can move neither his arms nor legs and is nearly deaf and almost blind, Yassin remained a charismatic figure. During the spring of 1998, he embarked on a tour of Arab countries, to raise money for Hamas. His popularity poses a threat to Arafat, whose stature among Palestinians has declined because of the languishing peace process and charges of corruption within the Palestine Authority. But Hamas has had problems of its own. There were reports of internecine feuding within the military cells.

Yassin was killed in March 2004 by an Israeli missile that fired on him as he was being wheeled from his early morning prayers. His killing also claimed the lives of his bodyguards and nine bystanders. Two hundred thousand Palestinians attended his funeral.

FURTHER READING

Economist p40 Dec. 19, 1992; *Middle East Affairs Journal* pi03+ Summer/Fall 1996, pl29+ Summer/Fall 1997; *Newsweek* p39 Oct. 20, 1997, with photo; *The New York Times A* pl2 Oct. 7, 1997, with photos, A pl2 Oct. 24, 1997, with photo; *Washington Post* A pl+ Oct. 7, 1997, with photo, pl8+ Oct. 26, 1997, with photo

---

BORIS N(IKOLAYEVICH) YELTSIN

Russian Prime Minister

Born: February 1, 1931; Sverdlovsk, Russia
Died: April 23, 2007; Moscow, Russia
Group Affiliation: Communist Party

INTRODUCTION

Not many years ago, only a handful of Westerners would have displayed any interest in the rise and fall of a first secretary of the Moscow City Communist Party Committee. The fact that the fate of Boris Yeltsin, an

Boris Yeltsin.

Kremlin.ru

occupant of that post, was followed so intently in the West and debated so heatedly and openly within the Soviet Union itself testifies to the changes wrought by the Communist party leader, Mikhail Gorbachev, and his policy of glasnost ("openness"). Yeltsin's case, however, is considered by many observers to be a bitter irony: a supporter of glasnost and perestroika (economic "restructuring"), he was punished for wanting to take Gorbachev's policies too far and too fast. Although he was demoted and publicly admonished, Yeltsin continued to enjoy wide popular support, among Muscovites in particular. In March 1989 he was elected to the Congress of People's Deputies as an at-large member for Moscow.

EARLY LIFE

Boris Nikolayevich Yeltsin was born on February 1, 1931 in Sverdlovsk, an industrial city in the Ural Mountain region of European Russia. He was, in his words, a "little bit of a hooligan" as a boy. When he was eleven,

he and two friends sneaked into a weapons warehouse and stole two hand grenades. "When we started to disassemble them, one of the grenades exploded," he told David Remnick in an interview for the *Washington Post* (May 21, 1989). Yeltsin lost the thumb and forefinger of his left hand in the accident. Trained as an engineer at the Urals M. Kirov Polytechnic Institute, he worked at various construction projects from 1955 to 1968.

LIFE'S WORK

Targeting for criticism the party bureaucrats who reveled in perquisites and privileges, such as shopping at special stores and riding around in chauffeur-driven cars, Yeltsin advocated the abolition of such special privileges and stressed that self-sacrifice rather than self-aggrandizement had to become the standard for party workers. He himself took to riding the city's buses and subways, talking to agitated commuters about the problems of the transport system. He began unannounced visits to city factories and stores, appraising their performance and noting what goods were in short supply. He gained great popular support when, early on in his tenure, he ensured that fresh vegetables would reach the capital by cutting through layers of middlemen and bureaucracy that had previously resulted in produce rotting in warehouses.

Yeltsin tried to beautify and personalize the city by encouraging street cafes and colorful fruit stalls. He formed an urban planning council, with a mandate to preserve historical buildings and restore architectural monuments, guided by his vision of a vibrant city, livable in the present and in tune with its past. Like the mayors of great urban centers everywhere, Yeltsin had to confront problems of overpopulation and housing shortages, crime, alcoholism, drug addiction, inferior education, and unemployment. What made his undertaking so different was that it involved a battle with the entrenched party machinery, the dislodging of self-satisfied bureaucrats, and the unprecedented firing of people who had considered their jobs and privileges an unalterable part of ideology and life.

Not surprisingly, Yeltsin made enemies, just as Gorbachev himself encountered resistance to his *glasnost* and *perestroika*. Nor did it help matters that Yeltsin was impatient and temperamental, pugnacious and undiplomatic. Even as he pressed for greater democratization in Moscow and in the entire Soviet Union, his subordinates considered him authoritarian, undemocratic,

Affiliation: Communist Party

He was thirty years old when he joined the Communist party, in 1961, at the height of Nikita S. Khrushchev's anti-Stalinist reforms, and from 1968 on he engaged in work for the party. In 1976 he was appointed first secretary of the Sverdlovsk District Central Committee, and over the next several years, he gained a reputation as an energetic, charismatic reformer. In July 1985 the new general secretary of the Communist party, Mikhail Gorbachev, brought Yeltsin to Moscow, as secretary of the Central Committee for Construction. When Yeltsin was promoted to first secretary of the Moscow City Party Committee in December 1985, he took over a post with responsibilities somewhat akin to those of an American mayor, with a clear mandate to reform the city bureaucracy, still rife with corruption from the previous administration of Viktor Grishin. In March 1986 he gained the status of a candidate (nonvoting) member of the Politburo, the Communist party's inner decision making body.

Wasting no time in asserting his new authority, Yeltsin clearly aligned himself with Gorbachev's reform wing of the Communist party and against the old guard. At the Twenty-seventh Party Congress, in February 1986, Yeltsin shocked party insiders, long accustomed to fulsome speeches of self-congratulation, when he took himself to task for his inaction and hypocrisy during the Brezhnev years. In a speech that he delivered to the Moscow City Party Committee later in the month, he advocated "pull[ing] out the roots of bureaucracy, social injustice, and abuses." Practicing what he preached, in April 1986 he announced the arrests of hundreds of corrupt trade officials and publicly castigated several city bureaucrats by name. "Moscow TV and radio programs are of no interest to Muscovites," he announced in another speech. "Muscovites—workers in particular—are straightforward folk," he told an interviewer for *Moskovskaya Pravda*, the Moscow party newspaper. "They call a spade a spade. And sometimes I feel ashamed and embarrassed in front of them because we officials could have done more, but we haven't."

and difficult to work with, but even his critics had to concede that he was hard-working and incorruptible.

On October 21, 1987 the Communist Party Central Committee met to hear Gorbachev outline the speech that he intended to deliver publicly at the seventieth anniversary celebration of the Russian Revolution. The session was held behind closed doors, as was customary, but because of the extraordinary happenings, accounts of the meeting leaked, first to the Western press and then to the Soviet public. According to a reconstruction of the session by Seweryn Dialer in *U.S. News & World Report* (March 28, 1988) that was based on interviews conducted in Moscow, Gorbachev had distributed a fifteen-page outline of his speech in advance of the meeting, and the agreed-upon ground rules of the session stipulated that there would be no comments or questions following Gorbachev's address. But when Gorbachev had finished speaking, Yeltsin suddenly requested the right to the floor. At first Gorbachev hesitated, but then granted Yeltsin permission to speak.

To a stunned audience, a nervous Yeltsin said that he had submitted a letter of resignation from both his Moscow Committee and Politburo posts. *Perestroika,* he said, was proceeding too slowly; it had given

virtually nothing to the people. He criticized the lackadaisical party leadership, singling out in particular Yegor Ligachev, the number-two man in the party hierarchy, whom he accused of adhering to old methods of leadership. Yeltsin contended that Ligachev was sabotaging his attempts to improve living conditions for the people of Moscow.

Bialer's account fails to mention any direct criticism by Yeltsin of Gorbachev himself, but early accounts in the Western press, in late October, centered on Yeltsin's reported accusation that Gorbachev was fostering a cult of personality that threatened to undermine the very programs he was striving to achieve. According to Bialer's reconstruction, when Yeltsin had finished speaking, Gorbachev opened the floor for others to respond. After a short period of silence, Ligachev countered, denying Yeltsin's accusations. Emboldened by Ligachev, twenty-two other party members followed in turn, denouncing Yeltsin and reproaching him for grandstanding. Yeltsin rebutted, standing by his charges against Ligachev but denying that he was threatening party unity or Gorbachev's integrity. Then Gorbachev reprimanded Yeltsin for his "petty-bourgeois outburst" and disclosed that this was not the first time that

Yeltsin's impatience had led to an uncalled-for confrontation. The Politburo had previously cautioned Yeltsin about his headstrong ways. He had submitted a letter of resignation once before, in August, but had agreed to defer the matter until after the anniversary celebrations. Bitterly castigating Yeltsin for not sticking to that agreement, Gorbachev labeled as "political adventurism" Yeltsin's appeal for accelerating the pace of *perestroika.*

Muscovites first learned of the "Yeltsin affair" from foreign journalists and news sources, for the domestic media were muzzled until after the anniversary observances. Consequently, rumors abounded. On November 11, Soviet television announced that the Moscow Party Committee had met on that day, with Gorbachev in attendance, and stripped Yeltsin of his post as first secretary. On November 13, *Pravda* printed a three-page spread about the November 11 party meeting, in which Gorbachev assessed Yeltsin's October 21 speech as "politically immature, extremely confusing, and contradictory" and accused Yeltsin of putting his personal ambitions before the interests of the party. Yeltsin, who had been hospitalized on November 8 for heart problems and who was brought directly to the meeting from the hospital, "confessed" to his party comrades that "ambition" had indeed gotten the better of him. "I am guilty before the Moscow city party organization, Moscow City Party Committee, before you, and, of course, I am very guilty before Mikhail Sergeyevich Gorbachev," he was reported to have said.

Yeltsin's abject confession, as widely reported in the Soviet media, had a chilling effect on many staunch supporters of Gorbachev's *glasnost.* The fact that the full proceedings of the November 11 meeting were released, but not Yeltsin's October 21 speech of accusation, led many to question the openness of "openness." Even corrupt party officials had not been subject to the type of humiliation meted out to Yeltsin. Many writers and other intellectuals conjured up images of the Stalinist show trials of the 1930s and their similar degrading expressions of contrition. No one expected Yeltsin to be sent to a prison camp or placed before a firing squad, but the parallels were eerie, nonetheless.

Most Western political analysts interpreted Yeltsin's firing as a victory for party conservatives over Gorbachev's reform wing. Although Gorbachev had joined in the chorus of denunciation, it was *glasnost* itself that seemed to have suffered a harsh blow. After all, as one of Gorbachev's most ardent promoters, Yeltsin had been trying to do for Moscow what Gorbachev had outlined as his goals for the Soviet Union: eliminate corruption, streamline the bureaucracy, modernize services, and reorganize production and distribution. Gorbachev was forced into the position of disciplining Yeltsin's hotheadedness, but as he himself said in an exchange with Soviet editors in January 1988, the "party's rebuff [of Yeltsin] was viewed by a certain part of the intelligentsia, especially young people, as a blow to *perestroika.*"

Reports of the November 11 party meeting put a damper on the Soviet public's belief in Gorbachev's commitment to *glasnost,* and the strong popular support for Yeltsin manifested itself in hitherto unheard-of demonstrations of protest. On November 17, several hundred students rallied at Moscow State University, demanding the publication of the text of Yeltsin's October 21 speech to the Central Committee. Police broke up a meeting of the "Club of Social Initiatives," assembled in a Moscow factory to debate the Yeltsin affair. At the November 15 "Moscow Forum," sponsored by the reform-minded magazine *Ogonyok,* several thousand people crowded in, asking why Yeltsin's October speech had never been published and "why," in the words of one participant, "Yeltsin, who until an hour ago was a leader of *perestroika,* turned by some secret accountings of the authorities into an enemy more wicked than those who for years brought shame to the country?"

Writing from Moscow for *The New York Times* (November 13, 1987), Francis X. Clines reported an atmosphere "close to political mourning" amongst Muscovites. People spoke freely to him, although anonymously, of their heartfelt esteem for Boris Yeltsin. "He would go to the people and listen" was a typical comment. Nor were the expressions of protest confined to Moscow, for demonstrations were held in Leningrad and Sverdlovsk as well. Authorities became so concerned about those manifestations of solidarity that notices were posted at all post offices in Yeltsin's hometown of Sverdlovsk to the effect that "communications of any kind for B. N. Yeltsin will not be delivered." Yeltsin, who returned to the hospital immediately following the November 11 meeting, was dismissed from his Politburo post in early 1988 and received a new assignment as first deputy chairman for state construction—a demotion but not a banishment to the provinces. In a reconciliatory gesture from the party leadership, he was retained on the party's Central Committee.

The fact that Yeltsin's October 21 speech remained unpublished continued to supply grist for the rumor mill. Several purported versions of the speech circulated underground in Moscow and Leningrad. One widely disseminated version, obtained by *Le Monde* in Paris, had Yeltsin criticizing the privileges of his fellow party bureaucrats as follows: "It's hard for me to explain to the factory worker why, in the seventieth year of his political power, he is obliged to line up for sausages in which there is more starch than meat, while on our tables there is sturgeon, caviar, and all sorts of delicacies." Soviet officials denied that the *Le Monde* text was accurate, but Lev Timofeyev, a Soviet intellectual and the editor of the unofficial journal *Referendum,* pointed out that Yeltsin's October 21 speech had already passed into the realm of "folklore." "It doesn't matter so much whether Yeltsin said these things," Timofeyev was quoted as saying in the *Washington Post* (February 13, 1988). "What matters is that Soviets want someone to have said them."

The German-language edition of the Russian paper *Moscow News* published in its inaugural issue of May 1988 an interview with Yeltsin that was conducted by the Soviet journalist Mikhail Poltoranin. The first Soviet report quoting Yeltsin since his ouster, it was remarkably free of the spirit of remorse and contrition that he had expressed in his "confession" of November 11, 1987. "I belong to those who are prepared to take the route with potholes, and have no fear of the risks," Yeltsin was quoted as saying. Yeltsin branded as forgeries some of the versions of his controversial speech of October 21, 1987 that were circulating in Russia and translated and published abroad, but he refused to give a full account of what he had said, explaining, "I don't want to talk about something I said a half-year ago. I could make a mistake." But, emphasizing the consistency of his position, he added, "I spoke out honestly and directly and said what I felt and thought was right."

In early May of 1988 Yeltsin was quoted in a mass-circulation publication within the Soviet Union called *Stroitelnaya Gazeta,* a daily publication of the construction industry. In it, Yeltsin both appealed to workers to help achieve *perestroika* and, at the same time, cautioned the party leadership on the importance of fulfilling the hopes and expectations of the people. Interviews that Yeltsin had conducted with the Novosti press agency and the journal *Ogonyok* were, however, not published, and in frustration Yeltsin took his case to the foreign media. In the midst of the Reagan-Gorbachev summit in Moscow, in late May of 1988, Yeltsin spoke to reporters of the BBC, once more assailing

Ligachev as an opponent of reform. Although the translation of Yeltsin's remarks into English had him calling for Ligachev's dismissal, Yeltsin later denied that he had ever suggested Ligachev's resignation. Caught off-guard and in the full glare of the summit spotlight, Gorbachev said he would make no comment until he had read the full text of Yeltsin's remarks, but he denied that there was any problem with Ligachev.

Yeltsin's penchant for dramatic public outbursts expressed itself in full force at the long-anticipated, well-publicized Nineteenth All-Union Conference of the Communist Party of the Soviet Union, which was held in Moscow during the last week of June 1988. Five thousand delegates from all over the Soviet Union attended the conference, which was historic in the openness of its delegate selection, of its conference debate, and of its media coverage. As Mikhail Gorbachev's show, it was virtually a referendum on *glasnost* and *perestroika.* On July 1, the last day of the conference proceedings, Yeltsin took the floor and made an emotional speech. Beginning with attacks on party corruption and privilege, he ended by appealing for his own political rehabilitation: "Rehabilitation after fifty years has now become habitual. . . . But I am asking for political rehabilitation while I am still alive."

Unrepentant, Yeltsin stated, in his publicly televised address, that the only mistake he had made in his October 21 Central Committee speech was one of timing, "before the celebration of the seventieth anniversary of the revolution." It soon became clear, however, that Gorbachev did not share Yeltsin's view of the affair, for in his closing address he denounced Yeltsin for both his emotionalism and his political mistakes. Obviously, the request for rehabilitation had been denied.

Early in 1989 neighborhood organizations in Moscow nominated Yeltsin for the city's at-large seat in the upcoming election for the Congress of People's Deputies. Casting himself as a populist candidate, Yeltsin attracted widespread support in the form of large, apparently spontaneous public demonstrations. At campaign rallies, he repeatedly called for greater political pluralism but denied that he was attempting to undermine Gorbachev. Two weeks before the election, in what some observers saw as an effort to discredit Yeltsin, the Communist party released to the press an official transcript of the Central Committee meeting on October 21, 1987 that had led to Yeltsin's dismissal from the Politburo. Repudiating Yevgeny A, Brakow, the candidate backed by the party, voters gave Yeltsin a landslide victory in the election on March 26, 1989, awarding him 89 percent of the votes.

When the Congress of People's Deputies convened, before live television cameras, late in May, Yeltsin was at first excluded from the 542-seat Supreme Soviet, but after two days of demonstrations in the streets of Moscow, he was named to the new legislature after a fellow reformist, Aleksei I. Kazannik, prevented a potential crisis by stepping down in Yeltsin's favor. Two weeks later the Supreme Soviet approved Yeltsin as head of its committee on construction and architecture. In that post, Yeltsin has argued for trimming the country's estimated $170 billion budget deficit by slicing large capital investments, even those proposed by foreign companies. "Any foreign company that plans a big project involving a lot of construction will have to come before our committee," he said, as quoted in *Business Week* (July 17, 1989).

In September 1989, shortly after he was chosen as the leader of the dissident legislators' opposition caucus, Yeltsin toured the United States, giving speeches—at about $25,000 a lecture, according to *The New York Times* (September 9, 1989)—on Soviet democracy in several major cities and meeting with American economic and business leaders, members of Congress, and, briefly, President George Bush, Vice-President Dan Quayle, and Secretary of State James A. Baker 3d. In his speeches and in interviews with the press, Yeltsin described the Soviet Union as being in a crisis and warned, as quoted in *Newsweek* (September 25, 1989), that Gorbachev had "not more than one year and probably about six months" to get his reform program moving. During his eight-day visit to the United States, *Pravda* reprinted in full an article from the Italian newspaper *La Repubblica* that portrayed Yeltsin as a drunkard who spent most of his lecture fees on liquor, video equipment, and clothing. Following considerable criticism from skeptical readers and from the weekly *Moscow News, Pravda* published a formal apology to Yeltsin.

On 4 March 1990, Yeltsin was elected with 72% of the vote to the Congress of People's Deputies of Russia representing Sverdlovsk. On 29 May 1990, he was elected chairman of the Presidium of the Supreme Soviet of the Russian Soviet Federative Socialist Republic (RSFSR), in spite of the fact that Gorbachev personally pleaded with the Russian deputies not to select him. He was supported by both democratic and conservative members of the Supreme Soviet, which sought power in the developing political situation in the country.

In June 1991, Yeltsin won 57% of the popular vote in the democratic presidential elections for the Russian republic, defeating Gorbachev's preferred candidate, Nikolai Ryzhkov, and four other candidates. In August 1991, a coup was launched against Gorbachev by government members opposed to perestroika. Gorbachev was held in Crimea. Yeltsin raced to the White House of Russia (residence of the Supreme Soviet of the RSFSR) in Moscow to defy the coup, making a memorable speech from atop the turret of a tank. The White House was surrounded by the military but the troops defected in the face of mass popular demonstrations. By August most of the coup leaders had fled Moscow and Gorbachev was "rescued" from Crimea and then returned to Moscow. Yeltsin was hailed by his supporters around the world for rallying mass opposition to the coup.

Although restored to his position, Gorbachev had been destroyed politically. Neither union nor Russian power structures heeded his commands as support had gone to Yeltsin. Taking advantage of the situation, Yeltsin began taking what remained of the Soviet government, ministry by ministry—including the Kremlin. On November 6, 1991, Yeltsin issued a decree banning all Communist Party activities on Russian soil. In early December 1991, Ukraine voted for independence from the Soviet Union. A week later, on December 8, Yeltsin met Ukrainian president and the leader of Belarus, in Belovezhskaya Pushcha. The three presidents announced the dissolution of the Soviet Union and the formation of a voluntary Commonwealth of Independent States (CIS) in its place in the Belavezha Accords.

According to Gorbachev, Yeltsin kept the plans of the Belovezhskaya meeting secret with the main goal of the dissolution of the Soviet Union to get rid of Gorbachev. He also accused Yeltsin of violating the people's will expressed in the referendum in which the majority voted to keep the Soviet Union united. On December 12, the Supreme Soviet of the RSFSR ratified the Belavezha Accords and denounced the 1922 Union Treaty. It ordered the Russian deputies in the Council of the Union to cease their work, leaving that body without a quorum. In effect, the largest republic of the Soviet Union had seceded.

On December 17, in a meeting with Yeltsin, Gorbachev accepted the fait accompli and agreed to dissolve the Soviet Union. On December 24, the Russian Federation, by mutual agreement of the other CIS states (which by this time included all of the remaining republics except Georgia) took the Soviet Union's seat in the United

Nations. The next day, Gorbachev resigned and the Soviet Union ceased to exist—thereby ending the world's oldest, largest and most powerful Communist state. Economic relations between the former Soviet republics were severely compromised. Millions of ethnic Russians found themselves in the newly formed foreign countries.

After the dissolution of the Soviet Union, Yeltsin resolved to embark on a program of radical economic reform which sought to expand democracy in the socialist system. His regime aimed to completely dismantle socialism and fully implement capitalism—converting the world's largest command economy into a free-market one. During early discussions of this transition, Yeltsin's advisers debated issues of speed and sequencing, with an apparent division between those favoring a rapid approach and those favoring a gradual or slower approach.

In January 1992, Yeltsin, acting as his own prime minister, ordered the liberalization of foreign trade, prices, and currency. At the same time, Yeltsin followed a policy of 'macroeconomic stabilization,' a harsh austerity regime designed to control inflation. Under this program, interest rates were raised to extremely high levels to tighten money and restrict credit. To bring state spending and revenues into balance, Yeltsin raised new taxes, cut back sharply on government subsidies to industry and construction, and made steep cuts to state welfare spending.

By early 1992, prices skyrocketed throughout Russia, and a deep credit crunch shut down many industries and brought about a protracted depression. The reforms devastated the living standards of much of the population, especially the groups dependent on state subsidies and welfare programs. Through the 1990s, Russia's GDP fell by 50 percent, vast sectors of the economy were wiped out, inequality and unemployment grew dramatically, while incomes fell. Russian commentators and even some Western economists blamed Yeltsin's economic program for the country's disastrous economic performance and many began to distance themselves from the program.

Also throughout 1992, Yeltsin wrestled with the Supreme Soviet of Russia and the Congress of People's Deputies for control over government, government policy, government banking and property. Yeltsin announced in a televised address to the nation on March 20, 1993, that he was going to assume certain "special powers" in order to implement his program of reforms. In response, the hastily called 9th Congress of People's

Deputies attempted to remove Yeltsin from presidency through impeachment on March 26, 1993. Yeltsin's opponents gathered more than 600 votes for impeachment, but fell 72 votes short of the required two-thirds majority.

On September 21, 1993 Yeltsin, in breach of the constitution, announced in a televised address his decision to disband the Supreme Soviet and Congress of People's Deputies by decree. In his address Yeltsin declared his intent to rule by decree until the election of the new parliament and a referendum on a new constitution, triggering the constitutional crisis of October 1993. On the night after Yeltsin's televised address, the Supreme Soviet declared Yeltsin removed from presidency, by virtue of his breaching the constitution, and Vice-President Alexander Rutskoy was sworn in as the acting president.

Between September 21-24, Yeltsin was confronted by popular unrest. The demonstrators were protesting the new and terrible living conditions under Yeltsin. Since 1989 GDP had declined by half. Corruption was rampant, violent crime was skyrocketing, medical services were collapsing, food and fuel were increasingly scarce and life expectancy was falling for all but a tiny handful of the population; moreover, Yeltsin was increasingly getting the blame. By early October, Yeltsin had secured the support of Russia's army and ministry of interior forces. In a massive show of force, Yeltsin called up tanks to shell the Russian White House, Russia's parliament building. The Supreme Soviet was dissolved, in December 1993 and elections for a new parliament were held. A referendum, held at the same time, approved the new constitution, which significantly expanded the powers of the president, giving them a right to appoint the members of the government, to dismiss the Prime Minister and, in some cases, to dissolve the Duma.

In December 1994, Yeltsin ordered the military invasion of Chechnya in an attempt to restore Moscow's control over the republic. Nearly two years later Yeltsin withdrew federal forces from the devastated Chechnya under a 1996 peace agreement brokered by Alexander Lebed, then Yeltsin's security chief. The peace deal allowed Chechnya greater autonomy but not full independence. The decision to launch the war in Chechnya dismayed many in the West.

In 1995, as Yeltsin struggled to finance Russia's growing foreign debt and gain support from the Russian business elite for his bid in the early-1996 presidential elections, the Russian president prepared for a new wave of privatization offering stock shares in some of Russia's most valuable state enterprises in exchange for bank loans. The program was promoted as a way of simultaneously speeding up privatization and ensuring the government a cash infusion to cover its operating needs. The deals were giveaways of valuable state assets to a small group of tycoons in finance, industry, energy, telecommunications, and the media who came to be known as "oligarchs." This was due to the fact that ordinary people sold their vouchers for cash. The vouchers were bought out by a small group of investors. By mid-1996, substantial ownership shares over major firms were acquired at very low prices by a handful of people.

In February 1996, Yeltsin announced that he would seek a second term. The announcement followed weeks of speculation that Yeltsin was at the end of his political career because of his health problems and growing unpopularity. When campaigning opened in early 1996, Yeltsin's popularity was close to zero. Meanwhile, the opposition Communist Party of the Russian Federation had already gained ground in parliamentary. Panic struck the Yeltsin team when opinion polls suggested that the ailing president could not win; some members of his entourage urged him to cancel elections and effectively rule as dictator from then on. Instead, Yeltsin changed his campaign team, assigning a key role to his daughter. He recruited a team of financial and media oligarchs to bankroll his campaign and guaranteed favorable media coverage the president on national television and in leading newspapers.

Yeltsin campaigned energetically, dispelling concerns about his health, and maintained a high media profile. To boost his popularity, Yeltsin promised to abandon some of his more unpopular economic reforms, boost welfare spending, end the war in Chechnya, and pay wage and pension arrears. Yeltsin's campaign also got a boost from a $10 billion loan to the Russian government from the International Monetary Fund. Yeltsin won reelection but underwent emergency quintuple heart bypass surgery in November 1996, and remained in the hospital for months.

In 1998, a political and economic crisis emerged when Yeltsin's government defaulted on its debts, causing financial markets to panic and the ruble to collapse. During the 1999 Kosovo war, Yeltsin strongly opposed the NATO military campaign against Yugoslavia, and warned of possible Russian intervention if

NATO deployed ground troops to Kosovo. In televised comments he stated: "I told NATO, the Americans, the Germans: Don't push us toward military action. Otherwise there will be a European war for sure and possibly world war."

On May 15, 1999, Yeltsin survived another attempt of impeachment, this time by the democratic and communist opposition in the State Duma. He was charged with several unconstitutional activities, including the signing of the Belavezha Accords, the coup-d'état in October 1993, and initiating the war in Chechnya in 1994. None of these charges received the two-thirds majority of the Duma which was required to initiate the process of impeachment of the president.

On August 9, 1999 Yeltsin fired his prime minister, Sergei Stepashin, and for the fourth time, fired his entire cabinet. In Stepashin's place he appointed Vladimir Putin, relatively unknown at that time, and announced his wish to see Putin as his successor. In late 1999 Yeltsin and President Clinton openly disagreed on the war in Chechnya. At the November meeting of the Organization for Security and Cooperation in Europe, Clinton pointed his finger at Yeltsin and demanded he halt bombing attacks that had resulted in many civilian casualties. Yeltsin immediately left the conference.

On December 31, 1999, in an announcement aired at 12:00 pm MSK on Russian television and taped in the morning of the same day, Yeltsin said he had resigned and Prime Minister. Vladimir Putin had taken over as acting president, with elections due to take place on March 26, 2000. Yeltsin asked for forgiveness for what he acknowledged were errors of his rule, and said Russia needed to enter the new century with new political leaders.

Yeltsin maintained a low profile after his resignation, making almost no public statements or appearances.

PERSONAL LIFE

Six feet tall, broad-shouldered, and with a shock of white hair, Yeltsin was an imposing presence who radiated energy and forcefulness. As is so often the case with Soviet functionaries, little was known about his personal life. It is also reported that he was a workaholic who managed to get by on four hours of sleep a night. When he got up, usually at 5:00 A.M., he read for about two hours—most often books by contemporary authors who, in his words, "have public resonance," among them Anatoly Rybakov, Gavril Popov, and even Aleksandr Solzhenitsyn—then he did his morning exercises before heading off to work. In expressing his credo, Yeltsin once said: "Above all, I admire honesty, principle, and character. Correspondingly, I hate dishonesty and toadyism."

Boris Yeltsin died of congestive heart failure on April 23, 2007, in Moscow, at the age of 76. He was survived by his wife, Naina Iosifovna Yeltsina, whom he married in 1956, and their two daughters Yelena and Tatyana, born in 1957 and 1959, respectively. His body laid in repose in the Cathedral of Christ the Saviour in Moscow and he was buried in the Novodevichy Cemetery on 25 April 2007.

FURTHER READING

London Observer p13 Mr 26 '89; *Maclean's* 100:21 N 23 '87 por; *Manchester Guardian* W p9 F 26 '89; *The New York Times* A p3 N 23 '87; *New Statesman* 112:11+ N 7 '86; *Time* 133:44+ Mr 20 '89 por; *U S News* 102:29+ Je 29 '87 por, 104:30+ Mr 28 '88 por; *Washington Post* C p1+ F 18 '89 pors, A p1+ My 20 '89; *International Who's Who,* 1989-90; *Yeltsin: A Life,* Colton, Timothy J, Basick Books, Ap 2008

Z

ERNESTO ZEDILLO PONCE DE LEON (SAY-DEE-OH PONS DAY LAY-OHN)

Former President of Mexico; Economist

Born: December 25, 1951; Mexico City, Mexico
Party Affiliation: Institutional Revolutionary Party

INTRODUCTION

Since he became the president of Mexico, in late 1994, Ernesto Zedillo Ponce de Leon, the man once referred to as the "accidental" head of state, has brought a drastically new style of leadership—his detractors might say lack of leadership—to his country. An economist by training, Zedillo served in the cabinet of President Carlos Salinas de Gortari, and he was running the campaign of Salinas's handpicked successor, Luis Donaldo Colosio, when Colosio was assassinated, in March 1994. Salinas quickly named Zedillo, an unlikely, lackluster candidate who claimed to have first considered the possibility of becoming president on "the day that [he] was nominated," as Colosio's replacement. Winning a decisive victory after an initially shaky campaign, as president Zedillo immediately displayed an openness and a commitment to democratic principles unheard of in a country accustomed to being governed in an unyielding and notoriously corrupt manner. His critics have called him a weak leader while his supporters, pointing to the political reforms he has brought about, have described him as a positive force for change. Even his victories have been overshadowed, however, by an economic crisis that erupted shortly after the beginning of his term and that continues to plague Mexico.

EARLY LIFE

The second of six children of lower-middle-class parents, Ernesto Zedillo Ponce de Leon was born on December 27, 1951 in Mexico City. Published sources differ as to the occupation of his father, who has been described both as a construction foreman and as an electrician who installed movie screens and sound units; similarly, his mother has been variously identified as a teacher, a secretary, and a vendor of candy at movie theatres, which, according to one article, contributed to Zedillo's fascination with films. When Zedillo was three years old, his father moved the family to the town of Mexicali, adjacent to the border with California. There, he grew up in what has been called the "gritty" Pueblo Nuevo area, where he helped his family to make ends meet by selling cans and other items to junk dealers. He attended public schools and earned grades good enough to win him admittance to the National Polytechnic Institute, in Mexico City, where he studied economics.

While he was a student, Zedillo landed a part-time job in the president's office of economic policy. He found a mentor of sorts there in Leopoldo Solis, a highly regarded government economist. At the age of 19, perhaps as a result of Solis's influence, he joined the Institutional Revolutionary Party (PRI), the world's longest-ruling political party, which has controlled the Mexican presidency since 1929. Roughly a year later he completed his studies at the National Polytechnic Institute ahead of schedule, enrolling next at Yale University, in New Haven, Connecticut, on a scholarship. He received his M.A. degree in economics in 1977 and his Ph.D. degree four years later. In his doctoral dissertation, "External Public Indebtedness in Mexico: Recent History and Future Oil Bounded Optimal Growth," he contended that Mexico's staggering debt was a result of governmental irresponsibility, rather than of the inflexibility of foreign banks, as many preferred to believe.

LIFE'S WORK

After returning to Mexico, Zedillo secured a position under Solis at Banco de Mexico, the country's central bank, which was sympathetic to the point of view he had expressed in his dissertation. He was promoted rapidly and eventually took charge of the multibillion-dollar Ficorca fund, a resource for Mexican heads of industry who were grappling with foreign debt in the wake of the devaluation of the peso, Mexico's unit of currency. Under Zedillo's stewardship Ficorca "was an amazingly successful program that has not received much public attention," as one Mexican consultant told Anthony DePalma for *The New York Times* (April 1, 1994). "But for the business community it was very relevant, which explains why Zedillo has so much clout with business."

In 1987, when Carlos Salinas received the PRI's presidential nomination, Zedillo joined the government as deputy secretary for budget and planning. After Salinas was elected in the following year, he named Zedillo budget and planning minister. The young economist thus became one of a group of technocratic "yuppies," in Salinas's cabinet. Unlike older PRI officials, whose political base was Mexico's peasant class, Zedillo and other younger members were concerned with exports and other areas of international trade. (It was under Salinas, for example, that Mexico signed on to the North American Free Trade Agreement, or NAFTA.) As a result, the party became segmented into distinct factions. In the post of budget and planning minister, Zedillo was a major contributor to an agreement among businesses, unions, and the government to employ wage and price controls, a plan that has been credited with significantly reducing Mexico's rate of inflation. Zedillo's role in this endeavor made him popular among foreign investors.

In 1992 Salinas made Zedillo his education minister. It was apparent by then that Zedillo was on the short list of government officials being considered as Salinas's successor. (In Mexico the head of state, who serves a single six-year term, traditionally has sole authority in choosing his party's next presidential nominee.) One of Zedillo's major tasks as education minister, however, seriously reduced the likelihood of his becoming president. After having successfully transferred responsibility for public education from the federal government to the 31 Mexican states, he took on the job of issuing new, updated history textbooks for fourth-,

fifth-, and sixth-grade students. In the late summer of 1993, just before the new texts were to be distributed, Zedillo recalled them—an act that many believed to be the result of pressure from government officials who were displeased with the unflattering accounts of recent Mexican history given in the books. Zedillo suffered the brunt of the national controversy that ensued.

A few months later, in November 1993, Zedillo resigned as education minister to serve as the campaign manager for Luis Donaldo Colosio, the head of the PRI and the man chosen by Salinas as the party's nominee in the upcoming 1994 presidential election. The campaign represented Zedillo's first political activity, and his inexperience showed: he was roundly criticized for failing to keep his candidate's name in the press to a sufficient extent. Meanwhile, Colosio was amending his political philosophy. On January 1, 1994 the Zapatista National Liberation Army—a group of Maya Indian rebels—took up arms in the southern state of Chiapas, seized territory, and declared war against the Mexican government in the name of greater democracy and distribution of wealth. Colosio began to feel that the government needed to implement social reforms more quickly than Salinas had deemed necessary. On March 23, 1994, at a campaign rally in Tijuana, he was shot to death by Mario Aburto Martinez, a 23-year-old mechanic thought to have accomplices in the killing. Six days later Zedillo received the PRI nomination, promising to embrace the platforms on which Colosio had run. "We're not starting a campaign," he stated in his acceptance speech, "we're continuing it."

Whereas the PRI had previously been virtually assured of seeing its presidential candidate to victory in 1994, the events of the first three months of that year dimmed the party's optimism. Many Mexicans suspected that the PRI itself was linked to Colosio's assassination—a suspicion that, in turn, revived earlier speculation about possible fraud in the election of Salinas in 1988, and ultimately called into question the party's very legitimacy. In addition, the officials who made up the old guard within the PRI were unhappy with the selection of Zedillo, whom they saw as a technocrat with little ability to inspire the blue-collar Mexicans who had traditionally supported the party. The uprising in Chiapas, which had quieted down since the ceasefire of January 12 but had not been crushed, had shaken some voters' confidence in the ability of the PRI to maintain order. Finally, in contrast to the personable and gregarious Colosio, Zedillo appeared to be out of his element among crowds. His manner was called "wooden" and "boring," and a reporter for *The New York Times* (April 12, 1994) described him as exhibiting a "notable lack of charisma," resembling "a young high school principal more than a politician," and looking "naked without a tie." Another reporter pointed to Zedillo's "less-than-stirring" campaign slogan: "Well-being for your family." Polls taken during the spring of 1994 suggested that Zedillo, who had begun the race as the front-runner, was losing public support.

Over time, however, several factors began to work in Zedillo's favor: the PRI, as the candidate himself suggested, sought to win back the public's confidence by taking steps to guard against election fraud; the party decided to unite behind its nominee for the sake of holding on to the presidency; the Mexican media, which openly supported the PRI, devoted much more coverage to Zedillo's campaign than to those of the other candidates; and, not least, Zedillo himself started to appeal to voters. While he hardly developed into a firebrand over the course of the campaign, he demonstrated an ability to give clear, substantive answers to questions about economic, political, and social issues. He continued Colosio's call for democratic and social reform by promising to increase spending on the infrastructure, root out corruption in the justice system, and grant more power to Mexico's congress. In the election, on August 21, 1994, Zedillo received roughly 50 percent of the vote, easily defeating Diego Fernandez of the conservative National Action Party (PAN), who came away with 30 percent of the ballots, and the left-leaning Democratic Revolutionary Party candidate Cuauhtemoc Cardenas, who had come close to beating Salinas six years earlier but wooed only 16 percent of all voters in 1994.

Immediately upon taking office on December 1, 1994, as Mexico's 26th president, Zedillo showed every intention of trying to fulfill his promises to work for democracy and for the sharing of wealth within the country. To a degree unrivaled by any previous president, he lent an ear to the nation's opposition parties. He went so far as to name Antonio Lozano, a PAN member, attorney general, an appointment that marked the first time in the history of the PRI that an opposition member had been asked to join the cabinet. His announced plan to overhaul the justice system impressed the legal community. Citing the great disparity in income between the rich and poor in Mexico, he declared, as quoted by the Chicago *Tribune* (December 2, 1994), "My highest duty and my strongest commitment is the fight against the poverty in which millions of Mexicans live. Poverty is the most painful burden in our history."

The reforms initiated by Zedillo in the first few days of his presidency took a back seat to an economic crisis following his devaluation of the peso in mid-December. He had hoped that the measure would lead to an increase in exports and thereby correct Mexico's trade imbalance; instead, the result was a 16 percent drop in the value of Latin American stocks, which represented a loss of approximately $600 million to foreign investors—whose capital was crucial in boosting Mexico's economy. That disaster, coming so early in Zedillo's term, led many to question the competence of his administration. After protracted negotiations with business and labor leaders forced him several times to postpone a televised address on his plan for handling the crisis, there was widespread agreement that Zedillo lacked his predecessor's ability to exert control over such situations.

In a half-hour speech on January 3, 1995, Zedillo unveiled his strategy, which called for wage and price controls and budget cuts. (Later in the month, President Bill Clinton authorized a $20 billion bailout loan from the United States government to Mexico.) Explaining that the plan would entail "painful" sacrifices on the part of all Mexicans, Zedillo said, as quoted in the *Washington Post* (January 4, 1995), "Mexico's development demands that we recognize realistically that we are not a rich country, but a nation with serious needs and shortages. We cannot, therefore, identify ourselves with patterns of consumption in wealthy societies that have already resolved the disparities that still afflict us." He also blamed the economic crisis in large part on what he called financial mismanagement and overspending on the part of the Salinas administration.

The following month saw a fiasco of a different nature. In December 1994 Zedillo had won a minor victory over the Zapatista rebels in Chiapas, who claimed that the election of the new governor there had been conducted fraudulently and vowed to prevent the transfer of power; federal troops deployed by Zedillo dispersed the rebels without bloodshed. On February 10, 1995 the Mexican military, acting under Zedillo's orders, captured the rebels' headquarters in the eastern part of the state, again without firing a shot. Although the Zapatista leader, Rafael Sebastian Guillen, had escaped, the government appeared to be on the verge of quashing the movement. Military leaders were thus baffled when, days later, Zedillo offered amnesty and the opportunity for peace talks to the rebels. His apparent flip-flop struck more than a few observers as a sign of weakness, and, as was revealed later, Zedillo narrowly avoided losing control of the government in a military coup.

Zedillo's standing with the Mexican public rose sharply, at least for a time, after a shocking revelation in early March 1995 that involved the September 28, 1994 assassination of Jose Francisco Ruiz Massieu, the secretary-general of the PRI and an adviser to Zedillo. Appearing on television, Zedillo announced that the brother of former president Salinas had been arrested in connection with the killing. Salinas, in turn, publicly proclaimed his brother's innocence and also seized the opportunity to attack Zedillo's economic policies. Political experts called the scandal the most dramatic incident in the history of the PRI's control of the presidency. While some surmised that Zedillo had made the announcement in the hope of scoring a public-relations victory, it appeared that many citizens welcomed evidence that their leaders were no longer above the law. (By mid-March, Salinas was in what was called "virtual exile" in the United States.) The *Washington Post* (March 5, 1995) reported that Zedillo's approval rating after his televised address was higher than Salinas's had been at any point during his presidency—a fact that bewildered political analysts, given all that had gone wrong in Zedillo's term up to that point.

Mexicans were not alone, however, in viewing Zedillo favorably. For example, the columnist Thomas L. Friedman of *The New York Times* (March 12, 1995) devoted an Op-Ed piece in large part to Zedillo's accomplishments. "What has been obscured is that Mr. Zedillo, while stumbling around in economics, has simultaneously instituted an impressive series of political reforms—making Mexico more open [and] democratic and less corrupt than ever before—for which he has gotten no credit, at home or abroad," he wrote. "Since coming to office . . . Zedillo has sacked the entire corrupt Supreme Court, which he replaced with new judges and made independent of the presidency. ... He has empowered the traditionally rubber-stamp Mexican legislature with real oversight responsibilities. . . . He has begun instituting the rule of law, where arbitrariness used to reign. ... In the short run, Mr. Zedillo is calculating that because Mexico is about to go through a brutal recession, with massive unemployment, having a more open political system that allows for more demonstrations and channels discontent via the ballot box may enable this society to blow off steam without blowing off the lid."

Later in March Zedillo put forth a new plan to stabilize the economy. The strategy called for a flexible exchange rate, which, it was hoped, would drive up exports while avoiding the overvaluation of the peso that, in Zedillo's view, had caused Mexico's current fiscal problems. The plan also included a controversial 50 percent increase in the sales tax. "I know that this is going to be painful. I know that nobody is going to like it," Zedillo admitted in a conversation with Tim Golden for *The New York Times* (March 14, 1995). "But this is what the country needs. It was said that I am not a good politician to put it that way. But some of the most traumatic experiences that we have had in Mexico around financial crises have to do with the fact that people were not told the truth." At one point during the interview, which he conducted in English, Zedillo confessed, "I thought [being president] was going to be rough. But I must be honest—I never expected anything as complex as what we have lived through over these last three months." Not surprisingly, perhaps, Zedillo's economic measures met with disapproval among a large portion of the public, and even though the congress passed the tax increase, two PRI legislators voted against the president's plan, marking the first time representatives had refused to support their party's leader. In the months that followed, however, Zedillo's plan showed signs of working. The government was able to repay $700 million of its loan from the United States in October 1995 and $1.3 billion more in January 1996. By that spring, while the country's economy remained fragile, Mexican officials were cautiously optimistic, as the peso gained strength, interest rates dropped, and the stock exchange hit record highs.

On another political front, Mexico's opposition parties were gaining power, a situation seen by some as evidence of the growth of democracy and by others as a sign of a weak administration. In mid-January 1995 Zedillo and the leaders of the country's largest parties agreed to work together to bring about reforms in state and national election laws and create a fair electoral process. (The pact almost surely enabled the opposition PAN to sweep the February 13 election in the state of Jalisco, handing the PRI its worst defeat in its 66 years in power. By December 1995, when Zedillo had been in office for a year, the PAN had taken control of four states and more than 200 cities.) After difficult, protracted negotiations, the low point of which was the PAN's temporary withdrawal from the entire process, in late July 1996 Zedillo and four other party leaders signed a plan—approved days later by the Mexican congress—calling for

17 constitutional amendments and dozens of other measures designed to guard against electoral fraud.

Meanwhile, negotiations between the government and the Zapatista army were slowly moving forward. On March 10, 1995 the congress had granted a month-long amnesty to the rebels to encourage them to participate in peace talks. The two sides opened formal communication in late April. In February 1996 the Zapatistas agreed to sign a pact, approved by the government a month earlier, that would expand the rights of Mexico's 10 million Indians, including the right to form local governments in their communities, to pursue multicultural education (specifically, to be schooled in their own languages), and to have greater representation in the national legislature. Most political observers saw the agreement as a political gain for Zedillo. Since that time, however, the negotiations have faltered, and in September the Zapatistas broke off talks, stating that the government had failed to make good on many of its promises and that it must release rebels arrested months earlier before the peace process could continue.

Meanwhile, in August, a group calling itself the Popular Revolutionary Army attacked police and military posts in six southern states, killing more than a dozen people, as part of its announced plan to overthrow the government and install a socialist regime in its place. (There is no apparent connection between that group and the Zapatistas, who have publicly distanced themselves from the Popular Revolutionary Army.) In the wake of the killings, Zedillo promised to fight the terrorists but to do so within the confines of the law. "In our country and others in Latin America, there are still open wounds from the way that terrorist and guerrilla groups were pursued in the 1970s," he said, as quoted by *The New York Times* (September 1, 1996). "We are not going to make the mistake of trampling the rights of others in our search for them, because that's what they want."

PERSONAL LIFE

The bespectacled Ernesto Zedillo Ponce de Leon is married to Nilda Patricia Velasco, with whom he has five children. In his private time, he is said to enjoy long-distance running. His public persona was epitomized in an incident reported by *The New York Times* (December 28, 1995): "At a . . . concert in Mexico City, someone noticed [Zedillo] in the presidential box at intermission and started to applaud. In time, most of the well-heeled crowd was clapping. Confused and unsure about what to do, Mr. Zedillo just sat there. Finally he stood up and acknowledged the crowd." In the same article, the Mexican writer Carlos Fuentes was quoted as saying, "It is amazing to think that it has turned out to be this unprepared, accidental president who faces the greatest challenge in Mexico since the [1910] revolution. All of us hope he is up to it."

Since leaving office, Zedillo has held many jobs. He has worked as an economic consultant for international companies and organizations, and presently teaches economics at Yale University. He is on the editorial board of *Americas Quarterly*, a policy journal, and works on peace and human rights issues with the group *The Elders*, which he joined in 2013.

FURTHER READING

N Y Times A pl+ Mr 30 '94 por, D p2 Ap 1 '94 por, A pl+Ag 23 '94 por; Washington Post A p25 Mr 30 '94 por; International Who's Who, 1995-96

ZHOU ENLAI (CHOU EN-LAI)

First Premier and Foreign Minister of the People's Republic of China

Born: March 5, 1898; Huai'an, Jiangsu Province, China
Died: January 8, 1976; Beijing, China
Affiliation: Chinese Communist Party

INTRODUCTION

Zhou Enlai, who was the first Premier and Foreign Minister of the People's Republic of China (the most populous county in the world, which now has almost 1.4 billion people and covers 3.7 million square miles) continues to be venerated by many Chinese since his death in 1976 of bladder cancer. Despite the excesses of President Mao Zedong, most notably The Great Leap Forward and The Cultural Revolution, both unstable periods when millions of Chinese lost their lives, Zhou is remembered as China's most humane leader of the 20th century, and the Chinese Communist Party today pro-

Zhou Enlai.

Affiliation: Chinese Communist Party (CCP)

When Zhou went back to China in 1924 he joined the Kuomintang-Communist alliance formed under Dr. Sun Yat-sen in preparation for the National Revolution, which took place over the next three years. (Kuomintang was the name of the national and revolutionary party organized by Sun Yat-sen and later headed by Chiang Kai-shek.) Zhou helped to train officers for the Nationalist Army as political director of the Whampoa Military Academy, of which Chiang Kai-shek was chairman, and he organized a Communist corps among the cadets.

In the Northern Expedition, led by Chiang Kai-shek to wipe out the war lords, Zhou was given the assignment of organizing the workers of Shanghai in readiness for the seizure of the city by the Nationalists. By March 1927 he had captured Shanghai and had proclaimed a "citizens' government." The following month, however, when the Nationalist forces marched on the city, Chiang Kai-shek, an opponent of the Communist power in the Kuomintang, ordered the capture and execution of many left-wing leaders *(The New York Times Magazine,* August 31, 1952*; Saturday Evening Post,* March 27, 1954).

motes Zhou as a dedicated and self-sacrificing leader, who did his best to carry out Mao's directives as moderately as he could. Zhou was a brilliant diplomat and highly respected by Henry Kissinger (National Security Advisor and Secretary of State during the Nixon Administration) and former President Richard Nixon. He had the foresight to begin the long process of normalizing Chinese-U.S. relations after more than more than thirty years of hostility by hosting President Richard Nixon and the First Lady in China in 1972.

EARLY YEARS

Zhou Enlai was born into a Mandarin family in 1898 in Huai'an, Jiangsu (also known as Hwaiyin, Kiangsu) province, China, and spent part of his childhood in Manchuria. Growing up in a scholarly atmosphere, he received his early education from his well-read mother and aunt. His father and grandfather were officials in the Manchu dynasty, and when that rule was overthrown by revolution in 1911, Zhou Enlai's father moved the family to Tianjin and established a business there. His father

suffered many financial reversals, so Zhou spent most of his early years in the care of his uncles, one who adopted him before he died of tuberculosis to have a male heir.

In Tianjin, Zhou Enlai attended the Nankai Middle School—a "Western-style" school in which he learned English. He then spent a year and a half studying in Japan at Waseda University and other universities. He returned to Tianjin to take courses at Nankai University, where he became editor-in-chief of a student association daily paper and one of the founders of a radical youth organization, Awakening Society. In 1919 he was arrested and imprisoned for leading a student demonstration against the government.

Following his release a year later he signed up with a group of students for a work-and-study program in Europe. He spent most of the next four years in France and also visited England and Germany. After Mao Zedong founded the Chinese Communist party in Shanghai in 1920, Zhou gave much of his attention to organizing overseas branches of the party among Chinese students. According to Edgar Snow in "Red China's Gentleman

Hatchet Man" *(Saturday Evening Post, March 27, 1954)*, "In 1923 Chou [Zhou] had paid his first call on Comintern headquarters, where he had met Bukharin, Zinoviev and Stalin."

LIFE'S WORK

Zhou Enlai, having escaped, fled later in 1927 to Nanchang, where he conducted an uprising which marked the founding of the Chinese Red Army, later known as People's Liberation Army after World War II. During the next few years, while he was forced to work underground against Chiang, Zhou made occasional trips to the U.S.S.R. In 1932 he became political director to Zhu De, Commander in Chief of the Red Army; and later he was made Vice-Chairman of the Revolutionary Military Council. He participated in the "Long March" (1934-1935), in which the Red Army retreated from Chiang's troops 6,000 miles to northwest China (from Jiangxi to Yan'an in Shaanxi).

From their headquarters in Shaanxi the Communist leaders sought to bring their forces into alliance with those of the Kuomintang in order to present a united front against further invasion by Japan, which had occupied Manchuria in 1931. Their success in this aim was achieved in part as a result of the "Xi'an Incident" in December 1936, when Chiang Kai-shek was captured by his "Young Marshal" Zhang Xueliang, who had been won over to the Communist cause. Zhou, generally believed to have had a hand in securing the release of Chiang and of persuading him to agree to united resistance to Japan, served for the next nine years as the chief Communist negotiator with Chiang's government.

Japan's direct attack on China in 1937 was followed by publication of a united front manifesto. In the uneasy Communist-Kuomintang alliance Zhou was an adviser to Chiang as deputy head of the political training department of the military affairs council of the Nationalist government. Negotiations with the Kuomintang, however, failed to achieve legal status for the outlawed Communist party or to establish a coalition government or to solve problems relating to the Chinese Red Army, among other issues. Zhou's additional assignments in the war with Japan were to obtain and transport equipment for the Communist headquarters at Yan'an, to supervise propaganda efforts among Chinese inside and outside of the country, and wherever possible to incorporate military groups into the Communist organization.

During World War II, when conflict between the two leading political parties in China hampered Allied fighting against Japan, U.S. President Franklin D. Roosevelt sent General Patrick J. Hurley as his personal representative to China, in 1944, to try to break the deadlock in Communist-Kuomintang negotiations. Hurley was replaced the following year by General George C. Marshall in what eventually proved to be an unsuccessful mission. In meetings between Zhou and U.S. officials, according to press reporters and other Western observers, the Chinese diplomat gave the impression of sincerity and moderation.

Chiang Kai-shek became the first constitutional President of China in 1948. Since his new government did not include representatives of the Communist party, civil war continued—while Zhou Enlai again headed the Communist delegation for peace talks with the Nationalists. "In the Communists' postwar decision to make a bid for all-out power, Chou [Zhou] is believed to have had a decisive influence," Edgar Snow wrote *(Saturday Evening Post, March 27, 1954)*. Zhou's judgment that Chiang could not subdue the Communist forces was verified by the Red victory at Mukden, Manchuria, in November 1948 and at Guangzhou and Chongqing in 1949. Withdrawing from the China mainland, Chiang moved to Taipei, Taiwan, in December 1949 and from headquarters there directed the government of Nationalist China until his death in 1975.

In Beijing, the People's Republic of China was proclaimed in September 1949 by the Chinese People's Political Consultative Conference under Mao Zedong, the Communist party Chairman. Mao announced on October 1 that Zhou Enlai would head the State Administrative Council (cabinet) as Premier. Other positions that Zhou held were Foreign Minister, a general secretary of the Politburo and a secretary of the Central Committee of the Communist party, and deputy chairman of the Revolutionary Military Council. He ranked among Communist China's "big four"—with Mao Zedong, Zhu De, and Liu Shaoqi.

Communist China's chief propagandist and protagonist to the outside world, Zhou visited Moscow with Mao in early 1950, and on February 14 signed a 30 year friendship and mutual defense treaty with the Soviet Union, thus welding the two Communist nations, Zhou said, into a force "which it is impossible to defeat." India and Great Britain also extended early recognition to Communist China's government, but the United States continued to recognize Chiang's Nationalist government as the government of China.

Relations between Communist China and the United States deteriorated further during the Korean War when the armies of the People's Republic intervened in November 1950 as "volunteers" on the side of North Korea against South Korean troops and United Nations "police action." In broadcasts from Beijing, Zhou Enlai repeatedly accused U.N. troops of waging germ warfare against Communist troops. This was vigorously denied. The Korean armistice, signed on July 27, 1953, failed to bring real peace between the United States and the People's Republic, in part because of the Chinese refusal to release prisoners of war who the United States charged were held in violation of the armistice.

Zhou's anti-Western views were made clear during discussions on Korean and Indochinese problems at the Geneva conference which opened in April 1954. As head of his country's delegation he stated that Asian countries should consult among themselves to secure peace in their own area, and he denounced the United States as an aggressor "dreaming to impose upon the Chinese people the power of the Kuomintang remnant clique" on Taiwan. He also demanded the withdrawal of all foreign military bases and forces from Asia.

A year later at the Bandung (Indonesia) conference of African and Asian nations Zhou again accused the United States of creating tension in the Taiwan area and declared that the "will of the Chinese people to liberate Formosa [Taiwan] and the coastal islands is a just one." In late 1956 and early 1957 Zhou made a tour of seven Asian and four East European countries, during which he appeared as a spokesman both for unity among Communist nations and for anti-colonialism among Asian nations. Through many public statements he endorsed the Soviet Union's suppression of the Hungarian revolution and denounced President Eisenhower's Middle East doctrine as a means of replacing French and British "colonial" domination in that area with another.

While Zhou Enlai was visiting U Nu (the former Prime Minister of Burma, now Myanmar, before the overthrow of the government by a coup d'état) he was interviewed by CBS reporter Edward R. Murrow. This interview was filmed and broadcast to the American people on December 30, 1956. Philippine Ambassador Carlos Romulo, when invited to answer Zhou Enlai, said on the Murrow program that he found "many distortions" in Zhou Enlai's statements. "How can he say that he represents the Chinese people," asked Romulo, "when there has never been a free election there? The government was set up by force and is maintained by force." He also said that Zhou Enlai was following the straight Moscow line, and revealed how closely Zhou's government was tied to the Kremlin.

At the time of the Morrow interview, the U.S.S.R. and Communist China were close allies. However, the relations between the two counties began to sour in the 1960s when President Mao disagreed with the then Soviet Premier Nikita Khrushchev policies regarding "de-Stalinization," in which he downgraded the memory of former Soviet leader Josef Stalin. Mao purged the CCP of Soviet supporters during the Cultural Revolution. The rift escalated over Chinese-Soviet border disputes and into a 1969 military conflict between China and the U.S.S.R. that lasted seven months and the prospect of an all-out nuclear exchange between China and the Soviet Union. Soviet Prime Minister Alexei Kosygin averted further aggression when he visited Beijing for talks with Zhou Enlai. They agreed to return ambassadors that were recalled and to begin border negotiations, which were not finalized until 1991.

After this incident, the United States secretly sent National Security Advisor Henry Kissinger to China to strength Chinese and American relations. The resulting "ping pong diplomacy," when China and the U.S. exchanged table tennis players, paved the way for President Richard Nixon's visit to China in 1972.

The relationship between Premier Zhou Enlai and President Mao Zedong was a complicated balancing act on the part of Zhou. Both politicians relied on one another, yet Mao harshly criticized Zhou. Zhou, a skilled diplomat within the Communist party as well as internationally, placated Mao by apologizing for his faults and praising Mao, thereby avoiding the fate of thousands of Chinese who were either killed or imprisoned during the Chinese Cultural Revolution.

Mao was still cruel to Zhou, denying him permission for surgery for his bladder cancer until it had already metastasized and had become terminal, causing Zhou great suffering. However, he continued working throughout his illness until his death on January 8, 1976. The state funeral was a low-keyed affair held on January 15, with Vice-Premier Deng Xiaoping delivering the eulogy, because Mao degreed that there would be no wearing of black armbands, no mourning wreaths, no mourning halls, no memorial activities, and no handing out photos of Zhou. Mao also did not attend the funeral; instead he sent a wreath. Mao and the Gang of Four (a political faction composed of four Chinese Communist Party officials that came to power during the Cultural Revolution:

Mao's last wife Jiang Qing, Zhang Chunqiao, Yao We-nyuan and Wang Hongwen) where concerned that public mourning for Zhou would later be directed against Mao and his policies. Zhou's body was cremated and his ashes were scattered about the hills and mountains of his home-town, in accordance with his will. Vice-Premier Deng Xiaoping was persecuted because of his eulogy.

On April 4, 1976, a spontaneous event occurred, called the Tianamen Incident. On the eve of China's annual Qingming Festival, in which Chinese traditionally pay homage to their deceased ancestors, thousands of people gathered around the Monument to the People's Heroes in Tiananmen Square, Beijing, to remember Zhou. They laid wreaths, banners, poems, placards, and flowers at the foot of the Monument and criticized the Gang of Four and even Mao for their cruelty to Zhou. The following day, people rioted when they found these items cleared away. Some were arrested and later sentenced to prison work camps, and similar demonstrations were held in seven other cities, leading to Deng Xiapoing being stripped of all his power in the government. Deng Xiaoping, when he returned to power in 1980, released the people arrested in the incident.

In 1977, stamps were issued in Zhou's honor and again in 1998 to commemorate his 100th birthday.

Zhou's hometown in Huai'an restored his family home and his traditional family school, which are now major tourist designations. His hometown also opened a large park and museum in his honor on his 100th birthday, including a replica of Zhou's living and working quarters in Beijing. A museum also was established in Tianjin in Zhou's honor, and a memorial was erected in Nanjing.

PERSONAL LIFE
Zhou Enlai married Deng Yingchao, another political agitator, in 1925. The marriage was childless. Mme. Zhou Enlai, who passed away in 1992, was also a member of the Chinese Communist Party. Zhou adopted three orphans, two girls and one boy, during the Chinese civil war. Recently, a book has been published speculating that Zhou was gay: *The Secret Emotional Life of Zhou Enlai, 2015.* However, a December 29, 2015, *The New York Times* article by Michael Forsythe states that the author Tsoi Wing-Mui, "presents no proof that Zhou was gay."

FURTHER READING
Zhou Enlai: The Last Perfect Revolutionary, 2008

GENNADI A. ZYUGANOV (GEN-NAH-DEE TSYOO-GAHN-OFF)
Russian Communist Party Leader

Born: June 26, 1944; Mymrino, Russia
Affiliation: Communist Party

INTRODUCTION
A former midlevel apparatchik who had risen steadily but unobtrusively through the ranks of the Communist Party of the Soviet Union, Gennadi A. Zyuganov emerged from the crumbling Soviet regime in 1991 to lead what was left of the then-despised and repeatedly banned and reconstituted Communist Party. His party's strong performance in the parliamentary elections of December 1995, when the Communists won 22 percent of the vote and the largest bloc of seats in parliament, made him a formidable opponent of the enfeebled Russian president Boris N. Yeltsin in Russia's first free presidential election as an independent nation, in June 1996. But in the July runoff with Yeltsin, Zyuganov performed

weaker than expected, losing by 14 percentage points, in part because he failed to expand the Communists' appeal beyond their loyal cadres of aging pensioners, disaffected workers, and veterans—a group described by one Russian social democrat as a "gerontocracy." "Zyuganov is not a monster or a genius, and he is not an empty suit," Alessandra Stanley declared in her profile of him for The New York Times Magazine *(May 26, 1996). "Hand-picked by the party's Central Committee to be the human face of Russia's New Communists, he is neither an idealist nor a cynic. He is a loyal party man who rose to his position on the strength of one big idea—nationalism."*

EARLY LIFE
Gennadi Andreyevich Zyuganov was born in 1944 in the small farming village of Mymrino, in the Orel

Gennadi A. Zyuganov.

region of southern European Russia, where he and his older sister grew up. His father, Andrei Zyuganov, a World War II veteran, was a schoolteacher and a beekeeper; his mother also taught school. "The life was full of hardships, but we lived in peace and friendship, quite happily . . .," Zyuganov told Stanley. "Very often it was like having a holiday deep in your heart. Something new was happening all the time: a village restored after the war, a new school built, sport facilities opened. We had an amateur actors' theatre in which my parents played, too. It was normal life of normal people who could work, celebrate, and be happy."

At the age of 14, Zyuganov joined the Komsomol, the organization for Communist youth, in the nearby town of Znamenskoye. Four years later, in 1962, he enrolled at the Orel Pedagogical Institute, where he eventually headed the student union. A former classmate, Svetlana Voronina, told James Carney of *Time* (May 27,

1996) that Zyuganov was a voracious reader. "Every book I bought on trips to Moscow," she said, "he wanted to read," After taking three years off to serve in the army, where he joined the Communist Party, he returned to the institute with an air of authority. "When he came back, he was older, more experienced," Vladimir D. Selyutin, another former classmate, told Stanley. "He was elected Komsomol leader right away." Having taught at a secondary school from 1961 to 1965, Zyuganov embarked on a career as a physics and math teacher at the institute after he graduated. But his work for the Communist Party took precedence, and he applied himself to its demands with vigor.

LIFE'S WORK

Before long Zyuganov's diligence and energetic manner brought him to the attention of Albert P. Ivanov, the first secretary of the Communist Party's Orel regional organization, who tried to steer Zyuganov away from his preferred area of specialization: propaganda. In an interview with Stanley, Ivanov said that he had explained to Zyuganov, "You are competent, a good organizer; leave the ideology work to those fancy fellows who speak English and German and French." Zyuganov heeded only half of Ivanov's advice and, in the late 1960s, took on double duty as an organizer and a propagandist.

In the meantime Zyuganov continued to advance through the ranks of the Komsomol. As first secretary of the local Komsomol in Orel, he played a prominent role in arranging for the erection of a statue in honor of the young victims of the Nazi occupation of the Orel region, where 250,000 people died during World War II. Alessandra Stanley has observed that the 17,500 inhabitants of Orel who were arrested and convicted by Soviet leader Joseph Stalin's henchmen between December 1936 and July 1937 have not been similarly honored, and she quoted Zyuganov's "absurd" claim, given to a reporter for the German magazine *Der Spiegel,* that "today there are more victims of repression in the camps than there were under Stalin." In other sources Zyuganov has responded to queries about his stand on Stalin's crimes by saying that many of the dictator's victims were Communists and that the issue had been dealt with in the 1950s. In one of Zyuganov's recent books (one source cites *Beyond the Horizon,* while another mentions his *I Believe in Russia*) he went even further, asserting that Nikita S. Khrushchev, who succeeded Stalin after the latter's death in 1953, had impeded progress by initiating a cultural and political thaw. "Stalin needed five to seven more years to make his ideological perestroika irreversible and insure the revival of the groundlessly interrupted spiritual and statist tradition of Russia," he contended.

Seeming to have had even less respect for Khrushchev's successor, Leonid I. Brezhnev, who presided over the economic stagnation of the 1970s, Zyuganov reportedly ignored orders from the party's Moscow headquarters when he was working for Ivanov in Orel. "Between ourselves, we were disgusted by the stereotypical thinking and stupidity within the party," Ivanov told Stanley, adding that Zyuganov "took a huge risk." "He could have told on me, or disagreed, but he never did," Ivanov said. According to a review of Zyuganov's *I Believe in Russia* and Aleksandr Yanov's recent book *After Yeltsin* for the *Economist* (June 15,1996), Zyuganov "boasted" to Yanov "that he had been expelled from the Communist Party under Brezhnev for his nationalist views." (Zyuganov has not confirmed his expulsion from the party.) Andrew Nagorski of *Newsweek* (June 17, 1996) quoted Aleksandr Khokhlov, a party official who remembered Zyuganov's early career, as saying, "I never heard him say that he disagreed with any of the policies at the time."

In 1983 Zyuganov, who was by then running the propaganda and agitation department of Orel's Communist Party, was called to Moscow to work in the propaganda department of the Central Committee of the Communist Party. His new job entailed frequent and extensive travel to far-flung areas of the Soviet Union to monitor party work. In 1989 he advanced to the position of deputy head of the Central Committee's Ideology Division. In the summer of 1990, he became one of seven secretaries of the Central Committee of the new, more conservative Russia-based party that split off from Mikhail Gorbachev's Communist Party of the Soviet Union, which had launched an era of reform characterized by perestroika (economic and political reform) and glasnost (freedom to exchange political ideas).

Zyuganov emerged from obscurity in 1991 as the author of "Architect at the Debris," a diatribe against perestroika, which appeared in *Sovetskaya Rossiya,* then the official newspaper of the Communist Party. "What we can see today," he wrote, "can be called a national calamity, comparable with the civil war or the invasion of Hitler's fascism. Glasnost has grown into a hysteria

and has become a weapon of ideological war against the people." Such tough language ensured that he was noticed not only by the party's hard-liners but also by their future allies, the nationalists. Not long afterward Zyuganov was among the 12 politicians who were so disaffected by Gorbachev's reforms that they signed their names to an anti-Gorbachev article entitled "A Word to the People," which appeared in the July 1991 issue of *Sovetskaya Rossiya*. The author of the article was Aleksandr Prokhanov, the editor of the ultranationalist weekly newspaper *Zavtra* ("tomorrow").

A few of the signatories were later arrested for being among the plotters of an attempted coup d'etat against Gorbachev, who was placed under house arrest on August 19,1991 at his dacha in the Crimea, where he was vacationing. Fortunately for Zyuganov, he too was relaxing in the Crimea and thus did not take part in the putsch, which failed two days later after Yeltsin, then the president of the Russian republic, led hundreds of thousands of pro-democratic protesters in mostly peaceful resistance. Many of the military troops were not prepared to fire upon civilians, and some 10 tanks defected to Yeltsin's side to protect the White House, as the Russian parliament building is known. Although Gorbachev returned to Moscow on August 22, he was compelled to share power with the wildly popular Yeltsin. The banning of the Communist Party of the Soviet Union, on August 29, was followed by declarations of independence by various republics. In December 1991 the Soviet Union was formally disbanded, Gorbachev resigned, and Yeltsin assumed control of many formerly Soviet structures and functions as leader of the Russian Federation.

When Zyuganov returned to Moscow from the Crimea on August 27, 1991, he found himself orphaned from the only professional home he had known. Before long, he met Aleksandr Prokhanov, who told Alessandra Stanley that Zyuganov "was obviously shocked and looked perplexed." "He was looking for human and political support among those in the thin strata that opposed the regime," Prokhanov continued. "We received him as a companion in distress." Zyuganov and Prokhanov are friends, and each of them understands his own place in the opposition. Keeping in touch with his former Communist colleagues, Zyuganov in 1992 became chairman of the Coordination Committee of Patriotic Forces of Russia and co-chairman of the Duma of the Russian National Sobor.

Throughout 1992 and 1993 conservative forces in parliament became increasingly resistant to Yeltsin's economic reforms, which had set off hyperinflation and massive societal dislocation. A power struggle between Yeltsin and parliament escalated until Yeltsin decreed the dissolution of parliament on September 21, 1993. Ignoring the decree, parliament voted to impeach Yeltsin on the same day. Hundreds of Yeltsin's opponents in parliament, including his own vice-president, Aleksandr V. Rutskoi, attempted a coup by barricading themselves inside the Russian White House, and there ensued a 12-day standoff between the rebel forces and pro-Yeltsin military and police units. Although Zyuganov initially supported the hardliners, he began to advise his colleagues against further intransigence after rival demonstrations in support of the opposing forces hinted at the bloodshed that was to come on October 3, when police and anti-Yeltsin demonstrators clashed outside the parliament building. Yeltsin ordered tanks to fire on the White House, whose defenders were subdued and their leaders arrested by the following day. According to Stanley, some of Zyuganov's former supporters believe that by going on television to urge them to "stay calm" during the crisis he had "betrayed the cause, selling out for a perch in the establishment."

The Communist Party, which had regrouped in 1992, only to be banned once again in the wake of the October 1993 coup attempt, managed to persist, although its rolls had dwindled considerably from the 6.8 million members it had claimed before the 1991 attempted coup. (By 1996 the party had boosted its membership to 580,000.) In the parliamentary election of December 11, 1993, half of the 450 seats in the Duma, or lower house of parliament, were allocated on the basis of party preference and the other half were filled by candidates elected by their local districts in individual races. Vladimir Zhirinovsky's ultranationalist Liberal Democratic Party won 23 percent of the party-preference vote and 64 seats in the Duma; the reformist, pro-Yeltsin Russia's Choice Party, led by first deputy prime minister Yegor T. Gaidar, came in second, with 58 seats; and Zyuganov's Communist Party took third place, with 48 seats. In the process, Zyuganov was elected to parliament.

Two years later, when Russian voters went to the polls on December 17, 1995, they handed the Communists 22 percent of the party-preference vote and 157 seats—by far the largest bloc in the Duma. The Liberal Democratic Party won second place in the party-preference polling, with 11 percent of the vote, but the next-largest bloc of seats in parliament went to Yeltsin's Our Home Is Russia Party, which was allocated 55. The Communists' surprisingly strong showing in that election has been attributed to voters' unhappiness with the turmoil unleashed by Yeltsin's reforms. Although inflation had fallen from an annual rate of 2,525 percent in 1992 to 132 percent by 1995, the standard of living for most Russians had continued to decline. Real incomes had tumbled by 50 percent over the previous five years, and more than a third of Russians were living below the poverty line.

Zyuganov, the presumed front-runner in the presidential campaign of 1996, exploited the country's grim conditions in his stump speeches. Blaming Yeltsin, whose approval rating hovered at a mere 5 percent in January of that year, for the ruination of Russia, he repeatedly alluded to the lawlessness that Russians had come to identify with capitalism. Michael Kramer of *Time* (May 27, 1996) quoted Zyuganov as saying, "Russians have only three rights today: The right to steal, the right to drink, and the right not to be responsible." The candidate offered an ostensibly comforting message that focused on taking care of the people and restoring law and order. Although the Communist Party platform still contained hard-line planks—among them "Everything was right in Soviet history (industrialization, collectivization). All sacrifices are justified" and "Stop the spread of Western ideology, Americanism, and the psychology of easy profit"—Zyuganov lifted the party's ban on religion and dispensed with its "internationalist" creed. In interviews with Western reporters and in speeches before international audiences, he tempered his intention to renationalize certain industries with a nod to foreign investors, saying that some private property would be allowed and acknowledging that radical moves could plunge the country into civil war, as had happened after the Bolsheviks came to power in 1917.

Such reassurances seemed, in the wake of the presidential election of June 16, 1996, to have allayed many voters' fears of a return to totalitarianism, for Zyuganov garnered 32 percent of the vote—only three points behind Yeltsin's 35 percent. A runoff between the two men was scheduled for July 7. Rallying to the cause of preventing a return to Communism, Yeltsin, who had suffered two heart attacks in the past year, took full advantage of the considerable powers of his incumbency in a spate of feverish campaigning. Two days after the June voting, he made former general Aleksandr Lebed, who had finished in third place, with 15 percent of the vote, his national security adviser in an effort to take nationalist support away from Zyuganov. The president then moved the date of the runoff to Wednesday, July 3, to head off the possibility that many of his supporters would fail to go to the polls if the vote were held on the following Sunday, when they would likely be at their country homes. He made an estimated $10 billion in campaign promises to interest groups and individuals over the course of the campaign-equivalent to the amount of a loan to Russia made by the IMF in April 1996. The media, although technically free, gave exclusively favorable coverage to Yeltsin, fearing a return to censorship under the Communists.

In the days leading up to the July 3 vote, Yeltsin's campaign managers blanketed television time with alarming reminders of Communist repression, civil disorder, and economic stagnation in an effort to scare people into voting against Zyuganov, if not "for" Yeltsin. "This election will come down to a race between someone people hate and someone they fear," a Western adviser to the Yeltsin campaign told Kramer, who quoted a taxi driver named Roman as explaining that Russians "have no concept of freedom," which many tend to equate with rampant chaos. "They substitute freedom of action for freedom of thought," Roman continued. "They see freedom as license. They don't realize freedom requires self-discipline. They fear that freedom leads to anarchy. They view it as the ability, if one can, to lord it over those weaker than they are." A survey taken by a Scottish professor in January 1996 of some 2,500 Russians found that 77 percent believed that "order" was "more important for Russia now" than was "democracy," which was ranked first by only 9 percent of the respondents.

In a final campaign speech, broadcast on July 1, Zyuganov appealed to voters not to fear him or the Communist Party but to hold Yeltsin accountable for their misery and the loss of the country's former superpower status. "Our bloc and myself are for an original, strong, respected, dignified Russia," he said, adding, "Our main task is to start up production and to increase the purchasing power of all citizens. . . . Your vote will not be a choice between Zyuganov and Yeltsin, you will be voting for a strong and mighty Russia or a colonial

administration." Yeltsin, too, cast the choice as one not between two men but as one for or against the future, declaring that a vote for him would be a vote for Russia. On July 3 Yeltsin won by an unexpectedly wide margin—14 points—with 54 percent of the vote.

As though sensing his imminent defeat, in the final days of the campaign Zyuganov had been calling for a coalition government, an indication to many political experts that he expected to play the role of principal opposition figure in the new government. On the day of the election, Zyuganov told Michael Specter of *The New York Times* (July 4, 1996), "Nobody will lose today and nobody will win. In the current conditions, Russia itself will lose if our course continues. But it cannot continue, even if everyone wanted it to." Indeed, that view corresponds to many assessments of the Russian political landscape in the wake of the election, the results of which gave little confidence to foreign investors and others with an interest in what seems to many to be an impossible, but necessary, marriage of stability and reform. Another cause of concern was Yeltsin's frailty, which prompted speculation about whether he would survive his four-year term. If he does not, and if Russia follows constitutional procedures, Prime Minister Viktor Chernomyrdin would become acting president for 90 days, after which new elections would be held.

Contrary to many analysts' prognoses, the opposition bloc did not collapse in the wake of Yeltsin's reelection. At the first congress of the all-Russian nongovernmental movement, held on August 7, 1996, Zyuganov was elected leader of the People's Patriotic Union of Russia, which was founded by more than 30 parties and movements, among them the Communist Party of the Russian Federation, the Agrarian Party, the Russian Party, the all-Russian political and nongovernmental movement, the Agrarian Union of the Russian Federation, the "Spiritual Legacy," and trade-union workers of the "agro-industrial complex."

Zyuganov has been a harsh critic of Vladimir Putin. He ran in the presidential elections of 2000, 2008, and 2012, but he placed a distant second in all three elections.

PERSONAL LIFE
Gennadi Zyuganov and his wife, Nadezhda, an engineer, have a son and a daughter, both of whom are in their 20s. In 1996 Zyuganov joined the ranks of Cuba's

Fidel Castro and the Bosnian Serb leader Radovan Karadzic as a recipient of the Mikhail Sholokhov literary award. Adrian Karatnycky, the president of Freedom House, assessed Zyuganov's books in an interview with James Carney for his aforementioned article in Time. "He has a deep historical view of Russia's mission as the opposition to the dissolute West. He's a big believer in the decline of the West and the emergence of a new civilization." In the words of the *Economist* reviewer who evaluated Zyuganov's *I Believe in Russia*, the book "should be read and re-read by anyone who thinks that Mr. Zyuganov is really a social democrat who might

yet make a comfortable partner for the West. He takes a paranoid view of history in which Russia is a permanent victim of evil outside forces."

FURTHER READING

N Y Times mag p60+ My 27 '96 pors; *International Who's Who* p26+ My 26 '96 pors; *New Yorker* p40+ fl 22 '96; *International Year Book* and *Newsweek* p50+Mr 11 '96 por, p32+ Je 17 '96 pors; *Statesmen's Who's Who,* 1995-96

Appendixes

Appendixes

TIMELINE OF WORLD POLITICAL EVENTS 1940-2016

DATE	MILESTONE
1940	President Franklin D. Roosevelt wins an unprecedented third term.
	Prime Minister Winston Churchill of Britain blames Italy's Benito Mussolini for aligning with Germany in World War II.
	United States declares neutrality in the war.
1941	Japan attacks Pearl Harbor, leading Roosevelt and Churchill to form an alliance.
	Roosevelt delivers "Infamy Speech" and Congress passes declaration of war against Japan, officially bringing the United States into the war.
1942	Persecution and genocide of Jews continues all over Europe, and eventually six million Jews will be killed.
	Reinard Heydrich, a high-ranking German Nazi official, is assassinated by Chech and Slovak soldiers.
1943	President Franklin D. Roosevelt, Prime Minister Winston Churchill, and Generals Charles de Gaulle and Henri Giraud of France meet in Morocco to plan war strategy.
	Winston Churchill addresses a joint session of the United States Congress.
	Italy's Benito Mussolini is arrested, and he is replaced by General Pietro Badoglio – the new government sides with the Allies.
	President Franklin D. Roosevelt closes the Works Program Administration and the Great Depression officially ends in the United States.
1944	President Franklin D. Roosevelt wins reelection and becomes the only president elected to a fourth term.
	In the Battle of Normandy (known as D-Day), 155,000 Allied troops help to liberate France from Germany, weakening the Nazi hold on Europe.
1945	Yalta Conference is held by President Franklin D. Roosevelt, Prime Minister Winston Churchill, and Soviet leader Joseph Stalin.
	Italy's Benito Mussolini is executed by Italian partisans.
	President Franklin D. Roosevelt dies suddenly and Vice President Harry S. Truman becomes president.

Germany surrenders and the war ends, with many countries declared liberated.

Winston Churchill resigns as Prime Minister.

1946   First meeting of the United Nations is held in London.

Charles de Gaulle resigns as president of France.

Juan Perón is elected president of Argentina.

Ho Chi Minh is elected president of North Vietnam.

Miguel Alemán Valdés takes office as president of Mexico.

1947   Cold War begins when President Truman signs an Act of Congress granting military and economic aid to Turkey and Greece in an effort to fight the spread of Communism.

President Truman signs the National Security Act, creating the Central Intelligence Agency, Department of Defense, the Joint Chiefs of Staff, and the National Security Council.

Jewaharlal Nehru takes office as the first Prime Minister of India.

Pakistan and Yemen join the United Nations.

State of Israel is created when the United Nations Assembly votes to partition Palestine into Arab and Jewish regions.

1948   Burma gains its independence from the United Kingdom.

Christian Democracy Party wins majority of the vote when Italy holds its first democratic general election.

Democratic presidential incumbent Harry Truman defeats Republican Thomas Dewey.

Israeli Declaration of Independence is made.

1949   António Óscar Carmona is re-elected president of Portugal for lack of an opposing candidate.

Ireland leaves the British Commonwealth and becomes the Republic of Ireland.

The Federal Republic of Germany is established.

Transjordan changes its name to the Kingdom of Jordan.

Israel signs truce with Syria to end 19-month long war.

1950
President Harry Truman orders the development of the hydrogen bomb, in response to the Soviet Union's first atomic bomb.

Soviet Union signs mutual defense treaty with China.

Celâl Bayar becomes the third president of Turkey.

The United Nations ends the diplomatic isolation of Spain.

1951
United States signs mutual defense pact with Australia and New Zealand.

King Abdullah I of Jordan is assassinated by a Palestinian while attending Friday prayers in Jerusalem. He is succeeded by his son, King Talal.

Winston Churchill is re-elected Prime Minister of the United Kingdom in a general election.

René Pleven becomes Prime Minister of France.

1952
King George VI of the United Kingdom dies; Elizabeth II is proclaimed as Queen.

Prime Minister Winston Churchill announces that the United Kingdom has an atomic bomb.

President Truman says he will not seek reelection; General Dwight Eisenhower wins presidency after defeating a democratic candidate from Illinois.

The Jordanian Parliament forces King Talal of Jordan to abdicate due to his mental illness; he is succeeded by his son King Hussein.

Pandit Nehru forms his government in India.

1953
Soviet Union ends diplomatic relations with Israel after a bomb explodes at a Soviet embassy.

Greece, Turkey, and Yugoslavia sign the Baltic Pact.

The Korean War ends with the Armistice agreement; North Korea remains communist and South Korea remains capitalist.

David Ben-Gurion resigns as Prime Minister of Israel.

1954
President Eisenhower warns of intervention in Vietnam after authorizing millions of dollars in aid; the Viet Minh take control of North Vietnam.

Colonel Gamel Abdel Nasser becomes premier of Egypt.

Pierre Mendès France becomes prime minister of France.

Joseph Stalin dies and the Soviet Union starts releasing political prisoners and deportees from its Gulag camps.

1955   President Dwight Eisenhower sends his first U.S. advisors to Vietnam.

West Germany joins the North Atlantic Treaty Organization (NATO).

Vice President Nixon serves as acting president while President Truman recovers from a heart attack.

José Ramón Guizado becomes president of Panama.

Vietnam War begins.

1956   Pakistan becomes the first Islamic Republic.

Pierre Mendès France resigns as prime minister of France due to France's policy on Algeria.

Colonel Gamel Abdel Nasser becomes president of Egypt.

A joint resolution of Congress is signed by President Dwight D. Eisenhower, authorizing "In God we trust" as the U.S. national motto.

Fidel Castro and his followers land in Cuba.

1957   Eisenhower is inaugurated for a second presidential term; he announces a 2-year suspension of nuclear testing.

U Nu becomes president of Burma.

Paul-Henry Spaak becomes the new General Secretary of NATO.

United States military sustains first combat mortality in Vietnam.

Adnan Menderes of the Democrat Party forms a new government in Turkey.

1958   President Eisenhower signs the Federal Aviation Act, giving aviation authority to the newly created Federal Aviation Agency.

Tunisia and Morocco join the Arab League.

Soviet Union performs a nuclear test.

King Faisal of Iraq is killed.

1959   The United States and Soviet Union governments recognize the new Cuban government of Fidel Castro.

Singapore, with Lee Kuan Yew as Prime Minister, becomes a self-governing crown colony of Britain.

Makarios III is selected the first president of Cyprus.

Martial law is declared in Laos.

1960   Democratic Senator John F. Kennedy wins presidency in a close race against Vice President Richard Nixon, becoming the youngest president elected.

United States announces that 3,500 American soldiers will be sent to Vietnam.

Civil Rights Act of 1960 is signed into law.

127 people die in riots when French President Charles de Gaulle visits Algeria.

Ethiopian emperor Haile Selassie visits Brazil. While there his bodyguard leads a failed military coup against his rule, proclaiming the emperor's son the new emperor.

1961   United States severs diplomatic and consular relations with Cuba.

Hassan II is pronounced King of Morocco.

Nazi Adolf Eichmann is sentenced to death for his part in the Holocaust after a trial in Jerusalem.

In a national broadcast, Cuban leader Fidel Castro announces that Cuba will adopt socialism.

1962   Cuba and the Soviet Union sign a trade pact; the United States puts an embargo against Cuba.

Jawaharlal Nehru is elected Prime Minister of India.

Algeria becomes independent from France and adopts a constitution.

In a televised address, U.S. President John F. Kennedy announces to the nation the existence of Soviet missiles in Cuba.

1963   Kuwait becomes the 111th member of the United Nations.

Malaysia is formed through the merging of the Federation of Malaya and the British crown colony of Singapore, North Borneo (renamed Sabah) and Sarawak.

President Kennedy is assassinated and Vice President Lyndon Johnson becomes President of the United States.

New U.S. President Lyndon B. Johnson confirms that the United States intends to continue military and economic support of South Vietnam.

1964   Several Palestinian groups unite to form the Palestine Liberation Organization (PLO).

Malta gains independence from Britain.

President Lyndon Johnson and his top-ranking advisors meet to discuss plans to bomb North Vietnam.

U.S. military personnel announce that U.S. casualties in Vietnam have risen to 1,387, including 399 dead and 17 MIA.

1965   Winston Churchill dies.

Greek Prime minister Georgios Papandreou and his government are dismissed by King Constantine II.

U.S. President Lyndon B. Johnson signs the Immigration and Nationality Act of 1965, which ends quotas based on national origin.

Charles de Gaulle is re-elected as French president with over ten million votes.

1966   Italian Prime Minister Aldo Moro resigns due to a power struggle in his party.

President Johnson announces that the U.S. will substantially increase the number of its troops in Vietnam; anti-war demonstrations take place across the country.

Leonid Brezhnev becomes General Secretary of the Soviet Union, as well as Leader of the Communist Party of the U.S.S.R.

Fidel Castro declares martial law in Cuba because of a possible U.S. attack.

1967   West Germany and Romania establish diplomatic relations.

Joseph Stalin's daughter, Svetlana Alliluyeva, defects to the United States via the U.S. Embassy in New Delhi.

Greece is taken over by a military dictatorship led by George Papadopoulos.

Fidel Castro announces that all intellectual property belongs to the people and that Cuba intends to translate and publish technical literature without compensation.

The Soviet Union ratifies a treaty with the United States and the United Kingdom, banning nuclear weapons from outer space.

1968   A civil rights protest staged at a white-only bowling alley in Orangeburg, South Carolina is broken up by highway patrolmen; 3 college students are killed.

U.S. President Lyndon B. Johnson signs the Civil Rights Act of 1968.

Saddam Hussein becomes Vice Chairman of the Revolutionary Council in Iraq after a *coup d'état*.

The United States Department of Defense announces that the United States Army and United States Marines will send 24,000 troops back to Vietnam for involuntary second tours.

1969

Richard Milhous Nixon succeeds Lyndon Baines Johnson as the 37th President of the United States.

Yasser Arafat is elected Palestine Liberation Organization leader at the Palestinian National Congress.

Charles de Gaulle steps down as president of France after suffering defeat in a referendum.

The first U.S. troop withdrawals from Vietnam are made.

1970

In Washington, D.C., 100,000 people demonstrate against the Vietnam War.

In the United Kingdom general election, the Conservative Party wins and Edward Heath becomes Prime Minister, ousting the Labour government of Harold Wilson.

Israeli forces fight Palestinian guerillas in southern Lebanon.

President Richard Nixon begins a tour of Europe, visiting Italy, Yugoslavia, Spain, the United Kingdom and Ireland.

1971

The People's Republic of Bangladesh (former East Pakistan) forms, under Sheikh Mujibur Rahman, at Mujibnagor.

Austria and the People's Republic of China establish diplomatic relations.

The total number of American troops still in Vietnam drops to a record low of 196,700.

The Indo-Pakistani War of 1971 begins with Operation Chengiz Khan as Pakistan launches preemptive attacks on nine Indian airbases. The next day India launches a massive invasion of East Pakistan.

1972

Kurt Waldheim becomes Secretary-General of the United Nations.

Richard Nixon and Leonid Brezhnev sign the SALT I treaty in Moscow, as well as the Anti-Ballistic Missile Treaty and other agreements.

Libya and the Soviet Union sign a cooperation treaty.

Chilean president Salvador Allende forms a new government.

1973

The United Kingdom, the Republic of Ireland and Denmark enter the European Economic Community, which later becomes the European Union.

U.S. President Richard Nixon announces that a peace accord has been reached in Vietnam.

Leonid Brezhnev becomes the first Soviet leader to address the American people on television.

Egypt and Israel sign a United States-sponsored cease-fire accord.

1974

Following a hung parliament in the United Kingdom general election, Conservative prime minister Edward Heath resigns and is succeeded by Labour's Harold Wilson, who previously led the country from 1964 to 1970.

Isabel Perón is sworn in as the first female President of Argentina, replacing her sick husband Juan Perón, who dies 2 days later.

A bomb explodes on a train between Italy and West Germany, killing 12 and wounding 48. Italian neo-fascists take responsibility.

Richard Nixon resigns following the Watergate scandal; Vice President Gerald Ford succeeds Richard Nixon as the 38th President of the United States.

1975

Margaret Thatcher defeats Edward Heath for the leadership of the opposition UK Conservative Party. Thatcher is Britain's first female leader of any political party.

In the Watergate scandal, former United States Attorney General John N. Mitchell, and former White House aides H. R. Haldeman and John Ehrlichman, are sentenced to between 30 months and 8 years in prison.

King Faisal of Saudi Arabia is shot and killed by his nephew; the killer is beheaded on June 18. King Khalid succeeds Faisal.

Prime Minister Indira Gandhi declares a state of emergency in India, suspending civil liberties and elections.

Juan Carlos is declared King of Spain following the death of dictator Francisco Franco; he would reign until his abdication in 2014.

1976

Jimmy Carter is elected President of the U.S., defeating Gerald Ford, and becoming the first president from the Deep South since the Civil War.

Patrick Hillery is elected unopposed as the 6th President of Ireland.

José López Portillo takes office as President of Mexico.

Jacques Chirac resigns as Prime Minister of France; he is succeeded by Raymond Barre.

1977

The Australian parliament is opened by Elizabeth II, Queen of Australia.

Portugal and Israel establish diplomatic relations.

The Likud Party, led by Menachem Begin, wins the national elections in Israel.

A demonstration and coup attempt in Angola takes place, after which thousands were killed by the government and Cuban forces.

1978

The Soviet Union nuclear weapons stockpile exceeds the United States nuclear weapons stockpile.

Afghanistan President Daoud Khan is killed during a military coup; Nur Muhammad Taraki succeeds him, beginning the Afghan Civil War.

The Camp David Accords are signed between Israel and Egypt.

Tuvalu becomes independent from the United Kingdom.

1979

The United States and the People's Republic of China establish full diplomatic relations.

Vietnam and Vietnam-backed Cambodian insurgents announce the fall of Phnom Penh, Cambodia, and the collapse of the Pol Pot regime

Ayatollah Ruhollah Khomeini returns to Tehran, Iran, after nearly 15 years of exile.

In a ceremony at the White House, President Anwar Sadat of Egypt and Prime Minister Menachem Begin of Israel sign an Egypt–Israel Peace Treaty.

1980

U.S. President Jimmy Carter proclaims a grain embargo against the USSR with the support of the European Commission.

The International Court of Justice calls for the release of U.S. Embassy hostages in Tehran.

Pierre Trudeau returns to office as Prime Minister of Canada.

Republican challenger and former Governor Ronald Reagan of California defeats incumbent Democratic President Jimmy Carter for the U.S. presidency.

1981

Iran releases the 52 Americans held for 444 days within minutes of Ronald Reagan succeeding Jimmy Carter as the 40th President of the United States, ending the Iran hostage crisis.

In France, Socialist François Mitterrand becomes the first socialist President of the French Fifth Republic.

Mahathir bin Mohamad becomes the 4th Prime Minister of Malaysia.

1982

The United States places an embargo on Libyan oil imports, alleging Libyan support for terrorist groups.

The United Nations Security Council votes to demand that Israel withdraw its troops from Lebanon.

In Israel, 400,000 marchers demand the resignation of Prime Minister Menachem Begin.

Helmut Kohl replaces Helmut Schmidt as Chancellor of Germany through a constructive vote of no confidence.

1983   Soviet military officer Stanislav Petrov averts a worldwide nuclear war by correctly identifying a warning of attack by U.S. missiles as a false alarm.

The first democratic elections are held in Argentina after 7 years of military rule.

Brunei gains independence from the United Kingdom.

Turgut Özal, of ANAP forms the new government of Turkey (45th government); beginning of a new civilian regime

1984   Sinn Féin's Gerry Adams and three others are seriously injured in a gun attack by the Ulster Volunteer Force.

Liechtenstein becomes the last country in Europe to grant women the right to vote.

P. W. Botha is inaugurated as the first executive State President of South Africa.

Prime Minister of India Indira Gandhi is assassinated by her two Sikh security guards in New Delhi.

1985   The Economic Cooperation Organization (ECO) is formed.

Nelson Mandela rejects an offer of freedom from the South African government.

Israel begins withdrawing troops from Lebanon.

The Soviet Union performs a nuclear test in eastern Kazakhstan.

1986   Spain and Portugal enter the European Community, which later becomes the European Union.

Yoweri Museveni is sworn in as President of Uganda

The United States Senate approves a treaty outlawing genocide.

Former United Nations Secretary-General Kurt Waldheim is elected president of Austria.

1987   Hu Yaobang, General Secretary of the Communist Party of China, is forced into retirement by political conservatives.

The new Constitution of the Philippines goes into effect, including Spanish and Arabic as optional languages of the Philippines.

The Conservative Party of the United Kingdom, led by Margaret Thatcher, is re-elected for a third term at the 1987 general election.

During a visit to Berlin, Germany, U.S. President Ronald Reagan challenges Soviet Premier Mikhail Gorbachev to tear down the Berlin Wall.

1988   George H. W. Bush is elected over Michael Dukakis, becoming the first sitting Vice President of the United States in 152 years to be elected as President of the United States.

Voters in Pakistan choose populist candidate Benazir Bhutto to be Prime Minister.

Former Korean president Chun Doo Hwan publicly apologizes for corruption during his presidency, announcing he will go into exile.

In the Iran-Contra Affair, Lieutenant Colonel Oliver North and Vice Admiral John Poindexter are indicted on charges of conspiracy to defraud the United States.

1989   Carlos Andrés Pérez takes office as President of Venezuela.

Sōsuke Uno succeeds Noboru Takeshita as Prime Minister of Japan.

Jiang Zemin becomes General Secretary of the Communist Party of China.

President of South Africa P. W. Botha meets the imprisoned Nelson Mandela face to face for the first time.

1990   General Manuel Noriegais deposed as leader of Panama and surrenders to the American forces.

The League of Communists of Yugoslavia votes to give up its monopoly on power.

Patricio Aylwin is sworn in as the first democratically elected Chilean president since 1970.

Mikhail Gorbachev is elected as the first executive president of the Soviet Union.

President George H. W. Bush and Soviet Union leader Mikhail Gorbachev sign a treaty to end chemical weapon production and begin destroying their respective stocks.

1991   The United Nations Security Council votes unanimously to condemn Israel's treatment of the Palestinians.

President Bush declares victory over Iraq in the Gulf War and orders a cease-fire.

President of Poland Lech Wałęsa becomes the first Polish president to ever visit the U.S.

Prime Minister of Iceland Steingrímur Hermannsson resigns following an inconclusive parliamentary election; he is succeeded as prime minister by Davío Oddsson.

Boris Yeltsin bans and dissolves the Communist Party of the Soviet Union.

1992   The Assembly of Bosnia and Herzegovina (without the presence of Serb political delegates) proclaims independence from the Socialist Federal Republic of Yugoslavia.

Russian leaders in Crimea declare their separation from Ukraine as a new republic, but withdraw the secession shortly thereafter.

Arkansas Governor Bill Clinton is elected the 42nd President of the United States.

The Czechoslovakia Federal Assembly votes to split the country into the Czech Republic and Slovakia, starting on January 1, 1993.

1993

In Moscow, U.S. President George H. W. Bush and Russia President Boris Yeltsin sign the second Strategic Arms Reduction Treaty.

Václav Havel is elected President of the Czech Republic.

Lien Chan is named by Lee Teng-hui to succeed Hau Pei-tsun as Premier of the Republic of China.

Authorities announce the capture of suspected World Trade Center bombing conspirator Mohammad Salameh.

The Israeli Knesset elects Ezer Weizman as President of Israel.

1994

U.S. President Bill Clinton and Russian President Boris Yeltsin sign the Kremlin accords, which stop aiming nuclear missiles toward each country's targets, and provide for the dismantling of Ukraine's nuclear arsenal.

Nelson Mandela is inaugurated as South Africa's first black president.

Israel and the Vatican establish full diplomatic relations.

Israel and Jordan sign the Israel-Jordan Treaty of Peace, which formally ends the state of war that has existed between the nations since 1948.

Russia and the People's Republic of China agree to de-target their nuclear weapons against each other.

1995

U.S. President Bill Clinton invokes emergency powers, extending a $20 billion loan to help Mexico avert financial collapse.

Jacques Chirac is elected president of France.

Prime Minister of the United Kingdom John Major wins his battle to remain leader of the Conservative Party.

Israeli Prime Minister Yitzhak Rabin is assassinated at a peace rally in Tel Aviv.

1996

Jorge Sampaio is elected president of Portugal.

Yasser Arafat is re-elected president of the Palestinian Authority.

King Fahd of Saudi Arabia announces his medical recovery in the national press and assumes power again from his brother, Crown Prince Abdullah.

The Likud Party, led by Benjamin Netanyahu, wins a narrow victory in the Israeli general election.

Boris Yeltsin emerges as the winner in Russia's first round of presidential elections.

1997   U.S. President Bill Clinton is inaugurated for his second term.

Madeleine Albright becomes the first female Secretary of State, after confirmation by the United States Senate.

The Labour Party of the United Kingdom returns to power for the first time in 18 years, with Tony Blair becoming Prime Minister, in a landslide majority in the 1997 general election.

Mohammad Khatami wins the 1997 Iranian presidential election and becomes the first Iranian Reformist president.

1998   Pakistan tests medium-range missiles capable of hitting India.

The bombings of the United States embassies in Dares Salaam, Tanzania, and Nairobi, Kenya, kill 224 people and injure over 4,500, and are linked to terrorist Osama bin Laden.

The Government of North Korea adopts a military dictatorship on its 50th anniversary.

U.S. President Bill Clinton orders airstrikes on Iraq. UNSCOM withdraws all weapons inspectors from Iraq.

1999   King Hussein of Jordan dies from cancer, and his son Abdullah II inherits the throne.

U.S. President Bill Clinton is acquitted in impeachment proceedings in the United States Senate.

Ehud Barak is elected prime minister of Israel.

Boris Yeltsin resigned as President of Russia, leaving Prime Minister Vladimir Putin as the acting President.

2000   Vladimir Putin is elected President of Russia.

Israel withdraws IDF forces from southern Lebanon after 22 years.

Republican Governor of Texas George W. Bush defeats Democratic Vice President Al Gore in the U.S. presidential election.

2001   2,977 victims are killed in the September 11 terrorist attacks at the World Trade Center in New York City, The Pentagon in Virginia, and in rural Shanksville, Pennsylvania.

U.S. President George W. Bush announces the establishment of the Office of Homeland Security.

The People's Republic of China is admitted to the World Trade Organization after 15 years of negotiations.

During economic crisis in Argentina government effectively froze all bank accounts for twelve months which led to riots.

2002

The US State Department releases an updated report naming seven state sponsors of terrorism, which lists Iran, Iraq, Cuba, Libya, North Korea, Sudan, and Syria.

In Moscow, United States President George W. Bush and Russian President Vladimir Putin sign the Strategic Offensive Reductions Treaty to replace the Anti-Ballistic Missile Treaty of 1972 and the START II Treaty of 1993.

The United Nations Security Council unanimously approves UN Security Council Resolution 1441, forcing Saddam Hussein to disarm or face "serious consequences."

2003

The Iraq War begins with the invasion of Iraq by the U.S. and allied forces.

Saddam Hussein, former President of Iraq, is captured in the small town of Ad-Dawr by the U.S. Army.

The Czech Republic and Poland approve joining the European Union.

The United States announces the withdrawal of troops stationed in Saudi Arabia, and the redeployment of some at the Al Udeid Air Base in Qatar.

2004

British Prime Minister Tony Blair visits Libyan leader Colonel Muammar Gaddafi, after Libya dismantles its weapons of mass destruction program (the first time a major Western leader visited Libya in several decades).

Republican incumbent President George W. Bush is declared the winner over his Democratic challenger, U.S. Senator John F. Kerry, in a close election for the presidency.

The largest expansion to date of the European Union takes place, adding 10 member-states: Poland, Lithuania, Latvia, Estonia, the Czech Republic, Slovakia, Slovenia, Hungary, Malta and Cyprus.

2005

Iraq holds its first parliamentary election since 1958.

North Korea announces that it possesses nuclear weapons as a protection against the hostility it feels from the United States.

The President of Kyrgyzstan Askar Akayev is overthrown in a revolution and flees the country.

Pope John Paul II dies; over 4 million people travel to the Vatican to mourn him.

Angela Merkel assumes office as the first female Chancellor of Germany.

2006   North Korea claims to have conducted its first-ever nuclear test.

Israeli troops invade Lebanon in response to Hezbollah's actions; Hezbollah declares war against Israel.

The United Nations General Assembly votes overwhelmingly to establish the United Nations Human Rights Council.

Ariel Sharon, Prime Minister of Israel, suffers a severe stroke.

2007   The State of Israel releases $100 million in frozen assets to President Mahmoud Abbas of the Palestinian National Authority, in order to bolster the president's position.

Prime Minister of Latvia Aigars Kalvītis and Prime Minister of Russia Mikhail Fradkov finally sign a border treaty between Latvia and Russia.

Vladimir Putin, President of Russia, is *Time* magazine's Person of the Year.

Former Pakistani Prime Minister Benazir Bhutto is assassinated, and at least 20 others are killed, by a bomb blast at an election rally in Rawalpindi.

2008   Kosovo formally declares independence from Serbia, with support from some countries but opposition from others.

Fidel Castro announces his resignation as President of Cuba.

Democratic U. S. Senator Barack Obama is elected the 44th President of the United States, and becomes the first African-American President.

Bangladesh holds its general elections after 2 years of political unrest over the interim government.

2009   Israel announces a unilateral ceasefire in the Gaza War.

North Korean leader Kim Jong-il pardons two American journalists, who were imprisoned for illegal entry, after former U.S. President Bill Clinton meets with Kim in North Korea.

The Prime Minister of Belgium, Herman Van Rompuy, is designated the first permanent President of the European Council.

2010   The United States and the United Kingdom close their embassies in Yemen due to the ongoing security threat by Al-Qaeda.

WikiLeaks, an online publisher of anonymous, covert, and classified material, leaks to the public over 90,000 internal reports about the United States-led involvement in the War in Afghanistan from 2004 to 2010.

The President of Poland, Lech Kaczyński, is among 96 killed when their airplane crashes in Smolensk, western Russia while on their way to commemorate the Soviet Katyn massacre.

2011

U.S. President Barack Obama announces that Osama bin Laden, the founder and leader of the militant group Al-Qaeda, was killed during a military operation in Pakistan.

Occupy Wall Street protests begin in the United States, a movement that spreads to 82 countries.

Israel and the Palestinian militant organization Hamas begin a major prisoner swap; Israeli Army soldier Gilad Shalit is released by Hamas in exchange for 1,027 Palestinian and Israeli-Arab prisoners held in Israel, including 280 serving life sentences for involvement in terror attacks.

2012

The European Union adopts an embargo against Iran in protest of that nation's continued effort to enrich uranium.

Iran suspends oil exports to Britain and France, following sanctions put in place by the European Union and the United States.

The UN General Assembly approves a motion granting Palestine non-member observer state status.

President Barack Obama and Vice President Joe Biden are elected to a second term, defeating the Republican nominee, former Governor of Massachusetts Mitt Romney.

2013

North Korea conducts its third underground nuclear test, prompting widespread condemnation and tightened economic sanctions from the international community.

American Edward Snowden discloses covert operations engaged in by the U.S. government to news publications and flees the country, being granted asylum in Russia.

Croatia becomes the 28th member of the European Union.

2014

Nicolás Maduro, the President of Venezuela, severs diplomatic and political ties with Panama, accusing Panama of being involved in a conspiracy against the Venezuelan government.

United States President Barack Obama's new economic sanctions against Russia go into effect, targeting companies and individuals close to Russian President Vladimir Putin.

U.S. President Barack Obama announces the resumption of normal relations between the U.S. and Cuba.

2015

The United Nations Security Council adopts Resolution 2199 to combat terrorism, allowing nations to use economic sanctions against countries with terrorist ties.

Cuba and the United States reestablish full diplomatic relations, ending over 50 years of hostility between the nations.

A suicide bomber kills over 100 people at a peace rally in Ankara, Turkey, and injures more than 400 others.

Multiple terrorist attacks claimed by Islamic State of Iraq and the Levant (ISIL) in Paris, France, result in 130 deaths.

2016   North Korea launches a long-range rocket into space, violating several UN treaties and prompting condemnation from leaders around the world.

In a referendum vote, the United Kingdom leaves the European Union.

In July, an unsuccessful *coup d'état* was staged against Turkish President Recep Tayyip Erdoğan and his government by a faction within the Turkish Armed Forces.

POLITICAL PARTY WEBSITE DIRECTORY

Austria
Austrian People's Party
www.oevp.at

Canada
Liberal Party of Canada
www.liberal.ca

China
Communist Party
http://english.cpc.people.com.cn

Denmark
Venstre
www.venstre.dk

France
Socialist Party
www.parti-socialiste.fr

Germany
Christian Democratic Union
www.cdu.de/

Hungary
Christian Democratic People's
Party
http://kdnp.hu/

Iceland
Independence Party
www.xd.is/

Israel
Likud Party
www.likud.org.il/

Italy
Democratic Party
www.partitodemocratico.it/

New Centre-Right
www.nuovocentrodestra.it/

Japan
Liberal Democratic Party
www.jimin.jp

Mexico
Institutional Revolutionary Party
http://pri.org.mx/

Netherlands
Labour Party
www.pvda.nl/

People's Party for Democracy and
Freedom
www.vvd.nl/

Pakistan
Pakistan Muslin League
http://pmln.org/

Philippines
Liberal Party
www.liberalparty.org.ph

Portugal
Socialist Party
www.ps.pt

Russia
United Russia
http://er.ru/

Singapore
People's Action Party
www.pap.org.sg/

South Africa
African National Congress
www.anc.org.za/

South Korea
Saenuri Party
www.saenuriparty.kr/

Spain
People's Party
www.pp.es/

Turkey
Justice and Development Party
www.akparti.org.tr

United Kingdom
Conservative Party
www.conservatives.com/

United States
Democratic Party
www.democrats.org

Republican Party
www.gop.com

Venezuela
United Socialist Party
www.psuv.org.ve/

Vietnam
Communist Party of Vietnam
http://en.dangcongsan.vn/

Yemen
General People's Congress
www.almotamar.net

Indexes

Indexes

Geographical Index

INDEX